The XSL companion

The XSL companion

Neil Bradley

ADDISON-WESLEY

An imprint of **Pearson Education**

Harlow, England · London · New York · Reading, Massachusetts · San Francisco · Toronto · Don Mills, Ontario · Sydney
Tokyo · Singapore · Hong Kong · Seoul · Taipei · Cape Town · Madrid · Mexico City · Amsterdam · Munich · Paris · Milan

PEARSON EDUCATION LIMITED

Head Office:
Edinburgh Gate
Harlow CM20 2JE
Tel: +44 (0)1279 623623
Fax: +44 (0)1279 431059

London Office:
128 Long Acre London WC2E 9AN
Tel: +44 (0)20 7447 2000
Fax: +44 (0)20 7240 5771
Website: www.awl.com/cseng

First published in Great Britain in 2000

© Pearson Education Limited 2000

The right of Neil Bradley to be identified as the Author of this Work has been asserted by him in
accordance with the Copyright, Designs and Patents Act 1988.

ISBN 0 201 67487 4

British Library Cataloguing in Publication Data
A CIP record for this book can be obtained from the British Library

Library of Congress Cataloging in Publication Data
Applied for.

Many of the designations used by manufacturers and sellers to distinguish their products
are claimed as trademarks. Pearson Education Limited has made every attempt
to supply trademark information about manufacturers and their products mentioned in
this book. A list of trademark designations and their owners appears on this page.

Trademark Notice

Adobe™ and Postscript™ are trademarks of Adobe Systems Inc.
Aldus® is a registered trademark of the Aldus Corporation.
Apple® and Macintosh® are registered trademarks of Apple Computer Inc.
IBM™ is a trademark of International Business Machines Corporation.
Microsoft® and MS-DOS® are registered trademarks and Windows™ is a
trademark of Microsoft Corporation.
Sun™ is a trademark of Sun Microsystems Inc.
T_EX™ is a trademark of the American Mathematical Society.
UNIX® is a registered trademark in the US and other countries, licensed
exclusively through X/Open Company Ltd.

10 9 8 7 6 5 4 3 2 1

Typeset by the Author
Printed and bound in the United States of America

The Publishers' policy is to use paper manufactured from sustainable forests.

Preface

This book covers a family of standards developed by W^3C (the World Wide Web Consortium). These standards emerged out of a proposal for a stylesheet language, submitted in 1997, which was to be called '**XSL**' (*eXtensible Stylesheet Language*). However, during its gestation, this proposal was eventually pulled apart into three separate standards. The first of these, **XPath**, defines a mechanism for locating information in XML documents, and it has many other uses beyond its role in formatting documents. The second, **XSLT**, provides a means for transforming XML documents into other data formats, including (but not limited to) formatting languages. Finally, the term '**XSL**' is now properly used only to name a proposed standard for embedding formatting information in documents using XML elements.

These three standards are still related. Together, they provide a means to format XML documents. The XSLT standard includes XPath constructs in a number of places, and XSLT can be used to convert an XML document into an XSL document. But each can be used alone, or with alternative technologies. As the XSL formatting language is less mature than XSLT, and not yet well supported, it is recognised that XSLT will initially be used primarily to convert XML documents into **HTML** documents, possibly enhanced with **CSS** styling instructions. Both these formats are therefore explained in depth. However, the first half of this book concentrates on using XSLT as a general tool for processing XML, and the way that it uses XPath to find and manipulate components of an XML document.

Acknowledgements

Thanks to Rupert Benbrook and to Rubus (www.rubus.com), for support in developing this book, and once again to Andrew Dorward for encouraging me to write the first one. Also to Katherin Ekstrom at Pearson Education. The many individuals who have worked together to develop the standards covered in this book richly deserve acknowledgement. Finally, thanks once again to Adobe for FrameMaker+SGML (which was used both in the preparation and publication of this book).

Feedback

Comments and suggestions for a possible future edition are welcome. They should be sent to the author, who can be found at *neil@bradley.co.uk*. Updates, additions and corrections can be obtained from the author's Web page, located at '*http://www.bradley.co.uk*'.

Neil Bradley
May 2000

Contents

Formatting

1. Using this book

Book structure

The chapters in the first part of this book, *Transformations (XSLT)*, cover the features of the XSLT language. They should be read in the order provided, as they each build on examples from previous chapters. At the very least, Chapter 3 and Chapter 4 should be read first. The second part, *Formatting*, describes XSL, and alternative formatting languages and stylesheets (HTML and CSS). Finally, the part entitled *References* includes information on how to analyze XML document type definitions (DTDs) and full details on the XPath standard.

Some familiarity with XML markup concepts is assumed. The reader should at least be comfortable with the syntax, scope and purpose of elements and attributes, with comments and processing instructions, and, to lesser extent, with entities and DTDs.

Style conventions

Names or terms that appear in **bold style** have specific meaning within XSL, XSLT or related technologies, and appear in bold typeface on their first significant occurrence, and thereafter whenever their roles are further defined. Each highlighted occurrence is referenced in the *Index*.

Text appearing `in a mono-spaced font` represents example data, usually an XSL or XML fragment. Larger examples are separated from the text:

```
This is a sample line of text.
```

Though bold typeface may be used to emphasize part of an example, such as '`look at `**`this`**` word`', it does not have the significance described above.

Examples of presented material (printed or displayed output) appear as follows:

```
This is presented material.
```

Words displayed in *italic style* are either quotations or simple 'attention grabbers'.

For the sake of clarity, element and attribute names are capitalized in the text, such as 'the Name element contains a name', but are fully lower case in XML fragment examples, as in '`<name>Smith</name>`', despite the fact that names are case-sensitive in the XML standard. HTML elements are shown in upper-case (and are not case-sensitive).

Note that mid-Atlantic spelling conventions are used in the text, but some terms and keywords appear with US spelling when consistency with a standard described in this book is important. For example, 'centre' is used in the text but 'center' is a parameter value in the HTML table-formatting model.

2. Overview

Stylesheets

With the release of XML in 1998, the benefits of the **generalized markup** concept was brought to the attention of a wide audience. When used correctly, XML tags identify each portion of a document; allowing these fragments to be located, extracted, analyzed and reused. However, the one weakness of this approach is that a document tagged using XML is not ready to be presented. The tags do not specify the format to be applied to the text they contain. The following example clearly identifies the title, author and publisher of a book, but does not indicate how these items are to be presented:

```
<book>
  <title>My Life</title>
  <author>J. Smith</author>
  <publisher>ACME Publishing</publisher>
  ...
</book>
```

Formatting information therefore needs to be obtained from another source. This normally takes the form of a data file that contains a set of rules, each one specifying how a specific element in the document is to be presented. Such a file is called a **stylesheet**. Stylesheets have been around for many years. They take many forms, and differ in capability. At the very least, a stylesheet is able to specify the font to use, the size of the text, any styles to apply to the text (such as underlining, bold or italic), and the size of gaps between paragraphs. Typically, the foreground and background colours may also be specified. Most stylesheets are able to automatically number items in a list, add prefix text such as 'Warning:', and even specify the dimensions of a page, positioning header, body and footer regions. More advanced stylesheets are able to resequence and reuse information. Using a stylesheet, the XML fragment above could be formatted in the following way:

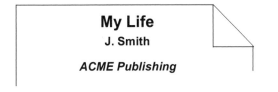

Even if stylesheets were not needed to format XML documents, they would still be very useful. An important benefit of using stylesheets is that one stylesheet can be substituted for another, in order to present the material in a different way. This may be done to take advantage of the features of a different publishing medium, to attract a new audience with different requirements, or to create a new product.

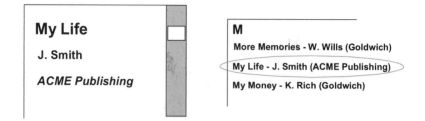

Proof that this is a desirable concept can be demonstrated by the fact that stylesheets have begun to be used with HTML documents, which (unlike XML documents) can also be presented without them. The **CSS (Cascading Style Sheets)** standard is a popular companion to HTML.

Most stylesheets are quite complex. They contain a number of rules, matching source elements to output formats. Even simple stylesheets need a mechanism for specifying where each new rule begins, and for identifying an element name and an output style. Stylesheets must therefore conform to a syntax specification, which is known as a **stylesheet language**. The generalized markup concept has a long history, going back far beyond the release of XML, and stylesheet languages of various flavours have existed to support them for a number of years. The 'official' stylesheet language for use with SGML (the father of XML), is **DSSSL** (Document Style and Semantics Specification Language). It is based on the SCHEME computer language, which is powerful but difficult to read.

An application-specific stylesheet language was used to format this book. It was formatted using FrameMaker+SGML, which uses an SGML-based stylesheet language. This paragraph was formatted by the following rule:

```
<Element>
  <Tag>Para</Tag>
  <Container>
    ...
    <TextFormatRules>
      <AllContextRules>
        <ParagraphFormatting>
          <PropertiesBasic>
            <ParagraphSpacing>
              <SpaceAbove> 9pt</SpaceAbove>
            </ParagraphSpacing>
            <LineSpacing>
              <Height>12.5pt</Height>
            </LineSpacing>
```

```
        </PropertiesBasic>
        <PropertiesFont>
           <Family>Times</Family>
           <Size>10pt</Size>
        </PropertiesFont>
           . . .
      </ParagraphFormatting>
    </AllContextRules>
  </TextFormatRules>
</Element>
```

The XSL standards

The title of this book refers to the acronym **XSL**, which stands for **eXtensible Stylesheet Language**. In the early stages of the development of this stylesheet language, this name was chosen to describe the specification. Since that time, things have become a little more complicated, and the final specification is actually an amalgamation of three standards: XSL, XSLT and XPath. The respective roles of these three standards can be explained in isolation. It is then possible to show how they work together to perform the task of formatting XML documents.

XSL

The original term 'XSL' is now used in a more limited way, to describe a way to specify output styles. The XSL standard defines an application of XML that deliberately breaks the golden rule for XML document structures. In this application, an element is used to describe the appearance of its content, instead of its meaning. In the following example, the element named 'block' contains a text block, such as a paragraph, and 'wrapper' contains a range of text to be styled in a specific way:

```
<block>This is an <wrapper style="bold">XSL</wrapper>
document.</block>
```

This is an **XSL** document.

XML documents should be self-describing, and so should not be created in this form. After all, an XML document that uses the XSL DTD is no more descriptive of its content than an HTML document. It is indeed analogous to an HTML page. The HTML equivalent of the example above is simply briefer (though HTML is a more limited format):

```
<P>This is an <B>HTML</B> document.</P>
```

This is an **HTML** document.

XSLT

XSLT (**XSL Transformations**) is an XML transformation language. Using XSLT, it is possible to convert XML documents into other data formats, including many of the formatting languages that are used to control the rendering of material onto a chosen medium. Such a language was originally part of the XSL standard but has now been extracted into a standard of its own. The XSLT standard specifies the format of the stylesheet document and includes definitions for the mapping rules. An XSLT document is actually an XML document that conforms to the XSLT DTD.

At the present time, the most popular use of XSLT is to convert XML documents into the data format recognized by Web browsers. The HTML format is an application of SGML, sharing ancestry with XML, and can therefore (with one or two caveats) be considered to be an XML format. This is convenient because XSLT is particularly good at converting one XML document into another XML document. The example below formats an XML fragment, containing a paragraph with an emphasized term, into equivalent HTML constructs:

```
<paragraph>A <emphasis>Highlighted</emphasis>
term</paragraph>
```

```
<template match="paragraph">
  <html:P>
    <apply-templates/>
  </html:P>
</template>
<template match="emphasis">
  <html:B>
    <apply-templates/>
  </html:B>
</template>
```

```
<P>A <B>Highlighted</B> term</P>
```

However, XSLT can be used for purposes other than formatting. XML documents can simply be transformed into new XML documents that conform to a different structure (perhaps conforming to a different DTD). Element content can be re-used, repositioned, sorted, split or merged with other content, and even transformed into attribute values.

A number of interesting benefits arise from the fact that XSLT stylesheets are XML documents. First, it is possible to use a DTD both to validate a stylesheet and, along with an XML-sensitive editor, to guide stylesheet authors. Second, a stylesheet can be stored in an XML repository, where it can be manipulated and versioned, down to the element level. Third, because XSLT stylesheets process XML documents, it is possible to write stylesheets that convert other XML/

SGML-based stylesheets into XSLT format, and to create stylesheet variants from another stylesheet. Finally, a stylesheet can be produced to format other stylesheets for presentation or printout.

XPath

XSLT can transform an XML document that conforms to one DTD into another XML document that conforms to a different DTD. At the simplest level, using techniques shown above, tags can be renamed to conform to element definitions in the target DTD. For example, a 'Paragraph' element can be output as a 'Para' element or 'P' element. But XSLT has much more powerful features that allow material to be moved or copied. Element content can become attribute values, and attribute values can become element content. Also, specific formatting can be applied to elements when they appear at a significant place within the document structure. This kind of advanced analysis and manipulation of data is performed using an **expression language**.

The original XSL proposal included such a language, but the XSLT standard now references a separate standard called **XPath**. This standard defines a general-purpose language for interrogating XML document structures. It is also used as a searching/query language and for advanced hypertext linking schemes. This language is not XML-based, but it has a compact syntax that has been designed to be suitable in a number of different circumstances. The following expression identifies 'Paragraph' elements within 'Chapter' elements that have a 'Type' attribute value of 'Important':

```
chapter//paragraph[@type='Important']
```

Once this expression language is understood, the skills gained can be utilized for querying XML structures (using XQL) and linking structures (using Xpointer).

Putting XSL, XSLT and XPath together

It can be seen that XSLT, with the assistance of XPath expressions, offers an ideal way to transform arbitrary XML documents into XSL documents, ready to be formatted for presentation. The following example shows an XSLT rule that maps a 'Paragraph' element in the source document to a bold paragraph in XSL format, but only when the paragraph is inside a 'Chapter' element and has a 'Type' attribute value of 'Important', as expressed using XPath:

```
<template match="Chapter//Paragraph[@type='Important']">
  <fo:block font-style='bold'>
    <apply-templates/>
  </fo:block>
</template>
```

Note that the focus of this book is on the XSLT standard for transforming XML documents. This standard makes significant use of the XPath expression language. The XSL standard itself is less vital to the whole package, as XSLT and XPath can be used together for many other purposes than to create XSL documents.

Naming confusion

The term 'XSL' is currently used to describe three different things, in one case more accurately than the others. First, it is correctly used to name the XSL standard itself. Second, more commonly but far less accurately, it is used to describe the standard properly named XSLT. Third, for historical reasons, it is used to describe the combination of XSLT (including XPath) and XSL, where an XSLT stylesheet is used to create XSL documents. Within this book, the third definition is used as well as the first, because no other term has emerged to describe the whole package (the context of the discussion should indicate which meaning applies).

The term 'XSL stylesheet' should perhaps refer to an XSLT document that outputs an XSL document, but is commonly understood to mean any XSLT document, no matter what output it generates.

XSL/XSLT processors

Software modules and applications are emerging to support each of the standards described above. An **XSLT processor** physically converts an arbitrary XML document into an XSL document, then an **XSL processor** interprets the XSL formatting instructions and renders the document content, typically to paper or screen, according to these instructions.

Some XSLT/XSL processors will be tightly integrated into a publishing application of some kind, such as a Web browser or a desktop publishing package, in which case the output from the processors is passed directly to the main application for rendering. The term **'embedded processor'** can be used for discussing this kind of processor.

However, some XSLT processors will not be tightly integrated into a presentation application and will instead produce an output data file that can be read by the application later. In this book, the term 'standalone processor' can be used to describe this kind of processor. A standalone processor may be used in several different ways; to create an XSL-styled document or a formatting file of another kind (such as HTML), or to create a new XML document.

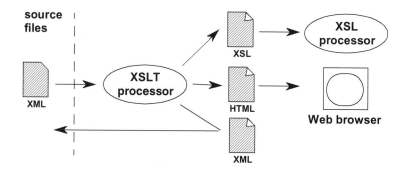

Why XSL?

With so many stylesheet languages already in existence, there has to be a good reason why a new one is needed. Indeed, some have argued that XSL is not necessary. However, there were valid reasons for the development of this language.

First, XSL has an obvious advantage over the vast array of product-specific stylesheet languages. As an industry standard, it is beginning to be supported by a wide range of tools, deployed on a wide range of computer platforms. A number of browser and publishing applications are being modified to accept XSL-styled documents for presentation, so removing dependence on a particular supplier. These are, of course, benefits complementary to the use of XML itself. However, this still leaves a small number of existing standards to discuss.

The **CSS** (Cascading StyleSheet language) format is widely used, in part as a consequence of the fact that the popular Web browser vendors have added support for this language. CSS was originally developed explicitly to complement HTML. At first sight this seems strange, as HTML comprises a large number of format-specific tags and so a stylesheet is not actually necessary. In fact, CSS was initially introduced to give Web page authors more control over format; it was simply a way to override the browser's default formatting settings, and in its simplest form the format instructions are not even stored in a separate stylesheet at all, but in an

HTML attribute called 'Style'. CSS can be used with XML, and some have argued that CSS is sufficient for this task. But XSL is far more powerful than CSS, as this book aims to show, and the task of learning both has been simplified by the adoption of CSS-style property names in XSL.

The **DSSSL** standard has been a major influence on the development of XSL, despite a dramatic difference in appearance. The initial impetus for the development of XSL came from a desire to replicate the power of DSSSL in a language that had a simpler, XML-based, syntax.

It is instructive to look back at XML and see why it has become such a success, as the stylesheet story may hold some interesting parallels. XML was introduced to fill a gap between the simple but limited HTML format and the powerful but complex SGML format. Likewise, XSL is intended to sit between the simple but limited CSS format and the powerful but complex DSSSL format.

Stylesheet example

For those keen to get started with XSLT, the following stylesheet is a simple but working example that can be modified and extended to test the concepts described in the following chapters:

```
<xsl:stylesheet
        xmlns:xsl="http://www.w3.org/1999/XSL/Transform"
        xmlns="http://www.w3.org/TR/xhtml1/strict">

  <xsl:template match="book">
    <HTML><BODY><xsl:apply-templates/></BODY></HTML>
  </xsl:template>

  <xsl:template match="title">
    <H1><xsl:apply-templates/></H1>
  </xsl:template>

  <xsl:template match="author">
    <H3><xsl:apply-templates/></H3>
  </xsl:template>

  <xsl:template match="publisher">
    <P><I><xsl:apply-templates/></I></P>
  </xsl:template>

</xsl:stylesheet>
```

This stylesheet can be used to process XML source documents such as the following:

```
<book>
  <title>My Life</title>
  <author>J. Smith</author>
  <publisher>ACME Publishing</publisher>
  ...
</book>
```

It converts these documents into HTML documents that can be viewed in any popular Web browser:

```
<HTML>
  <BODY>
    <H1>My Life</H1>
    <H3>J. Smith</H3>
    <P><I>ACME Publishing</I></P>
  </BODY>
</HTML>
```

3. Templates

The concept of the **template** is fundamental to XSLT. A template specifies the transformation that is to be applied to a specific part of the source document. Every stylesheet must contain at least one template if it is to achieve anything, and some stylesheets will contain a large number of them.

Template concepts

Template matching

Formatting using XSLT works by selecting an element in the source document, then choosing an appropriate template. The chosen template specifies an output format to apply to that element. A template is represented by the XML element **Template**:

```
<template>...</template>
```

The **Match** attribute is used to specify which element the template applies to. In the following example, the template is targetted at elements named 'para'. It is not used to process the 'title' and 'note' elements:

```
<template match="para">...</template>

    <title>The Title</title>
    <para>A source paragraph.</para>
    <note>A note.</note>
    <para>Another source paragraph.</para>
```

To be more precise, an element name appearing in the Match attribute is actually an example of a very simple expression (and an abbreviation of a more verbose instruction), indicating that all elements with this name that are children of the **current element** are to trigger the template (the term 'children' is commonly used to describe elements that are directly embedded within the element being discussed). When the XSLT processor selects an element in the source document, this becomes the current element. The name of the current element (and other information about it) will have been used to select the most appopriate template to process it.

Nodes and trees

However, it is not only elements that need to be processed. Although elements are very important, it must be recognized that XML documents also contain attributes, comments and processing instructions. Most importantly of all, they contain text. The term **node** is therefore used to refer to any significant item in an XML document, and it is more correct to state that the XSLT processor selects a **current node**.

The distinction between text within an element, and the element containing this text, must also be established. The following example XML fragment is represented by two nodes: one for the Paragraph element, and one for the text that it contains:

```
<para>This is a TEXT node in a PARA node.</para>
```

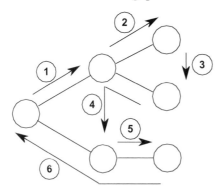

para ◯————◯ "This is a TEXT node in a PARA node."

This distinction is necessary because an element that may contain text is often able to contain embedded elements as well. When an embedded element is placed in the middle of a text string, then there are three nodes in the paragraph. The first represents the text before the embedded element, the second represents the sub-element itself, and the last represents the remaining text.

All nodes except one are attached to a another node, just as smaller branches of a tree are attached to major branches. Naturally, the structure this creates is called a **tree** structure. A single node in the structure sits at the '**root**' of the tree. This node does not represent the root element of the XML document, though it does directly this node, as other nodes may also be present that represent surrounding comments and processing instructions. Under normal circumstances, the XSLT processor works through the source document, in turn making each node the current node in what is termed a '**tree-walking**' process:

At any point, the next step to be taken is determined using a simple algorithm. First, if the current node has children, the first child is chosen, as in step 1 in the diagram above (also steps 2 and 5). Otherwise, if the current node has following siblings then the next sibling is chosen, as in step 3. Otherwise, the following sibling of the nearest ancestor with following siblings is chosen, as in step 4. If no such ancestor exists, then the process is complete, as in step 6. This is, of course, equivalent to stating that a template is chosen when the start-tag of an element is encountered while reading the source document in a simple linear fashion.

It is important to understand that the template is not fully processed until the accompanying end-tag has also been encountered. This means that several templates may be 'open' at the same time.

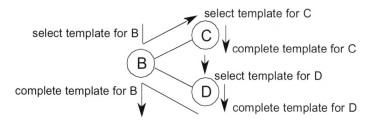

Consider the following example:

```
<chapter>
  <title>The Title</title>
  <para>A paragraph.</para>
  <para>Another paragraph.</para>
</chapter>
```

To process this sample, three templates may be needed; one for the Chapter element, one for the Title element, and one for the Paragraph elements:

```
<template match="chapter">...</template>

<template match="title">...</template>

<template match="para">...</template>
```

The first of these templates will be called when the processor reaches the Chapter element, but will not be complete until after the other templates have been called and processed.

Processing child elements

The processing of child elements is not automatic. It needs to be specified explicitly within a template, using the **Apply Templates** element. This is so named because it is used to indicate that appropriate templates should be applied to each of the child elements. In its simplest form, this element is an empty element. It acts as a place-holder, indicating the point where the processor should process child elements and output their content:

```
<template match="chapter">
  <apply-templates/>
</template>

<template match="title">
  <apply-templates/>
</template>

<template match="para">
  <apply-templates/>
</template>
```

Note that this instruction is added even to the elements that do not contain other elements. These are needed to process the text content of the elements.

Processing text

When an element directly contains text, the text is processed as a child of the element. This means that there must be a template to process text nodes. As this is such a common requirement, there is an implied template for this purpose built into every XSLT processor. Normally, it need not be entered explicitly into the stylesheet, but if present it would take the following form (the Value Of element is explained below):

```
<template match="text()|@*">
  <value-of select="."/>
</template>
```

Note that text nodes are represented by the 'text()' keyword, and that this template also processes all attributes, which are represented by '@*'.

The only reason to create this template would be to change the default behaviour (which is simply to output the characters).

Hiding content

The fact that it is necessary to include the Apply Templates element in a template in order to process the children of that element means that excluding the content of a specific element can be achieved simply by creating a template for it that does not contain this element. In the following example, even though there is a normal template for paragraph processing, this template is not triggered within Comment elements, because the template for the Comment element does not contain the Apply Templates element:

```
<comment><para>...</para><para>...</para></comment>

<template match="comment"></template>
```

```
<template match="para"><apply-templates/></template>
```

As text is only presented when the implied template for processing text nodes is called, omitting the Apply Templates element in the template for an element that contain text means that the text will not appear (but, as the example below shows, it is often advisable to include explanatory comments in templates):

```
<secret>This is secret text, do not show</secret>
```

```
<template match="secret">
  <!-- HIDE IT -->
</template>
```

Default child processing

When an element in the source document does not require specific processing or styling, no template needs to be created for it. The problem that arises is that this element may possibly contain other elements, for which templates exist. It would appear that these embedded elements would not be reached in the tree-walking process, as there is no Apply Templates element in the stylesheet that will trigger them. Consider the following example, where there appears to be no template to trigger the paragraph templates:

```
<book>
   <intro>
     <para>Embedded paragraph.</para>
     <para>Second embedded paragraph.</para>
   </intro>
   ...
</book>
```

```
<template match="book"><apply-templates/></template>

<!-- MISSING TEMPLATE FOR INTRO -->

<template match="para"><apply-templates/></template>
```

However, the paragraphs in this example will in fact be selected and processed as normal, because there is an implied template for element nodes that is triggered when there is no explicitly defined template. It can be made explicit, using the template shown below. This template matches any element, which is specified using the '*' symbol in the Match attribute, as well as the root node of the document ('/'):

```
<template match="*|/"><apply-templates/></template>
```

But there would only be a reason to do this if the default behaviour needed to be changed. For example, to prevent the display of elements that are normally formatted, when they appear within an element not recognized by the stylesheet, the following would be appropriate:

```
<template match="*|/"><!-- NO SHOW --></template>
```

Selective and repeated processing

In some cases, it is desirable to suppress the processing of most child elements but to ensure that child elements of a specific type, or types, *are* processed. The **Select** attribute can be used to indicate which children to process. In the following example, only the Title elements within the Chapter elements are processed (all others are ignored):

```
<template match="chapter">
  <apply-templates select="title"/>
</template>
```

There is no constraint that states that the Apply Templates element can occur only once within the Template element. It may be repeated. One reason to do this would be to ensure that the child elements are processed in a particular order, or processed more than once. In the example below, the title would be output before the paragraphs, even if it were not the first element within the chapter:

```
<template match="chapter">
  <apply-templates select="title"/>
  <apply-templates select="para"/>
</template>
```

In the following example, the title is output twice; the first time explicitly and the second time as part of general child processing:

```
<template match="chapter">
  <apply-templates select="title"/>
  <apply-templates/> <!-- ALSO PROCESSES TITLE -->
</template>
```

Note that the elements selected do not have to be children of the current element. Chapter 11 explains how this feature can be employed to reuse information from elsewhere in a document.

Prefixes and suffixes

The Apply Templates element actually defines the barrier between the part of the template that is processed before the content of the child elements and the part that is processed afterwards. In the following example, the only things that appear around the Apply Templates element are XML comments (which are not processed):

```
<template match="chapter">
  <!-- BEFORE CONTENT OF CHAPTER -->
  <apply-templates/>
  <!-- AFTER CONTENT OF CHAPTER -->
</template>
```

Entering text at these positions, however, specifies prefix and suffix text to appear around the content. The first example below adds a prefix to the content of the Note element, and the second encloses a quote in quotation marks:

```
<template match="note">NOTE:<apply-templates/></template>

<template match="quote">"<apply-templates/>"</template>
```

Such text may be enclosed in the **Text** element. In some cases, this element has no effect on the outcome, but it can be used to control more carefully what whitespace appears in the output and it has other benefits that are explained later:

```
<template match="note">
  <text>NOTE:</text><apply-templates/>
</template>
```

Tag replacement

The main purpose of XSLT is to specify how to convert an XML document into another XML document. In the simplest case, this could mean just replacing one set of tags with another. The start-tag and end-tag of the element that triggers the template are automatically discarded. Replacement tags can be included in the Template element, surrounding the Apply Templates element. The following example transforms the element 'title' into another one called 'ttl':

Note that the new tags may conform to the element set defined in the XSL standard. Other styling options include outputting to HTML format. As HTML is a well-known standard, it will be used in most of the examples in this chapter, and throughout the book.

Adding output elements to the template can be done in two very different ways, each having its own benefits and weaknesses. First, it is possible simply to add the output elements to the content of the template (though namespaces become very important when this approach is taken). The Namespaces standard is used to distinguish XSLT elements from output elements:

```
<xsl:template match="title">
  <H1><xsl:apply-templates/></H1>
</xsl:template>
```

Complex templates are at least relatively easy to read and understand with this approach:

```
<xsl:template match="book">
  <HTML>
    <HEAD><TITLE>The Title</TITLE></HEAD>
    <BODY>
      <xsl:apply-templates/>
    </BODY>
  </HTML>
</xsl:template>
```

When using a guided XML authoring package, a DTD must be created that contains both sets of elements.

Alternatively, XSLT includes an element called **Element** for this purpose. It identifies the output element using the **Name** attribute:

```
<title>This is a title</title>
```

```
<template match="title">
  <element name="H1"><apply-templates/></element>
</template>
```

```
<H1>This is a title</H1>
```

This approach avoids the namespaces issue and makes DTD-guided authoring more practical, but it makes the templates more verbose and more difficult to interpret:

```
<template match="book">
  <element name="HTML">
    <element name="HEAD">
      <element name="TITLE">The Title</element>
    </element>
    <element name="BODY">
      <apply-templates/>
    </element>
  </element>
</template>
```

The earlier, equivalent example is much clearer, even with the namespace prefixes on the XSLT elements (and this approach will be used in examples throughout the rest of this book).

Values of elements and attributes

Sometimes it is useful to be able to access the content of an element as a string, regardless of whether the element contains sub-elements or not. Instead of activating templates on the content of the current element, the content can be converted to a string and inserted into the specified output using the **Value Of** element. This element has a **Select** attribute, which in the simplest case is used to select the current element (although more advanced options are introduced later). The value '.' refers to the current element. Embedded element markup is ignored:

```
<para>All the <emph>text</emph> here is the value</para>

<value-of select="."/>


    All the text here is the value
```

This element can also be used to present the value of an attribute. Attribute names are distinguished from element names using the '@' symbol; so '@type' would be the name of an attribute called 'type'. An attribute name can be used in the Select attribute, in order to display its value:

```
<para type="secret">This is a secret.</para>

<xsl:template match="para">
  <P><xsl:text>[TYPE: <xsl:value-of select="@type"/>]
    </xsl:text>
    <xsl:apply-templates/>
  </P>
</xsl:template>


    <P>[TYPE: secret] This is a secret.</P>
```

Alternatively, the value of a sub-element can be 'dragged up' and inserted into the template. This is an interestingly different approach to selecting specific content for formatting, which does not require other templates to be present to process the content of the sub-elements. The name of the child element is simply entered in the Select attribute:

```
<name>
  <firstName>John</firstName>
  <lastName>Smith</lastName>
</name>

<template match="name">
  First: <value-of select="firstName"/>
  Last: <value-of select="lastName"/>
</template>
```

Later chapters show how the Select attribute can take other values that allow information to be copied from elsewhere in a document.

Breaking well-formed constraints

By default, the XSLT processor must output a well-formed XML document. This
is not a serious constraint, but in fact the reality is that the stylesheet itself, including the mixture of XSLT elements and output elements, must be well-formed too.
This is a more serious problem. For example, a list of alternating names and telephone numbers may need to be converted into a number of paragraphs, each containing a name and following number:

```
<name>J Smith</name>
<number>123</number>
<name>P Jones</name>
<number>321</number>
```

The obvious way to do this is to output a new Paragraph element at the start of each
name and end the paragraph after the following number, but this would make the
stylesheet itself invalid because the Paragraph element would then start in one
Template element and ends in another, crossing other element boundaries:

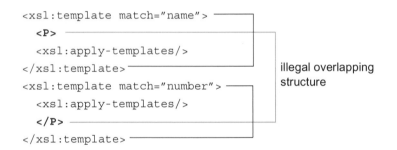

Note that it is also not possible to overcome this limitation by 'hiding' the markup
with the use of character entity references or normal entity references. The following does not work because the '<' references are output in this form, not as
actual characters, and so no application, not even a Web browser, will ever 'see' it
as a markup delimiter (and detect the element):

```
<xsl:template match="name">
  &lt;P&gt;    <!-- DOES NOT WORK -->
  <xsl:apply-templates/>
</xsl:template>
```

```
<xsl:template match="number">
  <xsl:text> </xsl:text>
  <xsl:apply-templates/>
  &lt;/P&gt;    <!-- DOES NOT WORK -->
</xsl:template>
```

```
&lt;P&gt;J Smith 123&lt;/P&gt;
&lt;P&gt;P Jones 321&lt;/P&gt;
```

However, this *is* a good way to demonstrate XML or HTML markup in a Web page. The example above would appear to the audience as follows:

```
<P>J Smith 123</P><P>P Jones 321</P>
```

Neither would it help to use CDATA sections, as in the following example. Again, the processor would either preserve the CDATA section in the output file, or convert the characters into references:

```
<xsl:template match="number">
  <xsl:apply-templates/>
  <![CDATA[</P>]]>    <!-- DOES NOT WORK -->
</xsl:template>
```

However, this problem can be overcome by using the **Disable Output Escaping** attribute, and setting its value to 'yes'. This attribute can be applied to the Text element and the Value Of element, and ensures that entity references are replaced by the characters they represent in the output file, even though the output file may then break XML well-formed rules:

```
<xsl:template match="name">
  <xsl:text disable-output-escaping="yes">
  &lt;P&gt;
  </xsl:text>
  <xsl:apply-templates/>
</xsl:template>

<xsl:template match="Number">
  <xsl:text> </xsl:text>
  <xsl:apply-templates/>
  <xsl:text disable-output-escaping="yes">
  &lt;/P&gt;
  </xsl:text>
</xsl:template>
```

```
<P>J Smith 123</P><P>P Jones 321</P>
```

These problems can be overcome in a similar but more efficient way if the XSLT processor supports the text ouput mode discussed later (see Chapter 14).

XSL format output

The XSLT standard was developed primarily to support the XSL formatting language (see Chapter 17 for details). In this case, it is necessary to create a file that contains formatting instructions, and the output must be an XML document that contains elements and attributes that hold this formatting information. The **Formatting Objects** namespace defines these elements and attributes. In the specification, and in all the examples in this book, the elements have a namespace prefix of '**fo**' (formatting object) to distinguish them from XSLT elements. For example, to format a Note element as a bold paragraph block, the 'block' element is required, with a 'font-weight' attribute that indicates bold styling:

```
<xsl:template match="note">
  <fo:block font-weight="bold">
  <xsl:apply-templates/>
  </fo:block>
</xsl:template>
```

This template would match the following XML document fragment:

```
<note>This is a note</note>
```

The output from the XSL processor, when encountering this fragment, would be:

```
<fo:block font-weight="bold">This is a note</fo:block>
```

It is interesting to note that this output, while it conforms to the requirements needed to qualify as well-formed XML, can hardly be described as adhering to the usual intent of XML markup to identify content rather than format. This does not matter so long as it is clear that the file produced is only going to be read by a formatting application and then be discarded.

XML transformation output

The XSLT processor does not have to produce an XML document that conforms to the Formatting Object namespace, or to any other formatting language. The output can instead be another XML document. The pattern-matching and resequencing capabilities described in later chapters can be used to manipulate the document into other forms, perhaps omitting or repositioning information. In the following source document, the name precedes the telephone number:

```
<employee>
  <name>J Smith</name>
  <number>123</number>
</employee>
```

A single template can rearrange the embedded elements and give the elements new names:

```
<xsl:template match="employee">
  <PERSON>
  <NUM><xsl:apply-templates select="number"/></NUM>
  <NM><xsl:apply-templates select="name"/></NM>
  </PERSON>
</xsl:template>
```

The result would be as follows:

```
<PERSON><NUM>123</NUM><NM>J Smith</NM></PERSON>
```

In this context, the name 'stylesheet' is a little misleading, as no actual styling is involved in the process. In fact, the name of the standard itself is equally misleading, as it incorrectly implies that XSLT can only be used to transform documents into the XSL format, when it can do so much more.

4. Stylesheets

An XSLT stylesheet contains instructions that an XSLT processor uses to transform an XML document into another format. Typical stylesheets consist of little more than a set of templates. However, there are a number of other instructions a stylesheet can hold that influence the way that source documents are converted into output documents. Also, stylesheets can be linked to XML documents in a number of different ways and may be constructed from instructions in a number of separate data files.

Using stylesheets

Assuming the existence of a stylesheet that is applicable to a particular source XML document, a mechanism is needed to indicate that this stylesheet is to be used to process the document. This can be done in a number of different ways, each with its own strengths and weaknesses.

Embedded stylesheets

Stylesheets can be embedded within the documents to process. This can be done because both the XSLT stylesheet and the document containing it are XML structures.

A later section describes how this approach works in detail. The main problem with the approach is that the same embedded stylesheet may be replicated across a large number of similar documents, which is inefficient and makes maintenance very difficult.

Referenced stylesheets

It is more common practice for a document to include a reference to the stylesheet. This reference is detected by the XSLT processor. The stylesheet is accessed and interpreted, then applied to the content of the document. In this way, the same stylesheet can be easily applied to a number of XML documents.

This is done using an XML processing instruction, with the name 'xml-stylesheet', a **Type** parameter that indicates the stylesheet language in use ('text/xml'), and a parameter holding a URL pointer to the stylesheet called **Href**:

```
<?xml-stylesheet type="text/xml"
                 href="styles/format1.xsl"?>
<book>...</book>
```

The obvious remaining weakness of this (and the previous) approach is that it is necessary to edit the XML declaration when a different stylesheet is to be applied to the document.

Unlinked stylesheets

Another possible approach is to pass the document and the stylesheet to the processor separately. This approach avoids any issues with applying different stylesheets at different times:

Using a command-line interface, the following example would be typical. It also includes the name of the file that the processor should create for the output:

```
C:\xsl> XSLProcessor MyStylesheet.XSL MyDoc.XML MyDoc.HTM
```

The Stylesheet element

An XSLT stylesheet is an XML document that conforms to the XSLT DTD. This means that common XML tools such as editors and parsers can be exploited to develop and validate stylesheets.

The root element of a stylesheet document is the **Stylesheet** element:

```
<stylesheet>
   ...
</stylesheet>
```

However, to emphasize the fact that a stylesheet can be used to simply transform one XML document structure into another XML document structure, an alternative element called **Transform** may be used instead. These two elements are completely interchangeable, and take the same attributes:

```
<transform>
   ...
</transform>
```

XSLT version number

Every stylesheet must include information on which version of XSLT the stylesheet conforms to. At present, only version '1.0' exists. The version number *should* appear in the **Version** attribute, but note that in practice some XSLT processors will accept the omission of this attribute and assume a default value of '1.0' when it is missing:

```
<stylesheet version="1.0"
           ...>
   ...
</stylesheet>
```

The specification includes a mechanism that allows an XSLT processor to work with stylesheets that include features it does not understand. A processor written to support the '1.0' specification would, if asked to interpret a stylesheet with a version attribute value of '1.1' or '2.0', ignore any element directly embedded within the Stylesheet element that it does not recognize, and it would also ignore any unknown attributes on remaining elements:

```
<stylesheet version="1.3" ...>
   ...
   <ignored-feature>...</ignored-feature>
   <template ignored-feature="...">...</template>
   ...
</stylesheet>
```

Namespace declarations

An XSLT stylesheet document may contain elements that do not belong to the XSLT DTD. The reason for this is to allow elements to be included as templates for the tags to be generated on output. The problem of how to mix elements from different DTDs in the same document has been addressed by a separate standard called **Namespaces in XML** (see Chapter 15). Each set of elements is a '**namespace**', identified by a URL. The namespace for XSLT is identified by the URL 'http://www.w3.org/1999/XSL/Transform'. An XSLT processor is not expected to follow this link. It is simply a unique, universally known identifying string. In principle, this identifier should be added as a prefix to each element from this namespace, but this would be both unwieldy and invalid. The namespaces standard therefore allows the URL to be mapped to a shorter, legal substitute string.

An attribute named '**xmlns:...**' is used to identify the namespace URL and map it to a substitute string. The value of the attribute is the URL. The rest of the attribute name is the substitute name. The example below identifies the Stylesheet element as belonging to the XSLT namespace, and the attribute declares the prefix string to be 'X'. The 'X' prefix must therefore appear on all the XSLT elements, including the Stylesheet element itself:

```
<X:stylesheet
      xmlns:X="http://www/w3/org/1999/XSL/Transform" ...>
   ...
</X:stylesheet>
```

The namespaces standard includes the concept of a default namespace. Any element with no prefix is deemed to belong to the default namespace. The attribute name '**xmlns**' identifies the default:

```
<stylesheet xmlns="http://www/w3/org/1999/XSL/Transform" >
   ...
</stylesheet>
```

Of course, it is not possible for two namespaces in the same document to both be the default namespace. The stylesheet author is therefore left with the choice of whether to use the default for XSLT elements or for output elements. For the benefit of clarity, examples of XSLT elements in this book use the default namespace except when output elements also appear in the example. The prefix 'xsl:' is used when this happens:

```
<xsl:template>
  <P><!-- OUTPUT ELEMENT --></P>
</xsl:template>
```

Fragmented stylesheets

The term 'stylesheet' implies a continuous 'sheet', represented by a single data file containing the Stylesheet or Transform element, and all the templates and other instructions. Indeed, this will often be the case, particularly for simple stylesheets. However, it is possible for a stylesheet to be pulled apart and divided into a number of separate data files. One reason for doing this is to make a huge stylesheet easier to manage and edit. A much better reason, though, is to make it possible to share parts of a stylesheet with other stylesheets. For example, an organization may create three stylesheets to format a series of books in three different ways (for different audiences or publishing media) yet discover that some typical components (such as tables, lists, and possibly the preamble) are to be styled in the same way in all three circumstances. It makes sense to extract these common components into separate files in order to avoid unnecessary repetition, and to simplify any updates to the formatting of these items.

XSLT includes two similar features to support this concept. Files containing templates and other instructions can be either 'included' or 'imported' into a stylesheet. These terms are not interchangeable, as in this context they have subtly different meanings.

Including external definitions

The definitions within one stylesheet can be referenced and used within another stylesheet using the **Include** element. The **Href** attribute is used to identify the stylesheet to include, and contains a URL:

```
<include href="/D:/xsl/tables.xsl" />
```

The URL may be relative, in which case the base location is the location of the current stylesheet. For example, if the remote file is in the same directory as the calling stylesheet, only the file name is needed:

```
<include href="tables.xsl" />
```

The Include element is only allowed directly within the Stylesheet or Transform element. Conceptually, this element is replaced by the contents of the stylesheet referenced. The templates inserted from a remote file are then treated exactly the same as templates originating within the current stylesheet.

When this feature is used extensively and a number of files are involved, care must be taken to avoid the possibility that the same file will be included more than once as this would introduce duplicate templates. In addition, it is not legal for a file to directly, or indirectly, include itself.

Importing external definitions

Material from another stylesheet can also be 'imported'. Importing is a subtle variant of including material, as described above. The mechanism is identical, except that the element name is **Import**. It uses the **Href** attribute in the same way:

```
<import href="tables.xsl" />
```

However, the Import element must, if present, appear before all other elements within the Stylesheet or Transform element:

```
<stylesheet ...>
  <import .../>
  <import .../>
  ...
</stylesheet>
```

The XSLT processor needs to move any Import elements it may find in the document being included to a position just after the native ones:

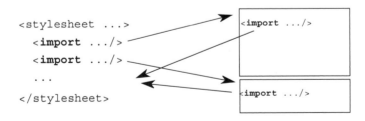

When imported templates or other instructions conflict with native instructions, the concept of 'importance' is used to resolve these conflicts. The exact meaning of importance levels varies, depending on the instruction. For Template elements, when the same template occurs in two or more files, only the one in the file with the highest importance is considered; all the others are ignored. This means that, after importing a set of templates, some of these templates can be overridden in the 'main' stylesheet. However, overriding of imported templates can be done in a more subtle way than simply replacing the imported template. Instead, the imported template can be 'extended'. The **Apply Imports** element is used to invoke the masked template:

```
<para>This is a paragraph.</para>


<!-- IMPORTED TEMPLATE -->
<xsl:template match="para">
  <P><apply-templates/></P>
</xsl:template>

<!-- OVERRIDE TEMPLATE -->
<xsl:template match="para">
  <DIV CLASS="P"><xsl:apply-imports/></DIV>
</xsl:template>


<DIV CLASS="P"><P>This is a paragraph.</P></DIV>
```

In complex cases, where imported documents also contain Import elements, the importance is calculated as follows, with (1) being the highest priority and (5) being the lowest. The priority increases as each file is imported, with the first one having the lowest priority of all:

Unlike inclusions, there is no issue with importing the same file twice. The following example is acceptable, though the lower-priority version will be ignored (although a stylesheet still cannot import itself):

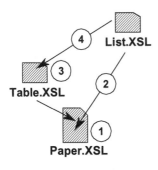

Embedded stylesheets

The opposite of splitting separate stylesheets into multiple units is the concept of embedding an entire stylesheet within an XML document to be formatted. The Stylesheet (or Transform) element can be embedded within other XML structures, allowing a document to contain the stylesheet that is to be applied to it.

This may not be a popular technique, as in practice it is usual for a single stylesheet to be applicable to many documents, and it would not be efficient for each document to contain copies of the same stylesheet. However, a document and an applicable stylesheet could be packaged for delivery to a publishing system using this technique.

It is not sufficient simply to embed a Stylesheet element in a larger document, because the XSLT processor still needs to be able to find it. When this is done using a stylesheet processing instruction, the URL in the Href parameter needs to point to the Stylesheet element. Using HTML linking conventions, a link can be made to an embedded element instead of a remote data file by giving the element a unique name. The '#' symbol precedes the name:

```
<?xml-stylesheet type="text/xml" href="#myStylesheet" ?>
<book>
   . . .
</book>
```

The Stylesheet element has an **Id** attribute to hold the unique element name. In theory, this will only be recognized as an element identifier if it is defined as such in an XML DTD, but in practice some software will assume it is anyway:

```
<?xml-stylesheet type="text/xml" href="#myStylesheet"?>
<!DOCTYPE book SYSTEM="..."> <!-- INCLUDES ID DEF -->
<book>
   ...
   <xsl:stylesheet xmlns:xsl="..."
                   version="1.0"
                   id="myStylesheet" >
   ...
   </xsl:stylesheet>
   ...
</book>
```

In most circumstances, the stylesheet itself should not be considered to be part of the formatted document, as its purpose is complete once the formatting has been applied to the rest of the document. Yet it is part of the document, and by default will be formatted along with the rest. This can easily be avoided, just by creating a template for the Stylesheet element that does not include the Apply Templates element:

```
<xsl:template match="xsl:stylesheet">
     <!-- SUPPRESS STYLESHEET -->
</xsl:template>
```

Stylesheet contents

Elements that may be inserted directly into the Stylesheet element are known as **'top-level'** elements. These elements may not be used anywhere else, and other XSLT elements may not be inserted at this location.

The Template, Import and Include elements have already been discussed. Other top-level elements are used to specify space preservation rules for output elements, specify the output format, and define linking schemes, the format of decimal numbers, sets of attributes for use in templates, variables and parameters:

```
<stylesheet ...>
    <import...>
    <include...>
    <strip-space...>
    <preserve-space...>
    <output...>
    <key...>
    <decimal-format...>
    <attribute-set...>
    <variable...>
    <param...>
    <namespace-alias...>
    ...
    ...
</stylesheet>
```

These elements can repeat, and can appear in any order (apart from the Import element described above). Most of these instructions are explained in later chapters; others are introduced or fully described below.

Output formats

Output from an XSLT processor can be customized in a number of ways. The **Output** element is an empty element, but has attributes that specify various requirements for formatting of the output:

```
<output ... />
```

The **Method** attribute controls fundamental formatting characteristics that are required for XML, HTML and text output. It holds the value '**xml**', '**html**' or '**text**' accordingly. The implications of these settings are described in later chapters. By default, the setting is 'xml', except when an HTML document is recognized by its root element name ('<HTML>'). The **Version** attribute supports this feature and is used, for example, to indicate which version of HTML to output:

```
<output ... method="html" version="3.2" />
```

The **Encoding** attribute specifies the character set to use for output, such as 'UTF-8' (the default) or 'ISO-8859-1' (the usual set used on the Web):

```
<output ... encoding="ISO-8859-1" />
```

The **Omit XML Declaration** attribute specifies whether or not an XML declaration is to be included in the output document and it has the value 'yes' or 'no'. When set to 'no', the declaration is created:

```
<output ... omit-xml-declaration="yes" />

   <book>...</book>

<output ... omit-xml-declaration="no" />

   <?xml ...?>
   <book>...</book>
```

When this attribute is set to 'no' (the declaration is to be created), the **Standalone** attribute can be used to specify whether or not the output document is a standalone XML document (ie, one that does not require the DTD for accurate interpretation). It also takes a value of 'yes' or 'no'. If the Encoding attribute is used, its content will also be copied into the XML declaration:

```
<output ... omit-xml-declaration="no"
          standalone="yes" encoding="ISO-8859-1" />
```

```
<?xml version="1.0" encoding="ISO-8859-1"
                    standalone="yes" ?>
```

The **Doctype System** attribute specifies that the output document should have an XML document type declaration, with a system identifier given in this attribute:

```
<output ... doctype-system="dtds/book.dtd" />
```

```
<!DOCTYPE book SYSTEM="dtds/book.dtd" >
<book>...</book>
```

The **Doctype Public** attribute specifies the public identifier to supply. If used, the Doctype System attribute must be given as well, in order to conform to XML rules, even if it only contains an empy string:

```
<output ... doctype-public="myBookDef" doctype-system=""/>
```

```
<!DOCTYPE book PUBLIC="myBookDef" "" >
<book>...</book>
```

The **Indent** attribute can be used to format XML output, by indenting embedded element structures. It takes the value 'yes' or 'no' (the default). When set to 'yes', whitespace is added to make the document easier to read:

```
<output ... indent="yes" />
```

```
<book>
  <title>The Book Title</title>
  <chapter>
    <title>The Chapter Title</title>
    <para>A paragraph.</para>
  </chapter>
</book>
```

There is a danger with this kind of formatting. For elements that have mixed content, unwanted space may be added, as in the following example:

```
<para>Do
  <emph>NOT</emph>
 add whitespace.</para>
```

Do **NOT** add whitespace.

The text content of selected elements can be output as character data sections (CDATA sections), '<![CDATA[...]]>'. These structures are used to avoid the need for '<', '&' (and other entity references) to represent significant markup characters when they appear in the text. The **Cdata Section Elements** attribute holds the names of the output elements. For example:

```
<software>if (6 &lt; 9) then ...</software>
```

```
<xsl:output cdata-section-elements="code ... ..." />
...
<xsl:template match="software">
  <code><xsl:apply-templates/></code>
</xsl:template>
```

```
<code><![CDATA[if (6 < 9) then ...]]></code>
```

If the text happens to contain the string '`]]>`', then this must be broken into two parts to avoid indication of an early end to the CDATA section. Two CDATA sections are created, with the '`]]`' sequence between them and the '`>`' in the second:

```
<![CDATA[ ... ]]>]]<![CDATA[> ...]]>
```

Finally, the **Media Type** attribute specifies the type of data output. For XML, this would be '**text/xml**' or '**text/application**'. Use of this attribute has no effect on the output document itself, and it is only of interest if the XSLT processor is able to transmit the output data directly over a network that uses the MIME scheme for indicating the data type of information transferred, such as over the Internet:

```
<output ... media-type="text/xml" />
```

With HTML documents, it has more widespread application, as described later.

Note that the attributes from multiple Output elements from different parts of a stylesheet that have been imported are merged, with the highest-importance definitions for each attribute used (except for the CDATA Section Elements attribute, which combines values from all definitions).

Space preservation

The XML standard defines the term '**whitespace**' to represent the invisible characters used to format text in a text file. These characters include the space character, the tab character, and the line-feed and carriage-return control characters (used to start a new line in the text file).

Sometimes, whitespace characters are included in an XML document only to make the markup easier to read. The following two examples are considered to be equivalent in terms of the information they contain, but the second is more legible:

```
<chapter><title>The Chapter Title</title><para>A para-
graph.</para></chapter>
```

```
<chapter>
  <title>The Chapter Title</title>
  <para>A paragraph.</para>
</chapter>
```

In both examples, the Chapter element appears to contain two children, namely the Title element and the Para element. However, the way that the second fragment is arranged means that whitespace characters appear between the child elements to create the new lines and indentations:

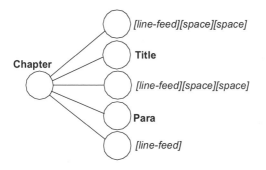

Note that even if the indents were to be removed, the same number of child nodes would be present, as there would still be a text node for each line-feed:

```
<chapter>[LF]
<title>The Chapter Title</title>[LF]
<para>A paragraph.</para>[LF]
</chapter>
```

By default, an XSLT processor does *not* treat text nodes that contain only whitespace characters differently from other nodes. It would retain all five child nodes of the Chapter element in the example above. The fact that the two XML fragments shown above are considered identical means that it should not matter that the XSLT processor will preserve them.

However, it is possible to instruct the processor to remove text nodes that only contain whitespace characters. The **Strip Space** element is used to indicate which elements to strip such text from. If the **Elements** attribute contains just '*', this (as usual) indicates that all elements are to be stripped of insignificant whitespace:

```
<strip-space elements="*" />
```

This is particularly useful when outputting a text file, rather than a new XML document, as many text file formats treat all whitespace as significant. In such circumstances, it is necessary to remove all whitespace that occurred only to make the source file easier to read.

Even when outputting XML structures, there are occasions when it is useful to remove whitespace, if only to reduce the size of the file.

Stripping whitespace from elements that have mixed content (a mixture of elements and text) can be dangerous. Consider the following example:

```
<para>Another <emph>great</emph> <name>ACME</name>
product</para>
```

In this example, there is a whitespace-only text node between the emphasized word and the company name. Stripping this space would cause these terms to be merged on output:

Another **great***ACME* product

Even when the Strip Space elements have been defined as described above, it is possible to make exceptions for such cases. The **Preserve Space** element also uses an **Elements** attribute to list elements that are not to be trimmed in this way:

```
<preserve-space elements="para" />
```

Recall that by default all elements are preserved, and so the following rule is implied:

```
<preserve-space elements="*" />
```

When both the Strip Space and Preserve Space elements are used, any conflicts are resolved using the same precedence rules as for template selections. For example, when one element contains '*' and the other contains an element name, the element name is more explicit than '*' and so overrules the general case. The Elements attribute is allowed to contain '*', or a space-separated list of element names (which can be qualified with a namespace, such as 'html:pre html:code').

Stylesheet whitespace

Spaces are often used in stylesheets to make them easier to read, just as they are in other XML documents (as described above). In this case, all insignificant whitespace is removed by the XSLT processor automatically. The two examples below would produce identical output:

```
<xsl:stylesheet match="para"><P><xsl:apply-templates/></
P></xsl:stylesheet>
```

```
<xsl:stylesheet match="para">
<P>
  <xsl:apply-templates/>
</P>
</xsl:stylesheet>
```

This is why the **Text** element is so important. It preserves whitespace that would otherwise be removed.

5. HTML output

Introducing the topic of HTML at such an early point in a book on XSLT and XSL (a competing formatting language) may seem premature. There should, over time, appear a number of typesetting systems, DTP packages and screen rendering browsers that can format data held in XSL format; and when this happens, XSLT and XSL will be used together to provide a complete formatting solution. But in the meantime, the most popular formatting language in use on the Web happens to be HTML. XSLT is currently most often employed to transform XML documents into HTML documents, for presentation in current-generation Web browsers. This chapter therefore covers the issues involved in outputting HTML. Readers not intending to use XSLT to format XML documents into HTML can safely ignore this chapter (though Chapter 18 provides an overview that may assist with understanding the examples in later chapters).

Pseudo HTML output

The HTML data format used to tag Web pages for presentation in browsers is, like XML, based on SGML. For this reason, there is enough similarity between HTML documents and well-formed XML documents that is is possible to output an XML file that will be accepted as an HTML document by existing Web browsers. The format of start-tags, end-tags, attributes and entity references are essentially the same. For example, the HTML tag '<P>' (Paragraph) can also be considered a valid XML tag. The following example replaces a Note element with HTML P (Paragraph) and B (Bold) elements:

```
<xsl:template match="note">
  <P CLASS="notepara1"><B> <xsl:apply-templates/></B></P>
</xsl:template>
```

It is important to note here that none of the markup minimization techniques allowed in HTML documents are permitted in XML. But this is only a minor inconvenience. For example, the following template is not legal for two reasons; the Paragraph end-tag is missing, and the attribute value is not quoted. The style-sheet itself is therefore an invalid XML document instance:

```
<xsl:template match="Note">
  <P CLASS=noteparal><!-- <<< MISSING QUOTES --><B>
    <xsl:apply-templates/>
    </B><!-- MISSING END PARA -->
</xsl:template>
```

Much more seriously, there is a discrepancy between HTML and XML formats concerning the format of empty elements. The XML specification allows empty elements to be represented by a single tag, ending with '/>'. HTML does not use this form, but does allow the end-tag to be omitted (and in some cases a browser may even insist on the end-tag being omitted). The next section discusses a clean way to generate true HTML; but that option may not be supported by the chosen XSLT processor, in which case the more primitive techniques described here must be used instead.

In HTML 4.0, the empty elements are:

- AREA (a clickable area of an image)
- BASE (a specified new base 'home' directory)
- BASEFONT (a specified font to use as the default)
- BR (break – start a new line)
- COL (definitions of various attributes for one column of a table)
- FRAME (specification for a single independent region of the browser window)
- HR (horizonal rule – a line across the page)
- IMG (image identifier)
- ISINDEX (query allowed)
- LINK (linked resource – including stylesheets)
- META (meta data)
- PARAM (applet parameter)

Usually, the most commonly needed of these are IMG and BR. Some current browsers object to the '/>' empty element markup, even if a preceding space is inserted, and retained by the XSL processor on output. Using end-tags is preferable, though some XSL processors may automatically reduce tags with no content to the single tag form. It may therefore be necessary to ensure that this does not happen by enclosing a single space within a text element:

```
<xsl:stylesheet match="newline">
  <BR><xsl:text> </xsl:text></BR>
</xsl:stylesheet>
```

Current browsers accept this approach, but in the latter case interpret this as two line-break instructions instead of one.

Where possible, these complications should be avoided using the technique described below.

True HTML output

The previous section outlines a number of issues that are raised when attempting to output an HTML document that conforms to the XML standard. To avoid these problems, the standard includes a mechanism for outputting documents that do not conform to the XML standard. The **Output** element is used to specify another format. Currently, the value of its **Method** attribute must be 'xml' (the default option), 'html' or 'text'. This element must appear directly within the Stylesheet (or Transform) element:

```
<stylesheet ...>
  <output method="html" ... />
  ...
</stylesheet>
```

To specify that the processor should output true HTML data, the value 'html' is used. When the '**html**' value is entered in the **Method** element, HTML tags are recognized and processed intelligently.

Note that the default Method value for the Output element should already be 'html' if the document element to be output is named 'html', 'HTML', 'Html', or some other variant, has no namespace prefix, and is preceded by nothing (or at most by whitespace characters).

HTML output characteristics

Perhaps the most significant change when outputting in HTML mode is that empty elements are reformatted to use HTML conventions. For example, the empty element BR is output as a normal start-tag, and the end-tag is omitted:

```
    ... first line<breakline/>second line ...
```

```
<xsl:template match="breakline">
  <BR/>
</xsl:template>
```

```
    ... first line<BR>second line ...
```

Special markup characters are the same in HTML as in XML and serve the same purpose. In HTML, '&' is used to represent '&', '<' is used to represent '<' and '>' is used to represent '>' wherever usage of the actual character could confuse the browser as it attempts to identify entity references and element tags. However, an HTML document does not use the escape sequences in some special cases, and so the XSL processor must output original characters in these circumstances. Specifically, the content of the SCRIPT and STYLE elements conform to formats other than HTML (typically JavaScript and CSS respectively).

```
<SCRIPT> ...  ( A < B ) ... </SCRIPT>
```

In HTML, an attribute is allowed to contain the '<' character. The entity reference '<' should therefore be transformed to '<':

```
<xsl:template ...>
  <IMG ... ALT="figure showing that 6 &lt; 7"></IMG>
</xsl:template>
```

```
      ... <IMG ... ALT="figure showing 6 < 7"> ...
```

Recognizing HTML elements

Even when HTML mode has been set using the Output element, this mode is only used for elements that have no namespace mapping to a URL. To distinguish HTML elements from XSLT elements, it is therefore usual to map the XSLT elements to a prefix (instead of the HTML elements):

```
<xsl:stylesheet ... xmlns:xsl="...">
  <xsl:template...>
    <HTML>
      <HEAD><TITLE>The Page Title</TITLE></HEAD>
      <xsl:apply-templates/>
    </HTML>
  </xsl:template>
</xsl:stylesheet>
```

There have been a number of HTML versions released since the introduction of this language in 1995. The number of tags differs between versions, with the general trend toward longer lists of allowed tags appearing in later versions. The **Version** attribute specifies the version of HTML to use for the output. A value of '4.0' (the default value) specifies HTML 4.0 output (where other valid options include '3.2' and '2.0'):

```
<output ... version="4.0" />
```

In future, this attribute value may be used to warn an XSLT processor that it is about to process a version of HTML that was released after the program was created, and which it therefore does not understand. In this case, it may warn the user of the problem, or even refuse to process the document.

Elements that are deemed to be HTML elements by their namespace designation (using the default namespace), but are not recognized as elements belonging to the specified version of HTML, are nevertheless treated as HTML elements. But, because they are unknown, they cannot be processed intelligently. The fallback behaviour is to treat such elements as in-line, non-empty elements:

```
<P>This paragaph contains an <UNKNOWN>unknown</UNKNOWN>
element.</P>
```

HTML element tag names are not case-sensitive. A tag in the stylesheet will be recognized as an HTML tag if the name matches, regardless of the case used. The following examples both produce BR elements (without the end-tag):

```
<xsl:template...>
  <BR></BR>broken text<br></br>
  <xsl:apply-templates/>
</xsl:template>
```

```
    ... <BR>broken text<br> ...
```

HTML processing instructions differ slightly from XML processing instructions. The question-mark delimiter is not needed at the end of the tag (the Processing Instruction element is discussed in Chapter 12):

```
<template...>
  <processing-instruction name="SPECIAL">some-
    instruction</processing-instruction>
  <apply-templates/>
</template>
```

```
    ... <?SPECIAL some-instruction> ...
```

When an HTML attribute can have only one value, and the presence or absence of the value acts as a simple switch, the convention is to include only the value in the element start-tag (omitting the attribute name, equals symbol and enclosing quotes). For example, the OL element (ordered list) may take the 'COMPACT' attribute to close up items in the list.

```
<xsl:template...>
  <OL COMPACT="compact"><xsl:apply-templates/></OL>
</xsl:template>
```

```
    <OL COMPACT> ... </OL>
```

DOCTYPE declaration

The HTML file produced can be given a document type declaration by specifying the **Doctype Public** and/or the **Doctype System** attributes:

```
<output ... doctype-system="html4.0.dtd" />
```

```
    <!DOCTYPE HTML SYSTEM "html4.0.dtd">
    <HTML>...</HTML>
```

```
<output ... doctype-public="-//html..."
            doctype-system="html4.0.dtd" />
```

```
    <!DOCTYPE HTML PUBLIC "-//html..." "html4.0.dtd">
    <HTML>...</HTML>
```

Characters

The **Encoding** attribute in the Output element specifies the output character scheme. Its value should be copied to the '**charset**' attribute of a suitable META element in the HEAD element (if the HEAD element has been created):

```
<output ... encoding="ISO-8859-1" media-type="text/html"/>


<HEAD>
  <META http-equiv="Content-Type"
        content="text/html" charset="ISO-8859" >
</HEAD>
...
```

Note that the **Media Type** attribute is also used, to populate the '**content**' attribute.

The HTML format allows for the possible use of entity references for many extended characters. The reference names are taken from sets defined by the ISO, and so are often the same as those defined in XML source documents. For example, 'é' is almost universally used to represent the e-acute character.

6. Contextual formatting

Good design practice exploits the hierarchical nature of an XML document to minimize the number of different elements needed to describe its component parts. It should never be necessary to invent new tags for content that is conceptually similar to existing material, when it can be unambiguously distinguished by its location within the document instead. For example, a Title element may be applied in a number of circumstances: to name a book, each chapter and section within the book, and to provide a heading for tables and legends for pictures. As this approach is common practice in XML documents, effective styling can rarely be achieved simply by assigning a single output style to each element type. The title of a book would normally look very different from the title of a chapter or table. The content of an element should therefore be formatted differently, depending on where that element appears, what it contains, or what attribute values are assigned to it. The stylesheet must be able to distinguish between each usage in order to apply appropriate formatting in each case. This is known as **contextual formatting**.

XML structures

Contextual formatting often involves selecting elements that occur in specific locations within a document's structure. It is therefore necessary to first understand what XML element structures are, and to appreciate the terminology commonly used to describe relationships between parts of an XML document. Note that not all of the concepts described in this section are relevant to contextual templates but are important for later discussions on locating elements for reuse.

An element may contain a number of embedded elements. These are termed **child** elements. These child elements share the same **parent** element. In the following example, the Title element and the Para element are both children of the Chapter element, and it follows that the parent of both these two elements is the Chapter element:

```
<chapter>
  <title>Embedded Title</title>
  <para>Embedded paragraph.</para>
</chapter>
```

In addition, the Title and Para elements in the example above are **sibling** elements, because they share the same parent. Siblings always have a simple sequential order. The first sibling in the example is the Title element as it occurs first in the data stream. The Para element follows the Title element, and it also happens to be the last sibling. The terms **preceding sibling** and **following sibling** are used to describe ordering relationships.

The family tree analogy is taken further, as the term **ancestor** is used to describe any element that contains the one under discussion, no matter how many levels may separate the two. The parent element is also an ancestor element. In the following example, the Para element has three ancestors, including its parent Warning element:

```
<book>
  <chapter>
    <warning>
      <para>Embedded paragraph.</para>
```

Similarly, the term **descendant** is used to describe all embedded elements, including children. In the example above, the Book element has at least three descendants, including its child Chapter element.

Finally, all XML documents must contain a single element that has no parent, as in the Book element above. This is known as the **root** element, as it is similar to the root of a tree (the ultimate source of all the branches).

Expressions

To meet the need to specify contextual relationships between elements and other markup constructs, the value of the **Match** attribute is actually an **expression** (as defined in the XPath specification). The Match attribute in the example below contains a simple expression (explained below):

```
match="warning/para"
```

Expressions are also used in other places in XSLT, but this chapter focuses on their use in the Match attribute, to specify a context for the template.

To be more precise, the Match attribute actually holds a particular type of expression, known as a **pattern**. A pattern is a context specification, against which the current node is compared. Only some parts of the wider expression language are relevant for this need.

Note that, when context is introduced, it is often possible for two or more templates to contain expressions that match the current element. In this case, a mechanism is needed to decide which template has 'priority'. A later section discusses prioritizing templates.

Most of the concepts described below involve analysis of the structure of the XML document within which the element resides, but the expression language syntax is not immediately easy to interpret. Illustrations are therefore used to show the conditions under which a test matches a particular element. The document hierarchy is shown as embedded boxes, with the element names appearing within the respective boxes. An element that will be selected by the expression is shown in a highlighted box, as in the 'X' element in the example below:

Alternative elements

When the same formatting needs to be applied to the content of a number of different elements, it is not necessary to create a separate template for each one. Instead, a pattern can be used that specifies a list of alternatives. The '|' symbol is used for this purpose, and is placed between the element names:

```
match="X | Y | Z"
```

This technique could be used to format names and foreign terms in the same way:

```
match="name | foreign"
```

```
<para>The <foreign>de facto</foreign> stylesheet
language is <name>XSLT</name>.</para>
```

The *de facto* stylesheet language is *XSLT*.

Simple location contexts

Typically, an element that has a significant context is identified simply by its location within the document structure. The name of the parent element, or some other ancestor element, determines the context.

Specific parent

In many cases, it is sufficient to specify what the parent element must be for the template to be applicable. In the following example, an X element is only to be selected when it is directly within a P element:

```
match="P/X"
```

The '/' symbol does not itself indicate that 'X' is the child of 'P'. This symbol is simply used to separate steps in a **location path**. When a particular step consists of only an element name, this is an abbreviation for the explicit statement 'child::X'. The following example is equivalent to the one above:

child::P/child::X

Note that the first occurence of 'child::' above is doubly redundant, as there is no requirement for 'P' to be the child of some other element (for it could be the document's root element).

Using this technique, specific formatting could be applied to paragraphs within a Warning element:

```
<para>A normal paragraph.</para>
<warning>
  <para>Warning paragraph one.</para>
  <para>Warning paragraph two.</para>
</warning>
<para>Another normal paragraph.</para>
```

```
match="warning/para"
```

A normal paragraph.
  WARNING:
  Warning paragraph one.
  Warning paragraph two.
Another normal paragraph.

Specific ancestors

Sometimes, knowledge of the parent of an element is not sufficient. The element containing the parent element may be significant, or an element at an even higher level in the hierarchy. To select an element that is the descendant of specific ancestors, more elements are named in the expression:

```
match="A/P/X"
```

This example makes it more clear that the pattern is read from left to right, and also that the verbose equivalent is in fact *very* verbose in comparison:

```
match="child::A/child::P/child::X"
```

Using this technique, specific formatting could be applied to a warning paragraph that appears within the introduction of a book:

```
<intro>
  <para>An introduction paragraph.</para>
  <warning>
    <para>Introduction Warning.</para>
  </warning>
</intro>
```

```
match="intro/warning/para"
```

An introduction paragraph.

Introduction Warning

Unknown ancestry

When several different elements could appear at a specific level, it would seem necessary to use several patterns, as in the following example, where paragraphs are to be formatted in a distinctive way within warnings, notes and errors, when these constructs appear within the Intro element:

```
match="intro/warning/para"
```

```
match="intro/note/para"
```

```
match="intro/error/para"
```

The need for three patterns can be avoided using a 'wildcard' that represents any element. The previous three expressions can be replaced by a single expression, using the asterisk character, '*', for the wildcard:

```
match="intro/*/para"
```

However, although the wildcard can be used repeatedly in the same pattern, this technique is quite limited because it is still necessary to know exactly how many levels deep the target element is. It would not be possible to identify a target element that appears at any point below another element without a large number of expressions:

```
match="intro/para"
```

```
match="intro/*/para"
```

```
match="intro/*/*/para"
```

```
match="intro/*/*/*/para"
```

To avoid this problem, it is possible to specify an unknown number of intermediate elements (including none). This is done using a double-slash, '//', as in the following example, which replaces the four above:

```
match="intro//para"
```

Advanced context

Context need not depend only on the location of the target element in the document hierarchy. The content of the element itself may need to influence the formatting to be applied. For example, an automatically generated prefix of either 'Warning:' or 'Warnings:' may be needed, depending on whether the Warning element contains a single paragraph or a list of warning items.

Specific children

It is possible to select an element that is the parent of another specific element, by placing the name of the sub-element within square brackets:

```
match="X[C]"
```

The square brackets actually enclose a '**predicate filter**'. A filter consists of a test to be made on the node to which it is attached. In this simple case, the test made is that the 'X' element (the current element) contains the 'C' element as a child.

Specific siblings

Predicate filters can be added to any element named in the pattern. For example, a filter can be added to the parent of the target element. It could be used to determine whether or not another element exists within the parent. It is therefore possible to select an element only when another specified element is present as its sibling. In the following example, the X element matches the pattern only if its parent, the P element, also contains an S element (and note that it does not matter how many times the S element occurs):

```
match="P[S]/X"
```

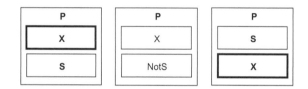

Attribute contexts

It is possible to select elements that have a particular attribute declared, or that have a given value for this attribute. Attribute names are distinguished from element names using an '@' prefix. While 'x' could be an element name, '@x' would be a quite separate attribute name. To specify that a particular attribute must be present, it is necessary to include the attribute name in the predicate filter:

```
match="X[@A]"
```

There is one complication that may arise when a DTD is referenced by the XML document being processed. The DTD defines the attributes which may be used with each element, and in some cases it provides a default value to be used when an explicit value is not provided in the tag. Many parsers are unable to distinguish between explicit and default attribute usage. The second example below would match a test for the presence of the Status attribute when the parser validates the document against the DTD but is unable to distinguish between explicit and defaulted attribute usage:

```
<!ATTLIST para Status (normal|secret) "normal">

<para status="normal">...</para>

<para>...</para> <!-- ALSO A NORMAL PARAGRAPH -->
```

It is perhaps more common for processing to depend on the value of a given attribute value, rather than just the presence of the attribute. To select an element that has a specific attribute value, the value is added between quotes, following an equals symbol. Note that different quotation marks must be used from those that enclose the entire attribute value:

```
match="X[@A='abc']"
```

XML is case-sensitive, and so the value must match exactly. In the following example, the template is activated by secret paragraphs:

```
match="Para[@Status='secret']"
```

Priorities

Only one template can ever be selected by an XSLT processor to format a specific instance of an element. In the expressions shown in previous chapters, there is one template for each element type, but the introduction of context-specific templates means that a number of different templates may be applicable. The following two templates both apply to a Para element. The first template matches paragraphs within the introduction of a book. The second matches paragraphs within a Warning element. It can be imagined that, in some circumstances, there will be a warning within an introduction. In this case, both templates would be applicable:

```
<template match="introduction//para">...</template>
```

```
<template match="warning// para">...</template>
```

When this possibility occurs, it is necessary to specify which of the candidate templates is to be chosen. This is done using the **Priority** attribute:

```
<template ... priority="2">...</template>
```

Priority values

One template is given precedence over another by assigning to it a higher priority value. In the following example, the warning paragraph takes priority over the introduction paragraph. The paragraph will therefore look the same in all warnings, regardless of whether or not they are also in the introduction section of the document:

```
<template match="introduction//para" priority="1">...

<template match="warning//para" priority=" 2">...
```

It does not matter where these two templates appear within the stylesheet, or which appears first.

Default values

It is not always necessary to use the Priority attribute. When it is not included, a default priority value is assumed. But the default value varies, depending on the content of the Match attribute.

Simple expressions that refer only to an element name, qualified with a namespace prefix, whether it includes the 'child::' prefix or not, have a default value of '0':

```
<!-- PRIORITY '0' -->
<template match="x:para">...</template>
<!-- PRIORITY '0' -->
<template match="child::x:para">...</template>
```

Other defaults are even less specific, so have values below zero.

An element name with no prefix has a default value of '-0.25'. This means that qualified names are more specific than unqualified names:

```
<!-- PRIORITY '0' -->
<template match="x:para">...</template>

<!-- PRIORITY '-0.25' -->
<template match="para">...</template>
```

Finally, the least specific form of all is a simple node test:

```
<!-- PRIORITY '-0.5' -->

<template match="*">...</template>
```

```
<template match="comment()">...</template>

<template match="text()">...</template>

<template match="processing-instruction()">...</template>

<template match="node()">...</template>
```

There is therefore a distinction between any element ('*'), and any element with a specific namespace qualifier ('abc:*'), which overrides the more general case:

```
<!-- LOWER PRIORITY (-0.5) -->
<template match="*">...</template>

<!-- HIGHER PRIORITY (-0.25) -->
<template match="abc:*">...</template>
```

All other cases default to a value of '0.5', and so a contextual template automatically overrides a simple element-matching template. It is not necessary to introduce the Priority attribute to distinguish between the general and special case in the example below:

```
<!-- LOWER PRIORITY (0) -->
<template match="para">...</template>

<!-- HIGHER PRIORITY (0.5) -->
<template match="warning/para">...</template>
```

However, when there is more than one contextual match, or when some contexts are more important than others, the Priority attribute is needed, and values should start from '1' to ensure that the default cases are overridden.

Conflict resolution

When two or more templates remain applicable (regardless of whether or not the Priority attribute has been used in some or all templates), this may be considered to be an error by the XSLT processor. The processor may report the problem and cease to function; but most will recover and, if they follow the standard, will simply select the template closest to the end of the stylesheet. If a processor that behaves in this latter way is chosen, then the order in which templates are placed in the file becomes a very important stylesheet design consideration:

```
<template match="book//para">...</template>

<!-- MORE SPECIFIC - APPEARS LAST -->
<template match="warning//para">...</template>
```

Finally, it would be a mistake to think that the length of an expression has any effect on default priority values. The two examples below both default to '0.5':

```
<template match="warning//para">...</template>

<template match="book/warning/para[@type='secret']">...
```

7. Expressions in attributes

The XSLT standard refers to a feature called '**attribute value templates**', which is actually a method for using expressions within output element attributes. These expressions are used to generate context-specific values to insert into the attributes. Without this feature, it would often be necessary to use the Element and Attribute elements instead of directly including output elements in the template.

Template markup

Before discussing the various ways in which attribute templates can be of benefit, it is necessary to establish how they are recognized and identify some repercussions of their possible presence.

Curly brackets

When an output element includes an attribute, the attribute is coded according to XML rules. It has a name, and a value enclosed in quotes. The value may be any text string allowed in attributes of the given type, assuming the use of a DTD to validate the output, or (when a DTD is not relevant) it can be any text string at all. The issue here is how to indicate to the XSLT processor that there is an expression embedded within the value:

```
TheAttribute="value ... expression ... value"
```

The expression is delimited using curly brackets. The left curly bracket, '{', begins the template, and the right curly bracket, '}', ends the template. The text between these brackets is intepreted as an expression:

```
="...{expression}..."
```

A single attribute can contain any number of expression templates:

```
="...{expression}...{expression}..."
```

With the curly brackets taking this special role, the obvious question that arises is how to represent these characters within a normal value. For example, the value 'a{b}c' may need to appear in an attribute, and the letter 'b' should not be interpreted as an expression. To solve this problem, the single character '{' is represented by the sequence '{{', and the single character '}' is represented by the sequence '}}'. For example:

```
="This is {{NOT}} an expression"
```

The XSLT processor removes the second bracket in both cases when outputting the string:

```
This is {NOT} an expression
```

String expressions

An expression may result in an object of any type allowed by the XPath expression language. But the need here is for a string value to be inserted into the attribute value. Therefore, the expression result is converted to a string, as if embedded within the XPath 'string(...)' function. This function is implied, and so the following two examples are equivalent:

```
="...{true()}..."
```

```
="...{string(true())}..."
```

In both cases, the function 'true()' resolves to the string 'true'. In the latter example, it is first explicitly converted to the string 'true', but this string is then also converted to a string (without effect). For the sake of brevity alone, the string function should not be included.

In order to avoid surprises, the XPath '**string()**' function needs to be fully understood. Software developers familiar with the DOM (Document Object Model) can be easily misled by this function as it does not necessarily return the string value of the object, such as the current element. The string value of an element is a combination (in document order) of the string values of all the text nodes within that element. An expression that refers to the current element ('.') actually returns all the text within that element and within the descendants of that element. The string value of an attribute is the normalized value (all whitespace converted to simple spaces, entity references replaced, and in some circumstances the removal of multiple and surrounding spaces).

Copy-through attributes

One of the most beneficial ways that expressions can be used here is to copy a value from a source attribute to an output attribute. Although the element and attribute names are different in the output document, the attribute values often remain the same. A typical example of this is the need to copy an image file name and the dimensions of the image. In this example, the source Image element uses Name, Y and X attributes for the purpose:

```
<image name="boat.gif" y="60mm" x="40mm"/>
```

This element needs to be converted to the HTML IMG element as follows:

```
<IMG SRC="boat.gif" HEIGHT="60mm" WIDTH="40mm"/>
```

To do this, the three values 'boat.gif', '60mm' and '40mm' need to be copied from the source attributes to the output attributes. The current element (the Image element) is the context for each expression, and so it is only necessary to refer directly to the source attributes:

```
<xsl:template match="image">
  <IMG SRC="{@name}" HEIGHT="{@y}" WIDTH="{@x}"/>
</xsl:template>
```

Element content to attribute

Almost as common as attribute value copy-through is the need to convert an element value to an attribute value. For example, in the source document the text to display if the image cannot be presented may be stored in the Image element, as element content:

```
<image name="boat.gif" y="60mm" x="40mm">
Picture of a boat.
</image>
```

In the HTML IMG element, this text needs to appear in the ALT attribute:

```
<IMG SRC="boat.gif" ... ALT="Picture of a boat."/>
```

The expression language makes this transformation almost as simple as copying-through attribute values. In this case, the value required is the text content of the element. The text node within the current element is represented by the 'text()' function:

```
<xsl:template match="image">
  <IMG ALT="{text()}" ... />
</xsl:template>
```

However, this approach is not infallible. The source element may contain child elements instead of (or as well as) directly containing text. The method shown above finds the first text block contained directly within the source element, if there is one, and ignores everything else. On the other hand, it would not be appropriate to copy child elements into the output attribute. The solution is to return the value of the current element ('.') (which means the concatenated values of all embedded text nodes):

```
<image ...>Picture of a <bold>BIG</bold> boat.</image>
```

```
<xsl:template match="image">
  <IMG ALT="{.}" ... />
</xsl:template>
```

```
<IMG ... ALT="Picture of a BIG boat."/>
```

Child element to attribute

Sometimes, an input structure will include child elements to hold discrete parts of a compound value. Each part may need to be converted to an attribute in the output document. For example:

```
<image>
  <name>boat.gif</name>
  <y>60mm</y>
  <x>40mm</x>
</image>
```

Again, patterns can be used to extract each part of the value into an attribute:

```
<xsl:template match="image">
  <IMG SRC="{name}" HEIGHT="{y}" WIDTH="{x}" />
</xsl:template>
```

This is safe, because the string value of the named element is inserted, including the values of any sub-elements.

8. Choices

Templates can be much more intelligent than previous examples have implied. The output specified by templates can vary, depending on relevant conditions. They can include portions that are enabled or disabled on a selective basis. This ability greatly increases the power of templates and can reduce the number of templates needed.

Introduction

XSLT is a declarative language. A stylesheet consists of a static set of instructions. Yet XSLT includes some instructions that will be familiar to software developers. If–then and choose–from features are included in all popular programming languages. Here, they are not used to control the flow of processing but to select optional portions of a template.

An 'if' statement isolates part of a template and only allows its content to become part of the template provided that some condition is met. A 'choose' statement is similar, but is more sophisticated. It is more efficient when the template output depends on a characteristic that has a wide number of options. It also allows a default value to be activated when none of the explicit circumstances tested is applicable.

If conditions

An **If** element encloses any fragment of a template that should only apply under special circumstances. The condition is defined using the **Test** attribute, which holds an expression:

```
<if test="...">
  ...
  <!-- OPTIONAL FRAGMENT OF TEMPLATE -->
  ...
</if>
```

The expression must return a boolean result. A value of 'true' unlocks the content of the If element for use in the template. A value of 'false' indicates a failed test, and the content of the If element is ignored.

A template fragment can therefore be marked, then explicitly included or excluded using the 'true()' and 'false()' expressions:

```
<if test="true()">
  ...
  <!-- REQUIRED FRAGMENT OF TEMPLATE -->
  ...
</if>


<if test="false()">
  ...
  <!-- IGNORED FRAGMENT OF TEMPLATE -->
  ...
</if>
```

This simple technique could be used during stylesheet debugging, to enable and disable parts of templates used to provide output that assists with this task.

The expression appearing in the Test attribute takes the current element, and the current element list, as its context. This attribute is typically used to make decisions based on attribute values of the current element, or the presence (or absence) of specified sub-elements, as in the following examples.

This example shows how different prefix text may be generated, depending on the value of an attribute:

```
    <note>Normal note</note>
    <note type="secret">Secret note</note>


<xsl:template match="note">
  <P>
    <xsl:if test="@type='secret'">SECRET </xsl:if>
    <xsl:text>NOTE: </xsl:text>
    <xsl:apply-templates/>
  </P>
</xsl:template>


    <P>NOTE: Normal note</P>
    <P>SECRET NOTE: Secret note</note>
```

This example shows how a default title can be generated if there is no explicit title within a note:

```
<xsl:template match="note">
  <xsl:if test="not(title)"><P>NOTE</P></xsl:if>
  <xsl:apply-templates/>
</xsl:template>
```

A good example of the use of this element is illustrated in the standard. When formatting a list of names, the punctuation following each name depends on its location in the list. Commas are appropriate after each name, except for after the last one. In the following example, the test is only true when the name is not the last one in the list:

```
<name>John</name>
<name>Peter</name>
<name>Lucy</name>
```

```
<if test="not(position() = last)"><text>, </text></if>
```

John, Peter, Lucy

The If element can be avoided by creating an additional template. The expression in the Test attribute is simply moved to both Match attributes, and in one case is enclosed by the 'not(...)' function. The following example avoids the If statement by testing for names at the ends of lists in a separate template. However, it can be argued that one of the main purposes of this command is precisely to avoid the need for additional templates:

```
<template match="name[not(position() = last)]">
  <apply-templates/><text>, </text>
</if>
```

```
<template match="name[position() = last]">
  <apply-templates/>
</if>
```

Other XSLT commands and output elements within the template must, as always, be well-formed. The If elements must therefore be placed with great care, both to fit into the well-formed structure and to avoid causing problems regardless of whether or not their content is enabled or disabled. Fortunately, the first requirement automatically takes care of the second. The following example is invalid, regardless of whether or not the test succeeds:

```
<xsl:template ...>
  <P>
    <xsl:if test="..."><B>...</xsl:test>
    <xsl:apply-templates/>
    </B>
  </P>
</xsl:if>
```

Finally, If elements can be nested within other If elements, to any number of levels.

Multiple choices

When one option is to be selected from a number of possible options, the If element can be used repeatedly. But, the fact that each If element is independent of the others can be inconvenient in some circumstances. It is not possible to prevent more than one of the tests from succeeding (if this is desired), and it is not possible to take specific action if none is triggered. Both of these constraints could be overcome if a set of tests could be treated as a group.

The **Choose** element encloses a number of alternative fragments of the template that should apply under different circumstances. Each alternative is defined using the **When** element, which works in exactly the same way as the If element described previously. The condition is defined using the **Test** attribute. At least one When element must be present within the Choose element, and these elements may not be used anywhere else:

```
<choose>
  <when test="...">
    <!-- OPTIONAL FRAGMENT OF TEMPLATE -->
    ...
  </when>
  <when test="...">
    <!-- OPTIONAL FRAGMENT OF TEMPLATE -->
    ...
  </when>
</choose>
```

Grouping of the When elements in this way makes it feasible for them to be treated as a whole. First, it becomes possible to ensure that only one is selected, even when more than one contains an expression that succeeds. It also becomes possible to recognize when none of the tests was successful, and to perform some default action when this is the case.

The order in which the When elements are placed within the Choose element can be very important, because only the first successful test is obeyed. In the following example, the two tests on the Colour attribute are only reached for elements that do not have a Type value of 'secret':

```
<choose>
  <when test="@type='secret'">
    <!-- ADD NOTHING - COLOUR NOT SIGNIFICANT -->
  </when>
  <when test="@color='blue'">
    <text>BLUE TEXT - NOT SECRET</text>
  </when>
  <when test="@color='green'">
    <text>GREEN TEXT - NOT SECRET</text>
  </when>
</choose>
```

The optional **Otherwise** element has no attributes, as its content is always selected when none of the When elements is relevant. It is never activated when a test succeeds.

```
<choose>
  <when test="@color='blue'">
    <text>BLUE TEXT</text>
  </when>
  <when test="@color='green'">
    <text>GREEN TEXT</text>
  </when>
  <otherwise>
    <text>DEFAULT TEXT - ALL COLOURS
    EXCEPT BLUE AND GREEN</text>
  </otherwise>
</choose>
```

The Otherwise element must appear after the list of When elements, immediately before the Choose element end-tag.

9. Sorting

The organizing of material into alphabetical or numerical order is a common requirement. For example, the index at the back of this book is sorted alphabetically. When the source material is not already in the correct order, XSLT is able to sort the data during the transformation process. Information can be sorted alphabetically, numerically, and repeatedly.

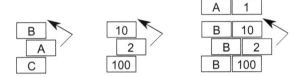

Simple element sorting

One good example of the need to sort elements is the task of creating a glossary. In the following example, the Glossary element contains a number of Item elements, which have not been arranged in any particular order:

```
<glossary>
   <item>XSL - ...</item>
   <item>XML - ...</item>
   <item>SGML - ...</item>
   <item>HTML - ...</item>
</glossary>
```

Using techniques described previously, it would be possible to convert this data into an equivalent HTML structure. However, as elements are normally processed in document order, the output shown below is in the same order as the source XML items:

```
<DIV>
   <P>XSL - ...</P>
   <P>XML - ...</P>
   <P>SGML - ...</P>
   <P>HTML - ...</P>
</DIV>
```

The **Sort** element can be used to override this default ordering. It is placed within the Apply Templates element, where it specifies that the elements matched by this instruction are to be output in sorted order. In the following example, the template for the Glossary element includes the Sort element, indicating that the Item elements embedded within the Glossary element are to be sorted:

```
<xsl:template match="glossary">
  <DIV>
    <xsl:apply-templates>
      <xsl:sort/>
    </xsl:apply-templates>
  </DIV>
</xsl:template>

<xsl:template match="item">
  <P><xsl:apply-templates/></P>
</xsl:template>
```

The Item elements are therefore transformed into paragraph elements that are output in the following order:

```
<DIV>
  <P>HTML - ...</P>
  <P>SGML - ...</P>
  <P>XML - ...</P>
  <P>XSL - ...</P>
</DIV>
```

Note that the Sort element can also be used in the For Each element (see Chapter 16). When it is used here, it must be the first element to appear:

```
<template match="addresses">
  <for-each ...>
      <sort ...>
      ...
  </for-each>
</template>
```

Correct ordering

Deciding what is the correct order is not as trivial an issue as may first appear. A number of factors, including language, capitalization and relative string lengths all contribute to this decision.

Sorting order will differ for each human language. The Roman alphabet used in English has an obvious order, with 'A' always appearing before 'B', and 'Y' always appearing before 'Z'. But it is far less obvious whether 'e' and 'é' are to be treated as the same characters or different, and if different which should appear first. This problem is even more obvious for different alphabets, such as Greek and Cyrillic. Fortunately, the UNICODE initiative (to create standard ways to store text electronically for all the world languages) covers sorting issues, and the XSLT standard recommends that processors use these recommendations. For this to work, however, it is important that the language of the text be recognizable by the XSLT processor. The **Lang** attribute is used for this purpose. The value 'EN' represents the English language. The standard states that when this attribute is absent, a default value is derived from the system environment. In practice, this may mean a derivation from the 'xml:lang' attribute in the source document, but when this is also absent, English will typically be assumed.

The simplest sorting algorithm imaginable would sort using the ASCII (American Standard Code for Information Interchange) codes of the characters. This would certainly ensure that words beginning with 'A' (ASCII code 65) would appear before words beginning with 'B' (ASCII code 66), and that terms that start with digits, such as '16-bit' would appear first ('1' has an ASCII value of 49). However, such an algorithm would also place all words beginning with an upper-case letter before the first word containing a lower-case letter, putting 'Zebra' before 'abacus' ('Z' is ASCII code 90, and 'a' is 97), which is rarely desired. XSLT therefore requires a more sophisticated approach that ignores capitalization (though not totally, as the order in which 'a' and 'A' must appear may still be important). By default, 'a' precedes 'A'.

The length of the text string is also significant. A shorter string that has the same characters as the first part of a longer string appears first. For example, 'the' appears before 'theory'.

A space character is deemed to be more significant than any other symbol. This means that 'a z' appears before 'abc', but the shorter-string rule takes precedence and so 'ab' also appears before 'a z'.

This example reflects the various rules described above:

```
<DIV>
  <P>1</P>
  <P>5</P>
  <P>55a</P>
  <P>a</P>
  <P>ab</P>
  <P>Ab</P>
  <P>a z</P>
  <P>abc</P>
</DIV>
```

Finally, when two items have exactly the same content, they must be output in their original order. This may seem a trivial point to make; if the strings are identical, then the order in which they are output should be irrelevant. However, it is possible to sort an item using only part of its content as the sort key, and in this circumstance the ordering becomes significant. XSLT can deal with this problem by assigning a secondary sort order for all items that have identical primary sort values.

Ordering options

Some options are available for changing the default sorting behaviour in some limited ways. Attributes on the Sort element are used to specify these changes.

Numerical ordering

It is possible to sort by numerical value. This is very different from sorting by characters when the characters happen to be digits. Normal sorting simply ranks digits by their ASCII value:

```
<P>1999</P>
<P>29</P>
<P>399</P>
```

In this example, '1999' is the first item because it begins with a '1'. But the numbers are clearly not ranked by value, as '1999' is larger than '29', which is smaller than '399'. Ordering by value can be achieved using the **Data Type** attribute. It has a default value of '**text**', but can be given an explicit value of '**number**'. The values are then ranked in ascending order:

```
<sort data-type="number" />


<P>39</P>
<P>299</P>
<P>1999</P>
```

Although the XSLT standard makes no comment on this point, a value test should not fail if the text string contains letters as well as digits, even if there is no space between them. The number should be constructed from the first unbroken series of digits:

```
<P>1xyz</P>
<P>22</P>
<P>333abc99</P>
```

Letter-case ordering

Capital letters can be placed above lower-case letters using the **Case Order** attribute. This attribute can only take two possible values; '**lower-first**' (the default) or '**upper-first**'.

```
<sort case-order="upper-first" />


<P>Abc - ...</P>
<P>abc - ...</P>
```

This attribute is only relevant when the Data Type attribute has an implied (or explicit) value of 'text'.

Selective sorting

The examples above all assume that the sort order value is the entire content of the elements to be sorted. The **Select** attribute can be used to identify a more specific item to be used as the sort value. The implied value of this attribute is '.', indicating the current element. The following examples are equivalent:

```
<sort/>
```

```
<sort select="."/>
```

The current element, in this context, means the element being sorted, and it applies to each one of these elements in turn.

As usual, this attribute can take any XPath expression, greatly improving the flexibility of the sort feature.

Child element selection

Elements that contain other elements can be sorted, and the sorting criteria can be specified to be the content of one of the sub-elements. In the following example, a list of countries consists of a name and population count (in millions) for each country. One interesting way to organize this list is to sort it by population size:

```
<countries>
  <country>
    <name>USA</name>
    <population>262</population>
  </country>
  <country>
    <name>UK</name>
    <population>58</population>
  </country>
</countries>

<xsl:template match="countries">
  <DIV>
    <xsl:apply-templates>
      <xsl:sort data-type="number"
                select="population"/>
    </xsl:apply-templates>
  </DIV>
</xsl:template>

  <DIV>
    <P>UK  <B>58</B></P>
    . . .
    <P>USA  <B>262</B></P>
  </DIV>
```

Attribute selection

Because the Select attribute can take any expression, it can be used to target an attribute instead of an element. For example, if the Country element has a Population attribute instead of an element, this attribute can be specified:

```
<sort data-type="number" select=" @population" />
```

```
<countries>
  <country population="262">
    <name>USA</name>
  </country>
  <country population="58">
    <name>UK</name>
  </country>
</countries>
```

Again, when deciding on the expression needed, it is important to recall that the current element is the element being sorted (in this case, each Country element), not the element from which the sort is specified (Countries).

Multiple sort criteria

The list of countries example above raises an interesting problem. Having decided to sort the countries by their population figures, what happens when two countries have the same population value? By default, they are simply output in document order. In the following example, Italy and the UK have the same count, and so the order in which they appear depends entirely on the order that they occur in the source file:

```
<countries>
  <country>
    <name>UK</name>
    <population>58</population>
  </country>
  <country>
    <name>Italy</name>
    <population>58</population>
  </country>
</countries>
```

It would probably be more desirable to sort countries with the same population count into alphabetical order, thus introducing a secondary sorting requirement. This can be achieved simply by repeating the Sort element in the template:

```
<xsl:template match="countries">
  <DIV>
    <xsl:apply-templates>
      <xsl:sort data-type="number"
                select="population"/>
      <xsl:sort select="name"/>
    </xsl:apply-templates>
  </DIV>
</xsl:template>


  <DIV>
    <P>Italy <B>58</B></P>
    <P>UK <B>58</B></P>
    ...
    <P>USA <B>262</B></P>
  </DIV>
```

The order in which the Sort elements appear is very important. The first occurrence is deemed to be the primary sort field. The secondary sort takes effect only on the items within each primary group.

There may, by the same principle, be more than two levels of sorting.

10. Numbering

Numbered lists and sequentially identified document components (such as chapter headings) are common features of many types of document:

1)	A)	i)	1.a.i) ......
2)	B)	ii)	1.a.ii) ......
3)	C)	iii)	......
4)	D)	iv)	55.g.xiii) ......
5)	E)	v)	55.g.xiv) ......

While these numbers can be entered as part of the text by document authors, there are good reasons why numbering is rarely done this way. One such reason includes the desire to style and position the numbers in a distinct way. Another is to facilitate the deletion, insertion and rearrangement of numbered items without having to edit the values in order to recreate the sequential order. Numbering is therefore commonly left to software that is capable of performing the relatively simple task of counting and generating values for these items. XSLT stylesheets are able to identify the elements to number, and insert the appropriate value.

HTML numbering

When transforming XML documents into HTML documents, it may not be necessary to use XSLT features at all. The simplest way to number items automatically is to use the OL (Ordered List) and LI (List Item) elements. In this scenario, the stylesheet does not actually number the items but leaves this task to the browser that will interpret the HTML tags. Take the simple example of a list of procedural steps:

```
<procedure>
  <step>walk to the door</step>
  <step>insert the key in the lock</step>
  <step>turn the key</step>
  <step>turn the handle</step>
  <step>push</step>
</procedure>
```

The following templates would suffice:

```
<xsl:template match="procedure">
  <OL><xsl:apply-templates/></OL>
</xsl:template>

<xsl:template match="step">
  <LI><xsl:apply-templates/></LI>
</xsl:template>
```

Advantage can be taken of HTML features for varying the style of the list by adding appropriate attributes to the OL and LI elements (see Chapter 18 for details).

When converting to HTML format, the stylesheet author has the choice of whether to use HTML list elements, or the XSLT numbering features described below.

Simple numbering

The **Number** element is replaced by a sequential value in the output. In its simplest form, using none of the attributes described below, this element is replaced by a value that represents the position of the element being processed within its list of sibling elements. The following template numbers each step in a list of procedures. Note that, although other elements may occur amongst the numbered elements, they do not interfere with the numbering process in any way:

```
<procedure>
  <title>Getting Through a Locked Door</title>
  <step>walk to the door</step>
  <para>Make sure you have the key!</para>
  <step>insert the key in the lock</step>
  <step>turn the key</step>
  <step>turn the handle</step>
  <step>push</step>
</procedure>

<xsl:template match="step">
  <P><xsl:number/>) <xsl:apply-templates/></P>
</xsl:template>

<H1>Getting Through a Locked Door</H1>
<P>1) walk to the door</P>
<P><B>Make sure you have the key!</B></P>
<P>2) insert the key in the lock</P>
<P>3) turn the key</P>
<P>4) turn the handle</P>
<P>5) push</P>
```

The first occurrence of the target element is given the number '1'. This means that numbering is automatically restarted within each list, as in the following example:

```
<procedure>
  <step>wake up</step>
  <step>brush teeth</step>
  <step>get dressed</step>
</procedure>
...
<procedure>
  <step>brush teeth</step>
  <step>go to bed</step>
  <step>sleep</step>
</procedure>
```

```
<P>1) wake up</P>
<P>2) brush teeth</P>
<P>3) get dressed</P>
...
<P>1) brush teeth</P>
<P>2) go to bed</P>
<P>3) sleep</P>
```

Number format

Some lists are sorted alphabetically, such as 'a. b. c.' or 'A) B) C)'. Others are sorted using Roman numbers (eg 'i ii iii iv'). The **Format** attribute is used to specify the method of numbering. The letter 'a' specifies lower-case alphabetic numbering, and 'A' indicates the use of capitals. The letter 'i' or 'I' represents Roman numbering (which uses lower-case or upper-case letters, including 'i' (one), 'v' (five) and 'x' (ten)):

```
<xsl:template match="item">
  <P><xsl:number format="a"/>. <apply-templates/></P>
</xsl:template>
```

```
<P>a. first item</P>
<P>b. second item</P>
<P>c. third item</P>
```

```
<xsl:template match="item">
  <P><xsl:number format="i"/>. <apply-templates/></P>
</xsl:template>
```

```
<P>i. first item</P>
<P>ii. second item</P>
<P>iii. third item</P>
```

Unlike digits and Roman numerals, which have no upper limit, alphabetically ordered items hit a problem after the letter 'z' or 'Z' has been reached. The solution recommended by the XSLT specification is to use additional letters at this point. After 'z', the next item would be labelled 'aa'. This would be followed by 'ab' and 'ac'. After 'az' comes 'ba' and 'bb'. Presumably, after 'zz', the next item would be 'aaa'.

The Format attribute can also contain surrounding punctuation. Typical examples would include '(A)' and '[i.]'.

```
<number format=" (A) "/>
```

At this point there appears to be little advantage in doing this, as the punctuation could just as easily appear around the entire Number element, without affecting the final result. However, this technique becomes more useful when discussing multi-part numbering later.

Expression values

The value to insert can be calculated using an expression, which is entered into the **Value** attribute. The expression must return a numeric value, as this is used as the count value. The most common expression seen here is simply '**position()**'. This function returns the position of the current element from among its siblings:

```
<number value="position()" format="A"/>
```

Under most conditions, adopting this approach has no effect on the result, but when the items are also sorted (see Chapter 9), and the final sorted list has to be numbered sequentially, this is the only way to achieve the desired effect. This is due to the fact that the expression is applied to the final, sorted list and not to the items in their original document order:

```
<list>
  <item>Z</item>
  <item>Y</item>
  <item>X</item>
</list>

<xsl:template match="list">
  <DIV>
    <xsl:apply-templates><xsl:sort/></xsl:apply-templates>
  </DIV>
</xsl:template>

<xsl:template match="item">
  <P>
    <xsl:number value="position()" format="i) "/>
    <xsl:apply-templates/>
  </P>
</xsl:template>

  <DIV>
    <P>i)  X</P>
    <P>ii)  Y</P>
    <P>iii)  Z</P>
  </DIV>
```

Even when not sorting, this technique raises some interesting new possibilities. For example, it is possible to create a reverse list by deducting the current position from the total number of items:

```
<list>
  <item>first</item>
  <item>second</item>
  <item>third</item>
</list>

<number value="last() + 1 - position()" />

<DIV>
  <P>3)  first</P>
  <P>2)  second</P>
  <P>1)  third</P>
</DIV>
```

See Chapter 20 for more information on expressions.

Elements to count

Previous examples have implicitly counted occurrences of the current element, using the sibling elements as context. However, it is possible to override this simple behaviour in various ways: only counting the element under certain conditions, adding other elements into the count, or separately counting other elements.

Selective counting

The **Count** attribute is used in the Number element to control counting. When this attribute is given a value that matches the current element name, this is equivalent to not including the attribute at all. The two examples below are therefore equivalent:

```
<xsl:template match="item">
  <P><xsl:number/>...</P>
</xsl:template>
<xsl:template match="item">
  <P><xsl:number count="item"/>...</P>
</xsl:template>
```

But the Count attribute actually contains an XPath pattern, not necessarily just an element name. For example, it would be possible to ignore Item elements that have a Status attribute set to 'ignore':

```
<list>
  <item>first</item>
  <item status="ignore">ignore this</item>
  <item>third</item>
</list>
```

```
count="item[not(@status='ignore')]"/>
```

```
<DIV>
  <P>1) first</P>
  <P>ignore this</P>
  <P>2) third</P>
</DIV>
```

Including other elements

Because the value of the Count attribute is a pattern, the 'l' symbol can be used to include other element names. For now, it will be assumed that the current element matches one of the elements named in the pattern (though this need not be the case). In this scenario, the other element or elements named are included in the count of previous siblings. For example, a step in the procedure that has been removed, but must continue to occupy a place in the sequence, could be represented by a Deleted element. The presence of Deleted elements could then be explicitly included in the calculation for the value of each Item element, by including a Count attribute with values of both 'step' and 'deleted':

```
<xsl:template match="step">
  <P><xsl:number count="step|deleted"/>...</P>
</xsl:template>
```

In the following example, as each Step element is processed, all previous Step and Deleted elements are included in the count:

```
<procedure>
  <title>Getting Through an Unlocked Door</title>
  <step>walk to the door</step>
  <deleted/>
  <deleted/>
  <step>turn the handle</step>
  <step>push</step>
</procedure>
```

```
<P>1) walk to the door</P>
<P>DELETED ITEM</P>
<P>DELETED ITEM</P>
<P>4) turn the handle</P>
<P>5) push</P>
```

Taking this example further, it is possible to include the same counter within the template for deleted items, thus recreating the full numbered list:

```
<xsl:template match="deleted">
  <P><xsl:number count="step|deleted"/>) DELETED ITEM</P>
</xsl:template>
```

```
  <P>1) walk to the door</P>
  <P>2) DELETED ITEM</P>
  <P>3) DELETED ITEM</P>
  <P>4) turn the handle</P>
  <P>5) push</P>
```

Using the value '*', it is possible to include all previous sibling elements in the count without having to list all their possible names.

Note that when counting elements that share the same parent element, as these examples all do, the current element name must be included in the list of elements to count. It is not possible to count only other elements. If the current element type is omitted, this is considered significant and triggers the feature described next.

Counting ancestor elements

It is possible to count occurrences of an ancestor element. One obvious need for this capability is to add a number to the title of each section of a document (such as the numbered chapter titles in this book). Although it is the Title element that is being processed and styled, it is the Section elements that precede (and finally enclose) the Title element that need to be counted. This can be achieved simply by inserting the name of the ancestor element into the Count attribute, in place of the name of the current element. When an XSLT processor analyzes the Count attribute value, it first establishes whether or not the name of the current element appears as a valid match in the pattern. If it does not, then the elements containing the current element are each analyzed until one is found that matches. The counting process then works at *that* level, generating a value that represents the number of previous siblings in the usual way. In the following example, there are two previous sections, and one enclosing section, so the value for the Title element is '3':

```
<book>
  <section>...</section>
  <section>...</section>
  <section><title>Section Three</title>
    ...
  </section>
</book>
```

```
<xsl:template match="title">
  <H1><xsl:number count="section"/>) <apply-templates/>
  </H1>
</xsl:template>
```

```
  <H1>3) Section Three</H1>
```

Note that the first match, working up the ancestor list from the current element, is the one that is used. If the three sections shown were all enclosed within another, outer section, the outer Section element would be ignored:

```
<book>
  <section>  <!-- IGNORE THIS ENCLOSING SECTION -->
    <section>...</section>
    <section>...</section>
    <section>
      <title>Section Three</title>
      ...
    </section>
  </section>
</book>
```

The number of levels searched up the ancestor list can be constrained using the **From** attribute. This attribute holds a pattern, naming the element or elements beyond which searching should not continue. For example, a Part element could be specified, preventing an enclosing section from being selected:

```
<number count="section" from="part" />
```

```
<book>
  <section>
    <part>  <!-- prevents access to Section -->
      <title>
```

It is difficult to envisage a scenario where this is actually useful. The nearest named element is selected, and so the only outcome of effective use of the From element would be an unsuccessful search. However, this attribute has a more significant purpose in other circumstances.

Multipart numbering

All previous examples have worked at a single level – either at the same level as the current element, or at some level higher in the document. A single list of siblings is counted, and numbered as required. However, there may be a need to present numbers that include several counters. Formal documents in particular tend to include such numbers as '1.2.7.3' or 'A–6–iv'. This effect can of course be achieved using multiple Number elements, arranged in sequence:

```
<xsl:template match="title">
  <P><xsl:number count="chapter" .../>.
    <xsl:number count="section" ..."/>
    <apply-templates/>
  </P>
</xsl:template>
```

However, this approach can be quite clumsy when dealing with several levels. As an alternative approach, the **Level** attribute can be used to indicate what type of numbering is required. Previous examples have illustrated the default setting for this attribute, with numbering being applied at a 'single' level (the list of siblings, at whatever level in the hierarchy). By including the attribute, and giving it the value 'multiple', the behaviour of the other attributes is changed to support multi-part numbering.

In 'multiple' level mode, the list of ancestors for the current element is searched for all occurrences of each of the elements in the pattern. Searching does not cease at the first occurrence found. For example, in a document that contains Section elements containing embedded Section elements, both levels will be applicable. For each level in the ancestor list for which a match has been made, the previous siblings of that element that match the pattern are counted. In the Count attribute, all matching elements at each level are included:

```
<number level="multiple" count="chapter|section" ... />
```

Each separate count is finally formatted into a single string (see below).

Restricting the search

The **From** element has a more significant role in this scenario. Unlike single-level numbering, searching up the hierarchy of elements does not stop at the first match, and so a blocking mechanism can be useful. For example:

```
<number count="section" from="chapter" />


    <book>
      <section> <!-- NOT INCLUDED -->
        <chapter>
          <section> <!-- INCLUDED -->
```

Compound number formatting

The issue that arises at this point is exactly how the compound string is to be organized. By default, the separate counts are just appended to each other, which is rarely desired. Quite apart from lack of visual appeal, a number such as '1234' could be interpreted in a number of ways, from a single value to such combinations as 'section 34 of chapter 12' or 'section 234 of chapter 1'. Typically, multipart numbers contain separating punctuation, such as a full-point as in '12.34' and '123.4'. The **Format** attribute is used to specify such effects. The punctuation is simply inserted between tokens that represent each level (from left to right):

```
<number ... format="1.a" />
```

```
1.a
1.b
1.c
...
7.m
7.n
7.o
```

When there are more levels in a generated number than there are tokens in the attribute, the last token (and preceding punctuation) is assumed to repeat. From the example above, values such as '3.c', '9.f.b' and '12.z.d.m' are all possible.

Document-wide numbering

The hierarchical structure of a document may be irrelevant to the counting scheme required. For example, if there is a requirement to provide each table in a document with a unique, sequential number, regardless of where each table occurs within the document structure, it is more appropriate to view the document as a simple data stream and count each table as it occurs in this stream. Setting the value of the **Level** attribute to '**any**' signifies this requirement.

```
<xsl:template match="table/title">
  <TITLE>
    <xsl:number level="any" count="table" ... />
    <apply-templates/>
  </TITLE>
</xsl:template>
```

```
<TITLE>(15) Table 15</TITLE>
```

Restricting the search

However, it would still be useful to be able to restart numbering from a significant point in the document. For example, tables may need to be numbered separately in appendices. The **From** element can play a very important role in this scenario, because in this case it does not simply eliminate upper levels in the hierarchy from consideration but instead blocks all elements *before* the named element or elements. The hierarchy is not important. For example, a Division element may be used to divide chapters into groups, with numbering restarting within each group:

```
<number count="chapter" from="division" />
```

```
<book>
  <chapter>
    <table>...</table> <!-- TABLE 1 -->
    <table>...</table> <!-- TABLE 2 -->
  </chapter>
  <chapter>
    <table>...</table> <!-- TABLE 3 -->
  </chapter>
  <division/>
  <chapter>
    <table>...</table> <!-- TABLE 1 -->
  </chapter>
</book>
```

However, the start-tag of an enclosing element still counts as occurring before the current element:

```
<number count="chapter" from="appendix" />
```

```
<book>
   <chapter>
    <table>...</table> <!-- TABLE 1 -->
    <table>...</table> <!-- TABLE 2 -->
  </chapter>
  <chapter>
    <table>...</table> <!-- TABLE 3 -->
  </chapter>
  <appendix>
    <chapter>
      <table>...</table> <!-- TABLE 1 -->
    </chapter>
  </appendix>
</book>
```

Advanced formatting options

The **Format** attribute provides a very flexible approach to formatting numbers. First, it is possible to make all numbers the same width by padding shorter numbers with leading zeros. This attribute contains the number of digits to be presented, with the zero digit used for all but the last, which must be a one (as in '0001'):

```
<xsl:template match="item">
  <P>
    <xsl:number format="01"/>. <apply-templates/>
  </P>
</xsl:template>
```

```
<P>01. first item</P>
<P>02. second item</P>
<P>03. third item</P>
...
<P>09. ninth item</P>
<P>10. tenth item</P>
```

Punctuation is often used within values to create groups of digits for legibility. But the actual mark used and the number of digits in each group may vary. Two attributes are available to specify the mark to use and the number of digits to place in each group. These are the **Grouping Separator** and the **Grouping Size** attributes. For example, in English documents, typical values for these attributes would be ',' and '3' respectively:

```
<number ... grouping-separator="," grouping-size="3" />
```

```
<P>1. one</P>
<P>2. two</P>
<P>3. three</P>
...
<P>999. nine hundred and ninety nine</P>
<P>1,000. one thousand</P>
...
<P>1,000,000. one million</P>
```

The **Lang** attribute allows a language to be identified, so that an appropriate sequence of characters can be used to label each item. When this attribute is not used, some other method must be used to determine the language to use. This may be the 'xsl:lang' attribute, when it is present in the source document.

It is widely known, and illustrated above, that in English there are two common ways in which alphabetic characters can be used to create an ordered list. These are the 'abcde' and 'i ii iii iv v' methods. Some other languages also have two options, but both options begin with the same letter. This means that putting the initial character in the Format attribute is not sufficient to identify which method to use. The **Letter Value** attribute is therefore used to identify the method. It has two possible values: '**alphabetic**' or '**traditional**'. There is no default or preferred value, and so when this attribute is not present an XSLT processor may not behave as predicted.

11. Reorganizing material

XML documents have a linear structure, and all material has a sequential location within the document. In addition, the philosophy of good XML document design includes the 'golden rule' that information should not be duplicated unnecessarily. When preparing material for publication, however, the original ordering may be inappropriate, and for convenience some material may need to be copied to another location in the document. Information can also be accessed from remote documents.

Information reuse

There are a number of reasons why information may need to be copied to another location in the output document. One typical example is the need to create a table of contents for a book. In this case, the chapter titles need to be copied to the beginning of the document.

Previous examples have shown how the Apply Templates element is normally used to select the children of the current element, so that the entire document can be processed in the correct order (in a tree-walking manner). However, it is also able to select material from elsewhere in the document, using the **Select** attribute. It has already been shown that this attribute can be used to select specific children of the current element, but as it can hold any XPath expression, it can also be used to select material from other locations. In the following example, instead of children of the current element, the chapter titles are selected:

```
<apply-templates select="/book/chapter/title" />
```

In this example, each chapter is selected in turn, and each title in these chapters is sought. Templates are applied to each matching Title element, and the output from these templates appears at the current location (whereby a table of contents is created).

Note that the ability to trigger templates to process material beyond the scope of the current element is potentially dangerous. It is possible to select the parent, or indeed any ancestor of the current element. This can lead to a processing loop that never ends. Some XSLT processors may detect and escape from this condition, but others may not.

It should be recalled that a template can hold more than one Apply Templates element. A single template may process the children of the current element, as well as grabbing material from elsewhere. The following template processes the content of a book, and also 'drags up' the titles from each chapter to build the table of contents:

```
<xsl:template match="book">
  <HTML>
    <HEAD><TITLE>A book</TITLE></HEAD>
    <BODY>
      <DIV>
        <xsl:apply-templates select="chapter/title" />
      </DIV>
      <xsl:apply-templates/>
    </BODY>
  </HTML>
</xsl:template>
```

When the structure and element names in the information to be copied does not alter on output, the **Copy Of** element can be used instead. The following example copies the Title elements in chapters directly to output (and does not change the names of the Title element, or any of the other elements):

```
<book>
  <chapter>
    <title>title one</title>
    ...
  </chapter>

  <chapter>
    <title>title <emph>two</emph></title>
    ...
  </chapter>
</book>
```

```
<xsl:template match="book">
  <out-book>
    <table-of-contents>
      <xsl:copy-of select="/chapter/title" />
    </table-of-contents>
    <xsl:apply-templates />
  </out-book>
</xsl:template>
```

```
<out-book>
  <table-of-contents>
    <title>title one</title>
    <title>title <emph>two</emph></title>
  </table-of-contents>
  ...
</out-book>
```

Context-specific formatting (modes)

The problem with the examples above is that the formatting of the copied material is not affected by its move to a new location. In many examples, including the building of a table of contents, there is a need to apply different formatting to the material at its new location. For example, the chapter titles should be larger than the table of contents entries (as they are in this book).

XSLT includes the concept of '**modes**'. Sets of templates can be assigned to specific modes, and the whole stylesheet can be switched between these modes to enable and disable templates that match the same element. The **Mode** attribute is added to the Template element to assign the template to a specific mode. In the following example, there are two templates that match the Title element, but one belongs to the 'contents' mode:

```
<template match="title">...</template>
```

```
<template match="title" mode="contents">...</template>
```

The title may be formatted in different ways, depending on which mode (in this case the 'default' mode or the 'contents' mode) is in effect at the time. Normally, the current mode is the default mode and all templates that have a Mode attribute are disabled. In the example above, the first template for the Title element is active and the second is inactive. To enable a specific mode, the Mode attribute is added to the Apply Templates element. The children (or other) elements processed as a result of this instruction are processed using the applicable templates:

```
<apply-templates mode="contents" />
```

This feature can be used to great effect when the need is to format copied material in a different way. Taking the table of contents example, the default mode can be used for normal rendering of the title at the top of each chapter, and another mode can be used to render the titles in a smaller point size within the table of contents. In the following example, H1 elements are used to format the Title element within the chapter, and H4 elements are used to format the Title element in the table of contents:

```
<xsl:template match="book">
  <HTML><HEAD><TITLE>A book</TITLE></HEAD>
  <BODY>
    <DIV>
      <xsl:apply-templates select="chapter/title"
                           mode="contents" />
    </DIV>
    <xsl:apply-templates/>
  </BODY>
</xsl:template>


<xsl:template match="chapter">
  <xsl:apply-templates/>
</xsl:template>


<xsl:template match="title">
  <H1><xsl:apply-templates/></H1>
</xsl:template>


<xsl:template match="title" mode="contents">
  <H4><xsl:apply-templates/></H4>
</xsl:template>
```

Note that there are built-in, mode-specific versions of the template that match elements with no explicit template definition. It is not necessary to create such templates as the following:

```
<!-- NOT NECESSARY (default behaviour) -->
<xsl:template match="*|/" mode="contents">
  <xsl:apply-templates/>
</xsl:template>
```

But it can be done, if the intention is to override the default behaviour (such as avoiding processing the descendants of unspecified elements):

```
<xsl:template match="*|/" mode="special">
  <!-- DO NOT PROCESS CHILDREN OF UNSPECIFIED ELEMENTS -->
</xsl:template>
```

Moving information

Moving information to another location in the output document structure can be achieved by first copying it, using the techniques described above, and then suppressing it at the original location. Again, the Mode attribute is used. The essential difference is that the default template does not contain the Apply Templates element, and so the information is not output in its original location:

```
<xsl:template match="title">
  <!-- SUPPRESSED OUTPUT AT ORIGINAL LOCATION -->
</xsl:template>
```

```
<xsl:template match="title" mode="new-location">
  <P><xsl:apply-templates/></P>
</xsl:template>
```

However, this technique is quite complex and should only be considered when the new location is far removed from the source. Reordering within a small structure can usually be achieved much more simply by selective child processing. Consider the following example, where the Name element first contains the title, then the first name, and then the last name:

```
<name>
    <title>Mr</title>
    <first>John</first>
    <last>Smith</last>
</name>
```

Assuming that the output ordering needs to be last name, first name then title, this can be achieved in one of the following ways:

```
<xsl:template match="name">
  <xsl:apply-templates select="last" />
  <xsl:apply-templates select="first" />
  <xsl:apply-templates select="title" />
</xsl:template>

<xsl:template match="name">
  <P><xsl:value-of select="last" /></P>
  <P><xsl:value-of select="first" /></P>
  <P><xsl:value-of select="title" /></P>
</xsl:template>
```

The For Each element may also play a significant role in reorganizing material. It is discussed in detail in Chapter 16.

Accessing remote documents

It is possible to access information stored in remote XML documents using the **document**() function. This function takes at least one, and possibly two parameters. The first parameter may be a string that consists of the URL for the remote document. The XSLT processor locates the document and then parses it to create an in-memory tree that can be accessed using XPath. For example, consider the following remote document:

`remote.XML`

```
<book>
  <title>The Remote Book Title</title>
  <para>Remote paragraph.</para>
</book>
```

If this document is stored in the same directory as the stylesheet, it can be referenced using the function 'document('remote.XML')'. This function could be used as the first part of an XPath location path. For example, the title of the book could be retrieved and inserted into the output document:

```
... and see <remotebookref/> for details...
```

```
<xsl:template match="remotebookref">
  <I>
    <xsl:value-of
         select=" document('remote.XML')/book/title" />
  </I>
</xsl:template>
```

```
...and see <I>The Remote Book Title</I> for details...
```

A node can be passed to this function instead of a string. In this case, the string value of the node is considered to be the URL. Perhaps the most obvious use of this feature is to open a document that is named in an attribute:

```
... and see <bookref name="remote.XML"/> for details...
```

```
<xsl:value-of select="document(@name)/book/title" />
```

```
...and see <I>The Remote Book Title</I> for details...
```

Using this technique, a change to the document title is automatically reflected in all referencing documents.

Note that relative paths are relative to the location of the stylesheet rather than the input document. It is possible to supply another base-URL address by including a second parameter. For example, if 'remoteXML' is actually found in '/D:/remote-docs', then this base path can be included:

```
/D:/remotedocs/remote.XML
```

```
select="document(@name, '/D:/remotedocs')/book/title"
```

Finally, it is possible to access information that could be in one of several documents. Instead of passing a single attribute value or element value to the function, a number of nodes can be passed instead. Each node represents a different document to be accessed. In the following example, a number of documents are referenced using DocRef elements. Using the expression '/doc/doc-ref', the document function receives all of these elements and therefore reads all the documents into memory. The title of the document that has an attribute value of 'secret' is accessed:

```
<doc>
  <doc-ref>remote1.xml</doc-ref>
  <doc-ref>remote2.xml</doc-ref> <!-- SECRET DOC -->
  <doc-ref>remote3.xml</doc-ref>
  ...
  <find-secret-title/>
</doc>

<xsl:template match="find-secret-title">
  <P>
    <xsl:value-of
            select="document('/doc/doc-ref')
                    /doc[@type='secret']/title"/>
  </P>
</xsl:template>

  <P>The SECRET Book Title</P>
```

12. XML output

One of the most significant tasks that XSLT is suitable to perform is XML-to-XML transformations. In many cases, this would be done to prepare a document for publishing (using HTML or XSL). Indeed, the primary purpose of XSLT is to create XML documents that conform to the XSL DTD. But there is no real reason why it should be restricted to this application. XSLT is a good, general-purpose XML transformation tool. It therefore includes a number of features for outputting XML structures, including elements, attributes, comments and processing instructions. It is also able to copy-through fragments of a source XML document directly to the output.

XML output format

An XSLT processor can be explicitly told that the transformation is to another XML document. Except in one special case, this is assumed in any case. But to be certain that output will be interpreted in this way, the **Output** element may be used. This element is a top-level element and so is directly placed within the Stylesheet element. The **Method** attribute contains the value '**xml**'.

```
<output method="xml" />
```

Elements

The **Element** element is used to generate element tags. The name of the element to output is specified in the **Name** attribute:

```
<element name="OL">
  . . .
  <!-- CONTENT OF OL ELEMENT -->
  . . .
</element>

  <OL>...</OL>
```

At first sight, this appears to be a less elegant alternative to simply embedding output elements within the stylesheet. Indeed, most people would agree that the stylesheet is less readable when using it. This can be demonstrated by the following examples, which are functionally identical:

```
<xsl:template match="book">
  <DOC>
    <TITLE>Test</TITLE>
    <MAIN>
      <xsl:apply-templates/>
    </MAIN>
  </DOC>
</xsl:template>


<template match="book">
  <element name="DOC">
    <element name="TITLE">Test</element>
    <element name="MAIN">
      <apply-templates/>
    </element>
  </element>
</template>
```

However, one good reason for using this technique is that an element can be created with a name that is generated from a computation. This is because the Name attribute may contain an expression. This expression could refer to a variable, or calculate the name of the element to output in some other way (see Chapter 16 for variable examples).

Another good reason for using this element is to avoid the problem that arises when attempting to use a DTD-sensitive XML editor to create the stylesheet. Incorporating output elements into the document requires that the DTD be updated to allow them to occur (and it is not sufficent simply to copy the original element and attribute declarations into the XSLT DTD, as their content models must be changed to allow embedded XSLT elements). When formatting the stylesheet on-screen to assist with authoring, it would also be necessary to create display formats for each of the elements. But the Element element is already part of the XSLT DTD. A reasonable editor will allow the Name attribute value to be presented at all times (as a prefix), at least partly overcoming the legibility issue:

Finally, as the comparitive examples above demonstrate, there is no need for namespaces when using this technique.

Attributes

The **Attribute** element represents a single attribute in the output. The **Name** attribute specifies the name of the attribute. The content of this element represents the attribute value:

```
<attribute name="author">J. Smith</attribute>
```

Usage with element definitions

The primary need for this element is to add attributes to output elements that are defined using the Element element described above. The Attribute element is placed within the Element element:

```
<template match="book">
  <element name="DOC">
    <attribute name="AUTHOR">J. Smith</attribute>
    <apply-templates/>
  </element>
</template>
```

```
      <DOC AUTHOR="J. Smith">...</DOC>
```

The attribute is attached to the nearest ancestor element definition (the nearest element that encloses it). In the following example, the first attribute is attached to the DOC element, but the second is associated with the P element (not the enclosing DOC element):

```
<element name="DOC">
  <attribute name="AUTHOR">J. Smith</attribute>
  <element name="P">
    <attribute name="TYPE">SECRET</attribute>
    <apply-templates/>
  <element>
</element>
```

```
      <DOC AUTHOR="J. Smith">
        <P TYPE="SECRET">...</P>
        ...
      </DOC>
```

Usage with output elements

This element can also be used when the element is defined as an explicit output element:

```
<xsl:template match"book">
  <DOC>
    <xsl:attribute name="AUTHOR">J. Smith</xsl:attribute>
    <xsl:apply-templates/>
  </DOC>
</xsl:template>
```

In most cases, this would be a clumsy way to add an attribute to an element when it can be more easily entered directly in the start-tag. The following example generates output identical to the one above:

```
<xsl:template match"book">
  <DOC AUTHOR='J. Smith'>
    <xsl:apply-templates/>
  </DOC>
</xsl:template>
```

But usage of the Attribute element in this scenario cannot be totally dismissed. This element can hold a wide range of other instruction elements, which can be useful when the attribute value needed depends on some complex contextual circumstance. For example, a paragraph could be designated 'secret' if it contains an embedded Secret element (and 'normal' otherwise):

```
<xsl:template match"para">
  <P>
    <xsl:attribute name="TYPE">
      <xsl:choose>
        <xsl:when test=".//secret">SECRET</xsl:when>
        <xsl:otherwise>NORMAL</xsl:otherwise>
      </xsl:choose>
    </xsl:attribute>
    <xsl:apply-templates/>
  </P>
</xsl:template>
```

However, it is also true to say that the previous example could be reformulated without the need for instructions within the Attribute element (by placing multiple attribute definitions within a Choose element).

Multiple definitions

When there are multiple definitions for an attribute with the same attribute name, only the last one is used. In the following example, the author name is 'J. Smith':

```
<xsl:template match"book">
  <DOC AUTHOR="M. Moore">
    <xsl:attribute name="AUTHOR">K. Jones</xsl:attribute>
    <xsl:attribute name="AUTHOR">J. Smith</xsl:attribute>
    <xsl:apply-templates/>
  </DOC>
</xsl:template>
```

```
<DOC AUTHOR="J. Smith">...</DOC>
```

Text

The **Text** element can be used to enclose each string of output text:

```
<text>some text</text>
```

Yet the XML standard does not define an explicit construct for blocks of text within the markup. Text is simply allowed to appear at given points in the document structure, typically mixed with embedded elements. Similarly, text intended to appear in the output can simply appear at appropriate points within a template. The following examples are directly equivalent:

```
<TITLE><xsl:text>A Title</xsl:text></TITLE>


<TITLE>A Title</TITLE>
```

The Text element therefore appears to be superfluous. However, spaces are often used in the construction of stylesheets to make them more legible, and these spaces should not affect the output generated. The following two templates are equivalent:

```
<xsl:template match="para">
  <P><xsl:apply-templates/></P>
</xsl:template>

<xsl:template match="para">
  <P>
    <xsl:apply-templates/>
  </P>
</xsl:template>
```

In both cases, typical output generated should be as follows:

```
<P>The content.</P>
```

In the second example above, there is a line-feed, and four spaces before the Apply Templates element, but none of this whitespace is expected to appear in the output. If leading spaces *are* required, the Text element must be used to make this explicit. In the following example, a single space is required:

```
<xsl:template match="para">
  <P>
    <xsl:text> </xsl:text><xsl:apply-templates/>
  </P>
</xsl:template>

  <P> The content.</P>
```

Comments

An XML comment can be created using the **Comment** element. When output, the start-tag is replaced with '<!--' and the end-tag with '-->':

```
<comment>This is a comment</comment>
```

```
<!--This is a comment-->
```

Content limitations

Because the '-' symbol is significant in the final comment markup, there are some constraints on its use in the text. An error may be reported if '--' appears in the text, as it would signify early temination of the comment. An error may also be reported if a single '-' symbol ends the comment:

```
<comment>The -- sequence is illegal, as is -</comment>
```

```
<!--The -- sequence is illegal, as is --->
```

Alternatively, a more sophisticated XSLT processor may recover from such problems on the user's behalf, by inserting spaces at vital points:

```
<!--The - - sequence is illegal, as is - -->
```

Copying-through comments

Comments in the source document can be copied-through to the output by creating a template to match '**comment()**' nodes. Both examples below will work equally well:

```
<template match="comment()">
  <copy-of select="."/>
</template>
```

```
<template match="comment()">
  <comment><xsl:value-of select="."/></comment>
</template>
```

But this will only work if the parser reading the source file on behalf of the XSLT processor has not discarded comments. A better method is described below, when discussing the Copy element.

Constructing comment text

The last example above shows the use of the **Value Of** element within a comment. This element can be used to do far more than simply copy an existing comment through to the output. In addition, a number of other instruction elements may be used within the Comment element. Although the final content of any comment must be a simple text string, this string can be constructed using advanced XSLT features.

For example, the Apply Templates element can be applied. This is useful for transforming an element in the source document into a comment in the output:

```
<author-note>Edit the following text</author-note>
```

```
<xsl:template match="author-note">
  <xsl:comment><xsl:apply-templates/></xsl:comment>
</xsl:template>
```

```
<!--Edit the following text-->
```

As another example, it is possible to insert the value of an attribute into a comment, and to generate content depending on a condition, such as the presence of this attribute:

```
<book author="J. Smith">...</book>
```

```
<template match="book">
  <comment><xsl:text>This is a book</xsl:text>
    <if test="@author"/>
      <text>, the author is </text>
      <value-of select="@author">
    </if>
  </comment>
</template>
```

```
<!--This is a book, the author is J. Smith-->
```

The elements that may be used within Comment elements (including several not yet introduced), include the Apply Templates, Call Template, Apply Imports, For Each, Value Of, Copy Of, Number, Choose, If, Text, Copy, Variable and Message elements (as well as the Fallback element).

Processing instructions

An XML processing instruction can be created using the **Processing Instruction** element. It has a **Name** attribute to hold the name of the target application (which becomes the first word in the processing instruction). The content of the element becomes the actual instruction. On output, the start-tag becomes '<?' and the end-tag becomes '?>':

```
<page-break/>
```

```
<template match="page-break">
  <processing-instruction name="ACME">
    {new page}
  </processing-instruction>
</template>
```

```
<?ACME {new page}?>
```

As a processing instruction ends with the characters '?>', it is illegal for the text in the instruction to contain this sequence of characters. An error may be reported if they occur.

Copying-through processing instructions

Processing instruction in the source document can be copied through to the output by creating a template to match '**processing-instruction()**' nodes:

```
<?ACME {new page}?>
```

```
<xsl:template match="processing-instruction()">
  <xsl:processing-instruction name="ACME">
    <xsl:copy-of select="."/>
  </xsl:processing-instruction>
</xsl:template>
```

```
<?ACME {new page}?>
```

But this will only work if the parser reading the source file on behalf of the XSLT processor has preserved such markup. Also note that the alternative way shown to copy-through comments (using Value Of) will not work for processing instructions, because it is also necessary here to copy-through the value of the Name attribute. However, a better method is described below, when discussing the Copy element.

Constructing an instruction

A number of instruction elements may be used within the Processing Instruction element, allowing an embedded instruction to be generated in a variety of ways. For example, the instruction may need to vary, depending on the value of a variable in the enclosing element:

```
<entry type="major">...</entry>
```

```
<entry type="minor">...</entry>
```

```
<template match="entry">
  <processing-instruction name="ACME">
    <if test="@type='major'"/>
      {new page}
    </if>
    <if test="@type='minor'"/>
      {new column}
    </if>
  </processing-instruction>
</template>
```

```
<?ACME {new page}?>
```

```
<?ACME {new column}?>
```

A large number of instruction elements may be used. See the list at the end of the Comments section above.

Copying source structures

When transforming XML documents into different XML documents, there may be times when some markup needs to be copied to the output without modification. Two instructions are available for specifying copy-through of XML constructs.

Copying document fragments

A document to be transformed may contain fragments that are to remain unchanged. The **Copy Of** element can be used to copy such structures directly to output. The **Select** attribute contains an expression to locate the fragment to copy-through. To copy the current element (and all its descendants), the expression needs to refer to the current element ('.'). For example, the source document may contain tabular structures that are already coded according to the HTML table standard, and the output document will also contain tables coded to this standard:

```
<template match="table">
  <copy-of select="."/>
</template>
```

Other expressions copy-through elements from elsewhere in the source document. For example, to copy to output as a single block all the Title elements in a source document, at the beginning of a book, the following would be needed:

```
<template match="book">
  <copy-of select="//title"/>
</template>
```

The fragment copied does not have to be an element. The examples below show how this instruction can be used to copy-through other markup, such as comments and processing instructions.

Copying nodes

A more limited variant of copying-through is available that only copies the current node. If the node is an element, its attributes and its children (text and sub-elements) are *not* copied. The **Copy** element represents the current node. For example, the templates to copy comments and processing instructions from source to destination files can be made much simpler than previous examples:

```
<template match="comment()">
  <copy/>
</template>


<template match="processing-instruction()">
  <copy/>
</template>
```

This works reliably because these node types have no internal structure, unlike elements. However, even element nodes can be usefully processed in this way.

The fact that the original node type is inferred means that the templates shown above can be combined into a single template. When it matches a comment, it is a comment that is created; when it matches a processing instruction, it is a processing instruction that is created:

```
<template match="comment()|processing-instruction()">
  <copy/>
</template>
```

13. Identifiers and links

Identifiers offer a way to target a single instance of an element, or group of related elements, for direct formatting in a distinctive fashion. They are useful when the choice of style depends on more than the element name, or even the context within which the element appears. When items are uniquely identified, it is also possible to create links to them, which a user may follow. This chapter describes two mechanisms for identifying elements in a more specific way, using identifiers, and then shows how to build hypertext links to uniquely identified items.

XML IDs

The XML language includes the concept of unique element identifiers, allowing a specific instance of an element to be given a name, so that it can be located when needed. This information can be used to provide a hypertext linking mechanism, or to identify an important item that needs to be formatted in a distinctive way. In this scheme, an attribute is used to hold the identifier. There is no restriction on what this attribute is called, as it is recognized by the attribute type assigned to it in a DTD. These attributes are given the type 'ID'. In the following example, the Name attribute of the Item element is assigned this special status. In a conforming document, this attribute must be present, and must be given a unique value:

```
<!ATTLIST item name ID #REQUIRED>
```

An XML parser is able to collect the values of all attributes of this type in the document, and report an error if any values are duplicated. The following fragment is valid, as each Name attribute value is different:

```
<item name="a">...</item>
<item name="aardvark">...</item>
...
<item name="zymurgy">...</item>
```

An XPath expression can exploit this feature using the 'id()' function. A selection can be made by reference to an ID value. In the following example, the template matches the item with an identifier of 'XSLT', for special formatting treatment:

```
<template match="id('XSLT')">...</template>
```

Alternatively, this same item can be reused at another place in the output document:

```
<apply-templates select="id('XSLT')"/>
```

The value of the function can be a space-separated list of identifiers. For example, if all items beginning with a single letter were to be formatted in the same way, the following template would be appropriate:

```
<template match="id('a b c d e f g h i j k l m n o p q r s
t u v w x y z')">...</template>
```

However, there are some severe limitations to be aware of:

- a DTD is required in order to identify attributes assigned to hold unique ID values, and this DTD must be read by the XSLT processor for the attributes to be recognized;
- the identifier must be stored in an attribute value (it cannot be element content)
- a single element can hold only one identifier (regardless of how many sets of relationships that element may participate in);
- only one element can have a particular identifier, and so it is not possible to use identifiers to group-related items;
- every identified item must have a completely unique identifier value, even when there is no relationship between one set of identifiers and another (perhaps distinguished by different element names);
- there are some severe constraints on the construction of the identifier: it must be a single word that conforms to XML name restrictions.

All these constraints can be overcome using the XSLT 'key' feature described below.

Keys

Within the XSLT standard, a powerful mechanism is included that overcomes the limitations of the XML ID scheme described above. XSLT can identify elements using a '**key**'. A key is a combination of three things. First, it includes a specific target element, and the purpose of the key is to retrieve this element when required. Second, it includes a value by which the element can be identified. Third, it includes a name that creates a distinct namespace for the value. This means that the same value can be used in different contexts, without causing any conflicts. For example, the value 'orange' would have one meaning in the 'colour' space, and a different meaning in the 'fruit' space. The names 'colour' and 'fruit' make this distinction, and the value 'orange' can be used in both without confusion.

While the key as a whole must be unique, any part of it does not have to be so. In the case of the name part, this is obvious. It is clear that the name 'fruit' may be used in many keys, with the value changing to identify elements that describe different kinds of fruit. However, it is also true for the value part of the key as well; more than one element may describe an 'orange' fruit. This flexibility allows a group of related elements to be formed and means that, when a key is used, it may locate more than one element:

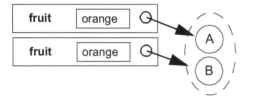

Furthermore, even the third part of the key, the element identified, does not have to be unique. This means that a single instance of an element may be involved in more than one key. For example, an element that describes an 'orange' fruit, may also be an element that describes an object of a specific colour (in the XML ID scheme, only one ID attribute can be defined for an element):

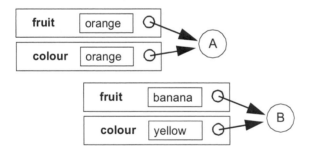

Using these keys, it is possible to apply specific formatting to all elements of a particular colour, or to all elements that describe a particular fruit.

Note that the illustration above also includes an example that demonstrates identical values in different namespaces ('orange' as a colour as well as a fruit).

Generating keys

Keys are defined by creating a namespace, then specifying which elements are to participate, and what part of these elements are to be considered an identifier value. The **Key** element is used to create keys:

```
<key .../>
```

The **Name** attribute specifies the name to give to each key created by this instruction. For example, it may be useful to create identifiers for every term in a glossary, and this list of identifiers could be called 'Glossary':

```
<key name="Glossary" .../>
```

It is then necessary to identify the element or elements that are to be included in this set of identifiable objects. This could be just the name of an element, or it could be a more complex XPath pattern. The **Match** attribute is used to do this, and the choice of name for this attribute is particularly appropriate as it has the same purpose and behaviour as when used in the Template element. For this example, Item elements will be selected, but only when they appear within a Glossary element:

```
<glossary>
  <item>...</item>
  <item>...</item>
  <item>...</item>
</glossary>
```

```
<key match="glossary/item" .../>
```

Finally, it is necessary to identify the text that will provide the unique value within each item. For maximum flexibility, this is done using an XPath expression. The **Use** attribute contains this expression. It is possible to select an attribute, the text content, or even the content of a sub-element. Assuming each Item element has the following structure, then the Subject child element is a good candidate for the key value:

```
<item>
  <subject>XSL</subject>
  <description>XML Stylesheet Language</description>
</item>
<item>
  <subject>XSLT</subject>
  <description>XML Stylesheet Language -
  Transformations</description>
</item>
```

```
<key use="subject" .../>
```

By putting these three attributes together in a single Key element, an instruction can be created to generate keys for all Item elements within Glossary elements, using the content of the embedded Subject elements as the key values:

```
<key name="Glossary"
     match="glossary/item"
     use="subject" ... />
```

In this case, there is a single Subject element in each Item element, so that the value is simple to determine. However, it is possible that there may be more than one matching element. When this happens, a key is created for each value. In the following example, two keys would be produced for the Item element, each with the same name but with different values ('XSL/XSLT' and 'XSLT/XSL'):

```
<item>
  <subject>XSL/XSLT</subject>
  <subject>XSLT/XSL</subject>
  <description>XML Stylesheet Language and
  Transformations</description>
</item>
```

When keys are present in the main stylesheet, and also in imported stylesheets, the keys defined in imported stylesheets for the same element are not ignored if there are multiple definitions at differing importance levels (according to the rules dictated by the import feature).

Using keys

Once generated, the keys can be used in similar fashion to XML identifiers, except that the function name is '**key()**' and takes two parameters instead of one. The first parameter is the key name, specifying the domain to search. The second parameter may be the value to search for, as in the following example. In this example, the Item element for 'XSL/XSLT' is located for formatting:

```
<template match="key('Glossary', 'XSL/XSLT')">
  ...
</template>
```

Recall that, because a key with a given name and value is not guaranteed to be unique, it cannot be assumed that such a reference will apply to a single element in the document.

Avoiding keys

A key does not offer anything that cannot be accomplished without this feature. As a key is constructed using expressions, these expressions could just as easily be used directly. The example above could be re-expressed as follows:

```
<template match="glossary/item[subject='XSL/XSLT']">
  ...
</template>
```

However, an XSLT processor may include advanced features for indexing elements and may build indexes from the information in the Key element, improving the performance of later searches. This feature also simplifies the expressions in the templates, making the meanings more clear.

Hypertext links

Many electronic documents contain **hypertext links**. These are links from references to the objects they reference, which users may follow if they desire. The popular Web browsers have been built around this concept from the start. But for a link to work, the destination object must have a unique identifier of some kind. In some cases, the source document will already have a unique identifier, identified as such within a DTD:

```
<!DOCTYPE book [ ...
<!ELEMENT chapter (para+)>
<!ATTLIST chapter ident ID #REQUIRED>
... ]>
<book>
  <chapter ident="ch1">
  ...
  </chapter>
  <chapter>
    <para>Link to chapter
      <linkto idref="ch1">one</linkto>.
    </para>
  </chapter>
</book>
```

No special effort is needed to convert such a document using XSLT, because the attribute values that link the reference to the destination are already in place in the source document and so simply need to be copied-through to the output:

```
<BODY>
  <DIV><A NAME="ch1"></A>
  ...
  </DIV>
  <DIV>
    <P>Link to chapter<A HREF="#ch1">one</A>.</P>
  </DIV>
</BODY>
```

A more significant problem is linking to an object that does not have a unique identifier in the source document. Using XPath expressions, it is possible to identify such elements, but not to assign identifiers to them. The **generate-id**() function can be used to create a unique identifier. This function is replaced by a unique value for the element, assigned by the XSLT formatter. For example, this function can be used to give every paragraph in the output document a unique identifier. The node to assign the identifier to must be passed to it, and in this case the '.' symbol is used to identify the current node:

```
<xsl:template match="para">
  <P ID="generate-id(.)">
    <xsl:apply-templates/>
  </P>
</xsl:template>
```

```
<P ID="N123456">...</P>
<P ID="N123457">...</P>
<P ID="N123458">...</P>
```

An element will always have the same unique identifier, even if this function is used to refer to the same element from elsewhere. This fact is very important. For example, every paragraph could be given a link to the chapter containing it, acting as a 'back-to-the-top' feature. It would be very important that all the generated identifiers are the same as each other, and as the chapter itself:

```
<xsl:template match="chapter">
  <DIV ID="generate-id(.)">
    <xsl:apply-templates/>
  </DIV>
</xsl:template>

<xsl:template match="para">
  <P><A HREF="#{generate-id(ancestor::chapter)">TOP </A>
    <xsl:apply-templates/>
  </P>
</xsl:template>


  <DIV ID="N987654">
     <P><A HREF="#N987654">TOP </A>...</P>
     <P><A HREF="#N987654">TOP </A>...</P>
     <P><A HREF="#N987654">TOP </A>...</P>
  </DIV>
```

14. Text format

Previous chapters have demonstrated how capable XSLT technology is at transforming XML documents into new XML structures, either to create new documents or to prepare material for publication. Yet XML data often needs to be processed for delivery to tools that are not XML-compliant. For example, there are a large number of very capable, text-based formatting languages, including RTF, TROFF and T$_E$X. XSLT is able to produce output that conforms to the syntax of such languages.

Non-XML output

It may seem to be obvious that it is not necessary for the output to be an XML document. When there is a need to transform an XML document into a proprietary format, it would seem to be possible simply to avoid entering any XML markup in the replacement text. With some limitations – which can be overcome – this assumption is correct. The following example produces RTF (Rich Text Format) output:

```
<template match="note">
  \pard\fs24<xsl:apply-templates/>\par
</template>
```

The only problem with this is that special characters are represented by XML entity references, due to the assumption that the output file will be read by an XML parser. In particular, if the characters '<', '>' or '&' appear in the replacement text, they will be output as '<', '>' and '&'. Only XML parsers recognize these as codes that are to be interpreted and replaced by single characters. If the output file is not going to be read by an XML parser, then these codes need to be replaced by the actual characters.

Earlier, it was shown that the Disable Output Escaping attribute may be used to overcome this problem, but this is a clumsy technique when the need is widespread. Consider the following example, which attempts to output data that contains a lot of '&' characters:

```
<template select="x">
  [<value-of select="x1"/>
  <text disable-output-escaping="yes">] &amp;[
  </text>
  <value-of select="x2"/>
  <text disable-output-escaping="yes">] &amp;[
  </text>
  <value-of select="x3"/>
</template>
```

```
[111] & [222] & [333]
```

Apart from the messy nature of this approach, it is also necessary to deal with special characters that occur in the source text. By default, when the Apply Templates instruction is applied to a text node, the characters '&', '<' and '>' are output as '&', '<' and '>'. To avoid this happening, it is necessary to override the default processing of text nodes as follows. The value of the current text node is output, with escaping disabled:

```
<company>Smith &amp; Son</company>
```

```
<template match="text()">
  <value-of select="."
            disable-output-escaping="yes" />
</template>
```

```
... Smith & Son ...
```

Finally, by default all output files have the namespace attached to the root output element. There should not be an issue here, as elements are not being output. But if there is any danger that something that looks like an element will be output, it is necessary to prevent the namespace attribute being attached. One way to do this is to configure the stylesheet to avoid having to use an explicit namespace for the output (by using the default namespace). The other is to ensure that the attribute is never created by setting the **Omit XML Declaration** attribute to 'yes' in the Output element. In addition, to avoid prefixes being added to the 'elements', the **Exclude Result Prefixes** in the Stylesheet element should be set to 'no'.

```
<stylesheet ...
            exclude-result-prefixes="no">
  <output ... omit-xml-declaration="yes" />
  ...
</stylesheet>
```

Text output mode

The techniques described above are complex and untidy. Fortunately, the XSLT standard includes a mechanism that makes output of non-XML data much simpler. However, this is an optional mechanism, and so a particular XSLT processor may not support it. In this circumstance, the techniques described above must be used instead.

Some XSLT processors (and hopefully most) will support the 'text mode' option. In this mode, none of the reserved escape characters is converted into its entity reference form ('&', '<' or '>'). This makes the Disable Output Escaping attribute redundant (if it is present at all). The main reason why this mode may not be supported is that some XSLT processors will not have control over the actual outputting of data.

The **Output** element is used to specify text format output. The **Method** attribute is given the value '**text**':

```
<transform ...>
  <output method="text"/>
  ...
<transform>
```

When the required output resembles XML, it is important to note that text that resembles element start-tags and end-tags is not copied to output. The first example below does not add any prefix or suffix to the content of the element. The second example works as expected:

```
<xsl:template match="title">
  <!-- DOES NOT WORK -->
  <TITLE><xsl:apply-templates/></TITLE>
</xsl:template>

<xsl:template match="title">
  &lt;TITLE&gt;<xsl:apply-templates/>&lt;/TITLE&gt;
</xsl:template>
```

The Media Type attribute can be used in this scenario. The default value is '**text/plain**':

```
<output method="text" media-type="text/xyz" />
```

The Encoding attribute can be used to specify how to represent special characters. If one or more characters in the source data cannot be represented by the format specified, the XSLT processor should report an error:

```
<output method="text" encoding="ISO-8859-1/" />
```

Extended characters can be specified in the template using the '&#...;' mechanism. This same mechanism is very useful in the following circumstance.

Line-ending issues

Line endings in ASCII text files have no relevance in XML, but in many formats they are very important. For example, in the TROFF (Text RunOFF) format, each formatting command must appear at the start of a text line. Line-end characters can be inserted into the output using XML character entity references. On Macintosh systems, the character Carriage Return (ASCII value 13) is used. On Unix sytems, it is the character Line Feed (ASCII value 10). On MS-DOS-based systems, both characters are used, in the sequence Carriage Return followed by Line Feed. But, depending on the parser underlying the stylesheet processor, either character alone may produce the platform-specific outcome required (so this needs testing). The following example outputs TROFF commands, with each command beginning a new line on a UNIX system (and '.PP' specifies a new paragraph):

```
<xsl:template match="warning">
.PP&#13;&#10;
WARNING:&#13;&#10;
.PP&#13;&#10;
<xsl:apply-templates/>
</xsl:template>


    .PP
    WARNING:
    .PP
    . . . . . .
```

Whitespace in the stylesheet can cause problems here. As previously described, nodes that consist only of whitespace characters, including the line-feed and carriage-return characters, are removed from the stylesheet when it is processed. The following example therefore does not work as intended:

```
    <name>John Smith</name>
    <name>Peter Jones</name>

<xsl:template match="name">
<xsl:apply-templates/>&#13;&#10;
</xsl:template>


    John SmithhPeter Jones
```

The obvious solution is to use the Text element to enclose the codes. This preserves them as required:

```
<xsl:template match="name">
<xsl:apply-templates/><xsl:text>&#13;&#10;</xsl:text>
</xsl:template>
```

Whitespace in the source document can also cause problems. A line-feed or carriage-return character in a source element is normally just copied through to the output:

```
<code>10 PRINT 'HELLO'</code>
<code>20 GOTO
10</code>
```

```
<xsl:template match="code">
CODE LINE: <xsl:apply-templates/>
</xsl:template>
```

```
CODE LINE: 10 PRINT 'HELLO'
CODE LINE: 20 GOTO
10
```

This problem can be solved by replacing the Apply Templates element with the Value Of element, ensuring that the string it selects (the content of the current element) is normalized before it is inserted into the output:

```
<xsl:template match="code">
CODE LINE: <xsl:value-of select="normalize-space(.)" />
</xsl:template>
```

```
CODE LINE: 10 PRINT 'HELLO'
CODE LINE: 20 GOTO 10
```

Finally, whitespace characters inserted into the source XML document to make the document easier to read could have unfortunate consequences if included in the output. Using the **Strip Space** element (within the Stylesheet element) ensures that this whitespace is removed prior to template processing:

```
<strip-space elements="*" />
```

However, this instruction must be used with caution, as described in Chapter 4.

15. Namespaces

Most of the examples in previous chapters have included a mixture of XSLT elements and HTML elements, and **namespaces** have been used to distinguish between them. The problem of mixing fragments of XML from different sources within a single data file is widely recognized, well beyond the application of XML being discussed in this book. The solution to this problem is the standard called '**Namespaces in XML**'. This standard was produced by W^3C and released as a recommendation on 14 January 1999. It can be found at http://www.w3.org/TR/REC-xml-names. It has already been described sufficiently to illustrate the previous examples, but this chapter explains the namespaces standard in more detail and also addresses the complex issues that arise when using namespaces in this application. In particular, the complications are discussed that arise from the fact that source documents, stylesheets and output documents may all use namespaces.

Namespaces in stylesheets

The need for namespaces

The concept of namespaces is very important to XSLT when a stylesheet contains a mixture of XSLT rules and output document elements. It is possible, for example, to imagine the need to create an XML document that contains an element named 'template'. Without namespaces, it would be very difficult for the XSLT processor to interpret the following markup:

```
<template match="...">
  <template>
    <apply-templates/>
  </template>
</template>
```

It is an incidental detail that HTML and XSL formatting elements do not happen to clash with XSLT elements in this way. In other cases, there may be such a conflict.

It is also important for the XSLT processor to be able to distinguish between element sets. A processor that understands XSLT 1.0 is expected to be able to interpret stylesheets that conform to a later version of the XSLT standard, and therefore the processor needs to be able to recognize XSLT elements that were invented later, so as not to treat them inadvertently as output elements.

Prefixes

At the heart of the namespaces scheme is the concept of an element prefix, which is separated from the element name using a colon, ':'. For example, the HTML element 'H3' could become 'html:H3', and the XSLT element 'template' could become 'XSLT:template'. Using this approach, the example above can be made valid, in this case by assigning the prefix 'XSLT' to all XSLT elements, and 'MyDoc' to all target document elements:

```
<XSLT:template match="...">
  <MyDoc:template>
    <XSLT:apply-templates/>
  <MyDoc:template>
</XSLT:template>
```

Namespace declarations

If prefix names were assigned by the same authorities that created the respective element sets, the same prefix could accidentally be chosen by both parties, and clashes would then still occur. To avoid this happening, namespaces must therefore be assigned an identifier that is guaranteed to be unique. A good, ready-made candidate for this is the URL standard. A URL provides a unique, globally recognized address for the description or DTD that defines the elements and attributes that a namespace covers. For example, HTML-4 is defined at http://www.w3.org/TR/REC-html40, and XSLT is defined at http://www.w3.org/1999/XSL/Transform.

While unique, these text strings would not be ideal as prefix names. First, they often contain characters that are not allowed in XML element names. Second, they are too long to be manageable. However, they can be mapped to *locally* defined prefixes that are both short and legal. The namespaces standard provides for this mapping using an attribute that includes the prefix '**xmlns**' followed by the assigned prefix name. For example:

```
xmlns:html="http://www.w3.org/TR/REC-html40"
```

```
xmlns:xsl="http://www.w3.org/1999/XSL/Transform"
```

In this example, the HTML-4 namespace is mapped, locally, to the prefix name 'html', and the XSLT namespace is mapped to 'xsl'. The document author (in this case the stylesheet author) decides what prefixes to use, so that conflicts can always be avoided. Note that for historical but now confusing reasons, the convention is to use 'xsl' for XSLT elements, and '**fo**' (**Formatting Objects**) for XSL elements.

The 'xmlns' attribute can be used on the Stylesheet element:

```
<xsl:stylesheet
        xmlns:xsl="http://www.w3.org/1999/XSL/Transform">
    ...
</xsl:stylesheet>
```

The XSLT standard contains examples that use namespaces for both the XSLT element set and the output elements:

```
<xsl:stylesheet
        xmlns:xsl="http://www.w3.org/1999/XSL/Transform"
        xmlns:fo="http://www.w3.org/1999/XSL/Format"  >
    ...
  <xsl:template>
    <fo:block><xsl:apply-templates/></fo:block>
  </xsl:template>
    ...
</xsl:stylesheet>
```

At first sight, DTD authors may think that these examples include two instances of the 'xmlns' attribute on the Stylesheet element, which would be illegal according to the rules of the XML specification. However, from the DTD perspective these are considered to be distinct attributes. The names 'xmlns:xsl' and 'xmlns:fo', for instance, are not the same. Creation of a DTD to validate stylesheets (to ensure correct usage of the XSLT elements), or to offer guided authoring of stylesheets, involves consideration of this and other issues.

Default namespaces

Using prefixes throughout reduces legibility and is unnecessary. One namespace can be assigned to be the default namespace. When no prefix is present, the element is assumed to belong to this default namespace. The following is therefore valid:

```
<xsl:stylesheet
        xmlns:xsl="http://www.w3.org/1999/XSL/Transform"
        xmlns="http://www.w3.org/1999/XSL/Format"  >
    ...
  <xsl:template match="para">
    <block><xsl:apply-templates/></block>
  </xsl:template>
    ...
</xsl:stylesheet>
```

The alternative approach is to make the XSLT elements the default set:

```
<stylesheet xmlns="http://www.w3.org/1999/XSL/Transform"
            xmlns:fo="http://www.w3.org/1999/XSL/Format">
  ...
  <template match="para">
    <fo:block><apply-templates/></fo:block>
  </template>
  ...
</stylesheet>
```

Theoretically, this method can even be used with HTML output, as the XSLT processor could be clever enough to recognize the HTML URL, realize from this that it is dealing with HTML, understand that current Web browsers cannot cope with output in the form '<html:HTML>...</html:HTML>', and therefore remove the prefixes on output. But some XSLT processors may not do this, and so it is worth testing first.

Attributes that have no prefix are assumed to belong to the same namespace as the elements they belong to, so that they have their own concept of 'default' namespace. A prefix is always needed on an attribute if it belongs to a namespace other than the one the element belongs to. Some XSLT attributes may be used in result elements. For example, the attribute 'use-attribute-sets' may be used in output elements to attach predefined attribute names and values to the element, but when used here they must include the XSLT namespace prefix:

```
<P xsl:use-attribute-set="common-set" version="1.3">
  ...
</P>
```

Namespaces in input documents

Documents to be processed using an XSLT processor may already conform to the namespaces standard, perhaps because they contain elements from more than one namespace.

The stylesheet needs to be able to distinguish between elements from different namespaces when selecting templates. This is simply done by including the prefix in the Match attribute:

```
    <widget>normal widget</widget>
    <acme:widget>an ACME widget</acme:widget>


<template match="widget">
  <!-- PROCESS NORMAL WIDGETS -->
</template>
```

```
<template match="acme:widget">
  <!-- PROCESS ACME WIDGETS -->
</template>
```

Although these prefixes are not attached to any elements within the stylesheet, the stylesheet must nevertheless contain a suitable namespace declaration (referring to the same URL as the equivalent declaration in the source document):

```
<xsl:stylesheet xmlns:="Widget-namespace"
                xmlns:acme="ACMEnamespace">
  ...
</xsl:stylesheet>
```

A declaration is not needed in the stylesheet for the input document's default namespace.

Namespaces in output documents

Namespace details may need to be added to the elements and attributes output by the XSLT processor. Indeed, this is vital when the created document contains elements from more than one namespace.

Multiple namespaces

It is a simple matter to include output elements in the stylesheet that have different prefixes, though it is of course necessary to include namespace declarations for each one.

When the output document contains elements from more than one namespace, the root element usually needs to contain multiple namespace declarations. All namespace declarations in the stylesheet are automatically copied to the output document, except for the XSLT namespace declaration and any others that are explicitly excluded (see below).

Avoiding namespaces

It is sometimes useful to be able to create output documents that do not use namespaces. Some simple XML-based applications may not be aware of the namespaces standard, and be 'hardwired' to expect specific element and attribute names. Such applications will not recognize names that include a namespace prefix. Namespaces also make XML documents harder to read, and more verbose.

The easy way to omit element name prefixes is to avoid using prefixes for these elements within the stylesheet (to make the output set the default namespace).

However, even the default namespace has a namespace declaration within the stylesheet, and normally this declaration is copied to the output. In this scenario, though, the declaration is not wanted. The **Exclude Result Prefixes** attribute can be used to suppress the namespace declaration. The value of this attribute consists of one or more space-separated prefix names, but in this case there is no prefix name (because it is the default). For the default namespace, the keyword '**#default**' is used:

```
<xsl:stylesheet xmlns="OUTnamespace"
                . . .
                exclude-result-prefixes="#default">
  . . .
</xsl:stylesheet>
```

The namespace declaration for the XSLT elements is not copied to output, but all other declarations in the Stylesheet element would normally be copied, including any that have been included just to refer to elements in the source document (as described above). These namespace declarations can also be suppressed in the output document using the Exclude Result Prefixes attribute:

```
<xsl:stylesheet
        xmlns:xsl="..."
        xmlns="OUTnamespace"
        xmlns:acme="ACMEnamespace"
        exclude-result-prefixes="#default acme">
  . . .
  <xsl:template match="acme:widget">
    <OUT-WIDGET><xsl:apply-templates/></OUT-WIDGET>
  </xsl:template>
  . . .
</xsl:stylesheet>


    <OUT>
        <OUT-WIDGET>...</OUT-WIDGET>
    </OUT>
```

Note that, because declarations are otherwise automatically copied to output from the stylesheet itself, attempts to copy-through the namespace declaration on the root element of the source document, using general techniques for copying-through attribute values, are not applicable in this special case.

It is important to appreciate that the Exclude Result Prefixes attribute alone cannot be used to create an output document that does not use namespaces. It excludes the namespace declaration but does not (despite its name) suppress prefixes attached to element names within the stylesheet. It is also necessary to use the default namespace for output elements.

Embedded namespaces

A large document may contain small fragments that conform to a different name-space, and the namespace declaration can appear on the 'root' element of each fragment, instead of on the root element of the entire document. The **Element** ele-ment has an optional **Namespace** attribute, which holds the URL of the name-space. An XSLT processor should be able to generate a prefix to use for the contents, such as 'ns1':

```
<template match="acme:widget">
  <element name="OUT-WIDGET" namespace="OutURL">
    <apply-templates/>
  </element>
</template>
```

```
<ns1:OUT-WIDGET xmlns:ns1="OutURL">
    <ns1:NAME>...</ns1:NAME>
    ...
</ns1:OUT-WIDGET>
```

The **Attribute** element may also use the **Namespace** attribute. If a document con-tains only a very small number of attributes from another namespace, this is a prac-tical option. Two attributes are actually created. First, the named attribute is created and given the stated value, as usual, but the name of this attribute includes a generated prefix. In addition, a namespace declaration attribute is also created on the element, including the URL given in the Namespace attribute, and the gener-ated prefix. For example, if a document occasionally contained a Currency attribute that conformed to the (fictional) 'Registered Currencies' format, and this format were to be assigned the namespace 'currencyURL', the following Name-space attribute would be appropriate:

```
<template match="price">
  <element name="PRICE">
    <attribute name="CURRENCY" namespace="currencyURL">
    <apply-templates/>
  </element>
</template>
```

```
<WIDGET>
  <PRICE ns1:CURRENCY="EN-pounds"
         xmlns:ns1="currencyURL">134</PRICE>
  ...
</WIDGET>
```

Outputting stylesheets (aliases)

Because XSLT documents are XML documents, they can be produced using another XSLT stylesheet. This approach might be used to convert other SGML/ XML-based stylesheet languages into XSLT equivalents. Consider the following example stylesheet rule (from a fictional language):

```
<rule trigger="warning">
  <style type="block" format="bold">
    <trigger-rules/>
  </style>
</rule>
```

The transformation required needs to convert this into an XSLT template (a quite trivial task in this example), and replace the product-specific formatting information with HTML equivalents (in this case bold and paragraph tags):

```
<xsl:template match="warning">
  <P><B><xsl:apply-templates/></B></P>
</xsl:template>
```

The problem that arises is that the output elements 'template' and 'apply-templates' must not get confused with the stylesheet rules. Yet the output document must refer to the XSLT namespace or it will not be later recognized as an XSLT document. At the same time, the XSLT namespace cannot be assigned to the output elements, as this would indicate to the XSLT processor that it should interpret these elements as instructions instead of output elements.

This problem can be overcome by using an alias for the URL used to identify output elements, and the **Namespace Alias** element to map the alias to the true output namespace. The **Stylesheet Prefix** and **Result Prefix** attributes hold the before-and-after names:

```
<xsl:namespace-alias stylesheet-prefix="alias"
                     result-prefix="xsl" />
```

This ensures that the correct URL is specified in the output document (the URL for 'xsl' in this case):

```
<xsl:stylesheet version="1.0"
        xmlns:xsl="http://www.w3.org/1999/XSL/Transform"
        xmlns:alias="ThisIsAnAlias" >
  ...
  <xsl:namespace-alias stylesheet-prefix=" alias"
                     result-prefix="xsl" />
  ...
```

```
<!-- CONVERT RULES TO TEMPLATES -->
  <xsl:template match="rule">
    <alias:template match="{@trigger}">
      <xsl:if test="style='block'">
        <P>
          <xsl:if test="format='bold'">
            <B>
              <alias:apply-templates/>
            </B>
          </xsl:if>
          ...
        </P>
      </xsl:if>
      ...
    </alias:template>
  </xsl:template>
  ...
</xsl:stylesheet>
```

The resulting output for the source rule shown above, and for the whole document, would be as follows:

```
<alias:stylesheet ...
       xmlns:alias="http://www.w3.org/1999/XSL/Transform">
  ...
  <alias:template match="warning">
    <P><B><alias:apply-templates/></B></P>
  </alias:template>
  ...
</alias:stylesheet>
```

16. Productivity features

XSLT includes some advanced features that assist with the construction of stylesheets (simplifying or reducing the effort needed to create them). None of the features described in this chapter affects what can actually be achieved using a stylesheet. Variables, attribute sets and named templates can be used to avoid needless repetition, and an advanced method of building a template can sometimes reduce the number of templates needed. Also, single template stylesheets can be abbreviated. Finally, debugging of stylesheets in development can be assisted using messages.

Variables

A variable is a named object that holds a value. A number of references can be made to the variable wherever that value is needed, and each reference is replaced by the value when the stylesheet is processed.

Use of a variable could be considered whenever the same value appears in two or more places in the stylesheet, and there is no reason to believe that the values in each place will ever be different from each other. For example, if important text is always presented on a red background, and there are a number of places where, for this purpose, the colour red is specified in the stylesheet, then the CSS instruction 'background-color:red' could be replaced with the variable name 'important'. There are two clear benefits. First, the value is replaced by a meaningful name ('important') that clarifies the purpose of the instruction. The stylesheet is therefore more legible, and is easier to maintain. Second, if the value needs to be changed, with a variable the edit is made in a single place (where the variable is defined), reducing the possibility of errors arising from forgetting to change one of the values, or from miskeying one of the updates.

Attribute definitions

The first way to define a variable is using the **Variable** element. The **Name** attribute holds the name of the variable. In the following example, a variable called 'important' is being defined:

```
<variable name="important" ...>
   ...
</variable>
```

Note that, unlike variables in programming languages, these variables do not actually '**vary**', in the sense that their values cannot change while the stylesheet is in use. However, it is possible to declare a new variable, with the same name but holding a different value, that overrides the original definition within a specific part of the stylesheet. A definition made within a template overrides a global definition. But it is not possible to override a variable that is already defined within a template, or a global variable with the another global variable of the same name. The first two definitions in the following example are therefore valid, but the third and fourth are not:

```
<variable name="blue" ...>
<!-- GLOBAL DEFINITION APPLIES HERE -->
<template...>
   ... <!-- GLOBAL DEFINITION APPLIES HERE -->
   <variable name="blue" ...>
   ... <!-- OVERRIDE DEFINITION APPLIES HERE -->
   <variable name="blue" ...> <!-- ILLEGAL -->
</template>
<!-- GLOBAL DEFINITION APPLIES HERE -->
<variable name="blue" ...> <!-- ILLEGAL -->
```

Simple variables

A variable can hold a simple text string. For example, the string 'background-color:red' can be stored in a variable called 'important'. This is done by entering the value into the Variable element:

```
<variable name="important">background-color:red</variable>
```

Variable references

The variable is used by referring to the variable name, and the name is replaced by the variable value when the stylesheet is processed. A reference to a variable is identified using a '$' prefix. For example, '$important' refers to the 'important' variable. Such references can appear wherever an XPath expression is allowed.

To insert a string attribute value into the middle of a text string, the Value Of element can be used. The variable name is placed in the Select attribute:

```
The style '<value-of select="$important"/>' is used for
important text.
```

The result is:

The style 'background-color:red' is used for important text.

At first sight, this approach may appear to be invalid. The value of the Select attribute should be an expression, but in the example above the replacement value for the variable reference is the string 'background-color:red', which is clearly not an expression. However, a variable reference within this element has an implied 'string('...')' function around it, so that the example below (using no variable) is equivalent:

```
The style '<xsl:value-of select="string('background-
color:red')"/>' is used for important text.
```

Variables can be referenced from most instruction elements, but cannot be used in the Match and Use attributes.

Variables in output attributes

The approach described above could be used to insert values into output element attributes, as in the following example where the important style definition is inserted into the STYLE attribute:

```
<xsl:template match="note[@type='3']">
  <P>
    <xsl:attribute name="STYLE">
      <xsl:value-of select="$important"/>
    </xsl:attribute>
    <xsl:apply-templates/>
  </P>
</xsl:template>


    <P STYLE="background-color:red">...</P>
```

However, there is a simpler way to achieve this effect. Variable values can also be inserted directly into output attribute values, using an expression:

```
<xsl:template match="note[@type='3']">
  <P STYLE='{$important}'>
    <xsl:apply-templates/>
  </P>
</xsl:template>
```

Result-tree fragments

Variables can also contain result-tree fragments. These are XML fragments that conform to the output format. For example, a copyright notice in HTML format may be enclosed within a paragraph element, and contain bold text.

When the value consists of an output element, as in the following example, it is considered to be a result-tree fragment:

```
<xsl:variable name="copyright">
  <P>(c) <B>ACME</B> Corp </P>
</xsl:variable>
```

This distinction is critical, because the way in which the value is output differs. When the value is a string, the Value Of element is used to reference it (discarding any embedded markup). When the value is a result-tree fragment, the Copy Of element should be used instead:

```
<xsl:template match="book"
  <HTML>
    <xsl:apply-templates/>
    <xsl:copy-of select="$copyright"/>
  </HTML>
</xsl:template>
```

In theory, the Copy Of element should work for simple strings as well as result-tree fragments, but it has been known to fail for simple text strings in some XSLT processors.

Expression values

An attribute value can be the result of an expression. The **Select** attribute is used to hold the expression. In this scenario, the Attribute element should be empty, as it is not possible for an attribute to have two values at the same time.

One use for this technique is to set flags that switch on and switch off parts of a stylesheet as desired. For example, consider a variable called 'debug', which holds an expression of either 'true()' or 'false()'. When the variable is given the value 'true()', all the debug paragraphs are to be output; when set to false, they are to be suppressed. This variable can be referenced in If tests:

```
<xsl:variable name="debug" select="true()"/>

<xsl:template match="para">
  <xsl:if test="$debug">
    <P>SOURCE WAS 'para' ELEMENT</P>
  </xsl:test>
  <P><xsl:apply-templates/></P>
</xsl:template>
```

However, in other circumstances it is important to understand that the expression is actually applied once the value has been copied over the references, not when the variable is defined. This means that context is important.

Attribute sets

Sometimes, the same set of attributes are attached to a number of output elements. For example, consider the possibility that Note, Warning and Danger elements are to be formatted in the same way, using XSL formatting attributes (explained in Chapter 17). If the specification were to change, all three of the templates below would need to be edited:

```
<template match="note">
  <fo:block color="blue" font-weight="bold">
    <apply-templates/>
  </fo:block>
</template>

<template match="warning">
  <fo:block color="blue" font-weight="bold">
    <apply-templates/>
  </fo:block>
</template>

<template match="danger">
  <fo:block color="blue" font-weight="bold">
    <apply-templates/>
  </fo:block>
</template>
```

But when the same attributes need to be attached to a number of output elements, they can be defined in a single place and referenced each time they are needed. The group of attributes concerned are defined using **Attribute** elements, but these elements are enclosed in the **Attribute Set** element. This set of elements is referenced by name, which is given in the **Name** attribute:

```
<attribute-set name="attention">
  <attribute name="color">blue</attribute>
  <attribute name="font-weight">bold</attribute>
</attribute-set>
```

The 'attention' set defined above can then be inserted by reference into the three templates, using the **Use Attribute Sets** attribute. This attribute can be used in the Element element:

```
<template match="note">
  <element name="block" use-attribute-sets="attention">
    <apply-templates/>
  </element>
</template>

<template match="warning">
  <element name="block" use-attribute-sets="attention">
    <apply-templates/>
  </element>
</template>
```

```
<template match="danger">
  <element name="block" use-attribute-sets="attention">
    <apply-templates/>
  </element>
</template>
```

This attribute can also be added to output elements, but the namespaces scheme requires a prefix that maps to the XSL namespace:

```
<xsl:template match="note">
  <block xsl:use-attribute-sets="attention">
    <xsl:apply-templates/>
  </block>
</xsl:template>
```

Conveniently, it is possible to override one or more of the attributes defined in the set, simply by specifying a new value in the output element:

```
<xsl:attribute-set name="attention">
  <xsl:attribute name="color">blue</attribute>
  <xsl:attribute name="font-weight">bold</attribute>
</xsl:attribute-set>


  <block xsl:use-attribute-set="attention" color="red">...
```

Expressions can be used in the attributes defined in an attribute set, without causing any problems as regards the appropriate definition of the current node and current node set. Variables may also be included, but only variables that are defined at the top level will be 'visible' within the attribute set definition.

When an imported stylesheet contains an Attribute Set element of the same name as one in the main stylesheet, the importing importance rules dictate that an attribute with the same name, but of lower importance, is ignored.

Named templates

When the same output structures are required in a number of circumstances, it is possible to create a template to hold them. This template can be named, and referenced from other templates.

Simple referenced templates

The template is given a name using the **Name** attribute. For example, a dividing line may need to be output above a number of different output structures:

```
<xsl:template name="divideLine">
  <BR/><HR/><BR/>
</xsl:template>
```

This template can be referenced from within other templates using the **Call Template** element. This element also has a **Name** attribute, which is used to name the template to use:

```
<xsl:template name="chapter">
  <xsl:call-template name="divideLine"/>
  <H1>NEW CHAPTER</H1><xsl:apply-templates/>
</xsl:template>

<xsl:template name="section">
  <xsl:call-template name="divideLine"/>
  <H2>NEW SECTION</H2><xsl:apply-templates/>
</xsl:template>
```

The named template does not change the current element, and if it contains Match, Priority or Mode attributes, they have no effect. It is simply a convenient wrapper for material that is needed in several places.

Parameters

As described above, named templates appear to be of limited value. It is not very common for exactly the same material to be needed in a number of different circumstances. For example, it is unlikely that a dividing line between chapters will be the same as between sections (it may be thicker or wider).

The following templates show how the Note, Warning and Danger elements have very similar formatting (only the background colour and prefix text differ):

```
<xsl:template name="note">
  <HR/>
  <DIV STYLE='background-color:blue'>
    <P><xsl:text>Note: </xsl:text>
      <xsl:apply-templates/>
    </P>
  </DIV>
  <HR/>
</xsl:template>

<xsl:template name="warning">
  <HR/>
  <DIV STYLE='background-color:yellow'>
    <P><xsl:text>Warning: </xsl:text>
      <xsl:apply-templates/>
    </P>
  </DIV>
  <HR/>
</xsl:template>
```

```
<xsl:template name="danger">
  <HR/>
  <DIV STYLE='background-color:red'>
    <P><xsl:text>Danger: </xsl:text>
      <xsl:apply-templates/>
    </P>
  </DIV>
  <HR/>
</xsl:template>
```

It would be useful to be able to use a named template, but to modify just part of its contents, depending on where it is applied. An approach familiar to software developers allows 'parameters' to be passed to a function, procedure or method; the **With Parameter** element provides this kind of feature in XSLT. This element can be used within the Call Template element. It has a **Name** attribute to name the parameter. The examples above can be reformulated in the following way. In the following example, the Note template passes two parameters to the 'NoteWarning-Danger' template, specifying the colour and prefix text to be used in this context:

```
<template name="note">
  <call-template name="NoteWarningDanger">
    <with-param name="colour">blue</with-param>
    <with-param name="prefix">Note</with-param>
  </call-template>
</template>
```

The named template needs to accept and use the two parameters. The parameters are defined within the template using the **Parameter** element. This element works in the same way as the Variable element. It has the same attributes and is referenced in the same way (by name, with a '$' prefix). The **Name** attribute is used to define the parameter, and the value is defined by the **Select** attribute or by the content of the element. The one big difference is that the value specified is only the default value, to be employed when a specific value is not passed to the template. In the following example, the color parameter is given a default value of 'white', and the prefix parameter is given a default value of 'Note':

```
<xsl:template name="NoteWarningDanger">
  <xsl:param name="colour">white</xsl:param>
  <xsl:param name="prefix">Note</xsl:param>
  <HR/>
  <DIV STYLE='background-color:{$colour}'>
    <P><xsl:value-of select='$prefix'>
      <xsl:text>: </xsl:text>
      <xsl:apply-templates/>
    </P>
  </DIV>
  <HR/>
</xsl:template>
```

Single-template short-cut

When only a single template is needed, and applies to the root node of the source document, the Template element is not required. Even the Stylesheet element is redundant. Instead, the root element of the 'stylesheet document' can be the root output element. However, namespaces are needed to support this feature. The root element needs to hold the XSLT version and namespace declarations:

```
<BOOK xsl:version="1.0"
      xslns:xsl="..." >
   ...
</BOOK>
```

Elements normally appearing within templates can be used freely, except for the Apply Templates element (as there are no other templates to apply):

```
<BOOK ...>
   ... <xsl:value-of.../> ...
</BOOK>
```

Direct processing

It is possible, under certain circumstances, effectively to embed templates within other templates. The **For Each** element is used for this purpose. It selects other elements and applies an embedded template to each occurrence. The number of templates needed can in this manner be radically reduced. Consider the following example, where information on a number of customers is present.

```
<customers>

  <customer>
    <name>J Smith</name>
    <order>123</order>
    <order>456</order>
  </customer>

  <customer>
    <name>P Jones</name>
    <order>987</order>
    <order>654</order>
  </customer>

</customers>
```

To create an HTML table from this structure, with one row for each customer, four templates would normally be required:

```
<xsl:template match="customers">
  <TABLE><TBODY><xsl:apply-templates/></TBODY></TABLE>
</xsl:template>

<xsl:template match="customer">
  <TR><xsl:apply-templates/></TR>
</xsl:template>

<xsl:template match="name">
  <TH><xsl:apply-templates/></TH>
</xsl:template/>

<xsl:template match="order">
  <TD><xsl:apply-templates/></TD>
</xsl:template/>
```

These four rules can be replaced by a single rule, which is both briefer and clearer in its intent. A template is created for the Customers element, and the table structure is built within it. Then each Customer element is selected using the For Each instruction, with each match building one row of the table, creating a header cell and placing the Name element content within it, and then activating a further For Each command that adds a table data cell for each Order element:

```
<xsl:template match="Customers">
  <TABLE>
    <TBODY>

      <xsl:for-each select="Customer">
        <TR>
          <TH>
            <xsl:apply-templates="Name"/>
          </TH>

          <xsl:for-each select="Order">
            <TD>
              <xsl:apply-templates/>
            </TD>
          </xsl:for-each>

        </TR>
      </xsl:for-each>

    </TBODY>
  </TABLE>
</xsl:template/>
```

Transformations that rely upon use of the Template element can be described as 'event-driven' processes. Individual templates in the stylesheet are triggered by events in the program. The document controls the order in which the templates are triggered (from the order in which the elements appear within it). With the direct approach described here, processing is controlled by the stylesheet instead. This approach is applicable when the output format is totally independent of the source document structure. The stylesheet may consist of a single template.

Many examples of this feature (including the one above) show its use in looping through child elements. However, the Select attribute can actually hold any expression. Consider the example of a complex document that contains a number of Name elements, some holding the names of people, others holding company names. When the requirement is simply to output all the individual names, then all the company names, in both cases as a list in document order, the direct processing approach is appropriate:

```
<xsl:template match="Document">
  <HTML><BODY>
  <H1>Individual Names</H1>
  <OL>
    <xsl:for-each select="//Name[@type='personal']">
      <LI><xsl:value-of select="."/></LI>
    </xsl:for-each>
  </OL>
  <H1>Company Names</H1>
  <OL>
    <xsl:for-each select="//Name[@type='company']">
      <LI><xsl:value-of select="."/></LI>
    </xsl:for-each>
  </OL>
  </BODY></HTML>
</xsl:template>
```

The Sort element can be used within For Each elements, but must appear first if present. The example above can be modified to list names in alphabetical order:

```
<xsl:template match="Document">
  <HTML><BODY>
  <H1>Individual Names</H1>
  <OL>
    <xsl:for-each select="//Name[@type='personal']">
      <xsl:sort/>
      <LI><xsl:value-of select="."/></LI>
    </xsl:for-each>
  </OL>
  <H1>Company Names</H1>
  <OL>
    <xsl:for-each select="//Name[@type='company']">
      <xsl:sort/>
      <LI><xsl:value-of select="."/></LI>
    </xsl:for-each>
  </OL>
  </BODY></HTML>
</xsl:template>
```

Messages

Many software developers will be familiar with the (now primitive) technique of adding 'print' statments to their programs in order to track down bugs. A similar technique is available to XSLT stylesheet developers, using the **Message** element. This element can be placed within a template and holds an appropriate message for display when the template is activated:

```
<template match="//warning/*/para">
  <message>Template //warning/*/para is activated</message>
  <apply-templates/>
</template>
```

This element has no effect on normal output from the stylesheet. Instead, the text content of the Message element is somehow presented to the user of the XSLT processor software. In a windows-based system, a pop-up window may appear. On a command-line system, the messages would appear as standard output:

```
D:\xslt> xslt In.xml Out.htm
D:\xslt> MESSAGE: Template //warning/*/para is activated
D:\xslt> FINISHED
D:\xslt>
```

The **Terminate** attribute, which has a default value of 'no', may be set to 'yes' in order to terminate document processing immediately:

```
<template match="problem">
  <message terminate="yes">Problem element detected
  correct the error and restart</message>
</template>
```

The Message element may be used within other elements that a Template element can contain:

```
<template match="para">
  <if test="@secret='yes'">
    ...
    <message>Secret paragraph found.</message>
  </if>
  ...
</template>
```

The Message element may in turn contain all these other elements, including the Value Of element, which is particularly useful for reporting on the current context. For example, the title of the chapter containing a secret chapter can be reported:

```
<template match="para[@secret='yes']">
  <message>Secret paragraph found in Chapter:
    <value-of select="ancestor::chapter/title" />
  </message>
  ...
</template>
```

As another example, a named template could be created that reports the name and identifier of the current element:

```
<template name="elementName">
  <message>
    ELEMENT: <value-of select="name()" />
    ID: <value-of select="@id" />
  </message>
</template>

<template match="para">
  <call-template name="elementName" />
  ...
</template>
```

17. XSL

At the heart of the original XSL proposal was a scheme for styling XML documents. Most of the discussion up to this point has focused on the now separate XSLT standard for manipulating content. While this capability can be used to format a document using other formatting languages (such as HTML), it was originally intended to prepare material for styling using XSL.

Note that XSL is a large and complex standard. While all XSL elements are introduced in this chapter, some of the more obscure attributes they may include are not completely described, are mentioned only briefly, or are not covered at all.

Background

XSL (eXtensible Stylesheet Language) is a markup language that is suitable for formatting material to screen and to paper. At the time of writing (early 2000), the XSL standard is still in draft form (http://www.w3.org/TR/2000/WD-xsl-20000301) and there is little software support for it. However, the details have changed little in recent versions, so that the information given here should be very close to the final standard (which will be found at www.w3.org/TR/xsl). Despite this, there are still gaps and questions outstanding, and so this description should be considered as a guide to the general shape and scope of the language, rather than a definitive reference to it.

XSL is a powerful, and therefore complex, language, with 51 formatting object types, including simple items such as blocks and inline areas, as well as lists, tables, dynamic features and links. The formatting objects are configured using some of the 231 properties also specified. While it is expected that XSL support will be added to many existing formatting products, including DTP (Desk Top Publishing) applications, typesetting engines and document browsers, it is unlikely that any of these products will have features that exactly match those defined in the XSL standard. However, competing products will have to reveal which features are supported, and product comparisons will soon therefore be easier to make than ever before.

Many of the formatting options are similar to, or identical to, CSS formatting properties. In such cases, CSS property names have been adopted by XSL in order to simplify transition between languages and reduce the effort needed to learn both. In general, a CSS property name is simply translated into an XML attribute name.

Note that an unofficial forum for discussing the implementation, use and future direction of XSL can be accessed by registering with the news group governed by majordomo@mulberrytech.com, including 'subscribe xsl-list' in the body of the message.

An archive of past correspondence can be accessed from the Web site http://www.mulberrytech.com/xsl/xsl-list.

XSL instructions

XSL formatting instructions are XML elements that contain the text they apply to. Attributes are frequently used to specify the styles to be applied to this text. For those familiar with CSS and other stylesheet languages, this is an unfamiliar concept. With these languages, the content is always separate from the styling instructions. The XSL approach more closely resembles traditional typesetting languages, where formatting instructions are embedded in the text.

XSL documents are therefore XML documents. Although no DTD is specified for XSL elements, one could be derived from the definitions in the draft XSL standard, and this DTD could be used to validate an XSL document. One possible reason why a DTD has not been defined could be to discourage that idea that XSL documents may be created directly by document authors. This would certainly be a bad idea, because XSL documents break the cardinal rule for XML documents; that they be self-describing. Instead, XSL documents should almost always be created from information in other formats, including other XML documents (but not excluding others forms, such as data stored in relational databases), and discarded after being used by an XSL formatting engine to create formatted output. Of course, one way to convert arbitrary XML documents into XSL documents would be to use XSLT.

The following example demonstrates the use of two of the most common instructions. It emulates the HTML fragment below:

```
<block>A <wrapper font-weight="bold" >bold</wrapper>
statement.</block>

<P>A <B>bold</B> statement.</P>
```

XSL formatting instructions are known as '**formatting object**' elements, or '**FO**' elements for short. In the event that these elements are mixed with elements from other document types, there is a namespace defined for them. The FO namespace is http://www.w3.org/1999/XSL/Format, which is commonly mapped to a prefix of 'fo':

```
<fo:block>A
<fo:wrapper font-weight="bold">bold</fo:wrapper>
statement.</fo:block>
```

This namespace is referenced from XSLT stylesheets:

```
<stylesheet ...
            xmlns:fo="http://www.w3.org/1999/XSL/Format" >

  <template match="para">
    <fo:block><apply-templates/></fo:block>
  </template>
```

Examples in this chapter dispense with the prefix, as they do not include elements from other namespaces and their absence makes the examples more legible. But it should not be forgotten that such prefixes are often necessary.

Templates and content

The root element of an XSL document is actually called **Root**. This element contains two major sections. First, templates are defined that specify the characteristics of the pages to display or print, including the size of these pages. More than one page template may be defined (for example, this book requires a different template for the preliminary pages than for the chapters, and the first page of each chapter differs from the remainder). The **Layout Master Set** element contains these templates:

```
<root>
  <layout-master-set>
    <!-- TEMPLATES -->
  </layout-master-set>

  <!-- CONTENT -->
</root>
```

Some templates may have header and footer regions, and the even-numbered pages may differ from the odd-numbered pages (as they do in this book). The **Simple Page Master** element is used to define each template, and so it may occur several times within the Layout Master Set element:

```
<root>
  <layout-master-set>
    <simple-page-master ...>
    <!-- TEMPLATE 1 -->
    </simple-page-master>
    <simple-page-master ...>
    <!-- TEMPLATE 2 -->
    </simple-page-master>
  </layout-master-set>
  ...
</root>
```

After the templates, the actual information to present is stored, including embedded formatting tags. This information may be divided into sections that will use different templates, or combinations of templates (there would be a separate section for each chapter of this book), and each section must therefore be linked to a specific template, or template combination. The **Page Sequence** element holds the content to associate with a particular template. It has a **Master Name** attribute to identify the template it is associated with. The Simple Page Master element has the same attribute, and so the two are linked by having identical values in these attributes:

```
<root>
  <layout-master-set>
    <simple-page-master master-name="Prelims">
    <!-- TEMPLATE 1 -->
    </simple-page-master>
    <simple-page-master master-name="MainContent">
    <!-- TEMPLATE 2 -->
    </simple-page-master>
  </layout-master-set>

  <page-sequence master-name="Prelims">
    <!-- CONTENT 1 -->
  </page-sequence>
  <page-sequence master-name="MainContent">
    <!-- CONTENT 2 -->
  </page-sequence>
</root>
```

Pages are created by selecting an appropriate template, and 'flowing' the content into areas that follow the page template rules. If there is too much content to fit the page, another page may be generated from the template, and the content then continues to flow into the new page. For example, in this book the number of actual pages produced varies for each chapter, depending on how much there is to say on each topic. But this can be prevented. For example, the first page of each chapter always uses a distinct template (this template is used for the content placed on the first page, but not subsequent pages).

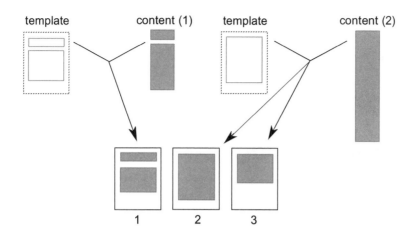

Pages

A template is used to define page characteristics. The dimensions of the page itself, and the margins that surround the area of the page that can be written to, are both specified using attributes on the **Simple Page Master** element.

Height and width

The height and width of the page is specified using the **Page Height** and **Page Width** attributes (an A4 page has a height of 29.7cm and a width of 21.0cm):

```
<simple-page-master master-name="Prelims"
                    page-height="29.7cm"
                    page-width="21.0cm">
    ...
</simple-page-master>
```

The value 'auto' is used when the page size is not known by the formatter. The value 'indefinite' specifies that the size of the page should be driven by the content. This is appropriate for the height dimension when the information is presented as an electronic page in a browser window.

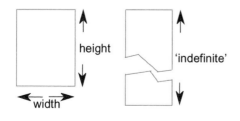

Note that when creating a stylesheet for presentation of material in an electronic product that creates a simple, scrollable interface (such as a Web browser), this can be considered to be a single (possibly very long) page and the following discussion on page sequences is not relevant. In this very simple case, a single page master template is created, and is referenced from a single page sequence object.

The height and width can also be specified using a single **Size** attribute, though the draft standard is still unclear on which direction is specified first.

Orientation

Most printers are able to print to a page in 'portrait' or 'landscape' orientation. In XSL, the **Reference Orientation** attribute can be used to specify what is to be considered the top and bottom of the page, irrespective of how the page is fed into the printer. Degree angles are entered in this attribute:

```
<simple-page-master reference-orientation="90" ... >
```

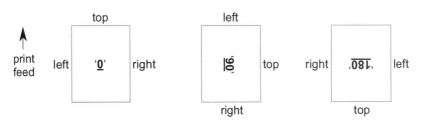

Writing direction

Text can be written left-to-right and top-to-bottom (as in English documents), or in any other combination, such as right-to-left and bottom-to-top. The possible values of the **Writing Mode** attribute are abbreviations of these settings, using 'l' for 'left', 'r' for 'right', 't' for 'top' and 'b' for 'bottom', so 'l**r-tb**' is appropriate for an English book:

```
<simple-page-master writing-mode="lr-tb" ... >
```

Note that the 'top' of a page is the side of the page defined to be at the top according to the page orientation described above. When the value is 'lr-tb', writing follows the paths shown below:

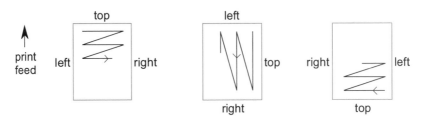

In English, when discussing objects that need to appear above a block of text, the term 'above' can be safely used. Likewise, when discussing objects that need to appear to the left of a line of text, the term 'left of' is unambiguous. But when lines can be written in either direction, and from bottom-to-top, these terms will often be inaccurate. Instead, the terms '**before**' and '**after**' are used to indicate position relative to blocks of text ('above' and 'below' in English), and '**start**' and '**end**' are used to indicate position relative to in-line objects.

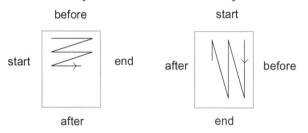

These terms are used frequently in the XSL standard. They are often part of an element or attribute name that is targetted at one of these positions (such as the attribute named 'border-start-style' and the element named 'region-after').

Margins

Most printing devices are unable to print text right up to the edge of a page, and even when this is possible it is usually undesirable. The area between the edge of the printable region and the edge of the paper is known as the 'margin', and margins for each edge are defined using the **Margin Top**, **Margin Right**, **Margin Bottom** and **Margin Left** attributes.

Each of these attributes takes a value that specifies the distance between the edge of the paper and the edge of the printable area. When printing double-sided for binding into a document or book, the left-side and right-side pages often have different margin widths (to cater for the space lost in the centre of the book due to the binding):

```
<simple-page-master master-name="left-page"
                    margin-left="1cm"
                    margin-right="1.5cm"
                    margin-top="1.5cm"
                    margin-bottom="2cm"  >
```

Again, the definiton of 'top' is taken from the page orientation:

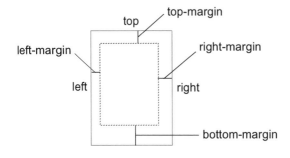

Page sequences

When a number of different templates are defined (using Simple Page Master elements), the way in which these templates are selected for the content flow needs to be defined. One way to do this is simply to assign each section of the content to a different master, as described above. But this technique is very limited.

In this book, for example, the text from each chapter would need to be flowed into three different templates. As much text as will fit on the first page needs to use a template that is only used for this page. Following this, as much text as will fit on the next page needs to occupy a page that follows the template for left-side pages.

It is not possible for the document author to determine in advance what text will appear on each page, and place this text in sections that refer to the relevant templates, as this depends on many factors, such as the font size, the column width, and the rules for hyphenation, all of which are determined by the templates and the pagination engine.

It is therefore possible to create a definition for a sequence of templates, including rules on which template to select in a given circumstance, using the **Page Sequence Master** element, which appears within the Layout Master Set element (by convention, below the page master templates but not restricted to this position). The content then links to this sequence, instead of to an individual template:

```
<root>
  <layout-master-set>
    <simple-page-master master-name="first-page">
      <!-- TEMPLATE 1 -->
    </simple-page-master>
    <simple-page-master master-name="left-page">
      <!-- TEMPLATE 2 -->
    </simple-page-master>
    <simple-page-master master-name="right-page">
      <!-- TEMPLATE 3 -->
```

```
    </simple-page-master>
    <simple-page-master master-name="blank-page">
      <!-- TEMPLATE 4 -->
    </simple-page-master>
    <page-sequence-master master-name="ChapterSequence">
      <!-- CHAPTER SEQUENCE DEFINITIONS -->
    </page-sequence-master>
  </layout-master-set>

  <page-sequence master-name="ChapterSequence">
    <!-- CHAPTER 1 CONTENT -->
  </page-sequence>
  <page-sequence master-name="ChapterSequence">
    <!-- CHAPTER 2 CONTENT -->
  </page-sequence>
  <page-sequence master-name="ChapterSequence">
    <!-- CHAPTER 3 CONTENT -->
  </page-sequence>
</root>
```

The Page Sequence Master element then contains references to the master templates, in the order that they are to be used.

Page numbering

The pages in a page sequence can be numbered. The **Initial Page Number** provides the number of the first page in the sequence, if a numeric value is entered in this attribute. Alternatively, the value 'auto' (the default) implies that the number should be automatically calculated as the next page number after the last page of the previous sequence (for instance, the chapters in this book do not restart page numbering). When the new sequence must begin on an odd or even page, the values 'auto-odd' or 'auto-even' may be used instead. If 'auto-odd' was selected, and the previous sequence ended on '27', then the new sequence would begin with '29' (like the chapters in this book, which all begin on an odd-numbered page):

```
<page-sequence master-name="Prelims"
               initial-page-number="1">
  ...
</page-sequence>
<page-sequence master-name="Chapter"
               initial-page-number="auto-odd">
  ...
</page-sequence>
<page-sequence master-name="Chapter"
               initial-page-number="auto-odd">
  ...
</page-sequence>
```

Sequences often need to occupy an even number of pages (such as the chapters in this book), regardless of how many pages are actually needed to hold the text. The **Force Page Count** attribute can be given the value 'even' to achieve this. Though generally less useful, the number of pages can also be forced to be an odd number. Later it is shown how a special template can be selected for the last page, if it has no content.

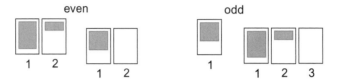

The default 'auto' value forces the last page to be even if the first page of the next sequence is odd, and odd if the first page of the next sequence is even, but has no effect when the initial page number of the next sequence is 'auto' (or when there is no next sequence), when it does not force any additional pages.

Other possible values are 'no-force', which does not generate any pages beyond those needed to hold the content under any circumstances, and 'end-on-even' and 'end-on-odd', which force the last page to be an even or odd number respectively, regardless of what the initial page number is.

Single pages

The **Single Page Master Reference** element is used to refer to a master page template, indicating that this template should only be used to generate a single page of output. This is ideal for referencing the 'first-page' template in the example above (each chapter in this book would only use this template once). This element has the **Master Name** attribute, which is used to reference the template needed:

```
<simple-page-master master-name=" first-page" >
  . . .
</simple-page-master>
  . . .
<page-sequence-master master-name="ChapterSequence">
  <single-page-master-reference master-name=" first-page" />
</page-sequence-master>
```

Repeatable pages

The **Repeatable Page Master Reference** element is used to refer to a master page template, indicating that this template should be used repeatedly. By default, the template is used as many times as necessary to encompass the content that uses it (this could, for instance, be used for the body pages of the chapters in this book, immediately following the simple reference described above for the first page of the chapter), as each chapter has an unknown number of pages to fill. But this would only be satisfactory if the headers on each page were the same.

The **Maximum Repeats** attribute may be used to specify a limit on the number of pages generated using this template. If more material is present, and no further templates are referenced, it is presumably truncated at this point.

This element has the **Master Name** attribute, which is used to reference the template needed:

```
<simple-page-master master-name=" body-page" >
  . . .
</simple-page-master>
  . . .
<page-sequence-master master-name="ChapterSequence">
  . . .
  <repeatable-page-master-reference
                    master-name=" body-page" />
</page-sequence-master>
```

Alternative pages

The **Repeatable Page Master Alternatives** element is far more complex than the options described above, and is able to perform sophisticated page master handling (of the kind needed to format this chapter):

```
<root>
  <layout-master-set>
    . . .
    <page-sequence-master master-name="ChapterSequence">
      <repeatable-page-master-alternatives>
        . . .
      </alternative-page-master-references>
    </page-sequence-master>
  </layout-master-set>
</root>
```

Each of these elements contain a number of **Conditional Page Master Reference** elements:

```
<page-sequence-master master-name="ChapterSequence">
  <repeatable-page-master-alternatives>
    <conditional-page-master-reference .../>
    <conditional-page-master-reference .../>
    <conditional-page-master-reference .../>
  </repeatable-page-master-alternatives>
</page-sequence-master>
```

Only one of the conditional references is selected for a particular page, and the order in which they appear within the Repeatable Page Master Alternatives element is significant, because it is the first appropriate reference that is chosen.

This element references a template that is to be used under the conditions specified in a number of attributes. These conditions all relate to the location of the page to be formatted next. First, last, even, odd and blank pages can all be recognized using these attributes.

The **Page Position** attribute can be used to activate a specified template when the page to be generated is the 'first', 'last', 'rest' (any page except for the first or last) or 'any' (the default). This is ideal for selecting the correct template for the first page of each chapter:

```
<conditional-page-master-reference
                  page-position="first"
                  master-name="first-page" />
```

The **Odd Or Even** attribute can be used to activate a specified template when the page to be generated is an odd-numbered page, such as '1', '3' or '5', or an even-numbered page, such as '2', '4' or '6'. The values '**odd**', '**even**' or '**any**' (the default) are allowed. This is ideal for selecting pages that have different headers or footers for left and right pages (such as the pages in this chapter). Every chapter in this book begins on a right-hand page, and as the first page is a right-hand page and is page number '1', then all right-hand pages are odd:

```
<conditional-page-master-reference
                  odd-or-even="odd"
                  master-name="right-page" />

<conditional-page-master-reference
                  odd-or-even="even"
                  master-name="left-page" />
```

These references should follow a reference to the first page, as the first page is a special case of an odd page and needs to be selected in preference.

The **Blank Or Not Blank** attribute can be used to activate a specified template when a page needs to be generated, even though there is no text to place on it (such as the left-hand pages at the end of many of the chapters in this book). The values 'blank', 'not-blank' or 'any' (the default) are allowed:

```
<conditional-page-master-reference
                   blank-or-not-blank="blank"
                   master-name="blank-page" />
```

Although described last, this reference would typically be placed before the odd-or-even references, if both are needed, because a blank page will also be an odd page or an even page but needs to be treated as a special case. Recall that the first valid conditional reference is selected from the list of options. Note also that the Force Page Count attribute needs to be used to create the blank page (typically with the value 'even'), as it would not otherwise be generated and the blank template would then never be needed.

Five conditional elements would be used to reference the five templates needed for the chapters in this book. The order in which they appear is significant:

```
<conditional-page-master-reference
                   page-position="first"
                   master-name=" first-page" />
<conditional-page-master-reference
                   blank-page="blank"
                   master-name=" blank-page" />
<conditional-page-master-reference
                   odd-or-even="odd"
                   master-name=" right-page" />
<conditional-page-master-reference
                   odd-or-even="even"
                   master-name=" left-page" />
```

Page regions

A simple page master is able to contain one or more regions to hold the element text. This can be static text that is to be repeated each time the template is used, or contain part of a text 'flow' that continues onto other pages.

Body region

One region, called the 'body region', must be specified. It is placed centrally within the page and is generally used for the main text flow.

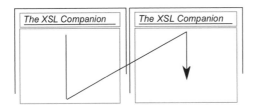

When some or all of the other, optional regions are also needed, they occupy space around the region body (beyond that already created by the page margins). The margin attributes can also be used on the **Region Body** element (borders and padding can as well, but will be ignored in this version of XSL):

```
<simple-page-master ...>
   <region-body margin-left="2cm"
                margin-right="2cm"
                margin-top="4cm"
                margin-bottom="3cm" />
</simple-page-master>
```

In effect, the body region margins are added to the page margins to position the region on the page:

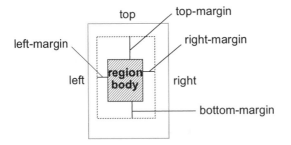

The body region can have multiple columns (other regions discussed below cannot). The **Column Count** attribute has a default value of '1', but this may be changed to a greater number. The document content flows from one column to the next. In an English document, the columns are ordered left to right. In a language that uses right-to-left writing, the column order is reversed. The **Column Gap** attribute indicates how much space to place between columns. The width of the columns is determined by deducting the sum of the intercolumn gaps, then dividing the remaining horizontal space by the number of columns:

```
<region-body column-count="3" column-gap="5mm" ... />
```

column-gap

The **Region Name** attribute identifies the region for later use. If not specified, the default name for the body region is '**xsl-region-body**'. Specific names are needed if the text flowing into the body region of an odd page is different from the text flowing into the body region of an even page (a typical example being a legal document that contains the same text in two languages).

The reference orientation for the body region may be changed relative to the page orientation. For example, all pages may be aligned vertically (as portrait pages), and all header and footer regions (see below) may inherit this setting, but in some cases the body text may need the additional horizontal space that landscape orientation provides. Tables with many columns typically need this additional space.

Overflows

A region or other area type may be too small to contain the information placed within it. This may not appear to be an issue from the description above; the text cannot be too wide as new lines are created as needed, and the text cannot be too long as new pages are generated as needed. Nevertheless, this issue does arise, even here.

When the content of an element is too large to fit in its containing box, some of the content will overflow. The extra material can be displayed as normal, removed, or (when presented electronically) can be accessed by scrolling either down or across. The **Overflow** attribute controls this behaviour with the values 'visible', 'hidden' and 'scroll' respectively. The value 'auto' is also available, but will often be interpreted as being the same as 'scroll':

The **Clip** attribute may be used to remove the edge of the content (when the overflow is not 'visible'). Clipping regions may in future take many different shapes, but for now it must take the form of a rectangle, 'rect(...)'. This shape takes four space-separated parameters that give the size of the clipped region above, to the right, below and to the left, in each case being the depth of the region from the relevant edge.

Viewports

As well as the region itself, a '**viewport**' is created. The viewport concept is only really relevant to electronic displays, where the user can view the content through an area that is smaller than the content but use scroll-bars (or other means) to bring other information into view. For those familiar with HTML frames, each viewport can be seen as a single frame in a frameset. The viewport for the body region is simply the area of the region itself. When creating a single large page, it will contain a scroll-bar to provide access to all the content. To work in this way, the Overflow attribute must be set to 'scroll' (and note that it is not compatible to have both multiple columns and scrolling).

Optional regions

Within the margins of the body region, other regions can be defined to hold headers and footers, or margin notes. Only one region can be placed on each side, and separate elements are used to define each one. These elements have the names **Region Before**, **Region After**, **Region Start** and **Region End**. They all have the same basic form as the Region Body element, and their names reflect their position relative to the body region, depending on the writing direction used (for English documents, 'before' is above, 'after' is below, 'start' is to the left and 'end' is to the right). The 'before' and 'after' regions will be the most commonly needed, as they are used to create headers and footers.

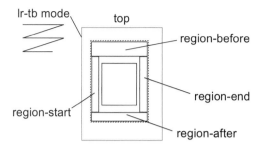

However, these regions cannot have multiple columns, so do not have the Column Count and Column Gap attributes described above for the body region.

Each of these areas has a viewport and a region. The viewport area is calculated by taking the **Extent** attribute value to give it depth, and stretches to the edges of the page area. If the **Precedence** attribute has the value 'true', the area takes precedence over other areas that overlap. If 'false' it is overlapped. The Region Start and Region End elements do not have this attribute (as it would otherwise be possible to create conflicting rules).

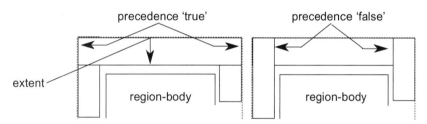

The region area lies beneath the viewport and is the same size, except when the Overflow attribute has the value 'scroll' (as for the body region).

Each region can use the margin attributes, and so the headers and footers can be reduced in size and more carefully positioned than the explanation above implies.

Borders

By default, the content placed in a region appears within the region defined by the inner-edge of each margin. However, it is possible to make room for a border line. The **Border Left Width**, **Border Top Width**, **Border Right Width** and **Border Bottom Width** attributes set the thickness of each side and are CSS-compatible. The writing-direction-based equivalents are **Border Start Width**, **Border Before Width**, **Border End Width** and **Border After Width**:

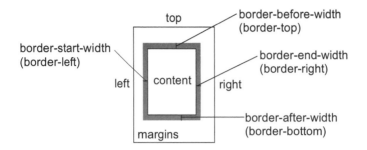

The **Border Width** attribute provides a shorthand method for specifying a simple width for all borders, or to separately define widths for top and bottom, followed by left and right, or to separately define widths for the top, the sides and the bottom, or to separately define widths for all four sides:

```
<!-- all sides 2pt -->
<block border-width="2pt">

<!-- 4pt sides -->
<block border-width="2pt 4pt">

<!-- bottom is 3pt -->
<block border-width="2pt 4pt 3pt">

<!-- top, right, bottom, left -->
<block border-width="1pt 2pt 3pt 4pt">
```

The border can have a colour. The colour is given using the **Border Color** attribute when all borders are the same colour, or by the **Border Left Color**, **Border Top Color**, **Border Right Color** and **Border Bottom Color** when the colours need to be specified separately. The Border Color attribute may thus take up to four values (with meanings the same as described above for border widths). Finally, the direction-sensitive variants **Border Start Color**, **Border Before Color**, **Border End Color** and **Border After Color** may also be used.

The border line can take a number of forms. The options are 'none', 'hidden', 'dotted', 'dashed', 'solid', 'double', 'groove', 'ridge', 'inset' and 'outset'. The **Border Style** attribute defines a style to use for the border, and may take up to four values (with meanings the same as described above for border widths). To give each side a different style, the **Border Left Style**, **Border Top Style**, **Border Right Style** and **Border Bottom Style** attributes may be used. As before, direction-sensitive variants **Border Start Style**, **Border Before Style**, **Border End Style** and **Border After Style** may also be used:

```
<block border-width="1pt 2pt 1pt 2pt"
       border-style="dashed"
       border-color="#FF0080" >
```

Finally, the **Border** attribute can be used to specify a single thickness, style and colour for all sides:

```
<block border="1pt dashed red" >...</block>
```

Padding

When a border line is present, some 'padding' space between the text and the border line is normally desired. The **Padding** attribute specifies how much space to insert. Different amounts of padding can be added to each side if desired. This attribute can take up to four values (as described for borders widths), or replaced by the **Padding Left**, **Padding Top**, **Padding Right** and **Padding Bottom** attributes, or by the writing-direction-sensitive variants **Padding Start**, **Padding Before**, **Padding End** and **Padding After**.

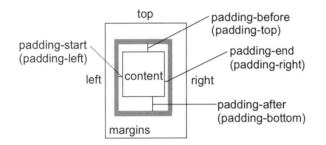

Background

Documents are not always printed or displayed on a simple white background. It is possible to specify a colour for the background, using the **Background Color** attribute. The value 'transparent' may be used to allow the background colours of enclosing objects to be seen behind the current object, and this is the default value:

```
<block background-color="red">
  <block background-color=" transparent">
   ...<!-- RED BACKGROUND -->
  </block>
  <block> <!-- ALSO TRANSPARENT -->
   ...<!-- RED BACKGROUND -->
  </block>
  ...
</block>
```

An image can be displayed behind the text, using the **Background Image** attribute, which uses a URL to identify the image file. A colour may be specified as well, and this colour appears beneath the image, showing through any transparent parts of the image and around the image. By default, the image appears in the top-left corner of the object that contains it (occupying the padding area, so immediately within any border lines), but can be offset horizontally and vertically using the **Background Position Horizontal** and **Background Position Vertical** attributes. When displaying electronic documents, the image may 'scroll' with the document, and this is the default value of the **Background Attachment** attribute, or it may be 'fixed', so that text scrolls over the image:

```
<block background-image="boat.gif"
       background-position-horizontal="1cm"
       background-position-vertical="3cm"
       background-attachment="fixed">...</block>
```

A small image can be repeated to fill the available area, and by default is repeated both across and down the area. The **Background Repeat** attribute has the default value 'repeat', but can be given the value 'repeat-x' to repeat only across the page, 'repeat-y' to repeat only down the page, and repeat can be switched-off with the value 'no-repeat':

```
<block background-image="boat.gif"
       background-repeat="repeat-x">...</block>
```

Content

The Page Sequence element contains any number of **Static Content** elements (including none), followed by a single **Flow** element. For the examples below, it will be assumed that there is a page sequence for each chapter of this book:

```
<root>
  <layout-master-set>
    <simple-page-master master-name="MainContent">
    <!-- TEMPLATE 2 -->
    </simple-page-master>
  </layout-master-set>

  <page-sequence master-name="MainContent">
    <static-content...>...</static-content>
    <static-content...>...</static-content>
    <flow...>...</flow>
  </page-sequence>
</root>
```

Static content

The **Static Content** elements hold the items that are repeated across a number of pages, such as the text 'The XSL Companion' on every even-numbered page in this book, and the text 'XSL' on every odd-numbered page in this chapter. Each element is mapped to a flow name, in order to identify which region of the master page selected is to receive the text held in this element. The value of the **Flow Name** attribute must match the value of a Region Name attribute of the region-defining element. When no explicit names are given, the appropriate default names can be referenced instead. The default names are the names of the region-defining elements but with an 'xsl-' prefix, such as 'xsl-region-body' and 'xsl-region-before':

```
<root>
  <layout-master-set>
    <simple-page-master master-name="MainContent">
      <region-body ... /> <!-- xsl-region-body -->
      <region-before ... /> <!-- xsl-region-before -->
      <region-after ... /> <!-- xsl-region-after -->
      <region-start ... /> <!-- xsl-region-start -->
      <region-end ... /> <!-- xsl-region-end -->
    </simple-page-master>
  </layout-master-set>

  <page-sequence master-name="MainContent">
    <static-content flow-name="xsl-region-before">
      <block>
        <xsl:text>Page </xsl:text> <page-number/>
      </block>
    </static-content>
  </page-sequence>
</root>
```

Default mappings are not adequate when wishing to place different text on odd pages to that which needs to appear on even pages. Two Static Content elements are needed (one for each piece of content), and they must map to different regions:

```
<root>
  <layout-master-set>
    <simple-page-master master-name="OddPage">
      ...
      <region-before region-name="BeforeOdd" />
    </simple-page-master>
    <simple-page-master master-name="EvenPage">
      ...
      <region-before region-name="BeforeEven" />
    </simple-page-master>
    <page-sequence-master master-name=" Chapter">
      <repeatable-page-master-alternatives>
        <conditional-page-master-reference
                      odd-or-even=" odd"
                      master-name=" OddPage" />
        <conditional-page-master-reference
                      odd-or-even=" even"
                      master-name=" EvenPage" />
```

```
          </repeatable-page-master-alternatives>
        </page-sequence-master>
      </layout-master-set>

      <page-sequence master-name="Chapter">
        <static-content flow-name="BeforeEven">
          <block><page-number/> The XSL Companion</block>
        </static-content>
        <static-content flow-name="BeforeOdd">
          <block>XSL <page-number/></block>
        </static-content>
      </page-sequence>
    </root>
```

Flow content

In most cases, the main content of a document will consist of large streams of information that need to be spread across many pages. As the information is formatted, it is said to 'flow' into pages generated from the master templates. The **Flow** element holds this information. There can be only one Flow element in a Page Sequence element, and its content is usually flowed into the body region of the master template (or templates) referenced from the sequence. This element must appear after any static content definitions. The **Flow Name** attribute references the region into which the content should flow, and this will usually be the body region (by default named 'xsl-region-body'):

```
    <page-sequence master-name="Chapter">
      <static-content ...>...</static-content>
      <static-content ...>...</static-content>
      <flow flow-name="xsl-region-body">
          <!-- FLOW CONTENT -->
      </flow>
    </page-sequence>
```

Blocks

Both static and flow content consists of one or more blocks of information. A small number of elements represent block-like information items, and these elements can be used in any order and quantity. They are used to create simple text blocks (such as paragraphs), lists and tables. The content of these elements is assigned to block areas that are stacked on top of each other (in the top-to-bottom writing direction).

Text block

The **Block** element is used to create paragraphs, titles and other simple text block objects. It can contain text, in-line objects, and even embedded blocks. Some blocks may contain all three.

In the following example, a block contains the title of a book ('The XSL Companion'), which is to be placed in the page header:

```
<root>
  <page-sequence master-name="Chapter">
    <static-content flow-name="BeforeEven">
      <block>The XSL Companion</block>
    </static-content>
    . . .
  </page-sequence>
</root>
```

When the body region is split into columns, blocks are normally placed in a single column at the next available position in the flow. The default value of the **Span** attribute is therefore 'none' (do not span across columns). However, it is possible for a block to span across all columns by setting the value to 'all'.

The formatting and style of text within the block is specified using attributes. There are a large number of attributes to choose from. It is possible to specify borders, padding within the borders, background colours, font characteristics, hyphenation rules, text colour, first- and last-line indentation, the height of text lines, strategies for dealing with page-breaks within blocks, column spanning, text alignment within lines, and the writing direction.

Blocks can be separated from each other using the margin attributes described above:

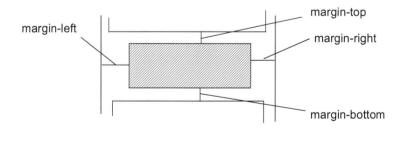

However, margins are quite limited (and are only included for compatibility with CSS), especially when deciding how much space to place between two blocks. For example, a value can be specified for the space needed above each paragraph, but if a paragraph begins a new chapter, this space should not appear. Also, a larger space would be specified after a title. While the after-title space could simply be added to the before-paragraph space, this is rarely desired. In this example, typically only the after-title space should be preserved. The 'space-before.xxx' and 'space-after.xxx' attributes are used for this purpose. Each is given a set value using the **Space Before** and **Space After** attributes (and note that Space Start and Space End are for in-line objects only), or an optimum value using the **Space Before Optimum** and **Space After Optimum** attributes (the default value for both is '0pt'). Spaces for adjacent blocks are merged if the **Space Before Precedence** attribute is not set to 'force' (which ensures the space given is preserved in all circumstances). In the following example, the title is given precedence, so the '12pt' of paragraph space is ignored:

```
<block space-after="16pt"
       space-after.precedence="1">The Title</block>
<block space-before="12pt">A paragraph.</block>
```

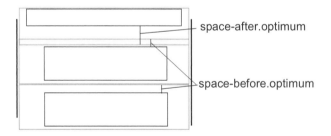

Note that if either element had a 'force' precedence, then this space is used in preference to the other one, no matter what its precedence value is and regardless of its size. Also, if both spaces have the same precedence value, then the larger space may be chosen (which would be appropriate for the example above, where the title-following space is more significant than the paragraph-preceding space).

When an optimum space is specified, it is also appropriate to include a mimumum and a maximum value. This can be done using the **Space Before Minimum**, **Space Before Maximum**, **Space After Minimum** and **Space After Maximum** attributes. This approach gives the XSL formatter more freedom to juggle what material appears on each page, while not breaking reasonable constraints on the size of gaps between blocks of various types:

```
<block space-before.optimum="14pt"
       space-before.minimum="12pt"
       space-before.maximum="16pt"
       space-after.optimum="5pt"
       space-after.minimum="3pt"
       space-after.maximum="8pt">...</block>
```

The **Space Before Conditionality** and **Space After Conditionality** attributes determine whether the space is preserved ('retain') or discarded ('discard') if the block is the first or last in its containing block (or page). If a paragraph has a before-space value, but happens to be the first item in a chapter that begins a new page, then usually the paragraph space will be unwanted:

```
<block space-before.conditionality="discard">...</block>
```

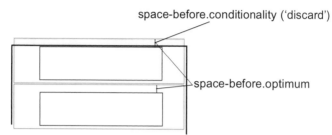

Similarly, blocks are indented within their surrounding areas (enclosing blocks or the whole page area) using the **Start Indent** and **End Indent** attributes, or the relevant margin attributes (but not Space Start or Space End, which are used for in-line objects):

```
<block start-indent="5mm"
       end-indent="15mm">...</block>
```

A block may be split into two or more separate blocks by the XSL formatting engine when it does not fit into the containing area (such as the current page):

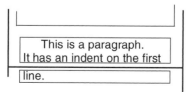

But it is possible to prevent this happening by setting the value of the **Page Break Inside** attribute to 'avoid' breaks within the block (in place of the default value of 'auto'). A more advanced version of this feature uses the **Keep Together** attribute to specify whether or not the entire block must be kept on one page (or column of the page), by giving it a value of 'always'. Yet more specific variants of this variable can be used to indicate whether or not the block can span columns, but not whole pages. The **Keep Together Within Page** and **Keep Together Within Column** attributes are used:

```
<block keep-together.within-page="always">...</block>
<block keep-together.within-column="always">...</block>
```

Furthermore, it is possible to ensure that the current block is always kept on the same page as the previous block using the **Keep With Previous** property. Given the value 'always', the **Keep With Previous Within Page** attribute ensures that the two blocks are not separated by a page-break, and the **Keep With Previous Within Column** ensures that the two blocks are not separated by a column break. The **Keep With Next Within Page** and **Keep With Next Within Column** attributes work in the same way to keep the current block with the next one (for example, a heading is typically kept with the first following paragraph):

```
<block keep-with-previous.within-page="always">...</block>
<block keep-with-previous.within-column="always">
...
</block>
<block keep-with-next.within-page="always">...</block>
<block keep-with-next.within-column="always">...</block>
```

Another way to do this is to use the **Page Break Before** attribute, giving it the value 'avoid'. The value 'always', on the other hand, ensures that there is always a page-break before the block. The value 'left' ensures that the page the block is placed on is a left-hand page, even if two page-breaks are needed to achieve this. Likewise, the value 'right' can be entered. The default value 'auto' does not force and does not forbid a page-break, but allows one to happen if the formatter wishes. The **Page Break After** attribute works in the same way for breaks after the block. A more advanced version of this capability is provided by the **Break Before** and **Break After** attributes, which take the values 'auto' (the default), 'column', 'page', 'even-page' and 'odd-page'.

Even when a block is allowed to span page boundaries, some control can be provided over how much text appears in each part. It is a common convention to avoid the situation of having a single line of text in either part. The illustration at the foot of the previous page shows what typographers call a 'widow' line. When a single line appears at the end of a page, this is termed an 'orphan'. The **Widows** and **Orphans** attributes specify the minimum number of lines that must occur in each of these positions. The default value is '2' in both cases, indicating that there must be at least two lines at each location. This value can be raised, or lowered to '1' (essentially having no effect). Lowering the value gives the XSL formatting engine more freedom to balance the objects on the page.

Block container

Blocks may be grouped within a container that specifies settings for all the enclosed blocks. The **Block Container** element performs this role. This element is usually used to define settings that are shared by a number of consecutive blocks. Typical changes made at this level include border and margin widths, background colour, and the orientation of text. The container can even have a fixed height or width, and be forced to override natural page-breaks:

```
<flow flow-name="xsl-region-body">
  <block-container margin-left="2cm" >
    <block>Related to next block</block>
    <block>Related to previous block</block>
  </block-container>
</flow>
```

This element may use the Overflow attribute to control how overflowing text is to be handled when the container is given a specific width and/or height.

Lists

Lists are more complex structures, composed of a number of items each divided into prefix and content portions. The **List Block** element contains one or more **List Item** block elements. Each row is vertically separated from the next by a size given in the **Space Between List Rows** attribute:

```
<flow flow-name="xsl-region-body">
  <list-block space-between-list-rows="12pt" >
    <list-item>...</list-item>
    <list-item>...</list-item>
    <list-item>...</list-item>
  </list-block>
</flow>
```

Each item is split into label and body parts using the **List Item Label** and **List Item Body** elements. Both must be present in every item, in the order shown below:

```
<list-item>
  <list-item-label><block>A) </block></list-item-label>
  <list-item-body>
    <block>first item, labelled A)</block>
  </list-item-body>
</list-item>
```

These two parts occupy adjacent areas on the page. The width of each part can be specified directly, using indentation attributes, but there will usually be ideal widths for each. This is specified on the List Block element, using two attributes.

The **Provisional Label Separation** attribute specifies the ideal gap between the item label and the item content, and the **Provisional Distance Between Starts** attribute specifies the ideal spacing beween the start of the label and the start of the content:

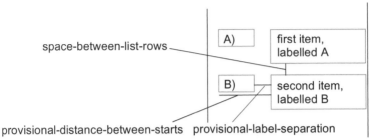

These two values are then used to help calculate two variables, called '**label-end()**' and '**body-start()**', which can be used in indentation attributes. For example:

```
<list-block provisional-distance-between-starts="20mm"
            provisional-label-separation="5mm" ...>
  <list-item>
    <list-item-label end-indent=" label-end()">
      ...
    </list-item-label>
    <list-item-body start-indent="body-start()">
      ...
    </list-item-body>
  </list-item>
</list-block>
```

It is also possible to indent the label from the left edge, and the body from the right edge, using other indentation attributes. (Note that the labels are indented in the illustration above.)

Tables

Tables are constructed from grids of areas, arranged primarily into rows, then into columns within the rows, creating individual cells. A table is identified using the **Table** element. However, the **Table And Caption** element may be used as a simple wrapper for the main Table element, which is preceded by a **Table Caption** element. By default the caption is placed 'before' the table but, using the **Caption Side** attribute, it can be placed 'after' or at one side ('start' or 'end'):

```
<table>...</table>

<table-and-caption>
  <table-caption caption-side="after">
    <block>The Table</block>
  </table-caption>
  <table>...</table>
</table-and-caption>
```

The grid is composed of cells within rows within body, header and footer blocks, using the **Table Header**, **Table Body**, **Table Footer**, **Table Row** and **Table Cell** elements:

```
<table>
  <table-header>...</table-header>
  <table-footer>...</table-footer>
  <table-body>...</table-body>
</table>

<table-body>
  <table-row>...</table-row>
  <table-row>...</table-row>
</table-body>

<table-row>
  <table-cell>...</table-cell>
  <table-cell>...</table-cell>
  <table-cell>...</table-cell>
</table-row>
```

An individual cell can be made to occupy space that would otherwise be occupied by adjacent cells. A cell can stretch across into cells further along the row, or down into cells below it. The **Number Rows Spanned** attribute specifies the number of rows encompassed, and has a default value of '1' (no spanning). Likewise, the **Number Columns Spanned** element specifies the number of columns spanned, and has a default value of '1' (no spanning).

The Table Row element is optional. When cells are not embedded in row elements, some of the Table Cell elements need to use **Starts Row** and **Ends Row** attributes:

```
<table-body>
  <table-cell starts-row="yes">
    <block>1,1</block>
  </table-cell>
  <table-cell ends-row="yes">
    <block>1,2</block>
  </table-cell>
  <table-cell starts-row="yes">
    <block>2,1</block>
  </table-cell>
  <table-cell ends-row="yes">
    <block>2,2</block>
  </table-cell>
</table-body>
```

The Table Row element includes the **Height** attribute, and the means to control page breaks before and after the row using the **Keep Together** attribute:

```
<table>

  <table-header>
    <table-row height="24pt">
      <table-cell number-columns-spanned="2">
        <block>Headings</block>
```

```
        </table-cell>
      </table-row>
      <table-row height="24pt">
        <table-cell><block>Head 1</block></table-cell>
        <table-cell><block>Head 2</block></table-cell>
      </table-row>
    </table-header>

    <table-body>
      <table-row height="16pt">
        <table-cell><block>cell 1</block></table-cell>
        <table-cell number-rows-spanned="2"
                    keep-together="always">
          <block>span down</block>
        </table-cell>
      </table-row>
      <table-row height="16pt">
        <table-cell><block>cell 2</block></table-cell>
      </table-row>
    </table-body>
  </table>
```

Often, table header rows are repeated at the top of each column or page that the table spans. This happens by default, but the **Table Omit Header At Break** attribute can be set to 'yes' to suppress this feature. The heading is suppressed in the example illustration above. Likewise, footer sections can be placed at the bottom of each page, or omitted, using the **Table Omit Footer At Break** attribute.

Borders and padding can be applied at all levels in this structure. A border is drawn around an empty cell by default, or if the **Empty Cells** attribute is set to 'show'; but if it is set to 'hide' then these borders are not drawn. Complete borders can be drawn around each cell, or the borders of adjacent cells can be shared (as in the diagram above). The **Border Collapse** attribute has a default value of 'collapse', but this can be changed to 'separate'. When borders for each cell are separate, the space between adjacent border lines is governed by the **Border Separation** attribute when the vertical and horizontal spacing is the same, or the **Border Separation Block Progression Direction** attribute and the **Border Separation Inline Progression Direction** when they differ. The **Border Spacing** attribute can be used instead, which takes two, space-separated values for horizontal then vertical settings:

```
<table empty-cells="hide" border-collapse="separate"
    border-separation.block-progression-direction="2pt"
    border-separation.inline-progression-direction="3pt" >
  ...</table>
```

The **Column** element is used to define in advance shared properties for cells that are in the same column of the table. For example, if all the cells in a column are right-justified, it is time-consuming to set this alignment value on every cell. But perhaps the most significant use of this element is to set the width of each column, using the **Column Width** attribute. The **Column Number** attribute identifies the column to apply the formatting settings to. It can be omitted for the first instance of this element, if it specifies formatting characteristics for the first column in the table. It can also be omitted for any instance that assigns formats to the next column in the sequence:

```
<table>
  <column column-number="1" column-width="3cm" />
  <column column-number="2" column-width="2cm" />
  <column column-width="1cm" /> <!-- IMPLIED COLUMN 3 -->
  <table-header>
    ...
  </table-header>
  <table-body>
    ...
  </table-body>
</table>
```

Individual cells refer to the settings in the Column element using the '**from-table-column**()' function. Therefore, not every cell in a column needs to adopt these settings (and for this reason, it is not a senseless option to include the Number Columns Spanned attribute in the Column element, when most (but not all) of the cells in the column span).

```
<table>
  ...
  <column column-number=" 2" text-align="right" />
  ...
  <table-body>
    <table-row>
      <table-cell>...</table-cell>
      <table-cell
          text-align=" from-table-column(text-align)">
        ...
      </table-cell>
    </table-row>
  </table-body>
</table>
```

In tables that have a large number of columns, there may be occasions when a series of columns have the same settings. Instead of simply repeating the Column element for each one, a single Column element may be used. The number of columns affected by the settings in this single element is given in the **Number Columns Repeated** attribute. But it should be noted that if the settings include the Columns Spanned attribute with a value greater than '1', then the spanned columns are skipped-over in this process.

It is not necessary to specify column widths if the table is formatted automatically to fit the available space. This is the default 'auto' mode, as specified in the **Table Layout** attribute, which can also take the value 'fixed'.

Lines

When text is flowed into a block, it occupies one or more lines within that block. Blocks may therefore contain line areas, which are adjacent to each other in the line-progression direction (vertically, working down the block, in English documents).

The number of line areas that are needed depends on how much text can be placed on each line. This will depend on the font chosen, and the size chosen to display characters in this font (such as 9pt Times Roman, or 12pt Helvetica). A major task of the XSL formatting engine is deciding how to arrange text over multiple lines (as well as how much material to place on each page). There is therefore no element to represent a single line, as the document author would not know how much text to place in each one. Thus:

```
<block>This is a paragraph. It is spread over a number
of lines.</block>
```

By default, line areas are simply stacked on top of each other (in English documents), with each line set to be the height of the font size chosen (or slightly greater). The **Line Height** attribute can be used to override the default value of 'normal', with a specific points size or other value.

First-line style

The first line of text can be given a different style to the remaining text, using the **Initial Property Set** element. Again, this element cannot surround the text it affects because the document author will not know how much text to include. It is therefore an empty element that must appear as the first item in a block:

```
<block font-size="12pt">
<initial-property-set font-size="14pt" />This is a
paragraph. It is spread over a number of lines.</block>
```

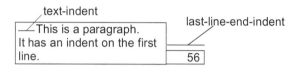

It is common practice to begin a new paragaph with an indent. The **Text Indent** attribute is used to indent the first line of text in a block, and the **Last Line End Indent** attribute similarly indents the last line of text, though a negative value is typically used here to create an 'outdent' for such items as page numbers in content lists:

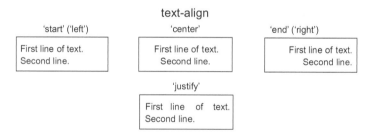

Text alignment

Text occupying a number of lines may be vertically aligned on one side or on both sides. The **Text Align** attribute takes the values 'start' (or 'left' in left-to-right mode), 'end' (or 'right' in left-to-right mode), 'center' or 'justify' (align to both edges). It is even possible to vary the alignment, depending on which side of the page is bound into a book (which will vary for alternating sides), with the values 'inside' and 'outside':

text-align

'start' ('left')	'center'	'end' ('right')
First line of text. Second line.	First line of text. Second line.	First line of text. Second line.

'justify'

First line   of   text.
Second line.

The **Text Align Last** attribute deals with the last line of text. Possible values are as described above for general text alignment, but an additional option of 'relative' operates as shown in the examples above (with 'start' being the default for the last line of justified text). Note that the last line of justified text is often only aligned on one side, because it is too short to pad with spaces without looking ridiculous.

Hyphenation

More care is usually taken in splitting words across lines on paper than on the screen, and hyphenation is a common way to balance the need to put as many words on each line as possible, while not reducing the space between words to such a degree that it is not possible to read the text. Moving the whole word down to the next line because it will not fit often creates large spaces when the text is justified on the line. The **Hyphenate** attribute defaults to 'false', but can be set to 'true', so enabling the hyphenation of words.

The character to be inserted by the formatter at the end of the line when hyphenating a word can be specified using the **Hyphenation Character** attribute. Normally, the hyphen character, '-', is specified.

Many typesetting systems and DTP packages have access to a hyphenation dictionary, showing acceptable break-points in each word. When such a dictionary is not available, the system must follow some simple rules instead, and one criterion that could be used involves placing a minimum number of characters at each side of the break. The **Hyphenation Push Character Count** attribute specifies the minimum number of characters that need to be pushed onto the next line, and the **Hyphenation Remain Character Count** attribute specifies the minimum number of characters to be retained on the original line. Typically, these values would both be set to '2':

```
<block hyphenate="true"
       hyphenation-character="-"
       hyphenation-push-character-count="2"
       hyphenation-remain-character-count="2">...</block>
```

The **Hyphenation Keep** attribute can be used to prevent the use of hyphens on words at the end of a line that is at the end of a column or a page. If set to 'column', a hyphen is not allowed at the end of a column. If set to 'page', a hyphen is not allowed at the end of a page. The value 'none' implies no restrictions.

Text can be difficult to read if a number of consecutive lines all have hyphenated words on them. By default, the **Hyphenation Ladder Count** attribute allows any number of consecutive hyphens, using the value 'none', but this can be changed to a number indicating the maximum number of hyphenated lines.

First line of text con-
tains some hyphena-
tion, as do two fur-
ther lines.

In-line objects

It is often not sufficient simply to break a block down into lines. Sometimes, a word or phrase within the text needs to be formatted in a different manner (such as the bold terms on this page), or a picture or page number (both current and referenced pages) needs to be inserted into the text at a specific point. These are all examples of 'in-line' objects. An in-line object may apply styles to a range of text within a line, or one starting on one line and ending on another. In-line objects are also used to format individual characters, and to insert leader dots ('....', commonly used in indexes).

In-line areas are stacked within a line area in the in-line progression direction. For English documents, this is left to right. When a formatted in-line element spans lines, additional in-line areas are created (one for each line occupied):

```
...<emph>first line</emph>...
```

The **Space Start** and **Space End** attributes are used on in-line objects to separate them from surrounding objects (recall that Space Above and Space After are used on block-level elements).

inline-progression direction

This is a paragraph.
It has an indent on the **first**
line.

space-start   space-end

This text is   spaced   out.

In-line text

The **Inline** element is the in-line equivalent to the Block element: a general-purpose container for a consecutive range of characters that need to share some formatting characteristic, such as a border, padding and background settings, or a change of font, font style or size. All of the characteristics shown below can be used in the Block element to set defaults styles for the entire block. The Inline element then acts as an override for the specific range of text it encloses; for example, the text it contains can be emphasized:

```
<block>A <inline font-weight="bold">bold</inline> word.
</block>
```

A **bold** word.

The baseline can be shifted up or down, the line height altered, and characters within the element can be forced to stay together within a single line (overriding any line breaks that the formatter would otherwise apply). The text can even be made invisible.

Basic character appearance can be specified. This includes the font family (such as 'sans-serif' or 'Arial'), the font size (such as '12pt'), the style ('normal', 'oblique' or 'italic'), the weight ('normal', 'bold', 'bolder', 'lighter'), stretch ('normal', 'wider', 'narrower' and others), and variant ('normal' or 'small-caps'). The **Font Family**, **Font Size**, **Font Size Adjust**, **Font Style**, **Font Variant** and **Font Weight** attributes performs these functions:

```
Some <inline font-family="Helvetica"
             font-size="12pt"
             font-size-adjust="none"
             font-style="italic"
             font-variant="small-caps"
             font-weight="bold" >Very Special
</inline>formatting.
```

Some *VERY SPECIAL* formatting.

The **Font Stretch** attribute allows characters to be stretched horizontally. The default value is 'normal', but it can be changed to 'narrower' or 'wider' (and a number of other subtle variations).

The single **Font** attribute replaces many of the attributes shown above, providing the style, variant, weight, size, line height and name. The following example is equivalent to the one above, except that the line height is also given ('14pt') and the stretch value is missing (as it cannot be provided in this form):

```
Some
<inline font="italic small-caps bold 12pt/14pt Helvetica">
Very Special</inline>formatting.
```

The **Text Decoration** attribute can be used to place a line under the text (an underline), but can also be used to place the line elsewhere, when taking the value 'overline' or 'line-through'. The **Score Spaces** attribute is used to decide whether or not to break the line where spaces appear, taking the value 'true' or 'false'.

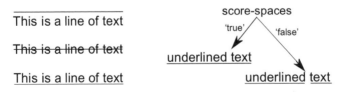

The **Vertical Align** attribute moves text up or down, and it takes the values 'baseline' (the default value), 'middle', 'sub' (subscript), 'super' (superscript), and a number of other, more subtle variations. The **Letter Spacing** attribute can take a value of 'normal', or any specific length of whitespace to insert between characters. The **Word Spacing** element does the same for the space between words (but is ignored when the line is justified, as spaces are then adjusted to make the right-hand edge of the last word reach the border of the content area). The **Text Transform** element is used to transform letters to all upper case ('uppercase') or to all lower case ('lowercase'), or to convert the first letter in each word to upper case and the rest to lower case ('capitalise'). The **Text Shadow** element allows shadows to appear around individual characters. It has a default value of 'normal', but it may take a multiple parameter value giving the horizontal then vertical length of the shadow, the blur angle then the colour:

```
Some <inline text-decoration="underline"
             vertical-align="super"
             letter-spacing="1pt"
             word-spacing="9pt"
             text-transform="lowercase"
             text-shadow="normal">Very Special</inline>
formatting.
```

some <u>very special</u> formatting.

Note that the Text Transform attribute is not generally recommended, as it does not apply to many languages. However, it can safely be used in languages such as English.

The **Color** attribute assignes a colour to the text. This attribute can be added to any element, and it would typically be used on the Block element or the Page Sequence element to set the default colour. For example:

```
<block color="red">DANGER: This is dangerous.</block>
```

In-line containers

The **Inline Container** element is the in-line equivalent to the Block Container element: a container for a consecutive range of in-line objects that need to share some formatting characteristics. It can be usefully employed to ensure that line ends do not occur within the embedded text, or to place a border around this text, or to change the direction of writing.

This element may use the Overflow attribute to control how overflowing text is to be handled when the container is given a specific width that is too small.

Characters

The **Character** element represents a single character that requires special formatting to be applied to it. The XSL processor treats all normal characters as if they were represented by the Character element, with the **Character** attribute set to the actual character. The two examples below are therefore equivalent:

```
<block>abc</block>

<block>
<character character="a"/>
<character character="b"/>
<character character="c"/>
</block>
```

This element is relevant when special formatting is required (though the Inline or Wrapper element can also be used instead in many circumstances). The Vertical Align attribute can be used to create superscript and subscript characters:

```
H<character character="2" vertical-align="sub"/>O is
water.
```

H$_2$O is water.

The **Apply Word Spacing** attribute specifies whether or not the character is considered to be a space between words. By default, the normal space character and the non-break space characters are considered to be word separators, and so they have a default value of 'yes'. All other characters have a default value of 'no'.

Text characters can be rotated using the **Glyph Orientation Horizontal** attribute, which takes a degree value, with '90' indicating a rotation of 90 degrees clockwise:

```
<block>ABC<character glyph-orientation-horizontal="90"
character="D">EFG</block>
```

ABCꓷEFG

The **Glyph Orientation Vertical** attribute works in the same way for vertically written text.

Graphics

The **External Graphic** element represents graphic data that is stored in a binary data file elsewhere. The graphic data is inserted at the location of this element. The **Href** attribute identifies the file to insert:

```
<block>Here is a picture of a boat:
<external-graphic href="boat.gif"/>.</block>
```

Here is a picture of a boat: .

While these elements are described as in-line elements, they can be separated from surrounding text simply by placing them in dedicated block elements:

```
<block>A boat is shown below.</block>
<block text-align="center">
<external-graphic href="boat.gif"/>
</block>
<block>The boat is shown above.</block>
```

A boat is shown below.

The boat is shown above.

The **Height** and **Width** attributes define a fixed area into which the graphic must be placed:

```
<external-graphic href="boat.gif"  width="5cm"
                                    height="7cm" />
```

As the image may not be this precise size, it may need to be scaled to fit. If the **Scale** attribute has the value 'maximum', the image is scaled in both directions to fit the given region. This means that the image may appear stretched in one direction or the other. As an alternative, the value 'maximum-uniform' may be used, which maintains the aspect ratio (and so avoids distorting the image) by scaling both dimensions until one dimension of the image reaches the given limit.

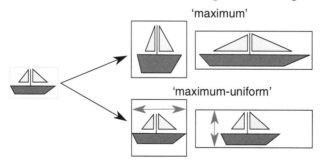

Alternatively, the scale can be given as a numeric value, such as '0.5' (reduce by half) and '2' (double in size). If two values are given, the first indicates the horizontal direction and the second indicates the vertical. The values '1.5 3' increases the size of the image by half horizontally, and by three times vertically. The default value for this attribute is simply '1.0', meaning that no scaling is to be performed in either direction.

The **Minimum Width**, **Maximum Width**, **Minimum Height** and **Maximum Height** attributes can be used to specify limits on the size of the image. The box is sized to fit the image (or the image scaled as described above), provided that it lies within these limits:

```
<external-graphic href="boat.gif" minimum-width="3cm"
                                  maximum-width="7cm"
                                  minimum-height="5cm"
                                  maximum-height="6cm" />
```

The **Instream Foreign Object** element represents graphic data that is part of the XML document (using a different namespace). It can also be used for other embedded data.

Leaders

It is common practice to put a row of dots between an item and its page number in the index of a book. This is done to ensure that the correct page number if noted when glancing across the page (though this book does not use this convention, because the two-column approach reduces the space between the item and the page number sufficiently to reduce the possibility of error significantly). The **Leader** element is used to insert a given character, repeating it as many times as necessary, in order to fill a gap.

The **Leader Pattern** attribute dictates the content of the leader area. The 'space' option is the default and implies no visible leader marks. The 'rule' option draws a simple line. The 'dots' option inserts dots (which is common in indexes). The 'use-content' option indicates that the text content of this element is to be used, and repeated as many times as necessary to fill the space.

```
<leader leader-pattern="dots" />
```

```
XSL .............................. 92
XSLT ........................... 155
```

```
<leader leader-pattern="use-content" >x</leader>
```

```
XSL xxxxxxxxxxxxxxxxx 192
```

Every leader occupies horizontal space. The **Leader Length** attribute holds a width value. However, as the first example above demonstrates, leaders are often used to justify the entire line. In this example, the leader dots repeat enough times to ensure that the page numbers are right-justified. The Leader element can therefore be given mimimum and maximum widths, as well as an optimum width, using the **Leader Length Optimum**, **Leader Length Minimum** and **Leader Length Maximum** attributes:

```
<leader... leader-length.optimum="5cm"
           leader-length.minimum="4cm"
           leader-length.maximum="7cm" />
```

When the Leader Pattern attribute has a value of 'dot' (or 'use-content'), by default the dots are spaced apart as they would normally be when appearing in the text ('.........'). But it is possible to widen the spacing using the **Leader Pattern Width** attribute, giving it a value such as '1mm' ('. . . . . .').

Finally, when the Leader Pattern attribute has the value 'rule', the rule style can be specified using the **Rule Style** and **Rule Thickness** attributes:

```
<leader leader-pattern="rule"
        rule-style="double"
        rule-thickness="2pt" />
```

Page numbers

Page numbers are used to give a unique label to the current page, and to reference another page from the current page. But actual page numbers cannot be known until the formatter has 'paginated' (made pages from) the source text. Instead, the position where the current page number must appear can be specified using the **Page Number** element:

```
This text is on page <page-number font-weight="bold"/>.
```

> This text is on page **123**.

Typically, this element is actually used in a static flow area, such as a header section (as at the top of this page).

The **Page Number Citation** element is used to reference an object that is (or may be) placed on another page. It is replaced by the page number of the page that contains that object. The **Reference Identifier** attribute provides the unique identifier of the object in question. Note that most objects can have **Id** attributes to facilitate the use of this feature:

```
Please refer to the summary on page
<page-number-citation ref-id="sum" font-weight="bold" />.

<block id="sum">To summarize, ...</block>
```

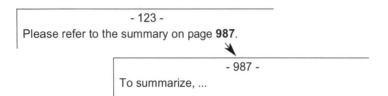

This element is particularly useful for creating content lists and indexes.

Hypertext links

Electronic documents are able to contain 'hot text' that acts as a link to other items in the same document or to items in another document. Web browsers commonly highlight such 'hypertext' links using underlined, coloured styles. The **Simple Link** element is used to create such a link:

```
See <simple-link...>Chapter 9</simple-link> for details.
```

See **Chapter 9** for detail.

The link should be either an internal link (to another object in the same document), or an external link (to an object in another document), using the **Internal Destination** attribute or the **External Destination** attribute respectively.

An internal destination is identified by the Id attribute on the other object:

```
See <simple-link internal-destination="CH9">Chapter 9</
simple-link> for details.

<block id="CH9">Chapter 9</block>
```

An external destination is identified by URL:

```
See <simple-link external-destination="ch9.xml">Chapter
9</simple-link> for details.
```

ch9.xml

The **Show Destination** attribute specifies how the link is to be followed. The value 'replace' indicates that the source text should be replaced by the destination text, by scrolling when the destination is in the same document and by document replacement when it is not. The value 'new' indicates that a new window should be opened for the destination text, leaving the source still visible.

When the destination text is presented, it may need to be highlighted, possibly by colouring the background. The **Indicate Destination** attribute has a value of 'yes' or 'no' (the default). Also, by default most browsers will show the first line of the destination text at the top of the window, but it may be desirable to show some preceding text. The **Destination Placement Offset** attribute can be given a size value to do this (the default is '0pt').

Object positioning

By default, block and in-line objects are positioned on the page, or within containing blocks, as described above. Each object is simply placed after the preceding object, either in the block-progression direction, or in the line-progression direction. However, the **Position** attribute allows for other options. Apart from the default value of '**static**', it can also take the values 'fixed', 'relative' and 'absolute'. The **Top**, **Right**, **Bottom** and **Left** attributes are used to position the object, though their relevance depends on which position option is chosen.

A '**fixed**' object is placed in a fixed location relative to the page edges or, when viewing on electronic media, relative to the viewport (which means that fixed objects never move, even if the viewport contains a scroll-bar). The '**absolute**' value indicates that the positioning attributes are to be used to position the object relative to the containing block. Such objects are removed from the flow, in the sense that they leave a space to be occupied by following objects. The '**relative**' value indicates that the positioning attributes are to be used to position the object relative to the position it would normally occupy if it were a 'static' object. The positions of following 'static' objects remains the same as they would be if this had not happened.

Out-of-line objects

There are times when it is convenient to remove an item from the normal text flow and place it at a new location on the page, or even on the next page. Large pictures often need to be moved to avoid leaving a significant gap at the bottom of a page, so that following text can occupy this space (preceding the image). Footnotes are moved to the bottom of a page, where they can be either read or ignored by the reader.

The major page regions can contain 'conditional' sub-regions at the top or bottom. These regions only appear if there is information to place within them, because a conditional sub-region grabs space from the region it is in. For example, the main body region may sometimes have footnote content. The body region has conditional areas at the starting edge and ending edge (top and bottom):

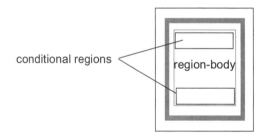

conditional regions

region-body

Floating objects

Large tables and figures are often moved to a location where they create the least possible disruption to the flow of text and the page balance, such as to the top of the next page or column. The **Float** element is used to contain such items, indicating to the formatting engine that it may move the content as appropriate. Only block-level elements can be used in the Float element:

```
<block>INLINE ITEM</block>
<float><block>FLOATING TEXT HERE</block></float>
<block>NEXT INLINE ITEM</block>
```

The formatting engine may move the enclosed items to the top of the current page, or to the top of a following page.

The **Float** attribute may be used to place the floating items to the 'left' or 'right' of the page. The default value is 'none', which the standard indicates as 'not floating'. It is difficult to believe that this is correct, as it means that in order to have a floating object it is necessary to use this attribute, and specify which side of the page it must appear on:

```
<float float="left"><block>LEFT TEXT</block></float>
<float float="right"><block>RIGHT TEXT</block></float>
```

Block-level elements, and the Float element itself, may contain the **Clear** attribute. This is used to move objects down beneath any previous floating objects. The value 'left' means that it must be moved below any floating objects on the left-hand side. The value 'right' means that it must be moved below any floating objects on the right-hand side. The value 'both' moves the object beneath all previous floating objects.

The **Span** attribute may be used, and given the value 'all' to span the object across multiple columns.

Footnotes

Similarly, a footnote is usually placed at the bottom of the first page that contains a reference to it, and it is of course not possible to determine in advance where a page-break may occur. The **Footnote** element contains the footnote text, which will float to the base of the page. This element can also contain a reference to the footnote:

```
<block>Here is a footnote reference<footnote>
<block>A reference to a footnote is usually a '*'</block>
</footnote>.</block>
<block>More text.</block>
. . .
```

> Here is a footnote reference*.
> More text.
> ...
>
> * A reference to a footnote is
> usually a '*'

Again, the **Span** attribute may be used, and given the value 'all' to span the object across multiple columns:

> Here is a
> footnote
> reference*.
>
> * A reference to a footnote is
> usually a '*'

Neutral objects

Some features may be employed both in-line and at the block level. These include the ability to swap-in and swap-out portions of the document dynamically, change the style of an object dynamically, and apply inherited styles to a range of items.

Switches

When publishing electronically, it is possible to hide and reveal portions of the document depending on user actions. The opening and collapsing of portions of a contents list can be supported using such a feature. The **Multi Switch** element contains a number of **Multi Case** elements. Each of these elements holds an alternative document fragment, and each alternative must be given a unique name, so that it can be referred to and activated later. The **Case Name** attribute holds this value:

```
<multi-switch>
  <multi-case case-name="first">...</multi-case>
  <multi-case case-name="second">...</multi-case>
  <multi-case case-name="third">...</multi-case>
</multi-switch>
```

Only one of these fragments is active when the page is initially presented to the user. The content of the first Multi Case element with a **Starting State** attribute value of 'show' (instead of the default value of 'hide') is presented first. The others can be revealed later:

```
<multi-case case-name="first">...</multi-case>
<multi-case case-name="second" starting-state="show">
  <block>THIS PORTION IS SHOWN FIRST</block>
</multi-case>
```

Within each document fragment, there may be any number of **Multi Toggle** elements, which are used to switch-in one of the other fragments. The text contained in these elements becomes 'hot' text that the user can select. When selected by the user, the associated case fragment replaces the current fragment. The **Switch To** attribute refers to the name of the fragment to swap in (the Case Name attribute of the relevant Multi Case element):

```
<multi-case case-name="closed" starting-state="show">
  <block>Heading
    <multi-toggle switch-to="opened" >
      [+]
    </multi-toggle>
  </block>
</multi-case>
```

```
<multi-case case-name="opened">
  <block>Heading
    <multi-toggle switch-to=" closed" >
      [-]
    </multi-toggle>
  </block>
  <block>- Item 1</block>
  <block>- Item 2</block>
</multi-case>
```

When multiple cases are embedded within other multiple cases, the user may change the selected case of the embedded case, then change the outer one, but later return to it. The question that then arises is whether the default case is shown for the inner multiple or the one that was last selected (ie does the browser 'remember' the previous state). The **Auto Restore** attribute can be added to the Multi Switch element. It takes a value of 'yes' or 'no' (the default). If set to 'yes', this attribute states that the default should be restored. Otherwise, the last one selected is restored instead.

Changing styles

The style of a range of blocks, or range of text, can be changed, depending on the current state of the environment. An example given in the XSL standard refers to the way that the colour of a hypertext link source may vary, depending on whether the link has been visited recently or is currently selected. The **Multi Properties** element contains a number of initial, empty **Multi Property Set** elements, each one providing the style to apply under a given circumstance, identified using the **Dom State** attribute. These elements are followed by the document fragment to be styled:

```
<multi-properties>
<multi-property-set dom-state="visited"
                    color="#FF0000" />
<multi-property-set dom-state="active"
                    color="#00FF00" />
<multi-property-set dom-state="inactive"
                    color="#0000FF" />
The colour of this text depends on the current state.
</multi-properties>
```

Only style changes that do *not* affect the placement of the text in the page should be included, as support for re-flowing the text may not be present in some systems, or may be an undesirable side-effect in any case.

The Dom State attribute refers to the DOM (Document Object Model), which is an in-memory tree-like representation of an XML document. DOM states, such as 'mouse-over', may be supported by the XSL formatter, but only if it is still active as the user is reading the document. Possible DOM states are not listed in the draft XSL standard and are yet to be determined.

Visibility

Block and in-line objects are normally 'visible', as specified in the **Visibility** attribute. These objects can be rendered invisible by setting this attribute value to 'hidden'. The objects then still exist, and still occupy the same amount of space they would normally do, but their contents are not presented. One reason to do this is to achieve unusual spacing effects. Another reason would be to add further interactive features, with software changing the value between 'visible' and 'hidden' as appropriate.

In a table, a cell that is set to 'hidden', when the Empty Cells attribute is also set to 'hide', will have no border lines (assuming separate border lines for each cell).

A third option is 'collapse'. In the circumstances above, this value is equivalent to 'hidden', but in table rows and columns it has a different effect. Unfortunately, the draft standard is not clear on what this difference is.

Wrappers

Sometimes, it is useful to be able to specify a style that is to be applied to a sequence of characters without creating an enclosing object. Although the **Inline** element can be used to specify character styles (which the characters inherit), it creates an inline object as well. The styles specified in an Inline element are actually applied to the inline object, and then inherited by embedded Character elements (which are implied when characters are entered directly). The Inline element is necessary when the intent is to add a border around the text, as the border is actually placed around the inline object created by this instruction. But when the intent is only to apply individual styles to each of the embedded characters, the **Wrapper** element is preferable. This element does not create an object on the page, but is simply used as a convenient 'wrapper' with inheritable properties:

```
<block>A <wrapper font-weight="bold">bold</wrapper>
word.</block>
```

This element can also be employed around block elements:

```
<wrapper margin-left="2cm">
  <block>...</block>
  <block>...</block>
  <block>...</block>
</wrapper>
```

Whitespace and line feeds

Most characters are simply rendered by formatting engines, but whitespace characters and line-feed characters can be treated in different ways. A number of attributes are available to control how they are handled.

Whitespace collapse

When there are consecutive whitespace characters, this may be due to the formatting of the source XML document rather than any intended document content. Many formatting engines and the popular Web browsers reduce sequences of whitespace down to a single space character, but allow this behaviour to be overridden in special cases (such as within the PRE (pre-formatted) element in HTML). By default, XSLT normalizes whitespace in this way, but the **Whitespace Collapse** attribute may take the value 'false' (instead of 'true') to prevent this action.

```
<block whitespace-collapse="false">This    text    is
widely          spaced.</block>
```

    This   text   is widely   spaced.

```
<block whitespace-collapse="true">This    text    is
widely          spaced.</block>
```

    This text is widely spaced.

Space and line-feed treatment

The **Space Treatment** attribute can be used to remove all whitespace characters, except for line-feed characters (which are described below). This attribute therefore affects the space character and the tab character. The default value is 'preserve', but can be set to 'ignore':

```
<block space-treatment="ignore">This text contains spaces
and    tabs.</block>
```

    Thistextcontainsspacesandtabs.

Similarly, the **Linefeed Treatment** attribute is used to 'preserve' or 'ignore' line-feed characters, but adds the 'treat-as-space' option. The 'preserve' option instructs the formatter to treat line feeds as line-ending instructions (to place the next character on the following line). The 'treat-as-space' option treats the line feed as a normal space character:

```
<block linefeed-treatment="ignore">Line one.
Line two.
Line three.</block>
```

Line one.Line two.Line three.

```
<block linefeed-treatment="preserve">Line one.
Line two.
Line three.</block>
```

Line one.
Line two.
Line three.

```
<block linefeed-treatment="treat-as-space">Line one.
Line two.
Line three.</block>
```

Line one. Line two. Line three.

The 'treat-as-space' option is the default, as it is used to format normal text in documents or books. The 'preserve' option is reserved for special cases, such as lines of poetry or lines of computer code that are *not* held in separate elements in the source document:

```
<block linefeed-treatment="preserve">
10 PRINT "Hello world."
20 GOTO 10
</block>
```

Wrap options

Normally, the formatter will wrap text onto the following line when the right edge of the content area is reached. The **Wrap Option** attribute has a default option of 'wrap', but changing this value to 'no-wrap' overrides this behaviour. This means that the text may occupy space outside of the content area. When this happens, the appearance of this text is governed by the value of the **Overflow** attribute (where it may be 'visible' or 'hidden', or in electronic documents it may be possible to 'scroll' in order to see it).

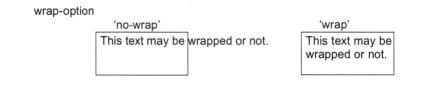

Whitespace short-cut

XSL has inherited the **Whitespace** attribute from the CSS property of the same name. XSL treats this attribute as a short-cut for setting a number of the properties described above to achieve a commonly required effect. This attribute has three possible values: 'normal', 'pre' and 'nowrap'. Note that in all three cases the equivalent Space Treatment attribute value is 'preserve'. Therefore, none of the options removes all spaces from the text (though some remove extraneous spaces).

A '**normal**' item has line-feed characters treated as spaces, whitespace normalized to single spaces, and text wrapped onto following lines by the formatter. The two examples below are therefore equivalent:

```
<block whitespace="normal">...</block>

<block line-feed-treatment="treat-as-space"
       white-space-collapse="true"
       space-treatment="preserve"
       wrap-option="wrap" >...</block>
```

A '**pre**' (pre-formatted) item has line-feed characters preserved and whitespace preserved, and text *not* wrapped onto following lines by the formatter. The two examples below are therefore equivalent:

```
<block whitespace="pre">...</block>

<block line-feed-treatment="preserve"
       white-space-collapse="false"
       space-treatment="preserve"
       wrap-option="no-wrap" >...</block>
```

A '**nowrap**' item has line-feed characters treated as spaces and whitespace normalized to single spaces, as for the 'normal' option, but text is *not* wrapped onto following lines by the formatter. The two examples below are therefore equivalent:

```
<block whitespace="nowrap">...</block>

<block line-feed-treatment="treat-as-space"
       white-space-collapse="true"
       space-treatment="preserve"
       wrap-option="no-wrap" >...</block>
```

Aural styles

XSL includes a large number of properties that assist with the audible presentation of material (taken directly from the CSS version 2 specification). Speech presentation is important, not just to those who are visually disabled but also to anyone who cannot switch visual attention from some other task, such as driving a vehicle.

The **Speak** attribute is used to render text audibly when given the value 'normal' (the default), or 'spell-out'. The 'spell-out' option is used to pronounce text such as XSL, by spelling out each letter; 'X', 'S', 'L'. A value of 'none' suppresses audible presentation of the content.

One of the most important properties of speech is volume. The **Volume** attribute can take a number of different types of value. A simple numeric value in the range 0–100 denotes a volume from barely audible to barely comfortable. A percentage value is used for volumes that are relative to inherited values:

```
<block speak="normal" volume="60">you should
<wrapper volume="150%">shout</wrapper> this and
<wrapper volume="50%">whisper</wrapper> this.</block>
```

The value 'silent' switches off sound (for recall that a volume of '0' does not indicate silence, just very quiet speech), and there are several named volume values that represent common requirements, including 'x-soft' (the same as a volume of 0), 'soft' (25), 'medium' (50), 'loud' (75) and 'x-loud' (100). Whatever value is specified, this is simply an initial value that the listener should be able to adjust.

Rate of speech can be defined with the **Speech Rate** attribute. This attribute takes a numeric value that represents words per minute, though some convenient named values are also available, including 'x-slow' (80 words per minute), 'slow' (120), 'medium' (180–200), 'fast' (300) and 'x-fast' (500). The values 'slower' and 'faster' adjust an inherited speech rate by 40 words per minute. As for volume, the listener should be able to override the initial setting.

Voices are also distinguished by type. The most obvious categories are 'male', 'female' and 'child', but it is also possible to refer to more specific categories (though the standard does not contain such a list of options), or even name an individual. Voice characteristics use an override system that is similar to the font specification, so that generic types can be chosen when specific types are not available on the local system. The **Voice Family** attribute is used. For example, a play may comprise a number of blocks with alternating voices:

```
<block voice-family="male-cockney, male">...</block>
<block voice-family="female-scottish, female">...</block>
<block voice-family="child">...</block>
<block voice-family="churchill, male">...</block>
```

When generic voice types are used, it is possible to add some variety by specifying the 'pitch', using the **Pitch** attribute. This attribute takes a value of 'x-low', 'low', 'medium', 'high' or 'x-high', or a numeric value giving the pitch in hertz. The named values do not have a pre-defined hertz equivalent, as it depends on the main voice characteristic chosen, such as 'male' or 'female' (the average pitch for a male voice is around 120 Hz, but for a female voice it is around 210 Hz):

```
<block voice-family="male" pitch="90Hz">...</block>
```

Some people speak with a steady pitch, and others vary the pitch even in normal conversation. The **Pitch Range** attribute specifies the degree to which the pitch can change during speech, from '0' (no change, a monotonous voice) to '100' (a wildly animated voice), with '50' representing a normal variance:

```
<block pitch="90Hz" pitch-range="20">...</block>
```

The voice can be further refined using **Stress** and **Richness** attributes that affect the inflection and the prominence or brightness of the voice.

Pauses between words are very important in speech. The ends of sentences, paragraphs, and larger divisions of the text are marked by pauses of different lengths. The **Pause Before** attribute creates a pause before the content of the element is presented. A set duration can be given, such as '20ms' (20 milliseconds), or a time span that is relative to the speed of the speech can be specified instead, such as '50%' ('100%' represents the time it takes to speak one word, on average, at the current speech rate). The **Pause After** attribute works in the same way but creates a gap *after* the content. When specifying a pause both before and after, a more convenient **Pause** attribute is available that takes two parameters, with the first parameter providing the before value, and the second parameter providing the after value. It can also take a single value, to represent both when they are of the same duration. The following two examples are therefore equivalent:

```
<block... pause="30ms 20ms">...</block>

<block... pause-before="30ms"
         pause-after="20ms">...</block>
```

In some cases, the pauses they produce may not be sufficient to identify punctuation, and it may be necessary to ensure that punctuation is clearly identified. The **Speak Punctuation** attribute takes a value of 'code' to specify that punctuation is to be read out. For example, 'this, and that' would be read out as 'this comma ...*(pause)*... and that'. The value 'none' (the default) disables punctuation speech.

Similarly, while numerals are normally spoken as 'continuous' digits, so that '237' is pronounced 'two hundred and thirty seven', it is possible using the **Speak Numeral** attribute to dictate that the digits are to be read out separately. The value 'digits' ensures that this example is pronounced 'two three seven':

```
<block...>The alarm code is
<wrapper speak-numeral="digits">1254</wrapper>.</block>

<block...>My age is
<wrapper speak-numeral="continuous">37</wrapper>.</block>
```

Sound effects can be played before or after the spoken content. The **Cue Before** attribute specifies a sound (identified by URL) to be played before the speech, and **Cue After** plays a sound afterward. The **Cue** attribute is more convenient if surrounding sounds are required, as it takes two values – one for before and one for after. A single value in the Cue attribute specifies that the given sound should be played both before and after the speech. Sounds can be inherited from parent elements, but existing sounds can be overridden using the value 'none' (to avoid playing a sound). A sound is identified by URL:

```
<block... cue-before="SOUNDS/BELL.WAV">...</block>
```

The **Play During** attribute allows a sound to be played throughout the speech. A value of 'auto' means that an existing sound, activated by an ancestor element, should continue to play throughout this fragment of the speech. If there is a possibility (or even a certainty) that the sound will end before the speech ends, it is possible to repeat the sound using the '**sound**' parameter. It is also possible to mix a new sound with one that is already playing, by adding the '**mix**' parameter. These two parameters must follow the URL value, and when both are present they must appear in the order described above:

```
<block... play-during="HUMM1.WAV repeat">...</block>
```

Advanced sound systems are able to provide stereo sound, and in some cases also surround-sound effects. When there are several people speaking, it can be useful to give each one a separate spatial location. Horizontal locations are specified using the **Azimuth** attribute, which accepts a value between '0deg' (zero degrees) and '360deg' (the same position). Values increase clockwise from the front-centre. For convenience, some named values are available to correspond to different degree settings, including 'center' (zero degrees), 'center-right' (20 degrees), 'right' (40), 'far-right' (60), 'right-side' (90), 'left-side' (270), 'far-left' (300), 'left' (320) and 'center-left' (340). The values 'leftwards' and 'rightwards' take an inherited value and move the sound left (by deducting 20 degrees) or right (by adding 20 degrees), though both appear to move sound in the wrong direction when it is behind the listener. The parameter 'behind' can be added to a value, moving the sound to the back:

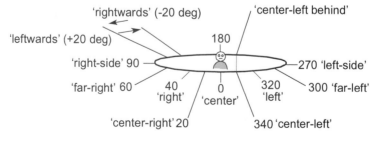

The following example places the judge at the centre-front, with prosecution and defence at each side:

```
<block... azimuth="center">JUDGE:...</block>
<block... azimuth="left-side">PROSECUTION:...</block>
<block... azimuth="right-side">DEFENCE:...</block>
```

Sound sources may also be located at different vertical locations. For example, a judge should perhaps be elevated above the other speakers. The **Elevation** attribute specifies a vertical location, from '0deg' (zero degrees) to '90deg' (overhead) or '-90deg' (beneath), with 'level', 'above' and 'below' also representing these extreme positions. The values 'higher' and 'lower' add and subtract 10 degrees respectively:

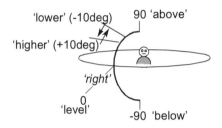

```
<block... elevation="75deg">JUDGE:...</block>
```

18. HTML 4.0

Although the primary impetus behind the development of XSLT has been to provide a mechanism for creating XSL documents, the reality is that most browsers in use today only understand HTML (along with CSS). Fortunately, XSLT is equally adept at converting XML documents into HTML documents (perhaps containing in-line CSS styles). This chapter explains HTML in sufficient detail to enable the formatting of XML documents for presentation in these browsers. HTML tags not used to format content are not discussed here. The most notable omission is elements used to build interactive forms.

The mechanism for producing HTML documents using an XSLT stylesheet is described in Chapter 5.

HTML

The concept of electronic links between text stored on computer systems is an old one, and many **hypertext** systems have been developed, though most have been confined to linking texts stored on the same system, and have used proprietory technologies.

It was only a matter of time before the Internet became an obvious candidate to support a hypertext system that spans systems and countries. With the infrastructure in place, it was only necessary to define two additional protocols: first, a new access protocol that would allow hypertext documents to be requested from a server; and, second, a document markup language that would be used to both style the received document and locate and enable any embedded hypertext links. The **HTML** (*HyperText Markup Language*) protocol performs the second of these roles, and was devised in 1990. HTML documents are transferred to the client browser.

The browser on the client system interprets the HTML document, removing the tags and presenting the content in an appropriate format. There are implied styles or behaviours associated with each tag. The HTML markup language takes a position half-way between format and structure. It includes style tags, such as the Italic element, where the output format is explicitly stated, but it also includes generalized objects, such as the Emphasis element, where output format is left to the browser.

The core feature of HTML – the very reason for its existence – is its ability to let readers follow links to other HTML documents anywhere on the Internet. When a **URL** reference to another file is selected by the user, the browser extracts the reference and sends a further request to the server (or to another server) for another HTML document, usually to replace the original but possibly to be presented in a new browser window.

HTML documents are also known as '**pages**'. The page first made available to users is known as the '**home page**', which usually has the default filename of 'index.html' (or 'index.htm').

Similarly, an HTML document may contain references to resources that conform to other data formats. In this way, image files and Java applets, amongst other objects, are downloaded to the browser and inserted into the presented version of the document.

HTML 4.0 is an application of SGML and is therefore defined by an SGML DTD. It is not possible for HTML to be considered an application of XML as it cannot be accurately described by an XML DTD. It uses advanced features of SGML, such as element and attribute minimization, and adopts SGML conventions for representation of empty elements. However, XHTML has just been announced as the next, XML-compatible version of HTML (but in terms of features is still essentially HTML 4.0).

HTML versions

There have been five versions of HTML, known as **HTML Level One**, **HTML Level Two**, **HTML+**, **HTML Level Three** and now **HTML Level Four**, of which HTML+ was an interim to Level Three that included tables. The respective DTDs are named **HTML 2.0**, **HTML 3.2** and **HTML 4.0** accordingly (level one predating full compatibility with SGML).

HTML 2.0 was the first version of HTML that conformed to the formal structures defined in the SGML standard, and has been supported by all browsers for so long that it is no longer necessary to discuss version 1.0. Version 2.0 added an interactive 'forms' feature and still forms the core of all following versions. The elements defined in this version are mostly still relevant. Nevertheless, some of the features of this (and the next) version of HTML have become deprecated or obsolete as more extensive or better-designed alternatives have emerged.

HTML 3.2, released in 1996, deprecated a few original elements but added numerous new elements for presenting tables, for styling text, for client-side image-based linking, and for document structuring. All popular browsers offer comprehensive support for this version.

HTML 4.0 is the current version and was released in December 1997. It was released by W^3C in December 1997. Some of its features have long been available in at least one of the popular browsers. In particular, the **frame** concept is in widespread use. There is an SGML DTD for this standard (http://www.w3.org/TR/REC-html40/). As with earlier ones this DTD is not XML-compatible (though the next version probably will be). Once again, the opportunity was taken to make obsolete a number of elements and attributes that have been superseded. New elements in this version allow the window to be split into frames, extend the table model, extend the forms model, add changed-content highlighting and a generalized non-HTML object identifier, and introduce some general text descriptions. Styles and scripts are also supported at last.

Basic document structure

An HTML-conforming document has a document element called **Html**. Unlike XML, element names are not case-sensitive, so the element may actually be named 'html', 'HTML' or 'Html' and does not need to match either the document type declaration or the end-tag.

The Html element encloses a **Head** section and a main **Body** section. The header contains a **Title**, which is presented in the title bar of the browser. The Body element may contain any of a number of other elements but will usually begin with the title repeated in a first-level-header element, **H1**. An **Address** element encloses details of the author of the document, and is usually inserted at the end of the document, where it is displayed in italic, possibly indented or centred:

```
<HTML>
   <HEAD>
      <TITLE>A Description of HTML</TITLE>
   </HEAD>
   <BODY>
      <H1>This is HTML</H1>
      ......
      <ADDRESS>Neil Bradley
      (http://neil@bradley.co.uk)</ADDRESS>
   </BODY>
</HTML>
```

The document background colour and foreground text colour can be specified in the **Body** element (though the following techniques are now deprecated), using the

Bgcolor (background colour) attribute and the **Text** attribute. In both cases, the format of the attribute value comprises either the name of a colour, or a coded RGB (red, green, blue) mix. Available colour names are 'aqua', 'black', 'fuchsia', 'gray', 'green', 'lime', 'maroon', 'navy', 'olive', 'purple', 'red', 'silver', 'teal', 'white' and 'yellow'. The RGB scheme uses three hexadecimal (two-digit) values preceded by a hash symbol, for example '#FF2250'. The first two digits indicate the amount of Red, the next two digits indicate the amount of Green, and the final two digits indicate the amount of Blue, to be mixed to create the desired colour. The example below produces a document with blue text on a yellow background:

```
<BODY BGCOLOR="#FFFF80" TEXT="blue">
```

As an alternative, the background can be composed from a picture, often in GIF format. The deprecated **Background** attribute provides a **URL** to the desired picture. When the picture is smaller than the display area, it is repeated across and down until it fills the display area:

```
<BODY BACKGROUND="images/background.gif">
```

A change to the document background or text colour may affect the visibility of **hypertext** links, so three additional attributes are available to set the colour of linking text (all now deprecated). The deprecated **Link** attribute sets the colour of a link that is not active and has not been visited. The deprecated **Vlink** (visited link) attribute sets the colour of all links that have been activated in the (recent) past. The deprecated **Alink** (active link) attribute sets the colour of the currently selected link. The format of the values is as described above for document foreground and background colors.

```
<BODY LINK="GREEN" ALINK="RED" VLINK="BLUE">
```

These attributes are deprecated because it is now possible to specify link styles using CSS:

```
A:link  { color:GREEN }
A:alink { color:RED }
A:vlink { color:BLUE }
```

The **Meta** element can appear in the header section, but is not used for document markup and is of most interest to those involved in browser/server communications. The Meta element is placed within the Head element to add meta-information not covered by attributes of other elements. The content of a Meta element is not to be displayed in the document, but may be read by the browser or server. It has three attributes, HTTP-Equiv, Name and Content. The **Name** attribute provides the name of the meta-information (almost an attribute name in itself). The **Content** attribute provides the current value for the named item. For example:

```
<META NAME="Index" CONTENT="cycle">
```

If more than one Meta element is present with the same Name attribute value, the various content values are accumulated into a comma-separated list; for example 'cycle, bus, car'. The third attribute, **HTTP-Equiv**, allows the content to be inserted into an **HTTP** header field (a topic not explored further in this book).

Differences from XML

HTML is currently an application of SGML, not XML, and unfortunately there are some minor differences in syntax. HTML takes advantage of a number of tag minimization techniques that SGML allows. In the early days of the Web, these were quite useful because Web page authors had to use standard text editors to create HTML documents and key every character in the tags. With the advent of WYSIWYG HTML editors that generate the tags automatically (behind the scenes), the issue of minimization is no longer relevant (this also being the primary reason for omitting such features from the XML standard).

Element minimization

The most obvious and widely used technique in HTML 4.0 is the omission of end-tags. Very often, the end of an element can be implied by the start of another. For example, it is not necessary to include an end-head tag, '</HEAD>', because its presence can be implied by the following Body start-tag, and the end-tag for the Body element is likewise not needed because the end-tag for the Html element implies this:

```
<HTML>
   <HEAD>
      <TITLE>A Description of HTML</TITLE>
   <BODY>
      <H1>This is HTML</H1>
      ......
      <ADDRESS>Neil Bradley
      (http://neil@bradley.co.uk)</ADDRESS>
</HTML>
```

Attribute minimization

Attributes can also be simplified significantly. When the attribute value must be a single value or word, the quotes can be omitted:

```
<BODY LINK=GREEN ALINK=RED VLINK=BLUE>
```

In some special cases, when the attributes that may be applied are very limited and the values that they have cannot conflict, it is also possible to dispense with the attribute name and equals symbol, as the presence of the value is sufficient.

Empty elements

The ability to omit end-tags leads to a perhaps more significant difference between XML and HTML. Empty elements in HTML are simply start-tags with no matching end-tags:

```
<!-- NO END TAG AND NO '/>' IN START TAG -->
<META NAME="Index" CONTENT="cycle">
```

This can cause some difficulties when attempting to include HTML tags within an XSLT document. While minimization in general does not cause any issues because it is an optional feature of HTML, the differences in the way that empty elements are represented cannot be so easily avoided. Chapter 5 describes how the **Output** element can be used to overcome this problem.

Text blocks

Except in one special circumstance, a browser will not obey any line breaks in the ASCII text file that contains the HTML document, but it will instead reformat the text to break at the right-hand margin of the window (or sub-region of the window) into which it is being displayed. This makes sense because fonts differ in respect of the widths of each character, and because the viewable area is determined by the size of the user's monitor and the size of the area assigned by the user to the browser window. Yet it is usually not desirable for an entire document to be reformatted into a single large text block. HTML therefore includes tags that break up the text into meaningful blocks. The most essential of these is the **P** (paragraph) element, which defines a single paragraph in the text. The browser begins a new paragraph on a new line and creates gaps between paragraphs:

```
<P>This is a paragraph.</P>
<P>This is another paragraph. </P>
```

With the advent of CSS and some of the common attributes described later, it is possible to use this one tag for almost all block-level formatting, though a number of other tags were defined in early versions of HTML and are still widely used for identifying headings, lists and other block-like structures.

Basic hypertext links

The **Anchor** element (**A**) is used to locate both the source and target ends of a hypertext link.

When used as a target element, the Anchor element usually contains the title of the referenced text (in order that it may be highlighted on completion of a link to that item) within the **Name** attribute:

```
<P><A NAME="details">The Details</A> are
here. ...</P>
```

When used as a source element, the Anchor contains a **Hypertext Reference** attribute (**Href**) which contains a **URL**.

```
<P>See <A HREF="#details">the details</A> for
the details</P>
```

A single Anchor may be both the source of a link and the target of a link:

```
<A NAME="summary" HREF="#details">See details</A>
```

When inserting links to other documents, the target document does not require an Anchor element, because the entire file is the target. However, it is possible to link to an anchored item in the other file by appending the hash symbol and item name:

```
<A HREF="../myfiles/detail.htm#part3">See
details, part 3</A>
```

If the path ends with a forward slash, '/', the target Web server supplies the name of the default home page:

```
HREF="http://www.myserver.com/myfiles/"
```

To target a browser at a home page held on the reader's own system, or another system visible over a local area network, the protocol becomes 'file:' (this is not officially a protocol name, and so should not be followed by the double slash):

```
<A HREF="file:/myserver/myfiles/me.html">
See My Server Home Page</A>
```

A **Title** attribute may be used to hold a brief description of the target resource, to be displayed by the browser when the mouse is over the link.

When relative paths are included in the URL, the starting-point is normally the address of the page containing the link. The **Base** element can be used to provide a new fixed point in the directory structure from which relative links should be calculated. It uses an **Href** attribute to specify the replacement path.

The **Link** element identifies other resources that are connected to this Web page, such as a style sheet. To identify the resource, it has an **Href** attribute, and the **Title** attribute holds a brief description of the resource:

```
<LINK TITLE="big print"
      HREF="bigprint.css"
      TYPE="text/css" >
```

The A and Link elements may contain a **Rel** (relationship) attribute, which identifies the relationship between the target object and the current page. The **Rev** attribute identifies the previous (reverse) relationship when the links form a chain. A browser could (in theory) style these links differently from others to indicate to the user that there is a preferred path to follow. These attributes are not widely used, but may be useful to Web search engines. The following is a Rel example:

```
<LINK REL="alternate stylesheet"
      TITLE="big print" HREF="bigprint.css"
      TYPE="text/css" >
```

Common attributes

Some useful attributes have now been added to almost every HTML element. The most ubiquitous are four core attributes, **Style**, **Class**, **Title** and **Id**. There are few elements that do not have them, the exceptions being structural tags (Html, Head, Title), background scripts (Script, Style and Area), applet tags (Applet and Param) and meta-data (Base, Basefont and Meta). In addition, many elements have new language attributes (Lang and Dir), and many others have attributes that allow scripts to be activated when the user interacts with the element in some way (Onclick, Ondblclick, Onmousedown, Onmouseup, Onmouseover, Onmouseout, Onkeypress, Onkeydown and Onkeyup).

In-line styles

The **Style** attribute allows **CSS** in-line styles to be applied. See Chapter 19 for general details on this standard. These in-line styles consist of CSS properties and values, separated by semi-colons (the curly brackets are not used):

```
<P STYLE="color: yellow ; background: black">This paragraph
will be styled in yellow on a black background.</P>
```

Element classes

The **Class** attribute introduces a measure of the generalized markup concept to HTML by allowing category names to be added to element instances. For example, some Paragraph elements may be more important than others:

```
P:{ color: black ; font-size: 10pt }
P:important{ color: red ; font-size: 14pt }

<P>This is a normal paragraph.</P>
<P CLASS="important">This is an IMPORTANT paragraph.</P>
<P>This is another normal paragraph.</P>
```

Note that the CSS style definitions in the example above may appear in the Head section of the document, and this approach to including CSS in HTML documents is discussed later.

Note also that it is the introduction of the two attributes described above that makes it possible to achieve so much with just the Paragraph element.

Element identifiers

The **Id** attribute (identifier) gives the element a unique name that may be used for various purposes, such as to provide a target for a hypertext link, to allow a style defined in a separate style sheet to be applied specifically to this element, or to be manipulated in a specific way by an ECMAScript procedure. The following paragraph is given a red colour by the style sheet and is also the target of a link.

```
P:#Scarborough { color: red }
...
<P ID="Scarborough">This is a paragraph about
Scarborough, a seaside resort in the north of
England.</P>
...
... See <A HREF="#Scarborough">Scarborough</A>...
```

This technique is familiar to XML users and is certainly a less clumsy way to identify the target of a link than wrapping the paragraph text within an A element (using the Name attribute to identify it). However, some of the currently popular browsers do not yet support this feature.

Element titles

The **Title** attribute allows a brief description of the content of the element to be included. Normally not visible, this text would only be revealed on user request. It can be used to build a simple table of contents, and it may be presented in the status bar. Thus:

```
<P title="HTML document">This is a paragraph about
HTML documents.</P>
```

Language

The **Lang** attribute describes the human language used for the textual content of the element:

```
<P LANG="EN">This is an English paragraph.</P>
```

The **Dir** attribute (directory) describes the direction of writing that is conventional for the human language concerned. It takes a value of 'ltr' (left to right) or 'rtl' (right to left):

```
<P LANG="EN" DIR="ltr">This is an English
paragraph read left to right.</P>
```

Event triggers

The 'On...' attributes all specify an ECMAscript function that is to be activated when the user interacts with the element in some given way.

The **Onclick** attribute activates the named function when the user clicks the mouse button over the element:

```
<P ONCLICK="MyParaClickFunction()">Click here!</P>
```

Similarly, the **Ondblclick** attribute activates the named function when the user double-clicks the mouse button over the element and **Onkeypress** activates when a key is pressed (and released). The **Onmousedown** and **Onmouseup** attributes detect the pressing and release of the mouse button while it is over an element. The **Onkeydown** and **Onkeyup** attributes work in the same way, but for key presses. Movement of the mouse pointer over the element is detected by the **Onmouseover** and **Onmouseout** attributes.

Alignments

Several elements have an **Align** attribute, with a possible value of 'left', 'center' or 'right', including the Paragraph element. However, it is now deprecated because CSS can be used instead.

```
<P>Left!</P>
<P ALIGN="right">Right!</P>
<P>Left!</P>
```

Headings and Divisions

Headings

Headers can be used to create crude section and sub-section divisions in the document, or to define outliner levels. The heading elements, **H1** to **H6**, hold title text with varying degrees of highlighting. H1 is the most important, and is typically used only for the title of the document (perhaps in conjunction with the Center element, described later). At the other extreme, H6 is the least important header, and should only be used when six levels of heading are necessary. Each header element is a block, separated from preceding and following objects, including paragraphs and other headers. Although no specific formatting style is indicated, typically the header elements are all displayed in bold typeface and the point size of the text varies, increasing with the level of importance.

```
<H1>The Document Title</H1>
<H2>A Section Title</H2>
<H3>A sub-section title</H3>
```

Divisions

The problem with headers is that, although conceptually they give a title to the text that follows them, the tagging does not represent this relationship. For example, it would not be possible to give a unique style to all the paragraphs that 'belong' to a section that is given a title using an H3 element.

What is needed is a way to physically enclose a block of related elements, and then to apply styles to this new structure. The **Center** element can be used to enclose any other structure or group of structures, including possibly the entire document.

```
<CENTER>
<H1>A centered heading</H1>
<P>A centered paragraph.</P>
</CENTER>
```

However, this tag has now been deprecated in favour of a more general mechanism. The **Div** (division) element extends the idea. It can be used to replicate the functionality of the Center element because it can take an **Align** attribute, with a value of 'left', 'center' or 'right'.

```
<DIV ALIGN="center">
<H1>A centered heading</H1>
<P>A centered paragraph.</P>
</DIV>
```

But the real power of this element becomes apparent when the Style or Class attribute is applied to it.

```
<DIV STYLE="color: red">
<H1>A red heading</H1>
<P>A red paragraph.</P>
</DIV>
```

Horizontal rules

The **Horizontal Rule** element (**Hr**) draws a line across the screen. It is an empty element. It can be used to highlight divisions of a large document.

```
<P>The next para is in another section</P>
<HR>
<P>New section of the document</P>
```

It has additional attributes (all now deprecated) that specify: the thickness of the line (the **Size** attribute); the width of the line, measured in pixels or as a percentage of the screen width (the **Width** attribute); and the alignment of a line narrower than the screen width (the **Align** attribute). It also has attributes that dictate that the line must be solid (the **Noshade** attribute). The Noshade attribute has a single legal value of 'noshade', and the attribute name does not appear. In the example below, the line must be solid, occupy half the width of the window and be centred:

```
<HR NOSHADE SIZE="4" WIDTH="50%" ALIGN="center" >
```

Lists

HTML supports various types of list structure. In all cases, an element that expresses the type of list is used to enclose a number of others, each representing one item in the list.

The most basic type of list is the **Ul** (unordered list):

```
<UL>
...
</UL>
```

An unordered list is used when the items do not form a logical sequence or series of steps. It contains a number of **Li** (list item) elements. Each of these contains text, and is automatically preceded by a bullet, dash or other symbol:

```
<UL>
<LI>First Item</LI>
<LI>Second Item</LI>
<LI>Third Item</LI>
</UL>
```

   • First Item
   • Second Item
   • Third Item

The deprecated **Dir** (directory list) element is intended to hold directory listings, which are very short items that may be formatted in columns (as in UNIX file listings):

```
<DIR>
<LI>MYBOOK.DTD</LI>
<LI>MYBOOK.XML</LI>
<LI>PARSER.EXE</LI>
<LI>REPORT.DAT</LI>
</DIR>
```

```
MYBOOK.DTD    PARSER.EXE
MYBOOK.XML    REPORT.DAT
```

The deprecated **Menu** list is intended to be used to represent software menu selections. The content of each item is assumed to be short, and the browser is likely to indent them and omit the bullet:

```
<MENU>
<LI>Activate</LI>
<LI>Options</LI>
<LI>Help</LI>
<LI>Exit</LI>
</MENU>
```

```
        Activate
        Options
        Help
        Exit
```

The **Ol** element (ordered list) is similar to the unordered list, but each item is preceded by a sequential, automatically generated number. It is used in preference to
the Ul element when the items describe a series of steps, or are referred to individ-
ually elsewhere:

```
<OL>
<LI>Step 1</LI>
<LI>Step 2</LI>
<LI>Step 3 - Go To Step 1</LI>
</OL>
```

```
    1. Step 1
    2. Step 2
    3. Step 3 - Go To Step 1
```

A **Type** attribute is available on the **Ol**, **Ul** and **Li** elements (but is now deprecated
in the first two cases). An ordered list can take Type values of 'A' (capital letters),
'a' (small letters), 'I' (large Roman letters), 'i' (small Roman letters) or '1' (digits),
which is the default. An unordered list can take Type values of 'DISC' (bullet),
'CIRCLE' (hollow bullet) or 'SQUARE' (a square hollow bullet). The list item
can take the same values, depending which list type it is within, and overrides the
current setting for the list within all remaining items. In addition, the ordered list
has a **Start** attribute, which indicates a start value for the first item when it is not
'1' (or equivalent), and the list item has a **Value** attribute that can only be used
within ordered lists to reset the current calculated value:

```
<OL TYPE="A" START="4">
   <LI>First Item
   <LI VALUE="G">Second Item
   <LI>Third Item
</OL>
```

```
    D   First Item
    G   Second Item
    H   Third Item
```

Some lists consist of a keyword or term, followed by an explanation of that keyword or term. The **Dl** (definition list) element contains a number of items (but *not* Item elements), each one consisting of two parts, a **Dt** (definition term) element and a **(Dd)** (definition details) element:

```
<DL>
<DT>HTML<dd>HyperText Markup Language
<DT>DTD<dd>Document Type Definition
<DT>XML<dd>Extensible Markup Language
</DL>
```

> HTML HyperText Markup Language
> DTD   Document Type Definition
> XML   Extensible Markup Language

All of the list types described above may be condensed by closing the gap between items, using the **Compact** attribute (now deprecated in all but the Dl element). This implied attribute has a single value option of 'compact', and the attribute name does not appear:

```
<UL COMPACT>
```

HTML has inherited this minimization feature from SGML, and it is not available in XML (though the XSLT processor should be able to output this minimized structure).

In-line elements

A number of HTML elements are in-line elements, meaning that they do not break the flow of text onto a new line (except in one case). These elements modify the style of the text or identify the nature of a range of significant characters.

The **Tt** (teletype) element specifies a monospaced font such as Courier. The **B** (bold) element specifies a bold typeface. The **I** (italic) element specifies an italic typeface:

```
<P>This paragraph contains <B>bold</B>,
<I>italic</I> and <B><I>bold/italic</I></B> text.</P>
```

> This paragraph contains **bold**, *italic* and ***bold/italic*** text.

Strong normally maps to bold typeface and **Em** (emphasis) to italic typeface. The computer sample elements **Code** and **Var**, as well as the **Kbd** (keyboard) element, normally map to a monospaced font. The **Samp** (sample) element and **Cite** (citation) element may both map to italic typeface:

```
<P><EM>Emphasized text</EM>.
<STRONG>Strong text</STRONG>.
<CODE>Computer text</CODE>.
<KBD>Keyboard text</KBD>.
<VAR>Variable text</VAR.
<SAMP>Sample text</SAMP>.
<CITE>Citation text</CITE>.</P>
```

> *Emphasized text.* **Strong text**. Computer text.
> Keyboard text. Variable text.
> *Sample text. Citation text.*

The **Dfn** (defining instance) element encloses the first occurrence or most significant occurrence of a term used in the text. Potentially, this element may be used by search engines to determine keywords, and by style sheets to highlight new terms as they are introduced:

```
... Although <DFN>XML</DFN> is related
to <DFN>SGML</DFN>, XML is also related
to <DFN>HTML</DFN> as HTML is an application
of SGML.
```

The font size may be varied using the **Font** element (now deprecated). The **Size** attribute dictates the new font size, either absolutely, as a value between '1' and '7' (the default being '3'), or relatively as a size change from the current value. A relative size is given by inserting a '+' or '-' character:

```
This text is <FONT SIZE="-1">smaller</FONT> than
normal.
```

An additional **Color** attribute uses the scheme described above for changing the document colour in the Body element. Font elements can also be embedded within each other.

The deprecated **Basefont** element is used to specify a new default font size for the whole document and should therefore be placed at the top of the Body segment. It also uses a **Size** attribute to set the font size:

```
<BASEFONT SIZE="2">Text size is smaller than normal but
<FONT SIZE="+1">is now as expected</FONT>.
```

The **Big** and **Small** elements are complementary, and they specify larger and smaller text respectively, but the actual size is determined by the browser. The **U** (underline) element specifies a line under the enclosed text, and the **Strike** element specifies a line through the text (both elements are deprecated).

The **Sub** (subscript) and **Sup** (superscript) elements are complementary. The first encloses small text that appears below the baseline and the second encloses small text that appears above the baseline:

```
The W<SUP>3</SUP>C is responsible for HTML.
Water is H<SUB>2</SUB>O.
```

Formatted text

It is sometimes important to be able to control the way in which the browser formats a block of text into individual lines.

The **Br** (line break) element forces following text to be placed on a new line. This is very useful for semi-formatting text, such as lines of poetry. It is an empty element:

```
<P>Break this line here <BR>so this is line 2.</P>
```

The **Preformatted** element (**Pre**) composes the content in a monospaced font. All spaces and line-feed characters are retained, making it possible to use these characters to create simple character-based diagrams or columns of text. The **Width** attribute (now deprecated) can be used to give the browser a hint as to the maximum length of the lines of text, so that it can choose an appropriate font size to render it:

```
<PRE WIDTH="30">
Here is a face:   ---
                 /   \
                [ o o ]
                 \ - /
                  ---
</PRE>
```

To use this element, the source XML data must already be in the necessary format. The Preserve Space attribute must be used, or each text line must be distinguished by separate elements (that can be removed during the transformation process). Also, if vertical alignment is important, the document author must have used a monospaced font.

The **Plaintext** and **Example** (**Xmp**) elements identify text that should be presented exactly as it is stored in the file, including preservation of line breaks. They are therefore indistinguishable from the Pre element (and are now deprecated or made obsolete).

Images

The **Img** (image) element identifies an image file, the content of which is to appear at the current location. This is an empty element; there is no end-tag. A **Src** (source) attribute specifies the name and location of the image file:

```
...there is a GIF file <IMG SRC="myimage.gif"> here.
```

The image name alone, as shown above, is sufficient when the image resides in the same directory as the HTML document. The rules for specifying an image file stored in another location are the same as for hypertext links (described later), so need not be covered here. By default, the base of the image is likely to be aligned with the baseline of the text. Image alignment can be made specific using the **Align** attribute (now deprecated), which takes a value of 'top', 'middle' or 'bottom'. As some browsers are not able to display images, an **Alt** (alternative) attribute may be used to display alternative text. The second example below demonstrates its use:

```
...there is a GIF file
<IMG SRC="myimage.gif" ALIGN="top" ALT="no Piccy"> here.

...there is a GIF file  --------   here.
                        |        |
                         --------

...there is a GIF file [no piccy] here.
```

This element takes additional alignment options using the **Align** attribute. In addition to the standard 'middle', 'top' and 'bottom' options, the new 'left' and 'right' options create floating images in the left or right margin. New attributes include **Border**, which specifies the thickness of the image border line, the **Vspace** (vertical space) attribute and the **Hspace** (horizontal space) attribute, which create extra space around the image, and **Width** and **Height**, which tell the browser the dimensions of the image to speed up downloading:

```
<IMG BORDER="2" VSPACE="3" HSPACE="4" ALIGN="left">
```

Due to the new floating images described above, the **Br** (line break) element has been extended to allow the break to force the next line to appear below large, horizontally adjacent floating images. Account can be taken of images that appear in just one of the margins. The **Clear** attribute (now deprecated) takes a value of 'all' (an image in either or both margins), 'left' (an image in the left margin only) or 'right' (an image in the right margin only):

```
<BR CLEAR="left">
```

A popular feature of HTML is its ability to attach links to parts of an image. This is called an image map. For example, a map of the world could be linked to other

HTML documents that describe characteristics of each country. The source of the link is therefore an area of the image. In the well-supported concept of a 'server-sided' image map, the browser simply passes the coordinates of the mouse-click to the Web server, which calls a script that decides, depending on the coordinate values, which HTML document to return to the browser. The **Img** element takes an additional attribute, **Ismap**, to indicate that the coordinates of the mouse-click should be sent to the Web server. This implied attribute has a single legal value of 'ISMAP' (the attribute name never appears):

```
<IMG SRC="myimage.gif" ISMAP>
```

However, the Web server must also be told which script to activate when the mouse is clicked on this image. To do this, the Img element is enclosed in an **A** element, which uses a **URL** to locate the appropriate script:

```
<A HREF="/cgi-bin/imagemap/my.map">
<IMG SRC="myimage.gif" ISMAP>
</A>
```

This scheme relies upon the use of the HTTP protocol, a Web server and CGI scripts, and so it is not particularly suitable for simple intranet solutions or for publishing HTML files on a CD-ROM. The concept of 'client-side' image maps overcomes this problem. The browser uses HTML tags to identify image areas and associated URLs to other documents or other parts of the same document. This approach provides the benefits of less interaction with the server (making the process more efficient) and independence from the HTTP protocol (making it suitable for simple intranet use, when a Web server may not be needed, and more efficient Internet use), as well as giving prior warning of the effect of clicking on any part of the image (the target URL being displayed as the pointer is moved over the image). The **Usemap** attribute is added to the Img element and holds the name of a **Map** element that defines areas of the image:

```
<IMG SRC="/images/myimage.gif" USEMAP="#mymap">

<MAP NAME="mymap"> ..... </MAP>
```

Within the Map element, each area and associated URL is defined using an **Area** element. This element contains attributes to define the shape of the area, the coordinates of the area and the URL associated with the area. The **Coords** attribute defines the coordinates of the area and the **Href** attribute provides the URL. The **Alt** attribute contains a textual equivalent to the area, to be used by applications that cannot support this feature. The **Nohref** attribute indicates that this area is not active, and it has a single possible value of 'nohref'. Consider an example of an image showing a new model of motor car. Each area of interest, such as the wheels or the engine, could be located and attached to an appropriate HTML document:

```
<MAP NAME="mymap">
   <AREA SHAPE="circle"
         COORDS="50, 150, 150, 250"
         HREF="wheels/back.html"
         ALT="Back Wheels">
   <AREA SHAPE="circle"
         COORDS="350 200 50"
         HREF="wheels/front.html"
         ALT="Front Wheels">
</MAP>
```

The default shape is assumed to be a rectangle, with four coordinates representing in pixels the left edge, top edge, right edge and bottom edge of the area. The first example above defines an area for the back wheel – '50' pixels in, '150' pixels down for the left and top edges, and (as the diameter of the wheel is 100 pixels), '150' in and '250' down for the right and bottom edges. The optional **Shape** attribute may be used to make this area type explicit, 'shape="rect"'. Another shape option is 'circle', which requires three values, namely the horizontal and vertical coordinates for the centre of the circle, followed by a radius value. The second example defines the area of the front wheel as a circle with a radius of '50' pixels, '350' pixels across and '200' down.

Backward compatibility can be provided for the benefit of browsers not able to use this facility. Both schemes for creating image maps (client-side and server-side) can coexist by including both the Ismap attribute and the Usemap attribute in the same Img element. In the example below, a browser that does not support a client-side map scheme uses the Anchor to pass coordinates to 'myscript.cgi':

```
<A HREF="myscript.cgi">
   <IMG SRC="/images/myimage.gif"
        USEMAP="#mymap" ISMAP>
</A>

<MAP NAME="mymap">
<!-- image mapping commands -->
</MAP>
```

Tables

The **Table** element encloses a table grid. The cells may be separated by border lines, using the **Border** attribute. A number of pixels value may be applied, such as '3' pixels, and a value of '0' indicates no border and no space for a border (which is different from the effect of not including the attribute). Alternatively, the tag may simply include the word 'border', which can be considered the same as a border value of '1':

```
<TABLE>            no borders, space for them remains

<TABLE BORDER="0">  no borders, no space for them

<TABLE BORDER>     same as 'border=1' using 'dummy'

<TABLE BORDER="10"> very thick border lines
```

The space between cells can be adjusted. The **Cellspacing** attribute takes a numeric value that states how much space there is between cells (including their borders). If a value of zero is used, the border lines overlap each other. It has a default value of '2':

```
<TABLE BORDER>              <TABLE BORDER CELLSPACING=8>
```

The space between the cell contents and the borders of the cell can also be adjusted using the **Cellpadding** attribute, which takes a numeric value. The default value is '1':

```
<TABLE BORDER>              <TABLE BORDER CELLPADDING=8>
```

The width and height of the table are often left under the control of the browser, which composes the table within the restrictions of the available window area. The **Width** attribute may be used to 'encourage' the browser to take into account the wishes of the document author. This attribute takes a numeric value that dictates how many pixels wide the table should be, or what percentage of the available screen width it should occupy. A pure number is interpreted as a pixel value. A percentage symbol indicates a proportion of the screen dimensions.

```
<TABLE BORDER WIDTH=800>
```

The table may have a title, which is contained within a **Caption** element. This element is placed within the Table element but before the elements described later. The content is by default displayed above the main table grid, but it may be explicitly displayed below the table using the **Align** attribute, with a value of 'bottom':

```
<TABLE>
   <CAPTION ALIGN="bottom">Title Below</CAPTION> ...
</TABLE>
```

The table structure is row-oriented, which means that the grid is built by first defining each row and then separating each cell within a row. Each row of data is enclosed in a **Table Row** element (**Tr**), and each cell is enclosed in either a **Table Header** element (**Th**) or a **Table Data** element (**Td**), the only difference being one of emphasis – the Th element content is usually displayed in bold (and centred). Th and Td elements may be mixed within the same row, possibly to create side headings:

```
<TR><TH>Colour<TH>Status<TH>Level</TR>
<TR><TH>Red<TD>Danger<TD>1</TR>
<TR><TH>Green<TD>Normal<TD>3</TR>
```

Colour	Status	Level
Red	Danger	1
Green	Normal	3

As shown above, a cell may directly contain text. But it may also contain any document body elements, including a complete embedded table. The Line Break element is particularly useful for formatting text within the cell. If a cell is empty, no border lines are drawn.

The width and height of a cell can be 'suggested' in the Td and Th elements, using the **Width** and **Height** attributes. The browser is not however required to obey these instructions.

The content of individual cells, or all the cells in a row, may be aligned horizontally and vertically in various ways. The default horizontal alignment is 'left' in Td elements, and 'center' in Th elements, as shown in the example above. The default vertical alignment is 'middle' for both types of cell. The **Align** attribute allows horizontal alignment to be set to 'left', 'right' or 'center'. The **Valign** attribute allows vertical alignment to be set to 'top', 'middle', 'bottom' or 'baseline' (where all cells in the row are horizontally aligned by last line, after the cell with the most lines is aligned to 'top'). An alignment set in the Tr element provides a default for all cells in the row, but individual cells may override this setting.

By default each cell occupies an area dissected by one column and one row, forming a simple position within the table grid, but may be expanded across or down using the **Colspan** and **Rowspan** attributes. These attributes take numeric values, and have implied values of '1' (zero is not a legal option). Higher values than '1' stretch the cell over adjoining areas:

```
<TR><TH>Colour<TH>Status<TH>Level</TR>
<TR><TH>Red<TD>Danger<TD>1</TR>
<TR><TH>Blue<TD COLSPAN=2>No Priority<TD>2</TR>
<TR><TH>Brown</TH><!-- NO CELL --><TD>3</TD></TR>
```

Colour	Status	Level
Red	Danger	1
Blue	No Priority	2
Brown		3

Note that the final row in the example above has only two cell elements, containing 'Brown' and '3', because the middle cell has effectively been replaced by the cell above it.

The content of a cell is normally formatted by the browser as it is composed to fit the available screen width. The **Nowrap** attribute may be used in the Th and Td elements to prevent lines being split. This is another example of a minimized attribute with a single possible value, in this case 'nowrap':

```
<TD NOWRAP>This line must not be broken</TD>
```

When presenting tables on paper, it is useful to be able to identify header rows, so that the pagination engine can repeat the headings at the top of each page. Similarly, footer rows can be repeated at the base of each page containing a reference to a footnote. When presenting to a scrollable window, a large table body may be collapsed to just a few scrollable rows, sandwiched between fixed, permanently visible headers and footers. The new elements **Table Head (Thead)**, **Table Body (Tbody)** and **Table Footer (Tfoot)** enclose rows of each kind.

Only the Tbody element is required, and for backward compatibility both its start-tag and end-tag may be absent (its presence then being implied). The Thead and Tfoot elements are optional because not all tables have rows that fall into these categories. When present, the Thead element must occur first, as would be expected, but the Tfoot element must *also* precede the body. The reason for this unusual arrangement is that it allows the rendering package to collect the content of a footer and then place it at the base of each page, without needing to process the table twice:

```
<TABLE>
    <THEAD>...</THEAD>
    <TFOOT>...</TFOOT>
    <TBODY>...</TBODY>
</TABLE>
```

In addition to the usual array of core, event and language attributes, these three elements also contain the **Align** and **Valign** attributes, so introducing another level of cell content alignment overriding, above the row level. In a table containing mostly currency values, it may be suitable to state that all header cells are centred, that all body cells are aligned on full-point, and that all footer cells are left-aligned.

It is not uncommon to find tables where all the cells in a particular column are aligned in the same way. For example, a price table in a catalogue may have two columns, the first being a description of each product, with the text left-aligned, and the second being the price of that item, aligned on a decimal point. Using the table model described in the previous section, each Td element would need to contain an Align attribute:

```
<TR>
<TD ALIGN="left">Red coat</TD>
<TD ALIGN="char" char=".">12.4</TD>
</TR>
<TR>
<TD ALIGN="left">Green coat</TD>
<TD ALIGN="char" CHAR=".">12.6</TD>
</TR>
```

Clearly, when many rows are involved, this is very time-consuming to produce, and also wasteful of memory and bandwidth. It is now possible to define a style for all cells in a column, using the **Column** element (**Col**). In the example below, the first Col element specifies an alignment of 'left' for the first column, and the second Col element specifies an alignment on the decimal point for the second column, so removing the need to specify these alignments in individual entries:

```
<COL ALIGN="left">
<COL ALIGN="char" char=".">
<TR>
<TD>Red coat</TD>
<TD>12.4</TD>
</TR>
<TR>
<TD>Green coat</TD>
<TD>12.6</TD>
</TR>
. . .
```

For horizontal alignments, the Col element overrides the Tr element, though individual Entry element styles are still the most significant:

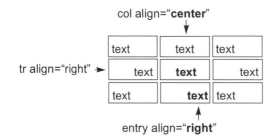

As indicated above, the first Col element is deemed to apply to the first column, the second applies to the next column, and so on. When several columns in a group have the same settings, only one Col element is required, and the **Span** attribute is used to specify how many columns are affected. The total number of columns in a table can be calculated by adding together the span values (when not present, a value of '1' is assumed). In the following example, the table has six columns (and it is assumed that if a Col element is used at all, then all table columns must be covered by these elements):

```
<COL ALIGN="left">
<COL SPAN="3" ALIGN="right">
<COL SPAN="2" ALIGN="center">
```

This element can also be used to predefine the width of each column, using the **Width** attribute, so that Web browsers and pagination engines can start building the table presentation before reading the entire table. In the following example, the column widths are '30', '40', '40', '40', '50' and '50':

```
<COL WIDTH="30" ALIGN="left">
<COL WIDTH="40" SPAN="3" ALIGN="right">
<COL WIDTH="50" SPAN="2" ALIGN="center">
```

The Width values may also be proportional, so that the table width can expand to the area available, and each column is assigned a 'fair' proportion of that width, based on the values in the Width attribute.

A value followed by an asterisk character denotes a proportional value. To make the column widths defined above keep their relative sizes but allow additional space to be exploited, it is only necessary to append the asterisk to the existing values, though the smaller values '3*', '4*', '4*', '4*', '5*' and '5*' would produce identical results. This approach is not yet universally supported.

When a large number of consecutive Col elements share some attribute values, but not others, a new and more efficient technique may be employed using the **Column Group** element (**Colgroup**). This element may enclose a number of Col elements, and has exactly the same attributes, which when used are deemed to apply to each embedded Col element that does not itself contain an explicit definition. In this example, both columns in the group are given a width of 55 pixels:

```
<COLGROUP WIDTH="55">
   <COL ALIGN="left">
   <COL SPAN="3" ALIGN="right">
</COLGROUP>
<COLGROUP WIDTH="50" SPAN="2" ALIGN="center">
</COLGROUP>
```

The other major benefit of column groups is that they define an identifiable vertical component of a table, consisting of several columns and regardless of any degree of commonality in style between these columns. This defined object may be the target of a hypertext link, or the trigger for an event, such as Onclick. A Colgroup element does not even have to contain Col elements if their presence is not appropriate. In this case, it has its own **Span** attribute:

```
<COLGROUP SPAN="3" WIDTH="35"></COLGROUP>
<COLGROUP SPAN="2" WIDTH="20"></COLGROUP>
```

It is not possible to mix Colgroup and Col elements. If just one Colgroup is needed, then all definitions must be applied using it. Another way to look at this restriction is to imagine that Col elements must always be contained within a Colgroup element; but, when there are only Col elements present, they are enclosed within an implied column group.

Descriptive markup

As stylistic elements are removed or deprecated, they are replaced by new descriptive elements. The following elements help stylesheet designers to develop more suitable formatting, and Web crawler search engines to perform more useful analysis of the document.

The **Abbreviation** element (**Abbr**) is used to identify an abbreviation in the text. It has a **Title** attribute, which is used to hold the full term:

```
...talk to <ABBR TITLE="Mister">Mr.</ABBR> Smith ...
```

Similarly, the **Acronym** element holds a form of abbreviation that substitutes each word in a name with one letter. The **Title** attribute is used in the same way:

```
... <ACRONYM TITLE="World Wide Web">WWW</ACRONYM> ...
```

The **Quote** element (**Q**) holds an in-line quotation:

```
... Shakespeare wrote <Q>To be or not to be...</Q> ...
```

The **Blockquote** element contains a block of text quoted from another source, which is typically indented by the browser.

The **Deletion** element (**Del**) identifies text that is to be considered as deleted, and is only present to bring attention to the fact that it no longer applies. Such text is typically presented with a line through it. Complementing this is the **Insertion** element (**Ins**), which identifies new text. Typically, new text is highlighted with a change bar in the margin. By convention, they should be used consistently as block-level elements, or as in-line elements, but not both, as it may be difficult to apply a suitable style for both types. They both contain optional **Datetime** and **Citation** attributes (**Cite**), indicating respectively the time the document was changed, and pointing to another document that contains comments on why the change was made, though the Title attribute may also be used to contain a short note on the reason:

```
... there are <DEL>fifteen</DEL><INS>nine</INS> days left
to Christmas ...
```

Styles and scripts

The **Style** element encloses stylesheet instructions. The **Type** attribute is required, and identifies the stylesheet language, such as 'text/css' or 'text/xsl'. The **Media** attribute identifies the type of media the stylesheet is aimed at, such as 'screen' (the default) or 'paper'. A **Title** attribute is also allowed to identify the stylesheet.

```
<STYLE TYPE="text/css" MEDIA="screen">
  p { color: green }
</STYLE>
```

A number of attributes have been added to the **Script** element, which is used to enclose script programs. The **Type** attribute describes the scripting language used, such as 'text/javascript'. The **Src** attribute identifies a remote file containing the scripts, using a URL. When Src is used, the **Charset** attribute may also be used to identify the character set used in the file that contains the scripts. The **Defer** attribute takes a boolean value of 'true' or 'false' to indicate whether or not the browser should defer executing the script. When set to 'true', this is a hint that the script does not alter the document in any way and so the browser can go ahead and render the document.

To prevent older browsers from simply displaying the scripts, it is necessary to surround them with a comment. Also, the **NoScript** element has been included to hold alternative information in the case that the browser is configured to prevent scripts from running or it is not familiar with the scripting language used.

Frames

Using frames, the screen is divided into areas, with each area possibly displaying a different document, each one scrolled independently. Among other uses, frames facilitate the use of table of contents and button bars that do not vanish as the user scrolls down the main document:

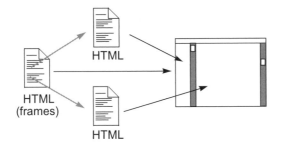

A frame-based document replaces the Body element with a **Frameset** element:

```
<HTML>
<HEAD>...</HEAD>
<FRAMESET>...</FRAMESET>
</HTML>
```

The Frameset element defines an area that generally fills the end user's screen. This area is divided into frames using the **Cols** or **Rows** attribute. These attributes take a value that specifies the width or height of the sub-areas. This value specifies the height or width using one of three methods, namely the number of pixels (not advised), proportion or percentage of the available space. Values are separated by commas, which also therefore implicitly specify the number of columns or rows in the set:

```
<FRAMESET ROWS="1500, 1000, 500">

<FRAMESET ROWS="3*, 2*, *">

<FRAMESET ROWS="50%, 33%, 16%">
```

The first example above specifies a height of 1,500 pixels for the first row, the second example reserves three proportional units for the first row (the asterisk character alone is equivalent to '1*'), and the third example specifies that the first row should occupy half the available height ('50%'). If the available height were 3,000 pixels, then all three examples above would be equivalent. These value types may be mixed:

```
<FRAMSET COLS="50%, 100, 2*, *">
```

When value types are mixed, fixed values have precedence, followed by percentage values, and then proportional values. In the example above, the second column is assigned exactly 100 pixels of horizontal space, the first column is then assigned half of the remaining space, and the remainder is divided among the proportional columns (the third column taking twice the space of the last column):

2nd (percentage) priority	**1st** priority	**3rd** (proportional) priority	
50% of remaining area	100 pixels	2*	1*

A Frame Set can contain further embedded Frame Sets. Each embedded Frame Set occupies the space reserved for it by the enclosing Frame Set. Taking the example above, a Frame Set embedded in the first column is restricted to the left half of the screen and will define subdivisions of this area:

```
<FRAMESET COLS="50%, 100, 2*, *">
   <FRAMESET COLS="60%, 40%">
   . . .
   </FRAMESET>
   . . .
</FRAMSET>
```

|-------- **60 %** -------|--- **40 %** ---|	100 pixels	2*	1*

A Frame Set may contain a **Noframes** element. This element is intended to hold information to be displayed by a browser that cannot interpret the frames. Its function is therefore similar to the Alt attribute in the Image element. Its content, which may include normal blocks such as paragraphs and lists, is not displayed in frames-aware browsers:

```
<NOFRAMES>
<P>If you CAN see this, then you can NOT see the Frames!
</NOFRAMES>
```

A frames-aware browser ignores this tag and all its contents. A browser that does not understand frames will not be aware of the Noframes element, but is most likely to remove the tags, while leaving the enclosed text intact for presentation to the user.

Finally, a Frameset element may contain a **Frame** element. This is an empty element, so has no end-tag. It is used to identify the document to be displayed within the frame, to identify the frame itself (so that it can be made the target of links from other frames or documents), to determine whether the width and height of the frame can be altered by the end user, to determine whether scroll-bars are used, and to specify margin widths. The Frame element has a **Source** attribute (**Src**) which contains the **URL** of the HTML document to be displayed in the frame. If no URL is provided, the area is left blank. The Frame element also has a **Name** attribute, which contains the name of the frame, so that it can be the target of a link from another frame or from another document:

```
<FRAME NAME="main" SRC="../areas/myarea.html">
```

By referring to the Name value of another frame, a new document can be requested, and displayed in that other area. This feature is ideal for changing the content of the main window as items are selected in a table of contents frame. The **A** (Anchor) element has a new **Target** attribute to refer to the actual frame in which the content should be displayed:

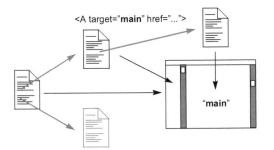

The Frame element also has a **Scrolling** attribute, which indicates whether horizontal and vertical scroll-bars are always present, present as required (when the height or width of the page exceeds the space provided on the screen), or never present. A value of 'yes' forces scroll-bars to appear even if not needed. A value of 'auto' displays scroll-bars when necessary and is the default value. A value of 'no' disables scroll-bars entirely.

The Frame element also has a **Noresize** attribute, which, if present, prevents the end user from changing the height or width of the frame. By default it is absent, and resizing is allowed. In XML terms, this must be seen as an attribute called Noresize that has an optional, single value of 'NORESIZE', and that minimization is in use to avoid stating the attribute name:

```
<FRAME SRC="../areas/myarea.html" NORESIZE>
```

Finally, the Frame element has **Marginwidth** and **Marginheight** attributes, which specify the space to reserve between the borders of the frame and the enclosed text. Width settings affect the space between the left and right edges. Height settings affect the space above and below the content. Values are in pixels and, if present, must be at least '1' and not so large that content cannot be displayed; if absent, the browser provides default settings.

Elements and attributes list

The following table shows the elements and attributes defined in the currently most supported, and the latest, version of HTML. Items marked with an asterisk, '*', are not supported by the latest version of at least one of the most popular Web browsers and so should be used with caution.

There are a very large number of attributes first defined in HTML 4.0. Many of them are defined using entities. To keep this table to a reasonable size, these groups are described here, and given the names 'Core' ('Id', 'Type', 'Class' and 'Style'), 'Events' ('Onclick', 'Ondblclick', 'Onmousedown', 'Onmouseup', 'Onmouseover', 'Onmouseout', 'Onkeypress', 'Onkeydown', 'Onkeyup') and 'Lang' ('Lang' and 'Dir') for reference under appropriate elements. However, note that when an attribute in one of these groups applies to the previous version of HTML, it is also included explicitly.

Elements and Attributes	HTML 3. 2	HTML 4.0
A	YES	YES
Core & Events & Lang		YES
accesskey *		YES
coords *		YES
charset *		YES
href	YES	YES
hreflang *		YES
methods	obsolete	
name	YES	YES
onblur *		YES
onfocus *		YES
rel	YES	YES
rev	YES	YES
shape *		YES
tabindex *		YES
target		YES
type *		YES
title	YES	YES
urn	obsolete	
ABBR		**YES**
Core & Events & Lang		YES
ACRONYM		**YES**
Core & Events & Lang		YES
ADDRESS	YES	**YES**
Core		YES

APPLET	YES	**deprecated** (use
align	YES	Object)
alt	YES	
archive		
code	YES	
codebase	YES	
height	YES	
hspace	YES	
name	YES	
object *		
title		
vspace	YES	
width	YES	
AREA	YES	**YES**
accesskey *		
alt	YES	
coords	YES	
href	YES	
nohref	YES	
onblur *		
onfocus *		
shape	YES	
tabindex *		
target		
B	**YES**	**YES**
Core & Events & Lang		YES
BASE	**YES**	**YES**
href	YES	YES
target		YES
BASEFONT	**YES**	**deprecated**
color *		
face *		
id *		
name *		
size	YES	
BDO		**YES**
Core		
dir *		
lang *		
BIG *	**YES**	**YES**
Core & Events & Lang		YES
BLOCKQUOTE	**YES**	**YES**
Core & Events & Lang		YES
cite *		YES
BODY	**YES**	**YES**
Core & Events & Lang		YES
alink	YES	deprecated
background	YES	deprecated
bgcolor	YES	deprecated
link	YES	deprecated
onload *		YES
onunload *		YES
text	YES	deprecated
vlink	YES	deprecated
BR	**YES**	**YES**
Core		YES
clear	YES	deprecated
BUTTON		**YES**
Core & Events & Lang		YES

accesskey *		YES
clear	YES	
disabled *		YES
name *		YES
onblur *		YES
onfocus *		YES
tabindex *		YES
type *		YES
value *		YES
CAPTION	**YES**	**YES**
Core & Events & Lang		YES
align	YES	deprecated
CENTER	**YES**	**deprecated**
Core & Events & Lang		
CITE	**YES**	**YES**
Core & Events & Lang		YES
CODE	**YES**	**YES**
Core & Events & Lang		YES
COL *		YES
Core & Events & Lang		
align		
char *		
charoff *		
span		
valign *		
width		
COLGROUP *		YES
Core & Events & Lang		
align *		
char *		
charoff *		
span *		
valign *		
width *		
DD	**YES**	**YES**
Core & Events & Lang		YES
DEL		YES
Core & Events & Lang		
cite *		
datetime *		
DFN *	**YES**	**YES**
Core & Events & Lang		YES
DIR	**YES**	**deprecated** (use UL)
Core & Events & Lang		YES
compact *	YES	YES
DIV	**YES**	**YES**
Core & Events & Lang		YES
align	YES	YES
DL	**YES**	**YES**
Core & Events & Lang		YES
compact	YES	YES
DT	**YES**	**YES**
Core & Events & Lang		YES
EM	**YES**	**YES**
Core & Events & Lang		YES
EMBED		YES
Core & Events & Lang		

FIELDSET		**YES**
Core & Events & Lang		
language *		
title *		
FONT	**YES**	**deprecated**
Core & Lang		
color	YES	
size	YES	
FORM	**YES**	**YES**
Core & Events & Lang		
action	YES	
accept-charset *		
enctype *	YES	
method	YES	
onreset		
onsubmit		
target		
FRAME		**YES**
Core		
frameborder		
langdesc *		
marginheight		
marginwidth		
name		
noresize		
scrolling		
src		
FRAMESET		**YES**
Core		
cols		
onload *		
onunload *		
rows		
H1	**YES**	**YES**
Core & Events & Lang		YES
align	YES	deprecated
H2	**YES**	**YES**
Core & Events & Lang		YES
align	YES	deprecated
H3	**YES**	**YES**
Core & Events & Lang		YES
align	YES	deprecated
H4	**YES**	**YES**
Core & Events & Lang		YES
align	YES	deprecated
H5	**YES**	**YES**
Core & Events & Lang		YES
align	YES	deprecated
H6	**YES**	**YES**
Core & Events & Lang		YES
align	YES	deprecated
HEAD	**YES**	**YES**
Lang		YES
profile *		YES
HR	**YES**	**YES**
Core & Events		YES
align	YES	deprecated
noshade	YES	deprecated
size	YES	deprecated

width	YES	deprecated
HTML	**YES**	**YES**
Lang		YES
version *		deprecated
I	**YES**	**YES**
Core & Events & Lang		YES
IFRAME		**YES**
Core		
align *		
frameborder *		
langdesc *		
marginwidth *		
marginheight *		
marginwidth *		
name *		
scrolling *		
src *		
width *		
IMG	**YES**	**YES**
Core & Events & Lang		YES
align	YES	deprecated
alt	YES	YES
border	YES	deprecated
height	YES	YES
hspace	YES	YES
ismap	YES	YES
langdesc *		YES
src	YES	YES
usemap	YES	YES
vspace	YES	YES
width	YES	YES
INPUT	**YES**	**YES**
Core & Events & Lang		
accept *		
accesskey *		
align	YES	
alt *		
checked *	YES	
disabled *		
langdesc *		
maxlength *	YES	
name *	YES	
onblur *		
onchange *		
onfocus *		
onselect *		
readonly *		
size	YES	
src	YES	
tabindex *		
type	YES	
usemap *		
value	YES	
INS		**YES**
Core & Events & Lang		
cite *		
datetime *		

ISINDEX	**YES**	**deprecated** (use INPUT)
Core & Lang		
prompt	YES	
KBD	**YES**	**YES**
Core & Events & Lang		YES
LABEL		**YES**
Core & Events & Lang		
accesskey *		
for *		
lang *		
language *		
onblur *		
onfocus *		
title *		
LEGEND *		**YES**
Core & Events & Lang		YES
accesskey *		YES
align *		deprecated
LI	**YES**	**YES**
Core & Events & Lang		YES
type	YES	YES
value	YES	deprecated
LINK	**YES**	**YES**
Core & Events & Lang		
charset *		
href	YES	
hreflang *		
media *		
rel	YES	
rev	YES	
title	YES	
LISTING	**deprecated**	**obsolete** (use PRE)
MAP	**YES**	**YES**
Core & Events & Lang		YES
name	YES	YES
MENU	**YES**	**deprecated** (use UL)
Core & Events & Lang		
compact	YES	
META	**YES**	**YES**
Lang		YES
content	YES	YES
http-equiv	YES	YES
name	YES	YES
scheme *		YES
NEXTID	**obsolete**	
N	obsolete	
NOFRAMES		**YES**
Core & Events & Lang		YES
NOSCRIPT		**YES**
Core & Events & Lang		YES
OBJECT *		**YES**
Core & Events & Lang		YES
align *		YES
archive *		YES
border *		deprecated
classid *		YES
codebase *		YES
codetype *		YES

declare *		YES
height *		YES
hspace *		YES
name *		YES
standby *		YES
tabindex *		YES
type *		YES
usemap *		YES
vspace *		YES
width *		YES
OL	**YES**	**YES**
Core & Events & Lang		YES
compact	YES	deprecated
start	YES	deprecated
type	YES	deprecated
OPTGROUP		**YES**
Core & Events & Lang		
disabled *		
label *		
OPTION	**YES**	**YES**
Core & Events & Lang		YES
selected	YES	YES
value	YES	YES
P	**YES**	**YES**
Core & Events & Lang		YES
align	YES	deprecated
disabled *		YES
label *		YES
PARAM	**YES**	**YES**
id *		YES
name	YES	YES
type *		YES
value	YES	YES
valuetype *		YES
PLAINTEXT	**deprecated**	**obsolete** (use PRE)
PRE	**YES**	**YES**
Core & Events & Lang		YES
width	YES	deprecated
Q		**YES**
Core & Events & Lang		YES
cite *		YES
SAMP	**YES**	**YES**
Core & Events & Lang		YES
SCRIPT	**YES**	**YES**
charset *		YES
defer *		YES
language		deprecated
src *		YES
type *		YES

SELECT	YES	YES
Core & Events & Lang		
disabled *		
multiple	YES	
name	YES	
onchange *		
onblur *		
onfocus *		
size	YES	
tabindex *		
SMALL *	YES	YES
Core & Events & Lang		YES
SPAN		YES
Core & Events & Lang		
align		
STRIKE	YES	deprecated
Core & Events & Lang		YES
STRONG	YES	YES
Core & Events & Lang		YES
STYLE	YES	YES
Lang		
media *		
title *		
type *		
SUB *	YES	YES
Core & Events & Lang		YES
SUP *	YES	YES
Core & Events & Lang		YES
TABLE	YES	YES
Core & Events & Lang		YES
align	YES	deprecated
bgcolor *		deprecated
border	YES	YES
cellpadding	YES	YES
cellspacing	YES	YES
frame *		YES
rules *		YES
summary *		YES
width	YES	YES
TBODY *		YES
Core & Events & Lang		
align *		
valign *		
TD	YES	YES
Core & Events & Lang		YES
abbr *		YES
align	YES	YES
axis *		YES
colspan	YES	YES
headers *		YES
height	YES	deprecated
nowrap	YES	deprecated
rowspan	YES	YES
scope *		YES
valign	YES	YES
width	YES	deprecated

TEXTAREA	**YES**	**YES**
Core & Events & Lang		
accesskey *		
cols	YES	
disabled *		
name	YES	
onblur *		
onchange *		
onfocus *		
onselect *		
readonly *		
rows	YES	
tabindex *		
TFOOT *		**YES**
Core & Events & Lang		
align *		
valign *		
TH	**YES**	**YES**
Core & Events & Lang		YES
abbr *		YES
align	YES	YES
axis *		YES
colspan	YES	YES
headers *		YES
height	YES	deprecated
nowrap	YES	deprecated
rowspan	YES	YES
valign	YES	YES
width	YES	YES
THEAD *		**YES**
Core & Events & Lang		
align *		
valign *		
TITLE	**YES**	**YES**
Lang		YES
TR	**YES**	**YES**
Core & Events & Lang		
align	YES	
bgcolor *		
valign	YES	
TT	**YES**	**YES**
Core & Events & Lang		YES
U	**YES**	**deprecated**
Core & Events & Lang		YES
UL	**YES**	**YES**
Core & Events & Lang		YES
compact	YES	deprecated
type	YES	deprecated
VAR	**YES**	**YES**
Core & Events & Lang		YES
XMP	**deprecated**	**obsolete** (use PRE)

19. CSS

CSS is a well-established stylesheet technology that may be considered to be a competitor to XSL, but not to XSLT. Indeed, there are a number of reasons why CSS could be of interest to XSLT stylesheet developers. When an XSLT stylesheet is used to convert XML documents into HTML Web pages, these pages can be enriched with CSS styles.

Background

CSS (Cascading StyleSheets) was developed for use with HTML and it has an important role in making Web documents more interesting. It is one of the core technologies that lie behind the marketing term DHTML (*Dynamic* HTML). With CSS, it is possible to control the appearance of most HTML elements: to define the font, size, style and colour to apply to the text content of a paragraph, table cell or list item.

CSS 1.0 was released in 1996 by W^3C, and it is reasonably well supported by current versions of the popular browsers. It is available from http://www.w3.org/pub/WWW/TR/REC-CSS1. A total of 53 properties are defined by this version of the standard, including properties that are used to define the style of the text (font, size, style), the colour of the text and background, layout information (line indents, alignments, spacing between letters and words), positioning (margins, borders, padding within borders) and generated constructs (lists and list items).

At the same time as early work began on XSL/XSLT, the same pressure for more control over the presentation of material within Web browsers led to further work on the CSS standard. Version 2 adds 77 new properties. These new properties fall into two main categories. Many are simply additions to existing areas of functionality. Others are used to provide new features, such as support for tabular layouts, aural output, and printed output. Unfortunately, CSS 2 is not yet well supported. The table at the end of this chapter lists all properties, and makes clear which ones were introduced with version 2.

Format primer

CSS consists of properties that defined formatting characeristics. Each property has two parts. First, the property name, such as 'color' or 'font-size'. Second, the property value, such as 'blue' or '14pt'. The name is separated from the value using a colon (and possibly also spaces):

```
color:blue


font-size : 14pt
```

When several properties are grouped together, the value of one property is separated from the name of the next property using a semi-colon (and possibly also spaces):

```
color: blue ; font-size: 14pt
```

These properties are possibly grouped into rules that assign the characteristics to an element. In the following example, the HTML H3 (header three) element is to be displayed as 14pt-in-blue style:

```
H3 { color:blue ; font-size:14pt }
```

A CSS document is an ASCII file that contains CSS rules. It is referenced from an HTML document using the LINK element:

```
<LINK HREF="CSS/MyStyles.CSS" TYPE="text/css">
```

However, a CSS stylesheet can also be embedded within an HTML document, using the STYLE element:

```
<STYLE>
H3   { color: blue ; font-size: 14pt }
</STYLE>
```

Finally, properties can be directly added to individual HTML elements, using the STYLE attribute:

```
<H3 STYLE="color:red;font-size:12pt">...</H3>
```

These in-line styles override general rules for the given element type, and styles defined at the top of the HTML file override those defined in an external stylesheet document.

CSS versus XSL/XSLT

As shown above, the syntax of CSS is far more compact than XSL (which uses XML syntax). It is therefore easier to write (both faster and without errors) when using standard text-editing tools, and transfers over networks more quickly. CSS is already well supported by popular Web browsers and Web-page authoring tools. It has gained acceptance, and it would certainly be difficult for another, similar stylesheet language to compete with CSS at this stage.

However, CSS was designed to format text blocks that have already been arranged in the correct order within an HTML document. It therefore lacks the transformation capabilities of XSLT. This is its major weakness.

Although it is possible to think of CSS as in direct competition to XSL/XSLT, many people who understand the strengths and weaknesses of each approach see that they can, and often do, complement each other. It is useful to know both when working on the Web, and to know when to apply one or the other, or perhaps both, to a given problem.

Finally, in an encouraging spirit of cooperation, the latest drafts of the XSL specification borrow the names of properties defined in CSS. This has been done for two reasons. First, the learning curve of moving from one to the other is reduced, making it more practical for both to continue to exist. Second, this agreement on the properties supported leads to a high degree of compatibility, which makes it easier for developers to create products that support both standards.

Relevance to XSLT and XSL

CSS has been one of the influences in the development of XSL. Indeed, as stated above, XSL has now adopted the names of properties defined in CSS. It is therefore possible to use existing experience of CSS, or a CSS textbook, to explain the behaviour and identify the attribute name needed in XSL to achieve a particular effect. For example, in CSS the property name 'font-size' defines the size of the text to present. This name has been adopted in XSL to achieve the same effect:

```
{ ... font-size: 12pt ... }
```

```
<xsl:inline font-size="12pt">...</xsl:inline>
```

When using XSLT to create HTML documents from XML documents, the HTML document can be enhanced by including in-line CSS properties. For example, the background colour of a note may depend on the importance of the note:

```
<xsl:template match="note[@type='danger']">
  <P STYLE="background-color:red">
    <xsl:apply-templates/>
  </P>
</xsl:template>
```

Rule constructions

It is useful to know how CSS stylesheet rules are constructed in order to create an XSLT stylesheet from an existing CSS stylesheet. The selector can be more than just a single element name, in the same way that the Match attribute value on the Template element can be more complex than a simple element name, though in CSS the options are not as extensive. There is no expression language in CSS, just a small number of specific options.

Merging rules

The first major difference is that there may be multiple rules in CSS for a given element. The properties in each rule are simply added together. When properties are duplicated across rules, the last rule has precedence. In the following example, the H3 element will be displayed in blue, 14pt text, with a word spacing of 3pt:

```
H3 { color: green ; word-spacing: 3pt}
```

```
H3 { color: blue ; font-size: 14pt }
```

There is no equivalent of this in XSLT. All properties must be collected together into a single template (though variables can be used to partially emulate the effect).

Shared rules

A single rule can apply to more than one element (so avoiding unnecessary repetition). Element names are separated by commas. In the following example, the highest three header levels will all appear in green text:

```
H1, H2, H3 { color:green }
```

The equivalent XSLT expression would be:

```
match="H1|H2|H3"
```

Context elements

A rule may only apply to an element when that element occurs within another specified element. In the following example, only table titles adopt the given style:

```
TABLE TITLE { ... }
```

This example can be deceptive. It represents a TITLE element that may occur within other structures inside the TABLE element. The equivalent XSLT expression would be:

```
match="TABLE//TITLE"
```

A number of variants of this have been added in CSS 2, making use of the '>', '*' and '+' symbols.

The '>' symbol is used to indicate direct descendants:

```
TABLE > TITLE { ... }
```

This is clearly equivalent to the following:

```
match="TABLE/TITLE"
```

Another option is to use the '*' as a wildcard that represents at least one level between the two elements:

```
BOOK * TITLE { ... }
```

The way to replicate this in XSLT is two use '*' *and* '//':

```
match="BOOK/*//TITLE"
```

Finally, it is possible to identify elements that immediately follow other elements, such as an initial paragraph after a title, using '+':

```
TITLE + P { ... }
```

Attribute context

CSS 2 also allows context to depend on the presence and possibly the value of an attribute, using square brackets to enclose the attribute name, or name and value.

```
P[type] { ... }

P[type="secret"] { ... }
```

This is one case where XSLT requires little translation of syntax (though quotes may need to be changed, as shown below, depending on the quotes used for the Match attribute):

```
match="P[@type]"

match="P[@type='secret']"
```

However, apart from '=' to check that the attribute value matches a given value, it is also possible to use '!=' (not equals) and '~=' (given value must be present within the attribute value as a distinct word). The first of these is easily converted (unfortunately, the XPath expression language has no equivalent for the '~=' feature):

```
P[type!="secret"] { ... }
match="P[not(@type='secret')]"
```

Properties

The following table shows all CSS properties, including which version of CSS they first appear in. Note that, beyond the values shown below, CSS 2 also adds the Inherit value to all properties. See the explanation at the end of the table for values specified in italic.

Property	Ver	Example values	Values
Font properties			
font	1	italic small-caps bold 18pt/22pt Helvetica, sans-serif	combination of six properties – font-style, font-variant, font-weight, font-size, line-height and font-family, with '/' between size and line height
	2	caption	... caption, icon, menu, message, small-caption, status-bar
font-style	1	italic	normal (the default), italic, oblique
font-variant	1	normal	normal (the default), small-caps
font-weight	1	bold	normal (the default), bold, bolder, lighter, 100, 200, 300, 400, 500, 600, 700, 800, 900
font-size	1	18pt larger	*Length*, xx-large, x-large, large, medium (the default), small, x-small, xx-small, smaller, larger
font-family	1	Helvetica, sans-serif 'Times New Roman'	comma separated alternative font names, first has preference; can be generic name (serif, sans-serif, cursive, fantasy, monospace); quote name with spaces, "Times New Roman" (but use single quotes in Style attributes)
font-size-adjust	2	0.58	*Number*, none (the default)
font-stretch	2	narrower	normal (the default), wider, narrower, ultra-condensed, extra-condensed, condensed, semi-condensed, semi-expanded, expanded, extra-expanded, ultra-expanded

Color and background			
color	1	blue #FF0	*Color*
background	1	red url(boat.gif) no-repeat scroll 10% 10%	combination (background-color, background-image, background-repeat, background-attachment, background-position)
background-color	1	green	*Color*, transparent (the default)
background-image	1	url(boat.gif)	URL, none (the default)
background-repeat	1	repeat-x	repeat (default), repeat-x, repeat-y, no-repeat
background-attachment	1	fixed	scroll (default), fixed
background-position	1	top 10mm 15mm	top, center, bottom, left, right, *Percent*, (*Length* – x, y)
Text properties			
text-decoration	1	underline	none (the default), underline, over-line, line-through, blink
vertical-align	1	sub	baseline (the default), sub, super, top, text-top, middle, bottom, text-bottom, *Percent*
	2	2pt	... *Length*
text-align	1	center	left, right, center, justify
	2	"."	... *String*
text-indent	1	1cm	*Length* (default '0') (first line of text block, minus value gives hanging indent), *Percent*
letter-spacing	1	2pt	normal (the default), *Length*
word-spacing	1	normal	normal (the default), *Length*
text-transform	1	uppercase	capitalize, uppercase, lowercase, none (the default)
line-height	1	22pt	none, (default), *Number*, *Length*, *Percent*
text-shadow	2	3px 3px red 2pt 4pt, -2pt -4pt 1pt blue	normal (default), *Length* (across) *Length* (down), and optional *Length* (blur angle) and optional *Color* (plus more optional shadows separate by commas)
Box properties			
margin	1	.3cm	*Length*, *Percent*, auto – repeated ('x' = all margins, 'x x' = vertical and horizontal and 'x x x x' = top/ right/bottom/left)
margin-left	1	.3cm	*Length* (default 0), *Percent*, auto
margin-right	1	.3in	*Length* (default 0), *Percent*, auto
margin-top	1	9pt	*Length* (default 0), *Percent*, auto
margin-bottom	1	10%	*Length* (default 0), *Percent*, auto
padding	1	1pt	*Length* (default 0), percent*** – repeated ('x' = all edges, 'x x' = vertical and horizontal and 'x x x x' = top/right/bottom/left)
padding-left	1	1pt	*Length* (default 0), *Percent*

padding-right	1	auto	*Length* (default 0), *Percent*
padding-top	1	1em	*Length* (default 0), *Percent*
padding-bottom	1	5pt	*Length* (default 0), *Percent*
border	1	1in	*Length* – repeated ('x' = all borders, 'x x' = vertical and horizontal and 'x x x x' = top/right/bottom/left) or URL (or, from v2, also set width, color and style – see below)
border-left	1	.3cm	*Length* or URL (or, from v2, also set width, color and style – see below)
border-right	1	.3in	*Length* or URL (or, from v2, also set width, color and style – see below)
border-top	1	9pt	*Length* or URL (or, from v2, also set width, color and style – see below)
border-bottom	1	10%	*Length* or URL (or, from v2, also set width, color and style – see below)
border-width	1	thick, thin 2pt 4pt 2pt 4pt	thin, medium, thick, *Length* – repeated ('x' = all borders, 'x x' = vertical and horizontal and 'x x x x' = top/right/bottom/left)
border-left-width	1	thick	thin, medium (default), thick, *Length*
border-right-width	1	thin	thin, medium (default), thick, *Length*
border-top-width	1	medium	thin, medium (default), thick, *Length*
border-bottom-width	1	3pt	thin, medium (default), thick, *Length*
border-color	1	blue green	*Color* – repeated ('x' = all borders, 'x x' = vertical and horizontal and 'x x x x' = top/right/bottom/left)
	2	transparent	as above, plus transparent
border-left-color	2	red	*Color*
border-right-color	2	black	*Color*
border-top-color	2	white	*Color*
border-bottom-color	2	red	*Color*
border-style	1	solid ridge solid ridge	none, hidden, dotted, dashed, solid, double, groove, ridge, inset, outset – repeated ('x' = all borders, 'x x' = vertical and horizontal and 'x x x x' = top/right/bottom/left)
border-left-style	2	dotted	none, hidden, dotted, dashed, solid, double, groove, ridge, inset, outset
border-right-style	2	ridge	none, hidden, dotted, dashed, solid, double, groove, ridge, inset, outset
border-top-style	2	dashed	none, hidden, dotted, dashed, solid, double, groove, ridge, inset, outset
border-bottom-style	2	dotted	none, hidden, dotted, dashed, solid, double, groove, ridge, inset, outset
width	1	50px	*Length*, *Percent*, auto (default)
min-width	2	50px	*Length*, *Percent*
max-width	2	50px	*Length*, *Percent*, none (default)
height	1	auto	*Length*, auto (default)
	2	15%	as above, plus *Percent*
min-height	2	50px	*Length*, *Percent*
max-height	2	50px	*Length*, *Percent*, none (default)
float	1	left	left, right, none (the default)

clear	1	left	left, right, both, none (the default)
overflow	2	hidden	visible (the default), hidden, scroll, auto
clip	2	auto	*Shape*, auto (the default)
visiblity	2	visible	visible, hidden, collapse (default is 'inherit')
z-index	2	12	auto (the default), *Integer*
Generated content			
content	2	open-quote "My prefix" close-quote	*String*, URL, *Counter*, attr(...), open-quote, close-quote, no-open-quote, no-close-quote (and any combination)
quotes	2	none "«" "»" "‹" "›"	none, *String String* (repeating)
counter-reset	2	section -1 imagenum 99	none (the default) or *Identifier*, then optional *Integer* (repeating)
counter-increment	2	section 10 item 1	none (the default) or *Identifier*, then optional *Integer* (repeating)
list-style	1	decimal outside	combination of list-style-type, list-style-image, list-style-position
list-style-type	1	circle	disc, circle (the default), square, decimal, lower-roman, upper-roman, lower-alpha, upper-alpha, none
	2	circle	as above, plus decimal-leading-zero, lower-greek, upper-greek, lower-latin, upper-latin, hebrew, armenian, georgian, cjk-ideographic, hiragana, katakana, hiragana-iroha, katakana-iroha
list-style-position	1	inside	inside, outside (the default)
list-style-image	1	url(boat.gif)	URL, none (the default)
Paged media			
size	2	8cm 12cm	auto (the default), protrait, land-scape, *Length* (one or twice)
marks	2	crop cross	none (the default), crop cross
page-break-before	2	left	auto (the default), always, avoid, left, right
page-break-after	2	always	auto (the default), always, avoid, left, right
page-break-inside	2	avoid	auto (the default), avoid
page	2	auto	auto (the default), *Identifier*
orphans	2	3	*Integer* (default '2')
widows	2	3	*Integer* (default '2')
Tables			
caption-side	2	left	top (the default), bottom, left, right
table-layout	2	fixed	auto (the default), fixed
border-collapse	2	separate	collapse (the default), separate
border-spacing	2	3pt 3pt 5pt	*Length* (default '0'), optional *Length*
empty-cells	2	hide	show (the default), hide
speak-header	2	always	once (the default) always

User interface			
cursor	2	crosshair, default url(eggtimer.gif), wait	auto (the default), crosshair, default, pointer, move, e-resize, ne-resize, nw-resize, n-resize, se-resize, sw-resize, s-resize, w-resize, text, wait, help, or URL() (repeating?)
outline	2	red dashed 2pt	combination of outline-color, outline-style, outline-width
outline-width	2	2pt	thin, medium (the default), thick, *Length* – repeated ('x' = all borders, 'x x' = vertical and horizontal and 'x x x x' = top/right/bottom/left)
outline-style	2	dashed	none (the default) , hidden, dotted, dashed, solid, double, groove, ridge, inset, outset – repeated ('x' = all borders, 'x x' = vertical and horizontal and 'x x x x' = top/right/ bottom/left)
outline-color	2	red	invert (the default), *Color*
Aural styles			
volume	2	medium	*Number*, *Percent*, silent, x-soft, soft, medium (the default), loud, x-loud
speak	2	spell-out	normal (the default), non, spell-out
pause	2	12ms 9ms	combination of pause-before and pause-after
pause-before	2	12ms	*Time*, *Percent*
pause-after	2	9ms	*Time*, *Percent*
cue	2	url(squeek.gif) url(go.gif) url(stop.gif)	combination of cue-before and cue-after
cue-after	2	url(squeek.gif)	url(...), none (the default)
cue-before	2	url(squeek.gif)	url(...), none (the default)
play-during	2	url(squeek.gif) repeat auto	auto (the default), none, url(...) mix? repeat?
azimuth	2	far-right behind 240deg	*nnn* deg, leftwards, rightwards or left-side, far-side, left, center-left, center (the default), center-right, right, far-right, right-side followed by behind
elevation	2	far-right behind 240deg	*nnn* deg, below, level (the default), above, lower, higher
speech-rate	2	faster 120 *(words per minute)*	*nnn*, x-slow, slow, medium (the default), fast, x-fast, faster, slower
voice-family	2	churchill female	male, female, child, (specific voice such as 'comedian')
pitch	2	low 200Hz	x-low, low, medium (the default), high, x-high, *number*Hz
pitch-range	2	44	0–100 (default 50)

stress	2	53	0–100 (default 50)
richness	2	70	0–100 (default 50)
speak-punctuation	2	code	code, none (the default)
speak-numerals	2	digits	digits, continuous (the default)
Classifications			
display	1	inline	none, block (**default**), inline, list-item
	2	block compact table-row	none, block, inline (**default**), list-item ...*PLUS*... run-in, compact, marker, table, inline-table, table-row-group, table-header-group, table-footer-group, table-row, table-column-group, table-column, table-cell, table-caption
marker-offset	2	section 10 item 1	*Length*, auto (the default)
position	2	relative	static (the default), relative, absolute, fixed
top	2	2pt	*Length*, *Percent*, auto
bottom	2	2pt	*Length*, *Percent*, auto
left	2	2pt	*Length*, *Percent*, auto
right	2	2pt	*Length*, *Percent*, auto
direction	2	rtl	ltr (the default), rtl (right-to-left)
unicode-bidi	2	embed	normal (the default), embed, bidi-override
white-space	1	pre	normal (the default), pre (pre-formatted), nowrap (single line)

Length – inches (in), centimetres (cm), millimetres (mm), points (pt), picas (pc), ems (em), x-height (ex), pixels (px). A '+' or '-' prefix is allowed.

Percent – '+' or '-', followed by number, then '%', e.g. 200% = twice size.

Color – black, navy, blue, aqua, purple, maroon, green, red, gray, fuchsia, teal, lime, yellow, white, olive, silver, #rgb (hexadecimal), #rrggbb (hexadecimal), rgb(r,g,b) (each value decimal or percentage).

Number – digits, optionally prefix with '+' or '-', may include decimal point.

Integer – digits, optionally prefix with '+' or '-', not including decimal point.

Time – Number plus 'ms' (milliseconds) or 's' (seconds).

String – Quotes characters, single or double, no embedded quotes of same type, use '\"' or '\'' instead. Newline is '\A' and just '\' to split text over lines in style-sheet.

20. Expressions

Earlier chapters have introduced the expression language used in the XSLT standard to trigger and configure templates, locate and reuse information, define keys, and for other purposes. Mostly, these expressions are defined in a separate standard called XPath; though XSLT adds some functions and defines a subset of XPath for use in special circumstances. This chapter provides a thorough examination of the XPath standard and the XSLT enhancements.

The XPath standard

Version 1.0 of the **XML Path Language** (**XPath**) was developed by W^{3}C and released as a recommendation on 16 November 1999. This standard can be found at 'http://www.w3.org/TR/xpath'.

Some parts of this standard form discrete subsets that are referenced from XSLT and other standards. XSLT makes much use of **patterns** (which are in fact defined in the XSLT standard). A pattern is a restricted form of **location path**, which in turn is just part of the full expression language.

Expressions in attributes

The syntax of the XPath expression language was carefully crafted to be applicable in a number of circumstances. For example, in some applications of XPath it is useful to be able to add an expression to a URL, and so the syntax needed to be both brief and consistent with the characters allowed in URLs. Similarly, for its use in XSLT, expressions need to be valid attribute values.

Quotation marks often appear in expressions. There must be no conflict between these quotes and the quotes that enclose the attribute value containing the expression. Either single or double quotes can be used, and so when the expression only contains one set of quotes it is a simple matter to avoid using the same quotes as used for the attribute value:

```
match="id('abc123')/..."
```

```
match='id("abc123")/...'
```

When the expression contains quotes within quotes, however, this solution is not sufficient. Fortunately, the entity references '**"**' and '**'**' may also be used.

If an expression contains a left chevron character, '<', this must be avoided by using '**<**', as the chevron character is not allowed in attribute values:

```
match="... position() &lt; 6 ..."
```

Patterns

A pattern is a limited form of location path (described next). Patterns are used in XSLT when the need is to decide whether the current element appears in a given context. Patterns are only allowed to contain some expression constructs. As the need for patterns is limited to matching XSLT templates, the definition of patterns is actually provided in the XSLT standard, not the XPath standard.

Where patterns are allowed

Patterns are used in the Match attribute within the Key and Template elements, as well as the Count and From attributes within the Number element:

```
<template match="pattern">...</template>
```

```
<key match="pattern">...</key>
```

```
<number count="pattern" from="pattern">...</number>
```

Matching elements to patterns

Unlike other expressions, patterns are read from right to left. Consider the following Match attribute in the Template element:

```
<template match="book/warning/para">...</template>
                 3       2       1
```

In this example, the first part of the pattern (part (1)) is compared against the current node. If the current node is a Para element, as required, then the next part of the pattern (part (2)) is compared against the parent of the current element. Providing that the parent is a Warning element, the final check is that this element is in turn enclosed by a Book element. In this example, the template is a candidate for the current element provided that the pattern accurately describes the current context.

Multiple patterns

A pattern can be divided into several distinct sub-patterns, separated by the vertical bar symbol, 'I'. If any of the sub-patterns is valid, the entire pattern succeeds. For example, the following template matches Note, Warning and Danger elements. If the current element is any of these, then the template is triggered:

```
<template match="note|warning|danger">...</template>

    <para>...</para>
    <note>...</note>
    <para>...</para>
    <danger>...</danger>
    <warning>...</warning>
```

Steps

Many patterns consist of a number of steps. Each step is separated from other steps using '/'. The following example has two steps, and it matches paragraphs within chapters:

```
match="chapter/para"

    <chapter>
      <para>This is a chapter paragraph.</para>
      <para>This is another chapter paragraph.</para>
        <section>
          <para>This is a section paragraph.</para>
```

When a step is empty, there are two adjacent '/' symbols, '//', indicating any number of intermediate elements of any kind. This example matches all of the following paragaphs:

```
match="book//para"
```

```
<book>
  <para>This is a book.</para>
  <chapter>
    <para>This is a chapter paragraph.</para>
    <section>
      <para>This is a section paragraph.</para>
```

A pattern must begin with a document root identifier, '/', a root and unknown-number-of-descendants identifier, '//', or an element identifier keyword, '**id()**' or '**key()**':

```
match="/..."
```

```
match="//..."
```

```
match="id('link99')/..."
```

```
match="key('color', 'yellow')/..."
```

Each step in the pattern is usually an element name or an attribute name (prefixed with '@'), or an element or attribute name prefixed with the keywords '**child::**' or '**attribute::**':

```
match=".../chapter/..."
```

```
match=".../child::chapter/..."
```

```
match=".../@author"
```

```
match=".../attribute::author"
```

The symbol '*' represents any element or any attribute, depending on whether or not it is preceded by '@' ('@*'):

```
match=".../*/..."
```

```
match=".../@*"
```

However, other node types can be included, and element names may have a namespace prefix.

```
match=".../*/..."
```

```
match=".../acme:price/..."
```

```
match=".../comment()"
```

```
match=".../text()"
```

```
match=".../processing-instruction()"
```

```
match=".../node()/..."
```

But most of these are only relevant as the final step in the pattern, as they cannot include children. For example, it does not make sense to ask whether a Para element is within a comment (because XML rules do not allow this).

In addition, one or more predicate filters are also allowed (see below):

```
match="…/chapter[@author='J Smith'] /…"
```

It is not possible for a pattern to include relative paths, including '.' and '..' instructions. A pattern must also not include direction keywords beyond 'child::' and 'attribute::'. For example, 'ancestor::' may not be used. This is because a pattern is used to 'zero-in' on the current node from the document root or an identified element. It does not make sense to allow the path to 'meander' around the document structure.

Location paths

Patterns are a limited form of **location path**. The general form of a location path has therefore already been described above. The main features of a location path beyond those adopted in patterns are the ability to make steps in directions other than downward into the structure of the document, and the ability to begin the path at the current location:

To support the taking of steps in various directions, a number of additional keywords are needed beyond 'child::'. A further 12 keywords are available, allowing navigation to parents and higher-level ancestors, descendants below the level of children, and material that simply precedes or follows the current element.

The '**parent::**' keyword selects the parent of the current node. As this is usually done simply to step back out of the node, as a preliminary step to moving elsewhere in the document, it is commonly used with the node() keyword ('parent::node()') in order successfully to match the parent, whatever node type it is or element name it has. Indeed, this is such a common requirement that there is a shorthand equivalent, '..', which should be familiar to users of some command-line operating systems. The location path '../title' selects a Title element that is a sibling of the current element. This is known as a **relative path**, as the target node selected by this expression actually depends on the location of the current node.

Note: Those familiar with the use of '..' (and '.', which is described below) from MS-DOS and UNIX operating systems should realize that the analogy with directory paths can be stretched too far. Operating systems always require that sibling directories have unique names, so that a path identifies a single target directory. XML documents have no such restriction, and so a location path will often match many target elements. For example, '//chapter/para', activated in the Book element template, will select every paragraph in every chapter, and '../title' may select more than one title.

The '**self::**' keyword, followed by node(), identifies the current node. This can also be useful when specifying relative paths, particularly when the target node is a descendant of the current node but the number of intermediate levels is not known. In this scenario, the '//' instruction is needed; but if this appears at the start of an expression, it indicates a descendant of the root node, not the current node. Therefore, the current node needs to be the first part of the expression, as in 'self::node()/ /...'. As this is a common requirement, the single character '**.**' is used as an abbreviation for 'self::node()'. For example, the expression './/title' finds descendant Title elements of the current node. The XSLT function '**current()**' can also be used but sometimes differs in meaning from '.' (see *XSLT Extensions* below).

The '**descendant-or-self::**' keyword represents zero or more steps down into the document structure. When used with node(), this represents any number of intermediate objects (including none). If this concept seems familiar, it is because this is the longhand equivalent of '//'. The expression fragment '/descendant-or-self::node()/' means the same thing but is far more verbose. This step only makes sense when it precedes another step that is more specific, such as '//para', as the actual number of steps into the document structure taken varies, depending on how many are needed to reach the element specified in the next part of the path. The 'or-self' part of the name is significant, as it indicates that if the current node matches the following element name, then no actual step needs to be taken.

The '**descendant::**' keyword is similar, but does not include the current node as a possible match. If the expression is 'descendant::para', and the current node is a Para element, this node will not be considered a match; it must contain another Para element for this test to succeed.

The '**ancestor::**' and '**ancestor-or-self::**' keywords work in the same way, but outwards from the current element instead of into its contents. For example, the expression 'ancestor::chapter' selects the chapter containing the current element.

The '**following-sibling::**' and '**preceding-sibling::**' keywords represent elements that follow or precede the current element within the parent element that they all share. To select the paragraphs that follow the current element, within the same parent, the expression 'following-sibling::para' is used. (Note that a count is maintained of the elements encountered in the direction taken. The significance of this is explained later.) Thus:

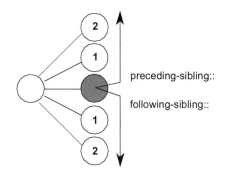

The '**preceding::**' and '**following::**' keywords are extensions of the sibling-specific versions described above. Preceding elements are all elements that have occurred before the current element, and have been closed before the current element has been opened (their end-tags occurring before this element's start-tag). Preceding siblings are included, but ancestors are therefore not included, because they are still open. Following elements are all elements that have not begun at the point of the current element, and so ancestors are again not included, but following siblings are:

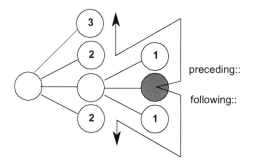

The following example demonstrates the kind of path that can be built using these concepts. In this example, all elements that precede the title of each chapter are selected:

```
//child::chapter/child::title/preceding-sibling::*
```

```
<book>
  <chapter>
    <author>J Smith</author>
    <title>Chapter One Title</title>
    ...
  </chapter>

  <chapter>
    <version>1.3</version>
    <date>12/4/2000</date>
    <title>Chapter Two Title</title>
    ...
  </chapter>
</book>
```

Expressions

The complete expression language includes the locations paths and patterns described above, but it also contains a wider set of features built around the use of **functions** to manipulate and analyze data items of various types, and **operators** to compare objects and perform various calculations.

Where expressions are allowed

XSLT allows full expressions to be used in a number of places. They are used in the Select attribute of the Copy Of element, Parameter element, Sort element (so long as it returns a string), Variable element, Value Of element (so long as it returns a string), and the With Parameter element:

```
<copy-of select="expression">...</copy-of>

<param select="expression">...</param>

<sort select="expression">...</sort>

<variable select="expression">...</variable>

<with-param select="expression">...</with-param>
```

They can also be used with the Test attribute of the If element (so long as it returns a boolean value) and the Value attribute of the Number element (so long as it returns a numeric value):

```
<if test="expression">...</if>

<with-param value="expression">...</with-param>
```

Expressions may be used in the predicate filters within patterns:

```
<template match="...test[expression]...">...</template>
```

Finally, expressions may be used in attribute value templates:

```
<IMG SRC="{expression}.gif" />
```

Data types and functions

The expression language handles boolean values, numeric values, strings and nodes. A number of functions are supplied to transform data items from one type to another, and to compare, manipulate and analyze them.

Functions

Functions perform a specific operation and return a value. A return value effectively replaces the function at its position within the expression. Functions have names that represent their purpose, such as 'round' and 'string-length', followed by brackets:

```
function()
```

In most cases, functions operate on supplied information, passed to the function as comma-separated parameters placed within the brackets:

```
function(parameter1, parameter2)
```

There are a number of functions available to support each of the data types discussed below. However, the examples in this section are generally not very useful except to illustrate the form and behaviour of particular functions. The later discussion on the use of operators shows how these functions may be put to more practical use.

Boolean values

A boolean value must be either '**true**' or '**false**'. This type of value is used in tests, such as in the If element, to decide whether or not to take an action. The function '**true**()' simply returns the value 'true', so the following If element is always triggered:

```
<if test="true()"><!-- ENABLED --></if>
```

The function '**false**()' always returns the value 'false'. The following test is never enabled:

```
<if test="false()"><!-- NOT ENABLED --></if>
```

The '**not**()' function reverses a boolean value, from 'true' to 'false' or 'false' to 'true':

```
<if test="not(true())"><!-- NOT ENABLED --></if>

<if test="not(false())"><!-- ENABLED --></if>
```

When a boolean test is needed but the expression does not return a value of this kind, the value is automatically converted to a boolean as if it were enclosed within the '**boolean**()' function, which converts values to 'true' or 'false' according to the following rules.

A number if considered to be 'true' if it is not zero (and is definitely a valid number). The value zero is therefore 'false', as is **NaN** (**Not a Number**):

```
<if test="1"><!-- ENABLED --></if>

<if test="0"><!-- NOT ENABLED --></if>

<if test="1bad"><!-- NOT ENABLED (NaN) --></if>
```

A string is considered to be 'true' if it contains at least one character. An empty string is 'false':

```
<if test="'x'"><!-- ENABLED --></if>

<if test="''"><!-- NOT ENABLED (empty string) --></if>
```

A set of nodes is true if there is at least one node in the set. A list of zero nodes is false. This is demonstrated by the simple test for the presence of elements of a specific type. In this example, if at least one Title element is present as a child of the current element, then 'true' is returned:

```
<if test="title">
  <!-- ENABLED (if embedded title(s)) -->
</if>
```

Numeric values

A numeric value can be any positive or negative real number, such as '3', '+55.5' and '-9999'. Numbers must be stored as binary values in eight bytes (64 bits), and so there is a (very high) limit on the values allowed.

A number of functions are included for manipulating numeric values. First, other data items can be converted to numbers using the '**number**()' function. Boolean values are converted to '1' when true, and '0' when false:

```
<if test="number(true())"><!-- ENABLED --></if>

<if test="number(false())"><!-- NOT ENABLED --></if>
```

Strings are converted to numbers if their contents are pure numbers, optionally surrounded by whitespace. If the string does not conform to these constraints, it is converted to NaN (Not a Number) (which is then considered 'false' as a boolean value):

```
<if test="number('1')"><!-- ENABLED --></if>
<if test="number(' -1 ')"><!-- ENABLED --></if>
<if test="number('-0')"><!-- NOT ENABLED (zero) --></if>
<if test="number('99 bad')"><!-- NOT ENABLED (NaN) --></if>
```

Other functions, described below, take parameters that need to be numeric values. But it is possible to pass other data types to them without having to use the number() function described above. This function can be omitted, as its presence can be implied. The two examples below are functionally identical, but the latter is preferable as it is more legible:

```
<if test="function(number('0.5'))">...</if>
<if test="function('0.5')">...</if>
```

The '**floor()**' function returns the nearest positive integer that is smaller than the value passed to it. For example, the floor of '3.2' is '3'. The '**ceiling()**' function rounds real numbers up to the nearest higher integer value, so '3.2' become '4'. The '**round()**' function rounds real numbers up or down to the nearest integer, with '0.5' rounded up to '1', and '0.4' rounded down to '0':

```
<if test="ceiling(0.5)"><!-- ENABLED (1) --></if>
<if test="floor(0.5)"><!-- NOT ENABLED (0) --></if>
<if test="round(0.5)"><!-- ENABLED (1) --></if>
<if test="round(0.4)"><!-- NOT ENABLED (0) --></if>
```

The '**sum()**' function returns the result of adding all the parameters, which must be nodes. The values to sum are the values extracted from each node. These values are first converted to strings (as described below), then the strings are converted to numbers. Finally the numbers are added together.

String values

A string value is a sequence of characters that is enclosed by quotes. Other data types can be converted into strings using the '**string()**' function. When a number is converted into a string, the string consists of characters that represent each digit of the number, plus any decimal point or leading '-' symbol (though minus zero becomes just '0'). An invalid number becomes the string 'NaN'. When a boolean value is converted to a string, the string holds the word 'true' or the word 'false'.

Strings can be analyzed using the '**string-length()**', '**starts-with()**' and '**contains()**' functions. The first of these returns a number representing the number of characters in the string. The second and third return a boolean value indicating whether or not the string starts with, or contains, the given series of characters:

```
<if test="string-length('1')"><!-- ENABLED (1) --></if>

<if test="string-length('')"><!-- NOT ENABLED (0) --></if>

<if test="starts-with('the', 'the boat')">
  <!-- ENABLED (true) -->
</if>

<if test="starts-with('the', 'a boat')">
  <!-- NOT ENABLED (false) -->
</if>

<if test="contains('boat', 'the boat is yellow')">
  <!-- ENABLED (true) -->
</if>

<if test="contains('boat', 'the car is yellow')">
  <!-- NOT ENABLED (false) -->
</if>
```

Other functions are used to create new strings from parts of existing strings. The '**substring-before()**' function and the '**substring-after()**' function extract initial or trailing characters from a string, with the cut-off point given as a character in the second parameter to the function:

```
substring-before('abc-123', '-')">

substring-after('abc-123', '-')">
```

If the given character is repeated in the string, only the first occurrence is relevant.

A more flexible version of this feature, called '**substring()**', specifies an offset and range for the characters to extract. In the following example, four characters are selected starting at the fifth character of the string:

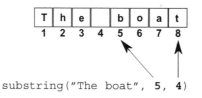

```
substring("The boat", 5, 4)
```

Characters within strings can be replaced. The '**translate()**' function takes three parameters. The first parameter is the string containing characters to be replaced. The second parameter is a list of characters that must be converted to other characters. The third parameter is the list of replacement characters. A specific character in the second string is replaced by the character at the same position in the third string. For example, values of 'abc' and 'xyz' for these two parameters specify that 'a' is to become 'x', 'b' is to become 'y', and 'c' is to become 'z'. Each occurrence in the first string is replaced; for example, 'translate('abc abc', 'b', 'x')', returns the string 'axc axc'. The following example returns the upper-case version of any string of alphabetic characters:

```
translate('Convert This',
           'abcdefghijklmnopqrstuvwxyz',
           'ABCDEFGHIJKLMNOPQRSTUVWXYZ')
```

The '**normalize-space**()' function returns a string that removes unnecessary whitespace characters from the parameter string. For example, ' the   boat ' becomes 'the boat'.

Node-set values

Every node has a value, which is represented by a string. The string value of a node is determined in different ways, depending on the node type. The value of the root node of the document is the concatenation of all the text nodes in the document (which is not generally useful). The value of an element node is also the concatenation of all the text nodes within that element, and within all descendant elements. For example, the value of the following Para element is the text in the paragraph, including the text in the embedded highlighted section ('All the text here is the value'):

```
<para>All the <emph>text</emph> here is the value</para>
```

Note that, for this reason, the Value Of instruction in XSLT can be useful for extracting the text from an element for reuse elsewhere, ignoring any embedded tags.

The string value of an attribute node is its normalized value (tabs and line-feeds are converted to spaces first).

The string value of a comment node is the entire content of the comment, not including the surrounding markup '<!--' and '-->':

```
<!--All the text of the comment -->
```

The string value of a processing instruction node is the instruction part of the code and so does not include the target name. It is not possible to retrieve the target name. However, processing instructions can be selected on a target-specific basis, by including the target name in the node function, as in 'processing-instruction('ACME')':

```
<?ACME page-break?>
```

The string value of a text node is all the characters in that node. A text node cannot be empty as it only exists in order to hold one or more characters.

Unlike the simpler data types described earlier, a node already exists at a specific location in the document. Therefore, to use a node in an expression it must first be found. A location path is used to find the required node. The other issue this raises is that location paths often target multiple nodes. For example, '//title' returns a list of all Title element nodes. Some of the functions described below work on a single node. When a list is passed to them, only the first node is processed.

When no location path is included, the default location is the direct content of the current node. For example, a test can be made for the presence of child nodes, of any kind (except attributes), using the '**node()**' function. If there are any children, such as text blocks, comments or processing instructions, these objects will have string values, and a string containing any characters at all is considered 'true'. Otherwise, the string will be empty, and therefore 'false':

```
<if test="node()">...</if>
```

This test, made on the Para elements below, has the following effect on the If element:

```
<para></para> <!-- NOT ENABLED -->

<para/> <!-- NOT ENABLED -->

<para>some text</para> <!-- ENABLED -->

<para><!-- a comment --></para> <!-- ENABLED -->
```

More specific variants use the '**text()**', '**comment()**' and '**processing-instruction()**' functions, and specific or general ('*') element names.

Context positions

The current node is always part of a current node list, though it is possible for this list to only contain the one, current node. The length of the node list, and the position of the current node within this list, can be important. After each step in a location path, the list contains all the nodes selected by this step.

The '**position()**' function returns a number that indicates the position of the node amongst the current list of nodes. In the simplest case, this is the position of the node amongst its sibling nodes:

```
<if test="position()">
  <!-- ENABLED (current list must be at least 1) -->
</if>
```

The position value is not always calculated in the same direction. In a location path, it depends on the direction of the step to be taken. The simple rule underlying the various directions illustrated below is that when the direction is forward, searching for elements that start after the start-tag of the current element, then counting is in document order. Otherwise, it is in reverse order.

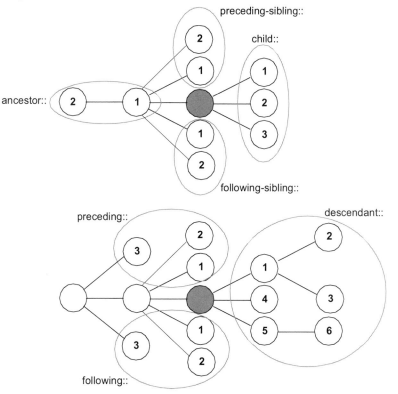

The 'last()' function returns the number of nodes in the current context list. The position will always be a value between '1' and this maximum:

```
<if test="last()">
   <!-- ENABLED (current list must be at least 1) -->
</if>
```

The 'count()' function returns the total number of nodes passed to it. For example, 'count(para)' returns the number of paragraphs, such as the number of paragaph children of the current element, and 'count(*)' counts all elements:

```
<if test="count(para)">
   <!-- ENABLED (if embedded paragraphs) -->
</if>
```

```
<if test=" count(*) ">
    <!-- ENABLED (if embedded elements) -->
</if>
```

The 'id()' function returns the node with the given unique identifier, if such a node exists. The function 'id('xyz')' returns the node with the unique identifier 'xyz'. Unique identifiers are only recognized if a DTD is used, and it assigns to one or more attributes the attribute type ID. This is typically used to apply formatting or to reuse the content of a specific element:

```
<xsl:template match="id('JSmith')">
    <P>J. Smith details:</P>
    <P><xsl:apply-templates/></P>
    <P>J. Smith works for company -
        <xsl:value-of select="id('company19')"/>
    </P>
</xsl:template>
```

The 'name()' function returns the string value of the name of the given node. The name returned is the qualified name, with a namespace prefix where appropriate. For example, 'name(.)' returns the name of the current node. This could be used in a named template to debug a stylesheet:

```
<xsl:template name="debug">
    <P>NAME = <xsl:value-of select="name(.)"/></P>
</xsl:template>
```

Operators

The expression language includes a number of operators, which are used to perform calculations and comparisons. Operators give purpose to the functions described above, allowing the returned values to be compared with each other and with fixed values. Comparisons for equality, for inequality and for comparative size can be made.

Addition and subtraction ('+' and '-')

Numeric values can be added together using the '+' operator, and subtracted using '-':

```
<if test="0 + 1"><!-- ENABLED (1) --></if>

<if test="1 - 1"><!-- NOT ENABLED (0) --></if>
```

Note that, to avoid confusion with hyphens in names, the '-' symbol is recognized as a minus by adding whitespace before it:

```
test="first-node - second-node"
```

Equality and inequality ('=' and '!=')

The '=' operator compares two items for equality. If they are equal, the boolean value 'true' is the result. Otherwise, the value 'false' is the result. Boolean values, numeric values and strings can all be compared using this operator:

```
<if test="true() = true()"><!-- BOOLEAN COMPARE --></if>

<if test="3 = 3"><!-- NUMERIC COMPARE --></if>

<if test="'Hi' = 'Hi'"><!-- STRING COMPARE --></if>
```

In the following example, two strings are compared. Some action is taken if the text content of the current element contains '234' at position three:

```
<number>123456789</number>]

test="self::node()[substring(text(),3,3) = '345'"]
```

Before making the comparison, however, the two sides must be made to be of the same object type (if they are not already). This is done automatically. If one side is a boolean value, the other side is converted into a boolean value. Otherwise, if one side is a number, the other side is converted to a number. Otherwise, if one side is a string, and the other is not, it is made into a string. In the following example, a string is compared with a number. As one of the items is a number, the other one (the string) is converted into a number. The two numbers are then compared:

```
<if test="'3' = 3"><!-- ENABLED --></if>

<if test="7 = '3'"><!-- NOT ENABLED --></if>
```

The opposite of equality is inequality. Placing an exclamation mark before the equals symbol, '!=', indicates the need for the compared items to be different rather than the same. This test can be made wherever a test for equality can be made. The result is 'true' if the compared items differ:

```
<if test="3 != 3"><!-- NOT ENABLED --></if>

<if test="'3' != 7"><!-- ENABLED --></if>
```

Larger and smaller ('<' and '>')

When two values are different, it is sometimes useful to know which of the two values is greater. The '<' symbol between two values tests whether or not the first value is smaller than the second, returning 'true' if it is. However, the rules of XML mean that this symbol must be replaced by the sequence '<' (less than):

```
<if test="9 &lt; 3"><!-- NOT ENABLED --></if>

<if test="3 &lt; 9"><!-- ENABLED --></if>
```

Similarly, the '>' symbol between two values tests whether or not the first value is larger than the second. In this case, the equivalent entity reference can be used ('>' (greater than)), but it is not necessary:

```
<if test="9 > 3"><!-- ENABLED --></if>

<if test="3 &gt; 9"><!-- NOT ENABLED --></if>
```

Numeric comparisons are made, provided that neither value is a node or set of nodes (explained later). Strings and booleans are converted to numbers ('0' or '1' in the latter case) prior to making the comparison.

At least ('<=' and '>=')

A slight variation of less-than and greater-than comparisons allows a different question to be asked. Is is sometimes useful to know whether a value is at least as great as another, or at most as great as another. This is done simply by combining the '<', '>' and '=' symbols.

The combination '>=' means 'greater than or equal to'. It is important that these symbols appear in this order:

```
<if test="4 >= 3"><!-- ENABLED (greater) --></if>

<if test="3 >= 3"><!-- ENABLED (identical) --></if>
```

The combination '<=' (actually '<=') means 'less than or equal to'. Again, the ordering of the two symbols is important:

```
<if test="3 &lt;= 4"><!-- ENABLED (smaller) --></if>

<if test="3 &lt;= 3"><!-- ENABLED (identical) --></if>
```

And

The 'and' operator is used to connect two expressions. Both sub-expressions must return a boolean value, and both must be true for the complete expression to be true. If the first part of such as expression is false, the processor does not need to bother to evaluate the second part, as the whole expression must be false:

```
<if test="9 > 5 and 5 > 1"><!-- ENABLED (both OK) --></if>

<if test="9 > 5 and 1 > 5"><!-- NOT ENABLED --></if>

<if test="5 > 9 and 5 > 1"><!-- NOT ENABLED --></if>

<if test="5 > 9 and 41 > 5"><!-- NOT ENABLED --></if>
```

Or

The 'or' operator is also used to connect two expressions. Either sub-expression can be true for the complete expression to be true. The four examples below are identical to the ones above, except for the operator in use. In this case, though, three of the tests are successful instead of just one:

```
<if test="6 > 5 or 5 > 4"><!-- ENABLED (both OK) --></if>
<if test="6 > 5 or 4 > 5"><!-- ENABLED (left OK) --></if>
<if test="5 > 6 or 5 > 4"><!-- ENABLED (right OK) --></if>
<if test="5 > 6 or 4 > 5"><!-- NOT ENABLED --></if>
```

Precedence

When an expression contains a number of operators, interpretation depends on the precedence assigned to each operator type. This is important because it would otherwise be possible to interpret the same expression in a number of different ways. For example, '5 < 6 and 9 < 8' would, if simply read from left to right, compare '5 < 6' (true), then test the 'and' condition against '9' (true, as 'true' and '9' are both true), before checking that the result is smaller than '8' (true, because 'true' is equivalent to '1', which is smaller than '8'). Interpreted this way, the expression would be true, but interpreted with '<' as a higher precedence than 'and' gives a different result. '5' is smaller than '6', so this is true, but '9' is not smaller than '8', so this is not true, and the two halves of the expression are not both true. The expression therefore returns 'false'.

The '<', '>', '<=' and '>=' operators have highest precedence, followed by '=' and '!=', and finally 'and' and 'or'. The examples above therefore work as intended. In the example below, six is greater than five, so this part of the expression is true, and three is smaller than four, so this part of the expression is also true. Therefore, the left part equals the right part (they are both true), so the whole expression is true:

```
<if test="6 > 5 = 3 < 4"><!-- ENABLED (both true) --></if>
```

The '+' and '-' operators described earlier have lower precedence than any of these:

```
<if test="1+1 > 9-8">
  <!-- ENABLED (2 greater than 1) -->
</if>
```

Predicate filters

Location paths often select a number of elements. For example, consider the expression '/book/chapter/para'. When used in a Match pattern, all paragraphs in all chapters match the pattern. When used in a Select expression, all chapter paragraphs are selected. Often, especially in the latter scenario, the actual requirement is to locate a single element, or at least take into consideration factors beyond simple contextual location. A **predicate filter** can be added to 'filter out' unwanted nodes. Filters are expressions enclosed in square brackets, '[' and ']', which return a boolean value. When the value returned is 'true', the node is accepted; when the value returned is 'false', it is rejected. Only accepted nodes are retained and form the basis of the next step in the expression.

Numeric comparisons

The simplest kind of predicate filter is a numeric value. This value represents a specific sequential location in the list of matching nodes. For example, the expression '//chapter/para' may, in one particular chapter, identify 23 paragraphs. Paragraph '1' will be the first paragraph in the chapter, and paragraph '23' will be the last. By entering a value in the predicate filter, only the paragraph at that position is valid. The others are discarded. The following example therefore selects the fifth paragraph in the third chapter of the book:

```
/book/chapter[3]/para[5]
```

The expression 'following-sibling::*[2]' likewise selects the element after the element following the current element. However, the direction of the count is important, and not always immediately obvious. When taking a direction outward or backward ('ancestor::', 'ancestor-or-self::', 'preceding::' and 'preceding-sibling::'), the count is in reverse order. For example, 'preceding-sibling::*[1]' selects the element immediately before the current one (not the first element within their shared parent). The easy way to remember this is to appreciate that the value '1' will always be the element nearest to the starting point.

Expressions in filters

Filters can contain any expression. This is an important point because they are used in patterns, which are otherwise constrained to a limited subset of the expression language. Patterns are much more flexible when they include filters.

First, though, it should be understood that the placing of simple numeric values in filters is a shorthand version of the '**position()**' function. The examples below are equivalent:

```
/book/chapter[3]/para[5]
```

```
/book/chapter[position() = 3]/para[position() = 5]
```

In the following example, paragraphs are only selected if they are in chapters that have no titles:

```
/book/chapter[not(title)]/para
```

```
<book>
  <chapter>
    <para>No title in this chapter.</para>
  </chapter>
  <chapter>
    <title>Chapter With Title</title>
    <para>There is a title in this chapter.</para>
  </chapter>
</book>
```

The shorthand version is provided because it is a common requirement to target a specific element by its contextual location (when it has no unique identifier), such as the fourth paragraph of the seventh section of the second chapter of the book:

```
match="/book/chapter[2]/section[7]/para[4]"
```

Multiple filters

More than one filter can be added to qualify a step in the expression:

```
node[...][...]
```

Normally, this is not an essential feature as multiple expressions can be combined into a single expression using the 'and' operator. However, it is not possible to use numeric values for node positions within a filter that contains other tests. For example, while '[position() = 3 and not(title)]' is legal (the element is the third one, and does not contain a Title element), the shorthand version '[3 and not(title)]' is not allowed. Using separate filters overcomes this limitation:

```
[3][not(title)]
```

The order in which multiple filters are presented is very important. The examples below are *not* the same:

```
//chapter[3][not(title)]
```

```
//chapter[not(title)][3]
```

The reason why they mean different things is explained by the fact that the first filter is applied to create a subset list of matching nodes, and then the second one is applied to this subset. The first example selects the third chapter, then selects or eliminates this chapter depending on whether or not it contains a title. The second example selects all chapters that do not have a title, then selects the third of these chapters.

XSLT extensions

XSLT adds some functions to those defined in the XPath standard. These functions are used to access other documents, find indexed elements, generate unique element identifiers, format numbers, refer to the current node, retrieve URLs from unparsed entities, and discover information about the XSLT processor and the vendor of the software.

Document function

This function is discussed in Chapter 11.

Key function

This function is fully described in Chapter 13.

Generate id function

This function is described in Chapter 13.

Format number function

Numeric values copied from source attributes can be reformatted using the **format-number()** function. For example, the number '12345.6' may be formatted as '12,345.600'.

This function takes at least two parameters, and it returns a string representation of the number that contains appropriate symbols and padding. First, the number to be formatted is given, and then a formatting template, which uses conventions copied from a Java class (the DecimalFormat class, which is part of the 'java.text' package). For example, to reformat a number to ensure that the decimal point appears, and that there are at least two digits after the point, the pattern '0.00' can be used:

```
format-number(123.4, '0.00')

    123.40
```

To pass an attribute value as the first parameter, it is only necessary to enter the attribute name, as it is automatically converted to a number before it is passed to the function:

```
<price val="123.4"/>
```

```
<xsl:template match="price">
  <P>Price:
    <xsl:value-of select="format-number(@val,  '0.00')"/>
  </P>
</xsl:template>
```

<P>Price: **123.40**</P>

The second parameter is a template for the formatting operation. The characters '0', '#', '-', '%', ',' and '.' have special meanings in this template

The character '**0**' indicates a placeholder for a digit that must be present. If the number to format has no digit at this position, '0' is output. This is demonstrated in the example above. The mimimum template pattern is a single '0' character, indicating that the formatted number must be at least a single digit value (anything less is not a number).

But most templates are divided into two major parts: the required integer part and the optional fractional part. The '.' symbol is a placeholder for the decimal point, which indicates the division between these two parts. The number to format is aligned on this point. For example, '123.4' becomes '123.40' when using the template '0.00', as shown above, but remains '123.4' when using the template '00.0'. It is an error for a pattern to include two '.' symbols.

The '#' symbol is also a placeholder for a digit, but in this case is not replaced by '0' if the digit is absent. It can be used before zeros in the integer part of the number (there must be at leat one '0' here), and after any zeros in the fraction part of the number, as in the following example:

###00.0###

The '#' symbols in this example appear to be superfluous, as they have no effect on the output, but are useful when mixed with grouping separators, which are indicated using a comma, ','.

Also, the '0' and '#' characters in the fraction part of the number indicate how many digits are allowed. So '.0#' indicates two digits only, and a longer fraction is reduced to this length by rounding the last valid digit up or down. Using the example pattern, the value '1.123' becomes '1.12', while '1.12999' becomes '1.13'. This rule does not apply to the integer part of the number, so '##0.' does *not* truncate the number '123456' to three digits:

```
            12
           123.4
           123.456 78
           876.543 21
          1234.56
     123456789.12
```

```
###,###,000.00#
```

```
           012.00
           123.4 0
           123.457
           876.543
          1,234.56
     123,456,789.12
```

A separate pattern can be specified for negative values and is separated from the first pattern using a semi-colon, ';'. In the following example, negative numbers are padded to six digits, preceded by a minus sign:

```
###,##0.00;-000000
```

The percent symbol, '%', is used to indicate a percentage. The value is automatically multiplied by 100. A fraction is thereby converted to a percentage:

```
    0.1
    0.99
```

```
%0
```

```
    10%
    99%
```

Similarly, the '?' symbol represents 'per mille' (per thousand). The value is multiplied by 1000. Also, the '¤' symbol (currency symbol) stands in for the current currency symbol, such as '$' or '£'.

It is important to recognize that the '0', ',', '%', '¤' and '-' symbols are only the default characters used in patterns in English. An optional third parameter to the function identifies a **Decimal Format** element that is used to control the formatting and override the default settings. This element is identified by the value of its **Name** attribute:

```
<decimal-format name="England" ... />
```

```
... format-number(123.4, '###,##0.00', England) ...
```

A number of other attributes on this element specify characters for each role. The **Decimal Separator** attribute and **Grouping Separator** attributes indicate which characters take these roles (defaulting to '.' and ',' respectively). For example, in

France the full-point character is the grouping character, and the comma is the decimal point:

```
<decimal-format name="France"
                decimal-separator=","
                grouping-separator="." />
```

```
'###.##0,00'
```

When a number if formatted, it may be an infinite number, an illegal number or a negative number. The symbol for infinity is given in the **Infinity** attribute, and this attribute may contain a string of characters. Likewise, the **NaN** attribute holds the string that should be presented when the supplied number if not valid. Remaining attributes must have a single character value. The minus symbol for negative numbers is specified using the **Minus Sign** attribute (default '-'):

```
<decimal-format name="England" ...
                infinity="INFINITY AND BEYOND!"
                NaN="NOT A NUMBER"
                minus-sign="M" />
```

Within the pattern template, reserved symbols are used to indicate digits ('#') and the separator when there are two templates (';'). The **Digit** attribute specifies the symbol to use to represent a digit, and the **Pattern Separator** attribute provides the separator character:

```
<decimal-format name="England" ...
                digit="D"
                pattern-separator="+" />
```

Finally, a number of attributes are used both to define special characters in the template and, at the same time, to define the output characters for the percent symbol, the per-mille symbol and the zero digit. The **Percent**, **Per Mille** amd **Zero Digit** attributes are used:

```
<decimal-format name="England" ...
                percent="P"
                per-mille="?"
                zero-digit="Z" />
```

Current function

While the **current node** is normally represented by the full-point symbol, '.', it can also be represented by the **current()** function. The following tests are directly equivalent (as they both test for the occurrence of at least one paragraph somewhere within the current element):

```
<if test=".//para">...</if>
```

```
<if test="current()//para">...</if>
```

However, their meanings can differ in a subtle way in some circumstances. When location paths are used in an expression, the concept of the 'current' element can be ambiguous.

In one sense, the current element is still the element selected by the template, regardless of where it is referenced from within an expression in the template. In another sense, the current element is the one selected by a previous step in an expression, as each step identifies a new current element from which the remaining steps take their context. It is sometimes useful to be able to distinguish between these two meanings.

The current() function always refers to the element selected by the template, so that the node it represents does not change in an expression. The '.' symbols, however, refers to different nodes, depending on where it is used in the expression. In the following example, the first test matches any directly embedded paragraphs that include (directly or indirectly) a Secret element. The second test selects the paragraph if there is a Secret element anywhere in the book:

```
<template match="book">
  <if test="para[.//secret]">PARA WITH SECRET</if>
  <if test="para[current()//secret]">PARA IN BOOK WITH
  SECRET</if>
</template>
```

A perhaps more realistic example of the need for this function is to compare attribute values. The following example compares the revision number of all embedded paragraphs with the revision number of the book itself; and only the latest paragraphs are processed:

```
<book rev="3">
  <para rev="1">Old paragraph.</para>
  <para rev="2">Still an old paragraph.</para>
  <para rev="3">New paragraph.</para>
</book>

<template match="book">
  <DIV>
    <apply-templates
        select="para[./@rev = current()/@rev]" />
  </DIV>
</template>

  <DIV>
    <P>New paragraph.</P>
  </DIV>
```

Note that this function cannot be used in a pattern, and so it must not be used in the Match attribute of the Template or Key element, or the attributes on the Number element.

Unparsed entity uri function

XML DTDs may contain entities that refer to external non-XML data, such as image files. The **unparsed-entity-uri()** function is used to obtain the system identifier (or public identifier) when an attribute value contains a reference to an entity name. Consider the following example, where the DTD defines an Image element that uses a Name attribute to hold the entity name. The example instance refers to an entity called 'Boat':

```
<!DOCTYPE book [
  <!NOTATION GIF SYSTEM "GIFviewer.EXE">
  <!ENTITY Boat SYSTEM "/images/boat.GIF" NDATA GIF>
  ...
  <!ELEMENT image EMPTY>
  <!ATTLIST image name ENTITY #REQUIRED>
]>
<book>
  ...
  <image name="Boat"/>
  ...
</book>
```

When converting such an example to HTML, which does not use entities, the output attribute must hold the path to the image instead of the entity name (so '/images/boat.GIF' must replace 'Boat'). When the name of an unparsed entity is passed to the function, it returns the URL for that entity:

```
    <image name="Boat"/>


<xsl:template match="image">
  <IMG HREF="{unparsed-entity-uri(@name)}" />
</xsl:template>


    <IMG HREF="/images/boat.GIF">
```

System property function

Information about the version of XSLT in use, and the vendor of the XSLT processor currently processing the stylesheet, can be obtained using the **system-property()** function. A specific processor may provide access to a large number of additional items. A string parameter passed to the function determines what item is wanted. For the core items, the parameters needed are '**xsl:version**', '**xsl:vendor**' and '**xsl:vendor-uri**'. For example, a comment could be constructed, to be placed in the output document, recording the technology and tool used to create the document:

```
<template match="book">
  <comment>
    <text>XSLT version: </text>
    <value-of select="system-property(xsl:version)" />
    <text>XSLT Processor vendor: </text>
    <value-of select="system-property(xsl:vendor)" />
    <text>XSLT Processor vendor Web site: </text>
    <value-of select="system-property(xsl:vendor-uri)" />
  </comment>
  ...
</template>
```

```
<!-- XSLT version: 1
XSLT Vendor: Apache Software Foundation
XSLT Vendor Web site: http://xml.apache.org/xalan
-->
```

21. DTD Analysis

There are a large number of XML books that describe how to build a document type definition (DTD). This chapter does not cover DTDs in enough detail to easily construct an efficient DTD, but it does explain enough to analyze an existing DTD for the clues needed to develop an appropriate stylesheet.

Introduction

The presence of a DTD is not required for a stylesheet to be developed for use with a document collection. But creating XSL stylesheets for documents that are not controlled by a DTD would be a very dangerous task. Templates must be created for all elements that are to be presented (or hidden), and so the names of these elements must be known in advance and with certainty. With no DTD, document authors are able to create new elements as required, and the stylesheet will have no mappings for new elements.

Assuming the presence of a DTD, it can of course be ignored by the stylesheet designed. However, it is an ideal source of information as it explicitly describes all the elements that may appear and all the contexts in which they may appear. This knowledge can save a lot of effort. For example, it would be wasteful to create a template for a Title element that appears within a Note element, if the definition of the Note element in the DTD does not include the Title element as a possible child or descendant. Studying a DTD is also much faster than studying all the documents in the collection to determine what has been used (and this technique is not adequate in any case, as allowed options that may be used in the future may not have been used up to the point of the investigation).

Each stylesheet created should therefore be associated with a particular DTD. It should be designed to style documents that conform to this DTD. Of course, there may be more than one stylesheet for a given DTD, each designed to style documents that conform to this DTD in a different way.

In order to study a DTD, it is necessary to know how to interpret the instructions it contains. In particular, the way that elements and attributes are defined must be understood.

Elements to style

To gain a list of all the elements that may occur in a compliant document, it is simply necessary to read the names appearing after the ELEMENT declarations. In the following example, the DTD defines just four elements, called 'Book', 'Title', 'Chapter' and 'Para':

```
<!ELEMENT Book     (Title, Chapter*)>
<!ELEMENT Title    (#PCDATA)>
<!ELEMENT Chapter  (Title, Para*)>
<!ELEMENT Para     (#PCDATA)>
```

The following is a conforming document instance:

```
<Book>
  <Title>The Book Title</Title>
  <Chapter>
    <Title>Chapter One Title</Title>
    <Para>First paragraph.</Para>
    <Para>Second paragraph.</Para>
  </Chapter>
  <Chapter>
    <Title>Chapter Two Title</Title>
    <Para>First paragraph.</Para>
    <Para>Second paragraph.</Para>
  </Chapter>
</Book
```

A template could be created for each of these elements.

```
<template match="Book">...</template>

<template match="Title">...</template>

<template match="Chapter">...</template>

<template match="Para">...</template>
```

However, it is usually necessary to study the possible content of the element to determine the role each element plays. Several templates, or perhaps no templates, may actually be necessary for a given element. In some cases, an element may not play any direct role in the styling of its content. In the example above, the Chapter element may not need to be processed (though its presence can be useful in creating context-sensitive styles for other elements). In other cases, more than one template may be needed for a given element. In the example above, the Title element may be used to give the whole book a name, and to give each chapter a name, and it is not likely that these two classes of title are to be styled in the same way.

Hierarchical context

When the style of an element depends on its location in the document, it is necessary to understand what contexts are allowed by the DTD. The ELEMENT declarations provide this information.

In the example above, the Book element definition specifies that a book may contain a Title element, followed by any number of Chapter elements. One possible parent of the Title element is therefore the Book element. However, the Chapter element definition also names the Title element as its first child, and so a Title element may instead have a Chapter element parent. The Para element does not mention the Title element in its definition, and so a Title element cannot have a Para element parent. The following two templates are therefore appropriate for this mode:

```
<template match="Book/Title">...</template>

<template match="Chapter/Title">...</template>
```

Required and sequential context

Optional elements

An element may be optional in some (or even all) contexts. This can be a factor in stylesheet design. For example, it would not be a good idea to arrange for a chapter Title element to force a page-break to start the new chapter, when the Title element is optional. If an element name is followed by a question mark, it is optional. In the following example, the title is optional within a Note element:

```
<!ELEMENT Note (Title? ...)>
```

The asterisk symbol is used to indicate that an element is repeatable but also optional. The Para element in the example below is therefore optional, and the note could be empty:

```
<!ELEMENT Note (Para*)>
```

Element Ordering

An element model may include elements that can appear in any order, or elements that must appear in the order shown. Ordering is predefined when the comma is used to separate element names in the model. In the following example, the Title element must appear first within a Note. As it is also required, it is possible to format the beginning of the note from the Title element template, and it may not be necessary to have a Note template at all:

```
<!ELEMENT Note (Title, Para*)>
```

```
<template name="Note/Title">
  <html:H3>NOTE: <apply-templates/></html:H3>
</template>
```

Block and in-line elements

When formatting text, the concept of 'block' and 'in-line' elements is an important distinction. Block elements have content that is to be separated from neighbouring blocks, usually by starting a new line and by creating a gap above and below the block. Titles and paragraphs are typical examples. The XSL 'block' property is used to create a new block (and the DIV element can be used in an HTML document). In-line elements have content that is to be simply appended to previous text, without creating a new line. Bold and italic phrases are typical examples. The XSL 'inline-sequence' property is used to create an new in-line region (and the SPAN element can be used in an HTML document). It is possible to identify block and in-line elements from studying the DTD content models.

It is important to discover which elements are block elements, and which are in-line elements, not only to apply appropriate formatting to them but simply because they are the elements that are most likely to require templates to be defined for them.

Text content

Both block and in-line elements share a common property; they may directly contain text. Elements that directly contain text are in any case good candidates for requiring a template, as this is the last chance to define a style for the embedded characters.

The **#PCDATA** keyword in the content model indicates this possibility. The 'Emph' element defined below is allowed to contain only text:

```
<!ELEMENT Emph (#PCDATA)>
```

```
<Emph>This is important text.</Emph>
```

When the definition includes other elements as well, further templates will probably be needed to cater for the text content of these other elements:

```
<!ELEMENT Emph (#PCDATA|Important)>
```

```
<Emph>This is <Important>not</Important> very important
text.</Emph>
```

This is **not** very important text.

In-line elements

In-line elements can be detected by studying the model for the parent element(s). If the parent element is allowed to contain text, as well as the given element, then it is almost certainly an in-line element. The Important element below is an in-line element:

```
<!ELEMENT Para (#PCDATA|Important)>
```

```
<!ELEMENT Important (#PCDATA)>
```

The case is strengthened further if the given element may itself directly contain text, as in the example above.

Some in-line elements may be present only for the purposes of allowing the enclosed text to be located (for searching purposes, for extraction and reuse, or for some other purpose), so it cannot automatically be assumed that the content needs to be styled in some way, though this is usually the case.

Block elements

Block elements are elements that can directly contain text but are not themselves used within other elements that can directly contain text. The Title and Para elements described above are good examples of this type. In the example above, they are used in Chapter and Book elements, which cannot contain text.

```
<!ELEMENT Chapter (Title, Para*)>
```

```
<!ELEMENT Para (#PCDATA|Important)>
```

Attributes

Attributes may play an important role in selecting elements by context. Attributes may also contain values that need to be presented, or used to determine what is presented. In some cases it is necessary to know whether an attribute is required to be present, or is optional, or to determine what possible values the attribute may hold. The ATTRIBUTE declaration defines one or more attributes for a given element. The element name follows the declaration keyword. In the example below, the

Para element has four attributes assigned to it, namely an 'ID' attribute, a 'Type' attribute, an 'Author' attribute and a 'Status' attribute:

```
<!ATTLIST Para   ID      #REQUIRED
                 Type    (Normal|Secret)  "Normal"
                 Author  #IMPLIED
                 Status  "draft">
```

If the attribute name is followed by the keyword #REQUIRED, then the element will always have this attribute present and it will always have a value. It is therefore not necessary to test for its presence in a template. However, if the attribute name is followed by the keyword #IMPLIED, then the attribute may be absent and it is appropriate to test for its existence.

```
<template name="Para[@Author]">...</template>
```

```
<template name="Para">
  <if test="@Author">...</if>
</template>
```

When a list of values is given between brackets, separated by vertical bar characters, this is the allowed list of values. The values 'Normal' and 'Secret' for the Type attribute above are typical. Again, these are case-sensitive.

Sometimes, a following default value is given, as in 'Normal' and 'draft' above, indicating that when a value is not present in the element tag, this value should be assumed. Depending on the parser used by the XSLT processor, the default may or may not be passed to the processor as an attribute value that is present. It is safer to test for its existence.

DTD construction features

Analysis of element and attribute declarations may be hindered if the way that DTDs use entities and marked sections is not understood.

Entities

Just as XML document authors may use general entities to aid construction of a document, DTD authors may use parameter entities to assist with the construction of a DTD. Whenever a set of attributes or a particular element model is needed in more than one place, the DTD author may use an entity to store the information in a single place, and an entity reference at each point where the information is relevant.

For example, if the Title and Para elements have the same attributes, the following may appear (the four attributes appearing in both elements):

```
<!ENTITY % standardAttributes  'ID         #REQUIRED
                  Type    (Normal|Secret) "Normal"
                  Author  CDATA           #IMPLIED
                  Status  CDATA           "draft"' >

<!ATTLIST Title  %standardAttributes; >

<!ATTLIST Para   %standardAttributes; >
```

A content model can be duplicated in the same way:

```
<!ENTITY % textBlock   '(#PCDATA|Emph)*' >

<!ELEMENT Title  %textBlock; >

<!ELEMENT Para   %textBlock; >
```

Marked sections

A DTD author may use marked sections to create multiple varieties of the DTD. Specifically, parts of a DTD can be switched off and switched on, perhaps to swap between alternative models. When creating a stylesheet that must cope with all the documents that comply with a given DTD, marked sections can often be ignored.

If the stylesheet does not need to cater for elements that are not part of the application of the DTD, then all statements within marked sections that contain the IGNORE keyword (or an entity reference that is set to 'IGNORE') can be safely ignored.

```
<![IGNORE[
  ...
]]>

<!ENTITY % ignoreThis 'IGNORE'>

<![%ignoreThis;[
  ...
]]>
```

22. XSLT DTD

Introduction

An XML DTD exists to describe the elements and attributes allowed in an XSLT stylesheet. XML editor software can use this DTD to provide a guided environment for the authoring of stylesheets. It can also be used by XML parsers to validate a stylesheet received from elsewhere. The DTD is listed in annex C of the standard. For those unfamiliar with XML DTDs, it is recommended that a book on XML be consulted before reading this chapter. Alternatively, Chapter 21 provides a brief overview of DTD markup.

The default DTD includes the prefix 'xsl:' on all XSLT element names, such as 'xsl:template'. This can be changed to whatever is appropriate (including no prefix at all if XSLT elements are assigned to the default namespace).

Top-level elements

The **Top Level** entity defines the elements that can occur within the Stylesheet (or Transform) element. It forces all Import elements to appear first (if any occur at all), and then allows any mixture of other allowed elements:

```
<!ENTITY % top-level "
    (xsl:import*,
      (xsl:include | xsl:strip-space |
       xsl:preserve-space | xsl:output |
       xsl:key | xsl:decimal-format |
       xsl:attribute-set | xsl:variable |
       xsl:param | xsl:template |
       xsl:namespace-alias
       %non-xsl-top-level;)*) ">
```

Note that the Template and Variable elements shown in this list are described in the next section. The other elements are described below.

A mechanism for adding non-XSLT elements to this group is provided by the entity reference at the end. But the **Non-XSL Top Level** entity is initially empty:

```
<!ENTITY % non-xsl-top-level " " >
```

The Top Level entity is referenced from two places, namely from the Stylesheet element definition and from the **Transform** element definition:

```
<!ELEMENT xsl:stylesheet %top-level;>

<!ELEMENT xsl:transform %top-level;>
```

For example:

```
<xsl:stylesheet ...>
  <xsl:import .../>
  <xsl:import .../>
  <xsl:template ...>...</xsl:template>
  <xsl:template ...>...</xsl:template>
</xsl:stylesheet>
```

There are also a number of attributes that these two elements can take, and these are grouped within the **Top Level Attributes** entity:

```
<!ENTITY % top-level-atts "
      extension-element-prefixes CDATA       #IMPLIED
      exclude-result-prefixes    CDATA       #IMPLIED
      id                         ID          #IMPLIED
      version                    NMTOKEN     #REQUIRED
      xmlns:xsl                  CDATA
            #FIXED "http://www.w3.org/1999/XSL/Transform"
      %space-att;

<!ATTLIST xsl:stylesheet %top-level-atts;>

<!ATTLIST xsl:transform %top-level-atts;>
```

Import element

The **Import** element is defined as follows:

```
<!ELEMENT xsl:import EMPTY >
```

The attributes are as follows:

```
<!ATTLIST xsl:import href  %URI;   #REQUIRED >
```

With the entity replaced, the true model is as follows:

```
<!ATTLIST xsl:import href  CDATA   #REQUIRED >
```

For example:

```
<xsl:import href="./library/styleTables.xsl" />
```

Include element

The **Include** element is defined as follows:

```
<!ELEMENT xsl:include EMPTY >
```

The attributes are as follows:

```
<!ATTLIST xsl:include href  %URI;   #REQUIRED >
```

With the entity replaced, the true model is as follows:

```
<!ATTLIST xsl:include href  CDATA   #REQUIRED >
```

For example:

```
<xsl:include href="commonStyles.xsl" />
```

Strip Space element

The **Strip Space** element is defined as follows:

```
<!ELEMENT xsl:strip-space EMPTY >
```

The attributes are as follows:

```
<!ATTLIST xsl:strip-space  elements  CDATA   #REQUIRED >
```

For example:

```
<xsl:strip-space elements="book title para" />
```

Preserve Space element

The **Preserve Space** element is defined as follows:

```
<!ELEMENT xsl:preserve-space EMPTY >
```

The attributes are as follows:

```
<!ATTLIST xsl:preserve-space
                    elements  CDATA   #REQUIRED >
```

For example:

```
<xsl:preserve-space elements="example preformatted" />
```

Output element

The **Output** element is defined as follows:

```
<!ELEMENT xsl:output EMPTY >
```

The attributes are as follows:

```
<!ATTLIST xsl:output
           method                        %qname;      #IMPLIED
           version                       NMTOKEN      #IMPLIED
           encoding                      CDATA        #IMPLIED
           omit-xml-declaration          (yes|no)     #IMPLIED
           standalone                    (yes|no)     #IMPLIED
           doctype-public                CDATA        #IMPLIED
           doctype-system                CDATA        #IMPLIED
           cdata-section-elements  %qnames;           #IMPLIED
           indent                        (yes|no)     #IMPLIED
           media-type                    CDATA        #IMPLIED  >
```

With all the embedded entity references replaced, the true model is as follows:

```
<!ATTLIST xsl:output
           method                        NMTOKEN      #IMPLIED
           version                       NMTOKEN      #IMPLIED
           encoding                      CDATA        #IMPLIED
           omit-xml-declaration          (yes|no)     #IMPLIED
           standalone                    (yes|no)     #IMPLIED
           doctype-public                CDATA        #IMPLIED
           doctype-system                CDATA        #IMPLIED
           cdata-section-elements  NMTOKENS           #IMPLIED
           indent                        (yes|no)     #IMPLIED
           media-type                    CDATA        #IMPLIED  >
```

For example:

```
<xsl:output method="HTML" version="4.0" />
```

Key element

The **Key** element is defined as follows:

```
<!ELEMENT xsl:key EMPTY >
```

The attributes are as follows:

```
<!ATTLIST xsl:key
           name          %qname;          #IMPLIED
           match         %pattern;        #IMPLIED
           use           %expr;           #IMPLIED  >
```

With all the embedded entity references replaced, the true model is as follows:

```
<!ATTLIST xsl:key
           name          NMTOKEN          #IMPLIED
           match         CDATA            #IMPLIED
           use           CDATA            #IMPLIED  >
```

For example:

```
<xsl:key name="nameKey" match="name" use="name/first"/>
```

Decimal Format element

The **Decimal Format** element is defined as follows:

```
<!ELEMENT xsl:decimal-format EMPTY >
```

The attributes are as follows:

```
<!ATTLIST xsl:decimal-format
          name                %qname;      #IMPLIED
          decimal-separator   %char;       "."
          grouping-separator  %char;       ","
          infinity            CDATA        "infinity"
          minus-sign          %char;       "-"
          NaN                 CDATA        "NaN"
          percent             %char;       "%"
          per-mille           %char;       "&#x2030;"
          zero-digit          %char;       "0"
          digit               %char;       "#"
          pattern-separator   %char;       ";" >
```

With all the embedded entity references replaced, the true model is as follow

```
<!ATTLIST xsl:decimal-format
          name                NMTOKEN      #IMPLIED
          decimal-separator   CDATA        "."
          grouping-separator  CDATA        ","
          infinity            CDATA        "infinity"
          minus-sign          CDATA        "-"
          NaN                 CDATA        "NaN"
          percent             CDATA        "%"
          per-mille           CDATA        "&#x2030;"
          zero-digit          CDATA        "0"
          digit               CDATA        "#"
          pattern-separator   CDATA        ";" >
```

Attribute Set element

The **Attribute Set** element is defined as follows:

```
<!ELEMENT xsl:attribute-set (xsl:attribute)* >
```

The attributes are as follows:

```
<!ATTLIST xsl:attribute-set
          name                %qname;       #REQUIRED
          use-attribute-sets  %qnames;      #IMPLIED >
```

With all the embedded entity references replaced, the true model is as follows

```
<!ATTLIST xsl:attribute-set
          name                NMTOKEN       #REQUIRED
          use-attribute-sets  NMTOKENS      #IMPLIED >
```

For example:

```
<xsl:attribute-set name="standardSet" >
  <xsl:attribute...></xsl:attribute>
  <xsl:attribute...></xsl:attribute>
  <xsl:attribute...></xsl:attribute>
</xsl:attribute-set>
```

Parameter element

The **Parameter** element is defined as follows:

```
<!ELEMENT xsl:param        %template; >
```

This expands to the following:

```
<!ELEMENT xsl:param ( #PCDATA |
          xsl:apply-templates | xsl:call-template |
          xsl:apply-imports | xsl:for-each |
          xsl:value-of | xsl:copy-of |
          xsl:number | xsl:choose | xslif |
          xsl:text | xsl:copy | xsl:variable |
          xsl:message | xsl:fallback |
          xsl:processing-instruction | xsl:comment |
          xsl:element | xsl:attribute )* >
```

The attributes are as follows:

```
<!ATTLIST xsl:attribute-set
          name                 %qname;      #REQUIRED
          select               %expr;       #IMPLIED >
```

With the embedded entity references replaced, the true model is as follows:

```
<!ATTLIST xsl:attribute-set
          name                 NMTOKEN      #REQUIRED
          select               CDATA        #IMPLIED >
```

Namespace Alias element

The **Namespace Alias** element is defined as follows:

```
<!ELEMENT xsl:namespace-alias EMPTY >
```

The attributes are as follows:

```
<!ATTLIST xsl:namespace-alias
          stylesheet-prefix    CDATA        #REQUIRED
          result-prefix        CDATA        #REQUIRED >
```

Templates

Template element

Templates are defined by the **Template** element.

```
<!ELEMENT xsl:template (#PCDATA %instructions;
                        %result-elements; | xsl:param)* >
```

The keyword '#PCDATA' refers to text that can be inserted directly into the Template element:

```
<xsl:template ...>REPLACE WITH THIS</xsl:template>
```

A template can also contain various instruction elements. Apart from the Param element, and the content of the Result Elements entity (described later), the **Instructions** entity is used to group the instruction elements, because they are also allowed in other locations (the For Each element and the Template entity):

```
<!ENTITY % instructions " %char-instructions; |
                          xsl:processing-instruction |
                          xsl:comment |
                          xsl:element |
                          xsl:attribute ">
```

This entity encompasses all XSLT instructions. However, most of the instructions allowed are further referenced from another entity, called **Character Instructions**:

```
<!ENTITY % char-instructions " |
             xsl:apply-templates | xsl:call-template |
             xsl:apply-imports | xsl:for-each |
             xsl:value-of | xsl:copy-of |
             xsl:number | xsl:choose | xsl:if |
             xsl:text | xsl:copy | xsl:variable |
             xsl:message | xsl:fallback ">
```

This is done because these instructions are also referenced from another entity. The **Char Template** entity also uses this entity, and is in turn referenced from the Processing Instruction, Comment and Attribute element definitions:

```
<!ENTITY % char-template "
             ( #PCDATA %char-instructions; ) ">

<!ELEMENT xsl:comment                (%char-template;)>

<!ELEMENT xsl:processing-instruction (%char-template;)>

<!ELEMENT xsl:attribute              (%char-template;)>
```

The reason for splitting the instructions in this way is to avoid the possibility of some elements containing other elements, such as comments containing either comments or processing instructions (which would be illegal). Character instructions are therefore instructions that can contain characters *and* further instructions.

Attributes

The XSLT attributes specified for the Template elements are as follows:

```
<!ATTLIST xsl:template
                match       %pattern;    #IMPLIED
                name        %qname;      #IMPLIED
                priority    %priority;   #IMPLIED
                mode        %qname;      #IMPLIED
                %space-att;>
```

With all the embedded entity references replaced, the true model is as follows:

```
<!ELEMENT xsl:template
                match       CDATA              #IMPLIED
                name        NMTOKEN            #IMPLIED
                priority    NMTOKEN            #IMPLIED
                mode        NMTOKEN            #IMPLIED
                xml:space   (default|preserve) #IMPLIED >
```

For example:

```
<xsl:template match="title" priority="2"
              mode="SpecialMode" >...</xsl:template>
```

Template instructions

A number of instructions may appear within a template, including comments, processing instructions, elements and attributes.

Template entity

The instructions allowed directly within a Template element are in some cases also allowed within the instructions themselves (with the exception of the Param element). For convenience, the Template entity is defined to group these elements:

```
<!ENTITY % template " (#PCDATA %instructions;
                %result-elements;)* " >
```

Elements that refer to this entity include the If, When, Otherwise, With Parameter, Variable, Parameter, Copy, Message and Fallback elements.

Comment element

A **Comment** element is defined as follows:

```
<!ELEMENT xsl:comment %char-template; >
```

With all entities replaced, the true model is as follows. The fact that all these elements can occur within a comment shows how the content of the comment does not have to be specified as a simple text string; its content can be determined using the full power of XSLT:

```
<!ELEMENT xsl:comment ( #PCDATA |
          xsl:apply-templates | xsl:call-template |
          xsl:apply-imports | xsl:for-each |
          xsl:value-of | xsl:copy-of |
          xsl:number | xsl:choose | xsl:if |
          xsl:text | xsl:copy | xsl:variable |
          xsl:message | xsl:fallback )* >
```

The attributes are as follows:

```
<!ATTLIST xsl:comment %space-att; >
```

With the entity replaced, the true model is as follows:

```
<!ATTLIST xsl:comment
          xml:space (default|preserve) #IMPLIED >
```

For example:

```
<xsl:comment xml:space="preserve">
This is a comment.
</xsl:comment>
```

Processing Instruction element

The **Processing Instruction** element is defined as follows:

```
<!ELEMENT xsl:processing-instruction %char-template; >
```

With all entities replaced, the true model is as follows. It is not clear why these elements are allowed to occur here, as they can have no purpose within a processing instruction:

```
<!ELEMENT xsl:processing-instruction ( #PCDATA |
          xsl:apply-templates | xsl:call-template |
          xsl:apply-imports | xsl:for-each |
          xsl:value-of | xsl:copy-of |
          xsl:number | xsl:choose | xslif |
          xsl:text | xsl:copy | xsl:variable |
          xsl:message | xsl:fallback )* >
```

The attributes are as follows:

```
<!ATTLIST xsl:processing-instruction
               name      %avt;    #REQUIRED
               %space-att; >
```

With all entities replaced, the true model is as follows:

```
<!ATTLIST xsl:processing-instruction
          name      CDATA                  #REQUIRED
          xml:space (default|preserve) #IMPLIED >
```

For example:

```
<xsl:processing-instruction name="ACME">
new_page
</xsl:processing-instruction>
```

Element element

The **Element** instruction is defined as follows:

```
<!ELEMENT xsl:element %template;>
```

With all entities replaced, the true model is as follows (with any output elements to be added). Note that an element can contain another element, which is necessary to build element hierarchies for output within a single template:

```
<!ELEMENT xsl:element ( #PCDATA |
          xsl:apply-templates | xsl:call-template |
          xsl:apply-imports | xsl:for-each |
          xsl:value-of | xsl:copy-of |
          xsl:number | xsl:choose | xslif |
          xsl:text | xsl:copy | xsl:variable |
          xsl:message | xsl:fallback |
          xsl:processing-instruction | xsl:comment |
          xsl:element | xsl:attribute )* >
```

The attributes are as follows:

```
<!ATTLIST xsl:element
          name                %avt;        #REQUIRED
          namespace           %avt;        #IMPLIED
          use-attribute-sets  %qnames;     #IMPLIED
          %space-att; >
```

With all entities replaced, the true model is as follows:

```
<!ATTLIST xsl:element
     name                CDATA              #REQUIRED
     namespace           CDATA              #IMPLIED
     use-attribute-sets  NMTOKENS           #IMPLIED
     xml:space           (default|preserve) #IMPLIED >
```

For example:

```
<xsl:element name="TITLE">
  A <xsl:element name="EMPH">Title</xsl:element>
</xsl:element>
```

Attribute element

An **Attribute** instruction is defined as follows:

```
<!ELEMENT xsl:attribute %char-template;>
```

With all entities replaced, the true model is as follows (with any output elements to be added). Note that an element can contain another element, which is necessary to build element hierarchies for output within a single template:

```
<!ELEMENT xsl:attribute ( #PCDATA |
         xsl:apply-templates | xsl:call-template |
         xsl:apply-imports | xsl:for-each |
         xsl:value-of | xsl:copy-of |
         xsl:number | xsl:choose | xsl:if |
         xsl:text | xsl:copy | xsl:variable |
         xsl:message | xsl:fallback )* >
```

The attributes are as follows:

```
<!ATTLIST xsl:attribute
         name                %avt;        #REQUIRED
         namespace           %avt;        #IMPLIED
         use-attribute-sets  %qnames;     #IMPLIED
         %space-att; >
```

With all entities replaced, the true model is as follows:

```
<!ATTLIST xsl:attribute
      name                CDATA                    #REQUIRED
      namespace           CDATA                    #IMPLIED
      use-attribute-sets  NMTOKENS                 #IMPLIED
      xml:space           (default|preserve) #IMPLIED >
```

For example:

```
<xsl:attribute name="author">J. Smith</xsl:attribute>
```

Apply Templates element

An **Apply Templates** instruction is defined as follows:

```
<!ELEMENT xsl:apply-templates (xsl:sort|xsl:with-param)*>
```

The attributes are as follows:

```
<!ATTLIST xsl:apply-templates
         select              %expr;       "node"
         mode                %qname;      #IMPLIED >
```

With all entities replaced, the true model is as follows:

```
<!ATTLIST xsl:apply-templates
         select              CDATA        "node"
         mode                NMTOKEN      #IMPLIED >
```

Call Template element

A **Call Template** instruction is defined as follows:

```
<!ELEMENT xsl:call-template (xsl:with-param)* >
```

The attributes are as follows:

```
<!ATTLIST xsl:call-template
         name                %qname;      #IMPLIED >
```

With the entity replaced, the true model is as follows:

```
<!ATTLIST xsl:call-template
             name                  NMTOKEN        #IMPLIED >
```

Apply Imports element

The **Apply Imports** instruction is defined as follows:

```
<!ELEMENT xsl:apply-imports EMPTY >
```

It has no attributes.

For example:

```
<xsl:apply-imports />
```

For Each element

A **For Each** instruction is defined as follows:

```
<!ELEMENT xsl:for-each (#PCDATA %instructions;
                        %result-elements; | xsl:sort )* >
```

With all entities replaced, the true model is as follows (with any output elements to be added). Note that an element can contain another element, which is necessary to build element hierarchies for output within a single template:

```
<!ELEMENT xsl:for-each ( #PCDATA |
         xsl:apply-templates | xsl:call-template |
         xsl:apply-imports | xsl:for-each |
         xsl:value-of | xsl:copy-of |
         xsl:number | xsl:choose | xsl:if |
         xsl:text | xsl:copy | xsl:variable |
         xsl:message | xsl:fallback |
         xsl:processing-instruction | xsl:comment |
         xsl:element | xsl:attribute | xsl:sort )* >
```

This model does not capture the precise requirement when the Sort element is used. If it occurs, it must precede all other elements and text.

The attributes are as follows:

```
<!ATTLIST xsl:for-each
             select                %expr;      #REQUIRED
             %space-att; >
```

With all entities replaced, the true model is as follows:

```
<!ATTLIST xsl:for-each
     select                CDATA               #REQUIRED
     xml:space             (default|preserve)  #IMPLIED >
```

For example:

```
<xsl:for-each select="item">
  <xsl:comment>There was an item here.</xsl:comment>
</xsl:for-each>
```

Value Of element

The **Value Of** instruction is defined as follows:

```
<!ELEMENT xsl:value-of EMPTY >
```

The attributes are as follows:

```
<!ATTLIST xsl:value-of
          select                     %expr;   #REQUIRED
          disable-output-escaping  (yes|no)  "no" >
```

With the entity replaced, the true model is as follows:

```
<!ATTLIST xsl:value-of
          select                     CDATA    #REQUIRED
          disable-output-escaping  (yes|no)  "no" >
```

For example:

```
<xsl:value-of select="@price" />
```

Copy Of element

A **Copy Of** instruction is defined as follows:

```
<!ELEMENT xsl:copy-of EMPTY >
```

The attributes are as follows:

```
<!ATTLIST xsl:copy-of   select    %expr;     #REQUIRED >
```

With the entity replaced, the true model is as follows:

```
<!ATTLIST xsl:copy-of   select    CDATA      #REQUIRED >
```

For example:

```
<xsl:copy-of select="table" />
```

Number element

The **Number** instruction is defined as follows:

```
<!ELEMENT xsl:number EMPTY >
```

The attributes are as follows:

```
<!ATTLIST xsl:number
          level      (single|miltiple|any)   "single"
          count      %pattern;               #IMPLIED
          from       %pattern;               #IMPLIED
          value      %expr;                  #IMPLIED
          format     %avt;                   "1"
          lang       %avt;                   #IMPLIED
          letter-value           %avt;       #IMPLIED
          grouping-separator %avt;           #IMPLIED
          grouping-size          %avt;       #IMPLIED >
```

With the entities replaced, the true model is as follows:

```
<!ATTLIST xsl:number
          level      (single|multiple|any)   "single"
          count      CDATA                   #IMPLIED
          from       CDATA                   #IMPLIED
          value      CDATA                   #IMPLIED
          format     CDATA                   "1"
          lang       CDATA                   #IMPLIED
          letter-value           CDATA       #IMPLIED
          grouping-separator CDATA           #IMPLIED
          grouping-size          CDATA       #IMPLIED >
```

For example:

```
<xsl:number level="multiple"
            count="chapter|section"
            from="part"
            format="1.a.i" />
```

Choose element

The **Choose** instruction is defined as follows:

```
<!ELEMENT xsl:choose (xsl:when+, xsl:otherwise?) >
```

The attributes are as follows:

```
<!ATTLIST xsl:choose %space-att; >
```

With all entities replaced, the true model is as follows:

```
<!ATTLIST xsl:choose
              xml:space (default|preserve)   #IMPLIED >
```

See below for a description of the content of this element.

If element

The **If** instruction is defined as follows:

```
<!ELEMENT xsl:if %template; >
```

With the entity replaced, the true model is as follows:

```
<!ELEMENT xsl:if ( #PCDATA |
          xsl:apply-templates | xsl:call-template |
          xsl:apply-imports | xsl:for-each |
          xsl:value-of | xsl:copy-of |
          xsl:number | xsl:choose | xsl:if |
          xsl:text | xsl:copy | xsl:variable |
          xsl:message | xsl:fallback |
          xsl:processing-instruction | xsl:comment |
          xsl:element | xsl:attribute )* >
```

The attributes are as follows:

```
<!ATTLIST xsl:if
          test            %expr;            #REQUIRED
          %space-att; >
```

With all entities replaced, the true model is as follows:

```
<!ATTLIST xsl:if
     test              CDATA              #REQUIRED
     xml:space         (default|preserve)  #IMPLIED >
```

For example:

```
<xsl:if test="@type='secret'">
  <xsl:message>Found secret paragraph</xsl:message>
</xsl:if>
```

Text element

The **Text** template instruction is defined as follows:

```
<!ELEMENT xsl:text (#PCDATA) >
```

The attributes are as follows:

```
<!ATTLIST xsl:text
          disable-output-escaping (yes|no) "no">
```

For example:

```
<xsl:text disable-output-escaping="yes">
create HTML &lt;P&gt; (paragraph) &lt;/P&gt;
</xsl:text>
```

Copy element

The **Copy** instruction is defined as follows:

```
<!ELEMENT xsl:copy %template; >
```

With the entity replaced, the true model is as follows:

```
<!ELEMENT xsl:copy ( #PCDATA |
         xsl:apply-templates | xsl:call-template |
         xsl:apply-imports | xsl:for-each |
         xsl:value-of | xsl:copy-of |
         xsl:number | xsl:choose | xsl:if |
         xsl:text | xsl:copy | xsl:variable |
         xsl:message | xsl:fallback |
         xsl:processing-instruction | xsl:comment |
         xsl:element | xsl:attribute )* >
```

The attributes are as follows:

```
<!ATTLIST xsl:copy
          use-attribute-sets     %qnames;    #REQUIRED
          %space-att; >
```

With all entities replaced, the true model is as follows:

```
<!ATTLIST xsl:copy
     use-attribute-sets NMTOKENS          #REQUIRED
     xml:space          (default|preserve) #IMPLIED >
```

For example:

```
<xsl:copy>
  <xsl:message>Copied source element -
  but no attributes</xsl:message>
</xsl:copy>
```

Variable element

The **Variable** instruction is defined as follows:

```
<!ELEMENT xsl:variable %template; >
```

With the entity replaced, the true model is as follows:

```
<!ELEMENT xsl:variable ( #PCDATA |
         xsl:apply-templates | xsl:call-template |
         xsl:apply-imports | xsl:for-each |
         xsl:value-of | xsl:copy-of |
         xsl:number | xsl:choose | xsl:if |
         xsl:text | xsl:copy | xsl:variable |
         xsl:message | xsl:fallback |
         xsl:processing-instruction | xsl:comment |
         xsl:element | xsl:attribute )* >
```

The attributes are as follows:

```
<!ATTLIST xsl:variable
          name      %qname;    #REQUIRED
          select    %expr;     #IMPLIED >
```

With all entities replaced, the true model is as follows:

```
<!ATTLIST xsl:variable
                name        NMTOKEN      #REQUIRED
                select      CDATA        #IMPLIED >
```

For example:

```
<xsl:variable name="Copyright">
  <xsl:text>(c) ACME Productions</xsl:text>
</xsl:variable>

<xsl:variable name="BookTitle" select="/book/title" />
```

Message element

The **Message** instruction is defined as follows:

```
<!ELEMENT xsl:message %template; >
```

With the entity replaced, the true model is as follows:

```
<!ELEMENT xsl:message ( #PCDATA |
         xsl:apply-templates | xsl:call-template |
         xsl:apply-imports | xsl:for-each |
         xsl:value-of | xsl:copy-of |
         xsl:number | xsl:choose | xsl:if |
         xsl:text | xsl:copy | xsl:variable |
         xsl:message | xsl:fallback |
         xsl:processing-instruction | xsl:comment |
         xsl:element | xsl:attribute )* >
```

The attributes are as follows:

```
<!ATTLIST xsl:message
                terminate        (yes|no)        "no"
                %space-att; >
```

With the entity replaced, the true model is as follows:

```
<!ATTLIST xsl:message
    terminate           (yes|no)             "no"
    xml:space           (default|preserve)   #IMPLIED >
```

For example:

```
<xsl:message>Error in processing</xsl:message>
```

Fallback element

The **Fallback** instruction is defined as follows:

```
<!ELEMENT xsl:fallback %template; >
```

With the entity replaced, the true model is as follows:

```
<!ELEMENT xsl:fallback ( #PCDATA |
          xsl:apply-templates | xsl:call-template |
          xsl:apply-imports | xsl:for-each |
          xsl:value-of | xsl:copy-of |
          xsl:number | xsl:choose | xsl:if |
          xsl:text | xsl:copy | xsl:variable |
          xsl:message | xsl:fallback |
          xsl:processing-instruction | xsl:comment |
          xsl:element | xsl:attribute )* >
```

The attributes are as follows:

```
<!ATTLIST xsl:fallback          %space-att; >
```

With the entity replaced, the true model is as follows:

```
<!ATTLIST xsl:fallback
     xml:space            (default|preserve)    #IMPLIED >
```

Instruction constructs

Some of the instructions described above have a very specific internal structure, including references to elements not described above.

Apply Templates element

The **Apply Templates** element has the following content model:

```
<!ELEMENT xsl:apply-templates
                         (xsl:sort|xsl:with-param)*>
```

Note that the With Parameter element is discussed later (see *Call template*).

The **Sort** element is defined as follows:

```
<!ELEMENT xsl:sort EMPTY >
```

The attributes are as follows:

```
<!ATTLIST xsl:sort
          select       %expr;            "no"
          lang         %avt;             #IMPLIED
          data-type    %avt;             "text"
          order        %avt;             "ascending"
          case-order   %avt;             #IMPLIED >
```

With all entities replaced, the true model is as follows:

```
<!ATTLIST xsl:sort
            select      CDATA           "no"
            lang        CDATA           #IMPLIED
            data-type   CDATA           "text"
            order       CDATA           "ascending"
            case-order  CDATA           #IMPLIED >
```

For example:

```
<xsl:apply-templates>
   <xsl:sort select="firstname"/>
</xsl:apply-templates>
```

Call Template element

The **Call Template** element has the following content model:

```
<!ELEMENT xsl:call-template (xsl:with-param)* >
```

The **With Parameter** element has the following definition:

```
<!ELEMENT xsl:with-param %template; >
```

The expanded model for this element is as follows:

```
<!ELEMENT xsl:with-param ( #PCDATA |
            xsl:apply-templates | xsl:call-template |
            xsl:apply-imports | xsl:for-each |
            xsl:value-of | xsl:copy-of |
            xsl:number | xsl:choose | xsl:if |
            xsl:text | xsl:copy | xsl:variable |
            xsl:message | xsl:fallback |
            xsl:processing-instruction | xsl:comment |
            xsl:element | xsl:attribute )* >
```

The attributes are as follows:

```
<!ATTLIST xsl:with-param
            name    %qname;     #REQUIRED
            select  %expr;      #IMPLIED >
```

With all entities replaced, the true model is as follows:

```
<!ATTLIST xsl:with-param
            name    NMTOKEN     #REQUIRED
            select  CDATA       #IMPLIED >
```

Choose element

The **Choose** element has the following content model:

```
<!ELEMENT xsl:choose (xsl:when+, xsl:otherwise?) >
```

The When element must occur at least once, and may repeat any number of times. It is defined as follows:

```
<!ELEMENT xsl:when %template; >
```

The expanded model for this element is as follows:

```
<!ELEMENT xsl:when ( #PCDATA |
        xsl:apply-templates | xsl:call-template |
        xsl:apply-imports | xsl:for-each |
        xsl:value-of | xsl:copy-of |
        xsl:number | xsl:choose | xsl:if |
        xsl:text | xsl:copy | xsl:variable |
        xsl:message | xsl:fallback |
        xsl:processing-instruction | xsl:comment |
        xsl:element | xsl:attribute )* >
```

The attributes are as follows:

```
<!ATTLIST xsl:when
        test            %expr;                  #REQUIRED
        %space-att; >
```

With the entity replaced, the true model is as follows:

```
<!ATTLIST xsl:when
        test            CDATA                   #REQUIRED
        xml:space       (default|preserve)      #IMPLIED >
```

The **Otherwise** element is optional, but if present must occur at the end in the following format:

```
<!ELEMENT xsl:otherwise %template; >
```

The expanded model for this element is as follows:

```
<!ELEMENT xsl:otherwise ( #PCDATA |
        xsl:apply-templates | xsl:call-template |
        xsl:apply-imports | xsl:for-each |
        xsl:value-of | xsl:copy-of |
        xsl:number | xsl:choose | xsl:if |
        xsl:text | xsl:copy | xsl:variable |
        xsl:message | xsl:fallback |
        xsl:processing-instruction | xsl:comment |
        xsl:element | xsl:attribute )* >
```

The attributes are as follows:

```
<!ATTLIST xsl:otherwise    %space-att; >
```

With the entity replaced, the true model is as follows:

```
<!ATTLIST xsl:otherwise
        xml:space       (default|preserve)      #IMPLIED >
```

For example:

```
<xsl:choose>
  <xsl:when test="@colour='red'">...</xsl:when>
  <xsl:when test="@colour='green'">...</xsl:when>
  <xsl:when test="@colour='blue'">...</xsl:when>
  <xsl:otherwise>...</xsl:otherwise>
</xsl:choose>
```

Result elements

A template may also contain result elements, such as HTML or XSL FO elements. Because the nature of these elements is potentially infinite, it was not possible for the XSLT DTD creators to include them directly. Instead, a mechanism to make them easy to include in variants of the XSLT DTD has been included.

The **Result Elements** entity is used to name output elements to be added to the XSLT elements. The value of this entity depends on the result elements needed. This could be the complete set of HTML elements, the FO elements from the XSL specification, or some other set of elements:

```
<!ENTITY % result-elements "...">

<!ENTITY % result-elements "html:P | html:H1 |
                            html:H2 | ..." >
```

As already shown above, this entity is referenced from the Template element definition. It is also referenced from the For Each element definition, and from the Template entity:

```
<!ELEMENT xsl:template  (...%result-elements;)*>

<!ELEMENT xsl:for-each  (...%result-elements;...)*>

<!ENTITY % template  "(...%result-elements;)*">
```

However, it is not sufficient to enter the element names in this entity. It is also necessary to add declarations for the elements in the result elements DTD. However, the original definitions should not be used. Instead, declarations that allow XSLT elements to be mixed in with these elements are needed. Reference to the Template entity is sufficient, as this entity in turn refers to the XSLT instruction elements as well as all the result elements.

```
<!ENTITY % template " (#PCDATA %instructions;
                  %result-elements;)* " >
```

For example, if adding the HTML paragraph element, as shown above, it is necessary to add the following declaration as well:

```
<!ELEMENT html:P (%template;) >
```

Note, however, that this approach removes any restrictions on the use of result elements in relation to each other that will typically be included in the original DTD.

In addition, at least four attributes need to be added to an element. This is in addition to any attributes the element normally has. These are the **Use Attribute Sets**, **Extension Element Prefixes**, **Exclude Result Prefixes** and **Version** attributes:

```
<!ATTLIST html:P  ...
        xsl:extension-element-prefixes CDATA    #IMPLIED
        xsl:exclude-result-prefixes    CDATA    #IMPLIED
        xsl:use-attribute-sets         %qnames; #IMPLIED
        xsl:version                    NMTOKEN  #IMPLIED>
```

To assist with adding these attributes to each result element, an entity called **Result Element Attributes** is included in the DTD:

```
<!ENTITY % result-element-atts   "
        xsl:extension-element-prefixes CDATA    #IMPLIED
        xsl:exclude-result-prefixes    CDATA    #IMPLIED
        xsl:use-attribute-sets         %qnames; #IMPLIED
        xsl:version                    NMTOKEN  #IMPLIED ">

<!ATTLIST html:P  ...
        %result-element-atts;>

<!ATTLIST html:H1  ...
        %result-element-atts;>

<!ATTLIST html:H2  ...
        %result-element-atts;>
```

This entity can be empty, in the case where no output elements are needed, and the Element element is used to declare output elements:

```
<!ENTITY % result-elements " ">
```

23. XSLT extensions

Although this book focuses on the inherent capabilities of XSLT version 1.0, this standard includes some features for handling enhancements to the XSLT standard itself, as well as product-specific enhancements that tool vendors may add, with the purpose of preventing errors when a stylesheet with such enhancements is processed using an XSLT processor developed to support an earlier version of the standard, or developed by another vendor. But it is the responsibility of the stylesheet author to be aware of these features and to implement the safeguards described in this chapter.

Extension functions

A vendor may add more functions to the expression language. As these would not be XSLT or XPath functions, they must be defined using a different namespace. For example, a vendor may add a function that is able to reverse the characters in a text string, called reverse():

```
<reverse>abcdefghijklmnopqrstuvwxyz</reverse>

<xsl:template match="reverse">
  <P><xsl:value-of select="acme:reverse(.)"/></P>
</xsl:template>

  <P>zyxwvutsrqponmlkjihgfedcba</P>
```

New functions must have a prefix, or they will be assumed to be extensions to those defined by XPath or XSLT (in a later version of these standards).

While an XSLT processor that does not understand the new function must raise an error if an attempt is made to use it, the processor will *not* raise the error merely because it is present in the stylesheet. This allows the stylesheet to contain such functions, but also to include a mechanism to avoid them when they will not be understood. The **function-available()** function returns 'false' if the function name passed to it is not supported. It can be used in If and Choose elements to avoid calling unknown functions, and to take some other 'fallback' action instead:

```
<xsl:template match="reverse">
  <P>
    <xsl:if test="function-available(acme:reverse)">
      <xsl:value-of select="acme:reverse(.)"/>
    </xsl:if>
    <xsl:if test="not(function-available(acme:reverse))">
      <xsl:value-of select="."/> (NORMALLY REVERSED)
    </xsl:if>
  </P>
</xsl:template>
```

When the function returns 'false', the following would be output:

```
<P>abcdefghijklmnopqrstuvwxyz (NORMALLY REVERSED)</P>
```

Extension elements

A vendor may add some new instruction elements to those allowed within a template. As these would not be XSLT instructions, they must be defined using a different namespace. For example, a vendor may add an instruction that is able to reverse the characters in a text string, called Reverse:

```
<reverse>abcdefghijklmnopqrstuvwxyz</reverse>
```

```
<xsl:template match="reverse">
  <P><acme:reverse select="."/></P>
</xsl:template>
```

```
<P>zyxwvutsrqponmlkjihgfedcba</P>
```

Note that this mechanism only applies within templates. Top-level elements that are not recognized are simply ignored (see below).

Recognizing extension elements

An XSLT processor needs to know which elements are extension elements so that it will not treat these elements as simple output elements. All XSLT processors can be informed that an element is an extension element, rather than an output element, by registering its namespace as an extension namespace. The **Extension Element Prefixes** attribute may be used on the Stylesheet element, and it holds a space-separated list of namespace prefixes used for extension elements:

```
<xsl:stylesheet ...
                  extension-element-prefixes="acme" >
  ...
  <xsl:template match="reverse">
    <P><acme:reverse select="."/></P>
  </xsl:template>
  ...
</xsl:stylesheet>
```

Note that the keyword '#default' can be entered in this attribute if the extension elements use the default namespace.

Testing for functionality

When an XSLT processor does not support a particular extension element (developed by another vendor), it can detect and avoid it. Unknown instructions can be avoided by first asking the processor if it understands the instruction, then stepping over the instruction if the processor does not understand it. The function **element-available**() returns 'true' if the element name passed to it is supported by the XSLT processor. This function can be used in the If and Choose elements:

```
<P>
  <xsl:if test="element-available('acme:reverse')" >
    <acme:reverse select="." />
  </xsl:if>
  <xsl:if test="not(element-available('acme:reverse'))" >
    <apply-templates/> (NORMALLY REVERSED)
  </xsl:if>
</P>
```

When the function returns 'false', the following would be output:

```
<P>abcdefghijklmnopqrstuvwxyz (NORMALLY REVERSED)</P>
```

Fallback processing

An alternative mechanism embeds 'fallback' instructions within the new instruction itself. If the processor does not understand the instruction, it must implement the instructions embedded within the **Fallback** elements. Multiple Fallback elements are normally only needed when extension instructions are also embedded within the main instruction. Thus:

```
<acme:reverse select=".">
  <xsl:fallback><apply-templates/></xsl:fallback>
  <xsl:fallback>(NORMALLY REVERSED)</xsl:fallback>
</acme:reverse>
```

If the processor recognizes the extended instruction, it ignores the Fallback elements embedded within it.

Forward compatibility

XSLT processors developed to support XSLT version 1.0 should be able to cope with stylesheets developed to conform to a later version of this standard. When the stylesheet contains a **Version** attribute with a value other than '1.0', the processor should adopt a '**forwards-compatible**' mode to help it cope with unexpected features.

When the processor has adopted this mode, it is given permission to ignore any top-level elements that it does not recognize:

```
<xsl:stylesheet version="1.3">
  <xsl:import.../>
  ...
  <xsl:new-feature /> <!-- 1.0 processors IGNORE -->
  ...
  <xsl:template>...</xsl:template>
  ...
</xsl:stylesheet>
```

Also, any unexpected elements appearing within a template do not cause an error. It is possible to step over such elements by testing the version of XSLT that the processor understands. The **system-property()** function can be used to request the supported version number by passing the parameter value '**xsl:version**' to it (as described in Chapter 20). The return value can then be compared with the version that supports the feature:

```
<xsl:template>
  <xsl:if test="system-property('xsl:version') >= 1.2">
    <xsl:new-template-feature />
  </xsl:if>
  ...
</xsl:template>
```

Alternatively, the 'fallback' feature described above can be used:

```
<xsl:template>
  <xsl:new-template-feature>
    <xsl:fallback>...</xsl:fallback>
  </xsl:new-template-feature>
  ...
</xsl:template>
```

Finally, unknown attributes are simply ignored.

Index

NOTES: This index identifies terms introduced in the main text (where they are displayed in bold). All entries are shown in the present tense, singular form (except where the term is a syntactic token name or keyword, or is always used in another form). Entries with an initial capital letter, such as 'Text,' are DTD-specific element or attribute names. HTML element and attribute names have the suffix '(HTML)' to distinguish them from XSLT and XSL element and attribute names. For example, there is an entry for 'Text' and another entry for 'Text (HTML)'.

The Making of
Modern British Politics
1867–1939

MARTIN PUGH

Basil Blackwell · Oxford

First published 1982
Reprinted 1983
Basil Blackwell Publisher Limited
108 Cowley Road, Oxford OX4 1JF, England

British Library Cataloguing in Publication Data
Pugh, Martin
The making of modern British politics 1867—1939.
1. Great Britain — Politics and government — 1837—1901
2. Great Britain — Politics and government — 1901—1936
I. Title
320.9'41'08   JN216

ISBN 0—631—12919—7
ISBN 0—631—12985—5 Pbk

Typesetting by Cambrian Typesetters
Farnborough, Hants.
Printed in Great Britain by
The Pitman Press, Bath

Contents

Preface

This book is designed to meet a need among students and teachers in the field of modern British history. Few areas of historical study can have generated as much scholarly work over the last twenty years, and the result has been a barrage of books and articles directed at the academic territory between the 1860s and the Second World War. Not surprisingly undergraduate and 'A level' students, who are often asked to cope with quite sophisticated questions of interpretation these days, frequently wear a slightly shell-shocked expression beneath the torrent of material. While the quantity of original, specialist work is difficult to handle, the traditional textbooks seldom take the student beyond a basic chronological account of the rise and fall of ministries. It is depressing to find how rarely even recently published general works reflect the central contributions made in books like Peter Clarke's *Lancashire and the New Liberalism* (1971) or John Vincent's *The Formation of the British Liberal Party 1857–68*, published as long ago as 1966, which have indisputably changed our view of the period. I hope that this volume will, if nothing else, help students to get to terms with some of the important and interesting questions raised by the study of British political history between 1867 and 1939, though I am conscious that it is a rash undertaking on my part. Readers should be warned that while I provide a guide to alternative views, especially in the bibliographies, I have made no attempt to act as a neutral referee on matters of controversy. Students who believe that an academic approach means refusing to commit oneself to anything definite ('safety first') might remember Lloyd George on Sir John Simon: 'The Rt. Hon. Gentleman has spent so long sitting on the fence that the iron has entered his soul.'

Although the treatment in this volume has been influenced strongly by the published and unpublished work of other historians, I have also tried to indicate areas where our knowledge is still relatively thin. My own research for the book has been deliberately directed upon areas in which it seemed likely to do most good. For example, while the archives of the Labour Party are, in general, rather thoroughly worked, certain parts, like the material relating to municipal elections, appear to be less used, although most relevant to the interpretation of Edwardian politics; I have also made considerable use of the Ramsay MacDonald papers which were unavailable for a considerable period. The popular basis of Conservative support remains a relatively un-trodden field, despite some stimulating contributions in recent years, and here I have given more than usual prominence to the evidence of Primrose League activity.

Naturally in preparing a volume of this kind I have been unusually grateful for the earlier efforts of other scholars – some indication of which is given in the bibliographies and notes. But I have a particular debt to those who read and commented on the book at various stages. Henry Pelling very kindly brought his critical gaze to bear on the whole manuscript with, I hope he would agree, beneficial results. I have also been greatly helped by David French who scrutinized chapters 8, 9 and 10; by Bill Purdue on chapters 5, 6 and 7; and by Maureen Calcott on chapters 11, 12 and 13. All of them would rightly dissent from much of what has been written here, and in thanking them I do not shirk my responsibility for the flaws of judgement and errors of fact which may persist.

Several academics have generously given me permission to make use of material published in tabular form in their own work: Hugh Berrington in 'Partisanship and Dissidence in the Nineteenth Century House of Commons', *Parliamentary Affairs*, 21 (1967–68); J. P. Cornford in his essay 'Parliamentary Foundations of the Hotel Cecil', Robert Robson (ed.), *Ideas and Institutions of Victorian Britain* (Bell, 1967); Michael Kinnear in *The British Voter: an Atlas and Survey since 1885* (Batsford, 1968); and Alan J. Lee in *The Origins of the Popular Press 1855–1914* (Croom Helm, 1976). I am also very grateful to Peter Liddle for allowing me access to his 1914–18 Personal Experience Archives presently held at Sunderland Polytechnic; and to Mr Leslie Gould of Leeds and the Librarian of the Leeds Library who made material available to me. I have been assisted in various other ways. The Research Fund of Newcastle University made a grant towards the costs of the research. In the early stages Robert Baldock gave valuable support and encouragement; and in the later stages Janice Cummin typed a number of the chapters expertly and rapidly. I would like to express my thanks to all those friends and relations who provided me with accommodation, without which it would be difficult to cover the archival resources of the country from Newcastle; and finally to my wife who was consistently supportive and tolerant of the moodiness of a pregnant author.

I am grateful to the proprietors of *Punch* for permission to reproduce the cartoons on pages 34, 115, 145, 163, 198, 237.

Part One 1867–1900

Chapter 1

Party and Participation
1867-1900

We have only to imagine, if we can, a Pitt or a
Castlereagh stumping the provinces, and taking
into his confidence, not merely a handful of electors, but any crowd he could collect in any part of
this island.
The Times, *26 December 1879, on the first Midlothian campaign*

Between the 1860s and the turn of the century, British politics, in
the constituency, party and parliamentary spheres, took on
recognizably modern characteristics. Although the transition
necessarily proved a lengthy and patchy process, the 1880s stand
out as the key decade of change. Indeed the general election of
1880 may, with some justification, be regarded as the first modern
election. It was a *general* election in that five-sixths of the constituencies were actually contested, and in that it produced a
national campaign as distinct from the sporadic, localized contests
typical of mid-Victorian elections. Voters were offered an unusually
clear-cut choice largely through the initiative of the *de facto* leader
of the opposition W.E. Gladstone who promised to reverse the
imperial and foreign policy of Disraeli if he was returned with a
majority. In contemporary eyes the novelty of the Midlothian
campaign, that 'ten days' waterspout dealing with all human
affairs' as *The Times* put it, consisted in a prospective Prime
Minister taking voters so seriously as to deliver to them lengthy
speeches on weighty subjects more properly addressed to the
Houses of Parliament. The year 1880 brought to a climax that
polarization of loyalties between the two party leaders which,
since Gladstone's championing of franchise reform in 1866, had
begun to transcend the local and personal patterns of allegiance;
and which imprinted upon British politics for decades thereafter

MR. GLADSTONE ATTACKING THE FRONT BENCH.

Harry Furniss, Pen and Pencil in Parliament *(1897).*

two stereotyped party positions in both foreign and domestic affairs.

Moreover, the 1880 election physically resembled a modern one. Hitherto the leaders had usually avoided speaking in other men's constituencies after nominations lest they be seen to interfere in a community's private affair; now they found ever more excuses to permit the electorate the novelty of oratory from outside. Gladstone pioneered the nearest approach to a whistle-stop tour as he journeyed up to Edinburgh descending from his train at Grantham, York and Newcastle to deliver short harangues, somewhat to the annoyance of the ordinary passengers, thence proceeding to an intensive programme of two daily speeches for a fortnight on his second campaign in Midlothian. Though many of the thousands who attended his progress around the constituency could not hear his speeches, Gladstone's every word at West

Calder or Dalkeith was caught up by eager journalists to be reprinted in the dense black columns of the provincial and national press, to be bandied about by the more obscure participants up and down the country. 'This duty of making political speeches,' Lord Salisbury complained to Queen Victoria in 1887, 'is an aggravation of the labours of your Majesty's servants which we owe entirely to Mr Gladstone.' One should not allow Salisbury's weary cynicism to obscure his own successful adaptation to a variety of political practices, including regular speech-making, of which he disapproved. It would be rash to conclude that the mass of voters felt moved to return Gladstone to power in 1880 because they shared the same concern with the affairs of Afghanistan and the Balkans. The impact of the controversy that had begun in 1876 over the Bulgarian atrocities and culminated in the Midlothian campaigns fell more forcefully upon the partisan activists and local backers of Liberalism, that vital intermediate group whose voluntary efforts and high morale were increasingly indispensable in harnessing the voters at large; but these party workers comprised a characteristic and central element in the political transition of late Victorian Britain.

Voting and Non-Voting

Victorians did not claim that their system was democratic, a term that smacked of continental abstraction and implied an excess of equality characteristic of American society; rather, it produced effective government, it guaranteed 'liberty', and it was representative. What it represented directly was those considered fit by reason of their independence, their material stake in society, their education and political knowledge to exercise the parliamentary franchise with beneficial effects upon political life. Men wholly absorbed in the daily struggle for existence were unlikely to develop the capacity for political judgement, still less the opportunity to exercise it freely. Conscious of the defects of even the existing electorate, radicals of the 1860s accepted that drastic and ill-considered extensions of the franchise would only open further opportunities for corruption; the business of a reformer was to find a form of words in law which in practice would define those who were beyond corrupting pressures. Moreover, the late Victorian conception of corruption extended beyond the traditional individual type to the more formal, institutional forms practised in the United States in which politicians offered groups of voters specific pledges of material gain in return for support. Political integrity required that a man who depended upon the state for his maintenance should be ineligible to vote for the government; hence in Britain men in receipt of relief from the Poor Law Guardians remained disqualified until 1918.

In fact an election was not primarily about the individual's rights, but about the representation of his community, from which it followed that the interests of non-electors could be represented quite adequately by the leaders of their community. Thus a land-owner spoke for his labourers politically as an extension of his other duties towards them; similarly the interests of the largest single group of non-voters, women, were upheld by their fathers and husbands. In a family, as in any other community, there was no special merit in every individual member voting in person, for 'mere numbers' provided no guarantee of efficiency or morality. Women were generally perceived by male politicians to be deficient in the intellectual and temperamental qualities appropriate for politics, to lack the independence, inclination and even the energy which was devoted instead to the vital task of child-birth.[1] 'Woman' in short was equated with married woman despite the fact that nearly a quarter of adult females were actually spinsters or widows in the 1860s, many of whom paid local rates and managed property; even wives were permitted, under the Married Women's Property Acts 1870, 1874 and 1882, to retain their property instead of surrendering it to their husbands on marriage. Faced with the fact that some women were 'fit', even on men's terms, for the franchise, politicians allowed female partici-pation, in discreet numbers, in municipal elections, on school boards and on boards of guardians. However, despite the growing similarity between local and national government in the late nine-teenth century, most politicians stuck to the view that the great parliamentary issues of Empire, war and national security ought not to be exposed to the vacillating and emotional judgements of women. Moreover, once a majority of men had obtained enfranchisement after 1884, the impetus behind Victorian reform waned noticeably; the remaining male non-voters stood pat upon their superior status as *men*, and eschewed making common cause with women.

The male non-voter himself was by no means uninvolved in the political process. Particularly in smaller boroughs elections were characterized by popular participation if only in the form of processions, rioting and intimidation. This attendant disorder obliged the authorities to extend the poll over two to three weeks (as in modern India) in order to allow the police to transfer scarce resources from one group of constituencies to another; not until 1918 did they feel confident enough to risk one-day polling. However, popular involvement also took on a political tone. Since the days of the Chartists non-electors had made a practice in some towns of gathering at the hustings when nominations were due, proceeding thence to elect, on a show of hands, an 'MP' as an alternative to the formal poll. Also, disfranchised radical working men in such towns as Rochdale, Stockport, Warrington, Stoke and Morpeth took to boycotting the shops and pubs of their political opponents, thereby playing a more independent role than some enfranchised workers who were more subject to employers' pressure at elections.[2] In addition the disfranchised invariably shared with the electors themselves a vicarious sense of participation in elections by aligning themselves with one candidate or party; millions of people wore ribbons and rosettes in party colours, or sported primroses on Disraeli's birthday. For a generation not yet in thrall to the personalities of football, films or popular music, political leaders and their contests provided a great entertainment or spectacle, a cause to belong to, and a link with the lives of the great.

Although the debate over franchise was conducted on the high ground of principle, the translation of 'fitness' into law proved to be severely limited by sheer ignorance of the numbers involved, by the exigencies of parliamentary management, and by assumptions about the help or hindrance newly enfranchised groups would lend to the legislating party. Disraeli's inability to patch together a temporary majority in the Commons in 1867 except by offering concessions to radical Liberal backbenchers produced a dramatic increase in the borough electorate, extending the suffrage to householders and to occupiers and lodgers paying an annual rent of £10, while leaving the county electorate but slightly modified. This lopsided, typically English pattern proved indefensible, and led to the rationalization of 1884 when the new borough franchises were extended by Gladstone to counties. The numerical effect of these changes provided the underlying dynamic to late Victorian political evolution (see table 1.1).

Under this system the proportion of adult males entitled to vote fluctuated usually between 63 and 66 per cent; the more imminent a general election the greater incentive for the parties to ensure that their supporters were on the register. However, the figures overstate the true proportion since half a million men were registered more than once; therefore, no more than six out of

TABLE 1.1. *Parliamentary electors in the United Kingdom*

1866	1,364,000
1869	2,445,000
1883	3,152,000
1885	5,708,000
1911	7,904,000

every ten men, at most, were parliamentary voters before 1914. Industrial towns, where enfranchisement had traditionally been much lower than that in medieval boroughs and counties, experienced particularly dramatic rises: in Blackburn 1,800 voters became 9,700 in 1868; Newcastle's 6,600 voters had increased to 21,400 by 1872. However, considerable unevenness persisted until 1914 in that residential towns (Oxford 75 per cent) and counties (Cornwall 80 per cent) enjoyed substantially higher enfranchisement than industrial boroughs (Oldham 63 per cent), the extremes being characteristic of large conurbations (Glasgow 52 per cent, Bethnal Green 42 per cent). This pattern was in fact a built-in consequence of the system adopted in 1884. For although the third Reform Act rationalized the existing pattern it nonetheless bequeathed a complex structure of seven distinct types of qualification (see table 1.2).

TABLE 1.2. *Parliamentary franchises 1885–1918*

		Proportion of the 1911 electorate (%)
Household	franchise for inhabitant occupiers, whether owners or tenants, of a separate dwelling house	
Occupation	franchise for those who occupied as owners or tenants, any land or tenement of £10 annual value	84.3
Lodger	franchise for those who rented rooms valued unfurnished at £10 p.a.	4.6
Property	franchise for 40s freeholders and other freeholders, copyholders and leaseholders (almost wholly confined to counties)	8.4

TABLE 1.2 *continued*

		Proportion of the 1911 electorate (%)
Service	franchise for inhabitant occupiers of a separate dwelling house through their employment or office, not as owner or tenant	1.8
University	franchise for graduates	0.6
Freemen's	franchise for freemen by birth or apprenticeship in boroughs where the qualification had existed before 1832	0.3

Source: Parl. Papers 1911, LXII, pp. 679–700.

Those who were expressly excluded by the electoral law fell into three groups; first, women who had been eliminated since the 1832 Act which adopted 'male persons' for the first time; secondly, such categories of men as lunatics, aliens, criminals, peers, receivers of poor relief, those guilty of corrupt practices in elections, and some officials involved in elections; thirdly, men such as sons living in their parents' home and servants residing with their employers who were effectively excluded as they could not claim to be householders. In this way some 1.5 million men (by 1914) found themselves excluded. However, this still left a much greater number — 3.75 million by 1914[3] — who failed to make good their claim (usually as householders or lodgers) simply because of the complicated process of registration. To introduce his name on to the register a potential householder or lodger had to demonstrate continuous residence for 12 months at a given address from July of one year to June of the next. On this basis his name could be entered on the preliminary list in April or May, and if it survived the scrutiny in September–October, would appear on the new parliamentary register in December, which became operative in January of the next year — an 18-month cycle. If the voter moved outside his borough or county constituency, or if his move involved a change of qualification, say from householder to lodger, he had not maintained continuity of residence for 12 months and forfeited his place. Since in working-class boroughs in the large conurbations up to 30 per cent of the population commonly moved each year massive disfranchisement was inevitable.

The system was also less than democratic in allowing the opportunity to vote many times. Joseph Chamberlain apparently possessed six qualifications, though this was by no means a record; given the leisurely spread of polling some men claimed to cast as many as ten votes. Overall the plural voters amounted to over half a million or 7 per cent of the total,[4] concentrated in commercial seats, in London and in county seats adjacent to or surrounding parliamentary boroughs. Supporters of plural voting argued that it properly reflected the stake a man had in each particular community. However, if every piece of property a man possessed fell within a single parliamentary borough or in a single division of a county he could vote but once; plural voting was possible only if his property was spread over different constituencies. Moreover, under the anachronistic convention that a borough was part of a county, freeholders in parliamentary boroughs exercised this vote in a neighbouring county seat with which they often had no interest or connection.

The final dimension of inequality lay in the marked variation in constituency size despite the effect the 1885 redistribution had in correcting the historic over-representation of the south and south-west. By adopting a basic population unit of 50,000 to justify new seats it proved possible to grant 39 additional metro-politan representatives, 15 to Lancashire and 13 to Yorkshire. Some 36 constituencies whose population was above 15,000 but below 50,000 lost one of their two members, while 72 boroughs under 15,000 were simply merged into surrounding counties. However, this still left many small boroughs returning their own members, for example Windsor, Durham, St Andrews and Salisbury, all with around 3,000 actual electors. At the other extreme the largest electorate by 1910 was the Romford division of Essex (61,000). An imbalance, moreover, remained marked between certain areas of the British Isles, notably Ireland whose 103 members represented an average electorate of 6,700 by contrast with the English average of 13,000. Ireland's exaggerated representation at Westminster had profound effects upon British politics before the First World War. In abandoning the traditional two-member constituencies for the more geographically restricted single-member seats in 1885 the legislators hoped to preserve the community basis of politics. However, the effect in the mature industrial society of late Victorian Britain was a system of con-stituencies frequently characterized by one dominant class; this was the reality behind what seemed to MPs rather artificial entities — North-East Norfolk, North-West Manchester — that were deficient in the prestige previously attaching to the representation of a county or major borough. This was symptomatic of the changing orientation of politics from the local to the national level, and from community to class.

Electoral Practice and Malpractice

Victorian elections were expected as a matter of course to be punctuated by excessive drinking, mob action ranging from exuberance to intimidation, an exchange of cash and a judicious application of the 'screw'. However, 'influence' covered a multitude of practices and forms, many of which were regarded as perfectly natural and proper. By tradition county politics was the preserve of landed gentlemen who both provided candidates and effectively determined the outcome through the loyalty they commanded among farmers and smallholders. The exercise of such influence could be effortless and inconspicuous, not necessarily coercive or unwelcome to the lower levels of rural society. So long as party politics remained a remote and intangible concept the typical county elector would act within the ambit of his local community; it was the county or community that his MP represented rather than either individuals or a party. Moreover, as the person who remitted rent in bad years, provided work in inclement weather, and contributed financially and socially to the life of the village or estate, the squire could legitimately expect political support; the relationship between squire and local electorate rested upon a mutual sense of duty and responsibility. In so far as voters anticipated a flow of benefits from an election it was these regular, tangible ones rather than legislative programmes at Westminster. Studies of politics in counties such as Lincolnshire from the 1830s to the 1880s suggest that 'politics' comprised certain agricultural matters, notably the malt tax and the tariff, which tended to unite farmers and landowners thus offering few openings for genuine party alternatives.[5]

However, this is to describe an ideal situation of rural stability characteristic of the capital-intensive and profitable agriculture of the mid-nineteenth century; it could not survive unscathed the contractions and changes in ownership brought on by falling agricultural profitability after 1875.[6] As unprofitable estates were disposed of and the gentry rented out a number of country houses to families without local, traditional connections, influence inevitably waned or, at least, required to be more deliberately exercised than before. While a landowner who was resident or played a full part in the life of the community might legitimately command loyalty, one who attempted to exercise it as an absentee or negligent owner encountered opposition and resentment.[7] This had always been the case; influence had never been easy to extend to a second candidate connected merely by party not by ties of family or county.[8]

Nor was a coercive element entirely absent, though it had always been more prevalent in Wales and Ireland than in the English counties, at least in the obvious form of eviction of tenants after elections. As late as 1894, however, Northamptonshire farmers took reprisals against agricultural labourers who had shown the temerity to stand successfully for election in the new parish councils.[9] On the whole influence was most effective when no active steps were necessary to exercise it; in the 1860s it was still regarded as bad form, as well as being futile, to canvass a landowner's tenants without first seeking his permission. Significantly the formal canvass seems to have become more normal from 1885, and was widely associated with undue pressure; Joseph Arch (founder of the Agricultural Labourers Union and Liberal MP for N.W. Norfolk) carried his inbred fear of the canvass to the extent of refusing to adopt it when himself a candidate, describing it as a 'mean subterfuge. Its object is to get at a man's vote in an indirect way.'[10]

It is often asserted that the apparently slight impact of the secret ballot, introduced by Gladstone in 1872, is an indication of the general absence of undue pressure. This is by no means consistent with the actions of many politicians themselves. In order to arrest their declining control in rural areas Conservative landlords often stationed an estate manager or agent outside the polling station to take down the names of those who voted;[11] and since ballot boxes were separately counted one observed how many votes each village had cast for the other side.[12] It was thus not difficult to undermine the rural elector's confidence that the ballot really was secret as the radicals claimed. Naturally voters who were habitually deferential towards their social superiors did not suddenly change their practice in the absence of strong political pressures to do so. Ireland provided a dramatic explosion following the introduction of the secret ballot in the form of 57 Home Rulers elected in 1874. In Wales 1874 brought gains for the Liberals, despite a national tide against them, but this was no more than a continuation of a well-established trend. In both these countries the basis of political revolt lay in the fact that landlord and rural voter were frequently not of the same community; a well-developed alternative community of a cultural–religious type generated an early break with political practice. In Scotland large landowners were often Liberal, albeit Whiggish, in allegiance and therefore pulled in the same direction as their tenants wished to go. In England the ballot made little impact under the restricted franchise before 1884; but it was a different matter under the reformed electorate and the subsequent widespread politicization of the counties. It is unlikely that Liberal gains in hitherto Conservative counties in 1885 would have been so extensive had the poll remained open, or that the rebellious Crofter candidates would have prised Highland seats from Whig control.

Influence in the boroughs had for long been more obviously corrupt and coercive. Small boroughs often saw an election as the best means of attracting money to the town. Indeed, an immediate objection to the Ballot Act was that it facilitated the taking of bribes from *both* sides by electors. Contemporary alarm over excessive levels of expenditure during the elections of 1868, 1874 and 1880 stimulated the Gladstone government to enact a Corrupt and Illegal Practices Prevention Act in 1883 which set maximum expenditure limits according to size of electorate, imposed upon a single designated agent the responsibility for making a complete return of his candidate's expenses, and made it the duty of the Director of Public Prosecutions to initiate cases where corruption had occurred. Although this appears to have been relatively effective in setting limits to spending during campaigns, it would be optimistic to think that it radically altered attitudes. Neither a politician guilty of corrupt practices nor a voter who took bribes were ostracized for what were regarded as minor peccadilloes. In ancient parliamentary boroughs bribery amounted to a tradition rather than a venal sin; as late as 1911, for example, when Worcester was investigated by a Royal Commission, no less than 500 electors emerged guilty; by this period bribery had settled at an unspectacular level of 2s 6d or 5s plus a few drinks per vote, and the Worcesters had ceased to be typical. Such practices dwindled essentially because they ceased to be efficacious; in substantial boroughs with 10–20,000 voters large-scale bribery was hardly worth the cost and was too blatantly obvious.

However, politicians circumvented the Act of 1883 to a considerable extent by spending money outside the election campaign period and by allowing others to spend it on their behalf, or in their interest. For the public still regarded it as a proper function of the MP to assist the borough, notably as an employer, and as a regular investor in community projects, charities and sporting clubs. MPs frequently distributed coal and blankets in winter, showered sweets upon the children, and saw that tea parties and 'knife and fork' suppers were thrown on suitable occasions. In addition the member's postbag would be full of begging letters from individual constituents seeking money or jobs. On top of this came the costs of being in Parliament. After 1885 expenditure of £800 to £1,000 was typical for a campaign; the candidates paid the, often exaggerated, costs of the returning officer; and the member commonly provided a salary of £100 to £300 per annum for his agent, plus additional sums for registration work each year. Thus the fact that by the First World War petitions alleging electoral malpractice had shrunk to a handful cannot obscure a certain continuity of practice and of attitude in the relation between a politician and his constituents.

Victorian reformers who hoped that judicious expansion of the electorate would foster a mature and informed debate on political issues in place of corruption and influence invariably lived to be disillusioned. Historians have rightly grown sceptical about any quick emergence of a 'politics of opinion' based upon the thinking individual voter after 1867. Indeed good evidence has emerged to suggest that the pattern in new industrial boroughs often repeated in certain respects that of county or medieval borough seats. Some employers, for example, appear to have mobilized the votes of their workers as effectively as any rural squire, and many a self-made manufacturer was known to give his men breakfast on polling day before marching them off to cast their votes for himself or his candidate. A number of medium-sized towns made it a practice to return the largest employer of labour — J.J. Colman the mustard manufacturer at Norwich, Joseph Pease the Quaker ironmaster at Darlington, or Charles Mark Palmer whose shipyards supported the economy of Jarrow; similarly industrialized county seats such as Northwich (Cheshire) returned the local chemical magnate Sir John Brunner, and the Mansfield division of Notting-hamshire elected the coal-owner Arthur Markham. Detailed study of Blackburn and Bury has demonstrated a distinct pattern in which working-class voters who resided near and worked in a factory owned by an active Liberal or Conservative reflected overwhelmingly his allegiance.[13] In such circumstances the result of an election could be as predictable from the relative strength of Liberal and Conservative employers as in a county from the number of the landlords' retainers. This is explicable especially in 1868 if one envisages the 1867 Act as enfranchising urban villages in which the factory served as the rural estate; here the pressures for unity around one's place of work against rival, external forces could be stronger than the individual's political opinion. Though dismissal of the politically rebellious introduced an occasional coercive element it was apparently the exception; coercion was more likely to be applied by a voter's own workmates than by his employer.[14]

Lest this should be seen as the universal pattern of urban politics in the late nineteenth century certain qualifications may be entered. Employer influence was characteristic of medium-sized towns where the range of employment was limited to one or two trades, and where the owners still resided near their workers in the 1880s. Where there existed a more varied economy and no dominant employers, a more rapid emergence of political opinion was a natural consequence.[15] Also the greater likelihood of residential separation of owner from worker in the larger conurbations, and even in the smaller Lancashire and Yorkshire towns by the 1890s, undermined the paternal relationships of the 1860s. Nor was the voter–employer relationship merely a passive, non-political one on the worker's part. In the constant shifting of house and job a workman of, say, Liberal views could deliberately seek a connection with a radical mill-owner. Just as a rural magnate who changed his politics did not expect the tenantry to switch allegiance automatically, so the employer had to recognize the existence of loyalties that were political or party as distinct from personal. Finally, the exercise of influence was naturally marked in the election following immediately upon the 1867 Reform Act when large numbers of working men voted for the first time but under the old conditions of open voting. By the 1880s even entrenched MPs were vulnerable to political issues; Brunner lost his seat in 1886; Palmer found himself almost unseated by a socialist in 1900. Moreover, any owner had to be known as a good employer or face a battery of criticism and innuendo during a campaign. As a result of personal and political considerations, by the turn of the century entrepreneurs with political ambitions were migrating away from the seats of their business: Richard Holt of Liverpool found a constituency at Hexham in Northumberland; Walter Runciman of Tyneside sat for Dewsbury; Alfred Mond of Cheshire represented Swansea. Such movements reflected the fact that it was no longer enough to be a local employer; allegiance to a political party furnished the safest guide to a constituency's representation.

The Rise of the Party Activist

One of the most striking features of mid-Victorian elections is that barely half the constituencies actually experienced a contest; and where seats were contested a third or more of voters normally split their two votes across party lines — an indication that Whig and Tory were not sharp political divisions but amorphous and overlapping groupings. Since two members had to be returned, Whigs and Tories frequently agreed to nominate a single candidate each with a view to avoiding the trouble and expense of a contest. Thus an election was often the result of a split *within* one side, between Radicals and Whigs or on personal grounds, rather than between parties. Such cosy arrangements were, of course, anathema to the dedicated party activists of the late Victorian era whose objective in manning the constituency organization on a permanent basis was to ensure a fight at every election. After 1885 single-member constituencies[16] eliminated traditional Whig Tory collusion, and the advance of formal party organization, stimulated by franchise extensions, may be measured from the decline in unopposed returns (see table 1.3). As the table shows 1885

TABLE 1.3. *Uncontested seats at general elections*

1857	333	1880	109	1900	243
1859	383	1885	43	1906	114
1865	302	1886	225	1910 (Jan.)	75
1868	212	1892	63	1910 (Dec.)	163
1874	188	1895	189		

marked the nearest approach to the mid-twentieth century practice in which virtually every constituency is contested; around 30 of the unopposed returns occurred in staunchly Nationalist areas of Ireland which the Unionists found it futile to fight. Even so, the large totals for 1886, 1895 and 1900, when the Liberal organizations were either split or starved of resources, indicate how incomplete the evolution remained.

Hitherto parliamentary election campaigns had rested in the hands of small groups of landowners, professional men or employers who used solicitors to organize the poll and the registration. However, an alternative approach based upon the assumption of a regular party conflict evolved particularly in those towns whose government had been reformed under the 1835 Municipal Corporations Act;[17] the municipally inspired prototype did not generally displace the improvisations at parliamentary level until politicians had to face the challenges and problems raised by the new franchises, the redistribution, and the restrictions upon expenditure in the 1880s, which generated a permanent, institutional framework eventually covering the whole country.

Three major manifestations of organized party activity may be identified. First the professional party agent began to displace the solicitor for whom electoral work was just a sideline. This was no more than a natural consequence of the complexity of the franchise and registration process after 1885. The agent's responsibility was to ensure that his party's supporters appeared on the preliminary list of voters in May, to put in further claims and defend them before the revising barristers in the autumn, and particularly to lodge objections against the names of known opponents. Such work could make all the difference to the lodgers' vote since they had to make a fresh application every year; if they or householders shifted house the party agents pursued them in an annual charade. Some found that lodging objections paid higher dividends than making claims. In Newcastle the Conservatives objected to 9,500 names between 1888 and 1891, and in nearby Gateshead where the population rose by 16 per cent between 1885 and 1891 the electorate dropped by 301![18] In 1908 the Leeds Liberals secured a net advantage from registration of 257 (98 claims, 159 objections) over their opponents; in Keighley the Conservative agent claimed net gains ranging from 69 in 1892 to 238 in 1897.[19] In dozens of seats a turnover of these proportions was enough to determine the result of an election, and the party that neglected registration work for a year or two suffered badly. Where both agents were alert and thorough they habitually met privately before the revising courts got to work for a mutual withdrawal of objections; there is thus no little substance in the view that the parties, as much as the law, determined the franchise before 1918. Agents had also to keep abreast of legal cases which modified the interpretation of the Act; for example the 'latchkey' decision of 1907 by which 'lodgers' who held a front door key to the building could qualify as 'householders' produced a sudden influx of new voters. Sensible of their role in winning elections the party agents asserted their status by establishing professional associations, the Liberals in 1882 and the Conservatives in 1891; they adopted examinations for full membership, endeavoured to impose minimum salary levels upon the parties, set up benevolent funds, and published semi-secret journals to brief members on the latest tricks of the trade.

A second characteristic of the post-1867 system was the local party-sponsored club. Especially in Lancashire and Yorkshire working men's clubs were a long-standing feature, but politicians felt so apprehensive of losing touch with the urban electors of 1867 that they threw considerable resources into extending the network. A typical neighbourhood club was a modest affair of two or three rooms, one for lectures, one for reading, drinking, billiards or smoking; even a strongly radical town like Keighley boasted 13 such Conservative clubs in 1907. A popular extension of club activity during the summer involved mass picnics and excursions by train to the country home of the MP, candidate or other party dignitary; in September 1900, we learn, 600 North Salford Liberals picnicked at Matlock Bath in Derbyshire by day and enjoyed a Venetian fete on the river by night.[20] On a more regular basis urban party associations developed their own brass bands and football clubs which the MP was expected to subsidize. In such ways the parties helped to fill the role nowadays occupied by a vast and varied entertainments industry. Their motives in moving deliberately beyond strictly political activity were to inculcate the values of the parliamentary system among the new voters, to impart political education at least to the activist elite, and to foster an habitual loyalty on the part of those who were uninterested in or ignorant of politics. In addition the parties frequently sponsored benefit societies, friendly societies, sick and burial societies, and even building societies; according to one Liverpool Tory in 1879: 'working men in the north country always wanted to see some return for their money, and would therefore more willingly join a benefit club than an association for a purely abstract object'.[21] The success of the clubs and the Primrose League shows how misleading, in the British context, is the assumption that traditional parliamentary parties were simply parties of 'individual representation' that failed to involve their supporters except intermittently at election times; the evidence suggests that the Conservatives, rather than any of the extra-parliamentary socialist or labour bodies, approximated to a party of 'social integration' in that they permeated the daily lives of their members.

Finally, party growth manifested itself in the emergence of formal constituency associations based upon individual member-ship running into hundreds or thousands, divided between branches for each ward or polling district. This provided the centre for volunteer activists whose time and efforts now provided free much of the canvassing, transport and propaganda work previously paid for on an *ad hoc* basis. Representative constituency bodies were pioneered by radical Liberals — it was dubbed the 'caucus' system — who gave it central institutional form in the National Liberal Federation (NLF) of 1877. Rank and file Conservatives encountered greater opposition from landed and parliamentary patrons who sensed a threat to their own control, and eschewed the Liberals' pretensions to policy-making and selection of candidates; nonetheless, after a slow start in 1867 the National Union of Conservative and Constitutional Associations (NUCCA) attained official approval and spawned affiliated associations across the country during the mid 1880s. By this stage few candidates stood without benefit of an agent, a permanent association, or backing of a network of social organizations which gave them links with the mass of voters no longer attainable simply through the personal connections of leading families. By building up habitual party loyalty the politicians themselves helped to replace older forms of community and group influence with institutional, political ones.

Party, Parliament and the 'Independent Member'

By 1900 observers of British politics had begun to draw certain conclusions, often pessimistic ones, from the experience of the reformed system since 1867. Graham Wallas in his *Human Nature in Politics* (1908) highlighted the irrationality of a mass electorate in contrast to the liberal ideal. Also in 1908 the American academic A. L. Lowell in *The Government of England* dwelt upon the centralization of power in the Cabinet and the corresponding decline in the authority and independence of the House of Commons. The roots of this change had already been identified in M. Ostrogorski's *Democracy and the Organisation of Political Parties* (1902), which drew attention to what he saw as the debilitating effects of caucus politics upon Parliament. Seen in perspective Ostrogorski's pessimism seems exaggerated, even misplaced, since, despite the pretensions of Victorian party organizations in the 1870s, by 1900 both Liberal and Conservative parliamentary leaders had harnessed their extra-parliamentary forces to serve their ends; they appealed directly to the voters over the heads of their critics for the 'mandate' as the fashionable term had it; their command of patronage and policy was rarely challenged successfully even in the Labour Party whose roots and strength lay, as yet, outside the House of Commons. Very few politicians used the party organization as their highroad to power; even Joseph Chamberlain and Lord Randolph Churchilll merely toyed with it before reverting to playing the game by the existing rules.

However, this should not obscure the very real changes that took place in the career and functions of the backbench politician in the late nineteenth century. Until this time membership of the House of Commons was still widely regarded less as a career than as a part-time activity undertaken along with other unpaid duties towards the community. This was held to be no small advantage in deterring carpetbaggers and in attracting to public service representatives of independent means. 'Once pay a member for his votes collectively,' declared Sir William Harcourt, 'and he will very soon make a market for his individual votes.'[22] Yet both tighter party discipline and the growing demands made by governments upon MPs undermined the conventional conception of the MP in our period. By tradition membership of the Commons impinged lightly upon the MP's time. Government business occupied only a fraction of the time of the House; attendance was frequently fitful and whipping slack, even unnecessary, for a ministry rested upon administrative rather than political support. Each August Parliament rose for the shooting season, members displaying a marked reluctance to return until the following February.

However, under Gladstone and his successors the parliamentary year grew longer. Governments appropriated sittings hitherto reserved for backbench legislation; and severe pressure upon government business caused by regular Irish Nationalist obstructionism prompted Gladstone in 1882 to pioneer the procedure for closure of debate by simple majority vote, a practice ritually condemned but nonetheless adopted by all governments anxious to squeeze legislation through. With the burgeoning scope of official activity came both lengthier and more complex legislation and financial proposals. Both the Public Accounts Committee of 1861 and the Estimates Committee of 1912 represented attempts to maintain the principle of Commons' scrutiny and control of finance without absorbing excessive amounts of time on the floor of the House. In practice Commons debates on Supply evolved into a largely ritual aspect of Parliament's work; in 1896 A.J. Balfour simply fixed the number of Supply days after which all remaining votes were taken by closure; they ceased to be opportunities for criticism of expenditure in detail and became instead occasions for general discussions initiated by the opposition. Thus governments grew to dominate the timetable and members to depend upon the party whip to keep them in touch with business from hour to hour. As attack by the opposition became normal practice so the whips displayed increasing intolerance of non-attendance or revolt. Life gradually ceased to be congenial for what Lord Salisbury described as 'the old judicial type of Member who sat rather loose to his party'.

Whereas the governments of the 1850s regularly suffered 10 to 15 defeats each year, by the 1900s their successors experienced only one per session on average. We may measure the growth of disciplined party behaviour by the number of Commons divisions in which 90 per cent of a party's representatives went into the same lobby (see table 1.4). Two features are particularly striking.

TABLE 1.4. *'Party votes' in the House of Commons 1850–1903*

	No. of divisions	Conservatives (%)	Liberals (%)
1850	321	45	37
1860	257	31	25
1871	256	61	55
1881	199	71	66
1883	253	65	52
1890	261	87	64
1894	237	92	84
1899	357	91	76
1903	260	83	88

Source: H. Berrington, 'Partisanship and Dissidence in the Nineteenth Century House of Commons', *Parliamentary Affairs*, 21 (1967–68), p. 342.

First, the Conservatives in office and in opposition displayed tighter discipline or cohesion than the Liberals. This is quite at odds with contemporary criticism of the caucus for supposedly subjecting the politicians to its dictates; in practice the NLF invariably lent encouragement to MPs in rebellion against the leadership. Secondly, the lax discipline prevailing up to the 1860s tightened up after 1868, but weakened somewhat during the early 1880s when the party leaders were inclined to seek co-operation from their opponents against their own rebellious supporters. However, the great divide on Home Rule in 1886 drove both sides towards greater cohesion than ever before, reaching a peak under the management of Salisbury and Balfour. A fundamental alteration had taken place since mid-century when government and opposition had been more fluid and relaxed, and neither side represented rigid parties. After 1886 governments ceased to be able to rely upon support from oppositions which now criticized everything but without prospect of defeating anything. All now turned upon maintaining the allegiance of one's own party majority; the older traditions of cross-bench voting by a large proportion of members gradually died out. Thus when Edwardians looked back nostalgically to a golden age of the 'Independent Member' they had in mind what we would think of as a House of 'moderates' whose fluctuating votes reflected the blurred and ambiguous lines of party demarcation.

Such developments seemed to many contemporaries to undermine the status of the MP while encroaching upon his time and freedom. Life in the Commons began to lose its attractions for young gentlemen. This is not to say that landed families did not continue to play a prominent role in both parties; simply that they had to make more deliberate efforts than before and acquiesce in the restrictions of parliamentary life. But the social composition of the Commons underwent a steady modification during the late Victorian era. It has been found that between 1868 and 1910 landowners fell from 46 to 26 per cent as a proportion of Conservative members and from 26 to 7 per cent among Liberals;[23] in the same period those whose livelihood lay in industry and trade rose from 31 to 53 per cent of Conservatives and from 50 to 66 per cent of Liberals; while those from legal and professional occupations grew from 9 to 12 per cent among Conservatives and from 17 to 23 per cent among Liberals. The dominance of lawyers in particular at Cabinet level was a noticeable feature of the Liberal governments of 1906–14 which included very few industrialists. This march of the middle classes, which some Edwardians professed to abhor as an invasion by 'wirepullers', professional politicians and men on the make, reminds us how very protracted was the process of penetration initiated by the famous 'middle class' victories of 1832 and 1846.

In fact by 1900 many a rising bourgeois had discovered a short cut if not to power at least to prestige by obtaining a knighthood, baronetcy or peerage, often after (though not necessarily because of) generous contributions to party funds, aid to ailing party newspapers and services at elections. The rate of creation of peerages during the 1880s and 1890s was twice that of the 1830–60 period. Moreover the proportion of industrial and professional middle-class men among the newly ennobled reached 43 per cent

during 1897–1911 by comparison with 14 per cent during 1867–
81.[24] Certain types of recruit, notably brewers and newspaper
proprietors, attracted criticism for their prominence; Guinesses
were elevated in 1880 and 1891, and a Bass and an Allsopp both
in 1886; Lord Glenesk arose from the *Morning Post* in 1899, Lord
Burnham from the *Daily Telegraph* in 1903, and Lord Northcliffe
from the *Daily Mail* in 1905. Yet the solid centre of British
industry was well represented by Lords Armstrong (armaments) in
1887, Inverclyde (shipping) in 1897, Joicey and Allendale
(mining) in 1906, and Mount Stephen (railways) in 1891 to take
only a few examples. Though both parties, especially the Liberals,
were under more pressure to raise central funds from wealthy men
by the 1880s, financial contributions were not the sole factor.
After 1886 Gladstone had to fortify the depleted Liberal ranks in
the Lords. Conversely Salisbury, whose 1885–86 ministry was a
turning-point in rapid creations, felt obliged to dispense honours
as an alternative to posts now thinly spread between Conservatives
and Liberal Unionists.

In the quest for office the new men competed under the old
rules in that until 1911, when MPs were awarded a £400 salary,
the backbencher had to live off a fortune amassed before his entry
into politics; by 1900 of course many a second-generation indus-
trialist could use his father's business to launch him into politics
in his youth. But party loyalty now demanded that aspiring
members should first tackle one or two hopeless or marginal
constituencies before being nominated for a safe seat for life. For
the politician's essential lifeline lay through his party rather than
in his roots in his locality. As Augustine Birrell remarked to
Asquith and Haldane one day as they gazed out across the Firth
of Forth to the country beyond: 'What a grateful thought that
there is not an acre in this vast and varied landscape that is not
represented at Westminster by a London barrister!'[25]

Chapter 2

The Evolution of the Gladstonian Liberal Party 1867–1895

A Liberal reform is never simply a social means to a social end, but a struggle of good against evil.
Sidney Webb, Nineteenth Century, *September 1901*

Emergence

'Like the Kingdom of Heaven,' Sir William Harcourt could say as late as 1891, 'the Liberal Party is a house of many mansions.' Indeed before the 1870s the 'Liberal Party' was so amorphous and diverse both politically and organizationally as to be quite unlike a twentieth-century party. Mid-Victorian parties were primarily loose parliamentary parties, and such cohesion as the Liberals possessed derived initially from their role as the normal governing party of the period, and, subsequently from Gladstone's dominating effect from 1866 until his retirement in 1894. Yet although diversity and dispute attended the party during these years, historians simplify too much if they overlook the steady and emphatic evolution of Liberalism towards a cohesive modern party framework and approach. The 1850s had seen the emergence of the parliamentary party under Palmerston; the 1860s brought new links between Liberals in the country and politicians like Bright and even Gladstone. In the 1870s formal party organization began to characterize the constituencies; and during the 1880s came the climax of political radicalization and a purging of the ranks which left popular Liberalism closer to parliamentary Liberalism than ever before. Gladstone's last government, 1892–94, saw the nearest approach to a programmatic party government and a drastic departure from the Palmerstonian era.

The origins of the parliamentary party may be traced back to 1850 when the death of Sir Robert Peel released his free trade followers to find permanent homes. Aberdeen's Coalition of 1852—55 provided a vital step in the transition by permitting the absorption of the Peelites into the Whig—Liberal governing group. Although this ministry came to grief in the Crimean War it provided the formula that was repeated with greater success by Palmerston in 1855—58 and 1859—65. On this latter ministry, which is usually thought of as the first Liberal one, Palmerston stamped his leadership effectively enough to ensure that the Whig—Liberal—Peelite combination would be more than a mere stop-gap. Its breadth of support and its range of leading administrators made it the natural ruling party of the time.

However, Palmerston's party was essentially a parliamentary one quite unrepresentative of many of the people who regarded themselves as Liberals in the country. Half of its members were landowners or gentlemen with private incomes; indeed, despite the famous victories over reform in 1832 and the Corn Laws in 1846, government remained largely in the hands of the traditional landed men. Yet if the middle classes had not acquired power they showed an increasing interest in penetrating the world of politics; and what made the Liberals more of a national party than their rivals was that they embraced much more of commercial and industrial Britain. They also incorporated many of the most active politicians who devoted themselves to causes, to public speaking in the country, and to building links with the press and pressure groups. In contrast politics for most politicians remained a part-time affair rather than a profession, and a local rather than a national or party matter. The other 'professionals' were the frontbenchers, often Whig peers like Granville, Kimberley, Spencer and Ripon, who, immersed in the great departments of state, addressed their energies more to administration than to a party audience outside Parliament; they resembled civil servants as much as modern politicians. In 1880 Gladstone still packed five earls, a duke and a marquess into his Cabinet of only 12 members. Later in the century many Whig peers abandoned politics, or at least Liberal politics; but those like Ripon and Spencer who chose to adapt continued to play a major role even on the Liberal side. However, their hold on cabinets was relaxed in favour of men who were typically party politicians such as Joseph Chamberlain, Sir Charles Dilke and John Morley. As the 1880 Cabinet shows, Gladstone had no prior intention to advance these men, convinced as he was of the virtues of government by disinterested gentlemen.

Yet the talents of Chamberlain, Dilke, Morley, W.E. Forster, Sir William Harcourt, John Bright, Henry Fawcett and H.H. Asquith won them posts under Gladstone notwithstanding their radical views; in fact after 1886 a Liberal cabinet could hardly be formed without such men.

Until the 1870s few MPs had to deal with organized parties in their constituencies. But whatever the Liberal forces lacked, as yet, in formal organization they made up for in vociferousness. Most had been drawn into political activity for a specific objective or cause often through a pressure group such as the United Kingdom Alliance (temperance), the National Education League (free, undenominational, state education), or the Liberation Society[1] (Church disestablishment); the outstanding common element here was Victorian Nonconformity engaged in a prolonged campaign to eliminate other grievances such as the payment of Church rates, denial of burial rights in churchyards and exclusion from the ancient universities. Other causes, represented by the Ballot Society, the Reform Union and the Peace Society, were fragments of the anti-Corn Law movement of the 1840s. Still others catered more specifically to radical working men organized in radical clubs, the 'new Model' unions and in the Reform League which harked back to Chartism. In addition there were the campaigns for moral improvement including not only temperance but the abolition of the Contagious Diseases Acts (which permitted the army to license prostitutes in certain garrison towns), the trade in child prostitution and capital punishment. The foot soldiers in this phalanx of pressure groups ranged from self-made manufacturers and merchants through the lower middle class of shopkeepers, teachers and journalists to craftsmen and miners. Where the parliamentarians were typically landed, Anglican and Whig, provincial Liberals were more commonly urban–industrial, Nonconformist and radical.

Disparate as these elements appear, they did in fact provide the fabric of local Liberalism; and although much of their energy was devoted to fighting Whigs rather than Tories, during the 1860s and 1870s they were harnessed to parliamentary Liberalism so effectively that by the 1890s it had come to reflect their views fairly well. Articulate in its incoherence, pressure-group Liberalism was much more cohesive than it appears at first sight. For its forces were concentrated socially and geographically in the towns of midland and northern England, Scotland and Wales. Membership of the groups overlapped so much that there was a natural attraction in the idea of an institutional umbrella such as the

Liberal Party. This was especially true for middle-class Nonconformists whose desire to become integrated into national political
life and throw off the stigma attaching to them led them to the
parliamentary Liberal Party, which, for all its imperfections,
provided the best quick route to power. It is no exaggeration to
say that Nonconformity was the factor that turned many
Victorians into active politicians, for those who neglected to
exercise their political influence were, in the words of the Congre-
gationalist Minister R.W. Dale, 'guilty of treachery both to God
and man'.

Unity also arose from a common perception of the means and
purpose of radical politics. While some objectives could be realized
at municipal level or by pressure applied through bodies like the
Trades Union Congress, all were hindered by the essential un-
responsiveness of Parliament. By the 1860s it seemed plain that
the key to further advance lay, as Cobden and Bright had perceived
years before, through extensive reform of the franchise and the
ballot. Political reconstruction invested Liberal politics with an
elevating and unifying theme; its business was the removal of
privilege and artificial restriction and the opening up of political
opportunity to the talents of every man. Herein lay the basis for
common action through the identification of common enemies by
middle- and working-class radicals which had been pioneered in
such places as Birmingham and Rochdale. Radicals discerned a
model and a moral reinforcement in the politics of the United
States.[2] Working men were encouraged by reports from emigrants
who dilated upon the greater opportunities there, the social
equality and the absence of a dominant landed elite. Similarly for
middle-class radicals a system that was democratic in being open
to energy and talent at the grass roots represented their ideal.
America played an important role in drawing together not just
popular radicals of Bright's stamp, but also many of the intellectuals and academics of the 1860s. James Bryce, Henry Fawcett
and John Stuart Mill were all drawn towards Liberal politics at this
time partly through their sympathy for the North in the American
Civil War;[3] this gave them not only contact with urban radicals,
but also a sympathetic appreciation for working men who
appeared to take a moral view of politics by their advocacy of
the Northern cause. Indeed, along with Oliver Cromwell and the
Italian nationalists Mazzini and Garibaldi, Abraham Lincoln
remained for years a hero to British radicals; and 'John Brown'
and other American tunes served as rallying songs for reformers
right through to Edwardian times.

This need for leadership and unity was also appeased to some extent by the provincial press, which in its Victorian heyday was highly political and disproportionately Liberal in sentiment. Papers like the *Leeds Mercury, Manchester Guardian* or *Newcastle Chronicle* provided a focus for radical activity, and by extensive reproduction of major speeches built a vicarious bridge between the people and leading politicians. The keystone of this arch was undoubtedly Gladstone. For until his emergence as a popular figure in the 1860s Liberalism continued to run on two parallel lines; the movement in the constituencies looked to parliamentarians like Bright who was only a backbencher remote from the seats of power. Thus when Gladstone began to speak on franchise reform and to visit industrial centres like Tyneside (which led to his abandonment of his university seat in favour of a popular constituency in 1865), he found a huge reservoir of 'virtuous passion' waiting to be tapped. As Chancellor of the Exchequer and destined Liberal leader Gladstone was the first major figure to take the trouble to come to the people; the experience proved immensely flattering for both sides.

However little Gladstone shared with Nonconformists he was highly attractive to them for his moral integrity and the almost puritanical incorruptibility that they discerned in his alienation from the existing condition of politics. It was precisely this capacity to articulate a sense of religious and political outrage – as was demonstrated during 1876–80 in the campaign over the 'Bulgarian Atrocities' – that equipped Gladstone to be the foremost spokesman of what was dubbed the 'Nonconformist Conscience'. But there was a price to be paid for harnessing the Nonconformist Conscience. Erring politicians (notably those tainted by adultery such as Dilke in 1885 and Parnell in 1890) provoked a storm sufficiently strong to sweep them to rapid political extinction.

This underlines the fact that Gladstone retained his control of the popular and parliamentary strands of Liberalism more by inspiration than by skilfull management, and showed an alarming penchant as leader for withdrawing altogether in times of difficulty. Eschewing the vulgar arts of party management he tried to hold to the higher ground of national interest. No doubt this reluctance to become involved was a useful tactic for keeping him above the sectional interests, and indeed reflected his own distaste for pressure-group politics, which he thought would lead to mediocrity among politicians and the corruption of class legislation. This was a characteristic view for a man of his generation; yet

Gladstone also levelled criticisms of self-interest at the 'upper ten thousand', and cultivated the lower classes because he discerned in them a capacity for moral and responsible behaviour that would improve political life. He therefore engaged in a dual enterprise of trying to govern through the best representatives of the traditional ruling class, while involving the lower classes in morally improving issues rather than pandering to their material welfare. The collapse of Whiggery and the aggrandizement of the 'caucus' had defeated these aims well before his retirement, but his struggles decisively influenced the development of Liberal politics. Although Gladstone's reputation for radicalism was exaggerated, he made the Liberal Party a vehicle for a certain kind of reform during 1866—74 and gave the radicals their best means of determining government policy; yet his evident alienation from many specific items in the radical programme commended him to the Whigs as a bulwark against drastic change until the 1880s. So long as both sides accepted his leadership and manoeuvred for his support Gladstone could play a pivotal and unifying role in the evolution of the party.

The Programme versus the Single Issue

Although Gladstone's followers were often captivated by the novelty of participation in national politics they also expected their support to be translated into precise reforms; yet their expectations were bound to be dashed because neither Gladstone nor the MPs as a whole approved of demands for Church disestablishment or temperance reform. Instead of allowing his priorities to be influenced by the rank and file Gladstone intended rather to use their 'virtuous passion' to strengthen his case in Parliament for the changes he did believe necessary. This strategy hinged upon his ability to create a single transcending issue which both Parliament and the constituency activists would accept as the priority. In this process the Reform Bill promoted by him and Lord John Russell in 1866 formed a vital step. For when the Bill perished as a result of Whig opposition Gladstone declined to carry on in office as, on past precedent, he might have been expected to do. His resignation meant that although the Whigs had won a limited victory over that particular Bill, they were going to lose the wider battle for control of future Liberal policy; the incoming minority Conservative administration would sooner or later be driven to an election that Gladstone intended to fight on the franchise question, thereby purging the rebels and producing a majority pledged to reform.

Since in the event Disraeli managed to pass a bill of his own by making concessions to radical backbenchers, Gladstone promptly found another overriding cause — disestablishment of the Church in Ireland and Irish land reform. On this basis he won a majority in 1868 which enabled him to impose both Irish reforms and several other measures during 1868–73. In this period of reform the authority of the gentry was curtailed by Forster's elected school boards and by the secret ballot; upper-class privilege was limited by reforms in the civil service and the army; and the status of the Church and the rights of property were encroached upon in Ireland. This was all of a piece with franchise reform itself as far as the radicals were concerned in that it attacked the sources of privilege and inefficiency which many had been criticizing since the Crimean War and even earlier. By 1874 the Palmerstonian mould had been decisively broken.

However, while the attack upon privilege furnished a fine theme, the omissions and shortcomings in detail strained the loyalty of Gladstone's supporters sufficiently to produce his defeat over the Irish Universities Bill in 1873. Many radicals believed that Irish disestablishment should lead rapidly to Welsh and Scottish; temperance men were highly irritated by the Licensing Act which regulated public houses and thus made drinking more acceptable not less; trade unions gained legal standing but their right to picket was left in doubt; and Nonconformists felt outraged at the use of ratepayers' money for subsidizing Anglican schools through the new school board system. The 1870 Education Bill best demonstrates the divisive tendencies in the party, for 132 Liberal members voted against it, while 133 abstained; it passed only with Conservative support. These examples show Gladstone's difficulties in trying to govern in the general interest on the strength of sectional interests, many of whom he believed to be propagating unpopular 'fads'; these he pronounced 'unripe' and urged their proponents to convert a majority in the country before expecting the government to risk adopting them. Unfortunately for Gladstone he could not easily command the country without the active assistance of the pressure-group radicals. Temperance fanatics and militant Nonconformists were the quintessential volunteer workers whose withdrawal could cripple the party locally; and the Liberal defeat in 1874 was widely ascribed to the recalcitrance of disappointed groups like the National Education League. No doubt the NEL deliberately fostered the impression that without them victory was impossible, and they overlooked the loss of support from those who considered that Gladstone had been far too sweeping. Eventually the 1874 defeat sobered many of the 'faddists'; they applied themselves to filling the gap left by conservative defections because the Liberal Party was still their best route to power.

However, the erosion of upper- and middle-class support was a more permanent phenomenon because they did have a political alternative. In 1874 many urban seats returned Conservatives, while in the counties — another portent — Whigs often withheld money and influence from Liberal candidates. The fact is that although in retrospect Victorian Liberalism may seem basically the party of free trade, individualism and self-help, by the 1880s contemporaries were more aware of the growing emphasis on state intervention and compulsion at the expense of individual rights. Temperance and education were two major spheres in which radicals had rapidly concluded that the inadequacy of individual effort could be remedied only by state compulsion. And during Gladstone's second ministry the 1880 Employers Liability Act and the 1881 Irish Land Act, which introduced tribunals empowered to revise rents, were seen as an even graver threat to private property than his earlier measures. Consequently the 1880s saw the resignation of men like the Duke of Argyll from the Cabinet and the creation of the Liberty and Property Defence League. By 1885, with Joseph Chamberlain in full flood against those 'who toil not, neither do they spin', many a traditional Liberal was inclined to take seriously the warning of the jurist A.V. Dicey that if one gave up individual freedom 'you can find no resting place until you reach the abyss of Socialism'.

In fact Gladstone's tactics in 1874 had been to offer abolition of the income tax, an idea nicely calculated to reassure the middle classes. Instead he retired for two years before re-emerging in September 1876, 'pamphlet in hand', to assume the leadership of the provincial crusade against Disraeli's pro-Turkish policy in the Balkans. This campaign was a classic illustration of his capacity for drawing the radicals from their narrow concerns by an appeal to moral righteousness. He began by condemning the Prime Minister for condoning the massacres of Bulgarian Christians merely because he thought it in Britain's interest to back up the Ottoman Empire; and by the time of the two Midlothian campaigns of 1879 and 1880 he had widened the attack to one on 'Beaconsfieldism', that is the use of military power for imperial aggrandizement as in South Africa and Afghanistan. In fact the policy of their governments was much closer than the rhetoric suggested. Disraeli had been drawn unwillingly into the conflicts with the Boers and the Afghans by British representatives on the ground, Sir Bartle Frere (high commissioner) and Lord Lytton (viceroy) respectively. Gladstone was to encounter the same problems, especially in Egypt and the Sudan.

Nevertheless, as an expedient for polarizing politics and re-capturing the leadership of radicalism the campaign against 'Beaconsfieldism' proved a triumph; but it was no solution to the problem that led to 1874. Others had begun to consider how to overcome the incoherence endemic in Liberalism. In particular Joseph Chamberlain, Mayor of Birmingham 1873–76, diagnosed the problem in terms of the dispersion of radicalism over innumerable causes. To be successful radicals had to concentrate on a single question as Cobden and Bright had done over the Corn Laws; the trouble was that their success had led to the disintegration of the forces that had brought it about, and ever since 1846 Bright had vainly sought a similar rallying point. Initially Chamberlain himself believed that either disestablishment or education would serve to concentrate radicalism and tighten its grip on the party, but 1874 had shown him the inadequacy of such causes when it came to rousing the electorate. Making a virtue of necessity, therefore, he abandoned the single-issue strategy in favour of programme politics. His main vehicle for this, the National Liberal Federation, was established in 1877 from the ruins of the National Education League with the object of radicalizing both the policy and the organization of the Liberal Party. It would represent the active, democratic constituency Liberals in the country who would select candidates who reflected their views. The annual assembly of the NLF would become a kind of Liberal Parliament in the country especially when the party was out of office; and being representative of the party's supporters it could legitimately prepare a programme of measures and indicate the priorities to the leaders. In this way it was hoped to harness radicalism's scattered forces to the governmental machine.

The basis of the NLF's claims to represent Liberalism lay in local parties whose membership was open to all supporters. The Birmingham Liberal Association, two-thirds of whose membership was reckoned to be working class, provided a model for others to emulate. Although middle- and working-class co-operation had long been a feature of Birmingham politics, similar systems had been pioneered in Oldham and Rochdale which inspired popular organization in places like Newcastle in the 1870s.[4] Every Liberal in the city was entitled to attend his local ward meetings which elected representatives to a 'Liberal 600', and this in turn chose an executive committee. At its inauguration in 1877 the NLF drew representatives from 95 such organizations.

Initially Gladstone's dislike of the pretensions of the caucus and programme politics was obscured; for when the NLF timed its inaugural meeting in May 1877 to catch the wave of excitement over the Bulgarian issue the Liberal leader graced the occasion with a speech at the Bingley Hall, Birmingham. Each believed they had caught the other. By hitching Gladstone's prestige to the NLF Chamberlain calculated that he was bound to strengthen radicalism at the expense of the Whigs who were undoubtedly embarrassed by the Bulgarian campaign. Ultimately this proved a shrewd assessment. But in the short run the NLF found itself swept along in Gladstone's crusade in which its own objectives were obscured. By maintaining his grip on radical affections, especially in imperial and foreign affairs, Gladstone succeeded for some years in checking the programmatic form of politics desired by Chamberlain. The year 1877 thus began the process of driving the two men apart.

As a result the Liberals swept home in the 1880 general election on a wave of moral righteousness with a negative mandate to undo Disraeli's policy but little else. The victory seemed unrelated to the issues of radical politics, and as the new administration staggered on without achievement the whole Midlothian strategy began to appear as a ruse designed to sidetrack radicalism. In fact Gladstone's difficulties during 1800–85 were partly due to the engrossing problems of South Africa, Afghanistan and Egypt; to the coercive measures for Ireland and the consequent obstructionism of the Nationalist MPs; and to time-consuming controversy over the entry into the Commons of the atheist MP, Charles Bradlaugh, who had refused to take the oath. However, the Prime Minister had no priorities for legislation, and important reforms of land and local government were frustrated. Consequently the faddists grew voluble again, and their clamour was stilled only by the introduction of a major measure, the 1884 Franchise Bill, which was passed before the government broke up over its defeat on the budget in June 1885.

In fact the two leading radical ministers, Dilke and Chamberlain, had already resigned in May, the latter to concentrate on a ferocious campaign against the landed upper class which was designed to win the newly enfranchised county voters for radicalism at the 1885 elections. In interpreting Chamberlain's proposals (dubbed the 'Unauthorised Programme'), one has to disentangle the ideological element from the tactical objective. His list included free elementary education, elective county government, land reforms, graduated taxation, death duties, disestablishment, devolution-all-round, manhood suffrage and payment of MPs. In part this grew out of Chamberlain's municipal experience in Birmingham where the council had shown its middle-class ratepayers the virtues of public enterprise in the provision of such services as gas, water, sewerage and lighting. This willingness to extend the collective element in economic and social matters marked Chamberlain out as what was often called a 'constructive radical'; conversely, eminent 'radicals' like John Morley shrank from 'construction' on both economic and political grounds, the more so as it was increasingly coupled with the demand for graduated taxation.

In other respects, however, Chamberlain's approach was less radical. The idea of local government reform or devolution was really to allow divisive matters such as temperance or education to be settled outside Parliament. Nor did he wish to offend the middle-class belief in private enterprise as his cautious approach to housing suggests.[5] For him the chief issue was land because it served to concentrate the attack upon the upper classes and to pre-empt any separate working-class onslaught on property in general. In the long run, he believed, middle-class radicals had to mobilize the new mass electorate before some one else did.

The tactical significance of the Unauthorised Programme is less obvious. On the face of it Chamberlain's object was to gain such a preponderance of radical MPs in the new Parliament that it would be impossible for Gladstone to repeat the experience of 1880—85. Historians have therefore tried to calculate the number of his supporters. One study suggests a growth from 80 in 1874 to 120 in 1880 and 160 after the 1885 election when 333 Liberals were returned altogether.[6] Another writer suggests 180, using as the criterion for radicalism an MP's support for even one point in the programme;[7] but this contrasts sharply with the chief whip's estimate of only 101 'Chamberlainites'. Retrospective assessments exaggerate Chamberlain's strength because they define radicalism in domestic terms and forget that the foreign—imperial dimension was equally important. Most radicals had inherited their creed from Cobden and Bright: trade not rule was the virtue of Empire: Britain should abstain from entanglements abroad and avoid expenditure on armaments. The irony is that on these matters the two leading radicals, Dilke and Chamberlain, were out of step with most radical opinion; they resented the failure of Gladstone, as they saw it, to stand up for British interests as much as the Whigs. Consequently Chamberlain could never prise radicalism away from Gladstone. During the early 1880s he began to recognize this: for many radicals now looked to Morley — a staunch 'Little Englander' — as a more suitable leader than Chamberlain; and the first working-men MPs such as Thomas Burt also followed the Gladstonian line on foreign affairs. Thus 'Chamberlainites' should not be equated with 'radicals'. There was little prospect of a takeover of the party by him in 1885; and herein lies the explanation for his otherwise extraordinary abandonment of the Liberal Party in the company of Lord Hartington and the Whigs in 1886.

1886: the Radicalization of the Party

The fall of Gladstone's government over the 1885 budget was followed by a minority Conservative administration and a general election in which the Liberal lead of 86 over the Tories was matched by the election of 86 Irish Nationalists. The deadlock was resolved by the launching of the 'Hawarden Kite' in December 1885 when Gladstone's son, Herbert, released the news of his father's conversion to Irish Home Rule. Thereupon Liberals and Nationalists combined to eject Salisbury from office; Gladstone introduced a Home Rule Bill which failed owing to the opposition of 93 Liberal MPs who withdrew under Hartington and Chamberlain to stand as Liberal Unionists at the ensuing general election of 1886.

This crisis reflected much more than a simple division of opinion over the principle of Home Rule. It was easy for men like Sir William Harcourt, who disliked the Bill intensely, to remain loyal to Gladstone. In so doing he had opted for one strategy; Chamberlain in withdrawing had opted for another. Having absorbed the lesson of 1880 he had no intention of allowing the Grand Old Man to lead the party off on another crusade, and thus forget the real business of radical politics. Since the 1885 election had confirmed that he could not dominate the party Chamberlain had sought a short cut by co-operating with Hartington and the Whig elements to topple Gladstone. The basis for a Hartington–Chamberlain government existed in their common dislike of Gladstone's supine and unpatriotic foreign policy; within such a

THE IRISH "VAMPIRE."

From Punch, *24 October 1885.*

government Chamberlain believed that Hartington, lacking Gladstone's influence with the radicals, would be obliged to allow him to determine the pace of domestic reform. This prospect of an alternative Liberal ministry posed a dilemma for Gladstone from which he escaped successfully by seizing the initiative over Home Rule. The joint withdrawal of Hartington and Chamberlain was a logical consequence in that it reflected their common failure to ditch Gladstone, and Chamberlain's inability to win control of the radical forces.

The ultimate significance of this turning-point in politics is as much misunderstood as its origins. Superficially the Home Rule crisis appears merely a divisive, weakening factor that deprived the party of its radical strength. The reality was different. It clarified Liberal politics by introducing a simple test of orthodoxy, and completed the process initiated unwittingly by Gladstone in 1866 when he refused to abandon franchise reform. The purging of the Whig elements had been proceeding apace during 1880—85 when the Dukes of Argyll and Bedford and the Marquess of Lansdowne, to name only the most illustrious, had left the party. Of the 73 Liberal Unionist MPs who survived the 1886 election only 20 were radical supporters of Chamberlain; by 1892 only 11 of the latter remained and several had rejoined the Gladstonians. In short 1886 virtually completed the radicalization of Liberalism. Although only 191 Gladstonians were returned in 1886 they comprised a much more cohesive party than ever before. For the first time Gladstone appointed radicals such as Tom Ellis and Arnold Morley as party whips, and when next he came to form a government in 1892 he had no option but to draw upon radicals to fill the cabinet posts.

The fact that the majority of radical politicians chose to stay with Gladstone reflected the loyalties of Liberals in the country. Evidence of the attitudes of the three layers of Liberalism suggests that Home Rule sentiment was at its weakest among parliamentarians, stronger among the electors, and at its strongest among the activists. It is easy to exaggerate the electoral unpopularity of Home Rule. Rebellious Liberal Unionists secured election in 73 seats because the Conservatives stood down in their favour, thus presenting them with around two-thirds of the former Conservative vote to add to a quarter to a third of the old Liberal vote. They managed this most easily in areas where the development of party organization had lagged, and where it proved difficult to obtain and finance a new Gladstonian candidate at short notice. In such cases the prestige of the sitting member served to carry sufficient support, particularly in parts of the south-west and western Scotland where the strategic implications of Home Rule seemed to lend force to the Liberal Unionists' case. On the other hand, in a straight contest between a Gladstonian and a Conservative the loss of Liberal votes was much slighter; in fact many Liberals improved their poll over 1885 and actually regained seats in such places as Huddersfield, Leeds East, Liverpool Exchange,

Manchester South-West, Wednesbury and Wolverhampton West.

These victories in the towns constitute further evidence of the strength of Home Rule sentiment where Liberalism was well organized. Indeed one study suggests that only 5–10 per cent of party activists felt sufficiently opposed to Gladstone's policy to leave the party.[8] To them Home Rule appeared an eminently radical issue on which they could sympathize with the Irish for fighting a common enemy. The swiftness with which the caucus fell into line behind Gladstone undoubtedly surprised Chamberlain. Following the introduction of the Home Rule Bill on 10 April 1886 the local organizations selected delegates for an NLF council meeting on 5 May: the 'Newcastle 600', the Nottingham 800', the 'Leicester 500' and many others declared emphatically for Gladstone; even at Birmingham the 'Two Thousand' dissented only on details. At the NLF meeting a motion mildly critical of the Bill was thrown out by 575 votes to 25, which led to the resignation of Chamberlain and his Birmingham loyalists Jesse Collings and Powell Williams. Moreover, sitting members who were prevaricating at Burnley, Nottingham West, Buckingham and Hastings found their local caucuses insisting that they endorse official policy; those who remained obdurate like G. O. Trevelyan and George Goschen were denied renomination; other prominent figures were ejected by a vote of the local party, notably Hartington at Rossendale and Sir Henry James at Bury. In general the wealthier Liberal supporters were more prone to withdrawal, so that the local parties became notably poorer if more cohesive politically. The year 1886 actually helped to reunite Liberal associations formerly in disarray at Bradford, Dewsbury and Newcastle. As many as 50 associations affiliated to the NLF for the first time, thus making its hold more complete than ever. In September 1886 it shifted its headquarters to London next door to the Liberal Central Association so that the two bodies could enjoy a common secretary, Francis Schnadhorst, and put an end to the rivalry between them.

The crystallization of the radical forces as a result of Home Rule is particularly noticeable in Scotland, which, though strongly Liberal, had been sharply divided between a Glasgow-based organization of radicals and an Edinburgh-based association of Whigs and moderates. The former vigorously propagated the two central issues of Scottish politics – land reform and disestablishment – and were conciliated by a new Secretaryship of State for Scotland in 1885 and the Crofters Bill of 1886. The radicals had long felt that a reformed county franchise would expose the inability of the Whigs to mobilize public opinion; they therefore established an NLF for Scotland on the English pattern and put up candidates against Whiggish Liberals in 28 of the 72 Scottish constituencies in 1885. Home Rule finally alienated the Scottish Whigs who had been trying to hold on to Gladstone during the 1880s, though the immediate price was the loss of 23 Liberal MPs opposed to Home Rule of whom 17 secured election in 1886. On the other hand the disestablishment radicals and land reformers who had grown impatient with Gladstone saw the futility of leaving and rallied to the Irish cause; Gladstone was now thrown into their arms.

Similarly the English pressure groups appreciated the tactical advantages of sticking to the Grand Old Man. The loss of so many local patrons plainly left the party more dependent than ever on the network of Nonconformity in the provinces. Even before 1886 the faddists had steadily reconciled themselves to long-term work within the party. The National Education League had actually disbanded after 1874 to channel its energies through the NLF and into school board elections, thereby becoming an integral part of Liberal electoral machinery. Similarly the Liberation Society dropped its coercive tactics after 1874 in the hope that loyalty would bring its reward, which it did in the shape of a Welsh Disestablishment Bill in 1894. The more closely these groups associated themselves with the Liberals the more their opponents backed the Conservatives; then the faddists could plausibly argue that Liberal candidates could not poll the full potential radical vote unless they aroused the enthusiasm of their own adherents. On balance the changing relationship between the party and the pressure groups between the 1860s and 1890s was to the advantage of the former. After the franchise extensions and introduction of the secret ballot it was much more difficult for the proponents of any cause to claim credibly that the abstention of their supporters had brought about the defeat of a candidate. By the 1890s, therefore, 'faddism' was for the most part neatly marshalled in the annual programmes of the National Liberal Federation.

One major element of weakness hampered the post-1886 Liberal Party: the absence of an effective radical leader in the front rank of parliamentarians who could succeed Gladstone whose age and intellectual rigidity increasingly limited his usefulness. It was indeed an irony that Chamberlain should have left the party at the very moment when it became the embodiment of programmatic radicalism. Initially he expected his severance from the party to be temporary, which is why the Liberal Unionists tried to avoid voting with the Conservatives in the Commons; this was intended to facilitate their return to Liberalism when Gladstone retired. In fact he stayed on, and the overtures for reunion in 1887 were easily rebuffed by those like Morley who disliked Chamberlain's brand of politics. While the Grand Old Man remained leader until 1894 Chamberlain gradually learnt to work with Salisbury whose government he joined in 1895. Gladstone and Morley were content to await the gradual return of the lesser figures embarrassed by association with Salisbury. The drift would have been faster but for Chamberlain's ability to secure certain reforms during 1887–92, particularly those for land and education.

Some writers still regard Home Rule simply as the 'most potent divisive force' in Liberalism after 1886;[9] this is a natural conclusion to be drawn from the correspondence of a few leading politicians who disagreed on the details of Home Rule as on the details of every policy. However, this is scarcely applicable to the party as a whole which, as we have seen, rallied round the principle of Home Rule. By 1888 the Conservative coercion policy in Ireland had given Gladstone a useful angle on the Irish Question because it allowed him to avoid discussing details and concentrate his fire on a simple moral issue. Resistance to government oppression dramatized the Irish Question for English audiences; 'Justice to Ireland does not arouse enthusiasm,' observed the cynical Labouchere, 'unless it be wrapped up in what they regard as justice to themselves.'[10] English working men were therefore urged to see the threat to their own rights of combination and organization inherent in the suppression of similar bodies in Ireland.

In time, however, Home Rule assumed a less prominent role in Liberal politics. The destruction of Parnell's career in 1891 as a result of a divorce scandal sapped the will of many British Home Rulers; and the inevitable rejection of the second Home Rule Bill by the peers in 1893 followed by Gladstone's retirement in 1894 turned the issue into a cul de sac for ambitious Liberals instead of the highway to office that it had been for Morley in the 1880s. Since the party had to have a post-Home Rule policy, programme politics enjoyed a heyday encouraged by Harcourt and the faddists. The culmination of this process occurred at the NLF's Newcastle conference in 1891 which endorsed the full range of reforms: taxation of land values, ground rents and royalties, death duties, free elementary education, Welsh and Scottish disestablishment, a 'direct popular veto' on the liquor traffic, parish councils, home-rule-all-round, the 'free breakfast table', and reform of the franchise and the House of Lords.

This had been the staple radical diet for some years. What made the 'Newcastle Programme' significant was its apparent endorsement by Gladstone only a year before his victory in an election fought on its provisions. In fact Gladstone paid only cursory attention to the items on the list at Newcastle, ignoring those he disliked and concentrating on Ireland. Regardless of his real attitude, the programme's importance became evident when his Home Rule Bill suffered rejection at the hands of the peers. Their action posed a dilemma for the Cabinet. If Home Rule was so vital then they must resign and ask the country to overrule the House of Lords. But Gladstone's colleagues declined to take this course. In 1892 they had compelled him to embody much of the party programme in the Queen's Speech, and it seemed to them that after six years out of office they must press ahead with the reforms on which they had recently won election. The ministers, in short, now thought along the same lines as the NLF. Hence 1894 brought Harcourt's famous 'Death Duties' budget and the establishment of parish and district councils, as well as unsuccessful attempts at legislation for employers' liability and Welsh disestablishment.

It would, therefore, be beside the point to say that the Cabinet never allowed the NLF to dictate its policy, for the two had moved so close together that as a rule aggressive tactics were not necessary. The 1892–95 Liberal government represented an important stage in the party's evolution in so far as it showed the absorption of programmatic radicalism both in principle and in detail. Where the rank and file chose to adopt aggressive tactics, as on Welsh disestablishment, it was not because of disagreements on the merits of the issue but because the leaders felt that the peers' hostility made it a futile cause; they nonetheless went ahead with a bill. Undoubtedly the party still had major unresolved problems, notably a solution to the House of Lords question, the emergence of independent working-class politics, and the resurgence of imperial sentiment. Yet it had substantially resolved the problems of the 1860s; and in the process it had abandoned the passive, parliamentary form of politics and shaken free from the upper-class control that had inhibited both its role as assailant of privilege and its evolution as a modern political party.

Chapter 3

The Conservative Revival
1874–1900

It is significant that . . . the reformed constituency
of Westminster should have preferred the unknown
Conservative who sold books (W.H. Smith) to the
famous Liberal — JOHN STUART MILL — who wrote
them.

The Times, *7 October 1891*

At the death of Disraeli in 1881 the Conservative Party stood in
some apprehension about its future. Since the repeal of the Corn
Laws in 1846 it had not won a majority at a general election
except for 1874, and, in view of the drastic reforms made and
anticipated, no one could feel confident that the pattern had been
decisively broken. Before 1846 the Conservatives had established
themselves as a national party representing agriculture while also
promoting the economic innovation desired by urban, industrial
England. But for the defection of the Peelites in 1846 they might
have gone on to perform the role subsequently filled by Victorian
Liberalism. Instead they lingered for 30 years a sectional rump,
suspect in the eyes of the electorate for their inexperience of
office, the prominence of the distrusted Disraeli, and the protectionist tendencies of the country gentlemen. As late as 1874
Queen Victoria noted with evident relief that Disraeli's new
ministers included only one duke and were 'not at all retrograde'!

Yet the Conservative reputation for wildness and instability
was somewhat exaggerated. Their dilemma really lay in the
absence of any distinctive policy with which to win the electorate.
There was little that a mid-Victorian Conservative government
might do with respect to Empire, economy, property or monarchy
that one under Lord Palmerston could not do better.[1] Not until
the forces of popular radicalism gained the ascendancy in the

Liberal Party, and Palmerston's chauvinistic conservatism gave way to Gladstone's moralistic reformism, did the Conservatives begin to appear a better vehicle for the aspirations of 'respectable' England once again. Disraeli was lucky, if rather late in life, in the events of the 1860s; but he knew how to exploit his opportunities. He saw how to divide and rule the House of Commons in 1866–67 by taking up franchise reform; and how to appropriate Palmerston's mantle by seizing upon the radical 'conspiracy' to dismember the Empire, and by pursuing the Crimean War policy in 1875–78.

Yet Disraeli's contribution to the Conservatives' restoration as a governing party and as a majority in the country has been much exaggerated. Although the transition coincided with franchise reform there is little evidence that the new voters gave the Conservatives an additional advantage; rather their existence helped indirectly by crystallizing the radicalization occurring within Liberalism, thereby allowing the Conservatives under Lord Salisbury to inherit the naturally conservative forces in the country. In the long run the party grew less in a 'Disraelian' mould than a 'Peelite' one. Disraeli's own pilgrimage from impecunious notoriety to the peerage left intact his fondness for pre-industrial society united by the deference of the labourer and the duty of the landowner. He could not easily accommodate an urban middle class or an organized proletariat and like Gladstone he regretted the explosion of wealth in the hands of men who did not recognize it as a duty 'to endow the Church, to feed the poor, to guard the land, and to execute justice for nothing'. For him government was best conducted by disinterested gentlemen through local communities not central bureaucracies. This reluctance to come to terms with industrialization restricted the scope for an active policy for the working classes because this implied bureaucracy and taxation; instead Conservatism returned to an accommodation with middle-class industrial wealth. The return of the latter-day Peelites, though not at all what Disraeli envisaged, nevertheless gave the party its increasing strength and much of its organization and policy in the late nineteenth century.

The Impact of Middle-Class Conservatism

In 1865 the Conservatives' strength lay in England where 221 of their 294 MPs held seats, particularly in counties and small boroughs. Their representation even in counties was threatened by urban expansion. Yet their perilously narrow electoral base was to be modified in three ways. First, the Liberal hold on Scotland strengthened slightly, and on Wales greatly, while in Ireland the Home Rulers mopped up 80 per cent of the seats after 1874. In this way the Conservative position as the English party was considerably accentuated. Second, the Liberals extended their base in the counties following the 1884 franchise reforms. Thus, whereas in 1868 Conservatives had won 115 out of 154 English county seats, in 1885 they held only 105 out of 239; counties had become a key element in an overall Liberal majority.

Conservatives were saved only by their growing support in large boroughs and suburban seats, which reached a climax in 1900 when they took 177 English boroughs as against 162 English counties. There were indications of this trend in Lancashire after 1852 and in London after 1859; and in 1868, despite its overall defeat, the party gained 34 seats in boroughs whose population exceeded 20,000. Loss of formerly radical constituencies like Middlesex and Westminster was a warning to the Liberals that urbanization had created middle-class residential communities whose aspirations were not those of radical artisans.

However, the large towns remained under-represented in the Commons, and, since they returned two members from undivided consituencies, the improved Conservative poll frequently left the party a larger minority but still unrepresented. If Conservatives were to realize their strength, tactics required a drastic redistribution based upon equal constituencies and a single-member system. This is why one finds such radical notions being urged by Salisbury and Sir Michael Hicks-Beach in 1884–85; they seized their opportunity when Gladstone, hoping to close a somewhat barren term of office, with a radical triumph, introduced a bill to extend the household suffrage to the counties. This the peers could plausibly reject unless a redistribution scheme were attached. In the ensuing compact between the party leaders the Conservative desire for equal single-member seats coincided with the objectives of the Chamberlainites who hoped to eliminate Whigs in small boroughs. Thus, boroughs with a population under 15,000 lost their separate representation, while those with under 50,000 lost one of their two members. This drastically reduced the representation of the south-west to the advantage of London and Lancashire, both of which proved to be Conservative for 20 years. All counties and all but 23 boroughs were divided into single-member seats along boundaries that were designed to reflect 'the pursuits of the people'. This scheme helped the Conservatives, first, by increasing the scope for plural voting in the divided constituencies at a time when the propertied classes were coming adrift from Liberalism. Second, the Conservatives believed that by keeping agricultural areas separate from mining or urban areas they could maintain the territorial influence of the landowners. Third, in conurbations the same principle involved creating separate working-class, commercial, and residential middle-class seats. This would at least save the Conservative minority from being swamped. Liberals like Leonard Courtney and Sir John Lubbock argued in vain that minority representation would best be secured by a proportional system. At the time few politicians perceived that in a mature industrial society characterized by residential separation the effect of trying to preserve homogeneous communities would be to facilitate class-based voting. The consequences were obvious in formerly radical cities like Leeds where Conservatives subsequently won two of the five seats, and Sheffield where they took three of five. London, however, provided quite the most striking example of Conservative gains (see table 3.1). Redistribution could not, of

TABLE 3.1. *Conservative MPs in London*

Pre-1867 (total 18)		Post-1867 (total 22)		Post 1885 (total 59)	
1859	0	1868	3	1885	35
1865	0	1874	10	1886	47
		1880	8	1892	36
				1895	51
				1900	51

course, have had this effect without shifts of allegiance, but it facilitated the translation of urban votes into new members. Indeed his work in 1884–85 alone entitles Salisbury to be considered a major architect of his party's revival; in combination with the Home Rule crisis of 1886 the redistribution of 1885 made these years the decisive turning-point for Conservatism.

The broader base of Conservatism gradually modified the party's social composition in Parliament; an analysis of the MPs according to the date of their election to the Commons brings out the extent and timing of the change (see table 3.2). Only among MPs elected in 1885–86 who had previously sat in Parliament was the landed element the predominant one; in each new set of recruits after 1885 a substantial majority were drawn from the industrial and professional middle classes, a reflection of the fact

TABLE 3.2. *Social origins of Conservative MPs*

Parliamentary group		Landed classes	% from Industry and commerce	Professional and public service	Other
1885–86	Old	54.8	28.7	15.2	1.4
1885	New	34.1	34.2	26.5	5.1
1886	New	36.7	27.5	29.2	6.7
1892	New	41.9	32.0	19.6	6.0
1895	New	36.0	28.0	24.9	10.9
1900	New	28.7	42.5	18.1	10.6

Source: J.P. Cornford, 'Parliamentary Origins of the Hotel Cecil', in R.Robson (ed.), *Ideas and Institutions of Victorian Britain* (1967), p. 310.

that suburban seats, which were likely to adopt bourgeois candidates, had become safer for Conservatives than many counties.

On the other hand an examination of the entire parliamentary party after each election brings out the continuity (see table 3.3).

TABLE 3.3. *Social origins of Conservative MPs 1885–1900 (%)*

	1885	1886	1892	1895	1900
Landed classes	45.8	43.3	46.2	41.2	38.5
Industry and commerce	31.1	29.5	28.1	28.3	32.0
Professional and public service	19.9	23.2	20.7	23.2	21.3
Others	2.9	4.0	4.7	7.3	8.6

Source: J.P. Cornford, 'Parliamentary Origins of the Hotel Cecil', in R.Robson (ed.), *Ideas and Institutions of Victorian Britain* (1967), p. 310.

Clearly the composition of the party changed rather gradually. For whereas the sons of the upper classes normally entered the Commons before the age of 30, the businessman had first to establish his financial independence by building up his company, so that a seat in Parliament crowned his career in his fifties. Professional men, especially barristers, could enter earlier, but were apt to treat politics as an aid to their legal careers rather than as the prime objective. Both groups were more likely to take on marginal or hopeless constituencies, and to die or retire after short periods as MPs. The squires elected before 1885 enjoyed particularly long terms as MPs, but began to drop out in substantial numbers only after 1900.

Consequently the ultimate reward of cabinet office, being the due of men who had established their reputation in the House, fell disproportionately to the landed gentlemen. A businessman could be caught between the need to attend his business and to devote time to a minor role as parliamentary private secretary or junior whip, which was a necessary step on the ladder of office. It is not surprising that both Disraeli and Salisbury drew criticism for neglecting the claims of middle-class supporters, though the latter quickly learnt to make lavish use of honours to compensate for shortage of jobs. Despite the competition a number of bourgeois recruits obtained major office under Disraeli and Salisbury as a result of the dearth of administrative talent and debating skills to combat the Liberal heavy artillery. The 1874 ministry saw Richard Cross as Home Secretary, Gathorne-Hardy at the War Office, Sclater-Booth at the Local Government Board, and W.H. Smith whose elevation to the Admiralty in 1877 caused a flutter at the Palace and W.S. Gilbert's satirical creation 'Sir Joseph Porter' in *HMS Pinafore*. Salisbury appointed C.T. Richie to three ministries, George Goschen to the Exchequer, and relied heavily on Smith as Leader of the Commons from 1886 until his death in 1891. Smith and Cross, derided by Lord Randolph Churchill as 'Marshall and Snelgrove', reached the top through personal ability rather than as representatives of urban middle-class Toryism, though business expertise was, perhaps, a factor in Goschen's appointment as Chancellor in 1887. Yet it took more than a few pioneers to kill Lord Randolph's snobbery or the ingrained condescension of the traditional leaders. Witness Arthur Balfour's advice to Salisbury on the choice of a new Postmaster-General in 1891 in which he commended W.L. Jackson (MP for Leeds North) who,

has great tact and judgement — middle class tact and judgement I admit, but good of their kind . . . he is that *rara avis*, a successful manufacturer who is fit for something besides manufacturing. A cabinet of Jacksons would [be] rather a serious order, no doubt: but one or even two would be a considerable addition to any cabinet.[2]

What is clear is that middle-class ministers were chosen, apart from the special cases like Chamberlain, on the strength of administrative competence and forensic talent. The epitome of urban Conservatism and the National Union, Sir John Gorst, conspicuously failed to make the Cabinet; however, Gorst, who largely ruled himself out by rebelliousness over labour questions, was never dangerous enough to command a place at the top. Indeed the only politician who can in any sense be said to have used the National Union to advance himself to the Cabinet, Churchill, was an aristocrat without a real following.

Organizing the Democracy

As the Conservative leaders contemplated the growth of urban political organization on the Liberal side they realized that they would have to match it eventually; yet it was Salisbury rather than Disraeli, who actually came to terms with this distasteful necessity.

Since the 1830s the party had made do with a rudimentary organizational structure emanating from the Carlton Club whence amateur officials attempted to stimulate registration work in the constituencies. However, continued electoral failure and the establishment of the Liberal Registration Association in 1861 were so worrying that by 1867 Disraeli was ready to respond to John Gorst's passionate demand that the party should deliberately consolidate its traditional links with the people. One expression of these links already existed in working men's Conservative clubs, and the first modest gathering of these – the National Union of Conservative and Constitutional Associations (NUCCA) – in 1867 received Disraeli's blessing. Whether through dismay at the election defeat of 1868 or through being apprehensive of the popular body, he also created in 1870 a separate Conservative Central Office which was designed to stimulate new associations, maintain contact with them and compile lists of candidates. Since these functions duplicated those of the NUCCA the dual system inevitably produced friction. Initially, however, both bodies made progress in the declining years of Gladstone's administration; and by 1872 Central Office and the National Union were closely linked through a common headquarters and Gorst's position as both principal agent and honorary secretary of the National Union.

The objects of the National Union were modestly conceived. As Gorst had reminded the approving delegates in 1867, it was 'not a meeting for the discussion of Conservative principles on which we are all agreed, it is only a meeting to consider by what particular organization we may make these Conservative principles effective among the masses'.[3] Initially the task of extending Conservative associations through the country proved congenial; and by 1877 some 791 bodies had affiliated, though many of these were clubs and registration societies not constituency associations. The victory of 1874, when 65 of the 74 Conservative gains in England and Wales occurred under the auspices of active Conservative associations, encouraged the National Union to ignore the indifference and hostility exhibited by much of the party which preferred to rely upon traditional *ad hoc* committees of solicitors and gentlemen to organize elections. Particularly in the rural areas local dignitaries disliked anything that smacked of the 'caucus'. They were also deeply suspicious of the voluminous body of literature eulogizing Disraelian reforms generated by the National Union in the 1870s; the Conservative case, they believed, should never be based upon programmes of exceptional legislation for the working class.

Gladstone's surprise victory in 1880 emboldened the National Union delegates to offer the party advice on the shortcomings of its attitude towards organization. They demanded more attention to speeches in the country by parliamentary leaders, and greater expenditure on new Conservative clubs which considerably facilitated registration work; and they condemned the habit of leaving organization in the hands of amateur 'gentlemen who practically knew nothing of election matters and undertook the management merely as a professional duty in their capacity of lawyers'.[4] In addition they pointed out that the 1883 Act on expenses and illegal practices would curtail the practice of paying for canvassing and conveyancing to the poll, and leave the party greatly handicapped against the radicals.[5] The expectation of an extended county franchise at this time was one of the considerations that impelled Lord Randolph Churchill to champion the party organization.

He was not the only one who was alive to the dangers posed by the rapidly changing rules of the electoral battle. Gorst, aware that the associations often existed only on paper and lapsed between elections, tried to encourage them to contest the municipal elections regularly and to find extra money for the building of clubs. But although the National Union took pains to dissociate itself from the National Liberal Federation and to abjure pronouncements on policy, its conferences eventually became the scene of lively debates, and not simply on organization. After

1885 the rank and file showed enthusiasm for various issues that the parliamentary leaders studiously avoided – alien immigration, women's suffrage, state subsidies for house purchase, and an imperial tariff policy; indeed the successful battle for protectionism waged in annual conferences during the 1880s and 1890s prepared the way for the Chamberlainite takeover after 1903.

Despite these undercurrents the National Union never directly confronted the leadership except in the early 1880s and then not over policy but over organization and the role of urban middle-class Conservatism. By 1880 Gorst, frustrated by Disraeli's neglect of the machine and by personal chagrin at not being offered a major post, sought a leader for his cause. Through his membership of the 'Fourth Party' (a self-appointed group of four MPs who tormented the Gladstone government), he found one in Churchill; it is significant that it took someone of Churchill's rank to spearhead the campaign. After securing election to the Council of the National Union in 1882 he proceeded to attack the practice of co-opting on to the Council 12 members nominated by Central Office which had little interest in improving organization in the country. He railed against the Central Committee, which Disraeli had established and was dependent on the leader for funds and personnel, for effectively reducing the National Union to an impotent, advisory role. Churchill demanded that control of organization and funds be removed from the irresponsible body to the elected Council. Culminating in a meeting with Salisbury in 1884 Churchill's campaign produced a face-saving compromise. The Central Committee was abolished, the Council freed of co-opted members and a little more money was granted to the National Union. None of these details, however, materially improved the power or status of the National Union.

Beneath the rhetoric Lord Randolph Churchill had never shared Gorst's objectives, and certainly not his hostility towards the traditional leaders of the party from whose ranks he came.[6] In 1882 he declined an invitation to contest Manchester, preferring to remain safely in the family borough of Woodstock until its abolition in 1885. He made a single foray on behalf of urban Conservatism by fighting a Birmingham seat against John Bright, but thereafter reverted to a safe seat at Paddington. Churchill had no intention of putting his career at risk for the cause of middle-class Conservatism, which is why, once he felt he had done enough to win a place in the next government, he dropped the National Union. It would be flattering both Churchill and the National Union to suppose that he endeavoured to use it as a power base from which to secure the party leadership, for was too young, too inexperienced in office and too lacking in support in Parliament. Salisbury pandered to Churchill's pretensions because he appreciated that his campaign was not directed against himself but against Northcote, and because he recognized that Churchill's platform oratory was an asset to the party. There was consequently no objection to elevating him to cabinet rank in 1885 provided that nothing of substance had to be conceded to the National Union. Churchill was safe because he was no Chamberlain.

Thus, after 1884 the National Union settled down to its functions of branch-building, propaganda and speech-making; and from 1885 all Conservative associations were automatically affiliated to it. A signal indication of the leadership's control over the organization was Salisbury's ability to ensure the withdrawal of Conservative candidates in all but a handful of the 93 seats held by Liberal Unionist MPs in 1886. Local constituency interest was simply over-ruled by parliamentary strategy. The party in the country was tended by 'Captain' R.W.E. Middleton, the principal agent from 1885 and honorary secretary of the National Union from 1886, who co-ordinated his work smoothly with Salisbury and the chief whip. Where Gorst had been prickly and ambitious Middleton was loyal, tactful and ready to accept the subservient role of the organization. This was congenial to Salisbury who enjoyed consulting him both over election statistics, of which he became a keen student, and over the awarding of honours in the party, which he was determined not to neglect. Much of Middleton's work consisted in creating a network of professional agents that covered half the constituencies by 1900 with an intermediate layer of officials in each region. They provided headquarters with electoral intelligence, and the public's reaction to legislation, particularly Liberal legislation that might be safely rejected by the Lords if it was not really popular. In retrospect the electoral successes of the Middleton era seemed to prove the advantages of a professional corps of organizers over the larger but more troublesome structure of associations represented by the National Union.

The Importance of the Primrose League

Late Victorian Conservatism presents an interesting paradox. On the one hand there is a strong impression from the improved electoral fortunes that the party adapted more successfully than its opponents to the conditions of a mass electorate. On the other hand this seems inconsistent with the leaders' patent distaste for popular organization, and their determination to keep the National Union strictly within bounds; indeed, although constituency associations became the norm after 1885, the organizations were often a mere formality, as small and remote as ever. The need to match the radicals in practical political skills was only partly met by the Conservatives' superior finances and the creation of full-time constituency agents. For they could by no means dispense with the efforts of a large corps of volunteer workers. In this respect the deficiencies of the formal party structure in the National Union and the constituency bodies were more than compensated for by the Primrose League, a key political institution in this period which has been remarkably neglected by the historians of the Conservative Party.

Founded in November 1883, the 'Primrose Tory League', as it was originally known, claimed to promote 'Tory principles – viz the maintenance of religion, of the estates of the realm, and of the Imperial Ascendancy of Great Britain'; by adopting both the primrose – supposedly Disraeli's favourite flower – and such slogans as 'True Union of the Classes', its leaders sought to emphasize the Disraelian source of their inspiration. The League Offered one class of membership at a guinea a year for 'Knights' and 'Dames', and another for associate members whose much lower dues went to their local branches; these branches were actually known as 'Habitations', the honorary president as the 'Grand Master', the ruling body as the 'Grand Council', the executive head as the 'Chancellor', official notices as 'Precepts', and subscriptions as 'Tribute'. All this delightfully anachronistic escapism made the Primrose League as appealing as a masonic lodge or a collegiate university, and it reminds us that the members created a political role that was as enjoyable as it was useful. By 1886 membership had reached 237,000, by 1891 it exceeded 1 million, and by 1910 2 million. These figures, no doubt, exaggerate because the League invariably added new members to the total while making no deductions for losses. However, the pattern of its growth broadly reflected Conservative fortunes. Membership more than doubled in 1886–87 under the stimulus of the Home Rule crisis, slackened in the early 1890s as Salisbury's government ran out of steam, quickened dramatically before and during the Boer War, and stagnated thereafter until 1910. By that year some 2,645 Habitations existed in the British Isles. Far from being a purely rural phenomenon the League entrenched itself in industrial Britain too, and claimed that nine-tenths of the members were working class.

Why was the Primrose League such an asset to the Conservative Party? Fundamentally because it provided a practical application of class and rank as a unifying force in society. Part of the difficulty with a body like the National Union was that Conservatives had felt uncomfortable with an organization designed for working men or the urban middle class. 'I have never been myself at all favourable, 'Disraeli once said, 'to a system which would induce Conservatives who are working men to form societies confined merely to their class.'[7] Whereas the National Union suffered embarrassment at the lack of participation by working men, the League adopted a frankly hierarchical structure that not only mirrored the gradations of society but dramatized them; by accepting class as a virtue not as a matter for apology the League comfortably embraced the Conservative view of social unity.

In the same way the League enjoyed an advantage over the National Union in that though it was a popular body it never appeared a threat to the leadership. Its relationship with the party remained spiritually close but organizationally loose. By confining its politics to fairly general principles like the Empire which would endure beyond the passing excitements of legislation, the League avoided either taking sides on divisive issues or presenting programmes to the parliamentary leaders. This is why Salisbury and Balfour were quite content to accept roles as 'Grand Master' and to present annual addresses. This arrangement gave them a friendly alliance with a large body of like-minded people who, by remaining separate, could not make unreasonable demands upon them.

As an electoral machine the League served the party in several crucial ways. It deluged the constituencies with its own and Central Office propaganda. The Warden of a Habitation was frequently entrusted with responsibility for preparing annually lists of voters and canvassing those on the register; its dense network of local contacts especially in rural areas enabled the League to mobilize the Conservative vote efficiently at elections. However, it was the League's regular round of activities *between* rather than during elections that gave Conservatives the edge over their Liberal rivals whose activity and vote was apt to fluctuate much more according to the ebb and flow of national political issues. By avoiding a formal 'Conservative' title the League also made it easier for non-Conservatives to participate in their events. Indeed they offered a great deal more than mere politics: Habitations readily accepted the warning that meetings should not be 'so distinctly elevating as to be pronounced dull'. They offered cheap dances, their own brass bands, and evening entertainments involving singing, conjurors, ventriloquists, jugglers, wax works, marionettes and pierrots. Such programmes available in each locality formed an irresistible attraction especially in country areas where they might be the only form of regular social event. In this way the League often integrated itself into the fabric of a community more effectively than political parties could do. Frivolous League activities provoked much hilarity and contempt from Liberals and socialists who were not convinced that politics was meant to be enjoyable. However, they saw that the teas, fetes and visits to country houses served a real function by providing a coveted opportunity for the lower ranks to mingle briefly with the great. Nor was the mixture purely social, for a fete or evening entertainment usually included its political address. A political message was delivered less directly though doubtless more effectively by techniques that were a novelty in themselves such as magic lanterns and *tableaux vivants* which displayed a series of images of imperial splendour such as the Queen enthroned as Empress of India, Gordon at Khartoum, Nelson on the *Victory*, Lords Roberts or Kitchener in Afghanistan or South Africa. This blend of patriotic history with recent controversial incidents was more shrewdly aimed than many more cerebral pieces of propaganda.

Another merit of the Primrose League lay in its capacity for involving women in the political process. From 1883 women had been admitted as members, and sometimes formed their own Habitations. Middle- and upper-class ladies threw themselves enthusiastically into arranging League functions, canvassing, contacting the outvoters, conveying electors to the polls in private carriages, raising funds and generally keeping the grass roots of Conservatism vigorous. By the 1890s the sight of the Primrose Dame speeding through villages on her 'safety' bicycle or descending *en masse*, as the 'Primrose Cycling Corps' at by-elections became a painfully familiar sight to radicals. Here again, it suited the men of the party that women should involve themselves so constructively but without pressing for power or for their enfranchisement. Nonetheless both Salisbury and Balfour followed Disraeli's example in indicating personal sympathy for votes for wealthy women. This early association between women activists and the Conservative Party doubtless laid the foundations for the party's organizational superiority in the twentieth century. More immediately the Primrose League generated the voluntary labour so necessary under the reformed electoral system of the 1880s and challenged the radicals' political skills effectively. By extending the Conservative influence beyond small groups of partisans the League succeeded where politicians invariably failed in keeping the cause healthy between elections, which goes some way to explaining the stability of the Conservative vote between the 1880s and 1914 by comparison with the more volatile Liberal performance.

Salisbury and Liberal Unionism

The third Marquis of Salisbury who led no less than four governments between 1885 and 1902 from the lonely eminence of Hatfield and the House of Lords, was a most unlikely leader in a democratic age of which he thoroughly disapproved. This period of dominance has long been neglected by historians; even by Conservatives his accomplishments have been ignored in favour of the more superficially attractive figure of Disraeli whose impact has generally been exaggerated. This is not altogether surprising; Disraeli does have a contemporary appeal where Salisbury seems inflexibly old-fashioned; Disraeli's name is easily linked with a creed and with a watershed in history where Salisbury seems to have left no permanent tradition; most of all, Salisbury basically despised his party, accepting it merely as the best available vehicle for his objectives; with his austerely intellectual approach he detested any pandering to the sentimental nostrums of Conservatism.

His opportunity to become leader arose after Disraeli's death in 1881 which inaugurated an unhappy experience in dual leadership by Sir Stafford Northcote in the Commons and Salisbury in the Lords. The outcome of this period — Salisbury's premiership in 1885 — was not expected in 1881. For Salisbury's record suggested the dangerously ideological backwoodsman; Northcote was safer, and was for some time the Queen's first choice. This failed to materialize because as Leader of the Opposition Northcote, by his conciliatory and lacklustre performance, threw away his main advantage over Salisbury, that he could directly confront Gladstone in the Commons. This was repeatedly emphasized by the lively attacks made by the 'Fourth Party' comprising Churchill, Gorst, Arthur Balfour and Sir Henry Drummond Wolff. It is now clear that one object of Churchill's activity in the Fourth Party as in the National Union was to facilitate Salisbury's attainment of the leadership in place of Northcote. [8] For his part Salisbury appreciated that Churchill's popular oratory obscured his traditional Conservatism, and welcomed a compromise that weakened Northcote's supporters in the National Union. The effect of the protracted controversy was to focus attention upon Salisbury as the one who could handle the popular body, and to edge Northcote off stage as an irrelevancy.

However, if the rumpus served to elevate Salisbury, it also drew attention to his political rigidity. Unlike most politicians he thought seriously about the long-term development of society. A quintessential conservative, Salisbury believed that the defects in man's condition were to a large extent congenital and consequently not susceptible to new ways of ordering society. Since what could be achieved through politics was quite limited it was desirable to restrain the state from trenching too far upon the private sphere as most reforms threatened to do. In government one should concentrate on administration rather than mere 'politics'. Like several other late Victorians with experience of India (Secretary of State 1874–78), Salisbury absorbed a firm belief in the superiority of strong, just, arbitrary government by a highly qualified elite compared with systems in which authority hinged upon representation and efficiency was hampered by political parties and assemblies.

Herein lay the menace of contemporary British society. In 1867 Salisbury had resigned from the Conservative government in disgust at franchise reform, and spent much of his nervous energy composing withering attacks upon Disraeli for his unprincipled opportunism and betrayal of Conservative principles – much as Disraeli had once berated Peel. The slide towards a democratic franchise seemed to him destructive of a stable and unified society. For once the Commons had, in the name of the people, aggrandized all power at the expense of the other elements in the mixed constitution (the monarchy and aristocracy) government would fall into the hands of men without property and lose its impartiality. Britain could easily slide into an American type of corruption in which politicians gained office by offering specific rewards to distinct groups or classes, thereby helping their society towards eventual disintegration.

Although these sentiments were never far from the surface they reflect the younger Salisbury, a man who had not yet acquired the mellow confidence that political success and a happy marriage gradually gave him. In practical terms, much as he preferred the 1832 system, he accepted that he could never hope to reverse the drift away from it.

Salisbury's apprehensions had materially abated by the time he became Prime Minister. He grew to appreciate Disraeli's desire to make Conservatism the British national party rather than the organ of a sectional interest. He realized, too, that the defence of 'liberty' could be accomplished within the framework of democracy; even the United States took on a more attractive appearance, for its federalism, its Senate and its judiciary imposed admirable curbs on the power of central government. The problem was how to extend the role of local against central government in Britain without simply handing over power to the radicals as had happened with the school boards. The best substitute for an American arrangement of checks and balances lay in reliance on the House of Lords and the Conservative Party.

Therefore Salisbury set himself to master some of the arts of party leadership, gratefully relying on his chief whip and principal agent. Yet he resented the obligation to immerse himself in the trivia of political life: 'Why should I spend my evenings being trampled upon by the Conservative Party?' He retreated to Hatfield as often as possible and kept social contact to a minimum. Fortunately his chief whip, Aretas Akers-Douglas, a congenial country gentleman from Kent, helped to save him from the consequences of his own aloofness, and managed efficiently an increasingly loyal parliamentary party. Though Salisbury could never attain popularity, his followers were in a sense grateful, for, as one historian has put it: 'A nobleman from a Tory family with illustrious forbears, Salisbury came from the class among which Conservatives wanted but rarely managed to find a leader.'[9]

His practical strategy was determined by the knowledge that his party had won a general election only in 1874 followed by what appeared to be traditional Liberal victories in 1880 and 1885. This, he believed, was simply because the party alignment still reflected the divisions of 1832 and 1846 — now irrelevant. Since the Liberal reforms had been absorbed into the system the Whigs ought logically to join the Conservatives in defending the status quo. Eventually Salisbury's major achievement was to facilitate the post-1886 realignment without forfeiting his own control. For him the detachment of the Whigs would ensure either a Conservative government, or, still better, a radical government with such a small majority that it lacked the authority to force through drastic changes; in such circumstances the House of Lords would step in as the guardian of the national will against sectional interests entrenched in the House of Commons.

The critical point in the unfolding of this strategy came after

December 1885 when Gladstone's commitment to Irish Home Rule became public knowledge, and began to alienate a substantial section of Liberals under Lord Hartington's leadership. However, Salisbury had to move skilfully, for Hartington had ambitions of his own. He seemed acceptable to a sufficiently wide range of opinion in both Liberal and Conservative camps to form his own government, which would have been tantamount to a restoration of the Palmerstonian alliance in the centre. Since this made him a threat to both Salisbury and Gladstone they endeavoured to prevent any coalescence in the centre. Gladstone forced the issue by preparing a Home Rule Bill, speedily dissolving Parliament after its defeat and elevating Home Rule as the test of Liberalism. For his part Salisbury contributed a strident anti-Home Rule speech in May 1886 in which he derided the Irish as comparable with the Hottentots in their unfitness for self-rule, and advised them to emigrate to Manitoba to alleviate their hardship. This inflammatory speech was calculated to polarize the debate between himself and Gladstone so as to drive Hartington to one side or the other, thereby losing the centre ground.

What was to be the relationship between the 93 Liberal Unionists, of whom 78 survived the general election, and the Conservatives? It was no part of Salisbury's intention in 1886 to absorb them immediately. Co-operation in the constituencies had served its purpose by reducing the Gladstonians to 191 while leaving 316 Conservatives. In view of the dangerous concatenation of Joseph Chamberlain and Lord Randolph Churchill he refused to bring the Liberal Unionists into his government; their joint energies harnessed to programmes of reform would certainly disrupt the Cabinet or take it out of his own hands. When in 1886 Churchill rashly offered his resignation as Chancellor of the Exchequer in protest at the Cabinet's refusal to accept economies the Prime Minister made a tentative offer to Hartington because he felt confident it would be declined; thereupon the vacancy was filled by recruiting another ex-Liberal, Goschen, leaving the party relationship unchanged. Similarly the Liberal Unionists declined to throw in their lot fully with the Conservatives. Susceptible to their Liberal critics in the country who had rebelled solely over Home Rule in many cases, they seized every chance to distance themselves from the new government by refusing to vote for it except over Ireland or when it stood in danger of actual defeat, which was rare.

However, the Gladstonian revival prior to 1892 convinced Salisbury that it was unwise to take Liberal Unionism for granted.

'JOEY'

In his wonderful Balance Trick, to be seen nightly at the St. Stephen's Circus, Westminster.

Hartington   Chamberlain   Salisbury   Balfour

Harry Furniss, Pen and Pencil in Parliament (1897).

He therefore determined to incorporate them into his next government by offering four cabinet posts. His belief that Chamberlain would accept the limitations of a Conservative cabinet was vindicated when the ex-radical asked only for a committee of investigation on old age pensions, and, for himself, the Colonial Office. In the long run this led to new problems, but for the time being it served to draw the two together and harness Chamberlain to a cause that was dear to the Conservative Party. Technically Salisbury, with 341 members in 1895, could have dispensed with a coalition. Yet he found some advantage in diluting his embarrassingly large majority with Liberal Unionist elements. For one thing he had discovered that the Nonconformists brought in by Chamberlain were not necessarily subversive radicals; and even radicals contributed to the checks and balances within the coalition. In practice major measures like the 1896 Education Bill succumbed entirely to Conservative attack; and the 1897 Bill for Workmen's Compensation only reached the statute book emasculated by the peers. While this process created friction on particular matters, Salisbury could at least rejoice that it served the higher purpose of setting limits on central government.

Salisbury and Social Reform

Though Salisbury's approach to domestic affairs sprang from a cynical distrust of government, it was softened by fear of adopting an entirely negative policy and by a modicum of compassion towards the poor. Fortunately elections could be won without stooping to 'class legislation' at the expense of the propertied section, for, as Churchill's meteoric rise had demonstrated, the working classes would respond to quite traditional Tory appeals in defence of Church, Empire and monarchy. However, this strategy succeeded best only when the opposition co-operated by concentrating on such questions as Home Rule. When in office after 1886 Conservatives felt obliged to adopt a constructive attitude on domestic matters if only to disprove the Gladstonian argument that all progress was blocked by the refusal to concede Ireland's demands. This accounts for the quantity of minor legislation, designed to be economical and undisturbing, enacted under Salisbury's premierships.

This policy should not be interpreted, as it sometimes is, as a resurrection of a Conservative tradition for strong paternalist government, unhampered by liberal individualism, which developed into a pragmatic collectivist ideology.[10] The origins of such a view lie in the historic Tory preference for strong government which had been characteristic of the revolutionary and Napoleonic war period and which did reassert itself in exceptional circumstances such as the First World War; but this is not to be confused with or causally linked with collectivism. Conservatives of the 1880s inherited the prevailing Victorian preference for curtailing government in favour of local autonomy and economy where this was seen to be effective. The basis of Salisbury's *laissez-faire* convictions was more political than economic; they sprang from his veneration of private property and hostility to interfering government rather than from the business liberalism that inspired many of his colleagues. Though he did not shrink from a little judicious state assistance for the poor, he believed that little could be accomplished by this means without causing financial and social damage; on the whole, therefore, he prescribed self-help as a general rule, but without the optimism that an early-Victorian liberal might have displayed. Conservatives also accepted the inevitability of free trade, though their candidates in agricultural constituencies still pandered to protectionism;[11] but as free traders they lacked the intense moral conviction with which many Liberals invested the issue. Salisbury, like many Conservatives, seems to have been undogmatic about free trade, accepting in principle by the 1890s the idea of retaliation against other countries.

As a social reformer Salisbury has suffered by comparison with Disraeli's achievements. In fact there was considerable continuity between the two periods. Disraeli himself had usually opposed social reforms in the 1840s and 1850s — 'those Gallic imitations' — as extentions of bureaucracy at the expense of local authority. Hence, as Richard Cross complained, he came to office with no precise social policy. The reforms of his administration in public health, food and drugs, factories and education were in fact essentially administrative not political in inspiration in that they merely extended or improved the legislation of previous governments; other legislation, like the Artisans Dwellings Act, was permissive in character, allowing municipalities to demolish slum housing more easily but not obliging them to replace it.[12] The Conservatives' claims as paternalists defending the workers against rampant capitalism rested upon traditional support for the ten-hour day and opposition to the new Poor Law. However, by the 1880s these traditions had begun to wither from neglect. Conservatives were increasingly to be found among those who defended the principles of 1834, while the critics of the Poor Law were radicals and Fabians who looked to the county councils and central government to shoulder its responsibilities. Similarly the demand for an eight-hour day often met a stony response in the 1880s from the middle-class employers who were now joining the Conservatives. In fact by 1892 the official party view condemned the eight-hour day for raising prices and lowering efficiency, as well as for interfering with the worker's freedom to determine his own conditions of work;[13] in short the party was preaching the arguments of classical economics more readily than their opponents. Nor was Disraeli's recognition of the right to picket in 1871 followed up by his successors who were more impressed by unions and militancy; indeed the Salisbury–Balfour era culminated with the Conservatives putting themselves at odds with labour by refusing to reverse the Taff Vale judgement of 1901 (see p. 121). The working man now seemed too assertive and powerful to fit the Disraelian conception.

By the 1880s the remnants of Disraelian Tories, Lord John Manners and Lord Cranbrook, were old and uninfluential. The real reformers were C. T. Ritchie (at the Local Government Board, the Board of Trade and the Home Office successively); A. J. Balfour, at least on education and Ireland; and Chamberlain from outside. Yet Chamberlain's influence proved less formative than that of men like George Goschen who, in becoming Chancellor in 1886, intended to help 'purge them of the cant of Tory Democracy', and irritated even Salisbury in his defence of the rights of property and hostility to social reform. Goschen's career demonstrates the crystallization of the naturally conservative forces around Salisbury and the abandonment of Disraelianism; he epitomized the middle-class recruits who had not quit Liberalism in order to pay higher taxes or suffer more legal regulation under the Conservatives.

Consequently the party effectively opted for a mid-Victorian liberal approach to finance much as it had adopted a Palmerstonian policy in external affairs. By 1892 their appeal was couched in terms of pure Gladstonian retrenchment: tea duty reduced and sugar duty abolished; in six years Goschen had contrived a budget surplus every time; the average rate of income tax had come down to 6½d, and £18 million had been given in relief of taxation.[14] Neither the 1880–85 nor 1892–95 Liberal governments could make such claims; Sir William Harcourt had raised income tax to 7¾d and added £9 million to taxation.

Land reform epitomized the Conservatives' dilemma, for radical propaganda among agricultural labourers threatened electoral disaster, while legislation for Scottish Crofters and Ireland provided precedents. Hence the passage of an Allotments Act in 1887 (extended in 1890), which empowered local authorities to purchase land for letting at economic rents, and the 1892 Small-holdings Act. Salisbury resisted these measures on the grounds that compulsory purchase was tantamount to confiscation, and that infringement of the rights of property owners would be economically counter-productive; yet his colleagues forced him to give way.[15] Some anticipated that the legislation would be relatively ineffective in view of the reluctance of landowner-dominated county councils especially in the south to make use of their powers.

Indeed the establishment of county councils in 1889 and the peers' amendments of the Liberals' Parish Councils Bill in 1893 proved an effective check on social reform. Though loath to disturb the existing management of county affairs through the Courts of Quarter Sessions by JPs appointed by the Lords Lieutenant, Salisbury knew that reform was a radical priority from which the 1880–85 government had narrowly been deflected;[16] further radical attempts had to be forestalled. Many Conservatives resisted direct elections for county councils because they would be expensive and, by introducing a political element, would exclude the best men — an argument typical of Salisbury. How-ever, Ritchie, backed by Chamberlain who saw this as a test of his influence with the Conservatives, managed to scotch the idea of indirect election. Yet the county franchise was restricted to occupiers, and a quarter of the membership of the councils was reserved for co-opted aldermen; in addition special restrictions on expenditure were imposed, and the poor law administration was withheld from them for fear that the radicals might gain control.

Fear of popular involvement also inspired educational reform in this period. Salisbury himself largely lacked sympathy with the idea of education for the masses which would deprive employers of child labour; but he failed to stop the extension of free elemen-tary education in 1891 by Balfour and his ally Chamberlain for whom it was a long-standing objective. The problem lay in the school boards, always seen as subversive bodies, which had taken to widening the range of subjects taught and had established secondary schools in many places. Apart from the cost to rate-payers it was thought to be destructive of social harmony to educate people beyond their station in life. The 1896 Education Bill, which proposed to remove control to county councils, proved abortive due to opposition within the Cabinet. Thereafter other ways were found of undermining the school boards. In 1899 the Board of Education instigated a case against the London School Board for spending money from the rates on science and art schools; the resulting 'Cockerton Judgement' made higher grade education illegal. Balfour's famous Act of 1902 finally ended the school boards by placing responsibility for education with committees of the county councils.

In contrast, housing did engage Salisbury's interest to the extent that he personally initiated the 1885 Royal Commission on Housing. Nonetheless his government refused to allow any infringement of the urban landlords' and landowners' rights over their property; they resisted any state involvement in house-building, though permitting the London County Council to act; and they adhered to permissive legislation in the bleak hope that market pressures would disperse population away from over-crowded urban centres.[17]

In Ireland dire necessity pushed the Conservatives well beyond what was thought safe for England. After 1881 when a shocked Salisbury found that the landowners did not want him to save them from Gladstone's Land Act, the rights of property were effectively thrown overboard. A combination of rents lowered by tribunals, agricultural depression and rural violence gradually destroyed the landowners' resolve to the extent that by 1900 they were ready to sell their land given attractive terms. During the 1880s the Conservatives had begun to appreciate the idea of creating peasant proprietors (at least in Ireland) in the conviction that to turn tenants into small owners was tantamount to convert-ing agitators into supporters of stable government, and thereby undermining 'Home Rule'. Beginning with the £5 million allocated for land purchase in Ashbourne's Act of 1885 and continuing with similar measures in 1888 and 1891, this policy culminated in Wyndham's Land Act of 1903 under which a quarter of a million Irishmen bought farms before 1914. As Salisbury observed dole-fully in 1887, 'It is the price we have to pay for the Union, and it is a heavy one.'[18] It is significant that those Conservatives most closely associated with this policy, Horace Plunkett, Lord Dunraven and George Wyndham, suffered a permanent check to their careers.

Ireland also afforded more scope for experiments in social inter-ventionism than England. As Chief Secretary Balfour applied state funds to pay wages for relief work in the most distressed counties and for the construction of light railways. His Congested Districts Bill of 1890 created boards in the west of Ireland (where the people were too poor to take advantage of land purchase schemes) with resources to acquire land, amalgamate uneconomic holdings, distribute seed potatoes and assist tenants to migrate from congested districts or to emigrate. The nearest approach to a similar policy in England came in 1905 in the form of Walter Long's Unemployed Workmen's Act, which involved using rate finance for relief work schemes in London. However, Balfour, now Prime Minister, retreated from the radical implications of the measure by limiting it to a three-year experiment only, and by appointing a Royal Commission on the Poor Law to avoid the necessity for further action.

This reluctance to deal boldly or constructively with social problems brought the Salisbury–Balfour era to an unimaginative end. Throughout these years Conservatives had been caught in the dilemma of financing social policies under a free enterprise system. Although this is sometimes seen as a Liberal problem it afflicted the Conservatives more, partly because they found themselves more frequently in office, but also because, in the absence of the political reform espoused by the Liberals, they felt an obligation to pass safe social legislation. Paradoxically Chamberlain's influence was probably greater during 1886–92 when he remained outside the government and felt anxious about justifying his co-operation by means of the measures for county councils, education and allotments. Later he sought influence through a vigorous imperial policy and a formidably long list of social reforms which he presented to Salisbury in a memorandum of 1894: compensation for industrial injuries, amendment of the Artisans Dwellings Act, loans to working men for house purchase, an eight-hour day for miners, reduction of alien immigration, old age pensions, labour exchanges, arbitration courts to settle industrial disputes, earlier closing for shops, and cheaper train travel for workmen. In fact his colleagues were amenable to action on several of these items, notably immigration and workmen's compensation. But by now Chamberlain had reconciled himself to playing a limited role. Although pensions did receive official sanction in the *Campaign Guide* for 1895, there was agreement only on a contributory scheme that would have omitted those most in need. The Cabinet drifted into the South African War and lost its opportunity to outflank the Liberals. Its whole approach to social questions was crippled by its addiction to retrenchment and inhibited by apprehension about the pressure of organized labour and the social investigations of the 1890s. Innovation was to be adopted only where it would forestall a more radical change. In this way Conservative thinking stagnated until the explosive reappraisal triggered by Chamberlain's disastrous tariff campaign of 1903.

Chapter 4

The Social Roots of Political Change in Late Victorian Britain

When you stand in the voting booth with your card and your pencil in your hand, think of this: I am going to vote either for robbing God or against it.
Warwickshire clergyman, quoted in The Nonconformist, *3 December 1885*

Up to 1841 British general elections remained essentially parochial in character: that is, the shifts of opinion from one constituency to another fluctuated over a wide range that reflected the multitude of local factors at work. Thereafter the range narrowed as more general influences common to the whole country made an impression. However, historians have characterized this as a regional rather than a national pattern which reached its height around 1868–85.[1] Using Dr Pelling's calculations[2] of the Conservative and Unionist share of the poll we may distinguish the broad party loyalties of the regions as they appeared in 1885 (see table 4.1).

TABLE 4.1. *Conservative and Unionist % vote 1885*

Strongly Conservative		Intermediate		Anti-Conservative	
S.E. England	54.5	East Anglia	49.2	Northern	
Wessex	51.5	Bristol region	48.7	England	41.7
Lancastria	51.4	Yorks region	45.8	Peak-Don	41.5
London County		West Midlands	45.5	Wales	39.6
Council area	51.0	Central Eng-		Scotland	36.3
		land	44.7		
		Devon and			
		Cornwall	44.3		
		East Midlands	43.7		

To a considerable extent these regional loyalties already reflected the uneven distribution of social classes in each area. But classes had by no means come to behave in a uniform fashion across the country. Working men in London and Lancashire were much less inclined to Liberalism than working men in north-east England or Wales; the middle classes of Scotland and Yorkshire were far more likely to vote Liberal than those of south-east England.

In terms of party fortunes the period from 1865 to 1900 falls into two phases with the watershed in 1885−86: the first saw a continuation of the mid-Victorian Liberal dominance interrupted only in 1874; and the second from 1886 saw it replaced by Conservative predominance with the partial exception of 1892 (see table 4.2).

TABLE 4.2. *General election results 1865−1900 (seats won)*

	1865	1868	1874	1880	1885	1886	1892	1895	1900
Conservative	294	274	356	238	250	316	268	341	334
Liberal Unionist						78	47	70	68
Liberal	364	384	245	353	334	191	273	177	184
Irish Nationalist			51	61	86	85	81	82	82
Labour							(ILP) 1		(LRC) 2

Broadly two kinds of changes are at work here; there are certain underlying movements in the allegiance of social, religious and cultural groups, in the entry of new groups of voters, and modifications of the constituency boundaries; and there are also short-term factors to be considered − the impact of particular issues and controversies, the timing and tactics of each election, and switches by the leading personalities. We have already noted one important long-term trend, namely the shift of middle-class and propertied interests towards Conservatism from the 1860s culminating in the schism of 1886. However, long-term group loyalties never entirely account for fluctuating election results, for every group has its soft, wavering fringes that respond to the ebb and flow of events and personalities. It would be too much to claim that the great Victorian issues, however passionately debated by the politicians, actually influenced more than a fraction of the electorate directly; party loyalty tends to be an impervious thing. But a small turnover of votes always produced drastic effects; as Lord Salisbury observed, a mere 2,000 strategically placed votes made 1880 a Liberal victory instead of a Conservative one. In addition, although economic questions had not yet become the staple of election debates, it does seem that party fortunes were vulnerable to sudden economic fluctuations; the downfall of Disraeli in 1880 and of Rosebery in 1895 was sealed by a slump immediately preceding each election, while Salisbury was saved from heavy losses in 1900 in part by the sudden buoyancy in the economy.

In 1868 Gladstone rallied radical sentiment with his bold programme of Irish reform; but the election, despite the extended electorate, essentially confirmed the traditional Liberal majority, marred only by a distinct ebbing of middle-class Palmerstonians. Coming after a plethora of innovations, 1874 exacerbated this trend; essentially a reaction by those whose interests seemed to have been threatened by Gladstone's reforms, this election saw both a suspension of Whig support for Liberalism in the counties, and a subsidence of radical—Nonconformist enthusiasm owing to dissatisfaction with recent legislation. In the long run the regular school board elections necessitated by Forster's Act probably consolidated the Nonconformist habit of voting Liberal, while also strengthening Conservatism among Anglicans and Catholics; for Conservative defence of independent religious schools was one means of neutralizing the Liberal appeal to the Irish. After 1875 the prevailing sense of economic depression, though exaggerated, shook Conservative loyalties especially among farmers suffering bad harvests and high grain imports; and social distress doubtless told more forcefully with the lower classes than the scarcely perceptible benefits of Disraelian social legislation. Although ostensibly the election turned upon the Midlothian onslaught on 'Beaconsfieldism', the outcome reflected this issue only indirectly in that the anti-imperial campaign restored radical morale and thereby helped the Liberals to poll their full strength again.

The election of 1885 appears more complicated. That it was less of a victory for the Liberals than 1880 was due primarily to Parnell's decision to withhold the Irish vote in England, to the unpopularity of Gladstone's imperial policies culminating in the death of General Gordon at Khartoum in 1885, and to renewed alarm among the urban middle classes at the radical tone of Chamberlain's 'Unauthorised Programme'. Yet Conservative urban consolidation was balanced by Liberal gains in the counties now under a new franchise. The question of Church disestablishment attained considerable prominence in England in 1885. For many years Nonconformists had been strenuously engaged, through the

Liberal Party, in removing the obstacles to their participation in national life, so much so that religious assignation had become central to party loyalty; wherever the 'free churches' were thickly distributed (as in Wales, Scotland, the north-east, Yorkshire, Cornwall and the midland and East Anglian towns), Liberalism was very strong. But the party still commanded much Anglican support too; the MPs were still mostly Anglicans and led by a prominent Anglican. However, this proved to be a waning asset in this period. Gladstone steadily eliminated Nonconformist grievances such as church rates in 1868; he disestablished the Church in Ireland in 1870, passed the University Tests Act in 1871, and the Church Burials Act in 1880. The next obvious step was disestablishment for Wales and Scotland, and the Liberation Society hoped to exploit the new county franchise to generate sufficient pressure to oblige Gladstone to take action. Since Chamberlain gave prominence to disestablishment the Conservatives raised the cry of 'the Church in danger' in 1885, hoping to win over middle-class Anglicans from Liberalism. Even Nonconformists, once their keenest grievances were rectified, showed some tendency to side with Conservatism as the embodiment of the *status quo* to which they now belonged. In fact the political behaviour of the Free Churches did increasingly reflect the social class of their members; furthest down the social scale — and highest in political radicalism — were the Primitive Methodists, followed by Baptists, Congregationalists, and finally, Wesleyan Methodists. The latter were longer in existence, more comfortably middle class, nearer to Anglicanism, less antagonistic to the established Church, and more receptive to a national political outlook. Hence Wesleyans displayed some reluctance to join radical campaigns by comparison with other Nonconformists; and by the 1890s many of them preferred Rosebery's brand of Liberal imperialism to Gladstonianism, and provided recruits for the Conservatives.

The Home Rule crisis of 1886 proved to be a watershed because it crystallized the attitudes of many Liberal followers already wavering for other reasons, and enabled them to take a coherent position as Liberal Unionists. Yet the impact of Ireland varied greatly from region to region. Western Scotland was considerably stirred because of the promixity of both Ireland and the Irish, while eastern Scotland remained relatively unmoved; north-east England and Yorkshire stayed largely Gladstonian while Lancashire moved even further to Unionism; in East Anglia the question seemed remote, yet in the south-west Home Rule seemed strategically relevant, and the St Ives division of Cornwall manifested the most marked shift to Unionism. Today it seems remarkable that for years afterwards the Irish Question provided a staple item in constituency campaigns; both parties clearly thought it worth keeping the issue alive. When taking the high ground of principle the Gladstonians urged the virtues of self-determination, and the Conservatives the threat to imperial unity and security. However, on the low ground of self-interest it was articulated differently. Conservatives repeatedly urged English working men to remember that a Dublin Parliament would destroy business confidence and thereby cause an even greater influx of destitute immigrants into English cities. The Gladstonians countered by warning that the bloody suppression of Irishmen's rights implied a threat to those of English workers too, and by arguing that an independent Ireland would in fact retain the population presently compelled to seek its livelihood abroad. While the Liberals plainly forfeited working-class support notably in the north-west, they enjoyed the compensation of a solid and organized Irish vote which gave them the edge in many urban constituencies right up to 1914.

By 1892 the Gladstonians had managed to effect a limited recovery from the debacle of 1886, but one based more upon county seats, a sign that they had revitalized the issues of 1885 but could not restore their full 1880 strength. Three years later after expectations had been dashed by the inability of both Gladstone and Rosebery to deliver the innovations promised the party went down to a heavy defeat. Essentially a negative reaction, the election saw Liberal abstentions and Conservative victory by default. The year 1895 also brought into general prominence the local veto on alcoholic sales (or 'Local Option') partly because it was taken up by Sir William Harcourt as he cast around rather desperately for fresh issues. Although temperance reform had acquired some political salience as long ago as 1871 as a result of Bruce's Licensing Bill, there had not been as sudden or complete an alienation of the drinking classes to the Conservatives as contemporaries often alleged. For years Gladstone fended off demands for the Local Veto in the belief that free trade and competition would eventually reduce the harmful effects of alcoholic consumption; also a number of brewers and publicans remained in the Liberal camp despite its connection with temperance; and in any case temperance became an election issue only where a candidate adopted a belligerent attitude on the subject. Although it was undoubtedly advantageous to the Conservatives in working-class seats to be able to defend a man's right to his beer, the party's association with the drink interest could not be too vociferously asserted. For one thing the improving working man was often a keen abstainer; for another, the party actually incorporated much middle-class temperance sentiment in the shape of organizations like the Church of England Temperance Society. Moreover, 1886 had brought many Liberal Unionists to their side who would merely be driven back to the Gladstonians if they were antagonized over licensing or education. Despite these qualifications, however, it is true that many a Liberal candidate risked alienating his staunchest backers if he remained lukewarm about temperance.

Between 1895 and 1899 the Liberals again appeared to claw back much of their support; but the by-election trend in their favour was suddenly interrupted shortly after the outbreak of the Boer War. There can be little doubt that the preservation of the 1895 Conservative majority was due to the shrewd timing of the 1900 general election fought in an atmosphere of embattled patriotism and an economy stimulated by the demand for war production. The government lost only ten English and four Welsh seats while gaining five in Scotland. In fact, in terms of votes there was a swing in their favour elsewhere except in Wales where foreign adventures seemed less relevant, and traditional issues, which favoured the Liberals, reasserted themselves. To a lesser extent the same was true of the remoter parts of England; Conservatives benefited most in the big towns especially London which was always quick to grow excited over international crises.

Rural Radicalism

The introduction of the secret ballot in 1872 produced little immediate impact upon English county politics; 1885 when the electorate was trebled proved to be the turning-point in that it led to an attempt to politicize areas hitherto somewhat insular and remote from national politics. Whether the traditional, conservative and Conservative pattern of rural politics could resist the new depended upon certain underlying social characteristics, notably the type of settlement pattern and the prevailing religious affiliation. For radical politics flourished only where it could establish roots in an alternative community to that epitomized by the joint authority of the squirearchy and the Church. The links between politics and religious figures — Anglican, Nonconformist and Catholic — were often active and blatant; one Lincolnshire vicar piously informed Lord Salisbury in 1885:

> I am canvassing the labourers here in Mr. Stanhope's interest, and find that a Liberal canvasser has been endeavouring to gain votes with the false assertion that the Conservatives are the enemy of the agricultural labourers, and wish to give the country a dear loaf. . . . As it is part of my duty to protect my parishioners from false doctrines of all kinds and from the father of lies and his progeny, I shall be glad to receive your reply on Saturday so that I may be able to state the truth publicly on Sunday.[3]

Political management by parson and squire attained maximum effectiveness in the 'closed' villages typical of the southern and midland counties and great estates in which all who lived depended upon the landowner for their cottage and employment. However, over the years the surplus population drifted to the 'open' villages which, in consequence, often grew into small towns. Here housing and sanitation were sometimes inferior and more expensive, while employment was irregular. Yet the residents, freer from the influence of their social superiors, tended to deviate in social and religious behaviour, often becoming islands of radicalism.[4] Nonconformists had frequently worsted the Church of England in the struggle for the allegiance of such communities; and the prevalence of their chapels in the small towns and villages of Wales, East Anglia and the south-west underpinned radicalism there. Nonconformity thrived also in areas of more scattered settlement based upon small farms and holdings remote from villages; this was typical of much of the heath and fenlands in eastern counties such as Norfolk, Cambridgeshire and Lincolnshire, of Cornwall and parts of Devon, and in the vast upland chain of Pennine country stretching from Derbyshire north to Yorkshire, Durham and Northumberland.

The significance of settlement and religion is very evident in a highly agricultural and traditionally Conservative county such as Norfolk, where less than half the agricultural population resided in closed villages and where the chapels were vigorous. Enfranchised in 1884, the labourers promptly delivered four of Norfolk's six county seats to the Liberals in 1885. Realization that the county electorate was not so amenable as previously led the Conservative chief agent to advise Salisbury in both 1892 and 1895 that the election should ideally coincide with harvest time when the labourers would be distracted and less politically involved.[5]

From the 1870s rural radicalism was being integrated with national politics at several levels. It enjoyed national leadership from Gladstone, through whom Liberalism spoke for the small man against the Establishment, and from Chamberlain's three-acres-and-a-cow approach. Radical newspapers like the *Daily News* also took a keen interest, for example by assisting the new agricultural trade unions in the 1870s by writing up the story of their strikes and encouraging urban radicals to provide funds urgently needed to sustain their action. Urban workers such as dockers often thought it worth while subsidizing land reform propaganda on the grounds that this would eventually retain the population on the land and thus mitigate the overcrowding and wage-cutting caused by migration to the towns. Similarly during the 1880s all kinds of essentially external organizations propagandized the counties often through mobile vans bearing lecturers, leaflets and lantern shows; the Land Restoration League's Red Van, the Land Nationalisation Society Van, the Sunrise Radical Van, the Beaconsfield Van, the Church Association Van, and the Home Rule Van were some of the entertainments from both parties at this time.

However, neither pressure groups nor national leaders could make lasting inroads against the underlying Conservatism without a network of sub-contractors able to link the party cause with the lives of the people. Without missionaries from small towns or chapels it was often difficult to find speakers and chairmen for village meetings, and a small shopkeeper or merchant, Nonconformist minister or even a travelling lecturer would fill this role. When parish councils were established in 1894, many labourers did come forward as candidates, though it was felt safer for an independent entrepreneur to take the risk of offending his superiors. One valuable source of stump orators was the agricultural labourers trade unions which sprang up especially in Warwickshire, Oxfordshire, Norfolk and Suffolk during the 1870s. Regular union activity proved very difficult to sustain for even in the strongest counties only a third of the men became members; farmers could therefore draw upon plentiful supplies of labour unless strikes were well co-ordinated and coincided with harvest time. Consequently, after initial successes the membership of the National Agricultural Labourers Union fell from a peak of 86,000 in 1874 to 10,000 by 1886. However, the experience increased the assertiveness of the labourers, and failure drove their leaders towards political solutions of which the first fruit was the county franchise of 1884. Like the union's founder, Joseph Arch MP, the labourers' leaders greatly strengthened radical Liberalism in this period.

While great national issues like Home Rule remained somewhat remote, the rural radicals worked the villages with a mixture of demands for political rights (county franchise, county and parish councils, disestablishment, the burials question), and material improvements; the latter included eliminating duties on basic food items (the 'Free Breakfast Table'), provision of allotments and smallholdings, poor law reform, and the local veto on licensed premises. The vicar frequently appeared as an obstacle due to his prominent role in vestry meetings which controlled charitable endowments and lands that were regarded as a potential source of new allotments.[6]

Despite the radical upsurge of 1885 the Conservatives managed to retain the bulk of their territory especially in the Home Counties and Wessex, though it could no longer be taken for granted. Whereas their strength had its roots in agriculture, radicalism had to be sustained by penetration from outside; and the continual migration, or even emigration, of the most active and discontented village radicals steadily enfeebled their cause. It was assumed that the reservoir of rural radicalism could be tapped only when the labourer was made more independent of his employer by possessing sufficient land to feed his family; yet this required more drastic local government reform than was provided either by county councils — still often under landowners' control — or parish councils which were starved of resources. Conservative strength lay among landowners and farmers; Gladstone made some efforts to win over the latter by repealing the malt tax, by compensation to tenants for improvements, and by the 1880 Ground Game Act. However, this was overtaken by the more radical proposals of the mid-1880s pitched primarily at labourers. Finally, as we have seen, the Conservatives produced a constructive response to the challenge in the shape of the Primrose League which gave a new lease of life to landed politics.

Working-Class Politics: Lib—Labs and Socialists

In 1852 Marx had optimistically forecast that the introduction of universal suffrage in England, with its large proletariat, would be 'a far more socialistic measure than anything which has been honoured with that name on the Continent. Its inevitable result, here, is the supremacy of the working class.[7] Of course neither 1867 nor 1884 ushered in universal suffrage, but the reforms did make working-class voters numerically dominant in at least 89 constituencies with 95 MPs;[8] had they been at all cohesive they could rapidly have emerged as a substantial and discrete force like the Irish. Yet such expectations were regularly dashed. While working men undoubtedly played a significant role at several levels, the emergence of an effective and independent political party for the working class proved to be a protracted, and even elusive, affair. Why was this so?

Certain quite practical obstacles restricted working men's participation. For example, polling stations were sparse in Victorian times and polling hours highly inconvenient (8.00 a.m. to 8.00 p.m. from 1884); most men were at work when the booths opened and could vote only in the last half-hour in the evening. The alternative was to lose pay by taking time off as the miners of Morpeth did in 1874 to secure the election of Thomas Burt. Working men could stand for Parliament from 1858 when property qualifications for MPs were abolished, though in the case of poor law boards of guardians not until 1894. Nevertheless the absence of salaries before 1911 made it all but impossible for a workingman to serve as an MP unless he was subsidized by his union or was prepared to eke out an existence by journalism and lecturing like Keir Hardie and Ramsay MacDonald. Even municipal councils and school boards, for which ratepayers were eligible as candidates, held meetings during working hours, so that a man sometimes sat for a single term only before passing on the burden to someone else.

However, the fundamental obstacles lay more in attitudes and expectations; until Edwardian times working-class voters lent negligible support to labour and socialist candidates because it was by no means obvious that they should or could sustain a party of their own; meanwhile they owed their loyalty to the two existing parliamentary parties. Working-class Tories will be considered separately. But radicals and socialists were, to a considerable extent, two sides of the same coin, their leaders engaged in a competition for the same support. In Britain Liberalism and socialism both tended to be moralistic and rationalist in character; their exponents displayed a similar confidence about improving society *both* by individual effort and by collective action; and consequently they suffered similar limitations in attempting to harness mass support.

Although from a twentieth-century standpoint it may seem inevitable that workers, once enfranchised, would take over or create a party devoted simply to raising their material conditions of life, this would be to exaggerate the nineteenth-century confidence in 'politics' and to underestimate the perceived drawbacks of reform and improvement. From the perspective of the working-class family 'improvement' was invariably intrusive or humiliating; it brought interference, inspection, regulation and taxation. For authority and government manifested themselves in such bodies as the boards of guardians through whom only 2–3 per cent of the population received relief in this period although ten times that number were in dire need of assistance according to the studies of Booth and Rowntree. People also shied away from beneficial measures like vaccination against contagious diseases which provoked stern individualist condemnation from working-class leaders like Burt and Arch who declared that he 'did not intend to have my children treated as if they were cattle'.[9] Benevolent legislation for slum clearance usually had the practical effect of reducing the total of cheap houses thereby raising rents and exacerbating overcrowding. Private bodies such as the Charity Organisation Society and the temperance groups also seemed rather to be an extension of authority chiefly anxious to save the working man from his own profligacy on drink and inessentials by imposing unwelcome restrictions on his conduct. In addition a whole pandora's box of friction was opened up by post-1870 educational reforms. Parents were antagonized initially by the lost earnings of children who, at ten years, seemed quite old enough to work, and by the fees payable for elementary schooling until 1891; then education brought with it inspectors to pursue truants and prosecute their parents, attempts to extract payment for meals from those who could afford it, and after 1907 medical inspection with its implied criticism of parents.

One should not exaggerate the negative attitude towards authority and improvement. Some skilled workers had been keen to pay for education well before 1870; and millions contributed to benefit schemes through friendly societies. Reforms such as old age pensions appear to have been immediately popular; and ultimately state-financed social welfare became a central part of the appeal of the Labour Party. But it was a gradual process in which innovation aroused suspicion and hostility until its value could be demonstrated. It is not, then, surprising that Victorian Liberal and Labour politicians were more voluble on free trade whose advantages were evident than on the principle of social reform. It would be fallacious to think that Gladstonian Liberalism inevitably lost the working class because it was too slow to offer them a welfare state; in so far as collectivist solutions aroused support before 1900 it was more middle-class than working-class in character.

The political impact of the working class inevitably reflected its lack of cohesion arising from the tremendous range of experience in terms of wages and relationships at work. A gulf had always existed between the skilled few and the unskilled majority, between a regular wage and casual labouring. Although the gap was narrowing there remained a world of indifference between the relative comfort of, say, Tyneside blastfurnacemen earning £2 or £3 a week and the precarious existence of an East London general labourer perennially searching for a day's work, or the Wiltshire farm worker on 14s a week. Men involved in irregular, casual or seasonal employment and those who remained dependent upon patronage and charity were least likely to generate either political aspirations or a supporting institutional structure. Even within the railway workers, for example, contemporaries identified a sharp distinction between 'the goods side and drivers and firemen not brought into touch with the public [who] are Radicals, [and] passenger guards and porters who are also underpaid but with funds augmented by tips and the patronage of the rich [who] are Conservatives'.[10]

Now the 'working class' reconstructed by historians has been unbalanced in that much more is known about highly unionized groups like the miners who left a record than about equally numerous groups like domestic servants who did not. And since miners were pioneers of independent political action it is easy to telescope the evolution of the labour movement. In fact the Victorian trade unionist was not a typical working man. As late as 1895 only 1.5 million men belonged to unions — about one in seven of the male workforce. It was not a practical proposition for most workers because by and large labour was so plentiful and employment unskilled that employers could usually resist strike action. Many of the firmly established unions were consequently among craftsmen whose skills had not been undermined by industrialization and in trades such as iron and steel or building where industrialization had greatly stimulated the demand for their labour. Even here it was difficult to recruit anything like a majority of the men for the union, and their agreed wage rates were always liable to be undermined by an influx of cheap, unskilled labour. Despite the emergence of the 'new unions' among less skilled workers in the 1880s and 1890s a sustained expansion of union strength did not occur in Britain until the

Edwardian and First World War period. Thus, there was not, as yet, a very large organized base for a working-class party — and what there was tended to be Gladstonian at least up to the 1890s.

For a craft union the emphasis was usually on establishing a regular bargaining procedure with employers, protecting their members through benefit schemes, and generally attaining a position of independence and self-respect. A Victorian working man often shared the same range of political views as his employer, if only in that they identified common enemies. Many a first-generation manufacturer in the northern towns retained close affiliations of residence and opinion with his roots, and experienced a similar sense of penetrating the hitherto closed world of politics. The skilled worker often hoped to raise himself in the same way by thrift, sobriety and industry as a small entrepreneur. Of course close master-and-man relations could not prevail in really large-scale factory production, yet workers' traditional allegiances plainly survived the transition to impersonal and unionized industry for many years. When a vacancy arose in the strong mining seat of Barnsley in 1897 the 'Liberal 300', of whom two-thirds were apparently working men, picked a mine-owner from Durham who comfortably won the election against both a Conservative and a working-class candidate nominated by the Independent Labour Party. For socialists it was a frustrating business to convince politically active trade unionists of the contradiction involved in voting for middle-class politicians. Many held firmly to their common belief in free trade and constitutional reforms, and often shared a commitment to Nonconformity and a conviction that temperance was the quickest route to improving the condition of the people. They found their political champions in Gladstone and Lincoln, in Charles Bradlaugh, the radical individualist and atheist MP, and in Henry George, the American land reformer whose book, *Progress and Poverty*, had sold 400,000 copies by the time of his triumphant tour of Britain in 1882.

Inevitably, perhaps, the late Victorian trade unionists have not generally been seen as heroes in the labour movement; rather they tend to be dismissed as passive and complacent, deficient in a sense of class consciousness and too concerned with safeguarding their position as 'labour aristocrats' to develop political objectives beyond their traditional function as appendages to Liberalism. Yet they were effective pioneers in several ways. By 1868 they had established the Trades Union Congress as a leading pressure group monitoring legislation affecting its members through Royal

Commissions and its own Parliamentary Committee. In 1874 the first working men — Thomas Burt (Morpeth) and Alexander McDonald (Stafford) — were elected to the House of Commons. Known as 'Lib—Labs' these members took the Liberal whip and espoused Gladstonian politics. Lib—Lab candidates were usually miners' union officials who stood in constituencies where their members were so concentrated as to enable them to bargain with the local Liberal associations over candidatures. Burt and McDonald were soon joined by other miners, notably William Abraham (the Rhondda), Charles Fenwick (Northumberland Wansbeck), John Wilson (mid-Durham), and Ben Pickard (Yorkshire Normanton). Rather less well known were the Liberal working men who represented London seats such as George Howell, a former bricklayer (N.E. Bethnal Green), Randall Cremer, a carpenter (Shoreditch) and James Rowlands, a watch-case maker (East Finsbury).

From the 1860s, then, the politically active working man was typically a Gladstonian, content to operate under the umbrella of Liberalism. Gladstone had led them within the pale of the constitution, and the Liberalism of this era enjoyed a powerful democratic reputation; it represented 'the people' in the sense of the artisans and small shopkeepers to whom it conveyed a gratifying sense of participation in a righteous struggle against their social superiors. 'What Gladstone was offering,' as one historian has aptly put it, 'was emotional subsistence level.'[11] His appeal was underpinned by the popular radical press, particularly the *Daily News*, and also by the mass circulation working-class Sunday papers, *Lloyds Weekly News, Reynold's Newspaper*, and the *News of the World* whose formula was domestic radicalism mixed generously with crime and sensation.

Thus for advocates of independent labour representation the problem resolved itself into how to wean the politically conscious working men away from radicalism rather than how to mobilize the entire working class, which seemed beyond the bounds of possibility. For many years labour leaders regarded the really impoverished slum populations as too passive and dependent to respond to their relatively sophisticated appeal. As Ramsay MacDonald put it in 1911: 'It is the skilled artisan, the trade unionist, the member of the friendly society, the young workman who reads and thinks who are the recruits to the army of socialism.'[12] Yet for many years socialist parties met with little success. The Social Democratic Federation, founded in 1883, represented the nearest approach to a Marxist socialist party. By the late 1890s the SDF claimed only 10,000 members through its true membership has been put at 2,600; it was always crippled by its inability to win more than a derisory vote at parliamentary elections, although it scored some successes in municipal contests. Like most organizations that took their socialism seriously the SDF attracted articulate middle-class people, but men like H.H. Hyndman, H.H. Champion and William Morris tended to reduce the Federation to disputatious fragments all energetically defining their ideological position in numerous journals rather than converting the working class. It has been calculated that no less than 800 Labour and socialist newspapers were published between 1890 and 1910, most of them with tiny circulations and very short lives. Even Keir Hardie's *Labour Leader* struggled against perennial losses. The only viable socialist paper, Robert Blatchford's *Clarion*, outsold all the rest of the socialist press put together with a circulation of 40,000. Blatchford's formula, not unlike that of other successful working-class papers, was a lively, readable blend of socialist radicalism combined with a vigorous, patriotic nationalism. It was Blatchford more than any of the politicians who articulated 'socialism' for the rank and file in pre-1914 Britain.

A far more realistic and pragmatic approach than that of the SDF was adopted by the Independent Labour Party founded in Bradford in 1893. Though socialist, the ILP displayed a certain flexibility absent from the SDF; for it espoused a shrewd mixture of radical Liberal causes and current trade union demands. Also its members reflected much more closely the working class of provincial England, and its leaders, especially Keir Hardie, spoke a socialism of a moralistic, humanitarian, revivalist kind. For some years the ILP-ers put their main emphasis on the local rather than the national sphere, working through municipal bodies, and also through trades councils which were often the most successful means of co-ordinating the efforts of the otherwise disparate elements in the labour and socialist movements. During the 1890s opportunities were seized, for example, in boards of guardians such as the one at Poplar in London to which George Lansbury and Will Crooks were elected; they were able to change policy locally by providing outdoor relief to the aged and fit working men temporarily unemployed, and even more importantly, to highlight the problems and thus concentrate the minds of the policy-makers elsewhere. London was also the source of a notable triumph for ILP tactics in 1898 when West Ham Borough returned a majority of Labour members, who proceeded to improve the conditions of council workers by introducing two weeks' annual holiday, a minimum weekly wage of 30s, and a working day of eight hours. Although there was little co-ordination of labour and socialist action around the country, in practice a common platform did exist. This comprised essentially a demand for the municipalization of basic utilities like gas and waterworks where they were still in private hands (this was advocated on grounds of economy — an important consideration to a ratepaying electorate — as much as for fairness and improvement). The second basic proposal was to establish a works department so that the council could be a direct employer of labour; by this means it might both alleviate unemployment locally, and, by inserting a 'fair wage' clause into its contracts, stimulate improvements in the conditions of men employed privately. Often this was accomplished by means of co-operation with Liberals and Fabians as in the case of the London County Council Progressives, but it certainly gave the labour movement a coherent political programme pitched towards working men. In the long run this experience proved to be immensely important. Local government in Bradford, Glasgow or London provided an invaluable apprenticeship in elections and office-holding that was eventually built upon at the parliamentary level; indeed it left Labour's mainstream in the twentieth century with a pronounced municipal flavour, and probably compounded the neglect of ideology.

Yet despite this progress the ILP found it all but impossible to break into national politics. Though Keir Hardie was briefly the MP for West Ham (1892–95), the ILP's membership fluctuated around 6,000 to 9,000 by the end of the decade; financially starved and without access to trade union strength, the party remained a somewhat ramshackle and diffuse organization which, after the early successes, seemed to stagnate in the face of the trend to Conservatism during 1895–1900. However, the ILP leaders had grasped the fact that the key to effective independent labour politics lay in tapping the funds and organization of the trade unions; and the events of the later 1890s and early 1900s enabled them to translate their strategy into practice in the form of the Labour Representation Committee. The emergence of the LRC at the turn of the century has sometimes been explained in terms of an outflanking of the traditional craft unions by the more socialist and radical leaders of the 'new unions'. Undoubtedly several groups like the Gas Workers and General Labourers Union succeeded in extending industrial organization to many semi-skilled and unskilled men hitherto outside the movement. Moreover, the successful strikes of 1888–90 threw up many new trades councils, and leaders such as Will Thorne and Ben Tillett who were ardent exponents of independent labour representation and critics of the TUC. With their advocacy of the eight-hour day they took the initiative in the TUC away from Henry Broadhurst, the Parliamentary Secretary and champion of Lib–Lab strategy; by the 1890s the Lib–Lab MPs were not, apparently, achieving much except respectability for themselves. Broadhurst himself served as an under-secretary in Gladstone's last government, but neither this nor his work on industrial legislation impressed the younger working-class activists with political ambitions who did not enjoy similar advantages. Lib–Labbery worked well enough for the miners but this no longer seemed sufficient.

Nonetheless too much should not be made of the new unions. They remained comparatively weak and soon lost much of their membership; by 1900 in fact only 100,000 of the one million affiliated to the TUC were members of the new unions. Thus the emergence of what was to become the Labour Party in 1906 could hardly have occurred at that time but for the willingness of the well-established unions who still dominated the movement to indulge in an experiment. They had been much influenced by the experience of economic stagnation during the 1890s which exposed hitherto well-placed skilled men such as shipwrights, ironfounders, steel smelters and blastfurnacemen to 10 per cent unemployment rates. Further, the employers now displayed a tendency to take advantage of higher unemployment by combining for concerted action to curb union activity as in the case of the Shipping Federation and the six-month lock-out of engineering workers in 1897. On top of this the legal status apparently achieved in 1875 now appeared to have been undermined by a number of legal decisions notably the *Lyons v. Wilkins* case in 1896 and 1899 which infringed the right to picket. All this seemed to point to the need for unions to be represented in Parliament on a similar scale to employers; industrial weakness, in short, stimulated a characteristic turn towards political remedies. It was in this spirit that in 1899 the TUC approved by 546,000 votes to 434,000 a resolution of the Amalgamated Society of Railway Servants to establish a new and independent political organization. As a result 129 delegates representing unions and socialist societies met in February 1900 to set up the Labour Representation Committee. Its leading supporters at this stage included printers, boot and shoe operatives, gasworkers and dockers, and those like the railway workers who were trying to win recognition from their employers. Their purpose may best be defined as 'Labourism', that is, to achieve a greater degree of direct working-class representation than was possible within the scope of existing Lib–Lab arrangements. The chief authors of the strategy, Hardie and MacDonald of the ILP, recognized the futility of attempting to commit the LRC to any distinctive left-wing ideology lest they play into the hands of the many unionists who were anxious to 'bury the attempt in good-humoured tolerance'. Hardie contrived to obscure the inconsistency between a wholly independent party, which the LRC nominally was, and the relationship with Liberalism, which the bulk of the unions still desired. Thus the new organization was not in 1900 expected by most participants to differ dramatically from earlier experiments in labour representation. The LRC had to begin life as a loose federal organization with an executive of twelve, comprising seven trade unionists, two from the ILP, two from the SDF and one Fabian, and with an unpaid secretary in Ramsay MacDonald. The unions continued to hold on to their money and declined any ideological innovation. It was a modest start for a party that was to form a government only 24 years later.

Working-Class Conservatism

Even today studies of voting behaviour suggest that around one-third of working-class voters consistently support the Conservatives. In the mid-nineteenth century when voters were offered two parties drawn from broadly similar social backgrounds and eschewing a class appeal there existed no neat general relationship between class and party allegiance. Investigation has always been difficult because working-class Conservatism largely lacked organization, and therefore a record, and also because of the somewhat equivocal attitude of the party itself. While recognizing the division of society into ranks as natural and desirable, Conservatives feared the potential for class conflict in an industrial society; their leaders were thus anxious to avoid being drawn into a competition for votes by appeasement of material demands. As a result Conservatives approached the matter in two distinct ways. One involved appealing to working men as working men by cataloguing the beneficial measures enacted by Conservative administrations since Disraeli's time, and reminding them of how badly the Liberals fell down on their promises. This approach was typical of the National Union which printed huge quantities of literature on the theme. The alternative was that usually adopted by the leaders and the Primrose League, which amounted to an appeal to working men as patriotic Britons, as soldiers-of-the-Queen, as English workers and as Protestants. To Salisbury the drawbacks of the former approach were only too obvious. National Union conferences were regularly troubled with complaints by working-class delegates that 'the time had come when the Conservative Party should have its Burts and its Broadhursts'.[13] Yet James Mawdsley of the cotton spinners enjoyed a lonely eminence as one leading Conservative trade unionist: he ran in harness with Winston Churchill in the double-member constituency of Oldham in 1899. But in the absence of payment of members, which the party thoroughly disliked, this experiment was unlikely to be repeated.

Two kinds of explanation are usually advanced to account for working-class Conservatism. The first is in terms of deference. This implies a willingness by the voter to be governed by his social superiors who are equipped to rule by birth and training, and a tendency to identify with the traditional values and institutions of his society, which invariably seem closely associated with the Conservative Party. This may well suggest the pattern for rural Conservatism; and is also consistent with the tendency noticed by some writers on local politics for Conservatives to do particularly well in both the wealthiest and the poorest wards.[14] There are signs of this in parliamentary elections, too, notably in the East End of London, and in strong Conservative seats such as Bristol West which combined the wealthy with the dependent poor. The other explanation sees the Conservative working man as a pragmatic or secular voter whose choice implies some assessment that his self-interest is best served by supporting the Conservative Party. In the nineteenth-century context the deferential and the pragmatic element was combined in the concept of Tory paternalism in the sense of government by hereditary leaders fully alive to their obligations, material and moral, towards the lower orders of society.

Although deferential attitudes were widespread in the nineteenth century they did not automatically make for Conservative voting. For until the 1860s the natural ruling elite in Britain – the Palmerstonian Whig–Liberal combination – was more closely identified with the symbols of national pride than the sectional and peripheral Conservative Party. However, there is a strong *prime facie* case for thinking that this changed during the Disraeli–Salisbury era as the Conservatives began to reap the benefit of association with patriotism and Empire. By his firmness over the Congress of Berlin, the Suez Canal, Afghanistan and South Africa Disraeli contrived to sharpen his disagreement with Gladstone who could plausibly, if inaccurately, be accused of planning the dismemberment of the Empire and of weakness towards the United States and Russia when British interests were threatened. Thereafter Conservatives ceaselessly propagated their claim to be the party of national interests, and cast aspersions on their opponents' patriotism; they catalogued the radicals' failures in the 1880s — defeat by the Boers at Majuba Hill, abandonment of Kandahar, death of General Gordon; and pinned the label 'Pro-Boer' indiscriminately on their rivals during 1899—1902. One conference speaker summed it up in 1905: 'in all those places where the enemies of England foregather, the advent of a Radical government would be hailed with undisguised rejoicing.'[15]

Some historians have gone to considerable lengths to exonerate the working classes from any sympathy with 'Imperialism', arguing that this was a sentiment of the lower middle and middle classes. However, this is tenable only if imperialism is fairly tightly defined, and if selective groups of working men are examined. The argument, for example, that the greater imperialism of the lower middle classes was manifested in their greater readiness to fight in the Boer War[16] is surely vitiated by the fact that, as in 1914, a huge proportion of working-class volunteers were rejected on grounds of physical unfitness to which others were less subject. There is more plausibility in the contention that working men regarded, or at least articulated, their patriotism in a different way, namely that they perceived a connection between vigorous imperial policies and material well-being. Such links obviously underpinned the popular Conservatism of centres like Woolwich, Newcastle and Sheffield where jobs depended on the fortunes of munitions manufacturers, and also in the dockyard towns of Plymouth, Chatham, Portsmouth and Southampton. However, Empire was hardly without its material advantages for other classes; and it would be rash to assume that the range of attitudes from patriotism to chauvinism was especially concentrated in any level of Victorian society. Many a working-class family felt a keen sympathy with the colonies whither they had so often dispatched their sons, and took an immense pride in the Royal Navy in which sons and brothers enlisted. Many also shared the widespread apprehension about an invasion of Britain so characteristic of the 1871—1914 period; and the undercurrent of xenophobia was easily stirred by the presence of Irish, Jewish and other east European immigrants.

THE ALIEN EMPLOYER (to British Workman): "You can go now. Mine friend, who has just arrived, will do your work for half your wages."

Protectionist propaganda 1906 from the Conservative pamphlet 'Topical Tips for Typical Tykes'.

Dislike of foreigners and defence of British interests formed complementary sides of a currency extensively coined by Conservative propagandists in the late nineteenth century at constituency level; they furnished the unifying theme behind the Irish Question, the aliens issue and the tariff. For example, it was argued that Home Rule would bring 'thousands of ruined and desperate Irishmen over to England to compete in our markets';[17] and much play was made with the common interests of the Irish Party, British Liberals and Britain's enemies. The pattern that had evolved in the Irish case was extended to the attack upon the immigration of aliens, usually described as 'pauper Jews' in the propaganda, who were similarly represented as undercutting wages, overcrowding accommodation and imposing a heavy burden upon the poor law authorities and ratepayers. The free trade in people was frequently blamed for conditions in the sweated industries; rather than advocating the imposition of minimum standards by law that would annoy small employers, Conservatives thrust the responsibility upon the influx of Poles and Russians.[18] That this struck a ready response even in radical working men is evident in Joseph Arch's disgust that Britain lost men through emigration every year while taking in immigrants who were 'the scum of their own countries, three of whom cannot do the work of one honest Englishman'.[19] When finally Balfour passed an Aliens Act in 1905 Conservatives continued to attack the new Home Secretary for not implementing it, and re-opening the door to 'the diseased and pauper aliens who are so dear to the Radical party'.[20]

Similar themes are evident in the tariff reform propaganda; material interests were articulated in the same emotive terms, namely the need to stand up for Britain by retaliating against inferior foreign goods produced by cheap labour which, owing to the spinelessness of the free traders, was depriving British workers of jobs. Protectionism characterized Conservatism locally well before Chamberlain's campaign was launched in 1903; in places like Sheffield where employment seemed threatened by imported German cutlery it became an integral part of the party's appeal and helped Conservatives to win three or four of the five seats throughout 1885—1914.

While these essentially nationalist themes provided the staple attack, more constructive elements were also included. Conservatives were keen to throw back at Gladstone the radical plea that Ireland blocked the way to reform by pointing to the combination of 'firm' government from Dublin with measures of improvement at home. Only a few of these produced tangible benefits, such as the elimination of elementary school fees in 1891, and the Truck Act of 1897 which placed limits on the much resented practice of paying workers in kind rather than in cash. On the whole, however, the Conservative Party stood to gain more by abstaining from too much costly improvement and allowing its rivals to provoke hostility to interference and regulation particularly in the fields of temperance and education. Even apparently constructive measures like the 1875 Artisans Dwellings Act assisted the Conservatives indirectly; for where energetic municipalities like Liberal-run Birmingham availed themselves of the powers in the Act for slum clearance they fuelled working-class resentment against themselves.[21] Thus, for late Victorian Conservatives the key to their appeal lay in capitalizing upon the unchanging and unifying issues like Empire and the foreigner, while leaving the radicals to suffer the consequences of dashed expectations and disturbing innovation.

Three major conurbations became notable bastions of working-class Conservatism in this period. In Liverpool and west Lancashire generally the party's predominance was inextricably bound up with the working-class Protestant backlash against Irish immigrants as Catholics, aliens and rivals for employment and homes. As early as 1868 Gladstone's burgeoning interest in Ireland contributed to his ejection from a Lancashire seat. As a result the Conservatives enjoyed a popular and organized base in the working class; by the 1890s the Liverpool Workingmen's Conservative Association claimed 6,000 members, and under Archibald Salvidge they held seven or eight of the city's nine constituencies after 1885, the only regular exception being the Scotland division where the Irish comprised a majority. Nor was this sectarian pattern seriously shaken until 1945. Glasgow and western Scotland, also a point of arrival for Irish immigrants, displayed similar tendencies, though with the difference that more here were Protestants from Ulster; even before 1886 the Glasgow Conservatives had successfully brought the Orange Lodges under the party's umbrella where, in combination with the Liberal Unionists, they made a formidable force.

Another region conspicuous for its popular Conservatism was Birmingham and the west Midlands. This was not simply the result of the detachment of Chamberlain and the Liberal Unionists from the Liberals, for even before 1886 Birmingham Conservatives had steadily raised their vote to 42 per cent by 1885. The party often ran working men and small tradesmen as municipal candidates and gained strength particularly in the poorer wards antagonized by the rule of the Chamberlainite machine.[22] Tariff reform won popularity among the west Midland metal trades, many of which were organized as small workshops where a close master-and-man relationship was more typical than large-scale production and unionization. After the amalgamation of Conservative and Liberal Unionist forces in 1886 Chamberlainite candidates were virtually unchallenged in every Birmingham constituency until 1929; and the west Midlands as a whole remained relatively resistant even to the Liberal revival of 1906. What is distinctive is the assertive, even populist character of Conservatism in both Birmingham and Lancashire.

By comparison the rural areas were more passive and deferential, as was the East End of London. In fact a formidable catalogue of poor East End constituencies elected Conservatives in the late nineteenth century: N.E. Bethnal Green, Walworth, Rotherhithe, Bow and Bromley, Mile End, Limehouse, Stepney, St George's (Tower Hamlets) and Deptford to take the best examples. Conservative strength here was, however, at least partly a reflection of Liberal and socialist weakness. London was notably irreligious, it was not strong on temperance, its workers were comparatively non-unionized; its population was quickly excited by the great imperial, war-and-peace issues; and alien immigration from eastern Europe assumed considerable proportions from the 1880s. The poverty of East End workers was the result of the casual and seasonal nature of their employment; and of the abnormal role of the service industries which fostered an abject dependance upon middle-class patronage. Also much of the population were catered to by a wide range of charitable enterprises. All of this was apt to undermine any spirit of independence and self-help, and to leave the working population comparatively indifferent to politics. The small size of the East End electorate facilitated the survival of the older pattern of politics in which constituencies looked to candidates as providers of employment or as distributors of largesse. This made for a working-class Conservatism of a more passive and less consciously political nature than elsewhere, lacking a strong organizational base, and able to win by default. Thus in London, even more than in other regions, popular Conservatism turned out to be very vulnerable in the Edwardian period when the Liberals posed a vigorous challenge with free trade and social reform which raised the level of participation and swamped the limited Conservative vote.

The Lower Middle Class

In Britain it has been easy to overlook those who fall between the 'working class' and the 'middle class', possibly because they seem to have played a less dramatic role than elsewhere in Europe, or because of an assumption that such groups tend to diminish. No doubt the lower middle class is far from being a cohesive section of society, but for our purposes its members are defined by the very ambiguity of their situation, frequently working class by origin yet precariously clinging to the bottom ranks of the middle classes by occupation and attitudes. They were a key element in Victorian political evolution, and a rapidly expanding, not a declining, group from the 1860s. In occupational terms the lower middle class falls into two categories: first the essentially pre-industrial group of small entrepreneurs, particularly shopkeepers, many of whom were hardly to be distinguished from the elite of craftsmen such as tailors and printers; second the administrative, technical and professional occupations whose numbers were greatly augmented in a mature industrial society, notably clerks, civil servants, elementary school teachers, journalists, travelling salesmen, insurance and friendly society collectors, and policemen.

The political significance of what Victorians often called the 'shopocracy' is readily apparent. For not only did its members enjoy the time and independence for local political activity, they also comprised a large proportion of the pre-1867 electorate; even in industrial towns the shopocracy often formed 30–50 per cent of the total, with craftsmen making another 25 per cent. In their ambitions and frustrations lay the seeds of formal political organization in boroughs. Municipal reform in 1835 presented an opportunity to challenge the exclusive control exercised by superior classes of merchants, landowners and lawyers. The basis of the controversy over parliamentary reform in 1866 lay in the Whig belief that, in view of the radicalism displayed by the urban shopocracy, the franchise had been extended as far as was safe, whereas Gladstone's proposal to lower the qualification from £10 to a £7 rental value was tantamount to a complete enfranchisement of small shopkeepers and craftsmen. Contemporary assumptions that they leant to radical Liberalism have been corroborated by evidence from surviving poll books for the mid-Victorian period which suggests that both shopkeepers and artisans supported the Liberals against the Conservatives by up to two-to-one, a markedly higher proportion than that of those immediately above or below them. During the 1870s local caucuses and the National Liberal

Federation opened up further avenues of participation for them and for journalists and teachers who were quick to appreciate the moral fervour and individualist tone of Gladstonian Liberalism.

Although franchise reform in 1867 and 1884 rendered the traditional lower middle class less numerically significant, non-manual jobs increased from 2 to 4 million in Britain between 1881 and 1914. In particular the number of clerks shot up from 100,000 in the 1860s to nearly 700,000 by the First World War; together with commercial travellers, teachers, central and local civil servants they numbered approximately 920,000. Moreover, since they increasingly resided in distinct suburbs somewhat apart from working-class or solidly middle-class communities, they often became a major element in the single-member constituencies. Conscious of having risen just above the working class and existing frugally on yearly incomes in the £75—£150 range, Victorian clerks were distinguished more by a belief in respectability and social mobility than by higher living standards. Frequently tee-totallers, active Nonconformists, and imbued with notions of self-improvement through individual industriousness and thrift, the new lower middle class was often as predisposed to Liberalism as the shopocracy. This is easily overlooked in the assumption that the urban clerk was typical of the sections detached from Liberalism in this period. There is, of course, a strong case for the view that their identification with their social superiors manifested itself in patriotic Conservatism and demonstrative loyalty to King and Empire on the part of those who volunteered to fight in the South African War. No doubt military service in such circumstances added zest and adventure to the lives of ambitious men confined to tedious jobs without prospects, just as it raised their status and self-regard. However, it remains unproven whether the lower middle class were especially prone to imperialism; and if the *Daily Mail* catered to the imperialists among them, the *Daily News* was read by their pacifists and Little Englanders.

Alternatively lower-middle-class politics may have been deter-mined by the pressures arising from a frustrating and ambiguous social position. Commercial salesmen were particularly vulnerable to economic fluctuations during 1875 to 1896. The supply of clerks and administrators, now beginning to be swollen by female recruits, was so plentiful as to make for stagnant wages and poor promotion prospects. Small shopkeepers, too, felt the competition of co-operatives and the rapidly spreading chain stores. These economic pressures coincided with an apparent loss of political clout as the organized working class claimed a growing share of legislative attention and esconced their representatives in Parliament. Some occupations — teachers, clerks and railway clerks for example — were driven to form trade unions though they endeavoured at first to be professional associations rather than militant bodies; otherwise unionization was eschewed as a sign of non-middle-class status.

Even in constituencies characterized by concentrations of lower-middle-class residents, such as Fulham, Hammersmith, Islington, Peckham, N. West Ham and Lewisham in London, and South Edinburgh, South Manchester and North Bristol, their political role is not clear. While these seats showed a shift towards Conservatism typical of the late nineteenth century, they also saw a reversion to the Liberals around 1906 as did most areas. In fact the three provincial seats mentioned above were more often Liberal than Conservative during 1885—1914, and South Edinburgh was never won by a Conservative. In London, where Liberalism was markedly weaker, Fulham, Hammersmith and Lewisham had already become Conservative by 1885; and where, as in Lewisham, the lower middle class was mixed with middle-class residents, the Conservative lead seemed unassailable. However, the early Liberalism of the four Islington seats and N. West Ham re-emerged by 1906, and this casts some doubt on the idea that the lower-middle-class electors were fundamentally alienated by the Liberal abandonment of individualism in favour of collectivist reform. If some propensity for radicalism was retained this may have been due to their Nonconformity, or may, alternatively, reflect their changing composition through constant recruitment. Literate, politically conscious young men rising into non-manual employment were often exponents of radical Liberalism and indeed of socialism as figures like Ramsay MacDonald and Herbert Morrison, the son of a Lambeth policeman, indicate; already by the end of the century the Labour movement was drawing upon clerks, journalists and teachers for activists and municipal candidates much as Victorian radicalism had previously done.

Part Two 1895–1914

Chapter 5

The Edwardian Crises
1895–1914

There are men who sit still with the fly-blown
phylacteries of obsolete policies bound round their
foreheads, who do not remember that while they
have been mumbling their incantations to themselves, the world has been marching and revolving.
Lord Rosebery, Chesterfield speech, 14 December 1901

The Waning of Radicalism

By the mid-1890s radical Liberalism had lost the drive and
purpose it had displayed between 1867 and 1885. No doubt this
was partly because so many radical reforms had been accomplished;
but it was also because some reforms, notably the franchise, had
not produced desirable results. Gladstone's modest victory in 1892
by no means reversed the disaster of 1886; and in 1895 the
Liberals won a mere 177 seats against 411 for the combined
Conservatives and Liberal Unionists, a performance that was only
marginally modified in 1900. It began to seem that the mass
electorate, subject as it was to crude appeals to chauvinism and
ephemeral emotions, fell well short of the mature, informed body
a stable democracy required. As a result many prominent Liberals
felt disinclined to transform the 1884 franchise into one-man-one-
vote, not least because this would now mean opening the
pandora's box of women's suffrage. Both older Liberals like
Gladstone and younger ones like H.H. Asquith often perceived
women as the epitome of a mass electorate — politically ignorant,
emotional, vacillating. They took refuge in the argument that since
women were characterized by Anglicanism and were likely to be
enfranchised on a property basis they would inevitably lean to

the Conservatives. Yet they felt embarrassed in this illiberal attitude by the pleas of the National Union of Women's Suffrage Societies, a rather Liberal and moderate organization, and by the Women's Liberal Federation which steadily and successfully worked to convert the MPs to suffragism. It was fortunate for the anti-suffragists that the Conservatives also remained too divided to formulate a policy, and were, as a group, even more resolutely hostile to women's suffrage. Thus by the end of the century the great Victorian reform crusade was in danger of petering out amid the manoeuvres to block the women's claim.

Disillusionment became evident too in the new regard for the American system of government on the part of such 'radicals' as James Bryce. Once the model for popular radicalism, America now served to demonstrate the viability of stable, conservative democracy, characterized by devolution of power, legislative inertia at the centre, and a strong second chamber.[1] It was no accident that despite their difficulties with the House of Lords the Liberals were so slow to produce a scheme for reforming the powers and composition of the upper chamber. In the 1860s the anti-Liberal majority there had been 60–70; this widened steadily even before the withdrawals of 1886, so that in the 1893 vote on the second Home Rule Bill the Gladstonians found themselves outnumbered by 419 to 41. Much of the work of the 1892–95 administration was crippled by the peers, more so than in the past. Yet the obvious response, an appeal to the country, required a more popular cry than was provided by any of the rejected measures. Indeed an unreformed House of Lords constituted a useful insurance for voters who felt it safe to vote Liberal as long as Home Rule remained an impossibility. Thus despite much rhetoric from Rosebery 1895 came and went without either a new issue or a determined plan to reform the chamber. Not until 1908 did the leadership think seriously about reform, and not until the budget of 1909 did the party risk linking a major social question with the constitutional issue. Meanwhile it seemed safer to accept the *status quo* than to challenge it; yet the consequence was to undermine the credibility of any Liberal social policies in the eyes of the electorate.

The electoral setbacks and inhibitions of post-1886 Liberalism have led some historians to argue that it was congenitally incapable of sustaining the role of a reforming party in a mass electorate. The grounds for such a view rest, first, on the party's inability to organize its following as effectively as its rivals, and secondly, on the individualism and rationalism that inhibited the Liberals from making the demagogic appeal required by an unsophisticated electorate.[2] This case appears convincing if based on the aloof, temperamental, parliamentary figures of Liberal Imperialism or on timid, faltering radicals like John Morley. However, it does tend to overlook the tough partisans such as Harcourt or Labouchere, the adept, manipulating whips such as Herbert Gladstone, J.A. Pease or the Master of Elibank, as well as the more obscure organizers like J. Renwick Seager of the Liberal Registration Department. The legendary organizer Francis Schnadhorst remained secretary to the Liberal Central Association until 1893 though evidently well past his peak; and the activities of the Society of Certificated and Associated Liberal Agents indicate no less professional an attitude towards organization than that of their opponents.[3] The difference between the two parties lay not in attitude so much as in resources. By the 1890s far less money fuelled the Liberal machine, but this by no means indicated a revulsion from this aspect of politics. Similarly the party of Lloyd George and 'Limehouse' can hardly be suspected of eschewing a demagogic approach; what is true, however, is that in the period between the defection Chamberlain and the emergence of Lloyd George the Liberals badly missed their former monopoly in popular platform oratory. The restoration of Liberal supremacy in all the coarser arts of politics by 1903–06 should warn us against portraying them as a special kind of party too encumbered by scruples to succeed. Their manifest weaknesses during the last 20 years of the century should not be mistaken for a congenital distaste or inacapacity for modern politics.

The attrition of Liberal strength may be discerned in the late Victorian press where the earlier predominance slipped somewhat. Many Liberal proprietors and editors no doubt liked to see their brand of political journalism as morally uplifting for the people while the Tories pandered merely to their baser emotions; radical papers were sometimes handicapped by proprietorial distaste for gambling and racing results which were a mainstay of the cheap evening press.[4] But the basic problem lay in the fact that it became increasingly difficult to sell strongly partisan newspapers of any variety by 1900 (see table 5.1). Moreover, the capacity of newer national newspapers to reduce their costs and draw a bigger circulation inevitably reduced the significance of the sober provincial press which had been disproportionately Liberal in sympathy; no major Liberal equivalent of the *Daily Mail* emerged. With its restricted audience and declining profitability the provincial radical paper stood in growing need of subsidies for survival; but at

TABLE 5.1. *Political loyalties of English daily newspapers*

	1868	1886	1900	1910
Liberal	26	66	71	57
Conservative	9	40	40	35
Independent	1	19	35	14
Neutral	8	13	25	15

Source: A.J. Lee, *The Origins of the Popular Press 1855–1914* (1976), p. 287.

a time when commercial wealth was drifting further towards Conservatism this naturally meant a thinning out of the Liberal press in relation to its rivals. Yet although by the Edwardian period the Liberal advantage had been narrowed by comparison with the 1860s it had not been destroyed by any means.

In another respects the transition from the 1860s to the 1890s involved a more drastic curtailment of the Liberal lead over the Conservatives. When the Liberal Unionists withdrew in 1866 they took with them not only wealthy and influential Whigs in the counties, but, more importantly, middle-class men in the industrial areas who gave Conservatism in the north and Scotland vital infusions of business and Nonconformist, especially Wesleyan, strength.[5] With far fewer subscribers constituency Liberal associations often had to neglect the costly annual work of maintaining the electoral register, and even to abandon contests; no less than 163 Unionists were returned unopposed in 1900 for example. Although local Liberal poverty was partly redressed after 1900 by infusions from central funds under Herbert Gladstone, the Edwardian party undoubtedly depended heavily for its finance on a small pool of really wealthy, progressive industrialists – Sir William Lever, Sir John Brunner, George Cadbury and Joseph Rowntree in particular.

A further consequence of the withdrawals was to leave the remaining subscribers in the constituencies with a greater influence over candidatures. The caucus system had never been as representative as its proponents had claimed; after 1886 it became increasingly a vehicle for the 'faddist' radicalism of the NLF which blocked the aspirations of working men to parliamentary representation. Usually a local caucus felt obliged to seek a candidate able to make annual contributions and pay his own election expenses; not only would a working man require support from the association, he would also be unable to administer the material assistance either to individual constituents or to the economy of the town itself which was expected of a middle-class politician. Hence it was often felt by working-class as much as by middle-class Liberals that a working man could not carry a radical constituency. The problem is well illustrated by Newcastle Liberalism. John Morley seemed an admirable candidate for this two-member seat in 1885; but as a journalist he had little money to devote to the association, which consequently succumbed to the temptation to adopt as his partner a wealthy but nondescript local businessman in preference to a working man like Arthur Henderson who would have widened the party's electoral appeal. Morley's defiant opposition to the eight-hour day compounded the alienation of organized workers thereby precipitating the loss of one of the Newcastle seats in 1892 and both in 1895.[6]

By contrast the concentration of miners in certain counties and the availability of financial support from the miners' federations facilitated the effective adoption of trade unionists by Liberal associations, especially from 1884 when miners benefited from the extension of the county franchise. In this way such seats could be economically secured for Liberalism; for the 'Lib–Lab' members were much appreciated by Gladstone as sound radicals quite independent of the Chamberlainite caucus. However, though the Lib–Lab experiment was a novel and significant asset, by the 1890s it seemed incapable of extension beyond a handful of constituencies dominated by the miners. Paradoxically the weakness of the strategy lay in the ease with which the miners' leaders were absorbed into the party establishment. Elderly men for the most part, who had sat at the feet of Bright and Gladstone, the Lib–Labs breathed life into traditional Liberal individualism; indeed the aversion of men like Burt for state intervention (outside the mines) made them more rigid Liberals than many of the younger middle-class politicians of the 1890s. Thus, although they symbolized the common interest of working men and radicalism, and contributed positively to labour legislation, the Lib–Labs failed to make a significant programmatic or intellectual contribution to Liberalism; lacking a distinctive impact they were bound to be outflanked eventually by more radical labour politicians.

These flaws in the infrastructure of radicalism were compounded by the absorption of the leading Liberals with in-fighting and the consequent vacuum in party leadership from 1894 to 1905. The adage that Gladstone became more radical with age has recently gained new support.[7] It is suggested, for example, that he perceived the Irish agitation as an aspect of the wider British working-class movement with which he increasingly sympathized. Certainly he deplored the suppression of workers' discontent in 1886 and 1887; but the Gladstonian defence of trade union liberties was individualist, and he could not embrace their economic demands as class representatives. Nor are there more than indirect indications of Gladstone's tentative sympathy for the radical social policies of graduated income tax and old age pensions. He strongly disapproved of Harcourt's Death Duties budget of 1894 and continued to hold that income tax facilitated extravagance and tended to the social disintegration of the community.

No doubt in the 1860s and early 1870s Gladstone had led Liberalism in a radical direction, but thereafter his energies were devoted more to restraining the forces he had unleashed; his tactics in 1886 obliged him ultimately to compromise with caucus politics to the extent of swallowing such previously unpalatable measures as Welsh disestablishment and land reform. But Gladstone's endorsement of the NLF's Newcastle Programme in 1891 was purely nominal. His reluctance to respond constructively to the social questions of the 1890s marked him as an essentially one-issue statesman who had become a liability to his party; and he found it hard to accept that he had been returned to power in 1892 *in spite of* Home Rule. Now growing deaf and tiring rapidly Gladstone absented himself increasingly from the Commons and whenever possible avoided meeting his Cabinet, which made his sudden reappearances all the more trying for his colleagues. He took little interest in the development of policy beyond Ireland, and preferred to deal with a few individuals, notably Morley, with whom he felt at ease. But for his negativism and temperamental infirmity Morley might have been groomed as the next leader. Yet, to rest on Morley as Gladstone did was only to advance deeper into the cul de sac of mid-Victorian radicalism, not to face the industrial society of the future.

Gladstone's colleagues took his somewhat pitiful retirement over increased expenditure and naval rebuilding in 1894 with relief mingled with apprehension; for they failed entirely to compensate for the inspiration he had long provided for Liberalism. 'Neither Harcourtian iconoclastic crusades nor Roseberian grand panjandrum secretiveness will do any good,'[8] as one Liberal put it. Now the party counted the cost of losing its two outstanding radical statesmen: Sir Charles Dilke, ruined by a divorce scandal in 1885, and Joseph Chamberlain, soon to become Lord Salisbury's Colonial Secretary. No one adequately filled the vacuum.

Rosebery, in many ways an attractive successor, rapidly proved congenitally unsuited to be Prime Minister and party leader; impaled upon a small, fractious Commons majority he did no more than inveigh ineffectually against the House of Lords in which he was himself incarcerated. In 1896 Rosebery threw up the leadership to spend the next decade exacerbating party divisions without making a determined attempt to regain his title. During 1896—98 Harcourt and Lord Kimberley shared the leadership in the two Houses; upon the former's retirement in 1899 Sir Henry Campbell-Bannerman attempted to consolidate a party rent by imperial controversies until he was rescued around 1904 by the discovery that he could win a general election. As a leader Harcourt was too narrow and negative, and too unpopular with his colleagues; Campbell-Bannerman and Herbert Gladstone were worthy but uninspiring; Morley and Bryce too detached, irresolute and pessimistic. Among the imperialists, apart from Rosebery, there was only Asquith, cold, remote and absorbed with his legal career; Grey, too dilettante; and Haldane, too much the intellectual and intriguer.

Liberal Imperialism

Absence of constructive leadership greatly exacerbated the discontent of young middle-class Liberals. For Herbert Samuel, Charles Trevelyan, Willoughby Dickinson and others of their generation the 1890s brought a heightened consciousness of the poverty and inhumanity of urban life. As sensitive young men growing to adulthood amid the dismal investigations of Charles Booth and Seebohm Rowntree they felt a certain guilt in the contrast between their own inherited wealth and privilege and the condition of the majority. Imbued with a Victorian sense of duty and public service many of this generation served a form of apprenticeship in social work connected with Toynbee Hall in the East End, or served on municipal councils, school boards and boards of guardians before entering the Commons. They admitted, too, the moral charge of socialism against the existing order of society even if they rejected its analysis and solutions. Moreover, they identified the danger of a mass electorate generating insatiable pressure for penal taxation and the confiscation of wealth, which threatened to reduce politics to a struggle between a party of property and a party of labour. Such a prospect was not to be avoided by Morley's dogmatic resistance or by faddism, but through the adoption of a constructive social policy. This explains why Rosebery was acclaimed and for years regarded as the white hope of younger Liberals; as the first chairman of the London County Council he seemed in tune with progressive politics and urban England.

Indeed Rosebery provided the link that bound up men like Trevelyan, Samuel and Runciman with 'Liberal Imperialism'. The label is a confusing one since the strength of Liberal Imperialism was by no means simply a reflection of imperialist sentiment; though it incorporated a right-wing element, it also included those who, rebelling against faddism, sought a positive social policy. This incoherence renders measurement of the number of Liberal Imperialists difficult. Analysis based strictly upon imperial issues indicates that in the parliamentary Liberal Party the Imperialists comprised one-eighth in 1892 rising to over a third by 1905.[9] This trend reflects the death, retirement and defeat of elderly Gladstonians and their replacement by younger men less committed to party traditions.

The Liberalism of free trade, self-help and non-interference did not drive them to open conflict, though it seemed an inadequate programme. However, the Gladstonian approach to foreign and imperial questions had always been contested, and it was this that crystallized the revolt. Strictly Liberal Imperialism was a coherent force only at the top where it comprised essentially Rosebery, Asquith, Grey, Haldane, Sir Henry Fowler and R. Munro-Ferguson. They criticized Gladstone for his obsession with Home Rule, which was undesirable in itself and had led him to pander to NLF programmes. 'Mr. G.,' said Haldane, 'thoroughly demoralised the Liberal Party by the policy of sop-throwing in the two years before 1892.'[10] As a result, they believed, the party had alienated moderate middle-class support and forfeited its claim as the national party; it had degenerated into a rabble of protesters and faddists unlikely to inspire the confidence of the country as a whole.

Shaking off Home Rule and the Irish Party thus seemed essential; for even if the policy was right it remained inexpedient because it could not be forced through the Lords, and presented the Tories with a useful cry. To some extent, however, this split could be obscured by merging the Irish issue into a home-rule-all-round approach and a wider policy of imperial federation for the Empire. They regarded further British expansion as an inevitable consequence of the competition of the great powers, though they do not seem to have argued the economic virtue of this. The Liberal

Imperialists shared with Chamberlain and many Conservatives a concern for drawing together the white colonies under an Imperial Parliament at Westminster so as to facilitate a closer defence policy. In the context of Imperial Federation the devolution of authority to Ireland would be less disturbing, while general devolution would enable Westminster to disperse many of the radical fads to the regions for settlement.

In foreign affairs the Liberal Imperialists desired continuity of policy between the parties. Although their disagreements with the Gladstonians began to manifest themselves during Rosebery's tenure of the Foreign Office in 1892–94, the split reached a climax only in 1899–1902 as a result of the Liberal Imperialists' support for Sir Alfred Milner in his negotiations with President Kruger; they adopted the somewhat naïve view that the conflict was about defending the rights of British settlers in the Transvaal, from which it followed that the South African War was just. However, the 'Pro-Boers' were so voluble that it seemed they would stamp their view upon the party in an election. To check this an Imperial Liberal Council was set up in April 1900 under Robert Perks MP, from which the frontbenchers stayed aloof lest they be charged with creating a faction. The Council claimed the allegiance of 109 MPs and 142 candidates, a considerable exaggeration. Most MPs adopted the compromise position that while the war had been forced on Britain, the government had been inept in diplomacy and negligent in its military planning. Until 1901 Asquith attempted to keep on the periphery of Liberal Imperialism so as to ease Campbell-Bannerman's task of holding the party together. He was dismayed, therefore, by the latter's celebrated speech in June of that year in which he condemned as 'methods of barbarism' Kitchener's use of concentration camps in South Africa. This seemed ominously to echo Midlothian and was interpreted as an abandonment of the middle ground by Campbell-Bannerman. When in September a Liberal Unionist candidate at the N.E. Lanark by-election was denied the party leader's support and that of other Gladstonians who preferred the ILP contender, they began to fear being squeezed out of the party. Their immediate response was to set up the Liberal Imperial League under Grey. However only Rosebery could mobilize their strength in the country, and he now took another of his fitful initiatives in a speech at Chesterfield in December which contained a striking appeal for Liberals to adopt a 'clean slate' and free themselves of the 'fly-blown phylacteries' in domestic as much as foreign politics. To this clear challenge Campbell-Bannerman responded simply by inviting Rosebery to define his relationship to the Liberal Party. By establishing a new Liberal League in February 1902 Rosebery virtually admitted that he was outside the fold.

Although divisions seemed to be crystallizing as the South African War approached its end Liberal Imperialism was in fact about to be submerged in the tide of Gladstonian revivalism. Asquith, Grey and Haldane did achieve high office in 1905, but the group had lost its coherence well before then. Rosebery finally parted company with his colleagues on account of their radical financial policies; but even before 1906 he had shown himself to be a handicap because of his steadfast failure to sustain his initiatives. At heart he had no desire to regain the Liberal leadership, preferring instead to lead a coalition; and for a time it was conceivable that the disintegrating Salisbury government and squabbling opposition would present him with the opportunity. However, the Liberal Imperialists failed to exploit the situation; always inept in the basic political arts they neither organized themselves in the Commons nor built up a grass-roots organization; remote and elitist they absorbed themselves with policy and office more than with in-fighting. Tactically the Liberal Imperialists sought the middle ground when the war was driving opinions to extremes; and their acquiescence in the policy of Milner and Kitchener proved genuinely offensive to Liberals who were not 'pro-Boers'. Nor did they compensate by launching a bold social policy; instead they conveyed only a distaste for programmes in general and Liberal fads in particular. Eventually they were wrecked by the ramifications of the war, particularly Balfour's 1902 Education Act which most Liberals attacked, and the revival of the free trade issue to which all rallied. Asquith in particular reworked his passage to Liberal affections by pursuing Chamberlain around the country. He appreciated that by 1902 the party was thoroughly tired of factionalism and anxious to unite on the causes presented by the Tories. Unity and revivalism swiftly made Liberal Imperialism irrelevant as a discrete force.

'National Efficiency' and Tariff Reform

The Liberal Imperialists were by no means alone in their attitude towards party politics, imperial and social questions. In a sense they simply represented a Liberal expression of the wider movement for 'National Efficiency' around the turn of the century which embraced Fabian socialists like Sidney and Beatrice Webb, as well as collectivist Conservatives like Milner, Chamberlain and, peripherally, Balfour. Though they sprang from every political tradition the enthusiasts for National Efficiency shared certain qualities and convictions. Fundamentally they were reacting to the perceived decline of industry and agriculture during the previous 20 years, and the corresponding enfeeblement of Britain as a world power, a process that appeared to culminate in the disasters of the South African War and subsequent revelations about the degeneracy of the British urban population in the Report of the Inter-Departmental Committee on Physical Deterioration in 1904. Apprehension about British decadence stimulated a variety of remedies including the improvement of secondary education, particularly technical and scientific, to enable Britain to complete with Germany. On the military side the critics fastened upon the crippling role of the Treasury, the lamentable amateurism of army officers and the inadequate training of their men; military training for civilians was commended for both its physical and moral advantages. Also typical of National Efficiency advocates was the bold application of state power in the field of social welfare, for Bismarckian rather than humanitarian reasons: a healthy population was a more efficient workforce and more stable politically.

The other unifying theme lay in the identification of the nineteenth-century system of parliamentary government as the underlying cause of Britain's decline. Critics argued that popular democracy had warped parliamentary politics by rendering it vulnerable to sectional pressures. Governments were run increasingly by amateurs adept at party warfare but incompetent in administration and the development of policy. They were obliged to indulge in sham conflicts on irrelevant issues that turned Parliament into an entertainment for a few partisans. 'Party is an evil,' declared Rosebery, 'its operation blights efficiency.' One striking consequence of this was held to be that too much authority had lapsed to the Treasury whose narrow retrenchment philosophy killed both military innovation and social reconstruction; it also tended to eliminate the contribution of the expert and businessman to administration. This debilitating process was evident too at local level where specialists like doctors and engineers were losing out to the generalist and bureaucrat. In addition local government was hopelessly fragmented among 133 county, county borough, district and parish councils, 643 poor law boards, and 2,500 school boards. In short there were too many elected authorities with insufficient powers and expertise for coherent, efficient administration. But Balfour's Education Act and the Webbs' proposals for poor law reform in the famous Minority Report of 1909 were very much in accordance with National Efficiency thinking. Ideally it was hoped to bypass the lackadaisical, garrulous 20-member Cabinet by cabinet committees fortified with specialists and the practical wisdom of businessmen as a means of curbing party and Treasury influence. The cult of the expert found typical expression in the Committee of Imperial Defence established by Balfour in 1902 as a vehicle for the evolution of defence policy unimpeded by parliamentary interference.

Despite such notable initiatives along National Efficiency lines Balfour could not as Prime Minister (1902–05) avoid reaping the political whirlwind of the South African War. While attempting to sort out the problems bequeathed by his uncle he was overtaken by the tariff reform wave set off by Joseph Chamberlain in May 1903. His tariff campaign was designed in the short run to restore the initiative to a government faltering between the need to reduce high wartime taxation and to raise revenue for social reform. But it sprang from a long-term concern for national decline. During the 1880s and 1890s the remnants of Conservative agricultural protectionism had begun to receive infusions of support from industry particularly steel and textile manufacturers subject to foreign competition. Whereas in 1860 only 5.5 per cent by value of British imports had been manufactured items, by 1900 this was 25 per cent.[11] Much impressed by what he took to be the effects of a protected domestic market upon Germany and the United States, Chamberlain argued that these powers were now using their system of mass production to dump goods so cheaply on Britain as to undermine our manufacturing sectors; unless checked the process would denude Britain of industry. Yet for Chamberlain the central virtues of a tariff policy were its contribution to imperial economic unification and its potential for the social regeneration of Britain. The first would be attained through preference for colonial goods in the British market and acceptance by them of our manufactured products; it seemed possible to make a start in 1902 by retaining the temporary levy of 2s a bushel on foreign grain but exempting Empire imports. The second object would be achieved through the increase in employment once the home market had been secured, but also through the application of the new source of revenue from tariffs to social welfare schemes. This desire for a constructive social policy reflected Chamberlain's long-standing belief that politicians must come to terms with the working class; yet while very many Conservatives were attracted by the commercial advantages of protectionism only a minority of imperialist–collectivists like L. S. Amery appreciated his wider vision and strategy.

However, this was the first time that the latent Conservative protectionism had been given a lead from the top, and it is no surprise that the bulk of the party fell into Chamberlain's lap after 1903, although ironically he himself was incapacitated by a stroke in 1906.[12] Before the election Balfour had attempted to hold a middle position between the free traders — 83 out of the 392 Conservative MPs[13] — and the protectionists on the basis of a retaliation policy, the idea being to force concessions from protectionist states and thus restore genuine freedom of trade. However tactically shrewd this failed to satisfy the emotional forces unleashed on both sides of the debate; moreover, the two wings of the party soon became so unequal that any compromise proved irrelevant. For in 1906 the free trade MPs shrank to a handful; a few joined the Liberals, some were denied renomination and others perished in the electoral holocaust; meanwhile the 'Whole Hoggers' came to comprise a majority in the parliamentary party. By 1910 the free trade elements reluctantly accepted that the overriding threat was now the 'socialism' of Lloyd George; and to defeat it they acquiesced in a tariff policy. However, the rallying of the middle classes between 1906 and 1910 failed to compensate for the unpopularity of protectionism with consumers in the country. Thus after failing in the January 1910 election the Conservatives made frenzied efforts to reconcile their major constructive policy with the voters' apparent dislike of dear food. By December Balfour had decided on a pledge that no tariffs would be introduced without popular approval in a referendum, a tactic that probably produced a few gains in Lancashire, but left the party out of office and still badly divided. Indeed, Conservative realization that by staking everything on the tariff they had opened up the House of Lords, the Union with Ireland and the Welsh Church to radical attack led many to judge the whole campaign a mistake. Although Chamberlain had regarded a constructive social policy as integral to his strategy, neither Balfour nor Bonar Law, his successor in 1911, felt inclined or able to develop this. Instead they allowed themselves to be impaled upon a narrowly protectionist case closely linked in the public mind with the peers' revolt against Liberal taxation and welfare proposals. This misjudgement lay at the heart of the Conservative dilemma throughout the Edwardian period.

The Crisis of Conservatism

The origins of the notion that a crisis of dire proportions erupted in Edwardian England lay in events during and after the First World War. An apparent concatenation of more or less violent challenges to authority before 1914 does convey an impression of a violent spasm in which the consensus on which the social and political system rested was disintegrating; it is tempting to see Edwardian governments rescued from this prospect by the outbreak of war, which, however, only interrupted the collapse of the economic, social and political pillars of the Victorian world. In order to substantiate such a thesis it would be necessary to demonstrate first that the manifestations of violence were in nature and in effect anti-parliamentary; and second, that they were all symptoms of a common underlying malaise not just a series of coincidental events. This has never, in fact, been done. Moreover, the thesis has suffered from a prevailing assumption, the understandable result of hindsight, that the Edwardian crisis was a crisis of Liberalism. Yet, as one recent writer has wisely observed, it would be quite as appropriate to discuss the period in terms of the crisis of Conservatism.[14]

The foundations of the Conservative dilemma were electoral, in the sense that the party proved unable to dislodge from power the Liberal–Labour–Irish alliance; and programmatic, in that the split over tariffs simultaneously restored the unity and morale of the Liberals. It was a misfortune for the Conservatives that their attempt to convert the country to protectionism in 1910 coincided with a distinct economic revival. No doubt this was a 'last innings' for traditional British staples like coal and cotton: shipbuilding would have been in grave trouble but for naval rebuilding programmes; and productivity continued to languish. But the buoyancy of the Edwardian economy undoubtedly took the steam out of protection and, incidentally, robbed it of its appeal to labour.

Much the most ominous aspect of the crisis was Ireland. In particular the appearance of private armies of Ulstermen and Nationalists and the inability of the government after the so-called Curragh Mutiny of 1914 to use the army to enforce its policy in Ireland presented a severe challenge to an elected administration especially in view of Conservative connivance with the Ulster rebels. Yet there is a danger of swallowing Unionist propaganda of the time. When the party disposed of Balfour in 1911 after his third election defeat, it took in Bonar Law a leader whose strength was of a brittle kind. Not only did he lack the patronage of the premiership, he enjoyed a status inferior to at least five colleagues in terms of both governmental experience and social standing.[15] Merely a compromise between Walter Long and Austen Chamberlain, Law had little hold on his party at first except as a vigorous debater on tariffs and Ulster. 'I shall have to show myself very vicious, Mr Asquith, this session: I hope you will understand,' he told the Prime Minister privately in 1912.[16] His tough 'new style' was appreciated by the party as a welcome contrast to Balfour's elegant but ineffectual philosophizing. They rallied to him, but only because he was doing what they wanted. Pandering to the extremists had led his predecessor to disaster, and, given his failure to dislodge the Liberals from their Home Rule policy, it was likely to achieve the same for Law. By 1914 he and Sir Edward Carson were anxious chiefly to find a way out of the Irish problem without shattering the confidence of their followers.

Bonar Law's defeat was implicit in the Asquith government's persistence. It could not renege on Home Rule without destroying the hold of the Nationalist Party in Ireland upon whom it depended for its Commons majority. As Asquith put it, 'An ungovernable Ireland is a much more serious prospect than rioting in four counties.'[17] To some extent both party leaders had to consider the question through English eyes, in that both were playing to win the next general election. The Cabinet believed that by offering Lloyd George's ingenious compromise of a six-year exclusion for Ulster from the Dublin Parliament they had shown themselves reasonable to the English voters, who were antagonized only by irresponsible Unionist interference with the army, and who viewed with relief the conclusion of the Irish Question at last. Hence they refrained from prosecuting Law, Carson and Captain James Craig since this would only be to rescue them from their dilemma. This impression is corroborated by the Unionists' own realization by 1913–14 that their attempt to stir the English constituencies over Home Rule was falling flat.[18] The Liberals were not to be caught out on a novel and perplexing policy as in 1886; they had long since lost what support they would ever lose on Home Rule.

Whether Bonar Law would have been rescued by a civil war can only be guessed at. However, one can look for connections between the Ulster controversy and the suffragette agitation or the industrial unrest. Comparison with the Women's Social and Political Union (founded in 1903 by Emmeline and Christabel Pankhurst) is illuminating, for while the authorities unhesitatingly used the law against the latter they treated the Ulstermen far more circumspectly. This reflected the inability of the women to mobilize mass support; by 1914 the Pankhurst militants represented no more than a shrinking rump of the women's movement increasingly isolated from potential adherents among working women and alienated from middle-class sympathizers.[19] Certainly the Pankhursts' antagonism to Labour and industrial action during 1911–14 runs against the idea of a general or connected revolt. The women's violence amounted to sporadic assaults upon property by a handful of activists designed to win publicity, which obscured the fundamentally conservative nature of the WSPU and the movement generally.

As for the wave of strikes, their basic causes lay in the price rises and stagnation of money wages after 1900. When to this was added the 1906 Trades Disputes Act which overthrew the Taff Vale judgement, and the increase in employment during 1910–14, it is clear that the major restraints on strike action had been removed. Much has been made of syndicalism as an underlying force at this time. While it is true that certain initiatives towards industrial unions and co-operation between unions such as the Triple Alliance of coal, railway and transport workers were consistent with a syndicalist strategy, the actual motives were of much more limited significance. Industrial unionism remained exceptional, and co-ordination of strikes was calculated to minimize the damage to the unions themselves; their object in bringing pressure to bear was invariably to secure from employers recognition and a regular system of collective bargaining, not to undermine the parliamentary system in favour of industrial democracy. If the authorities had adopted a strategy of unmitigated coercion towards labour unrest and had declined to appease workers' demands, it is possible that the strikes could have developed into revolution. But neither government nor union leaders intended to allow this to happen. Although there were several explosive points, notably the shooting of two miners at Ton-y-pandy in 1910 and the arrest of Jim Larkin during the Dublin transport workers' strike in 1913, these were exceptional. Frequently the unions found allies in ministers like Lloyd George and civil servants like Sir George Askwith of the Board of Trade whose object was to induce employers to engage in collective bargaining. In addition the Trades Disputes Act (1906), the Trade Boards Act (1909) and the Miners Minimum Wage Act (1912) demonstrated how Parliament could be used to further the aims of organized labour. The most striking endorsement of the Labour movement's parliamentary strategy came in 1914 when all but three of the 63 unions that balloted on the question of a political fund associated with the Labour Party supported the proposal; this was hardly the action of men alienated from the parliamentary process. The leaders remained keen to take what the system offered in representation and legislation, in terms of employment under the Labour Exchanges scheme, and as approved societies under the 1911 National Insurance Act. This tendency to become integrated into the system rather than to undermine it was typical of the pragmatic approach of British trade unionism, which showed no sign of diminishing before 1914. The handful of synidcalists undoubtedly won a certain prominence in 1911–14 when the average union member was moved by the recent decline in real wages; but they in no sense led or directed the working-class movement, and enjoyed a fleeting eminence only while the special circumstances of 1911–14 lasted.

Thus, with the exception of Ulster the Edwardian agitations cannot be represented as effectively anti-parliamentary in nature; nor did they comprise a single or interconnected phenomenon, apart from a little rhetorical and stylistic imitation of the Ulster Unionists by the WSPU and some unions. Each remained a discrete movement. It is significant that the new light thrown on this period by oral evidence has tended further to undermine the apocalyptic view by showing how little sense of crisis the ordinary, obscure person had.[20] This underlines the point that the concept of catastrophe was essentially an upper-middle-class one, and even then, characteristic of the political 'outs' after 1906. Their exaggerated apprehensions about the arrival of independent working men in the Commons representing their class, and the general assertiveness of labour, were compounded by the demagogy of Lloyd George. Not since Chamberlain had attacked those 'who toil not, neither do they spin' in 1885 had they heard the upper class pilloried from on high. 'They are forcing a revolution and they will get it, 'declared Lloyd George at Newcastle in 1909, 'the Lords may decree a revolution, but the people will direct it.'[21] However, it was not a revolution but graduated taxation and a modest redistribution of income that he intended; by preaching against the peerage he sought not to foment class conflict but to harmonize the potentially conflicting working class and middle class, for therein lay electoral salvation. Nor are there sound grounds for the old view that the people were in fact bored and disillusioned by the constitutional conflict of 1910. This is to miss the wider social dimension behind the constitutional argument; it also overlooks the actual evidence for turnout among voters: 86 per cent in January and 81 per cent in December 1910. Such figures have rarely been exceeded before or since; moreover, it is particularly striking that the second election of the year should have produced such a response for a reduction of 4 per cent was the unavoidable result of the staleness of the register by December. The elections of 1910 can hardly be seen as other than notable indications of popular involvement in the parliamentary process. Though Bonar Law might claim that there were things stronger than parliamentary majorities, the experience of the Edwardian years belies such alien sentiments. Unlike the opposition who stumbled from one problem to the next, the government confronted each obstacle and ultimately imposed their strategy by the strength of representative democracy. They played the parliamentary game with indications of conviction because within the rules it was a game they invariably won.

Chapter 6

Edwardian Progressivism

British Liberalism is not going to repeat the errors
of Continental Liberalism. . . . Let Liberalism proceed with its glorious work of building up the
temple of liberty in this country, but let it also
bear in mind that the worshippers at the shrine
have to live.
David Lloyd George, Swansea, 1 October 1908

Origins of the New Liberalism

The history of Victorian Liberalism has often been written as
though it is to be equated with *laissez-faire*. Clearly much of its
drive derived from an industrial middle class bent upon levelling
the privileges of the aristocracy and eliminating restrictions upon
individual enterprise. Yet 'economic liberalism' was always distinct
from party Liberalism whose primary achievement was political
democracy in Britain. In practice the period from the 1830s to
the 1880s was one of continuous experiment with state intervention in the economic and social affairs of individuals whose actions
were restrained in the interests of the community; in the process
the Victorians laid the foundations for the huge central bureaucracy of the twentieth century. Particularly at the municipal level,
where Liberalism was often the party of expenditure and interference not of retrenchment and abstention,[1] the notion gained
ground that certain economic functions, ranging from water and
gas to parks and libraries, were better performed by the community
than by the private entrepreneur.

Moreover the Liberalism of the Victorians was as subject as most
creeds to reinterpretation by its adherents; and the 1880s and

1890s constitute an especially important phase of this kind. Reinterpretation for politicians did now, however, imply any repudiation of essentials. The primary concern of Liberalism continued to be liberty defined by the law. Confidence in the virtues of the free play of individual energies and talents was qualified by knowledge of the consequences and also by an appreciation that the terms of competition must not be too unequal; where they were, the state might legitimately adjust them even though infringing the rights of some individuals in the process. In the last 20 years of the century the elements of interventionism waxed steadily stronger, and not only in Liberalism. Why was this so? Undoubtedly the perceived difficulties of the British economy, now facing severe international competition and shrinking profits, eroded the attractions of industrial growth as a panacea for society's ills. Whereas in, say, 1851, it seemed likely that another generation of economic expansion would absorb unemployment and poverty, by the 1880s few could be so confident. Far from being eliminated, poverty, as the investigations of Charles Booth and Seebohm Rowntree suggested,[2] had remained at a depressingly high level. The consequences of advanced industrialism were minutely observed in London where society seemed to fragment into social classes by residence. Aware of the strains on their society adherents of Liberalism tended to reaffirm their basic object of maximizing liberty as a means to individual moral improvement; some like Herbert Spencer sought to achieve this by advocating a reduced role for the state; others like T.H. Green, the Oxford philosopher, urged a greater and more positive use of interventionism. What is important historically is that by the 1900s it was those who thought along Green's lines who had come to typify active political Liberalism in Britain.

By the turn of the century an impressive body of academics and publicists were reinterpreting the Liberalism with which they had grown up. Green himself was no more than a representative, not the most advanced, of new Liberal thinking in the 1880s: while accepting the capitalist system as broadly consistent with social good, he justified state legislation in carefully limited areas to maintain the conditions for individual initiative. D.G. Ritchie, the collectivist radical, took a more emphatic view of the state as a positive agent of improvement. L.T. Hobhouse, the sociologist and journalist, argued that freedom was devoid of meaning to the victim of uncontrolled free enterprise and urged collective action for mutual advantage. J.A. Hobson, perhaps the best-known propagandist for the 'New Liberalism', urged that the state should maintain a minimum standard of life for all its citizens and operate certain economic functions for the community as a whole. Hobson was most conscious of the link between social and political change; the idea that 'politics had anything to do with industry or standards of living' was, he noted, somewhat novel. In his view Victorian politicians had endeavoured to keep social questions out of politics by agitating alternative issues; but by 1900 the broad divide in politics corresponded increasingly with the social divide, with possession and property on the Conservative side.

However, thinkers are not usually politicians, and in Britain especially there is great scepticism about the connection between the realm of ideas and actual historical events. Yet links there were, if only in the shape of the 31 Balliol College men who sat in the Parliament of 1906, four in the Cabinet. Take the apparently unpromising example of H.H. Asquith whose ministerial career spanned the Gladstonian and the Edwardian phases. Tutored by Green at Oxford, Asquith was a typical politician in being rather uninterested in abstract ideas and not apparently afflicted by a social conscience. Yet he acquired an enduring scepticism about the traditional party platidudes and was unencumbered by ideological inhibitions such as *laissez-faire*; it was he who, as Chancellor of the Exchequer 1906–08, initiated the financial and social radicalism that antagonized traditional Liberals. However, the 'New Liberals' were usually more intellectually curious than Asquith. A typical example is Herbert Samuel who combined writing on Liberalism, investigation into social conditions and active party politics. Like William Beveridge and R.H. Tawney he had been at Oxford at a time when young undergraduates were urged to go out and discover why so much poverty existed in British society, and did so. Characteristically the first stop was work in London's East End, often at Toynbee Hall, before moving on to wider political activity. For those who chose to operate through the party system the intellectual basis of their action was twofold. First, it showed the continuity of Liberal thought, a matter of some importance to men like Samuel and Hobhouse, anxious not to repudiate their traditions. Second, it demonstrated the existence of a real alternative, both theoretically and practically, to 'socialism' to which many young middle-class men would otherwise have been driven. As it was they enjoyed a fruitful relationship with the Fabians, particularly Graham Wallas, the Webbs and Ramsay MacDonald. Indeed, much of what in twentieth-century Britain is termed 'socialism' is no more than the 'New Liberalism' of 1900.

The starting point for the 'New Liberals' of this period was a belief that in the past liberty, while a proper concern of Liberals, had been too narrowly defined in terms of legal, political and religious liberties; yet it was now apparent that for most men the chief restraint upon their liberty was economic or social in nature. Thus the individual's material welfare should be of equal concern to the state as his moral condition. In this way the New Liberalism came, for many, to imply drastic social reform. In the words of J.M. Robertson MP, 'Laissez-faire is not done with as a principle of rational limitation of state interference, but it is quite done with as a pretext for leaving uncured deadly social evils which admit of curative treatment by state action.[3]

However, New Liberals looked beyond the symptoms of distress to the underlying distribution of wealth. Did a redistribution of resources threaten the traditional Liberal commitment to private property? The reformers were clear that while the state ought not to infringe what rightly belonged to individuals, what did not rightly belong was a different matter. Wealth was so often the result not of individual enterprise but of community development that society could properly differentiate between earned and unearned income, and tax the latter more heavily for the benefit of the community at large. The death duties introduced by Sir William Harcourt in 1894 were a harbinger of this theme in radical policy which increasingly divided the Liberals from Conservatives. The best target for taxing the 'unearned increment' was, of course, land. For as a result of the expansion of towns and the needs of local authorities urban land increased spectacularly in price in the nineteenth century. To radicals land was a monopoly of the privileged class which they had historically sought to 'free'. To levy a toll upon its increment, therefore, could provide resources for the state while leaving private ownership intact and stopping short of confiscation. In this way land reform provided both a practical expression for popular radicalism and a valuable bridge between Cobdenite traditions and New Liberalism.

New Liberalism also challenged the notion that taxation was inherently or necessarily an evil, and argued that the budget might become a positive instrument of social policy. This view was to be translated into practice by Asquith and Lloyd George as Chancellors in the period 1906–14, though Harcourt had pointed the way. Their policies offended orthodox economic wisdom which held that the uneven distribution of income in the community was both necessary and beneficial since its concentration in the hands of a few meant it would be channelled into future production; the

THE PATIENT ASS.

From Punch, 18 April 1896.

effect of diverting it to the masses whose expenditure was held to be essentially non-productive would be detrimental to business activity. Now death duties were defended on the grounds that they tapped resources not normally available for investment. However, Liberals, notably J.A. Hobson, began to dispute the conventional financial assumptions fundamentally. Hobson charged that the uneven distribution of income actually hindered the economy because it deprived the mass of the population of the capacity to consume goods while diverting the surplus into the hands of those who merely generated more goods for which there was an insufficient market. In short, the real weakness – underconsumption by the masses – could be remedied by a reallocation of purchasing power through taxation and social welfare; rising demand would stimulate economic growth. Underconsumptionist arguments enabled the New Liberals to justify their emphasis on social reform as a means of reducing the waste and inefficiency in society, for such expenditure need not be regarded as a cost or burden upon the productive economy. Thus the Edwardian governments were fortified by an assumption that one might helpfully raise the level of expenditure according to the condition of the economy and employment. It is not entirely accidental that in the 1920s Liberals were more inclined than their rivals to espouse Keynesianism.

Yet the New Liberals had to face the political implications of their ideas. Did not a programme of sweeping social reform and graduated taxation amount to a class policy at variance with the party's traditions? Some like Hobhouse frankly urged that the improvement in the conditions of the working class was now so overriding a priority that no party that claimed to represent national and not sectional interests could ignore it. Samuel argued that since any expenditure that raised the material condition of the poor was in the interests of the wealthy the latter should bear their share of the cost. This notion of a fair contribution from those best able to pay became a standard defence much favoured by Lloyd George during the controversy over his 'People's Budget' in 1909–10. By this stage the New Liberal orthodoxy held that the state must accept a wide responsibility for the welfare of the people financed by limited redistributive taxation; it broke with the traditional fondness for retrenchment and individual property rights; and it offended against the Gladstonian belief that taxation should not be a means of marking out different social classes or types of wealth. Even in Gladstone's time these principles had been infringed in special cases such as Irish land reform; and retrenchment had been gradually abandoned out of expediency. However, the New Liberals, fortified both by principle and by necessity, pushed financial and social policy unapologetically into its twentieth-century mould. Thereby they increasingly distinguished the Liberal Party from the Conservatives who still favoured indirect taxation, objected to graduated taxation on principle, and preferred to restrict government expenditure to basic administrative functions.

Between the 1880s and the First World War the New Liberalism gradually came to occupy the mainstream of Liberal politics. The critical decade was the 1890s when the 'New Liberal' title began to be applied to various groups and individuals such as the Rainbow Circle whose members included Samuel, Hobson, Charles Trevelyan, J.M. Robertson and Percy Alden. They were absorbed both with social policy and with a political strategy of co-operation between middle- and working-class radicalism, such as that pioneered by the Progressives on the London County Council. By the turn of the century Hobson, Samuel, Robertson, Hobhouse and Charles Masterman, all prolific writers, had generated a coherent revision of their creed and a programmatic refurbishment for the party (see bibliography). In 1896 the Rainbow Circle produced its own *Progressive Review*, but it enjoyed much wider support from radical editors such as C.P. Scott (*Manchester Guardian*), W.H. Massingham (*Daily Chronicle*), J.A. Spender (*Westminster Gazette*), and most importantly A.G. Gardiner of the *Daily News*, the cheap radical paper widely read by provincial activists which consistently promoted an alliance of Liberal and Labour forces.

Tension inevitably existed between the New Liberals and orthodox stalwarts among backbench MPs, local party chairmen, and municipal politicians who formed the warp and woof of the local party fabric. Impatient with existing organizations like the NLF 'merely reiterating its approval of the Newcastle Programme', New Liberals sought more direct approaches to power. Fortunately for them the electoral defeats of the 1890s and the withdrawal of some wealthy patrons left a vacuum for younger radicals: 1886 had prepared the ground; and by the 1900s those employers and other wealthy men who remained in the Liberal camp had generally accepted the need to come to terms with labour.[4] Indeed among the keenest advocates of old age pensions, graduated taxation and state intervention were industrial magnates like William Lever and Sir John Brunner (the leading manufacturers of soap and chemicals respectively), who along with the Cadbury and

Rowntree families continued to finance the party up to 1914. Industrialists like James Joicey, the north-east coal-owner, found radicalism excessive and quit the party; adherents of strict *laissez-faire* like Richard Holt, the Liverpool shipowner, remained MPs until 1918 but had dwindled in numbers and influence. After 1900 the older generation of social radicals — Sir Charles Dilke, Francis Channing or Sydney Buxton — were joined by younger men in Parliament. In London where the field was wide open Charles Masterman, Christopher Addison, T.J. Macnamara and Percy Alden gained seats; here as elsewhere Herbert Gladstone played a vital role as chief whip (1899–1905) in placing radical candidates in winnable seats and often assisting them financially. In the north a similar role was filled by Charles Trevelyan, himself elected in 1899, who helped to place Samuel, Robertson and Runciman in radical industrial constituencies. The steady transformation of the personnel of Liberalism grew into a flood in 1906, for of the 401 Liberals then returned to the Commons 205 had never sat in the House before.

This change was somewhat obscured by the aftermath of the South African War; none of the Liberal Party's leaders acted as midwife to the New Liberalism as Lloyd George, Asquith and Churchill did after 1906. Indeed the war divided radicals like Hobson and C.P. Scott who condemned British policy, from men like Trevelyan and Samuel. After 1902 Liberal rhetoric was diverted towards such tempting targets as education, 'Chinese Slavery' and free trade, and propaganda took the negative line of reversing Toryism. This inevitable attempt to exploit the government's difficulties culminated in the revivalist campaign of 1906. However, this obscures the underlying trend. Examination of the 1906 campaign material shows the general commitment of candidates to old age pensions, graduated taxation, poor law and land reform, which was soon reflected in backbench impatience for legislation after the election. The governments of Campbell-Bannerman and Asquith turned out to be more radical than the campaign rhetoric had suggested. Retrenchment had been a useful stick with which to beat the Conservatives but it was rapidly abandoned by the incoming administration. Asquith's 1907 budget proved to be a key point in the overthrow of financial orthodoxy. He asserted the principle of income differentiation by retaining the rate of tax on earned income at 9d while raising that on unearned to 1s in the £; he made compulsory personal declarations of every class of one's income; he forced the Treasury to accept the idea of a super-tax, and insisted that social reform obliged governments to plan for rising expenditure several years ahead. The widespread support for his non-contributory pensions scheme and the measures for the feeding and medical inspection of schoolchildren is some indication of changed attitudes in Britain; the individual was no longer seen as wholly responsible for his family's welfare; nor, significantly, was there any question of disfranchising the recipients of the new benefits as the recipients of poor relief were. In short the strength of the Liberals' position was that although they were reformers they were not dangerously in advance of opinion in the country. Similarly Lloyd George's 1911 National Insurance Act reflected Victorian self-help traditions in incorporating the contributory principle and by involving existing friendly societies and insurance companies in the scheme. His celebrated budget of 1909 embodied elements of redistribution in the shape of the £10 income tax allowance for children under 16, the super-tax on incomes above £5,000, the additional 2d on unearned income, the extra rates for death duties and the modest levies on land values; although the purchase tax increases on tobacco and spirits did bear upon poorer families. Of the £17 million deficit that Lloyd George intended to make up by these means £8 million arose from pensions, only £3 million for Dreadnought building and the rest from a fall in revenue as a result of reductions in trade. The emerging strategy for dealing with an economy subject to serious unemployment involved three items: the Labour Exchanges of 1909; the attempt to replace the income workers lost through ill-health, unemployment or old age; and thirdly the Development Commission. In the 1909 budget the Chancellor set aside £200,000, with a promise of any surplus accruing to the exchequer, for use by the Commission on experimental farming, forestry, rural transport and land reclamation. This reflected the thinking of radical industrialists in favour of state investment in those sectors of the economy that private enterprise failed to finance. Because fairly full employment returned from 1910 little use was made of the Development Commission, but it signified governmental intention to regulate expenditure as and when the state of the labour market made it desirable.

By the time of the campaigns on the 'People's Budget' in 1909–10 Lloyd George had reduced the New Liberalism to a tangible, popular form. He based his case squarely on a free enterprise economy under free trade. In this system, he contended, Liberalism represented the interests of those who created wealth, that is employers and workers, who were in conflict with a parasitic landowning class and their political agents. He often delighted to point to the wealth of the Liberal candidates on whose platforms he spoke, noting how much extra they would pay in taxation. What distinguished such men from their opponents, he claimed, was their willingness to shoulder a fair share of the cost of national defence and social reform, thereby proving the sincerity of their concern for the people's welfare, and also demonstrating that the Liberal Party was not bent upon the confiscation of wealth. Thus Liberalism served the vital function of unifying the social classes who worked for a living by seeing fair play between them in the national interest. The Liberal Party was the most efficacious vehicle for the working classes because it harnessed to their cause large sections of the middle class who would be frightened into reaction by a party based solely on labour. Here lay the political and intellectual rationale for the New Liberalism.

The Politics of the Pact 1903—14

Though never an outstanding politician either as orator or admini-strator Herbert Gladstone became a pivotal figure particularly in the decade after he became Chief Whip in 1899. As heir to his father's 'Little England' views he greatly appreciated the rapprochement of labour and Liberal forces as a result of the South African crisis. To Gladstone it was axiomatic that nothing of significance divided Liberals like himself from the mainstream working-class politicians: all parties, he believed, tended to develop a left, centre and right: the emergence of organized labour was thus essentially a natural expression of radical liberalism whose inclusion under the Liberal Party's umbrella was both logical and necessary if progressive Liberalism was to be strength-ened against the imperialist right now so much in evidence. To this end the Campbell-Bannerman—Morley—Gladstone leadership had declined to support an official Liberal candidate of imperialist views at the Mid-Lanark by-election of 1901 in favour of Bob Smillie the Independent Labour Party nominee. When another seat fell vacant at Dewsbury in 1902 they attempted, unsuccessfully, to secure the nomination of a working man, Sam Woods. In calling in the workers to redress the balance of middle-class Liberalism the party leaders clearly risked alienating their own local activists; however, without a large measure of common sentiment between Liberal and Labour forces in the country Gladstone's initiative in 1903 in seeking terms with Ramsay MacDonald, Secretary of the

Labour Representation Committee, would not have been practicable at all. This appeared to be the lesson of three by-elections at this time. When the safe Liberal seat at Clitheroe fell vacant in 1902 it was filled unopposed by David Shackleton, a trade unionist of essentially Liberal convictions standing for the LRC, because of the approval of local Liberals. Similarly Liberals abstained at Woolwich, where they were weak, on behalf of Will Crooks (LRC) who gained the seat from the Conservatives. But it was the Barnard Castle by-election in 1903 following the death of Sir Joseph Pease that caused the greatest stir, for in a three-cornered contest the seat went to Arthur Henderson (LRC) by 47 votes. Although a Liberal defeat the election's significance lay in demonstrating the vitality of Liberal–Labour sentiment among working-class voters. For Henderson won because he enjoyed the tacit support of the Liberal leaders; because as Pease's former agent he was well known locally as a *Liberal*: and because the local Liberal association blundered by nominating a tariff reformer at a time when free trade sentiment had been sharply aroused. Henderson, sound on free trade, was thus the best Liberal available. For Gladstone this underlined the dividends to be won by Liberal–LRC co-operation. For the elections did not indicate that the LRC was about to sweep the country in its own right. The Labour leaders appreciated this, though socialist activists often did not; at Norwich in 1904, for example, an ILP candidate obtained only 13 per cent while the Liberals gained the seat. This rubbed in the point that if socialists were unlikely to succeed as socialists, labour candidates of Liberal views would flourish.

For MacDonald this was by no means an unwelcome reading of events. His own inclinations and record as a candidate led him to seek accommodation with the Liberals, but to do so from a position of strength. However, in 1900 the newly launched LRC had been too weak. Only 376,000 union members had been affiliated (at only 10s per thousand) by 1901 although delegates representing 546,000 had voted for the creation of the LRC, and TUC membership was over three times this figure. However, the notorious Taff Vale judgement of 1901 which made the Society of Railway Servants, and therefore any union, liable for the financial losses arising from strikes, transformed the situation by stimulating union leaders to extend their political influence. By 1903, 861,000 had been affiliated, the fees had been raised, and a fund established to pay a £200 salary to MPs elected under LRC auspices thereby enabling the National Executive Committee to exert a degree of control for the first time.

As a result of these developments MacDonald found himself able to impose his strategy upon a labour movement now anxious to obtain rapid representation in Parliament, while at the same time he had something to offer Gladstone — not only votes, but the LRC's financial resources (this latter was important for hitherto a labour alliance had always appeared a financial liability to the Liberals). Thus by 1903 MacDonald and Gladstone had identified a common interest in victory over a crumbling Conservative government and the danger of jeopardizing it by splitting the Progressive vote. Later, when under attack from his own party, MacDonald tried to minimize his role in the pact by arguing that no formal bargain had been struck. But this was only because neither could guarantee to withdraw candidates in specific constituencies and both feared that a public announcement would provoke criticism. Gladstone's private papers show that there was nothing spontaneous about the pact; MacDonald made great exertions to kill Labour candidatures in Liberal seats not covered by the pact,[5] and, though he could not control the socialist societies he often emasculated their efforts by denying them the LRC ticket. For Gladstone it was relatively easy to secure a clear run for the LRC in derelict seats in Liverpool, Lancashire or Birmingham, and not difficult to share candidatures in double-member constituencies such as Preston, Bolton, Leicester, Derby and Newcastle, particularly as this was frequently marginal or Conservative territory. As a result 31 of the 50 LRC candidates in 1906 were unopposed by Liberals.

In retrospect the pact appeared an unnecessary mistake for the Liberals in that 24 of the 29 LRC MPs won by virtue of Liberal withdrawals, while the Liberals' own 401-seat landslide would not have been materially smaller in the absence of co-operation. However, in 1903 this had not been obvious. Labour had saved Gladstone a lot of money and tied the Conservatives down in all constituencies. Moreover, since the Labour members were for the most part 'sober, earnest Liberals' they reinforced the progressive drift of Liberal politics admirably. The significance of this strategy is underlined by the availability of an alternative during 1903—05. For Chamberlain's tariff campaign and the consequent hounding of free trade Conservatives from their constituencies after 1903 presented the Liberals with a golden opportunity to reverse the losses of 1886 by clawing back the centre ground. They largely succeeded in doing this among the electorate, at least temporarily, as their victories in southern and middle-class seats show. Yet how much of the personnel and programme of the rebel Conservatives should be absorbed? Those Conservatives who expected free trade and retrenchment to provide an adequate bridge between them and the Liberal Party were mistaken as Trevelyan reminded Winston Churchill:

> The Liberal Party is not a free trade party. It is only satisfied with Free Trade as an economic base to work from. . . . The whole raison d'etre of present day Liberalism is constructive reform. . . . What I want to know is how much common ground can you find with reforming Liberals on economic and social questions? . . . the reform forces in the party are vastly stronger than ten years ago and I am certain will never check themselves for the sake of a few Tory votes.[6]

As a result Liberal—Conservative co-operation in 1906 was limited to a few exceptional cases; 12 crossed the floor before the election, including Churchill and J.E.B. Seeley who won election in Manchester and Liverpool respectively; others like Arthur Elliott (Durham City) and Richard Cavendish (North Lonsdale) enjoyed a free run from the Liberals. But the pact with Labour pre-empted any general arrangement; Lancashire, the centre of free trade Conservatism, was already the scene of the most widespread application of the Gladstonian strategy.

Faced with the bleak prospect of an overwhelmingly radical House of Commons the tactics of the 157-strong Conservative opposition were initially rewarding. By employing their majority in the Lords to reject or emasculate legislation of concern to Liberal pressure groups especially on education, licensing and land, they shrewdly maximized discontent within the government's ranks. For while traditional radicals became exasperated at the failure of their huge majority to overawe the peers during 1906–08, the social radicals resented the time wasted on bills that were clearly doomed. This feeling was exacerbated by unmistakable evidence that the peers were studiously accepting measures like the Trades Disputes Bill and the feeding of schoolchildren for fear of antagonizing the workers. So long as the government ploughed the issues that left the country as a whole unmoved it deprived itself of the option of a successful dissolution and exposed itself to attack from backbenchers and Labour for neglecting social questions; the loss of two by-elections to Labour at Jarrow and Colne Valley in 1907 appeared to underline the point. Thus so long as the Conservatives applied their destructive tactics judiciously they could oblige the Cabinet to soldier on while indirectly encouraging Labour to loosen its ties; by redividing the radical forces the opposition could reasonably expect to return to power at an election around 1911—12.

Unhappily for the Conservatives they had not thought out their tactics quite so rationally, nor did they apply them so precisely. So much emotion, fear and pride underlay their politics that they failed to resist the provocation offered by Lloyd George in 1909. There are now no real grounds for thinking that the Chancellor deliberately prepared his budget with a view to its rejection by the peers. His object was rather to use the budget as a Trojan Horse that would gain legislative entry for such items as land and licensing reform rebuffed in ordinary bills.[7] Yet when he perceived in the rising antagonism of the Tory Party the possibility of a first-class constitutional—social controversy he grasped it quickly. His budget in fact raised two matters of longer-term significance. The first was not the land taxes themselves but the consequent provision to undertake a valuation of all the land in the country, a necessary preparation for an effective radical policy for the land. To avert this more distant threat many peers felt obliged to reject the immediate proposals, modest as they were. Secondly, the increase in revenue demonstrated that social reforms could be paid for without abandoning free trade and thereby knocked away a central prop of the tariff reform argument. Hence the particular prominence of protectionist Conservatives in the move to reject the budget. However, no one could be sure how far the Liberals would capitalize politically on the financial break-through, nor how soon. For the present their proposals were not self-evidently revolutionary in character; extra taxation could be justified by the need to pay for pensions, which the opposition dared not oppose because they were too popular and the Dread-nought programme for which they had loudly clamoured. In throwing out the budget, therefore, they placed themselves in a dilemma exacerbated by the weight of constitutional precedent that heavily favoured the government. Had they stuck to their original tactics and left the budget alone the Liberals would have borne the unpopularity for higher taxes which fell upon all sections to some extent, without any immediate compensation. Instead, by assailing the innovations with great passion they invested them with a revolutionary significance, thereby burnishing brightly the progressive credentials of the government in the eyes of labour — the key to continued power. They enabled the Liberals to claim, with some plausibility, that their opponents were a lot of rich men trying to evade their taxes, and were intending to renege on old age pensions now that they realized the cost, a point which, significantly, Conservative candidates tried to refute at length during the 1910 general elections.

The opposition did derive some immediate gain from the constitutional crisis in that they obliged the Liberals to go to the country twice during 1910 and, in the process, removed the overall Liberal majority of 1906. However, the circumstances of the elections so greatly reinforced the 1903 pact as to keep the Conservatives more firmly out of office. Many a northern town that had not seen the landed aristocrat of radical demonology for years was now treated to the spectacle of elderly peers gracing the platforms of Conservative candidates; even Lord Curzon let slip the typically arrogant aphorism that 'all civilisations are the work of aristocracies', a remark that was endlessly repeated by gleeful radicals. The effect of all this on Labour was of crucial importance. It could not but welcome the government's initiatives as a step in the right direction; if the peers condemned the budget as red socialism MacDonald had no desire to dispute it. The Labour leaders' only doubts, justifiable ones, were whether the Cabinet would shirk the ultimate task of curbing the powers of the Lords permanently. Driven both by sentiment and by tactical necessity, therefore, Labour threw its efforts more strongly behind the Liberals, even to the extent of reducing its candidates from 78 to 56 between the January and December elections. Thus the triumph of Lloyd George's tactics in 1910 was a dual one; he dictated the terms of the debate by forcing the Conservatives into wild negativism and Labour into loyal acquiescence.

The Chancellor's achievement was not simply a short-term rhetorical coup, however. The New Liberalism had not begun with the budget of 1909, nor did it end with it; for the Cabinet could not cease to deliver social reform for fear of disappointing expectations aroused in the country. This undoubtedly made for certain difficulties in the short run. For example the 1911 National Insurance Act seemed to threaten so many vested interests[8] that the opposition exploited their fears effectively in the by-elections of 1911–12. By 1913, however, when the insurance benefits began to be paid out, the credit redounded to Lloyd George. Indeed, for all their vehemence in public some Conservative leaders had seen from the start that national insurance would only consolidate the Liberals' reputation, and by 1913 the most they could do was to promise to improve, not to repeal it. In order to counter the negative siege mentality that fell over the Conservative Party in the reaction from protectionism prominent Conservatives like F.E. Smith established the Unionist Social Reform Committee in 1912. Yet it proved difficult to shift the party from its obsession with Ireland in these years. Pethaps there was truth in Bonar Law's characteristic comment that if the country wanted social reform it would not vote the Conservatives back into office. This prospect was enhanced because every stand the Conservatives took tended to compound their alienation from the bulk of the working-class vote which was what kept the Liberals in power. It is easily forgotten that even the Ulster question, on which the Labour Party remained as consistently nationalist as the government, helped to reinforce the electoral pact when it showed signs of breaking down. Hence the futility of a Conservative strategy that united their opponents instead of dividing them.

Despite this it is sometimes assumed that the New Liberalism was bound to destroy the Liberal Party by alienating the middle classes, or alternatively, that fear of a middle-class reaction would bring reform to a halt thereby losing the working-class vote. The electoral evidence bearing on this will be considered in chapter 7. Here it must be noted that the idea of a termination of social radicalism in terms of policy and programme around 1911 is largely theoretical; it is scarcely borne out by the empirical evidence. The budget of 1914 projected a record national expenditure of over £200 million; Lloyd George continued pushing out from the bridgeheads already established. Income tax relief for children was doubled; he introduced a graduated tax rising to 1s 4d in the £ on earned income over £2,500; super-tax now became payable at £3,000 instead of £5,000, and at steeper rates rising to a maximum of 2s 8d; and the scales for death duties were also increased to a maximum of 20 per cent on estates over £1 million.

These unmistakable signs of the government's intention to stick to its new course are all the more impressive in view of the criticism they continued to provoke in some quarters. Throughout 1906—14 there was evidence of middle-class protest against higher taxes and especially rates, which helps to explain Conservative municipal successes on the basis of ratepayers' revolts. Some industrialists also articulated their misgivings at the trend in policy; Alfred Pease, for example, explained his refusal to appear on a Liberal platform in Cleveland by his dislike of the

> disposition to multiply laws and restrictions. . . . The idea that the State can take from one class and give to other classes and take the place of individual enterprise is a very corrupting one.[9]

There was also a discernible feeling that too much legislation bestowed special advantages on labour. In 1908, for example, there had been pressure from colliery-owners and shipowners, reflected in Cabinet by Runciman, against minimum wages for miners as tantamount to 'truckling for miners' votes'.[10] However, the Liberal Party had already parted company with the Yorkshire coal-owners without, it transpired, impairing its grip on the Yorkshire constituencies. So long as sums of £5,000 and £10,000 at a time were donated by Lever and Rowntree the party did not need to fear the loss of the remaining Gladstonian businessmen.

However, the criticism made it all the more important not to neglect issues of traditional concern to Liberals: hence the time devoted to Welsh disestablishment, Home Rule and the franchise in 1911—14, in a shrewd attempt to balance the novel and the traditional elements in the programme. By 1912 the Cabinet was also well aware of the desirability of relieving the burdens of the lower ranks of the middle classes especially by sparing local rates from some of the cost of education, roads and the poor law.[11] This was one of the considerations that drove radicals and Lloyd George 'back to the land' in the last years of peace.

The Land Campaign, launched in October 1913, has often been misunderstood as an anachronism. Yet seen in all its ramifications it amounted to a drastic extension of social radicalism. Lloyd George capitalized on the widespread agreement that the previous 30 years had seen a disastrous weakening of British agriculture with serious social, economic and strategic consequences. His Rural Land Enquiry showed, as did official statistics, that 60 per cent of agricultural labourers earned only 18s or less per week, and that despite a reduction in the labour force housing conditions remained appalling since few landowners were now willing to invest in new cottages. Not only was it difficult for the opposition to deny the underlying case for action, but in addition land was an ideal means of arousing the enthusiasm of Liberals of all shades. Further, recent research into the distribution of wealth in Britain has undermined the old assumption that after the industrial revolution the chief source of great wealth was industrial in character; as late as 1900 the large fortunes in Britain were still to a remarkable degree concentrated in land, urban landholdings, and commerce.[12] In taking land as a target, therefore, the radicals were by no means mistaken. Finally they expected to derive a considerable short-term electoral advantage in the shape of extra votes from labourers and farmers in many rural seats in the west and north narrowly held by Conservatives. This potential was underlined by the by-election successes scored in 1912 and 1913 by candidates who concentrated on land reform to the exclusion of all else (E.G. Hemmerde at N.W. Norfolk and R.L. Outhwaite in the urban seat of Hanley).

While Lloyd George publicized the campaign much of the detailed preparation was undertaken by Runciman at the Board of Agriculture. Realizing that labourers tolerated low wages through fear of losing their cottages, Runciman planned for the construction of 90,000 houses by the state each with up to one acre of ground to give the labourer a measure of independence. This was to be undertaken by a new Ministry of Lands and Forests which would also enjoy compulsory purchase powers to acquire undercultivated and waste land, thereby bypassing the county councils which had proved useless for the purpose. It was to appoint commissioners to fix the price of land and wages boards to fix fair minimum wages in each locality; farmers faced with higher wages would be able to appeal to tribunals for revision of their rent.[13] The government had already adopted such methods to regulate wages in the sweated industries under the Trade Boards Act and for the miners; the extension of the idea of establishing a 'minimum standard' restored the initiative in social policy to Lloyd George. Invited to join his Land Campaign MacDonald and Keir Hardie admitted privately that land was the economic bedrock of reform, but feared a complete loss of their political independence.[14]

By the end of 1913 an equally important urban dimension had emerged partly due to the vociferousness of land taxers in Parliament, who wanted Lloyd George to offer precise policies for the towns. They urged in particular a national tax on land values so as to enable the government to relieve local rates; and also the rating of site values by muncipalities instead of the levying of rates on the value of buildings and improvements. Lloyd George was evidently keen to respond to the pressure for relief of small property-owning ratepayers and small businessmen; during the winter of 1913 he committed himself to a measure of site value rating and promised the Town Tenants League compensation for small businesses faced with exorbitant demands by landlords for renewal of their leases.

In short the Liberals embodied in the Land Campaign moves to shore up their exposed middle-class flank and simultaneously strengthen their standing with a number of working men. The expediency of this strategy is borne out by the Conservative reaction to it. After 1910 Austen Chamberlain had warned his colleagues that unless they could offer alternative policies on land they would not win back the urban support they had lost. Tactically the Party Chairman, Arthur Steel-Maitland and the Chief Whip, Lord Edmund Talbot, believed it wise to avoid provoking controversy and thereby giving Lloyd George more credit over land reform. Indeed, Leslie Scott MP, of the Unionist Social Reform Committee, offered Conservative co-operation over his legislation if only he would not 'Limehouse' the landlords again.[15] But with the opposition at a disadvantage the Chancellor pressed on with the campaign, and there are few grounds for thinking that the New Liberalism had been checked on the eve of war in 1914.

Edwardian Labourism

With hindsight the evolution of the Labour Party is easily depicted in terms of a deterioration in ideological purity as the socialist inspiration of Keir Hardie gave way to the pragmatic leadership of Ramsay MacDonald. However, studies of both men and of the Labour movement generally have entirely revised such a picture. MacDonald was remarkably consistent in his views and objectives, while Hardie differed from him in style and temperament rather than in ideology or programme. The careers of both were characterized by a history of radical Liberalism and a practical grasp of electoral collaboration combined with persistent advocacy, vehement in Hardie's case, of independent political action by working men. As with most Edwardian Labour politicians the mainspring of their action lay in the social condition of working people, but the form taken by it was moulded by the ideas and institutions prevalent in the 1880s, notably the chapel, the trade union and the municipal council. A survey of the reading of the 29 Labour and 24 Lib—Lab MPs elected in 1906 revealed that hardly any had drawn their ideas from explicitly socialist sources; only two mentioned any knowledge of Marx, and only two had read the *Fabian Essays* of 1889. Much more widely read were Henry George (author of *Progress and Poverty*, 1879), a bible for land reformers), John Stuart Mill and John Ruskin along with the Bible, Dickens, Scott, Bunyan and Tennyson. Keir Hardie, while by no means unaware of Marxism, made no serious study of it; he found attractive the notion of the historic struggle of the working class and the prospective degeneration of capitalism prior to a co-operative, classless society; but he had no patience with the idea of a revolutionary overthrow of capitalism or of the growing immiseration of the workers. For him the object of political action in the British context was to take advantage of the available means for improving the lot of working people. This meant enacting social reform; adopting allies outside the Labour movement; and (what was most distinctive) increasing the direct representation of the working class by working men – in short 'Labourism'.

The economic ideas of Edwardian Labour were an amalgam of three main strands. First, they shared many of the Victorian assumptions about the economy, particularly the necessity for wage levels to be regulated according to the price commanded by the products of labour in the market. They shared enthusiastically the Liberal loyalty to free trade. This is a striking indication of the basic orientation of the movement, for while cheap bread had obvious attractions, free trade had not been an obviously desirable policy to the Chartists; nor would it have been a natural policy for a party seriously contemplating socialism. Indeed the Edwardian tariff reformers and right-wing apostles of National Efficiency were a good deal closer to advocating an economy operating on socialist lines than most Labour politicians. In addition the Labour Party espoused the radicals' predilection for graduated taxation and using the unearned increment of land to finance social reform. Henry George's *Progress and Poverty* seems to have stimulated Hardie as much as it did the young Lloyd George. 'Land Nationalization' was also used loosely as shorthand for compulsory purchase powers for local authorities; in 1892 Hardie referred to 'nationalizing the land by taxing land values' much as a radical Liberal would have done. Finally Labour politicians adopted a range of trade union demands for employers' liability and workmen's compensation for accidents, a shorter working day to spread the available employment, amendment of the Truck Act, and recognition of unions by employers. There was nothing here that looked out of place in the manifestos of Liberals in the 1890s.

Before the First World War the Labour Party never accepted state ownership and operation of industry as a general principle, and even limited forms of control like tariffs were automatically ruled out. Neither MacDonald nor Hardie had more than the haziest notion of the administrative implications of nationalization, or of the bureaucracy necessary for a comprehensive system of welfare services. Indeed the only grounds that some writers have found for justifying the description of Hardie as a 'socialist' is his advocacy of the nationalization of coal mines. Yet the significance of this was quite limited. He believed simply that state control would facilitate the achievement of union objectives, the eight-hour day and minimum wages, which he had found from experience in the Ayrshire coalfield difficult to win. In short, coal nationalization was not part of an analysis of how industry should be run, but a special case. Consequently while the Edwardian Labour Party undoubtedly had coherent ideas about economic affairs they were hardly *distinctive*; and any description of Labour as socialist must be modified by the fact that its 'socialism' had no basis in economics. At this time it meant essentially humanitar-ianism and fraternity, a generous-spirited belief in co-operative action for and by the disadvantaged which owed its inspiration to Christianity as much as to politics. The same tendency led Labour towards a pacific, anti-imperial, Gladstonian approach to inter-national affairs. The South African War threw Labour and the radicals together in common outrage; hence J. Bruce Glasier of the ILP could say of John Morley, of all people, that he 'stood for much that [was] essential to a socialist state and international peace'.[16] In denouncing Kitchener's 'methods of barbarism' in 1901 Campbell-Bannerman rekindled the torch of Gladstonianism, and this was taken up by MacDonald in 1914 who stood thereafter as the heir to a common tradition.

While Hardie was not a systematic thinker, MacDonald gave Labour a more coherent, historical framework, and, perhaps confusingly, the language of socialism. Not only did he have no time for the class struggle; he never conceived of Labour as merely a working-class party. Not for nothing had he been secretary to a Liberal MP and an active member of the Rainbow Circle in the 1890s (as well as a member of the SDF in 1885, the Fabian Society from 1886, and the ILP from 1894). For him all that was wrong with the Liberal Party was that it had served its historic function and might obstruct the coming of the New Liberalism or socialism. Initially the ILP and later the LRC were seen by him as successors to the Liberal Party which would eventually take the form of a more effective alliance of middle-class and working-class radicalism. If there was a difference between him and Hobson or Hobhouse it was that he was trying to recruit the middle class and they the working class. Though MacDonald spoke of socialism it was not for him a policy but a vision that would evolve gradually not spring from the ruins of the present system. Society's progress in that direction was perceptible in small steps; when Balfour's government adopted the Unemployed Workmen's Bill in 1905, for example, this was worth having because it drove politicians closer to admitting an obligation to provide work or maintenance for every man, and thus made Labour's own Right To Work Bill seem much less utopian after 1906. Despite his talk of socialism MacDonald's own economic observations were apt to comprise a castigation of the deadweight of landownership and rent upon industry rather than an economic critique of capitalism. However, it has rightly been urged that the virtue of presenting socialism as an evolutionary growth from existing society lay in giving Labour its own objective which, if vague, did not frighten those who had to be won over; MacDonald's strength was a capacity to convey to radicals a reassuring sense of continuity and parliamentarianism and to Labour a comforting belief in ultimate, inevitable triumph.

Although MacDonald's approach clearly owed a great deal to his early Fabianism, it is significant that the Labour Party never availed itself of a Fabian programme before 1914. As a forcing house for investigation and ideas the Fabians inspired the respect of both Liberal and Labour politicians, but their claims to direct influence have been regarded as exaggerated by recent historians. The Fabian Society and the Labour Party were kept apart partly by the sheer elitism of the former, anxious not to waste time trying to build a new party based on what it saw as intellectually destitute trade unions. As a result, from the late 1880s much of the Fabian effort had been diverted into municipal affairs especially in London under the umbrella of the Progressives. The Fabian approach showed little of the humanity of the typical working-class politician but more of the hard-headedness of the National Efficiency school. Fabians believed that labour exchanges would facilitate the identification of shirkers; they criticized health insurance because it was wasteful to subsidize the sick; they welcomed the 1902 Education Act, which was generally condemned by Labour leaders; most of them supported the South African War and lacked sympathy with Home Rule and even with women's suffrage. They thus remained for long a middle-class pressure group largely isolated from the sentimental radicalism inherent in the working-class movement. However, this relationship began to change during the last two years of peace. Faced with the refusal of Lloyd George and Churchill to be guided by Fabian remedies as laid down in the Minority Report of the Royal Commission on the Poor Law and impressed also with the potential strength of the labour movement as demonstrated in the strikes of this period, Sidney and Beatrice Webb recognized that Labour could serve both as a vehicle and as a power base; the fruits of this were garnered during the war and afterwards.

Thus, what seems indisputable and central in the emergence of Labour as a separate party is not ideology so much as a struggle by politically conscious working men to achieve direct representation in Parliament. Consequently the MPs followed a course barely distinguishable from the Lib—Labs in the Commons before 1914 in that they threw their weight behind the Liberal causes and made a distinctive contribution only on strictly trade union issues. Hardie, despite the vehemence with which he sometimes attacked the Liberals, departed from the Lib—Lab approach only in seeking more seats for working men and in declining to take the Liberal whip. For most of the LRC MPs returned in 1906 the pact was perfectly consistent with long-held attitudes; they regarded the LRC as no more than a continuation of earlier efforts to elect working men so as to modify the law relating to them; few expected or wanted to transform the LRC's role as a separate pressure group into that of a governing party.

However, events conspired to eliminate the distinction between the Lib—Lab and the LRC contingents to the advantage of the latter. In the early 1900s the leading working-class politicians, John Burns, Ben Pickard, Thomas Burt, Richard Bell and Charles Fenwick, were Lib—Lab in sympathy but all elderly figures who had reached or passed their peak. Burns, the impassioned strike leader and SDF militant of the 1880s, had graduated by way of Progressivism on the London County Council and a parliamentary seat at Battersea from 1892 to an honoured position in the Liberal Party and cabinet rank in 1905. It is significant that when invited by Hardie to lead the LRC in 1903 Burns found it unattractive. Indeed before 1906 only two of the LRC MPs, Hardie and Crooks, stuck strictly to the independent line; Henderson, Bell and Shackleton became more or less identified with Liberalism. In 1903 there had been some danger that the Lib—Lab forces would persuade the LRC conference to allow the affiliation of bodies like the National Democratic League which would have stifled the independence of the LRC and kept it as a Liberal pressure group. However, attempts of this kind only provoked support for the ILP proposal for an extra levy on the unions to finance new candidatures. Yet in 1906 the Lib—Labs still numbered 24 in the Commons; but Burns, the symbol of the Liberal/working class alliance spent his declining years complacently enthroned as President of the Local Government Board, an object of attack by Hardie for his reluctance to initiate remedial measures for unemployment. Meanwhile changes in leadership and militancy led the Miners Federation to seek affiliation to the Labour Party in

1908, a step that virtually ended Lib—Labbery as a separate body. In so far as the miners were incorporated into the Labour Party they tended to undermine still further its political coherence and minimize its distinctiveness from Liberalism.

Although specific aims and policies had been avoided in 1900 at the foundation of the LRC, nonetheless the typical Labour candidate of the 1900s offered the electorate a battery of proposals including the eight-hour day, reversal of the Taff Vale decision, employers' liability, old age pensions, poor law reform, the feeding of necessitous schoolchildren, taxation of land values, free trade, Home Rule, nationalization of mine royalties, mines and railways, payment of MPs, curtailment of the powers of the House of Lords and universal suffrage. There was virtually nothing in this that was not acceptable to the New Liberals, or to Gladstonians for that matter. Nor was this merely a tactic to win Liberal votes. The annual conference in 1906, for example, apart from reaffirming many of the items already listed, pledged itself to the Local Veto, condemned the Education Act of 1902 and welcomed the entente with France provided it was not used against Germany. It is only fair to note that at least one delegate protested at 'tinkering with the out-worn pledges of the Liberal Party'. Occasionally, as in 1908, a resolution calling for the socialization of industry slipped through without debate apparently because it was not taken seriously enough to warrant the time, and served to encourage the socialists.

In the Commons, MacDonald demonstrated a clear idea of the appropriate tactics. 'Governments are not afraid of socialist speeches,' he observed, 'they are very much afraid of successful criticism in detail.'[17] This approach enabled Shackleton and MacDonald to play a useful role especially during 1906—08. The government proved quick to adopt Labour Bills on Trades Disputes and the feeding of schoolchildren, and compromised on the Workmen's Compensation Bill. For Campbell-Bannerman, Labour thus helped the government in the direction in which it was already going. But it is not the case that the pensions scheme was the result of by-election losses to Labour in 1907, for their introduction had been carefully planned well beforehand by Asquith. What is true is that when Labour members voted for motions critical of the Cabinet on such matters as pensions they usually did so in company with larger numbers of Liberal back-benchers, all impatient to drive the Cabinet in the same direction. Unemployment provided the best issue on which Labour could distance itself from the Liberals by means of its Right to Work

Bill and Hardie's dramatic interventions at Burns's expense. However, by 1908 the initiative was passing to the Liberals; after 1909 there were only occasional revolts by a handful of Labour members over the Insurance Bill and women's suffrage. Once the Liberals had lost their overall majority in 1910 Labour became nearly as reliable in the division lobbies as the Liberals: moreover, after the 1909 Osborne Judgement (which checked the rights of trade unions to use their funds for political purposes) Labour felt the need of cabinet help in changing the law. Eventually this concession was granted in 1913, and in 1911 Labour obtained payment of members.

Co-operation between the parliamentary party and the government naturally produced fierce criticism in the movement notably from Victor Grayson who had been elected as an Independent Socialist in 1907 and declined the Labour whip; there flourished a mutual antagonism between Grayson and the other Labour MPs who felt relieved at his defeat in 1910. A more persistent critic, the dockers' leader Ben Tillett, waged campaigns to make the parliamentary party responsive to conference, and published a famous pamphlet *Is the Parliamentary Party a Failure?* in 1908. Yet the leadership of MacDonald, Hardie, Snowden and Henderson — 'softly feline in their purrings to Ministers' as Tillett put it — always carried the conference with them; from 1909 when he became chairman of the parliamentary party, MacDonald went a long way to establishing himself as leader in a traditional sense, and to confirming the right of MPs to make party policy.

Chapter 7

The Electoral Struggle
1906–1914

> Nothing has hampered our movement in the coun-
> try more than this false idea of independence, that
> only Labour or Socialist votes should be given to
> Labour or Socialist candidates. It is humbug.
> *J. Ramsay MacDonald*, Labour and Electoral Reform, *1914*

The traditional view that Edwardian politics was characterized by
a Liberal Party too ideologically rigid and rooted in middle-class
radicalism to avoid being outflanked by a socialist party or to
survive the emergence of a working-class electorate has proved to
be virtually untenable. Yet the evidence that has destroyed the old
view has also generated an alternative interpretation whose
strengths and weaknesses will be considered in this chapter. Based
upon the concept of 'Progressivism' this view entails a number of
related propositions about the nature of political change in the
early twentieth century. It argues that the increasingly national
orientation of politics facilitated the regeneration of Liberalism in
terms of both programme and personnel by 1914, so that Liberal
politics was directed by a set of professional politicians and
intellectuals propagating a synthesis of Liberalism and Socialism
known as Progressivism, which restored its intellectual vitality
and popular appeal. The emergence of the Labour Party was less
a sign of a more radical type of politics than a reinforcement of
Progressive Liberalism. This is borne out by the electoral revival
based not on the traditionalist reaction in favour of free trade
and Nonconformity, but on the social and economic issues characteristic of twentieth-century politics. A shift had taken place in
the emphasis of political debate reflecting a move away from the
community and religious group basis of voting of the nineteenth
century towards the class-based voting of the twentieth century,

a change that had occurred substantially before the First World War rather than after it. Thus the party divide began to coincide with fundamental social cleavages for the first time. These last two points are worth immediate clarification. The 1906 Liberal landslide was plainly increased by infusions of voters influenced by tariffs, education and other aspects of traditional politics; however, these fell away by 1910 as is demonstrated by the loss of Liberal gains in the southern residential and county constituencies. Yet the withdrawal of this middle-class support still left the Liberals in power because of their retention of the working-class vote, especially in the northern and industrial areas including Lancashire and London where Conservatives had formerly been very strong. Indeed in 1910 the Liberals were still gaining working-class seats not won in 1906. Thus the 'Progressive' interpretation amounts to much more than the view that Liberalism survived the Edwardian elections; it suggests that it adapted to the chief trends of twentieth-century politics, flourishing on the basis of its social–economic appeal to the working class. The implication is that there was nothing inevitable in the rise of Edwardian Labour as a governing party.

The Containment of Labour

If the general election of 1906 had stood in isolation as the last Liberal victory before 1914 it might be regarded as a freak; it would still be a formidable task to explain why a party capable of winning 400 seats was in fatal decline, but the suspicion would be there. However, the two elections of 1910, while far less spectacular victories, provided corroboration that 1906 was part of a longer-term change. Seen in perspective 1910 was a more significant victory than that of 1892 for example, because the Liberal–Labour forces won a higher share of the poll, because they derived this more from the working-class seats, and because it was accomplished against the background of four years of Liberal government, whereas in 1892 they had enjoyed the advantage of having a Conservative government to attack (see table 7.1).

What was the relative position of Labour and Liberalism in the Edwardian period? Although the evidence is restricted by the very fact of their electoral co-operation, it is abundant enough to indicate relative strengths and a trend: 24 of the 29 Labour victories in 1906 were achieved in the absence of Liberal opposition

TABLE 7.1. *General elections 1892–1910*

	Conservative		Liberal		Labour		Irish Nationalist	
	% vote	No. of seats won	% vote	No. of seats won	% vote	No. of seats won	% vote	No. of seats won
1892	47.0	314	45.1	272	0.3	3	7.0	81
1895	49.1	411	45.7	177	1.0	0	4.0	82
1900	51.5	402	44.6	184	1.8	2	2.5	82
1906	43.6	157	49.0	401	5.9	29	0.6	83
1910(Jan.)	46.9	273	43.2	275	7.7	40	1.0	82
1910(Dec.)	46.3	272	43.8	272	7.2	42	2.5	84

under the pact; and the boost to Labour fortunes carried over into 1907 when the party gained seats at Jarrow and Colne Valley at Liberal expense. The year 1908, however, proved to be the turning-point, for the introduction of pensions in that year followed by Lloyd George's budget in 1909 restored the initiative to the government. Thereafter Labour experienced losses down to 1914. This is obscured by the affiliation of the Miners Federation to the Labour Party in 1909 as a result of which most of the Lib–Labs transferred to Labour giving the party a nominal total of 45 MPs; eight losses and three gains in January 1910 left 40 members. Common sentiment, stimulated by the challenge of the peers, made the two radical parties anxious to avoid splitting the Progressive vote in 1910; leading Labour figures like MacDonald, Hardie and Thomas had been elected in two-member seats with Liberal MPs and on the strength of Liberal votes, an arrangement they had no wish to terminate. As a result, despite an expansion of local organization between 1906 and 1910 the pact substantially held in that 78 Labour candidates stood in January, and only 56 in December, against 51 in 1906.

Moreover, among the voters the pact appeared to work even more effectively than in 1906; Labour candidates adopted all the Liberal issues and arguments, while the Liberal organization helped turn in the vote for them. Particularly impressive evidence for the effectiveness of the pact is provided by the cohesion of the Progressive vote in two-member constituencies such as Leicester. A negligible number of voters 'plumped' for a single candidate only, the vast majority preferring to 'split' their two votes between

Liberal and Labour and to ignore the Conservative (see table 7.2).

TABLE 7.2. *Leicester: general election December 1910*

Result	Crawshay-Williams (Liberal)	13,238	elected
	MacDonald (Labour)	12,998	elected
	Wilshere (Conservative)	7,547	
Plumpers	Crawshay-Williams	728	
	MacDonald	574	
	Wilshere	7,245	
Splits	Crawshay-Williams/MacDonald	12,316	
	Crawshay-Williams/Wilshere	194	
	MacDonald/Wilshere	108	

Thus within the confines of the pact Leader did well; outside it the party seemed to have a tenuous hold. In the 35 three-cornered contests in the two elections of 1910, its candidates came third in 29 cases, second in 6 and first in none. Attempts to break out of the pact against Liberals met with failure except in two special cases (West Fife and Gower) where Conservatives withdrew in Labour's favour. In addition the Liberals displayed an alarming capacity to win back seats lost in by-elections (Colne Valley and Jarrow) and to recover seats like Gateshead 'lost' as a result of the miners' affiliation to the Labour Party (see table 7.3). The strictly independent Labour vote was, as yet, rarely sufficient to elect MPs who necessarily depended heavily upon tactical support from Liberals.

TABLE 7.3. *Gateshead parliamentary elections*

1906		*1910 January*		*1910 December*	
Liberal–Labour*	9,651	Liberal	6,800	Liberal	8,763
Conservative	5,126	Conservative	6,323	Conservative	5,608
		Labour*	3,572		
	4,525		477		3,155

*The same candidate in 1906 and 1910.

Although 1910 appears to undermine decisively any idea of an irresistible advance by Labour in the country, these elections were undoubtedly conducted in circumstances that militated against any effective initiative by the Labour Party. In order to elucidate a longer-term pattern historians have scrutinized the various by-elections between 1911 and 1914, some discovering a decline and some an improvement in Labour strength. Mid-term by-elections naturally offered excellent opportunities for gains at the government's expense, but significantly it was the Conservatives not Labour who benefited. Clashes between Liberal and Labour candidates in working-class seats in this period do, however, shed light on their relative support. Vacancies in industrial constituencies coincided with severe industrial unrest and government unpopularity in 1911–12 over its National Insurance Bill, Labour also enjoyed the advantage of outside organization and abundant support from its MPs in most of the by-elections which was not so freely available at general elections. However, despite this, Labour came bottom of the poll in each of the 14 industrial seats it contested, polling 10–20 per cent in six and 20–30 per cent in eight. The Liberals held on to almost all their working-class strongholds (though more marginal seats were lost to the Conservatives), and, as one study has concluded, in no contest did as many as half the miners vote for a Labour candidate.[1] Some results were, on the face of it, quite good for Labour, such as that at Holmfirth (a West Riding mining constituency) where the party's poll rose from 14.9 per cent in January 1910 to 28.2 per cent in June 1912. Whether this would have been repeated in the more difficult conditions of a general election is perhaps doubtful. The only valid comparison is with the by-elections of the previous Parliament when, especially in 1907, Labour had actually been able to gain seats. Further, the worst results for the party occurred in the four Labour seats to be defended, all of which were lost, one in a straight fight with a Conservative and the others in three-cornered contests where Labour came bottom of the poll (Bow and Bromley, Hanley, Chesterfield and N.E. Derbyshire); the worst was at Hanley which the Liberals regained reducing Labour to 11.8 per cent of the poll in the process.

If there is a pattern during the Edwardian period these results suggest one in which Labour gained ground sharply in the early 1900s, reached a peak around 1906–07, and steadily, though not disastrously, fell back thereafter. Of course very few constituencies experienced regular three-cornered contests, but where there is a run of results the stagnation or decline of the Labour vote from around 1908 down to 1914 is fairly clear (see table 7.4.). In short, there are no real grounds, in the voting behaviour, for believing Labour to have been poised to take over from the Liberals by

TABLE 7.4. *Huddersfield: Labour % poll*

1906	1906 (by-election)	1910 January	1910 December
35.2	33.8	31.6	29.0

1914. On the contrary, without the protection of the pact the parliamentary party would have been reduced to a handful.

The Franchise Factor

Impressive as the evidence of parliamentary elections is, it may well be considered insufficient to support the argument because of its narrowness. For we have become conscious of how many men were excluded from the register before 1914: approximately four in every ten. By contrast the franchise reforms of 1918 produced an electorate equivalent to 95 per cent of the adult male population. In this structural change some writers have discerned the central explanation for Labour's ability to overtake the Liberals after 1918, and also the reason for their failure to dislodge the Liberal Party before 1914, the implication being that there was a large reservoir of working-class support that could not be tapped until the electoral law had been overhauled.

This is such an attractive and neat method of resolving the fluctuations in party fortunes over a long period that it is worth considering why it has not so far been demonstrated on the basis of evidence, and why it is almost certainly mistaken. The interpretation rests upon two assumptions, first that working-class non-voters before 1914 were different in certain respects from working-class voters, and, second, that these differences were such as to make the former more likely than the latter to support the Labour Party. Even the first assumption is no more than partly true. In 1911, a year in which the register was short because elections had recently taken place, some 42 per cent of adult males were excluded, but this figure comprised only 12 per cent who actually failed to meet one of the seven qualifications, and no less than 30 per cent whose names failed to appear only because the complications of the registration process and the residence requirement deprived them of their right to register as householders or lodgers.[2] Thus, the bulk of non-voters were not under permanent, legal disfranchisement, but would appear on the register from time to time according to their circumstances and the efforts made by the parties. Similarly the working men on the 1911 register could easily drop out next year owing to a change of address. One should not, then, exaggerate the difference between voters and non-voters, for their composition fluctuated constantly.

The second assumption involves a consideration of the social characteristics of the disfranchised which served to keep them temporarily or permanently off the register. Men in receipt of poor relief, for example, were specifically disbarred; those who rented rooms below £10 annual value fell outside the lodger qualification; those who moved frequently, often because of inability to pay their rent, interrupted the 12-month residence requirement – and up to 30 per cent of families did move each year in some of the big cities; those who lived with their parents could not qualify as 'householders' themselves; and servants residing with their employers and soldiers living in barracks were subject to the same disqualification.

Now the question arises whether such social characteristics made for political inclinations of a Labour kind. Both soldiers and domestic servants, for example, were taken by most politicians to be largely Conservative out of deference or personal interest; certainly such groups were isolated from the kind of political and social pressures that fostered Labour voting, or even Liberal for that matter. Again, those families constantly shifting between poor tenement accommodation or being forced on to the boards of guardians comprised the most impoverished section of the urban population whose vulnerability to charity, patronage and beer, and exclusion from the chief institutional pillars of radical politics, notably trade unions and Nonconformity, put them beyond the reach of the Labour movement. The Liberals drew traditional support from various poor immigrant communities particularly the Irish whose level of enfranchisement was abnormally low, and in the conditions of Edwardian Britain any increase in the Irish electorate would have helped them not Labour. Beyond this there are indications that much of the impoverished urban population lent support to Conservatism. Labour certainly found the problems of establishing an organization in such districts as Shoreditch, Whitechapel, Stepney and St-George's-in-the-East insuperable. As MacDonald put it in 1912: 'In places like the Potteries [of Staffordshire] where poverty and degradation is of the blackest kind, the Labour Party is bound to be weak.'[3] In contrast the Labour Party's ability to win and consolidate independent support in such areas as Colne Valley, Woolwich or Barnard Castle reflected a very different working-class population, one that was comparatively stable, skilled, highly unionized, affluent, literate and politically conscious. In many cases it was no doubt an advantage to Labour that the electorate was restricted to certain sections of the working class; for to have extended the electorate in, say, Bethnal Green, where only 42 per cent were voters, would have done little — in the circumstances — to improve the party's prospects.

This impression is corroborated by the attitude of both radical parties to the franchise. In 1911 the Liberal organizations through their federations tendered confidential advice to the chief whip to the effect that one-man-one-vote by means of simplified registration and shortened residential qualification would give them a significant advantage, especially if combined with the abolition of plural voting.[4] It is significant that exception was made to this only with regard to some parts of Scotland and certain Yorkshire seats (notably Bradford, Dewsbury, Colne Valley, Spen Valley, Shipley, Hull and Buckrose) where it was felt a wider franchise could give Labour extra strength from the younger voters. Generational differences may well have been the most promising aspect of the non-voters from Labour's point of view. For example, in the case of the miners 55 per cent enjoyed the franchise and it seems unlikely that the other 45 per cent had different political views, unless one takes into account that many of them were young men who may have been less wedded to Liberalism, more militant or more socialist than their fathers.[5] This may be reflected in the fact that although miners as voters appeared to remain loyal to Liberalism, the union leadership changed before 1914 and began to replace Lib–Lab collaboration with attacks upon Liberal seats. In general, however, the generation that grew to political consciousness amid the reaction against imperialism after 1900 and the Edwardian phase of Lloyd George radicalism was likely to be captured by the Liberals.

Thus, the distinctions between voters and non-voters, so far as they existed, were not on the whole such as to facilitate drastic changes in party support at this stage. Indeed, Labour never behaved as though an extended franchise was the key to success; though committed to the principle of one-man-one-vote the party never attempted to put pressure on the government on this question or to turn it into an issue. No doubt the Labour leaders appreciated that reform was not in their immediate interests; for their appeal was not as yet pitched to the amorphous collection of the disfranchised, nor did they yet possess the necessary organization to compete for them against the larger parties. Thus, although the non-voting working class may have been a potential source of Labour support, neither the political conditions prevailing before 1914 nor the party itself were favourable to the exploitation of this strength.

The Local, Municipal and Regional Dimension

By 1914 it was an open question whether the Gladstone–MacDonald pact, which lay at the heart of Edwardian politics, would survive the next general election, for it had been breached so frequently during 1911–14 as to raise the prospect that Labour was growing out of it. It is abundantly clear that for the voters and for the parliamentary leaders on both sides collaboration on Progressive lines represented a genuine and entrenched sentiment; however, its endurance at the intermediate level of party activists and local politicians appeared far more dubious. The strains were naturally greater at local, and perhaps regional, level. When in 1906 the politics of the pact were seen to operate nationwide, the effect on local Labour politicians, as one Liberal agent commented, was to make them see 'visions of themselves on the floor of the House of Commons, as they consider themselves as good as any Tom, Dick or Harry who are there at the present time'.[6] Instead of satisfying aspirations, except on the part of those actually elected, the arrangement showed the need for more pressure on the Liberals. However, Liberal associations saw no need for further concessions by 1910; and the result was a series of damaging three-cornered by-election contests beginning in November 1911 when Labour intervened in the Liberal-held seat at Oldham which the Conservatives consequently won. In July 1912 the Liberals triumphantly snatched Hanley from Labour, a humiliating result that provoked Labour retaliation at Crewe immediately afterwards. Altogether six Liberal and three Labour seats were lost as a result of three-cornered contests and many more were narrowly saved. Through the National Executive Committee the Labour leaders endeavoured to smother a number of potential Labour candidatures, but while they could withhold official sanction and money they lacked effective control over their constituency supporters. As a federal organization the party relied upon affiliated bodies, namely trade unions and socialist societies, to provide its steel frame in the country. In so far as the party possessed an electoral machine at all it comprised the branches of the Independent Labour Party who could not be prevented by the NEC from

THE TRIANGULAR TEST.

LIBERAL WHIP. "MY COW, I THINK." LABOUR PARTY LEADER. "MY COW, I THINK."
UNIONIST CANDIDATE (*milking*). "MY CHANCE, ANYHOW."

From Punch, 10 July 1912.

launching their own candidates occasionally. Only one constituency in ten had a Labour Representation Committee and then it was often inadequate as an electoral machine; the more numerous trades councils were frequently centres of Lib–Lab sentiment, reluctant in any case to run elections and preferring to rely upon the Liberals even in Labour-held seats.

For Ramsay MacDonald this posed an acute dilemma, heightened in 1913 when his supporters in Leicester demanded a fight for the vacancy arising from the death of the Liberal MP with whom he sat in harness. To the activists such by-elections presented a chance to prove that Labour MPs had not been elected merely by Liberal permission and an opportunity to demonstrate independence from the government, an attitude flatly repudiated by MacDonald as 'this false idea of independence'. In his view so long as the two parties had to combine at Westminster they must face 'actual Parliamentary conditions' in the constituencies too. Yet this strategy proved vulnerable to the charge of condemning Labour to a stagnant position, in view of Liberal obstinacy over seats. Though MacDonald had no intention of abandoning the pact he accepted the desirability of putting pressure on the Liberals, but he believed this to be futile where organization was inadequate or where a candidature was frivolous and merely calculated to antagonize. In practice this often meant stopping candidacies of socialists from the ILP or British Socialist Party whose influence within the party MacDonald was intent upon limiting. Yet he did not wish the party to be encumbered with the Lib–Lab elements whose primary loyalty was to Liberalism; and to this end he tried to manoeuvre them away from relations with Liberal associations and accepted also interventions by Labour in Liberal mining seats. He hoped he could hold his disparate forces together until the party was strong enough to resist the two other parties. But this was a long-term process dependent upon the development of a grass-roots organization; in fact the steady expansion in the number of affiliated constituency bodies up to 1909 had been checked and the slight decline was not arrested until wartime (see table 7.5). Like the electoral evidence this is inconsistent with the

TABLE 7.5. *The Labour Party: affiliated constituency bodies*

1901	1902	1903	1904	1905	1906	1907	1908	1909	1910	1911	1912	1913
7	21	49	76	73	73	83	92	155	148	149	146	143*

*Sometimes given as 158 (85 trades councils and 73 LRCs) because some constituencies are counted twice.

idea of a continuous or inexorable advance before 1914. Given this limited local base MacDonald determined to keep his bridges with Liberalism open until the time arrived when the radical rank and file would want to cross over to Labour and thereby convert a working-class pressure group into the non-class, national party he had always desired.

MacDonald's capacity for taking a long view was underpinned by the immediate pressure of Liberal retaliation. Their local associations had become alive to the disintegrating effects of having to withdraw candidates in favour of Labour. Twelve months after the Clitheroe by-election of 1902 the agent there, conscious, no doubt, of approaching redundancy, lamented: 'Our organisation is falling to pieces like a rope of sand, our subscriptions have fallen to 25 per cent, and we cannot get a meeting together except, perhaps, with a view to winding up the business of the Association.'[7] Consequently, by 1914 there was a tendency to replace retiring Lib–Lab MPs with Liberals rather than to allow their seats to be filled by Labour; and even sitting members like Henderson and Hardie were threatened by Liberal opposition. The problem was that constituency activists often wanted to emphasize the differences between parties rather than maximize the common ground; a separate candidate was the best means of doing this. After 1910 the Cabinet was under pressure from radicals in the country to concentrate on the traditional reforms obstructed by the peers, and to show less indulgence to the trade unions. All this is not to say that the Progressive strategy was not feasible, only that it proved more difficult to sustain at the grass roots than in London, and that it hinged upon continued control of power by the Liberals at Westminster.

Historians are beginning to suggest a relationship between the municipal and the parliamentary pattern of politics in the Edwardian period. It has been argued that the municipal evidence runs counter to the Progressive strategy in several ways; for example, the signs of Liberal losses in local elections could be symptomatic of a grass-roots decline well before the First World War; and Labour advances threatened to drive the Liberals into co-operation with the Conservatives at local level, thus undermining their parliamentary tactics and effectively preparing the way for the widespread Conservative–Liberal collaboration between the wars. However, it is easy to attribute too much significance to municipal contests. In general Edwardian local elections seem to have provided voters with an opportunity to punish the governing party at Westminster as they do today. In the early 1900s the

Liberals gained from the reaction against Balfour, only to suffer losses after 1906. In a sense, then, such elections were an ephemeral indication of improving Conservative morale, and should not be mistaken for a fundamental Liberal collapse.

Yet in some ways municipal politics were altogether different from national. All three parties frequently avoided formal involvement; thus contests were sometimes between brewers or publicans, who were usually Conservatives, and temperance reformers, who were inclined to be Liberals. Conservative–Liberal co-operation in the shape of ratepayers or municipal alliances was not a novel feature in the 1900s but a continuation of the older attempt to win middle-class Liberal votes by harnessing Liberal Unionists to policies of retrenchment. Such tactics were an inevitable consequence of the local government franchise; by comparison with the parliamentary franchise it excluded certain working men such as lodgers, while including women who possessed a £10 occupation qualification. Consequently the concerns of small property owners, shopkeepers and the lower middle class generally, upon whom the municipal rates pressed hardest, were of central importance. In contrast to the parliamentary electorate, most of which did not pay income tax, the municipal voters viewed retrenchment with a good deal of favour, and this obliged all parties to preserve the traditional cry of economy. This fact helps to explain long-term Conservative strength and also why radical Liberals and socialists saw national government as the more suitable vehicle for social policy; pending a thorough overhaul of local authority finance, they looked to Lloyd George to open up new sources of revenue by the taxation of ground values.

Labour's progress locally was surprisingly limited but more steady than in parliamentary elections. Table 7.6 shows, as one would expect, that 'Labour' locally was frequently represented by candidates of the socialist groups whose desire to drive a wedge between Labour and Liberalism was a long-standing objective. Whether this strategy was in decline rather than in the ascendant during the Edwardian years is still an open question. The nomination of known socialists usually alienated trades council support and tended to divide the Labour forces, which helps to account for the losses recorded in 1908. Following the success of Victor Grayson at Colne Valley local socialists took the offensive only to find that moderate Labour and Liberal support had been antagonized. This was the basis of Labour allegations in 1908 that there had been Liberal–Conservative collusion in a number of towns to defeat its own candidates.[8] In cases like Bradford Liberal–

TABLE 7.6. *Labour's municipal record*

	Candidates		Elected	Net gain/loss
	'Labour and Socialist'	SDF/BSP		
1907	274	66	86	10
1908	313	84	109	−33
1909	422	133	122	23
1910	281	49	113	33
1911	312*	32	157	78
1912	463†	95	161	42
1913	442	52	196	85

* +23 undefined   † +38 undefined

Socialist clashes were a traditional feature of muncipal and parliamentary elections; in others, such as Bolton, Progressive co-operation prevailed at both levels. Where Labour did lose as in 1908 this frequently reflected the temporary alienation of moderate Labour votes by socialists; in this sense the municipal pattern tends very often to complement the parliamentary alignment rather than to run against it.

However, it is evident that the Progressive pattern of politics had evolved more fully in some regions than in others. Lancashire and the north-west might be taken as the model in that it enjoyed the attentions of major exponents of the New Liberalism and the Labour alliance in C.P. Scott, radical entrepreneurs such as Sir William Lever and Sir John Brunner, and a prominent Cabinet exponent of social reform in Churchill. The traditional Liberal weakness in Lancashire facilitated electoral co-operation which produced no less than 13 Labour MPs in the region; by striking at working-class Conservatism the alliance delivered 47 of the 62 seats in 1906 and 42 and 35 in the two elections of 1910.

London provided a similar triumph for Progressivism in that the Liberals captured 49 of its 58 constituencies in 1906 and held 35 in December 1910, a dramatic reversal of the post-1885 pattern. London displayed most markedly the lapse of religious loyalties and the residential separation of the classes which had produced 38 seats with a working-class majority. Of these only two were Labour-held, for the structure of London's economy and the qualities of its working population made the capital very stony ground. Moreover, the entrenched tradition of joint Liberal—

Labour action through the London County Council Progressives, and the concentration there of the New Liberal writers and MPs (notably Charles Masterman, Sydney Buxton, Christopher Addison, W.H. Dickinson and T.J. Macnamara) gave Progressivism a more commanding hold than in Lancashire.

Other major urban–industrial regions displayed some of the features of London and Lancashire, but less conspicuously and with significant variations. For example the Midland coalfields of Derbyshire, Nottinghamshire, Leicestershire and Warwickshire were notable for their profitability and relatively good industrial relations, which also made for close political collaboration between owners and workers. It was here that after 1910 Labour seats were melting away fastest – a reflection of the Lib–Lab sentiments of the miners. Coal-owners like Sir Arthur Marshall were still prominent Liberal MPs, and this, together with the presence of radical land reformers like Josiah Wedgwood, R. L. Outhwaite and Edward Hemmerede, lent a more traditionalist tone to radicalism in the Midlands and East Anglia. More advanced social radicals were also present in the form of Francis Channing and his successor L. C. Money in East Northamptonshire. Conversely the West Midlands retained bastions of Conservatism still untouched by Progressive assaults.

In north-east England Lib–Lab attitudes were even more entrenched, especially among the Northumberland and Durham miners who had been pioneers of electoral participation but tended to maintain the partnership with the Liberal owners. The relative isolation of the region and the long-standing predominance of Liberalism made for far less change during the 1900s than elsewhere. The MPs remained a mixture of elderly trade unionists (Burt, Fenwick and Wilson) and local industrial magnates (Palmer, Joicey, Furness), though by 1914 many of these men had retired or were about to do so, to be replaced by career politicians from outside the region. Though Labour had received Liberal support in Sunderland, Newcastle and Darlington, the party had had to fight for Chester-le-Street, Barnard Castle and Jarrow. Independent Labour and socialist support was so weak by comparison with Lib–Lab sentiment that the Liberals triumphed in three-cornered by-elections at Houghton-le-Spring and N.W. Durham in 1914 and contemplated a counter-offensive against Labour seats.

Wales has also been seen as an homogeneous region steeped in traditional Nonconformist Liberalism, or 'sunk in the politics of nostalgia' in the words of Kenneth Morgan. Certainly Wales displayed fewer signs of the New Liberal impact despite the

THE ELECTORAL STRUGGLE 1906–1914

presence there of Lloyd George. This was largely a reflection of undimmed electoral success since the 1860s and a strong feeling that MPs should be local men; it also reflected the adherence of the South Wales coal-owners to the Liberal Party which, eventually brought the industrial conflict into politics with highly disruptive effects. By 1914 the great phalanx of Welsh Liberalism was faced with widespread clashes with Labour in Monmouth and Glamorgan, which up to that time had largely been beaten off.

Yorkshire was another bastion of Liberalism even through the years of Conservative rule. However, the county had long been strong in ILP branches too, especially in the West Riding towns; the result had been regular conflict, for Liberals saw little need to concede seats to socialists. In fact the West Riding saw nearly as many three-cornered contests as straight fights in industrial seats, and only Leeds East and Halifax (the only two-member constituency) were willingly conceded under the 1903 pact. Nonetheless, though the activists feuded the working-class electorate remained impressively loyal to the Liberals who retained 27 of the 38 West Riding seats in 1910. The vigorous Yorkshire Liberal Federation enjoyed some notable Progressives as MPs — Charles Trevelyan, Herbert Samuel, Herbert Gladstone and Walter Runciman. The key to the strength of New Liberalism here lay in the radical, politicized working class which was not divided by anti-Irish and Conservative sentiment as was the Lancashire working class.

Some of these tendencies were present in Scotland where Liberal strength coincided with an early and ideologically devout socialist organization, particularly in the west–central industrial belt. All but two of the eleven Labour candidates in Scotland in 1906 were considered by the Liberals there to be 'socialists' — an indication of trade union weakness and of an ideological divide which was absent in most parts of Britain. Hence the Master of Elibank (MP for Midlothian and later Liberal chief whip) warned against conceding anything to Scottish socialists[9] described by Churchill, himself MP for Dundee, as an 'obscure gang of malignant wirepullers', for fear of undermining the morale of their own supporters. Thus no pact ever operated and Labour obtained only two seats in Scotland (Glasgow Blackfriars and West Fife) despite its considerable underlying strength. A particular feature was that Scottish Labour candidates seemed to draw as much support from Conservatives as from Liberals, and socialists displayed a tendency to vote Unionist in the absence of their own candidate. There are indications of this in the beneficial effect on Unionists of Labour withdrawals in N.W. Lanark and Leith in 1910, and in the Labour gain at West Fife after a Unionist withdrawal. Thus in Scotland the 'Progressive' vote seems less of a reality than elsewhere in the country, and Labour stood much more on its own strength. If Scotland and to a lesser extent Wales were inconsistent with the Progressive pattern of politics, they were very much the exceptions; though some regions had obviously advanced much faster along the road to Progressivism they all exhibited a New Liberalism based upon working-class backing.

When the Lights went out

By 1914 all parties had begun to prepare seriously for the general election which, under the terms of the Parliament Act of 1911, had to take place by December 1915. There is sufficient evidence, without going into the realms of speculation, to estimate the likely outcome of a dissolution in peacetime.

Any easy assumption of a Conservative victory finds surprisingly little basis in the evidence. For example, the electoral trend has been deduced from the constituencies that enjoyed a Liberal–Conservative contest in December 1910 and in a by-election during 1911–14.[10] These show a very definite and intelligible pattern of slight swings against the government in February–August 1911 (0.8 per cent), a heavy swing between November 1911 and August 1912 (4.4 per cent), and a marked recovery in the shape of a smaller swing against the government from November 1912 to May 1914 (2.1 per cent). This cyclical fluctuation of opinion was of normal proportions, and indeed repeated the pattern of 1906–09 which had culminated in a Liberal victory; by 1914 Liberal support appeared to have returned to the level of 1909. Thus, there is no adequate electoral evidence for assuming a Conservative victory in 1915.

However, the political circumstances and issues of an election must also be taken into account. The Liberals were endeavouring to create advantageous conditions by means of a bill to abolish plural voting, which on the outbreak of war required only its third and final passage in the Commons; this move was calculated to deprive the Conservatives of the three-to-one advantage they were thought to enjoy among the 500,000 plural voters and thereby deliver into Liberal hands 30 seats won in December 1910. On policy the main initiative comprised Lloyd George's Land Campaign which as we have seen equipped the radicals with definite proposals on land-holding, minimum wages and house-building — all designed to retain the initiative from Labour, label the Conservatives as the party of privilege, recover support from small property owners in towns, and attract extra rural support among labourers and small farmers. Taken with the government's other reform measures this gave the Liberals a far wider appeal than the perilously narrow and negative cry of their opponents.

It was not surprising, then, that some Conservatives, feeling that they had run out of ideas, apprehensively contemplated a fourth election defeat. Naval scares had lost their credibility. Fears about the National Insurance Act had subsided. Tariff reform still presented a dilemma because of the reluctance of Lord Derby, the Cecils and Lancashire and Scottish Conservatives to accept it. In November 1912 Bonar Law had decided to risk repudiating Balfour's pledge to hold a referendum before introducing tariffs, but the reaction against this proved so strong that he agreed to surrender the 'food taxes' for the sake of party unity. The effect was to dismay the farmers who had always expected to benefit from higher prices;[11] and the wider result was that by 1914 the party had little definite to offer the electorate on its central economic philosophy. This left Conservatives marooned on Ulster as their only chance of upsetting the government. As we have already noted, by 1914 the voters were a good deal less agitated about this than the politicians; and in so far as the issue had any novel impact it was as likely to harm the opposition (in view of their inclination to tamper with the army and jeopardize national security for party advantage) as to assist them. This somewhat desperate situation led several MPs including F. E. Smith and Leslie Scott to demand a more positive appeal particularly to urban voters with social and land reform; as Austen Chamberlain put it after 1910, without some proposals on land 'we have no chance of winning the towns back'.[12] However, by 1912–14 the party was in full retreat from the interventionist social policies advocated by the more advanced tariff reformers; it now seemed that their obsession with economic novelties had led the party into the disasters of 1910–11. Instead Bonar Law hoped that by ignoring Lloyd George's proposals as far as possible they might deprive him of a popular cry. Yet the danger was that the radicals, unchallenged, would win over voters who assumed Conservative opposition to reform. The one course from which the party shrank was outright attack upon the proposals — an indication that some lessons had been learned from 1910.

Thus the only development that seemed likely to upset Liberal prospects was widespread conflict with Labour. Yet the more the

Conservative leadership played the Ulster card the closer they bound the Labour leaders to Asquith. It is easy now to overlook the overriding importance Ramsay MacDonald and his colleagues attached to maintaining Asquith in power so as to see Home Rule through to success. To this end in June 1913 MacDonald engaged in talks with two Liberal MPs, Josiah Wedgwood and Philip Morrell, on closer co-operation; it emerged that the idea of a firm alliance enjoyed the support of Snowden and George Barnes, the acceptance of even Hardie and W.C. Anderson, and the acquiescence of almost the entire parliamentary party who recognized that a formal alliance would be the logical conclusion of their position.[13] When, in March 1914, the government feared a rejection of the Annual Army Bill by the Conservative peers, Lloyd George offered on Asquith's behalf increased representation in return for Labour withdrawals in the constituencies, seats in the Cabinet and an agreed programme to follow an election.[14] Though this particular crisis failed to materialize it shows how MacDonald was under pressure to opt either for independence or for closer co-operation; by 1914 his predilection for the latter course threatened to dissolve the Labour Party into its main constituent parts, the Lib–Lab majority and the socialist minority.

By June 1914 according to Labour's chief agent the party contemplated contesting 37 seats with sitting Labour MPs, another 18 where candidates had been sanctioned, 22 where candidates had been selected but not sanctioned, and 40 where candidates were possible but uncertain. Allowing for the fact that four of the Labour seats were also listed (significantly) among the 'uncertain' category this represented a total of 113. It is by no means obvious whether this was incompatible with a working arrangement with the Liberals. It undoubtedly implied more three-cornered contests than in 1910, though, judging from the by-elections, the strongly working-class constituencies would not be lost to Conservatives. In the more vulnerable marginals MacDonald's influence would doubtless have secured sufficient withdrawals to placate the Liberals and bring the total nearer to the 78 candidates of January 1910. The most predictable outcome was a further reduction in the size of the parliamentary party given some local Liberal retaliation.

The more the Edwardian evidence underlines the fact that the Liberals were in no imminent danger of decline, let alone eclipse, the more importance must, apparently, be attached to the First World War as the decisive factor in their downfall. Yet while a chronological explanation of this kind may be basically sound it surely cannot be made to run too far; for the war in no sense constitutes a sufficient cause, taken in isolation, for the dramatic disruption of the 1914–26 period. Indeed, the impact of wartime can best be understood in relation to pre-war problems; for the seeds of Liberal decline, patently present before 1914, developed mightily in the conditions of 1914–18.

What were the pre-war sources of weakness? Plainly the Progressive strategy tended to falter at the point where local activists came under pressure from parliamentary leaders; thus any growing apart of the two such as began to occur after August 1914 was bound to be dangerous. Moreover, success hinged upon the Liberals remaining in office and delivering the full range of radical demands; the wartime collusion with the Conservatives from 1915, loss of office and of the radical initiative spelt disaster. In addition there were at least three areas of policy in which the pre-1914 Liberal government stood in danger of cutting itself off from its traditions; in each case they concerned not the social–economic purposes of Liberalism but its political- moral objectives, and in each case war fostered the conditions in which Labour could uphold these traditional Liberal causes.

First and most obviously, the drift of foreign and defence policy under Sir Edward Grey and the ex-Liberal Imperialists in the Cabinet during 1906–14 had offended Liberal sentiments reaching back to Gladstone and Cobden. Grey's obsession with the German threat had led him to cultivate the deeply detested regime of the Tsar, to pander to the cruel and corrupt policy of King Leopold of the Belgians in the Congo, to abet French imperialism in North Africa, and to instigate British military involvement on the Continent in their support. In their defence ministers were driven ultimately to the Disraelian argument that national interest must take precedence over sentiment and morality. But however moribund Gladstonian economics were by 1914 the GOMs approach to foreign affairs remained very much alive on the left; radical MPs had often spoken out against Grey in the realization that their silence would present to Labour 'the whole honour of voicing the best traditions of Liberal foreign policy'.[15] The dilemma was obscured by the Prime Minister's success in outmanoeuvring the critics in July and August 1914 and by the paucity of the resignations; wartime eventually forced the radicals to develop a complete critique of Grey's policy and to adopt an alternative vehicle for its propagation.

Another area of politics in which the Asquith governments parted from Liberal traditions was the franchise question, particularly as it affected women. Forcible feeding of suffragettes and their reimprisonment under the 'Cat and Mouse' Act were felt to be deeply humiliating however much provoked by the Pankhursts; by 1916 when the tangled question of parliamentary registration reappeared Asquith's previous stubborn obstructiveness over the women was seen as the reason for the party's failure to rationalize the franchise when it had had the opportunity. More serious in the long run was the demoralizing effect of Asquithianism upon Liberal activists, especially women, in the country, who by 1914 had grown tired of being taken for granted by their leaders. The Women's Liberal Associations, torn between loyalty to suffragism and to party, were dwindling for lack of purpose, as members looked elsewhere.[16] 'Every bright and clever woman in my Liberal society has left us,' one complained to Mrs Lloyd George. 'Can you wonder at our intense gratitude to men like Philip Snowden and Ramsay MacDonald and labour associations who value their women?'[17] This discontent was in 1912 turned into electoral collaboration between the Labour Party and the National Union of Women's Suffrage Societies (the largest and non-militant suggragist organization led by Mrs M.G. Fawcett), whereby the latter provided money and organizers for candidates at by-elections and in seats presently held by Liberal anti-suffragists like McKenna and Harcourt.[18] In this way even before 1914 a number of middle-class Liberals in the NUWSS were being brought into regular contact with the Labour movement. This limited shift was to grow significantly during wartime as constitutional women suffragists joined with various anti-war groups in permanent alienation from Liberal politics in favour of Labour.

The third area where war exacerbated existing weaknesses concerns the trade unions. The Asquith government had not given adequate support to its own moderate adherents against their critics in the unions, as is shown by their handling of the Osborne Case of 1909. In this case the House of Lords had upheld the plea of a Liberal trade unionist who had challenged his union's right to use its funds for political activities. One colleague at least advised Asquith to allow the judgement to stand,[19] a view strongly reiterated by Scottish Liberal miners in 1910;[20] and nothing was done for several years, during which the Labour Party's income dropped by £20,000. However, in 1913 the Osborne Judgement was overthrown in favour of a system whereby unions were permitted to establish a fund for political purposes provided their members approved in a ballot and individuals were allowed to contract out. These safeguards failed to have the anticipated effect. Not only did most unions vote to set up the fund, but relatively few members opted out of the levy. Thus, whereas previously a union's contributions had had to come from general funds in competition with other expenditure demands, now very large sums were to be built up for the sole use of the Labour Party. Taken in conjunction with the payment of a £400 salary to MPs from 1911 this gave a solid foundation for a parliamentary Labour Party not previously available. Moreover, membership of unions affiliated to the TUC, which increased from 1.6 million in 1910 to 2.6 million in 1914, continued during the war, thereby facilitating the adoption of far more candidates than had previously seemed feasible.

In addition the government stood in danger of alienating itself from the rank and file by the authorities' handling of militant strike leaders, particularly Tom Mann and Jim Larkin. Although few workers were syndicalists they sympathized with Mann who was prosecuted in 1912 for urging troops not to shoot at men on strike.[21] In 1913 the leader of the Irish Transport Workers strike, Larkin, was sentenced to seven months' imprisonment for seditious libel, an act that Lloyd George immediately recognized as a political blunder;[22] for by casting itself, through the Attorney-General, as Larkin's prosecutor the government tended to divide and embarrass the moderate pro-Liberal working men.[23] This pattern was to be repeated during the war when unrest, particularly in the South Wales coalfield and among Clydeside munitions workers, had the effect of alienating Lloyd George from much of labour and resulted in the deportation of shop stewards. Though alive to the danger before 1914 the radical politicians entirely failed during the war to arrest their party's gradual severance from the organized working class which had been a pillar of its Edwardian triumphs.

Part Three 1914–1920s

Chapter 8

The Impact of the Great War
on British Politics

No man who is responsible [for embarking upon
war] can lead us again.
C. P. Scott to David Lloyd George, 3 August 1914

Disintegration of the Progressive Alliance 1914—16

As if to prove the dictum that in politics the expected rarely
happens H. H. Asquith contrived to take Britain united into a
major war in August 1914 while preserving his Liberal—Labour—
Irish alliance apparently intact and unscathed. This step was of
such importance for subsequent developments that we must
examine how it came about.

The traditions of Midlothian and the 'Pro-Boers' were very
lively on the left in 1914. Ostensibly a formidable resistance to
European wars was entrenched in such bodies as the Liberal
Foreign Affairs Group under Arthur Ponsonby MP, which claimed
the allegiance of several hundred MPs; but in the crisis of July—
August 1914 it could rely upon no more than 20 or 30. Why did
the opponents of war fail to stop their own government? Over the
years the radicals had been so concerned to avoid the political
menace and the financial burden of a large conscript army that
they had usually placed their faith in the Royal Navy as a sufficient
defence that was also cheap and non-aggressive. However, naval
innovation in the era of the Dreadnought and Von Tirpitz's Naval
Laws had made the 'Blue Water' argument a much more expensive
one; nevertheless radical complaints about the naval estimates had
always been contained because extra taxation had obviated any
need to sacrifice social reform for the navy. Similarly, Haldane's
creation of the British Expeditionary Force had been approved

because he saved money through reorganization and because the force was originally seen in a colonial context rather than in a European one. Grey and Asquith had always been able to answer their radical critics by saying that Britain had given no undertakings to another European power for military support, which was true in the letter rather than in the spirit. For since 1906 both Foreign Secretary and Prime Minister had envisaged the prospect of a Franco—Russian war against the Central Powers in which Britain must participate because of the menace to her own security from the expected German victory. The creation of the British Expeditionary Force, the plan to convey it across to France (accepted even by the navy from 1911), the naval conversations with France, and the mutual reallocation of their fleets, all gave the government the immense political advantage of a precise strategy carefully worked out in advance.

Not only had the radicals failed to check the trend of foreign and military planning before 1914, they had also learnt to place confidence in Sir Edward Grey. His role at the London Conference of 1913 in settling the Balkan War, which could easily have involved the major powers, greatly reassured his critics about his desire and ability to keep the peace; hence in August 1914 it seemed to many that if Grey could not stop war it was indeed unavoidable. In fact during the vital week before Britain's declaration Ponsonby deliberately abstained from calling a meeting of the Liberal Party for fear of embarrassing the Foreign Secretary;[1] on his side Grey, by being conciliatory and ambiguous, kept the radicals waiting until the government was able to present the party with a *fait accompli*.

Further, one must remember that although in July 1914 half of Asquith's Cabinet of 20 were reckoned as opponents of British participation in a war, the ministers never gave a lead to the backbenchers. The most likely anti-war leader in the government, Charles Trevelyan, was trapped as an under-secretary, too junior to be privy to cabinet intentions yet obliged to be loyal until it was too late. Opposition to Grey at cabinet level had been more serious back in 1911 when Morley, Harcourt and Runciman led a revolt over alleged military undertakings given to France as a result of the Moroccan crises; this forced Asquith to establish a cabinet committee, including Lloyd George, as a guarantee that no British pledges would be given without specific approval by the Cabinet. Thereafter Lloyd George could not say, except in his memoirs, that he was either in ignorance of or basically in opposition to British foreign policy. Though he kept up pressure for naval economies and spoke publicly about improving relations with Germany these were merely token gestures; he never succeeded in altering policy. Indeed his personal weakness after the Marconi Scandal in 1912 left him unusually dependent on the Prime Minister who had saved him from resignation. Thus, although this was not always appreciated at the time, Lloyd George had become a most unlikely leader of an anti-war crusade well before 1914.

THE TRIUMPH OF "CULTURE."

From Punch, *23 August 1914.*

In the absence of a lead from Lloyd George other ministers hesitated to throw away their careers and jeopardize the government. In the event there were only two cabinet resignations, those of Morley and Burns, both of them exhausted volcanoes by this time, neither of whom attempted to mobilize opposition in party or country. Asquith was extremely fortunate to escape so lightly, and it is a tribute to his patience and shrewdness in allowing events to make their impression that he kept the Cabinet together. Several considerations during late July and early August contributed to this conclusion. An obvious one is the, to some, unexpected swiftness with which Germany implemented the Schlieffen Plan and marched into Belgium, thereby rapidly disabusing those ministers who had wanted to believe Germany basically a civilized power. This did not, of course, weigh with Grey, Haldane, Asquith or Churchill, whose case for British participation remained quite as strong if Belgium were untouched, but it helped weaken the resolve of their opponents. Further, it is now apparent from the diary of one minister, Sir Charles Hobhouse,[2] that they believed the German government deliberately kept its ambassador in London, Lichnowsky, in the dark about its intentions so that he would make a better job of convincing the British that their involvement was not called for; this sense of deception helped to close ranks. Secondly it seems that some of the reluctant ministers (Runciman, Simon, Pease, Harcourt) were under the impression that war implied embarking upon an essentially naval enterprise in support of the French; had they appreciated how promptly the BEF would cross the Channel and how dramatically the continental commitment would grow under Kitchener's appeal for men, they would probably have stood out. Thirdly there were important political considerations. If the Cabinet had failed to reach agreement Asquith, Grey and Haldane would have resigned thus breaking up the government. On 2 August Bonar Law and Lansdowne wrote to Asquith urging prompt support for France and offering 'our unhesitating support to the Government in any means they may consider necessary for that object'.[3] Asquith made a point of reading this to the Cabinet so as to underline the fact that they would be replaced by a Conservative or a coalition ministry. In short, a war was not to be avoided by a few Liberal resignations. Why should ministers, so recently battling to complete their legislation, surrender to the opposition what the electorate had denied them? Since war was expected to produce economic disruption and social distress it would enable the Conservatives to reverse the trend to social reform and make authoritarian innovations of all kinds. If there had to be a war, better that it should be a liberal one. In this way many Liberal and Labour politicians who on 3 August had prepared to join 'peace' meetings found themselves on the 4th reconciled to war by the consideration that Britain had done her best to keep the peace and could neither leave France in the lurch nor Belgium violated. This historic turnabout bears the hallmark of Asquithian statescraft. It would have been a blunder to have taken consent for granted. Given a short delay not only the Liberals but the Irish and Labour wings of the progressive alliance rallied strongly. The Irish leader, Redmond, astonished opponents and delighted allies with a bold speech backing Grey on 4 August. Given a short war and a Home Rule Bill on the statute book there was every reason for him to stick to Asquith and, by demonstrating Irish loyalty in England's moment of crisis, allay Unionist apprehensions.

Equally strikingly the Labour Party showed its patriotic instincts by voting to support the government and ousting its chairman Ramsay MacDonald in the process. Unlike most of his colleagues MacDonald seems to have perceived the significance of the war as a decisive interlude in which the Liberal alliance might be safely disrupted; but for the time being he had to make do with the ILP and the Union of Democratic Control[4] as bridges of anti-war sentiment by which middle-class radicalism would begin to cross to Labour. In retrospect the Great War provided Labour with an historic opportunity to cut adrift from the Liberal Party on a matter of liberal principle. A similar opportunity might have been exploited during the South African War had not Labour been too young and ineffectual to forestall the Liberal recovery in 1902; 1914 proved to be different because the party was sufficiently established to seize upon the dilemma created by the Liberal leaders' decision to take Britain to war; but most were slow to see the new possibilities.

In rallying to the government the supporters of the progressive alliance shared a determination that this must not be a war of aggrandizement or one fought by 'methods of barbarism'. H. G. Wells' brilliantly pithy phrase 'The War to End War' stuck because it expressed what many wanted to believe. Men of intellectual weight like Gilbert Murray and James Bryce wrestled with their liberal consciences and concluded that this was a just war. Masterman, the minister initially responsible for propaganda, was able to draw upon the talents of the Edwardian literary world: Arnold Bennett, John Galsworthy, John Masefield, H. G. Wells and Thomas Hardy were among those who averred publicly that

Britain was right to 'defend the rights of small nations, and to maintain the free and law-abiding ideals of Western Europe against the rule of "Blood and Iron" and the domination of the whole Continent by a military caste'.[5]

On the Conservative side, of course, all this dilatory manoeuvring for morally comfortable positions was regarded as irrelevant. The opposition responded to war with a single-minded patriotism unhampered by political scruples or traditions, and fortified by a conviction that they had been proved right in diagnosing the German threat. However, they soon realized that they were in an awkward tactical position. Conscious that their hour had come, the opposition believed that they ought to be running the war. The alternative was to join the armed forces, which some 98 Conservative MPs had done by January 1915; their action strengthened the government's parliamentary position, and exacerbated the frustration of those remaining on the backbenches increasingly susceptible to scaremongering. It was all too easy to ascribe military failures to government lack of determination and indulgence towards enemy aliens supposedly spying and sabotaging the war effort. If few leading Conservatives gave credence to the wild rumours that Prince Louis of Battenburg, the First Sea Lord, Sir Eyre Crowe of the Foreign Office, or Haldane the Lord Chancellor were German sympathizers, they did nothing to check them. For some months, however, the government's critics were held at bay by the inspired decision to appoint Kitchener Secretary of State for War. His reputation in the country made him hard to attack with any credibility, as the opposition soon discovered. The flaw lay in the fact that once appointed he proved difficult to remove, and that when victories failed to materialize it was his colleagues who were apt to bear the blame. This was the effect when Sir John French, casting about for an excuse for the failure of his offensive at Neuve Chapelle in 1915, blamed Kitchener for lack of high-explosive shells, though he had previously claimed to be amply supplied.[6]

The government's other temporary advantage lay in the 'party truce', which amounted to a suspension of by-election contests by the main parties and restraint by the Conservative leaders in Parliament. In fact Balfour, Bonar Law, Austen Chamberlain, Walter Long and Lord St Aldwyn were all involved, in Balfour's case quite closely, in official work by attending committees or giving advice. On the strength of this co-operation government spokesmen were apt to claim that the opposition were informed of and responsible for the decisions made, an interpretation apparently well received in the country but highly exasperating to Conservatives who felt the Liberals were taking advantage of their enforced good behaviour.[7]

This situation exacerbated the tendency already manifested in 1910–11 for the Conservative backbenches to organize in defiance of their leadership. Up to a point it was useful for Bonar Law to be able to channel backbench energy into a body like the Unionist Business Committee; indeed he encouraged one of his rivals, Walter Long, to take the chairmanship, for it provided a forum for criticizing the government without actually breaking the truce or being unpatriotic. However, when in May 1915 the Unionist Business Committee threatened to force a Commons debate on the alleged shells shortage, Law could not stay aloof except at risk of splitting the party and jeopardizing his own leadership. Having established himself since 1911 by his abrasive style he found it dangerous to abandon what now seemed an inappropriate tactic. Yet if he failed to give a lead it began to look as though Curzon, Carson or Long would fill the vacuum.

By the spring of 1915 Bonar Law faced three unpalatable courses of action. He could simply join his followers in attacking the Liberals, which would have led to the general election due in December, and probably a Conservative government. He ruled this out because it would push much of the Liberal and Labour forces into opposition to the war as in 1899–1902 but with far more serious consequences; also the Edwardian industrial revolt seemed to compound Conservative doubts about their ability to handle an organized working class in a crisis. An alternative was to form a coalition with the Liberals, but this was rejected by Law and virtually all leading Conservatives as calculated to silence necessary criticism.[8] Thus Bonar Law stuck to the third option, the 'party truce', until May 1915. At this point the split between Churchill and Admiral Sir John Fisher, First Sea Lord, at the Admiralty combined with the launching of the 'shells scandal' in the press created pressure that was too powerful for Law to resist. Anxious to avoid being driven to censure the government he was pleasantly relieved to discover that Lloyd George and Asquith himself were offering him a coalition. However, because Law accomplished this largely in isolation from and against the wishes of many of his colleagues, the Conservatives failed to confront Asquith with agreed terms either on policy or offices. Asquith retained in Liberal hands all the key posts except the Admiralty, and Law, despite his obvious claim to a major role, was relegated to the Colonial Office because it suited his own rivals in the party to devalue his status. Yet this underlined for the Conservatives that it was not a genuine coalition but a triumph for Asquith.

In the short run the coalition served to put off the election which the Liberals expected to lose and kept Asquith in office until the end of 1916. In a longer perspective, however, it proved a crucial point in the disintegration of the Liberal Party. It would be far too simple to think that war placed an intolerable strain upon Liberal susceptibilities, for like all political parties they had a strong inbuilt tendency to hang together regardless of policy as August 1914 shows. We have already noted that the Cabinet's pre-war difficulties in the party over foreign policy, suffrage and labour militancy left them exposed to attack from the left, and wartime conditions exacerbated this. Well before the war the Cabinet had envisaged a wide-ranging Emergency Powers Bill. In 1911 they had introduced the Official Secrets Act, and they now enacted the Defence of the Realm Act, a sign that they were not inhibited by philosophical scruples from eroding individual rights. The crisis was held to justify other infringements of political liberalism: the Aliens Restriction Act, strict censorship, the National Register Act, and the protectionist element in McKenna's 1915 budget were further evidence of this. The point is that such measures were accepted in the emergency; they only became dangerously divisive when the party experienced the demoralizing shock of May 1915 when Asquith announced the end of the Liberal government without the slightest consultation or preparation even among his closest colleagues. 'The more I contemplate this Coalition, the more I revel in the new sense of freedom it gives us all,' observed one MP. 'No one on earth can pretend that we were elected to support this Government.'[9]

From this moment the Liberals and their leadership were fatally divided. Predictions that under Conservative influence the war would now be fought by something closer to Prussian methods appeared to receive confirmation in Ireland and in conscription. On the eve of war Home Rulers had been dismayed at the shooting of Nationalists in the south while the army was not apparently to be used against Ulstermen. The Home Rule Act went on the statute book but was suspended for the duration of hostilities. Thereafter the Irish alliance collapsed progressively. Redmond refused cabinet office in 1915 but Asquith took the odious Carson in as Attorney-General. Yet the situation did not become irretrievable for the Nationalists until 1916 when the Easter Rebellion was put down with calculated brutality by the army, who acted as though administering a lesson to a colonial people.

The effect was compounded by the subsequent failure of the government to prevent the execution of Roger Casement. A rebellion that had begun with little support quickly gained retrospective sanctity with the result that by 1917 the country had thrown over the Nationalists for the Sinn Fein, and the Nationalist Party had become alienated from the Liberals. It was Asquith also who bore the blame for failing to obtain the acquiescence of Conservative ministers in Lloyd George's hastily negotiated settlement of the Home Rule question in the aftermath of the rebellion.

The drift to conscription had a similar effect. Asquith here prevaricated by opting for the Derby Scheme in October 1915 to give voluntaryism a last chance to produce sufficient men. When, inevitably, this proved inadequate he accepted conscription of single men in January 1916 and married men in June. His manoeuvring succeeded in keeping the government together. Yet the real strength of his position since 1914 had been that by continuing in office he provided the best guarantee against authoritarian measures; to retain that support he therefore had to make a stand on a matter like conscription which was so deeply offensive to many people. Instead his cleverness alienated so much support that by December 1916 most of the theoretically Asquithian forces resigned themselves to the Lloyd George Coalition on the grounds that the worst had already happened; there was no point in keeping Asquith as Prime Minister. Much of the confusion of First World War and subsequent politics arises from the fact that the right wing of Liberalism now looked to Lloyd George; while the left—centre had perforce to take Asquith for their leader. Bearing in mind his history of Liberal Imperialism, his sympathy for conscription at the time of the South African War, and his attitude to Grey's foreign policy this was clearly a false position for Asquith; he was no 'quintessential liberal', and thus never an effective leader in the circumstances arising out of the war.

Lloyd George and the Conservatives 1916—18

For the Conservatives the real value of the 1915 Coalition, not apparent at the time, was that it solved the Edwardian dilemma by dividing the progressive alliance. More immediately, coalition had the effect of altering the relationship between Asquith and Lloyd George to the latter's advantage in that it gave him allies in

Cabinet whom the Prime Minister could not ignore. For the strength of the Conservatives' position lay in the fact that the government's legal term would run out in December, and they agreed to no more than a bill prolonging Parliament's life for eight months. Consequently throughout the war the Unionist peers enjoyed the power of forcing a general election by declining to pass such a bill again. Through his skill in finding compromises Asquith lived with this situation until December 1916 when he made a major error of judgement. Appreciating Lloyd George's natural facility for responding constructively to immediate problems Asquith had rightly placed him at the new Ministry of Munitions. However, Lloyd George, conscious that he had to succeed, refused to be baulked by the obstacles to the manufacture of munitions; chief among these he identified the voluntary system of recruiting which deprived him of thousands of skilled engineering workers.[10] Though at the start of war Lloyd George had lent no support to Churchill's desire for conscription, he suffered no moral scruples over it, and proceeded to throw his weight behind those Conservatives who wanted compulsion.

Following Kitchener's death in June 1916 Lloyd George allowed himself to be manoeuvred into the War Office without any of the powers that he himself had helped to strip from the Secretary of State. Left thus with responsibility but insufficient control Lloyd George quickly grew frustrated and highly susceptible to schemes for reorganizing the machinery for running the war. His object in this was to eliminate the inefficiency arising from a dilatory Cabinet, civil servants and generals; though critical of Asquith he did not intend to drive him from the premiership, regarding him as essential for persuading the country to accept unpalatable measures – a view endorsed by Bonar Law. However, it proved difficult to bring pressure effectively to bear; he shrank from resignation which would leave him isolated and impecunious, and he feared Liberal hostility to him for scheming with the Tories. At first he found only Carson, who had left the Cabinet, and Sir Max Aitken, Bonar Law's *éminence grise*, to work with. Most Conservatives, however appreciative of Lloyd George's work at Munitions, had no desire to raise the untrustworthy 'little bounder' to the premiership. His strength came through Carson's role as leader of the 150-strong Unionist Business Committee. In November 1916 in a debate on the disposal of captured enemy property in Nigeria, during which the rebels demanded that it should be sold only to 'natural born British subjects' not to the highest bidder, Conservative MPs split 65 for Carson and 73 for

Bonar Law, the minister responsible for defending the government's policy. Just as in 1915 the incipient party split obliged Law to act. For in antagonizing the tariff reformers of the UBC over the Nigerian issue he was offending his own staunchest supporters in the party. He therefore joined with Lloyd George and Carson to present Asquith with terms for a reorganization of the machinery of war. Basically this involved removing the running of the war from the traditional Cabinet to a War Cabinet of three members, not including the Prime Minister, who would be freed from departmental duties by their deputies and thus able to sit from day to day making rapid decisions.

Asquith had always made the mistake of taking Bonar Law for granted; given the connivance of the other leading Conservatives he believed it safe to relegate him to a minor position. However, after the Prime Minister's rejection of the Lloyd George–Bonar Law proposals the Conservative ministers met on 3 December and decided to offer their resignations; when communicated to Asquith by Law this decision induced him at once to reach a compromise with Lloyd George over a War Cabinet. Yet it rapidly emerged that Law, whether by accident or by design, had failed to convey accurately his colleagues' intentions. Curzon subsequently explained that the resignations would facilitate the reorganization of the government by Asquith, if necessary without Lloyd George; they were thus helping him against the manoeuvres of Law and Lloyd George. This changing interpretation of the Conservative ministers' motives was the major reason for a swift withdrawal by Asquith from the compromise, which in turn forced Lloyd George into an unwelcome resignation. Thereupon the Conservatives also resigned and the government collapsed. When Bonar Law declined the King's invitation to form an administration Lloyd George had his chance. He would have failed at this point had the Conservatives refused to serve under him. Their puzzling behaviour can only be put down to their own confusion. They probably feared that if they simply restored Asquith he might kill off any real reorganization of government which they thought essential; he was only the lesser of several evils. Some like Curzon, who undoubtedly found Lloyd George repugnant, could not overcome the temptation to serve in any government; and Lloyd George might at least be more amenable to pressure.

That he could form a genuine coalition only became apparent when Liberal and Labour support materialized. A canvass of Liberal MPs by Christopher Addison revealed 49 firm supporters and many more who would be drawn by prime ministerial patronage. On the Labour side all the indications up to December 1916 were that the leading figures, Arthur Henderson and J. H. Thomas, preferred Asquith; yet he had exhausted his usefulness by now. After an entrancing appeal by Lloyd George, Labour MPs voted by 18 to 11 to back him, a decision confirmed by the NEC. Thus although Asquith had so recently seemed the indispensable Premier, there were sufficient elements of support in each party to make the new coalition feasible.

By his refusal to serve in the government Asquith became responsible in the first instance for the dire split in the Liberal ranks. For now the Liberals enjoyed two leaders, one the Prime Minister and the other Leader of the Opposition, along with two whips in the House. Though initially this was seen as a temporary and superficial division, it hardened during 1917–18 as MPs formed the habit of voting for or against the government. Though radicals and pacifists regularly attacked the illiberality of Coalition policies Asquith shrank from giving a lead, even on the question of British peace terms on which Lloyd George was very vulnerable. The sole exception was Asquith's intervention in support of General Maurice's allegations in May 1918 that the Prime Minister had lied to the Commons over the size of forces on the Western Front. Even here Asquith fumbled his opportunity by insisting on a select committee of investigation instead of accepting Bonar Law's rash offer of a tribunal of two judges. Though the Liberals' 98 to 71 split in favour of Asquith in the Maurice Debate seemed to formalize the division it only reflected a, by now, fairly well-established fact. There was little point in taking a risk over the Maurice issue if Asquith was not prepared to offer sustained, co-ordinated opposition. Instead he left it to back benchers, protesting that he wished essentially to support the war effort, a claim whose credibility would have been greater had he not refused to join the government. This absence of strategy had a disintegrating effect on parliamentary politics. Like Joseph Chamberlain in 1886 Lloyd George took with him a few radicals like Addison and Montagu; but the bulk of his support came from the Liberal right and those attracted by his powers of patronage; for some of these coalition was to be a stage on the road to the Conservative Party in the 1920s. Conversely many of the progressive radicals and pacifists were so dismayed by both Asquith and Lloyd George that they loosened their Liberal ties preparatory to a shift to Labour after the war. Many elderly, traditional Liberals drifted into retirement in 1918. The only feasible course for the Liberals after December 1916 lay in reasserting their leadership of the radical left by attacking the illiberality of the Coalition; Asquith's inability to do this not only in 1916—18 but until 1926 when he retired, doomed the party by leaving a vacuum for Labour.

For the time being the future appeared to lie in the special relationship growing up between Lloyd George and the Conservatives which, remarkably, endured for six years. Recognizing the Conservatives as the chief prop to his government Lloyd George promptly elevated Bonar Law to be Chancellor of the Exchequer and Leader of the House. In that capacity Law, not the Prime Minister, would manage the backbenchers. He also took care to install in his War Cabinet two influential leaders of party opinion, Curzon and Milner, and to tie Carson down as First Lord of the Admiralty. By thus restoring a measure of power and dignity to the Conservatives, and reassuring them over his commitment to the 'knock out blow' he made them more amenable than might have been expected. Law was never again in real danger of losing the loyalty of the party to a rival, and this was the essential underpinning to Lloyd George's Coalition.

Once committed to Lloyd George it seemed inconceivable to part with him, for the alternative was a renewed Asquith premiership that might lose the war or negotiate a humiliating peace. This prospect kept Conservatives loyal in the Maurice Debate when they rallied to Lloyd George despite a suspicion that he had been lying. Further, the original rationale for coalition in 1915, namely the difficulty of a purely Conservative government carrying the country during war, now seemed stronger. Much that occurred in 1917 underlined the point; industrial unrest, initially checked by the war, now began to rise sharply; the government, greatly fearing that the anti-war groups might infect industrial workers with pacifism, over-reacted by attempting to stop the activities of the UDC. With a man of Lord Lansdowne's stamp publicly urging a negotiated peace in November 1917 one can see why the danger of a collapse of the will to fight seemed to loom so large; Russia was going down in revolution, the French and Italian armies disintegrating in mutiny and defeat. In this situation Lloyd George's buoyant, well publicized oratory seemed ideal for rallying the nation for further efforts.

For although the domestic situation looked precarious the war had created opportunities for repairing the Conservatives' connections with the workers. Addressing a rather critical special party conference in 1917 Bonar Law reminded them that in the past the opposition of organized labour had been fatal to Conservatism and tariff reform; but now, 'gentlemen, this war has shown us that among the Leaders of Labour there is a body which is national and patriotic' (Hear Hear and applause) 'and feels these sentiments as strongly as we do'.[11] The implication was that certain concessions must be expected if a patriotic working class was to be harnessed to Conservatism. One means to this end was provided by Lord Milner's British Workers League established to provide working men with an alternative leadership to that of socialists or trade unionists. Designed to combine traditional Conservative policy with vigorous social reform the BWL furnished some 18 candidates in 1918 in industrial seats where the Conservatives felt they would have no chance, ten of whom were elected as the 'National Democratic Party'. Although the NDP soon lost credibility in the trade union movement once the war passed, it is significant as an indication of the Conservative mood during the last two years of war.

Milner was prepared to go to unusual lengths in terms of state intervention and social welfare to accommodate a wider social range of support; for a brief period in 1918–20 his colleagues paid what seemed a high price for mass backing. Yet before then the biggest gesture, and greatest risk, had already been made in the form of the Representation of the People Act which ushered in adult male suffrage. One of the most important manoeuvres of the fading Asquish Coalition had been the establishment in August 1916 of a Speaker's Conference on the franchise. Its report was inherited by Lloyd George in January 1917; with the firm backing of Henderson, Long, and an apprehensive Bonar Law he turned it into a bill. The Conservatives' fears were laid by various concessions, in particular the preparation of a scheme of postal and proxy voting designed to ensure that the men in the forces – on whose support they counted – would not be excluded from the election while the 'shirkers' and pacifists enjoyed the franchise. In addition they obtained a five-year disfranchisement of conscientious objectors, and a special franchise for 19 year olds on active service. The modified redistribution would, they hoped, help them in rural seats and in Ireland, as would the extension of plural voting in some areas, a few extra university seats, and most of all, the promise (never fulfilled) of a complete reform of the powers and composition of the House of Lords so as to rectify what Conservatives regarded as 'one-chamber government' since 1911.[12] Even so, much of the party was highly disgruntled at being forced by its leaders to accept a huge electorate amounting to 21 million (of whom 8.4 million were women) in 1918 compared with barely 8 million before the war. Conservative Central Office had repeatedly warned that a majority of the new male voters would be working men, and in their twenties.[13] One must remember that politicians at this time felt acutely conscious of the immaturity of the young who lacked considered opinions and judgement and were liable to be swayed by emotional appeals; this was one reason for imposing a 30-year age limit on women voters. The most dangerous moment would come if and when demobilized troops returned to temporary unemployment and caused a landslide on the lines of 1906. Now for the Conservatives alliance with Lloyd George clearly provided the safest means of effecting the transition from war to peace on the basis of a vast new electorate. He was pre-eminently the popular leader who could capture better than any of the staid and remote figures in their own party the support of the masses. With his Liberal and Labour followers Lloyd George would guarantee a popular majority for the Coalition, and the containment of the menace represented by an independent Labour Party. This was the electoral foundation of coalition strategy for the Conservatives until 1922.

Even in 1918 some right-wing Conservatives would have preferred to risk going it alone. Yet the leadership of the party would not let them do so. Working with Lloyd George became a habit; for Bonar Law particularly it proved an effective partnership; he shared with the Prime Minister relatively humble social origins and a lack of the grand panjandrum style of his colleagues. Balfour, Chamberlain and Birkenhead also relished the freedom from party cant that membership of a coalition gave them. Thus for rebel Conservatives separation of the party from Lloyd George would have been tantamount to separation from their own leaders.

Although by 1918 the prospect of American assistance and an improvement in food and shipping supply gave some confidence, it was generally expected that the Allies would have to fight on through 1919 for complete victory. It was therefore a wartime not a post-war general election that Lloyd George prepared for. Parliament was nearly three years beyond its proper term, and an appeal to the country for a mandate to finish the war would greatly simplify the government's work by purging the Commons of troublesome left-wing war critics. However, so much fuss had been made of the need to allow the troops to vote that an election was necessarily delayed until the autumn of 1918 when the new register was expected to be ready. But the real problem was to decide on what basis Lloyd George should appeal to the country. Though widely regarded as indispensable in wartime he had no real party, only a group of parliamentary followers. Characteristically Lloyd George did his best to keep his options open for as long as he could. He worked hard on polishing up his liberal and radical credentials, aided by the work of Addison on housing and Herbert Fisher on education; and by November he was able to hold out to Liberals the prospect of a fair peace settlement and a league of nations, and at home house-building, minimum wages, health and land reform, and even a reaffirmation of free trade and Home Rule. There was certainly an element of deception in this for he had already agreed a programme with the Conservatives that included some protectionist measures and a reform of the Lords; however he drew enough Liberals to him to serve his purpose which was to make him strong enough to bargain with the Conservative Party. As early as July 1918 his whip F. E. Guest, had embarked upon detailed negotiations with Sir George Younger the Conservative party chairman for a mutual withdrawal of candidates to avoid dividing the coalition vote. By 20 July Guest had secured Bonar Law's agreement to a free run for Lloyd George Liberals in 114 seats, for Labour in 15 and for the NDP in 17.[14] In fact Lloyd George was still toying with ideas of making an independent appeal, and luring Asquith into his government as Lord Chancellor when military events rapidly closed in. On 11 November the Armistice was signed, and on the 14th the Labour Party withdrew from the Coalition. He therefore fell back on the prepared plan of fighting in co-operation with the Conservatives, since if he did not win an election while his prestige was at its height the Conservatives would sooner or later wake up to the fact that they could manage without him. Consequently he and Bonar Law issued a letter of approval – dubbed the 'Coupon' by Asquith – to 374 Conservative, 159 Liberal and 18 NDP candidates, whose election would extend into peace the wartime Coalition government.

Labour's Change of Course

Superficially Labour's divisions over the First World War mirrored those of the Liberals: a minority adopted outright opposition; the bulk concluded reluctantly that it was a justified war; and some, in a natural culmination of the strategy of 1903, went to the extent of serving in government from 1915 to 1918. However, these divisions were far less damaging to Labour, and we must consider why this was so.

By the end of the war Labour managed to rally around a new programme, achieve a clearer sense of purpose than its rivals and attain greater coherence than before. Fundamentally this was possible because the movement was still more than just a parliamentary force, and a split at that level was less vital than for, say, the Liberals. Also, for much of the rank and file international affairs were still too remote to be acutely disruptive. Much of the credit for containment of the problem must be ascribed to Arthur Henderson's restraint; after succeeding MacDonald as chairman he made no attempt to purge the anti-war elements in the party. Nor did MacDonald wage his campaign primarily through the party, concentrating instead on the UDC and subsequently the ILP, which illustrates the advantage of the federal party structure adopted in 1900. Henderson, well attuned to the feelings of the average working man, simply supported the war effort by accepting a post as President of the Board of Education in 1915, and acted as a mediator between government and unions and a symbol of working-class co-operation. His inclusion had been expected to strengthen Asquith's hand against the Conservatives; for the voluntaryists, for example, had assumed that the labour movement would resolutely resist military conscription as tantamount to the direction of labour. This did not happen, and Henderson saw that on the whole the rank and file were too caught up in the war climate to worry much. He joined the new Coalition in December 1916 (as a member of the five-man War Cabinet) not because of any virtues of Lloyd George, but because working-class interests seemed, on balance, better served by working within the government than in opposition. Nor was this merely a matter of collaboration foisted upon the movement by MPs. At its 1916 conference at Bristol the party's delegates representing 73 unions, 39 trades councils, 41 local Labour parties, two socialist societies and one branch of the Women's Labour League approved by 1.5 million to 600,000 a resolution pledging assistance to the government in waging war, and by a similar margin backed Labour participation in the Coalition. The next conference endorsed membership of Lloyd George's administration by a margin of six to one.

Nevertheless Labour had to perform a precarious balancing act. Participation by Henderson and others in government undoubtedly boosted the party's confidence and status; yet at the same time it had to keep intact its role as a pressure group for the working class. That this was possible may be ascribed largely to the activities of the War Emergency Workers National Committee which contrived to maintain the links between the party's obligations to its grass roots and its responsibility to governments.

Though originally conceived in August 1914 as a peace protest committee, the WNC promptly faced Britain's involvement as an inescapable fact and constituted itself as a body representative of the working class devoted to defending their immediate interests. From nine nominated and six elected members it grew to 40. Its secretary was Jim Middleton, the assistant secretary of the Labour Party. Among its prominent members were patriotic trade union leaders like Will Thorne, Havelock Wilson and W. J. Davis, TUC MPs like James O'Grady and C. W. Bowerman, and near jingoes like Ben Tillett, John Hodge and H. M. Hyndman. Patriotic Labour was no mere figment of the Conservative imagination. At the other end of the spectrum the WNC included ILP representatives Fred Jowett, H. Dubery, W. C. Anderson and Ramsay MacDonald, and more moderate critics of the war like Bob Smillie of the Miners Federation. Most, however, were of the 'sane patriotic' persuasion personified by Henderson who believed Germany must be beaten, but refused to enjoy the war. In this category were Fred Bramley, J. A. Seddon and Sidney Webb who was a patriot as in the South African War, but thought it a mistake to elevate the war into a dominant political question when it could be made to serve longer-term purposes.

Indeed most Labour critics tried to abstain from involvement in great issues over which they believed they could exert little influence. This disengagement from the war was sometimes deliberate; socialists like the young G. D. H. Cole, for example, were anxious not to discredit their cause by association with anti-war movements. Disengagement never had a demoralizing effect because Labour found an alternative in the form of concentration upon a defence of the interests of working-class families during wartime. At national level the WNC served admirably as the focus of this activity, vigilantly intervening with the authorities over prices, housing, rent control, and benefits and pensions for soldiers and their families. In this way it was possible to indulge in political work which kept Labour's basic purpose alive at a time when most forms of politics were suspended or disrupted. Its achievements should not be exaggerated; it probably only edged the government in the direction in which it was moving already, and it firmly declined to put itself at the head of unrest that threatened the war effort, or to risk a serious challenge on matters like conscription. It concentrated on winning compromises, yet avoided being sucked into the official machine: Smillie refused to become food controller; Henderson resigned from the Committee on becoming a minister.

Even more importantly the activity of the WNC nationally was complemented at local level by the work of trades councils. War generated all kinds of local bodies such as food control committees and profiteering committees for which trades councils and Labour municipal groups were called upon to provide representatives. They attempted, too, to resist pressure for retrenchment in local government, to maintain the real level of council employees' wages, and to see that the families of servicemen did not suffer.[15] Perhaps the most important single issue was housing; from 1917 Addison as Minister for Reconstruction attempted, through the Local Government Board, to persuade local authorities to prepare detailed plans for house-building. The response was very patchy, but Addison's initiative enabled Labour councillors, where already well represented,[16] to impose their housing policy, albeit temporarily. Thus from the Housing Act of 1919 until its abandonment in 1921 there existed a situation in which a Liberal minister's national policy was readily grasped by Labour locally; in this way Labour inherited the social reform tradition at grass roots and actually resuscitated Addison's measure in the form of Wheatley's Housing Act when in office in 1924.

At Westminster Labour's loyalty to the Coalition was not shaken until Henderson's visit to Russia in June 1917 which had been intended to encourage the provisional government of Kerensky to maintain the war effort. However Henderson, who welcomed the new democratic regime, soon recognized how precarious it was; to persist with the war was to invite overthrow by the Bolsheviks, and he came home convinced that Russia would have to move towards a negotiated peace to forestall another revolution. A means to this end was at hand in the shape of an impending conference at Stockholm of socialists from belligerent countries on both sides which Henderson believed should be attended by Russia and by representatives of British Labour. This episode demonstrates the dramatic effect upon such a pragmatic, unideological person as Henderson of removing him from the isolation of British domestic politics. He began to see the implications for Britain of the demobilization of disillusioned troops unattached to parliamentary democracy and open to anarchy and revolution. However his new attitude towards Russia commended itself so little to his cabinet colleagues, obsessed only with military victory, that he was effectively sacked from the War Cabinet. Although George Barnes took his place this proved to be a major blunder by Lloyd George, for it forced Labour into formal defiance of government policy for the first time. The Labour Party

Conference sanctioned British representation at Stockholm, and foreign affairs seemed suddenly to facilitate a rapprochement between middle-class socialists of the ILP and UDC and moderate trade unionists.

By September 1917 work was in hand on several key areas of Labour Party activity. A statement of 'Peace and War Aims', largely the work of MacDonald, Webb and Henderson, appeared in October; a new party constitution and a programme entitled 'Labour and the New Social Order' were ratified by a special conference in September 1918; and during 1918 Henderson devoted himself to preparing the party to fight a general election. All these changes, whatever their intrinsic significance, marked Labour's emancipation from the politics of the pact that had prevailed since 1903. Confidence and will to do this sprang from three sources. In the first place the parliamentary alliance had plainly ceased to exist, more by Liberal ineptitude than through Labour's intention. Henderson and MacDonald were conscious of the potential Labour support from middle-class radicals disillusioned and detached from their old party loyalty; Liberal organization had been deteriorating in working-class strongholds and many Liberal MPs would retire leaving opportunities for Labour. With no Liberal government in power all the pressures that had been effective in keeping Labour in tow before 1914 had lapsed.

The second factor was the expansion of the party's resources. Of course, payment of members in 1911 and the settlement of the Osborne dispute in 1913 had put the party in a stronger financial position. During the war total trade union membership rose from 4.1 to 6.5 million, and that of TUC-affiliated unions from 2.6 to 5.2 million. The intention of the constitutional reforms was to translate this latent strength into actual constituency machinery in the form of an organized party in every seat; the number of affiliated constituency bodies (LRCs and trades councils) grew as shown in table 8.1.[17] While their rivals were stagnating or collapsing Labour made up ground. The fairly static pre-war position

TABLE 8.1.

1913	1914	1915	1916	1917	1918
143	179	177	199	239	389

changed significantly in 1917 and dramatically in 1918; the number of affiliated bodies for that year corresponds very closely with Labour candidatures at the election. Similarly with candidates the breakthrough was concentrated right at the end of the war. Although in January 1916 30 candidatures were sanctioned all but one of these were already on the list of 117 in 1914; by January 1917 four more had been sanctioned, though again two were on the 1914 list. Thus most of the 388 who fought in 1918 emerged in the closing stages. However, since 1914 the NEC had used two travelling organizers to tour constituencies to ascertain which should be fought, and this was stepped up in 1917 when 79 districts were visited.[18] Though the NEC adhered to the party truce, independent Labour candidates had appeared in by-elections at Salford North in February 1917 where a seat was gained from the Liberals, and at Wansbeck in May 1918 where the miners unsuccessfully contested Charles Fenwick's old constituency.

The third stimulating factor from the summer of 1917 was the realization by Henderson that the Cabinet would seriously press for the comprehensive electoral reform proposed by the Speaker's Conference. This was to assist Labour in several ways; by expanding the working-class vote at a time when the Liberals were in no position to exploit it; by limiting election expenses which made the contest with the Conservatives less unequal; and by revising constituency boundaries which in disrupting existing party organizations damaged the other parties more than Labour. In addition when Henderson contemplated fielding 500 candidates he did so on the assumption that the alternative vote (which prevents the election of a member on a minority of the votes), originally part of the Reform Bill, would obviate the danger of splitting the progressive vote to Conservative advantage; it was not until February 1918 that the alternative vote was dropped from the Bill; but though worrying for Labour, this came too late to have a significant effect on the number of candidates. Thus the pact was dead and Labour with 388 candidates could bid to form a majority for the first time. In retrospect, the concatenation of a Liberal split, the war, and electoral reform created such obviously favourable conditions for a fresh strategy by Labour that it seems remarkable that the party was so slow to seize its opportunity. However much importance one gives to working-class political consciousness as the explanation for Labour's emergence as a major political party, the fact remains that the *timing* appears to owe far more to parliamentary politics. The potential for a governing party based on the working class had existed unrealized for decades, but there are no good grounds for thinking that Labour would have attained this status in the 1920s but for the decisions and blunders of 1914–18.

Chapter 9

A Mass Electorate at War

No one can be really at peace in his own mind now until he has in some way offered his life to his country.
Gilbert Murray to J. L. Hammond, 17 November 1915[1]

Impact on Civilians

The experience and response of the mass of people during the First World War were of major importance in shaping the modern pattern of British politics. The year 1918 saw the majority of the adult population enfranchised for the first time, and produced an election that imposed a pattern for the next half century. What is striking is that the immediate impact of war seems to have been far less disturbing in Britain than in other countries. The explanation for the comparative stability and acquiescence of the population may be found first by considering the material—social conditions of wartime, and second by examining how attitudes towards the war were moulded and contained.

Against the immediate background of widespread industrial militancy the authorities not unnaturally took at face value the threats made by some socialist leaders to use the weapon of a general strike to stop international war. However, since the anti-war movement collapsed, on both political and industrial fronts, this danger failed to materialize. Yet the government greatly feared that a sharp rise in unemployment and an increase in food prices, as a result of hoarding and the interruption of imports, would generate mass disturbances; hence the need in the early months for 'business as usual', as Churchill put it.

In fact the government's difficulties on the industrial front were to arise not from a surplus of labour but from a shortage. The immediate effect of the war was to reverse militancy; the

972 stoppages of 1914 dropped to 672 in 1915, and the number of days lost fell from 9.8 million to 2.9 million; there was a further fall during 1916 followed by successive increases in strike action in 1917 and 1918, when 5.8 million days were lost, and a fivefold increase during the 1919—21 period. By and large men were anxious to take advantage of opportunities created by the desperate need for coal, munitions and other war supplies to work a full week, and their leaders were drawn into co-operation by politicians stressing the crucial nature of their contribution to the war effort. Strikes in the South Wales coalfield led eventually to the state running the entire industry and conceding national wage agreements. Under the 'Treasury Agreement' of March 1915, later embodied in the Munitions of War Act in July, the engineering unions accepted temporarily a dilution of skilled labour and waived their right to strike in return for concessions over wages and profits. Inevitably the amenability of union leaders exposed them to challenges at local level, hence the emergence of a major shop stewards movement in this period. The most serious disturbances were those led by the Clyde Workers Committee in 1915—16; however, this was a case in which a genuinely syndicalist leadership mobilized conservative craftsmen worried about the erosion of their position as skilled men but uninterested in a social revolution or in stopping the war. Clydeside was therefore of local importance, and untypical of the working population as a whole. The increase in strikes in 1917 reflected simply a desire to catch up with the price rises of the early part of the war. Walter Runciman, who had occasion to bargain with both sides of industry as President of the Board of Trade, concluded that the unions were far more susceptible to appeals to their patriotism than the employers who invariably insisted on guaranteed profit levels well above those of peacetime.

Since four-fifths of wheat, two-thirds of sugar and half of the meat consumed in Britain were imported some price rises were inevitable; however, shortages and inflation during 1914—18 were never serious enough to have demoralizing effects upon the population. Although the rationing system of the last year of war seems to have been popular and successful, it was never applied to potatoes and bread because the authorities believed the industrial population must be well supplied with energy-producing foods. Both middle-class and working-class families were bombarded with instructions about economic eating, but the latter were quite resistant to this pressure. The Edwardian generation had grown up on an improved and varied diet in which meat made regular appearances on the working man's table. Serious erosion of that standard was not necessary because the incomes of working-class families increased in real terms during the war. This was not primarily due to rises in wage rates, which fell behind price rises in the first two years, but to the movement out of low-paid employment such as domestic service into higher-paid jobs with plenty of overtime; women who had earned 10s as servants could earn from £2 to £5 in munitions factories. In addition many boys of 18 left home, freeing jobs as errand boys, barrow boys and newspaper boys for younger brothers and sisters who absconded from school. Thus the labour shortage during the war stimulated the purchasing power of many families and built up a demand for consumer goods. Cheap items like black pudding were de-rationed because demand slackened, while luxury goods like pianos were bought by thousands towards the end of the war. These manifestations of consumerism have much importance. They exacerbated the gulf between the civilian and the soldier who did not appreciate being told how lucky he was to be at the front. Also, in so far as civilian needs were satisfied there was no major build-up of discontent by the time of the 1918 election; only in the aftermath, 1919–20, when the civilian felt his gains slipping away, did he grow politically restive.

From the outbreak of hostilities the authorities had taken steps to persuade the civilian population that any hardships and sacrifices were well worth making. Initially they were unduly apprehensive about the panic and demoralization that news of military setbacks or zeppelin attacks might cause. They therefore adopted several techniques to maintain morale. Propaganda was directed from Wellington House by Charles Masterman, eventually superseded in 1918 by a Ministry of Information under Lord Beaverbrook; the Parliamentary Recruiting Committee flooded the country with posters and meetings; and the government, using its powers under the Defence of the Realm Act, censored closely all information pertaining to the war. However, the military reports emanating from the War Office and the Press Bureau were so bland and thin as to force the press to start bypassing the official machinery. There were absurd attempts to blot out outstanding events such as the German entry into Belgium on 3 August (reported in the *Daily Telegraph* but flatly denied by the Foreign Office), and the sinking of the *Audacious* by a mine (photographed for the American papers but censored in Britain). Yet there was a basis for official fears. Between 14 and 25 August the French armies had suffered no less than 300,000 casualties, a rate of

25 per cent; it was feared that knowledge of this would have shocked and possibly checked the flow of recruits.

However, when on occasion the truth slipped through — such as in *The Times'* report on Mons, headed 'Broken British Regiments Battling Against Odds' — the press were not very proud of their scoops. Most editors and proprietors wished to be loyal if only the authorities would feed them good rousing copy. This appears to have been widely reflected among their readers who often had no desire to read the unvarnished truth. *The Times* was denounced for its story on Mons, and the *Mail* and *The Times* were publicly denounced for criticizing Kitchener for shortages of shells in 1915. Therefore a compromise was devised in 1915 whereby a handful of journalists were allowed into France and had their articles censored on the spot and at the War Office before they reached their editors. The whole object was to protect the army from criticism and maintain domestic morale with unceasing streams of heroic tales. As one of the journalists later wrote:

> We identified ourselves absolutely with the Armies in the field. . . . We wiped out of our minds all thoughts of personal scoops. . . . There was no need of censorship of our dispatches. We were our own censors.[2]

Thus the press largely abdicated its function during the war at least as far as military events were concerned; it soaked up the grotesquely inaccurate information about Haig's battles, and regaled readers with stories of troops who loved nothing better than going over the top.

The public were probably more inclined to believe what they read in the press than is the case today, especially when presented in photographic form such as the *Daily Mail's* bogus official war postcards depicting 'Tommy' rescuing a comrade under fire. However, it must be remembered that to a large degree the troops co-operated by filling their letters home with reassuring platitudes about their good health and spirits in an effort to spare the feelings of their families. It was hardly surprising that when the men came home on leave they frequently found that an unbridgeable gap had opened up between them and the civilians, and they were often reduced to solitary brooding over their experiences.

However, as the lengthening lists of casualties appeared in the press during 1915 and 1916 telling a tale inconsistent with the official version, one might have expected signs of disillusion and questioning about the fight-to-a-finish. It may be that the sheer numbers of casualties were too difficult to take in, and that grief was concentrated on known individuals. Since so many families suffered losses their own grief could be partly assuaged in the general sense of loss; it soon became abnormal and humiliating *not* to have a close relative at the front. In these circumstances even to consider ending the war before the enemy had been defeated could seem a betrayal of those who had already died. This fear of disloyalty was instrumental in cutting off the anti-war organizations from most of the civilians who might have sympathized with them. Initially the flood of patriotism at home was so overpowering that the Union of Democratic Control (UDC), for example, feared even to make its views known to the public; this lack of any co-ordinated effort at opposing the policies connected with the war was never really overcome. Only when goaded by the right-wing press did the UDC articulate its interpretation of the war as a product of secret diplomacy, the arms race and the foolish pursuit of the balance of power. The implication that Britain was by no means blameless was treated with utter disbelief. To accept the UDC version of events would have been, for civilians and politicians alike, to admit that one had been wrong or deceived before 1914; and to concede the pacifists' argument would have been at allow them a higher moral standard than oneself. Although there was greater sympathy for bodies like the No Conscription Fellowship, social intimidation kept the number of applications for exemption by 'Conscientious Objectors' down to 16,000; even these were untypically middle-class, perhaps because the successful objector had to be articulate enough to face a tribunal keen to catch him out, and usually had to demonstrate pre-war membership of a group like the Quakers who were well known for pacifist sentiments.

The party truce in by-elections offered scope to independent candidates to mobilize discontent, but this was done successfully only by those who wished to push the government into more belligerent policies. When as a result of Keir Hardie's death in 1915 two 'Labour' candidates contested his old seat at Merthyr Tydfil, the pro-war C.B. Stanton easily defeated his anti-war rival. 1916 was probably the year in which the anti-war movement began to make an impression. The appalling British disaster of the Somme involving Kitchener's volunteer armies reinforced doubts about the possibility and purpose of a complete military victory. The demise of the Asquith government released more left-wing politicians from an uncomfortable position. And in turning its attention to a negotiated peace and future methods of maintaining

peace the UDC received indirect strength from similar pronouncements made in 1917 by President Woodrow Wilson and Lord
Lansdowne. In April 1918 a peace-by-negotiation candidate polled
a third of the votes at the Keighley by-election, a modest sign of a
potential anti-war party in the country.

However most people plainly regarded the origins of the war as
irrelevant and the 'knock-out blow' as the only possible strategy.
In the last resort this must be ascribed to the popular conception
of the enemy. For the Edwardian generation had absorbed a diet
of invasion literature and war scares fomented by the press, and
by 1914 they were so highly susceptible to the idea that German
spies and saboteurs were in their midst, especially among the alien
population, as to accept suggestions that war critics were paid
agents or sympathizers of the Germans. Moreover the circulation
of atrocity stories served to transform the 'German' into a sub-
human brute. Although quite without foundation atrocity stories
gained credibility partly by dint of repetition and partly by the
authority given them by Lord Bryce's committee of investigation
which pronounced thousands of 'atrocities' true despite its failure
even to interview witnesses. British propagandists enjoyed some
factual basis to substantiate their view that German ways of
waging war were inhuman; the execution of Nurse Edith Cavell,
the sinking of the *Lusitania* or the use of poison gas were
undeniable, though not without parallels on the Allied side. The
arrival of Belgian refugees was for many sufficient proof of the
inevitability of a fight to the finish.

The impact of wartime pressures upon political attitudes is not
easy to discern, though certain features are clear enough. In the
country party politics had been largely suspended as erstwhile
opponents joined together on the recruiting platforms. At Westminster too, normal debate subsided with the result that the press
stepped in to fill the vacuum. Right-wing proprietors and editors,
though vociferously loyal to the war effort, attempted the
systematic denigration of the Asquith governments, concentrating
particularly on individuals like Haldane, Churchill and McKenna
whom they presented as men of doubtful patriotism responsible
for military and naval setbacks. By contrast the press tended to
encourage the public to place its confidence in Kitchener and
Haig, Fisher and Jellicoe; it is significant that many people refused
to believe that Kitchener had gone down with HMS *Hampshire* in
June 1916, so much did they need a figurehead. In addition,
diaries and letters of the time suggest that many liked to see the
guiding hand of the King behind the 'strong' measures like the

Defence of the Realm Act; as one teenager put it in February 1916: 'We wish the King would turn all the Government out and give orders himself, and really beat the Germans properly.[3] This naïve longing for a leader is reflected in the enthusiasm of many middle-class people for the former radical menace Lloyd George. When he became Prime Minister in December 1916 his speeches on the 'knock-out blow' and his photograph were promptly pasted into the nation's scrapbooks — treatment usually accorded to soldiers but not to politicians.

Among the non-combatant population women were particularly vulnerable to the official view of the war. Private diaries written by women during the war, for example, tend to reflect the feeling that only as a man could one make a real contribution; this was relentlessly exploited by the recruiting campaigns and posters designed to challenge the manhood of the non-combatant male, and emphasize that the least, and most, that a woman could do was to ensure that her menfolk were dispatched to the front. Beyond this, officialdom approved most strongly of women as the bearers of the next generation of fighting men, hence the indulgence shown to mothers of the illegitimate 'war babies', offspring of thousands of Kitchener's volunteers in 1915. For middle-class girls nursing was still seen as the appropriate wartime occupation, while working-class girls had to face resentment and prejudice when national necessity forced farms and munitions factories to take them on. This ran against the trend of half a century in which women were eased out of supposedly inappropriate heavy and dirty manual labour — except in the home. It is significant that where women who undertook male tasks during the war have left a record of their feelings they seem to have taken for granted that they were stepping in on a purely temporary basis, and they vacated their jobs at the end of the war without protest. This is not so surprising in view of the relatively conservative, middle-class nature of the bulk of the pre-1914 women's movement, which had largely confined itself to the narrow question of the parliamentary franchise and neglected the wider social objectives that the vote might help them to attain.[4] In this light the grant of the franchise in 1918 to women over 30 years who were either local government electors themselves or the wives of local government electors is explicable. Both the Speaker's Conference and Parliament were determined to keep women in a minority among voters, and to enfranchise only those who as relatively mature, family women seemed likely to constitute a stable, loyal section of the community.[5] Although the 8.4 million women voters comprised 40 per cent of the total electorate, they were not expected to form a distinct group pressing their own claims, but rather a loyal, patriotic body reflecting the politics of their husbands.

Thus the civilian population, if longing for peace, seems to have wanted victory first. Any disillusion evident from 1916 onwards was held in check partly by buoyant standards of living, by the absence of a credible alternative analysis of the war to resist official and press propaganda, and by a simple faith in the King, Sir Douglas Haig and Lloyd George.

Impact on the Troops

During the war many politicians adopted a comforting view of the men in the trenches as dedicated patriots; not only did they extend the franchise to them, but insisted on the need for their participation in a general election. However, much of this misplaced confidence stemmed from a confusion between the troops of 1914–18 and the regular army; in understanding their attitudes one must bear in mind the broad distinction between the regulars, the volunteers of 1914–15, and the conscripted men of 1916–18.

Among professionals and upper-class officers one finds the most evidence of an uncomplicated response to war, and, as might be expected, the least questioning or disillusion. Their observations are replete with sporting metaphors of war, with hunting at the front, and with war as a decent honourable affair. This was characteristic of airmen whose favourite form of warfare – duels with enemy planes – appealed strongly to traditional, romantic notions. One of them protested against his sister's munitions work: 'if we can't win this war without our women coming down to manual labour of that description I'd just as soon we were licked.'[6] For such men war furnished an opportunity to prove their manhood and to simplify life's complexities; as Julian Grenfell, who had joined the army before 1914, enthused:

Isn't it luck for me to have been born so as to be just the right age and just in the right place – not too high up to be worried – to enjoy [the war] the most.[7]

Even in 1916 such men bore war's losses fairly stoically, followed their leaders uncritically, and interested themselves in simple patriotism and the status of their regiments. Indeed many felt only one doubt: 'I hope to God the politicians in England will not betray us and make peace before we have absolutely crushed our enemies.'[8]

On the other hand the vast majority of troops in 1914—16 were volunteers, 1,186,000 of whom came forward in the period from August to December 1914. By any standards this was a remarkable response. Although taught for a generation to expect an invasion and, since the early 1900s a German invasion, the bulk of the British people had remained stubbornly hostile to the idea of conscription. This reflected neither pacifism nor lack of patriotism, but status and pride. While the army was still associated with drunkenness, low company and exile, respectable working-class families were loath to allow their sons to join except out of dire necessity: 'I would rather bury you than see you in a red coat,' Field Marshall Sir William Robertson's mother had once told him. As a result even the Conservative Party, though agitating for extra expenditure on the navy, had declined to risk supporting Lord Robert's National Service League in urging compulsory military training. However, hundreds of thousands of men in all classes found respectable forms of military participation in the Volunteer Force, the Territorial Army and the Rifle Clubs which were sharply distinct from both the regulars and from 'Prussianism'. Against this background of voluntaryism the response to Kitcherner's appeal becomes explicable.

For many, of course, neither the personal nor the political implications of joining up involved much deliberate thought. Younger men often volunteered in a light-hearted way on the spur of the moment; for war offered a unique opportunity to get away from home to see foreign parts for a few months. For men without prospects Kitchener's army seemed a glamorous alternative. Yet although special factors such as the slump in the building trade during the summer of 1914 helped recruiting, it remains true that thousands left secure jobs as miners or engineers to join up.

Yet while September 1914 saw 450,000 volunteers come forward, October produced only 137,000; the first rush to the colours was already fading. In January 1915 the Board of Trade's Labour Department estimated that two-thirds of the males aged 17—45 were fit for army service, a total of 6 million; at this point roughly 2 million were already in the forces and at least 1 million working in vital industries, leaving perhaps 3 million possible recruits. During 1915 some 1.28 million men were taken, but it became more of a struggle to find them. In the months of

July, August, September and December less than 100,000 volunteered, and the tone of the recruiting campaigns grew sharp and
vituperative; the local press taunted the 'Shirkers of a National
Duty'. In October, under Lord Derby's recruiting scheme, men
were invited merely to attest their willingness to serve if required;
significantly the Prime Minister's alleged promise at this point that
all single men would be taken before married men prompted a
sudden spate of marriages. Although the Derby Scheme may have
stimulated the increase in October recruiting, by December the
monthly figure had fallen to 55,000 compared with the 30,000 a
week which some ministers were now demanding. After 16 months
of war the pool of willing men had clearly begun to dry up. Now
a man could calculate more coolly the costs and risks involved in
going to war; it was plainly going to be a more protracted affair
than originally thought; while casualty lists swelled ominously
the attractions of greater employment opportunities at home
increased. Consequently the authorities resorted to compulsion
from January 1916, thereby squeezing out another 1.2 million in
1916, 820,000 in 1917 and 490,000 in 1918.

By contrast with the widespread disaffection and collapsing
morale among the troops of France, Russia and Italy the British
appeared immune from mutiny or politically inspired discontent.
This led many contemporaries during the war and inter-war years
to characterize the troops as essentially passive, apathetic, shell-
shocked, disillusioned but unable to articulate their feelings. More
recently there has been a reaction against this approach to the
effect that the British 'Tommy' was basically cheerful and stoical
in temperament, a fact inexplicable to the educated middle-class
sensibilities of the anti-war writers. However, this version, which
is essentially part of the attempt to restore the reputation of Sir
Douglas Haig and the war of attribution, is not well grounded in
the source material. Certain aspects of the anti-war writers' case,
for example the idea of the 'lost generation', have now been
corroborated by research; while many of the features of war
experience identified by Robert Graves or Siegfried Sassoon may
now be studied in the contemporary records of ordinary, obscure
men. In the long run, war experience was to have a disillusioning
and a radicalizing effect for some working-class men and also for
some middle-class men who found themselves closer to and in
greater sympathy with the lower levels of society than they had
ever been in peacetime. What concerns us here is how far the
limited forms of discontent during 1914—18 had political implications.

It is perfectly clear that from the outset the spirit of the Kitchener armies was unusual; there was not the normal respect for the officers and only contempt for the training experienced in England. In the trenches keenness and discipline varied widely from one regiment to another. A common manifestation of discontent, recognized by the authorities, was for men to commit offences calculated to get them out of the front line to prison camps at base. In order to counter slackness and declining morale the army made great use of night-time patrols in no-man's-land, which the men often handled by sitting quietly and reporting 'all quiet', or even by mutual agreement with the enemy to ignore patrols. As one 21-year-old conscript wrote in August 1917:

> I'm doing properly whatever duty comes my way but I'm not going out of my way; I'm no longer interested in the Army; I'm only interested in finishing this ghastly war, and to that end I'll help.[9]

As for the cheerfulness shown by men going over the top, this was often the result of the very powerful rum ration or because of the greater chance of receiving a 'cushy' wound to send them home, as opposed to the likelihood of a fatal head wound in the trenches. There were also more deliberate manifestations of revolt, notably the mutiny by 10,000 British troops at the Etaples camp in the summer of 1917, an event concealed by the authorities at the time. Rates of desertion remained fairly high at around 10 per cent a year, worsening steadily after Passchendaele. Altogether there were 304,000 court-martial cases, of which 86 per cent resulted in conviction. The number of suicides and of men shot for cowardice in the trenches will never be known since they were officially recorded as deaths in action.

A major political implication of experience as a combatant was that the troops took a more balanced and relaxed view of the Germans than did most civilians. The army's intelligence broadsheets on atrocities were regarded as 'comic cuts' by men, who while often bitter at the loss of friends and acts of cruelty, accepted that the behaviour of their own side was very similar. This helped to set them apart from the wild conceptions of those at home. 'Don't be harsh in your judgements on them,' one man reproached his mother, 'we who are up against them cannot be.'[10] Indeed coming home on leave was often the catalyst of disenchantment; when the men wanted only a good sleep their families were bent upon parading them before an admiring locality and discussing the one thing they wished to forget. It could be infuriating to be told how lucky one was to have a 'crack at the Bosche', to be handed white feathers when in civilian clothes, or to contemplate the profits being made out of the war to which Horatio Bottomley's *John Bull* magazine regularly drew the soldiers' attention. Alienated from home men often found relief in rejoining their comrades who at least understood. Loyalty to comrades and to junior officers who shared the same dangers and privations was a major reason for the steadiness of the British troops. Even a man like Siegfried Sassoon who ostentatiously quit the army in July 1917 in protest against the prolongation of the war found himself driven back at his own wish in 1918. This underlines the important fact that the most dissatisfied soldiers were either isolated from a coherent alternative view of the war, or, like Sassoon, so antagonized by the pacifist spokesmen that no effective link was forged between critics at home and in the army.[11]

Consequently dissension tended to concentrate on specific material complaints such as poor boots, the pilfering of food on its way to the front line, and the 5s and 6s paid per day to colonial troops while the British received only 1s 6d. Some links grew up between these grievances and the Soldiers and Workers Councils in industry. In June 1917, for example, men in several southern county regiments formed the Home Counties and Training Reserve Branch of the Workers and Soldiers Council[12] and issued a number of demands such as examination by civilian doctors for wounded men before being sent back to the front; but they also made political complaints over their exclusion from citizenship, the failure of the government to indicate on what terms they would negotiate a peace settlement and the financing of the war by loans and the printing of money. However, although 'Soldiers Charters' were taken up by the ILP and some Labour politicians during 1918 there was never an effective attempt to harness the servicemen to the Labour movement let alone to the peace movement. Labour leaders often took at face value the confidence of the right wing in the troops, so that they suspected organizations of such men of being directed against trade unions, or even threatening the parliamentary system. Arthur Henderson's initiatives during the genesis of the Representation of the People Act in 1916–17 and during the organizational extension of the Labour Party in 1917–18 reflected a profound apprehension about the consequences of several million ex-soldiers being unemployed and unattached to parliamentary politics. Political safety seemed to lie in demobilizing the soldiers as quickly as possible so that their aspirations might be tackled as workers rather than as soldiers. It would be fatal, Herbert Morrison told the ILP, to attempt a unionization of the armed forces which would 'lead to the army being looked upon as a respectable profession'.[13] In this way the political potential of military discontent was never exploited during the First World War.

The Coupon Election 1918

The Coupon Election of 14 December 1918 in which no less than 21 million soldiers and civilians enjoyed the right to vote, proved to be a watershed in twentieth-century politics. It ushered in the inter-war era of Conservative dominance; it dealt the Liberals a blow from which they never fully recovered and thereby gave Labour the chance to become the parliamentary opposition.

The victory of the candidates of the Lloyd George Coalition in 526 seats out of 707 left it in a remarkably strong position, particularly in view of the failure of the largest opposition group, Sinn Fein, to attend Westminster (see table 9.1). Like most elections the 1918 result had been broadly determined well in

TABLE 9.1. *1918 General Election*

	Coalition			Opposition	
	Seats	*Vote* *%*		*Seats*	*Vote* *%*
Con	335(374)*	32.6	Lab	57†(388)	22.2
Con Uncouponed	48(75)	6.1	Lib	28‡(258)	12.1
			S Fein	73 (102)	4.5
LG Lib	133(159)	13.5	I. Nat	7 (60)	2.2
Nat Lab	10(18)	1.5	Others	16 (197)	5.3
	526			181	

*Figures in brackets denote number of candidates.
†Also Independent Labour at Anglesey and Aberdeen N., Co-operative at Kettering and National Socialist Party at West Ham (Silvertown) give the total of 61 sometimes quoted.
‡37 were elected as Liberals without the Coupon, but 9 of these took the government whip subsequently.

advance of the campaign. It is difficult to interpret the landslide other than as a long-delayed eruption of Germanophobia which could only redound to the benefit of the Conservatives. Not all government candidates actively stirred such emotions for it was unnecessary to do so. Lloyd George can be defended from the charge of intending to fight the election on a policy of making Germany pay 'until the pips squeak', for he had begun by speaking of a sanely negotiated peace and domestic reform. But he was too sensitive to audience reaction to stick to unpalatable topics, and it was not surprising that he ended the campaign pandering to popular desires for vengeance instead of using his prestige to counter them; on 11 December he put prime ministerial approval on the notion that Germany should pay the uttermost cost of the war and on an absurdly high estimate of what that was.

Candidates were made to feel that their soundness on this issue was under scrutiny; in London, for example, candidates received telegrams from the editor of the *Evening News* demanding:

> For the guidance of your constituency will you kindly state whether if elected you will support the following (1) Punishment of the Kaiser (2) Full payment for the war by Germany (3) The expulsion from the British Isles of all Enemy Aliens.

In a competition of this kind the Conservatives enjoyed a head start, for Liberal and Labour candidates, even those who had been staunch supporters of the government, could have their pre-1914 record thrown back at them. In Shoreditch Christopher Addison, despite having the coupon and his wartime ministerial record, found his Conservative opponent pointing to his votes against the naval estimates: 'It has not taken a war to teach me my policy.'[14] Since very few candidates were prepared to repudiate or question the cause or conduct of the war, the Conservatives could simply adopt the stance of men who had been proved right by events. Most politicians contrived to capitalize on their personal contribution preferably by military service; by way of compensation women were photographed with husbands in uniform, while older men drew attention to their part in the South African War or to their sons' role in the present one. It is not without significance that the only seat gained by an uncouponed Asquithian Liberal was at Leith where William Wedgwood Benn was able to quote from General Hamilton's dispatches on actions in which he had taken part.[15]

Some opposition politicians tried to turn the obsession with the forces to their advantage by widening the issue to the welfare of the troops and their families. They often criticized Lloyd

George for effectively disfranchising the men by rushing into an election while they were still abroad. C.P. Trevelyan warned against the maintenance of conscription after the war, and his 'Soldier's Fourteen Points' included rapid demobilization, state maintenance for discharged men, an increase in privates' pay to 6s and higher weekly pensions. But with his UDC record Trevelyan polled a derisory 5.6 per cent (admittedly as an independent against three party candidates); perhaps the most impressive poll by a 'pacifist' was Arthur Ponsonby's 22.6 per cent against Coalition Liberal and Labour at Dunfermline.

Our understanding of the outcome of the 1918 election is enhanced by comparing it with another landslide, that of 1945, which shows that the association of an election with a war does not necessarily produce a move to the right. In both cases the party in office at the start of the war proved highly vulnerable to blame for lack of preparation or of determination in conducting the war. Moreover in 1945 there was no question of branding the Labour opposition as unpatriotic, for the Conservatives were, if anything, more exposed because of their pre-war weakness in the face of the dictators. There is a further element of difference that bears strongly upon the results. During the Second World War it could be confidently assumed from 1943 onwards that Germany could not win, which relieved the people of much concern. There followed two years in which the sacrifices imposed upon civilians grew more irksome; in the process thoughts of revenge faded and attention turned towards domestic conditions after the war. Thus by the time of the election the issues of social reform in which the voters were primarily interested were precisely the issues that the Labour Party could most effectively exploit.[16] No such considerations applied in 1918. As late as the spring of 1918 the war was very nearly lost by the Allies, and it was assumed that hostilities would go on through 1919. When during the summer of 1918 the military tide suddenly began to turn, the Armistice and the general election followed rapidly while the emotions of wartime were still high. Thus the timing of the Coupon Election was vital; had it been postponed, however, until 1919 or 1920 it would instead have caught the angry mood of disaffection and produced a result far more favourable to the parties of the left.

While the underlying mood determined that 1918 would be a Conservative victory, it does not fully explain the scale of the victory. Naturally the result represented a distortion of the voting in that the Coalition won 74 per cent of the seats for 54 per cent of the poll. In the absence of the Liberal–Labour pact the opposition forces were bound to throw away much of the territory held in 1910. What perhaps requires consideration is why the one factor that might have been expected to tell in favour of the non-Conservative parties, the vastly increased franchise, did not apparently help.

To consider first the forces vote, it is evident that the government went to considerable lengths to allow them to participate in the election. This complicated and prolonged the preparation of the new register; men in Belgium and France were granted postal votes with a two-week delay in the count to give them time to reach the returning officers, and those further afield voted by proxy. Yet there are good grounds for doubting whether the soldiers' vote was a loyal government one. Out of the total electorate of 21 million, service voters numbered 3.9 million; of these 2.7 million were sent ballot papers but only 900,000 actually voted in the election. This low rate of participation reflected the physical difficulties and a certain isolation from politics in general and from local constituency conditions in particular. From what we know of the troops' resentment against domestic propaganda they were bound to find the Coalition's case less plausible than the civilians did, but the main factor was simply the difficulty of mobilizing their support in the chaotic conditions of 1918. Observers at the count noticed that soldiers had sometimes expressed their feelings by inscribing 'demobilize first' on the ballot, and that a high proportion of absent votes went to Labour candidates.[17] The private papers of a number of prominent pacifist politicians certainly contain letters from soldiers wishing them success and endorsing their views on the war.[18] And well before the election the UDC organizers had reached the conclusion that discharged men provided the most receptive material.[19] Thus there are indications that as in 1945 the troops would in fact lean to the left; however, it must be stressed that this was a latent tendency not fully realized in 1918; too many had to vote while still abroad; and the direct connections between politicians and soldiers such as Sassoon's work for Philip Snowden at Blackburn were very much the exception.

The evidence, impressionistic as it is, tends to suggest that civilian voters, particularly the women among them, were far more the backbone of the Coalition's majority. Isolated from the real war they were apt to want to prove their loyalty to the men who had fought by voting for a tough peace settlement; this was their vicarious blow against Germany. Candidates themselves formed the impression that women voters leant strongly to the

From Punch, *15 November 1922.*

Coalition,[20] voting as they believed their husbands or brothers would wish. This seems credible in the light of the finding of later studies that women as a whole give a consistently higher Conservative vote than men. If so, this is important because of the large role of women in 1918. For their effective part was rather greater than their 40 per cent share of the electorate suggests. Women frequently acted as proxies for sons and husbands who comprised one-third of the 3.9 million service vote. Also the overall turnout of only 59 per cent conceals wide differences; at York for example, it was found that 75 per cent of home electors had voted, but only 40 per cent of absent voters. Thus women as part of the domestic electorate seem likely to have had an effective ratio of 50:50 with men in 1918.

Inevitably the coupon arrangement attracted much contemporary comment, particularly from those who ascribed their defeat to the misleading effect it had had on voters. However, there are good grounds for thinking that the coupon was a handy excuse for those who would have been defeated in any case. Although 133 of the 159 Liberals who received the coupon won seats, this was because in most cases the coupon deterred local Conservative associations from opposing them; it was the free run that guaranteed success. This is corroborated by the successes of Conservatives who stood without the coupon: 25 of these were Irish Unionist MPs, but in Britain 37 Conservatives stood uncouponed with success in 23 cases. A number of these were in hitherto unfavourable constituencies; for example Barrow was gained after 12 years as a Labour seat; and Liberal seats fell at Bury (where the Liberal had the coupon himself), Rotherham, Derby, Salford West, Forfarshire and East Fife (Asquith's seat). It looks very much as though Conservatives were doing equally well with or without the coupon. It may however, have been decisive in tipping the result against prominent Asquithian ex-ministers who were within reach of victory, notably Runciman at Dewsbury, Samuel at Cleveland and McKenna at Pontypool. Here Conservatives won simply by maintaining their pre-war share of the poll while the non-Conservative vote was evenly split between Liberal and Labour. These are distinct from the really disastrous Liberal performances such as Sir Charles Hobhouse's 7.6 per cent at East Bristol or McKinnon Wood's 8.2 per cent at Glasgow (St Rollox), which reflect a widespread collapse of party organization during the war, deteriorating relations between MPs and local associations, and a failure to keep in touch with a vastly expanding electorate in these crucial years. The Asquithians had created a hopeless tactical position for themselves. By declining to attack the 'knock-out blow' approach to the war they cut themselves off from one section of opinion; yet by refusing to participate in Lloyd George's Coalition government they only emphasized their position as the men who could be blamed for the early failures. This was an untenable position simply because the public found it hard to understand.

In many ways the Labour Party's performance in 1918 is the

most interesting. The total of seats won, 57, is significant only by comparison with the pathetic performance of the Asquithian Liberals, for it represented only a modest advance on the 42 seats won in 1910. Moreover to a considerable extent the same ground was being held in the two elections: solid mining constituencies. There was a similar concentration of Labour MPs in Lancashire together with an expansion from bridgeheads already established in the coalfields of South Wales, the North-East and the Midlands. Of the MPs in 1918 51 had been nominated by trade unions, 25 of them by the Miners Federation. In terms of seats 1922 was to be the real point of breakthrough for Labour.

The other factor contributing to the successes of 1918 was the patriotic attitude adopted by many trade unionists. Prominent Labour figures like J.H. Thomas, who won comfortably against Conservative and Liberal opposition, and J.R. Clynes and Vernon Hartshorn, who were unopposed, took a line very similar to Lloyd George's over reparations and Germany. Conversely, candidates attempting to propagate the views of the UDC or ILP usually met overwhelming rebuff even in working-class seats, and local Labour parties did their best to avoid association with the ILP for fear of damaging their chances. Anti-war MPs, though not surprised at losing, were astonished at the scale of their defeat; at West Leicester MacDonald won only 23.6 per cent in a straight fight, while Snowden achieved 19.7 per cent at Blackburn in a three-cornered contest. Thus, the socialist/trade unionist rapprochement on foreign policy from the summer of 1917 appears not to have penetrated from the national to the local level. In the country Labour chose to present the war as a triumph for the working classes and made only token gestures towards ILP views of past and future foreign policy by talking vaguely of international co-operation in place of secret diplomacy. MacDonald and Snowden, like Ponsonby and Trevelyan, had been misled by audiences which 'listened spellbound' in private meetings or ILP gatherings. It proved difficult to translate their enthusiasm into an efficient canvass of a mass electorate. As MacDonald's agent explained: 'the root cause of lethargy among ILP'ers was the *fear* of personally defending an unpopular candidate. I mean having to encounter opposition on the doorsteps.'[21]

In the long run, of course, the seats won in 1918 were of less significance than the size of the Labour vote — 22.7 per cent of the total. This cannot be assumed to reflect the effect of the expanded franchise; it reflected the number of candidatures, now 388 compared with 56 in December 1910. Comparisons between the pre- and post-1918 franchise are virtually impossible because in most cases both the constituency boundaries and the number of candidates also changed. In the Wansbeck division of Northumberland where a by-election took place only five months before the general election, the same Labour and Liberal candidates enjoyed a straight fight on each occasion. The only major change was the doubling of the electorate; yet the Labour poll actually dropped slightly from 47 per cent to 43 per cent. This serves as a reminder that the new voters were by no means an automatic source of additional Labour strength.

The key to Labour's strength lay in taking over in 1918 part of the support and strength of the Liberal Party. Since for 707 seats there were only 258 Asquithian Liberal candidates compared to 388 Labour ones it is obvious that many former Liberals were obliged to choose between a Labour and a government candidate or stay at home; 1918 broke the habit, and thereafter the number of Liberal candidatures fluctuated wildly from one election to another. Both Liberal and Labour candidates in 1918 commented on the numbers of ex-Liberal constituency activists now running Labour campaigns.[22] Arnold Rowntree pointed out that those who had previously voted Liberal 'for traditional reasons but are not specially interested in policies' often went for the Coalition, while radicals, pacifists and the more politically involved were opting for Labour in 1918. This loss of local activists, which crippled Liberal work at constituency level in the inter-war years, was really the most dire consequence of 1918, for it meant that subsequent national Liberal revivals could never be made to survive at the grass roots. This development was less the result of the coupon itself than of Asquith's earlier abandonment of the pre-1914 Progressive alliance from 1915 onwards. Because at the time relatively little canvassing was done and because voters were sometimes reluctant to proclaim their alienation from their old party, the full extent of the leakage was not apparent until the count when candidates often blamed the coupon for the result. But the underlying importance of 1918 lay in a shift of existing Liberal support to Labour, and, of course, to Conservative candidates; in so far as the newly enfranchised made an impact it was probably to strengthen the Coalition government.

Chapter 10

Party, Ideology and the State
in the Great War

> . . . the substitution of public service for private
> profit is no new ideal for me who was brought up
> by my Father to believe in the Municipal Socialism
> of the London Progressive Party.
> *William Wedgwood Benn to A. Munro, 25 January 1927*

The Myth of Laissez-faire and Interventionism

There is a pervasive notion that the politics of the Great War in
Britain took the form of an ideological struggle between the forces
of *laissez-faire* and those of interventionism and collectivism in
which the former was decisively, and inevitably, defeated; December 1916 when the rigid adherents of economic liberalism were
displaced by the Lloyd George/Conservative Coalition is usually
seen as the turning-point in this conflict.[1] Now it has long been
obvious that this interpretation of 1916–18 is particularly
difficult to square with the economic attitudes of governments of
all kinds during the inter-war period, especially the 1920s, which
hardly reflect conversion to collectivism by the experience of the
war. Moreover, now that we are aware how far *laissez-faire* had
already been abandoned by the Liberals before 1914 we can only
be thoroughly sceptical of writers who assume that the prevalence
of this doctrine accounts for the difficulties encountered by the
governments of 1914–16.

The truth is that every main political school found interventionist
ideas acceptable in certain respects but repugnant in others;
sections of every party had already moved towards the modern
conception of the state; and the collectivist policies practised in
the 50 years after 1918 were essentially extensions of those

principles established before 1914. Liberals had characteristically come to see the state as a humanitarian agency of social welfare and a redistributor of surpluses for the benefit of society, but drew the line at protectionism and confiscation, and sought to make free enterprise work effectively rather than to eliminate it. The Labour Party shared these attitudes; it espoused state ownership of one or two special industries, but shrank from a state that threatened freedom of labour or freedom of trade, and was innocent of the role of a sophisticated modern bureacracy. Socialists, while being clear about the superiority of the common good, ranged all the way from Fabian confidence in a benevolent state to the Guild Socialist and syndicalist suspicion of it. Conservatives were willing enough to bow to state control in the civil and military spheres when pressing national interests required it, but in economic affairs they accepted the paraphernalia of control on a strictly temporary basis and retained intact their belief in minimal government and minimal taxation; while the bulk of the party had shifted closer to *laissez-faire* they had made trade a special exception, and one school of imperialists had embraced a Bismarckian concept of the state. The First World War did not so much modify any of these attitudes as rearrange the places of those who held them.

Up to 1914 it was the Liberals who, because of their restoration to office in 1906 and because of their relatively rich intellectual heritage, had done most to shift Britain away from nineteenth-century economic doctrines. The palpable dismay evinced by many of them at war in 1914 did not reflect economic ideology. Just as the government was prepared to play fast and loose with its political principles, so too it proceeded largely unencumbered by traditional economics. The Asquith Cabinet had in fact considered in advance of war what kinds of steps would be necessary to save the economy from collapse in time of war. Having identified food supply and disruption of internal communications as major problems they had prepared to intervene in the fields of railways and shipping insurance despite Treasury advice to the contrary; and they were quick, of course, to underpin the whole financial system in 1914. Hence there was no hesitation in using their powers under two Acts of 1870 and 1888 to impose control on the railways in August 1914. This was done by co-operation between the railway company directors and civil servants through the Railway Executive Committee, a typically pragmatic step that set the pattern for many subsequent extensions of control during the war.

In so far as the government's approach was governed by principle at all it was derived not from economics but from a military conception of the kind of war Britain would fight. If one started from the assumption that the careful pre-war plans based on a modestly sized Expeditionary Force and the Royal Navy were Britain's chief contributions then it followed logically that there would be no radical disruption of the economy and little need for additional controls beyond those already mentioned. The War Office would be able to rely upon its existing arrangements with the arsenals and with private munitions manufacturers to supply the army without imposing great strains upon the resources of the economy.[2] Nor was this contrary to military views; it was in fact underpinned by the government's military advice as to the quantity of ammunition required by the army; despite the experience of the South African War the experts continued to regard the artillery as basically a supporting weapon, and were content to use shrapnel rather than high-explosive shells, although the latter were later found indispensable on the Western Front.[3] Thus when a 'crisis' blew up in 1915 over a shell shortage the situation was the result of the government having acted on certain military judgements by military men, not because it was inhibited by economic doctrines.

The underlying reason why the Asquith government got into difficulties was that it allowed, almost unthinkingly, the original basis of its war policy to be drastically altered by Lord Kitchener's vast extension of the size of the armed forces. By January 1915, when some 2 million men had enlisted, business could no longer be run as usual, even with the navy keeping the trade lanes open, because of the huge demands made on our economic resources by the needs of the troops for supplies of all kinds, and because of the shortages of skilled labour particularly in mining, engineering and agriculture. An alternative strategy was articulated by Maurice Hankey, Secretary of the War Council, by ministers like McKenna and Runciman, and by civil servants like Hubert Llewellyn Smith of the Board of Trade; the latter argued in January 1915 that of the 3 million fit men of the right age still remaining at home no more than 1.1 million could be taken for the army without crippling British industry.[4] The implications of this were that Britain's best policy lay in using her industrial base to support the Allies, making maximum use of the Royal Navy militarily and economically, and restricting her offensive role on the Western Front. For reasons that need not detain us here this strategy was not followed; Kitchener's mass volunteer armies gave way to conscription and to a greater and greater British participation in the land war. What is important is that although these alternatives were hotly disputed, the disagreements sprang not from economic beliefs but from differing politico–military conceptions about how to fight the war.

The empirical evidence tends to show that even those who believed in a 'small' war were flexible and opportunistic in adopting appropriate policies; indeed it was a matter of trial and error with forms of intervention and control for all governments during the war years. A characteristic and important example of this is food supply. At the outset of the war the Asquith government stepped in to purchase wheat from the USA and Argentina and sugar from the West Indies, to control Indian wheat, and to secure an agreed scale of maximum retail prices with shopkeepers. This policy grew bit by bit until by 1918 no less than 80 per cent of Britain's food was passing through the government machine and subject to price control. The palpable intention of Asquith's government was to interfere with the free market by cutting out the middlemen whose competition raised prices, and by releasing their own supplies on to the market so as to keep the price level down. Thus, for example, a Board of Trade index that showed a 15 per cent price rise at the beginning of August 1914 showed a 5 per cent fall at the beginning of September.[5] However, not only was this activity done secretly, it was even denied by Walter Runciman, the President of the Board of Trade in the House of Commons;[6] the reason was the fear that private traders might be deterred from bringing in goods if they thought the government would undercut them. Thus official statements about the virtues of 'business as usual' should not mislead historians as they often did contemporaries as to the real policy being pursued.

In other spheres intervention came as and when a particular problem was identified. Politicians were not slow to involve themselves in the munitions question; as early as October 1914 Kitchener had a 'Shells Committee' forced upon him; in March 1915 a new cabinet committee known as the 'Treasury Committee' was given authority by Asquith to override the Secretary of State for War; under the Defence of the Realm (Amendment No. 2) Act 1915 the government armed itself with wide powers including the right to control factories for the production of munitions; and in May 1915 a fully fledged Ministry for Munitions was established under Lloyd George. Under its auspices during 1915 and 1916 the government imposed control over 250 factories and mines, and regulated prices and profits; the needs of migrating munitions workers helped produce the Rent Restriction Act; strikes in the South Wales coalfield led to control there in November 1916 which was extended to the whole coal industry in 1917.

This system of controls grew continuously throughout the war; there is little justification for seeing December 1916 as marking a particular shift from *laissez-faire* to interventionism. Lloyd George was, of course, not by nature moved so much by ideological considerations as by an appreciation of immediate problems. He certainly accepted certain aspects of the McKenna–Runciman approach to the war, particularly their view that there was a limit to the number of men who could safely be taken from industry: hence his concern to bring skilled men back from the front under conscription. He persevered with well-established experimentation; for most of the key decisions involving state intervention in the economy had already been taken before he became Prime Minister. What Lloyd George did was to dramatize the policy; for example the system of County Agriculture Committees devised in 1916 was incorporated in the 1917 Corn Production Act under which production targets were imposed upon farmers with the threat of losing their land if they failed to co-operate. Similarly he high-lighted the food question by appointing a food controller. Lord Devonport, the first appointee, made little impact but his successor Lord Rhondda did advance policy a stage further by a cautious experiment with sugar rationing, which was greatly extended in the closing stages of the war. On balance it would be hard to argue that Lloyd George's government was either more or less prone to approaching its problems from a coherent view of the state's proper role. The conventional picture of Lloyd George's arch-opponents McKenna and Runciman as doctrinaire exponents of *laissez-faire* is a gross caricature. It is significant that while Lloyd George himself was no radical as wartime Chancellor of the Exchequer, McKenna was responsible for a drastic increase in the income tax in 1915, broke with free trade in October 1915, and introduced the Excess Profits Duty at 50 per cent.

None of the wartime governments erected their system of controls deliberately in the sense that they thought out the principles involved. Policy developed in a piecemeal fashion as one sector of the economy came under strain and an *ad hoc* solution was found. Wartime intervention was a matter of expediency rather than of ideology; and because there was little sense of conversion on the part of the politicians of Lloyd George's Coalition, so, once the crisis had passed, there was correspondingly little inclination to preserve and perpetuate what had been erected in wartime. The immediate sequel was therefore a swift collapse of the elaborate apparatus of economic controls; and the framework of social reconstruction was no sooner erected than dismantled. For an explanation of these events we must look further at the Conservative Party and at the 'irregulars' brought in to man the machine of government by Lloyd George.

Conservatism, Capitalism and the State 1914–22

Not only has the Conservative Party been much less studied than its rivals, but such work as exists tends to look more at leadership and organization than at ideology; and it is easy to make the assumption that the Conservatives, whether out of patriotism, through sheer pragmatism or from an inherent collectivism, responded positively to the wartime phase of interventionism. A limited empirical basis for this assumption does exist in the party's keenness for conscription and various forms of control over civilian life in which their attitude contrasted with that of many Liberal and Labour figures. However, it would be a mistake to translate this political stance into the realm of economics and to project the Conservatives as natural interventionists. In the generation before 1914, as we have seen, the tendency had been for Conservatives to adopt the arguments of nineteenth-century economic individualism, and the struggle over tariffs had left the party very hostile to almost all forms of interventionism by 1914:[7] there must be some doubt whether this was really reversed by the First World War. In the Edwardian era the party had been in one of its periodic bouts of ideological in-fighting over protectionism; the other issues that really mattered to Conservatives at the time were Ulster and the House of Lords. That the tariff issue remained alive throughout the war was largely a reflection of the vigour of the Conservative backbenches. This was by no means new for since 1903 the 'other ranks' had been seizing the initiative, and in 1911 the party unceremoniously removed its leader, a tactic that became a habit for Conservatives during the twentieth century. But the war years certainly increased the scope for backbench activity particularly through the Unionist Business Committee, established in 1915, and the Unionist War Committee in 1916; the former pursued trade matters relentlessly and the latter agitated any question on which the government, and by implication the Conservative leadership, showed slackness. Part of their power arose from the leadership the two committees enjoyed by Long and Carson respectively which made them difficult for Bonar Law to ignore. The trend culminated in the famous party meeting at the Carlton Club in 1922 which killed the Lloyd George Coalition and bequeathed to the party a permanent organization in the 1922 Committee. In the last two years of peace Law had been checked on food taxes by a revolt of his free traders, and so it was by 1914 an open question what a Conservative government would attempt beyond a measure of imperial preference; thus the battle to push the party to a frank acceptance of protectionism was still to be won. Now wartime created fresh opportunities for protectionism as the UBC quickly saw. German colonial and overseas markets became available to British enterprise, while the elimination of industrial imports from the Central Powers stimulated new developments at home. The Balfour of Burleigh Committee on Commercial and Industrial Policy in 1917 endorsed the view that at the end of the war Britain's infant industries would require full protection. These possibilities stirred some sections of industry to exert pressure on the Conservative Party. In certain respects private industry's experience of wartime co-operation with the state had proved reassuring; many firms received large contracts and often abnormally high levels of profit; they were shielded from the usual competition and to some extent from the pressures of their labour force. These cushioning effects stimulated some industries actively to seek government help in the form of tariffs and subsidies, co-operation with the civil service and amalgamations designed to control the market.[8] The object was to extend such advantages into peacetime while sloughing off the high wartime levels of taxation and direct government intervention on prices and operations.

During the war attempts were made to stiffen the somewhat shaky Conservative commitment to protectionism, now compromised apparently by the entanglement with Lloyd George. However, the Federation of British Industry, not all of whose members saw great advantages in tariffs, tried to avoid a strong line on protectionism or close association with political parties. Consequently a new organization, the British Commonwealth Union, sprang up in December 1916, determined to prolong economic warfare with Germany and inspired by fear of socialism and revolution. The BCU promoted 24 Conservative candidates in 1918 of whom 18 were elected, although its influence through key figures like Sir Robert Horne was much wider than this suggests. By 1918 it was saying what most Conservatives thought, for the one essential condition for the preservation of the

Coalition at that time was the inclusion of protection for key industries and anti-dumping legislation in the manifesto. In this sphere at least the new government attempted to live up to its promises with the Safeguarding of Industries Act of 1921 which imposed a 33½ per cent duty on goods largely from Germany.

The general theme of Conservative policy arising from the war was that business must be set free — with a special exception for trade. Any consideration of the impact of the war on the party's attitude must take account of the fact that every aspect of control apart from trade protection had been dismantled by 1922 to vociferous approval. Food rationing lingered longest because of apprehension in 1919–20 about unrest among demobilized men and the trade unions; and the Ministry of Food proved itself by keeping supplies moving during the railway strike of 1919. But by the second half of 1920 when world food prices began to fall the government gladly ceased subsidies, scrapped the rationing apparatus, and abolished the Ministry itself in March 1921, followed by the sugar and wheat commissions. Less popular forms of control had been dismantled from 1919, and by 1921 Munitions, the Coal Control Department and the Railway Executive had all closed. Sir Eric Geddes, the Transport Minister, produced a plan to nationalize the railways in his 1921 Act, but the Cabinet rapidly dropped it in the face of backbench hostility, and the most he could achieve was amalgamation of the existing companies into four groups. On coal, where the war had generated some support for public control, the government prevaricated by appointing the Sankey Commission, but ignored the verdict of a majority of its members in favour of some form of nationalization, and proceeded to decontrol the industry in 1921 earlier than planned.

Such an emphatic and rapid reversal of wartime innovations reflected the absence of any intellectual conversion by most of the politicians concerned. There did exist a degree of support among some of the civil servants who relished a new and constructive role. For example, the pre-war use of trade boards and minimum wages by the Liberals was extended during the war to agricultural and munitions workers, and some 63 trade boards had been established by 1921. However, the move towards a general minimum wage was decisively checked in 1921 because the administration of trade boards conflicted with the Treasury's view that money spent on public purposes deprived productive industry of investment, and with its conviction that a minimum wage policy would hinder the downward movement of wages believed to be essential for a return to full employment.[9] In short, the Treasury, especially when led by the highly orthodox Austen Chamberlain, still held the whip hand over younger innovatory ministries like Labour, and managed to have centres of economic heresy like the Ministry of Transport abolished by 1922. In the absence of strong political support the new ministries that embodied interventionist thinking proved highly vulnerable.

Superficially the creation by Lloyd George of the Ministry of Reconstruction in 1917, which gave way to the Ministry of Health in 1918, represented a bolder commitment than Asquith's Cabinet Committee on Reconstruction. However, the new Ministry under Dr Addison suffered from the Cabinet's habit of delaying its plans, particularly for housing, throughout 1917—18 so that they ran into the post-war inflation; but Lloyd George's basic blunder lay in denying the Ministry executive powers and obliging it to persuade ministries like the notoriously unconstructive Local Government Board under the conservative Hayes Fisher to accept its proposals. That the two outstanding social reform schemes were the responsibility of Liberals — Addison for housing and H. A. L. Fisher for education — exposed them to much Conservative carping and obstruction. Conservatives came to resent not simply the large number of new ministries and departments spawned by Lloyd George, but his predilection for insinuating into them all kinds of 'experts' and businessmen from outside party politics whose virtue indeed was supposedly their freedom from party shibboleths. The most reviled were the press barons, Northcliffe, Harmsworth and Beaverbrook; Sir Joseph Maclay, the Shipping Controller, held Parliament in such low esteem as to refuse to sit in either House. Conservative politicians were not alone in feeling both worried and insulted; for the new ministers, as the personal creations of the Prime Minister, added to his patronage and power while sapping that of the party and Parliament. Not surprisingly there was a severe reaction against these practices after 1918. Even fairly liberal-minded Conservatives like Stanley Baldwin were inclined to assume a necessary connection between the extension of government controls and corruption; the dynamic figure of Lloyd George so personified economic interventionism as to make them recoil for some years from a repetition of war-time policies.

The introduction of experts and businessmen into the Coalition represented the culmination of the earlier movement for National Efficiency. Now this approach did involve certain Conservatives, notably Lord Milner and his flock of disciples, many of whom

were esconced in Lloyd George's personal secretariat in 1917 —
another form of prime ministerial government to its critics. While
other Conservatives sometimes lent support to an extended role
for the state, for example Salisbury over housing and Selborne
over agriculture, Milner was the only major figure who consistently
identified *laissez-faire* as an evil because it precluded full employment and social reform. In describing himself as a 'National
Socialist' Milner implied the use of state power in a Bismarckian
sense to regenerate Britain's industry and population. It is
significant that when in August 1920 the Cabinet considered the
preliminary verdict of the Sankey Commission on the coal
industry only five ministers supported nationalization — the two
Liberals, Addison and Montagu; the two Labour men, Barnes and
Roberts; and a solitary Conservative, Milner. Yet he was too
isolated from the mainstream of Conservatism now bent on a
return to nineteenth-century freedom. Among the younger men
there was a strong echo of Milnerite radicalism in Sir Oswald
Mosley, elected as a coalitionist in 1918; imbued with a similar
determination to raise the standards of the working people he
sought to take the tariff policy to its logical conclusion in an
economically united Empire under a strong benevolent state. Yet
to mention Mosley is to move to the periphery of Conservatism in
the 1920s, and to remember that he had abandoned the party as
hopeless by 1922. It is significant that a number of those
prominent Conservatives who joined Labour during the 1920s —
Mosley, Lady Cynthia Mosley (daughter of Lord Curzon), Lord
Sankey, Oliver Baldwin and Stafford Cripps — had been moved
to a strong policy of state action by their sympathy for the lower
classes engendered by wartime experience. They are very much
the exceptions that tend to prove the general Conservative trend
in the 1920s.

Finance and taxation were at the root of Conservative post-war
attitudes, particularly in the reversal of the promise to build half
a million 'homes for heroes'. As a central aspect of policy in 1918
housing shows clearly the ideological limitations of official thinking. In the first place the government would not consider building
the necessary houses itself, preferring to leave it to local authorities
to settle quotas, buy land and offer contracts to private builders.
As a result of the Cabinet's tardiness the housing programme was
eventually launched amid a post-war boom in which builders were
undertaking more profitable work than local authority housing;
as a result the government reluctantly offered them subsidies to
make it worth their while. In defence of the government it has

been argued that it was inconceivable to have imposed controls on the costs of the building industry at this time;[10] this of course is to overlook the fact that in 1918 the government had been doing precisely that in a vast range of industries.

By 1920 the subsidies had made the housing programme far more expensive than originally envisaged and it ran straight into the demand for retrenchment which was already growing loud by the end of 1919. For the 'anti-waste' campaigners within and without the Conservative Party, housing was seen as a prime cause of the high rate of income tax, still at 6s at this point. Led by Chamberlain, a very retrenchment-minded Chancellor, the government managed to reduce the tax to 4s, and in 1921 appointed the Geddes Committee to recommend cuts in expenditure. Its report in 1922 effectively put paid to major reforms in education and housing, while the strength of backbench feeling on the subject drove the Prime Minister to defend his Minister of Health by referring to his 'unfortunate interest in public health''![11] The interpretation of contemporary critics like Keynes of these reversals as the result of pressure by narrow and blinkered businessmen-in-politics does have considerable basis in the evidence. We have already noted the well-established means by which Conservative backbenchers exercised their strength, and how a government Bill on transport could be routed by its own supporters on the floor of the House of Commons. Research into the composition of the party has shown that the newly elected MPs, of whom there were 168 in 1918, were drawn more from the middle class and less from landed backgrounds than those sitting in 1914.[12] While the change in this direction predated the war it received a boost in 1918; over two-thirds of the entire parliamentary party were businessmen (39 per cent) and professionals (31 per cent), while those whose connections were with the traditional occupations — the land (15 per cent) and the services (15 per cent) — were a small minority.

The understandable groundswell of opposition among the rank and file to both pre-war and wartime taxation and intervention was not checked by a coherent economic philosophy among its leaders, who, in the case of men like Austen Chamberlain seem to have shared the prevailing conviction that the economy would right itself once the burdens and obstacles imposed upon it were lifted. Bonar Law, a fairly timid wartime Chancellor, had indicated sympathy for a levy on capital designed to lift the crushing burden of national debt payments; but when the idea was pronounced suicidal by the party chairman Sir George Younger Law promptly dropped it.[13] Even the comparatively liberal Stanley Baldwin, who had supported social reform before 1914, bowed to retrenchment as a member of the Geddes Committee. He went along with the capital levy to the extent of imposing a personal one on his own fortune when Financial Secretary to the Treasury in 1919; but as President of the Board of Trade he took his part in decontrolling the coal industry in 1921. Thus as the party approached the 1920s it seems to have been struggling to return to *laissez-faire* rather than move away from it, apart that is from its tariff policy which the war helped to strengthen. But beyond this the experience of 1914–18 appears to have produced a negative reaction against interventionism which had profound effects upon government handling of economic problems in the inter-war years; not until the 1930s was Conservative faith in the role of the state partially rekindled.

Labour's Socialist Commitment and the Liberal Inheritance 1914–29

Up to 1914 the relationship between the Labour Party and socialists had been one of mutual suspicion. While trades unionists often resented socialists as middle-class people who were merely milking them of their funds, socialists despaired of the absence of ideological coherence and the prevailing parliamentary 'opportunism' of the party's leaders. The First World War by no means destroyed these objections on either side. However it did provide an institutional means, through the Workers National Committee, for more constructive participation by socialists in the activities of the party than previously. The fact that middle-class socialists like Sidney Webb and R.H. Tawney supported the war facilitated their absorption, especially under the aegis of Henderson who pronounced himself keen to 'enlarge the bounds of the Labour Party and bring in the intellectuals as candidates'.[14] Because wartime collectivism produced a proliferation of committees requiring labour representation and joint boards of managers and workers such as the Whitley Councils, it seemed to the Webbs the ideal opportunity for the transmission of their ideas to the machinery of the state. In the long run the close involvement of Fabians in the party meant that when, a generation later, socialist programmes of nationalization became practical politics it was the Webbian brand of socialism that was adopted. However in the short and medium term the process of wartime collectivism alarmed socialists like Cole and Tawney who considered that it merely bolstered capitalism by making profits secure and by tightening the relations between business, civil servants and government. This pre-empted genuine socialism in the sense of greater control by workers in industry; and as a result many socialists were by 1918 more anxious to dismantle the controls of an autocratic state than to extend them.

On the face of it the Labour Party constitution of 1918 marked a major shift to a coherent left-wing position, including as it did the commitment in Clause IV to 'secure for the producers by hand or by brain the full fruits of their industry, and the most equitable distribution thereof that may be possible upon the basis of the common ownership of the means of production'. Yet this view has been strongly refuted by a number of historians in view of the party's record in the inter-war period; some argue that ideas are far less important than class and organization, others that statements of principle like Clause IV should not be taken literally.

The significance or insignificance of the socialist commitment becomes clearer if it is seen in the context of the other changes in the structure of the party centrally and locally at this time. Almost from the start of the war a distinct right-wing and patriotic reaction directed particularly against the ILP had manifested itself within the movement. By 1916 a group of union leaders under Havelock Wilson of the seamen were attempting to launch a strictly trade union Labour Party. In January 1917 these elements narrowly succeeded in persuading the party conference to modify the procedure for electing the National Executive Committee; whereas under the original constitution the unions and the socialist societies had chosen their own representatives separately, the new proposal was for selection by conference as a whole, thereby throwing the choice effectively to the big unions. This move was followed later in the year by Henderson's plans to harness middle- and working-class supporters to the party by means of a framework of constituency parties and ward branches based on individual membership (again a departure from the original federal pattern of 1900 involving predominantly indirect membership of the party through affiliated bodies). These innovations won the support of the TUC Parliamentary Committee in September 1917 as a realistic response to the expansion of the franchise. Now this reform of membership and constituency bodies also commended itself to socialists in some ways; individual membership was likely to draw in many middle-class recruits, and the 500 candidates envisaged by Henderson both implied a complete break with the Liberals and presented excellent opportunities for middle-class candidatures. In practice, however, the structural reforms did not always have this effect. In so far as the Labour Party created individual membership and proper constituency parties it deprived the ILP of the special role it had hitherto fulfilled in the movement. From 1909 to 1918 the ILP lost membership and suffered a breakaway to the British Socialist Party founded in 1911. Although the ILP picked up some new middle-class members after 1918 it was a much enfeebled body (in 1918 only three of the Labour MPs were nominated by the ILP whereas its members had dominated the 1906—14 party). But the clearest sign of the ILP's slackening hold had come in the conference decision in January 1918 to abolish the right of socialist societies to elect their own representatives to the party executive; instead the NEC was to comprise 11 trade union, 5 constituency party, and 4 women's section representatives all chosen by the entire conference.

In view of this tendency for power to shift to the right wing, one is bound to question the importance conventionally attached to the adoption of a socialist line in foreign policy statements and in Clause IV of the constitution. Clearly most unions regarded the constitution with some suspicion, and it took someone of Henderson's reputation to reassure them that they were not committing themselves to a radically new departure in policy. Since Clause IV was not translated into a precise or comprehensive socialist economic programme they were no doubt justified in thinking of it as, in substance, no more than the 'collectivism' of social reform and the 'socialism' implied in the nationalization of mines and railways which had been approved before the war; it did not imply centralized economic planning and particularly not of labour itself, which must, they thought, remain free to bargain. Party policy, as expressed in 26 resolutions of conference in 1918 and as put to the country in December, emphasized the development of social welfare, minimum standards of health, housing and education, extension of the unemployment insurance scheme to occupations presently omitted, consumer protection and attacks on profiteering, resumption of free trade generally and trade with Russia in particular, the restoration of civil liberties and complete industrial freedom, graduated taxation and a levy on war profits to pay off the national debt, Irish Home Rule and a just peace settlement. Apart from these traditionally radical policy pronouncements, the unions were reassured in their control of the party by a further concession proposed by the miners, textile and dock workers after the conference debate in January 1918: this raised the union representation on the NEC from 11 to 13. Thus on everything that mattered — policy, organization and electoral machinery — the unions saw no threat, and could afford to regard with some indulgence vague statements of ideology embodied in the constitution.

On the other hand, if the socialist commitment cannot be taken literally, it should not be regarded as being devoid of meaning. For it was at least an emphatic way of underlining the permanence of the party's break with Lloyd George in 1917, and its intention to become a truly independent party with a simple yardstick to distinguish it from Liberalism. It has been credibly suggested that the function of Clause IV was to provide the kind of political myth that most political movements cherish and around which they may rally. 'Socialism' both showed the party faithful where they stood in relation to previous historical development, and generated a necessary sense of inevitable progress towards a better state of things. Certainly MacDonald, by articulating this theme, endowed Labour with a formidable optimism and sense of purpose during the 1920s. Like 'Empire' for late nineteenth-century Conservatives, 'Socialism' was for Labour a symbol sufficiently vague to be impervious to mere day-to-day policies and events.

This idea of 1918 as a symbolic change rather than one of substance for Labour is certainly consistent with the empirical evidence that we have about the many recruits won by the party after the war. We have already noted the tendency for local Liberal activists to defect to Labour in 1918 and for Labour to champion social reform in local council chambers in 1917–18; an equally pronounced infusion of first- and second-rank politicians (particularly from Liberal but also to a lesser extent from Conservative backgrounds) took place between 1918 and 1929. Often people of middle- and upper-class status who were accused of betraying their class, these men and women palpably transformed Labour into the kind of national representative party that MacDonald had long envisaged.

In considering their impact intellectually upon the party one must bear in mind that the chief stimulus causing them to sever relations with their old party was the war, either its origins or its consequences. MPs such as E. T. John, H. B. Lees-Smith, Josiah Wedgwood, R.L. Outhwaite, Joseph Martin, Arthur Ponsonby and Charles Trevelyan had severed relations due to disagreement with their constituency parties before the coupon election, which they fought largely as independents or ILP members before joining the

Labour Party. Others waited to be defeated as Liberals before switching allegiance, notably Percy Alden, Sydney Arnold, Noel Buxton, Willoughby Dickinson, Edward Hemmerde, Joseph King, L.C. Money, J.D. White and R.C. Lambert. In general they rebelled against what they saw as a mandarin elite at the Foreign Office, which under Grey had foisted the war upon Britain, and also against the uses to which victory was being put, notably repression in Ireland and India, resistance to the new revolutionary regimes in Europe, exploitation of Germany for the benefit of a few capitalists and the defeat of trade unions at home. The disclosure by the Bolsheviks of the secret treaties demonstrated, in their view, how little British policy had been based on respect for self-determination and how much on cynical manipulation of territory in the interest of power politics.[15] Trevelyan, one of the most articulate, justified his transition to Labour by drawing a comparison with the moral leadership of Liberalism by Cobden and Bright after the Crimean War, which was taken over later by Gladstone; like most of the recruits Trevelyan plainly saw Labour continuing this tradition in foreign affairs.

Through their participation in Labour's Advisory Committee on International Questions Liberal and pacifist recruits rapidly made foreign and defence matters salient within the party. Their role in MacDonald's two governments was also significant. In 1924 they included Trevelyan (Education), Haldane (Lord Chancellor), Josiah Wedgwood (Chancellor of the Duchy of Lancaster), Noel Buxton (Agriculture), Ponsonby (Under-Secretary for Foreign Affairs) and Sir Patrick Hastings (Attorney-General). In 1929 Trevelyan again served at Education with, Addison (Agriculture), Wedgwood Benn (Secretary of State for India), Arnold (Paymaster-General), William Jowett (Attorney-General), Lees-Smith (Post-master-General), and Ponsonby in two successive under-secretary-ships and the Duchy of Lancaster.

Since all these apart from Addison, Haldane and Wedgwood Benn seem to have been prompted to change allegiance primarily by foreign affairs, one must consider how far the recruits were in tune with Labour on social and economic matters; did they inhibit or strengthen the demand for a left-wing economic policy? In many respects they plainly reinforced the existing tendencies of their new party, particularly Labour's predilection for free trade. They argued for the morally beneficial effect of free trade on international relations, and sought the reopening of commercial relations with Russia. They also believed that competition, which had been one means of checking the power of capitalists, had been curtailed by wartime protectionism and cartels; many ex-Liberals preferred state control to protectionism for private industry. Their conviction that Labour was a better champion of the free trade cause on which the Liberal leaders had reneged was confirmed by Snowden's 1924 budget which removed the McKenna duties. Other ideas received a strong boost from the recruits. The capital levy owed its conception to Sydney Arnold among others, and was regarded by J.A. Hobson as an important factor in his switch of loyalties. With the WNC's support for the 'conscription of wealth' Labour seemed the party most likely to adopt the levy. Though party conferences did indeed approve it, MacDonald and Henderson made it clear well before 1924 that they would not attempt to put such an 'extremist' policy into operation. A similar cause was land taxation which brought a vocal band of ex-radicals including Wedgwood, Trevelyan, Hemmerde, Outhwaite and White into the party, arguing that Lloyd George had betrayed them and that Asquith was useless. Although in 1925 conference endorsed their views and although there was strong support in the party for nationalization of the land, there was little chance of the 1929 government taking up either policy.

If there is any doubt about the heterogeneity of Labour's social and economic ideas in the 1920s Josiah Wedgwood provides further confirmation. A thoroughly old-fashioned radical–individualist moved by concern for Indian, Irish or aliens' oppression, he abhorred state interference: 'By Socialism, I suppose you mean Social Reform and inspecting babies' hair. By Socialism I mean a land (or a time) when we shall not need policemen.'[16] Wedgwood's immense popularity in the Labour Party — he was made vice-chairman of the parliamentary party — is a testimony to the strength of Gladstonianism there.

However, a number of men can be said to have seen in social questions a positive reason for joining Labour: for example, Leo Chiozza Money, the Liberal–Fabian, who, having served as an under-secretary in the Coalition, resigned in disgust at the rush to decontrol industry. Others such as Lord Haldane and Percy Alden were also appreciative of collectivism on Fabian lines; Haldane's enthusiasm for administration by a trained elite made him a willing nationalizer of the coal industry. In some ways the most central figure in Liberal–Labour politics proved to be Christopher Addison. When he broke with the Liberals in 1923 he identified in justification three areas where Labour's claims were superior: social reform (particularly housing and education), free trade, and disarmament.[17]   What   Addison   termed   'Practical Socialism' involved state intervention to raise standards where private enterprise was inadequate. In housing Labour adopted his policy of subsidizing council house building from national taxation. In agriculture he effectively wrote Labour's programme in the 1920s to reflect his desire for a system of agricultural marketing boards that would eliminate middlemen and offer guaranteed prices to producers. In support of this policy Addison attempted, though without success, to persaude the 1929—31 Labour Cabinet to abandon free trade in favour of import quotas on food imposed by the boards.[18] If a recruit like Addison was more accurately a collectivist than a socialist, nonetheless his Agricultural Marketing Act demonstrated a better grasp of the legislative route to socialism than any minister except Herbert Morrison. Though not likely to push the party much beyond the limited nationalization already contemplated, Addison and the other recruits strongly reinforced the predilection for socialistic progress through social welfare which typified mainstream Labour opinion. In this he personified the continuity between New Liberalism and Labour. 'All social reformers,' as Trevelyan put it, 'are bound to gravitate, as I have done, to Labour.'[19]

One of the few who considered economic as distinct from social questions was William Wedgwood Benn, who, when he joined in 1927 declared that he had for some time questioned 'the theory of private enterprise and free competition';[20] as competitive industry failed to revive in the 1920s and relapsed into combinations of capital, he increasingly saw workers' control as an alternative form of industrial organization; he saw this as a natural development from the municipal socialism of the late nineteenth century. Even among those like Trevelyan and Wedgwood Benn who were attracted by ideas there is no sense of dramatic conversion or any indication that the change of party implied a new position on economic and social policy. When Trevelyan referred to the 'minimum socialist programme' in the 1920s he included a package of the 'living wage', public works especially housing, nationalization of mines and railways, a levy on land values, a capital levy and free trade. In so far as there was an underlying theme it was the Hobsonian one of increasing the power of consumption of the mass of the people.

Thus Labour's transition from minor to major party status between the First World War and the 1920s provides a singular example of the continuity that underlies political change. For the Liberals did not collapse during the 1920s because of their addiction to discredited doctrines of free trade, social reform,

Irish Home Rule, Gladstonian views on armaments and international morality, civil liberties and self-determination in India; on the contrary they collapsed because Labour now enjoyed a stronger claim as champion of all these Liberal traditions than did the Liberal Party. Transition to Labour involved a reaffirmation of one's political principles rather than a surrender or infringement of them. Ultimately the war entailed not an intellectual or programmatic outflanking of one party by the other so much as the inheritance by Labour of the broad ground of pre-1914 Progressivism.

Part Four 1918–1939

Chapter 11

The Elevation of Labour and the Restoration of Party Politics 1918-1924

The Labour Government's main weakness is vanity;
they are all . . . delighted with the good impression
they are making on the middle class.
Diary of William Wedgwood Benn, 19 March 1924

Fragmentation of the Coalition

In view of the critical state of the war in 1916 the establishment
of Lloyd George's Coalition was not surprising; what is more
remarkable is that it survived until 1922. As hostilities drew to a
close Lloyd George seemed unshakeably ensconced in the premiership, an impression later reinforced by his pre-eminent role in the
peace settlement and the subsequent international conferences.
However, domestic affairs, where he relied upon his agents (first
Bonar Law and then Austen Chamberlain), proved to be his un-
doing. After four years of peace the Prime Minister embodied the
irregular, interfering spirit of wartime too well to be widely
acceptable, and in the absence of any permanent institutional
supports he proved vulnerable to the reassertion of party feeling.
Lloyd George fitfully perceived the unlikelihood of the Conservatives settling down permanently as his supporters, or, had he
wanted such a thing, of their making him their leader, which left
the alternative of launching a new centre or national party.
Rearranging the political kaleidoscope to produce new combinations was a favourite pastime for politicians in the immediate post-
war years because so many of them enjoyed a tenuous attachment
to party. Lloyd George might therefore reasonably have hoped to

draw from the Conservatives the ex-Liberal Unionist Chamberlain, those like Milner, Balfour, Birkenhead or Worthington-Evans who were apt to disparage the party and who relished the conditions of coalition government, and the ambitious and opportunistic like Curzon who would enrol with the dispenser of patronage. From the Labour ranks J.H. Thomas and J.R. Clynes were optimistically believed likely to join Lloyd George, while the Coalition Liberals furnished him with administrative talent if little political inspiration. However, in normal times such a collection could not cohere, as the government of coalitionists, businessmen and experts had done during the wartime emergency. Politicians need a common basis of sentiment or objective if only because without it they cannot maintain organization and loyalty in the country; this is why it is futile to study modern politicians purely as a group seeking power without reference to their ideology and popular following. In the absence of a coherent programme or philosophy the 'centre party' proved a chimera.

The insufficiency of power alone is demonstrated by the disintegration of Coalition Liberalism after 1918. The essential justification for their participation had been the reconstruction programme. Yet by 1921 reforms in housing, education and agriculture had been curtailed or abandoned for the sake of retrenchment. The Safeguarding of Industries Act of 1921 with its 33½ per cent tariff on certain goods provoked over half the Coalition Liberals to vote against their government or abstain. Even more offensive was the recruitment of the 'Black and Tans' to subdue Sinn Fein, a policy presided over by a Liberal Minister, Sir Hamar Greenwood. The only other Liberal influence lay in Indian policy as directed by Edwin Montagu: he pledged self-government in 1917 and pushed through the Montagu– Chelmsford reforms in 1919, while Conservatives roared their approval of repressive measures like the Amritsar Massacre carried out in India itself. Montagu's reward was bitter vilification which drove him to resignation in 1922. Christopher Addison had been obliged to give up as Health Minister in 1921, which served to underline Lloyd George's unwillingness or inability to stand by his Liberal ministers when they pursued a progressive policy. Thus by 1922 the Coalition Liberals, seeing no future in saving the Prime Minister from his reactionary colleagues, began to resolve their embarrassing dilemma by making overtures to the Asquithians for reunion; although some, such as Winston Churchill and Sir Alfred Mond, shifted towards a formal Conservative allegiance. This imminent disappearance of coalitionism had been heralded by electoral vulnerability. Between 1919 and 1922, when the Asquithians made five by-election gains, the Coalition Liberals lost nine seats, seven of them to Labour, a significant indication that their role as bulwark against the left was played out.

That the Coalition survived, despite this, for four years of peace reflected Conservative appreciation of the Prime Minister's positive achievements. He had been persuaded to take a strong line towards both Sinn Fein and the Bolshevik regime in Russia; by 1921 he had been led to financial retrenchment by pressure of the anti-waste campaigns; most importantly, he had managed to steer a course through the intense industrial militancy of 1919—20 culminating in the collapse of the 'Triple Alliance' of miners, railwaymen and transport workers in March 1921, and to do it by judicious concessions; for example he set up the Sankey Commission on the coal industry but resisted its majority recommendation for nationalization. By 1922 industry had been returned to private control with a measure of tariff protection.

Against this some Conservatives felt that the government merely prevaricated over tariffs and assistance for agriculture. Nor did the National Union feel it had been fairly treated over reform of the House of Lords, a Conservative objective since 1911, and a condition for acceptance of franchise reform in 1917. Despite investigation by the Bryce Committee and a pledge of reform by Bonar Law and Lloyd George in 1918 nothing was done to restore the powers or change the composition of the Upper House. From the start the core of criticism of the Coalition had been the 42 MPs dubbed 'Diehards' who were for the most part typical of the landowning and Ulster elements of the party, not of the business elements as were the coalitionists; and as elderly men unlikely to serve in government they enjoyed secure representation in safe Conservative seats;[1] on both counts therefore, they felt little need of coalition. The Diehards were specially antagonized by Indian reform, the Irish settlement and the reversal of policy towards Russia, all of which smacked of Bolshevik influence in public life.

However, only 58 MPs voted against the Irish Treaty, and Diehard opposition is by no means an adequate explanation of the overthrow of Lloyd George. By the time of the Carlton Club meeting disillusion extended well beyond mere items of legislation. Many backbenchers had never ceased to dislike Lloyd George as much on personal as on political grounds. Once the pressure of national crisis was lifted, their resentment at his irregular methods of government resurfaced. They believed that he undermined both the Foreign Office and the Treasury through his personal secretariat, and that he exploited incidents like the Chanak Crisis of 1922, when Britain almost went to war with Turkey, to perpetuate a presidential style of government. Though the War Cabinet and the non-political ministers had disappeared, he remained associated with unsavoury characters such as Sir William Sutherland and Maundy Gregory through whom honours were lavishly dispensed at inflated prices. Though the Conservative Party also benefited from the sale of honours, in the debates of 1921 critics chose to foist the guilt upon the Lloyd George fund. Thus it was in generalized fears about methods of government and corruption that a determination to sever relations festered; when Stanley Baldwin spoke of the 'morally disintegrating effect of Lloyd George on all whom he had to deal with', he reflected widespread Conservative sentiment.

In addition some Conservatives contemplated the cost of coalitionism in terms of their own careers. Since May 1915 the party had always been denied a share of office proportionate to its numbers. Even during 1919–22, when there were in total 21–2 cabinet ministers, Conservatives occupied only 10–12 of them.[2] This was most irksome for the rising junior figures whose promotion was blocked; it has been estimated that some 40 individuals were deprived of office in this period; notable among them were Lord Selborne and Sir Arthur Steel-Maitland, the former party chairman. Junior ministers outside the Cabinet, including W. C. Bridgeman, R. A. Sanders, Sir P. Lloyd-Greame, Edward Wood and L. S. Amery, also comprised a centre of opposition to the Coalition in 1922.

The New Strategy 1922

By 1922 these fears had been crystallized by the realization that it was no longer politically necessary to subject the Conservative Party to Lloyd George. For the tactical rationale behind coalition-ism consisted in the assumption that the advance of Labour could best be checked by using Lloyd George to harness Liberal and new, unattached voters to Conservatism. Between 1919 and 1922 this assumption broke down decisively in the eyes of most Conservatives. The coupon arrangement of 1918 had left Coalition Liberals defending working-class seats vulnerable to a Labour resurgence which swept Spen Valley and Dartford in 1919, Norfolk South, Heywood and Radcliffe and Southwark S.E. in

1920, and Leicester East and Pontypridd in 1922. Altogether Labour made 13 gains, including five from Conservatives, in these years, clear evidence that they rather than the Asquithians (five gains and one loss) were benefiting from the unpopularity of the Coalition. Hence the growing acceptance that the party must accustom itself to Labour as the permanent opposition party.

For a time right-wing resentment towards the government was harnessed by independent Conservatives fighting on a retrenchment platform led by Horatio Bottomley and Lords Rothermere and Northcliffe. By 1920 candidates of the 'Anti-Waste League' were snatching safe Conservative seats on a policy most Conservatives wished to make their own. Thus, not only was Labour's advance not being blocked, but the very elements that should have resisted were being superseded by breakaway groups. If the party continued to tie itself to Lloyd George, the argument ran, he would reduce it to the divided and demoralized condition in which he had left the Liberals. Such considerations induced weightier figures like Lord Salisbury to initiate the People's Union For Economy which was designed to absorb the retrenchment sentiment and unite working- and middle-class support thus avoiding a sharp polarization along class lines between Labour and the rest.[3] In the short run Salisbury lent respectability to the rebellion, while facilitating a shift in policy towards retrenchment; by the end of 1921 the electoral threat of the Anti-Waste League had been contained by the adoption of their platform by official candidates.

Once the Labour gains had undermined the Prime Minister's credibility as a radical leader the acceptance of him and his policies grew not merely irksome but futile in Conservative eyes. That he could be dispensed with was dramatically underlined by the by-election at Newport in October 1922. Here a Conservative, intervening in a Coalition Liberal seat, emerged top of the poll in a three-cornered contest. Newport thus reinforced those who argued that safety now lay in abandoning Lloyd George in favour of a straightforward appeal by an unencumbered Conservative Party; for if seats like Newport could be won they were well within reach of an independent majority. This emboldened Conservative associations to adopt candidates in Coalition Liberal seats, thereby forcing them to seek a return to the Asquithian fold.

March 1921 proved to be decisive in breaking up the Coalition in that Bonar Law's resignation through ill-health provided the rebels with an alternative Prime Minister 18 months later. Law's successor as party leader, Austen Chamberlain, wholly failed to conciliate the disgruntled Conservatives. Aloof and remote, Chamberlain treated the junior ministers somewhat contemptuously; with his Liberal Unionist origins he never felt as acutely as Law the strain of coalitionism on the party. Out of stubbornness and loyalty Chamberlain declined to give any indication that the premiership would not remain indefinitely in Lloyd George's hands.

Conscious of the danger, the Prime Minister contemplated snatching a quick election early in 1922 so as to enable him to create a new ministry and a new centre party on the strength of a full five-year term of office. However, the hint of this in January drew a sharp reaction from a phalanx of leading figures outside the government – Salisbury, Derby, Selborne and Law – as well as from Baldwin, Curzon and Griffith-Boscawen. But the party chairman, Sir George Younger, took the lead in announcing his refusal to stand as a coalitionist at a general election. However much Lloyd George might declare he would not be bullied by a 'second-rate brewer', he was deterred by Younger's initiative which stimulated local parties to adopt candidates in Coalition Liberal seats thereby confirming Law's and Baldwin's fear of an imminent split in the party caused by Lloyd George. He thus let slip an opportunity to quit his allies on an issue of his choosing, relying instead upon Chamberlain who, after consulting his colleagues about the next general election, consented to summon a meeting of the parliamentary party at the Carlton Club on 19 October.

Of the 286 MPs present at the Carlton Club only 86 voted to maintain the Coalition and 187 against. Analysis has suggested that a majority of the Chamberlainites not only held office but also represented somewhat marginal constituencies vulnerable to a loss of Liberal support.[4] In the absense of these pressures the bulk of the party failed to respond to Chamberlain's offer of an election without coupons but with co-operation. By failing to voice his own reservations about Lloyd George he played into the hands of Baldwin who condemned the Prime Minister as a divisive and demoralizing force. By holding out the prospect of fighting under a separate party programme Chamberlain could have kept the Coalition going for some time, but by adopting a tough response to a moderate motion he alienated himself from the moderate mass of the party who now took confidence in the presence of Bonar Law, clearly available as Conservative Prime Minister. Without him many of the rebels would have shrunk from cutting adrift from Lloyd George for fear of losing office altogether.

The consequences proved to be immense and long-term in nature. Within hours Lloyd George had resigned office, and the next day Law was elected party leader just before forming a new administration. He followed this up with a vital decision — to dissolve Parliament at once, the upshot of which was a comfortable Conservative victory with 344 seats out of 615. By quickly plunging into an election so recently resisted by the party Bonar Law shrewdly caught his opponents unprepared. Lloyd George, barely alive to being out of office for the first time in 16 years, could not quite decide whether to attack the Conservatives for having ejected him, or to attempt to keep open the option of a new coalition with the Chamberlainites who stayed aloof from the new government. Though designated simply as a Liberal he found himself proscribed as an alien by most Asquithians. All seemed suddenly anxious to dissociate themselves from him. By ditching him now that he was an electoral liability the Conservatives avoided the unpopularity they otherwise risked as the governing party; the left, too, was deprived of much of the momentum generated since 1919. Speed, in short, was Law's best weapon in 1922 and he used it to the full.

However, the real significance of the Conservative decisions in 1922 concerned long-term strategy. As in 1918 they sought to contain the emergence of organized labour under the widened franchise, but they adopted a different method. Instead of relying on Lloyd George they now hoped to destroy him along with the Asquithians by squeezing their support between themselves and Labour. By concentrating the debate on Labour and building it into a major force they would shake out enough right-wing and moderate Liberal support to give them a comfortable lead over Labour. The 1922 election demonstrated the feasibility of this strategy.

Baldwin and Normality 1923

No one grasped the new strategy more eagerly or exploited it more deftly than Stanley Baldwin who had emerged from the relative obscurity of the Board of Trade to the Exchequer in October 1922, thence to the premiership on Law's retirement in May 1923. For him practical wisdom in politics consisted, first, in so arranging matters as to exclude Lloyd George from office, and second, in keeping his party calm about the prospect of a Labour administration. He was wholly responsible for the next crucial decision that determined the political pattern of the 1920s, namely the plunge into a general election in November 1923 only a year after the previous contest with a fresh majority still intact. Ostensibly the reason was Baldwin's wish to introduce tariffs designed to reduce unemployment; but he was hampered by the pledge given by Law not to introduce them without the nation's express approval. Since the consequence was to turn the 344 Conservative members into a minority of 258 and to precipitate the first Labour government the whole exercise appeared to many contemporaries an unforced error of grave proportions.

This, however, was a superficial and short-term view. Any notion that the need for protectionism had grown so urgent as to permit no delay may safely be dismissed as an explanation for Baldwin's conduct. He had, if anything, become more lukewarm about tariffs during his term at the Treasury[5] and his willingness to offer the Chancellorship to McKenna in 1923 provides corroboration that it was far from the forefront of his mind. Baldwin's action had less to do with the economic merits of protection than with the political implications of its adoption. For he remained obsessed with the need to complete the restoration of normal party politics initiated by Bonar Law. So long as Chamberlain, Birkenhead, Balfour, Horne, and Worthington-Evans stood outside a Conservative Cabinet the prospect of a revived coalition could not be ruled out. Baldwin also recognized the palpable inferiority of his Cabinet by comparison with the team Lloyd George might still field; with a worsening economic situation and no clear policy he felt reluctant to stumble on while the critics waited confidently for the 'second-eleven' Cabinet, in Churchill's phrase, to collapse in discredit.

By announcing his wish for a mandate on tariffs in a speech at Plymouth on 25 October, Baldwin at once polarized politics. Since the Liberal Party was bound to declare for free trade Lloyd George could not escape an unequivocal stand, nor is there any good evidence that he had intended to opt for protectionism. For Baldwin the advantage consisted in the fact that Lloyd George, in nailing his colours to the free-trade mast, thereby facilitated Liberal reunion and simultaneously isolated himself from the Chamberlainites − permanently as it turned out. This served Baldwin's real purpose of restoring party unity, for regardless of the result of the election it emerged that the former coalitionists would now serve under him in a future Conservative government. But although he consciously placed his majority in jeopardy in 1923 Baldwin did not realize how great was the risk; though the tariff issue appeared suddenly it was hardly a novel proposal, and since the party had carried it through five elections there was no reason to anticipate catastrophic losses; the Conservative majority was expected to be reduced rather than destroyed.

When, on the contrary, a strong reaction in favour of free trade and cheap food produced 107 Conservative losses and only 18 gains the gamble was seen to have failed lamentably. Yet there was no great upsurge in favour of a coalition to check the dreaded advent of Labour to office. Baldwin certainly suffered much criticism for his miscalculations, but very few challenged his underlying strategy. Instead of being deprived of the leadership he was retained as a bulwark against men like Birkenhead who were so unpalatable to the rank and file. Thus Baldwin was able to steady the party while it came to regard Labour's entry into minority government as a safe and temporary experiment between two Conservative ministries. Such conclusions reflected the parliamentary arithmetic of 1923 in that the 258 Conservatives faced 191 Labour and 158 Liberal members. Labour could not govern for long alone; nor could they even take office without a measure of outside support. Therefore instead of resigning promptly after the election Baldwin remained in office to meet the new Parliament in January 1924, as he was fully entitled to do as Prime Minister and leader of the largest party. In this way he focused attention upon Asquith who was obliged to take the deliberate step of voting the Conservatives out of power, thereby earning the responsibility for putting MacDonald in. Had Baldwin quit immediately he would have given the King a measure of choice between MacDonald and Asquith. As matters turned out the arrival of a Labour administration, which squeezed Liberalism more drastically and rapidly than any alternative, served to advance the new strategy to Baldwin's ultimate advantage.

The 1923 election epitomized the failure of the Liberals to seize their opportunities through internal division and the absence of firm and constructive leadership. With Asquith out of Parliament from 1918 to 1920 Lloyd George could have had himself elected leader or chairman, but at that stage there must have seemed little point in attaching himself to the shattered remnants. As early as February 1919 some Liberal MPs, reflecting the feeling of the rank and file, began to hold meetings designed to lead to reunion of 'Wee Frees' and coalitionists. However, the Asquithians, still outraged at the Coupon Election, feared absorption by the more numerous Lloyd George supporters and declined all offers of the government whip. Asquith himself gave no impetus to the move for party unity; 'the old man is stoical to the point of indifference,' as McKenna put it. Unfortunately he displayed little beyond stoicism. After a remarkable by-election triumph in the working-class constituency of Paisley in February 1920 he failed to take any initiative either on policy or on reunion until, in 1926, the leadership of a much-enfeebled party finally slipped from his palsied hand. By 1920 the split within the party had worsened in that every coalitionist Liberal seat was now regarded as a legitimate target for independent Liberal candidates. Although the coalitionists published their own *Lloyd George Liberal Magazine* and set up their own local organizations, their position was extremely shaky in the country. In 1922 their 150–60 candidates contrasted with the Asquithians' 320; moreover their seats were very vulnerable. Of the 116 Liberals elected in 1922 only 47 were coalitionists and of these only four had won against a Conservative. With the renegades thus humbled Asquith should have shown magnanimity for the sake of the party and worked for reunion before it was too late. Instead he did nothing to check the factionalism of Lord Gladstone, Simon, Runciman, and others who professed to regard Lloyd George as an incubus upon the party. Their antagonism was only sharpened by the realization that they desperately needed subsidies from his political fund. In the surge of enthusiasm over free trade in 1923 Lloyd George did dispense £160,000 to the party, but thereafter he held on to his money as his one major bargaining weapon; rather than pour it out to help an organization under Asquithian control he chose to wait for his older rival's inevitable retirement. Having lost his seat at Paisley in 1924 Asquith carried on from within the House of Lords for no other purpose than to prevent the party succumbing to Lloyd George. He thus largely prevented the rejuvenation of Liberalism until after 1926, by which time too many radicals had been lost to Labour to permit even Lloyd George to restore the party's old strength.

Factionalism caused the Liberals to let slip their big opportunity in 1923 when all the leaders, except Churchill, apparently agreed on giving MacDonald his chance to become Prime Minister. Disintegrating tendencies were inherent in the situation, for in the country Conservatively inclined Liberals would inevitably blame the leaders for putting a Labour government in office, while left-wing Liberals would equally have resented any attempt to maintain Baldwin in power. Lloyd George's remark that 'if Ramsay were tactful and conciliatory I feel certain that the Party as a whole would support him in an advanced Radical programme'[6] looks particularly naive in view of the fact that MacDonald was very prickly towards the Liberals, had no such radical programme, and was not offered detailed terms in return for Liberal support. But it was characteristic of Lloyd George to think of constructive programmes while remaining blind to the effect of his proposal upon his party. As a party the Liberals' only viable strategy in 1923 lay in declining at once to vote for a MacDonald administration, thus obliging the King to summon Asquith rather than risk a third general election. Many Conservatives would have voted to keep Asquith in office for a short period as an acceptable alternative to Labour until they had regrouped. It would have been a risky course, but infinitely less hazardous and destructive for the party than the inept choice actually made. This was the last chance to restore Liberalism as an independent governing party, and it is still puzzling that such shrewd politicians missed it. The best explanation lies in their personality and recent history. Lloyd George, so recently ousted from the premiership, would not go out of his way to return too quickly, especially to his pre-1916 role as junior to Asquith; and Asquith had had too much experience of the Welshman's machinations to want to preside again over a ministry that included his rival.

The MacDonald–Baldwin Axis 1924

In the immediate aftermath of 1918 the Labour Party seemed unsure how to reap the benefit of its newly won position. In the eyes of MacDonald, temporarily in the wilderness, those who had survived the electoral holocaust were an uninspired set of trade union leaders who had not yet grown out of their subordinate relationship with Lloyd George; the party, he said, 'must forget the purple bondage and the flesh pots of Egypt which were its reward for the sorry part it played in the war'.[7] Though moved by bitterness MacDonald had a point; under William Adamson the parliamentary party conducted itself less like an opposition – and government-in-waiting – than as a pressure group seeking minor concessions from the rulers. As a result the parliamentary party tended to lose control in the movement between 1919 and 1922.

Yet these were vital formative years in several ways. As the reaction against the war and traditional diplomacy began to gather strength the Labour MPs were seen to have failed to offer serious opposition to the Treaty of Versailles. To the socialist and pacifist critics stolid trade unionists had nothing to offer on great moral issues; yet MacDonald both understood and could articulate their views. In addition this period saw a continuation of the dramatic wartime expansion of the industrial side of the movement and an outburst of militancy which reached a peak in 1921. Moreover, the success of many strikes tended to raise the prestige of the industrial as compared to the parliamentary movement. The alternative to the parliamentary strategy was cast not in terms of syndicalism but of 'direct action' which won the approval of party conference in 1919 and took practical shape in the Triple Alliance of miners, railwaymen and transport workers. 'Direct action' claimed its greatest success in May 1920 when the dockers refused to load the *Jolly George* with arms for use in Poland against the Bolshevik cause. The government's retreat gave some grounds for the belief that they had compelled it to abandon its interventionist policy. In fact there was nothing revolutionary in the objectives of the union leaders; direct action was no more than a means to limited, material objectives. In April 1921 when two elements in the Triple Alliance withdrew to leave the miners to strike alone, direct action crumbled and thereafter the parliamentary leaders regained the initiative. Although MacDonald had been highly apprehensive about direct methods in 1920 he kept on the right side by saying that the country had been saved from another war – a widely acceptable view of this episode.

Many politicians defeated in 1918 assuaged their pain with the thought that this was a good parliament to be out of; for Ramsay MacDonald this was not untrue. His exclusion left him free to articulate the sentiments of Labour activists in the country and served to emphasize his patent superiority as a parliamentarian to those presently encamped uneasily on the opposition front bench. Indeed his attraction as leader during the 1920s was strikingly similar to Gladstone's for the Liberals in the 1870s; outstanding in the Commons he appealed outside as leader of moral righteousness; because of the ambiguity of his politics the various elements within the party could look to him as their own spokesman. Thus MacDonald furnished a unifying force able to harness to the Labour cause the socialists of the ILP, the prickly idealistic ex-Liberals and the dour, respectable unionists. The later repudiation of MacDonald fostered the view that for the Labour Party an individual leader was less important than the ideology or class unity of the movement. Yet the party clove to MacDonald as a substitute for a clear philosophy; moreover, as a working-class party it exhibited remarkable fondness for its leaders, especially those drawn from the higher social classes, as the election of the radical baronets Sir Charles Trevelyan and Sir Oswald Mosley to the National Executive Committee suggests; conference always felt immensely flattered at the presence of such recruits.

Of course MacDonald's re-establishment in the leadership did not occur suddenly. Initially he seemed an electoral liability and his narrow defeat in a by-election in the Labour seat at Woolwich in February 1921 was cited as proof that his war record remained a bar. However, after Woolwich there appeared little mileage in scurrilous attacks on his patriotism, and in 1922 he was returned comfortably to the Commons for the South Wales mining seat of Aberavon. Further, MacDonald enjoyed a great advantage over his rival J.R.Clynes, whom he defeated 61 to 65 for the leadership after the election; he had a clear idea of the strategy appropriate for the party. Although Labour led the Liberals in Parliament by 142 to 116 their popular support was equal and there could be no certainty in 1922 that the Liberals would not succeed in making Labour again the third force in a two-party system. The new leader had no doubt of the urgency of keeping Labour's claims upon radicalism to the fore, and taking advantage of the factionalism in the Liberal camp. Hence his refusal, unlike Clynes, to be conciliatory over occupation of the opposition front bench which he declined to share with the Liberals. This was symptomatic of his intention to polarize politics around a Conservative–Labour struggle; an objective wholly shared by Baldwin and substantially realized during 1923–24.

In this task MacDonald derived an early advantage from the prominence of foreign affairs in 1922 and 1923. The crisis over the French occupation of the Ruhr and the incubus of reparations tended to vindicate left-wing criticism of Versailles and strengthen MacDonald's authority. In addition the Labour leader was a keener student of foreign affairs than either of the Conservative Prime Ministers and could handle them on relatively equal terms. In particular Baldwin's government, worthy but mediocre, served to undermine any notion that Labour was not in the same league.

When the election of 1923 made Labour, with 191 MPs, the second largest party MacDonald, though surprised at the sudden turn of events, grasped his historic opportunity without hesitation. He appreciated that if Labour failed to produce a ministry at this point the Liberals would probably do so, thereby forcing Labour off the opposition front bench in favour of the retiring Conservatives. He therefore proceeded to form his administration as though he enjoyed a majority and a full term of office ahead of him. Since he could at any moment be voted out by the Conservatives if the Liberals merely abstained, the logic of the parliamentary arithmetic called for formal co-operation with Asquith. Yet the latter asked for no agreement, while MacDonald for his part resolutely avoided any understanding. This was in part a reflection of personal vanity and sensitivity; he had no governmental experience and thought his opponents were waiting for him to make a fool of himself. However, it was also deliberate policy to kill the client relationship with the Liberals; any deal with Asquith would have antagonized the left, and it was actually advantageous to preserve his minority position as an excuse for the absence of socialist legislation. This was indeed necessary since MacDonald had no idea of a socialist programme and intended simply to demonstrate a capacity to run the administration quietly, so as to explode the myth that Labour was either 'unfit to govern' or dangerously radical.

Agreement with the Liberals would have tied MacDonald to office for much longer than he really wished to hold it. He certainly had no desire to invite immediate defeat, as some ILP members urged, by offering Parliament a full socialist programme; that would only have proved the critics right about Labour. It would also, in view of the King's reluctance to grant a third general election, have deprived MacDonald of a dissolution and led to a Liberal government. However he wished, after governing respectably for a short time, to find a way out before basic economic and social questions had to be faced. In this sense MacDonald was always seeking a defeat, but not too soon; he managed to achieve this with the tacit co-operation of Stanley Baldwin.

In pursuit of respectability and reassurance the new Premier strengthened his Cabinet with experienced figures from Liberal backgrounds — Haldane as Lord Chancellor, C.P. Trevelyan at Education, Noel Buxton at Agriculture, Josiah Wedgwood as Chancellor of the Duchy of Lancaster — and from the Conservative ranks — Lord Parmoor as Lord President of the Council and Lord Chelmsford at the Admiralty. The rest of the posts were filled by known moderates apart from Health and Works which went to two socialists, John Wheatley and F.W. Jowett. In so far as the Prime Minister faced pressure over posts it took a personal rather than a political form. Somewhat sobered by the magnitude of events the party felt reluctant to insist upon the claims of any particular groups or individuals. The overriding objective was to

RAMSAY THE UNRUDDY.

Sir Despard Murgatroyd—Mr. MacDONALD   *Mad Margaret—SOCIALISM.*

D. M.   "I ONCE WAS A VERY ABANDONED PERSON—"
M. M.   "MAKING THE MOST OF EVIL CHANCES."
D. M.   "NOBODY COULD CONCEIVE A WORSE 'UN . . . ." [*Dance.*
M. M.   "THAT IS ONE OF OUR BLAMELESS DANCES." —*Ruddigore*, Act II.

From Punch, *20 February 1924.*

launch the government, and the more it conformed to prevailing
notions of a proper administration the better the party liked it.
MacDonald's rigid insistence on the wearing of court dress by his
ministers and the eagerness of the new ministers' wives to be
coached by Beatrice Webb in the behaviour appropriate to their
role, were trivial but telling symptoms of the desire to win acceptance.

Matters of policy also reinforced the strategy. As his own Foreign Secretary MacDonald succeeded in improving relations with France as a necessary prelude to French withdrawal from the Ruhr and a reduction of reparations under the Dawes Plan. No one could fault this any more than they could attack Snowden's cautious free-trade budget or Wheatley's Housing Act based on Addison's earlier measure. The flaw lay in the absence of ideas on unemployment; Snowden granted a placatory £28 million for public relief works in July while MacDonald endeavoured to restore trade with Russia by granting recognition to the new regime.

For the most part the Conservatives remained content to grumble at Baldwin for his part in causing the advent of Labour to office, but were deprived of any sense of trauma. By avoiding anything controversial MacDonald facilitated the Conservative leader's desire to allow the new government a short period of office. As Neville Chamberlain observed, 'it would be too weak to do much harm, but not too weak to get discredited'.[8] Consequently there was no effort to turn Labour out, a fact obscured by Baldwin who launched himself on a series of speeches in the country during the summer of 1924 thereby conveying to his supporters a gratifying impression of a great ideological battle which bore little relation to the actual situation in Parliament. In fact Baldwin both liked and trusted the Prime Minister; he approved the continuity in foreign policy and continued to receive a selection of Foreign Office papers during the year.[9] In the Commons, of course, the 191 ministerialists theoretically stood in dire danger of defeat by the 258 Conservatives; however, government defeats on relatively minor matters helped to maintain the illusion that Baldwin was fulfilling the opposition's job, while on major issues there was sometimes a suspicious closeness between the government's margin and the number of Conservative members absent and unpaired. By keeping MacDonald in until September Baldwin hoped to allow time to reorganize and arouse his supporters in the constituencies; since the spring the party had been under instructions to work on the basis of a November election. Thanks to the common interest of the two leaders polling day was 29 October.

By September the Conservatives were ready to censure the government over the withdrawal by the Attorney-General of a proposed prosecution of a Communist editor, J. R. Campbell, under the Incitement to Mutiny Act; meanwhile the Liberals, patience exhausted at MacDonald's refusal to co-operate, put down a motion criticizing the Russian Treaty negotiated by MacDonald. His reaction was a mixture of delight and relief:

I am inclined to give the Liberals an election on it if they force it. I have no intention of deserting a post of difficulty but the conditions of office perhaps bribe me to take this chance of ending the present regime.[10]

As a private note in his diary this shows MacDonald's eagerness for speedy release. He particularly welcomed an attack upon the Russian Treaty because it lent a general political significance to the challenge and therefore justified a dissolution. Baldwin took a similar view; it was better to secure their defeat on the Treaty than over the Campbell case.[11] So determined was MacDonald not to let slip the opportunity for his government's defeat that when the Liberals put an amendment to the Conservative motion asking merely for a select committee of enquiry, he insisted on treating it as a resignation issue. This was quite unnecessary, and he knew that Asquith wanted to find a way out of the confrontation; nonetheless MacDonald secured his own defeat by 198 to 364 votes!

Yet there were entirely sound reasons for taking this course. After nine months his own supporters had grown increasingly unhappy both about rising unemployment and about the government's willingness to declare a state of emergency and use troops in the dock strike and in a London Underground strike. MacDonald could not go on much longer with so little of substance to show; nine months was sufficient to prove Labour's competence to the undecided voter. By surrendering office at this stage he lent plausibility to the view that lack of a majority had prevented him from tackling basic economic questions; that he perished defending left-wing causes like the Russian Treaty and the Campbell case also served to deflect criticism within the movement. The impression of reactionary forces ganging up to eject Labour was greatly reinforced by the so-called Zinoviev Letter during the election campaign. This document purported to be an incitement to class war in Britain from the President of the Communist International in Moscow. A gift to Conservative propaganda, released on the weekend before polling day for maximum effect, the Zinoviev Letter probably made no more than a marginal contribution to the Conservative victory; its importance lay rather in strengthening Labour's own impression that it had been deprived of office by capitalist conspiracies, and thereby helped to divert attention from the ideological shortcomings of the government itself.

It may be objected that no Prime Minister risks an early general election, let alone courts one, if he cannot be confident of winning it; yet that was not really an option for MacDonald since a Conservative victory fairly soon was inevitable. By-elections during 1924 reassured MacDonald that his own support would not collapse; Labour held Burnley and gained West Toxteth (Liverpool). More significant was the Liberal loss at Oxford to a Conservative through Labour intervention and the attrition of the Liberal vote at Glasgow Kelvingrove from 18.1 per cent to 4.9 per cent to Conservative advantage. Such results confirmed the shakiness of the swollen Liberal poll of 1923, and the prospect that Conservatives would recover many seats narrowly lost to the Liberals in that year. That the Conservatives were bound to be the major beneficiaries in the short run mattered little to MacDonald. For his main concern was the relative strength of Labour and Liberalism; while his party dropped from 192 to 151 seats in 1924, the Liberals' 158 shrank to 42; Labour candidates rose to 512 while the Liberals fielded only 340; consequently their respective share of the poll stood at 33 per cent and 17.6 per cent. In this way the 1924 election completed the joint objectives of Baldwin and MacDonald by squeezing out the Liberal Party and raising Labour to the status of government-in-waiting on a permanent basis. The return to two-party politics after the confusion of wartime was almost complete.

Chapter 12

Origins of the Conservative Electoral Hegemony 1918–1931

It is not surprising that the desire to put an end to this plague of annual elections should be uppermost in the minds of many voters.

The Nation, *1924*

Although the most striking feature of the 1920s was the sustained surge in popular support for the Labour Party, this should not obscure the Conservative preponderance which so characterized the period. Indeed, during 1918–39 the Conservatives formed or predominated in governments after five of the seven general elections, and were consistently the largest party except during the 1929–31 Parliament. How was this hegemony established and maintained at a time when the terms of the electoral battle had changed drastically and in ways that might have been expected to present the advantage to a rival party claiming to stand for the working-class majority? In this chapter we shall attempt to isolate the chief elements both in Conservative success and in Labour's growth which proceeded apparently unchecked until 1931.

The Impact of the Electoral System

It would be erroneous to assume that the Conservative parliamentary majorities of 1918–39 reflected their transformation into a natural majority in the country. A glance at the voting figures shown in table 12.1 indicates that the victories of the 1920s were attained on a fairly narrow basis, usually a bare two-fifths of the poll. It can be argued that Conservative strength is in fact underestimated by the figures because of the number of strongly Conservative seats not contested by the other parties and therefore

TABLE 12.1.

	Conservative		Liberal		Labour	
	% Vote	Seats	% Vote	Seats	% Vote	Seats
1922	38.2	345	29.1	116	29.5	142
1923	38.1	258	29.6	159	30.5	191
1924	48.3	419	17.6	40	33.0	151
1929	38.2	260	23.4	59	37.1	288

omitted. It is true that Conservatives enjoyed a disproportionate share of unopposed returns, largely in Northern Ireland and southeastern county divisions. However, the numbers were not large and were diminishing (see table 12.2). In fact the net loss of Conservative votes arising from this source is insufficient to make more

TABLE 12.1. *Unopposed returns*

	Conservative	Liberal	Labour
1922	42	10	4
1923	35	11	3
1924	16	6	9
1929	4	–	–

than a marginal impression on their share of the poll even in 1922.[1] In that year only 483 Conservatives stood and a portion of the party's support must have gone to National or ex-Coalition Liberals. But their share is also inflated by the smaller number of candidates fielded by the Liberals whose absence in 1924, for example, from 275 of the 615 constituencies, served to boost the Conservative share. One may generalize by saying that the Conservative– Liberal–Labour share changed from 4–3–3 in the early 1920s to 4–2–4 by the end of the decade.

That such a division generated comfortable Conservative majorities may be ascribed in the first instance to party relationships and the electoral system. Single-member systems invariably produce highly unrepresentative results in which slight shifts in votes lead to exaggerated changes in representation; but the effect is notoriously erratic when three, rather than two, evenly balanced parties are in competition. Whereas before 1914 the Lib–Lab pact had resulted in straight fights in five seats out of six, during the 1920s three-cornered contests became usual. Consequently the division of the 'Progressive' vote between Labour and Liberal gave the Conservatives a major advantage. This was dramatically demonstrated in 1922 when the comfortable Conservative majority of 345 (out of 615) was based on a percentage poll five points *below* that obtained in the disaster of 1906 which had yielded 157 seats (out of 670)! By contrast the Liberal and Labour parties managed 58.6 per cent in 1922 compared with 54.9 per cent in 1906, yet returned only 258 members instead of 430. In 1922 they divided the vote virtually evenly between themselves, though the seats fell out to Labour's advantage because the greater concentration of its vote in certain industrial counties and conurbations brought its candidates more frequently to the head of the poll. The erratic operation of the electoral system left a major impact on politics during the successive general elections of 1922, 1923 and 1924. Labour came to power with only 191 seats following the 1923 election when a modest loss of Conservative votes precipitated a net loss of 87 seats largely to Liberal candidates in constituencies where Labour did not stand. The bizarre logic was reversed the following year in that Labour's increased strength facilitated Baldwin's return to power; for the rise in Labour candidatures from 422 to 512 occurred largely in seats won by Liberals in 1923 thereby producing many of the 107 Conservative gains from Liberals. Labour itself won substantially fewer constituencies in 1924 despite an increased share of the poll.

The long-term effect of the electoral system emerges from a comparison between the 1922 and 1929 elections. Although the Conservative vote was similar in each case they won 85 seats fewer in the latter year. The reason for this lay in a realignment of the non-Conservative vote during the decade. For whereas in 1922 Labour and the Liberals took 29 per cent each, by 1929 they stood at 37 per cent and 23 per cent; despite their party's 'revival' during 1926–29 many erstwhile Liberals regarded Labour as the more probable or desirable winner against the Conservatives. The disproportion in seats − 288 to 59 − was far greater than previously.

Why did the non-Conservative politicians not attempt to deprive the Conservatives of their built-in advantage either by means of proportional representation using multi-member seats or by using the alternative vote in single-member seats? Before 1914 the Liberal Party, though tempted by the alternative vote, had neglected such innovations so long as the pact held. All parties tended to interpret Edwardian elections as meaning that the bulk of Liberal and Labour voters would use their second preferences to mutual advantage. Therefore when PR and the alternative vote were debated under the Representation of the People Bill in 1917–18 most Labour and Liberal MPs favoured the alternative vote while the Conservatives resisted both schemes. Although the radical parties still retained a majority in the Commons at this time, they lacked leadership on this point, and in deference to Conservative objections Lloyd George induced sufficient coalitionist Liberal and Labour members to reject all varieties of reform. Thus they missed their best opportunity to break out of the traditional system. After 1918, since the Conservatives were unyielding, the Liberal Party hoped to obtain reform from the minority Labour governments. At the Speaker's Conference of 1930 the Liberals proposed PR in urban areas and the alternative vote elsewhere, a formula that seemed likely to maximize their advantage; for they would gain Labour second preferences in rural counties while limiting Labour's clean sweep of industrial regions. Unlike many in his party MacDonald had always disliked PR, but in view of the vulnerability of his government he gave consideration to the alternative vote. Now according to the party's chief agent if this had been applied in the 313 constituencies whose MP had been elected on a minority vote in 1929 the representation would have been substantially modified: the Liberal total would have risen from 41 to 88, Labour's from 120 to 135–43, and the Conservatives fallen from 152 to 67–82.[2] Yet for MacDonald this would not have been an unmixed blessing; for the advantages of curtailing the Conservative strength were outweighed by the disadvantages of boosting the Liberals. Moreover the agent's calculations had to be made on the assumption that each party's first preference votes would remain the same. However the likelihood was that the new system would have encouraged wavering radicals to vote Liberal instead of backing Labour in order to keep the Conservatives out, and also relaxed the pressure on 'moderates' to vote Conservative rather than Liberal to stop Labour. Already the Liberals under Lloyd George's inspiration were dangerously near to a breakthrough; their 5 million votes in 1929, against 8 million for each of the other parties, threatened a return to three-party politics. MacDonald's whole strategy in the 1920s consisted in using the logic of the first-past-the-post system to drive the Progressive vote into Labour's camp, as the Liberals had used it before 1914. To allow the Liberals a guaranteed parliamentary base of 100–50 members — the inevitable consequence of electoral reform — would have been to destroy the prospect of a majority Labour government which was now within sight. A bigger Liberal representation would have led to coalition which, especially with Lloyd George's participation, foreshadowed a restoration of the Liberals as the senior partner in government. Thus although MacDonald humoured Lloyd George even to the extent of introducing a bill for electoral reform, he relied upon the Conservative peers to delay and destroy it for him; it was a reasonable assumption that his government would not last long enough to have to fight for the measure. The establishment of a National Government in 1931 killed off any prospect of reform, and also undid the Liberal revival of 1929 by shifting the Liberals into a closer relationship with the right, thereby completing the vacating of the left for occupation by Labour. Conservative predominance between the wars was, thus, for Labour a necessary price to be paid in the medium term for maintaining its own elevation as the major alternative at the expense of the Liberals.

The Conservatives and the Constituencies

The second key element in the Conservatives' success is to be found in the reorganization of the constituencies in 1918 and the Conservative response to it. The previous redistribution back in 1885 had left plenty of anomalies such as seats like Kilkenny with 1,700 voters, and the shifts of population since then had only exacerbated the disparities. By 1918 the average English constituency had twice as many electors as the average Irish seat and somewhat more than those in Wales and Scotland. This over-representation told against the Conservatives, though it was to some extent balanced by Conservative command of many small boroughs in England.

It seems obvious that the growth of population since 1885, especially in suburban areas around London, Birmingham, south Lancashire or Glasgow, would inevitably have produced Conservative gains under any redistribution that moved towards equal constituencies. One historian has estimated that if the 1918 redistribution had operated at the previous general election (December 1910) it would have had the effect of adding 3 to Liberal strength, 5 to Labour and 34 to the Conservatives (see

TABLE 12.3.

	Actual result December 1910	Effect of 1918 boundaries
Conservative	272	306
Liberal/Labour	314	322
Irish	84	79

table 12.3).[3] However, this calculation of a net Conservative gain of 26 should not be seen simply as the effect of equal constituencies. If one sets aside the 6 net gains in Ireland — for Ireland's representation was exempted from the general provisions in 1918 — one has 20 gains in England, Wales and Scotland; this includes four university-seat gains (also exceptions to the population rules), which leaves 16. The key to these in fact lies in the overall increase in the Commons to 707 members rather than to any strict application of the principle of equal constituencies. None of the parties had objected in principle to equalization at the Speaker's Conference in 1916; existing borough and county seats were to retain separate representation only if their population reached 50,000 and new ones were to be formed for every 70,000 and for remainders of 50,000. The redivision of residential constituencies, particularly in London, Middlesex, Surrey, Warwickshire and Lancashire, certainly generated additional Conservative seats. Before 1914 9 of the 13 largest seats had been Conservative, of which 7 were in London (Croydon, Ealing, Enfield, Harrow, Lewisham, Wandsworth and Wimbledon); Wandsworth, for example, became 4 separate seats in 1918 each returning a Conservative. However, much of this was offset by the disappearance of many small Conservative boroughs like Salisbury, Winchester, Windsor, Taunton, Canterbury, Hereford and Bury St Edmunds, which were merged into the surrounding county constituencies. These modifications contained a special significance within the party for they eroded still further the natural parliamentary base of the landed elements while extending that of the commercial and urban sections, a process discernible by 1900 but greatly speeded up in the twentieth century.

In fact the principle of equal constituencies was circumscribed in ways calculated to assist the Conservatives, such as the increase in university representation from 9 to 15,[4] which the party had expected to lose altogether.[5] In addition the rules for constituency size were always interpreted flexibly because of the assumption that parliamentary boundaries should coincide with administrative ones. In 1918 the Boundary Commissioners' room for manoeuvre was significantly widened by a Conservative amendment to the Instructions to the effect that they should avoid creating constituencies of an inconvenient size or character.[6] This could not save sparsely populated (Liberal) counties like Caithness and Sutherland or Radnor and Brecon from amalgamation; but it did allow a number of English agricultural seats to be given the benefit of the doubt where their population was not too far below the limit laid down in the Act. According to private Conservative estimates at least 17 county seats, which on a strict interpretation should have been abolished, were thus preserved.[7] This was possible only at the cost of inflating the membership of the Commons from 670 to 707, something that the House, though very critical, was prepared to tolerate on the assumption that before very long the Irish element was bound to shrink as a consequence of Home Rule. Thus, so far as England, Scotland and Wales are concerned, the 1918 redistribution gave the Conservatives a modest gain, not so much through the application of equalization as by certain judicious modifications of it.

Ultimately, however, their major gain came from Ireland where Conservatives had long been anxious for redistribution, in view of the huge Nationalist preponderance. In fact in 1918 the total of Irish seats was raised by two to 105 with a slight internal rearrangement. But since the 73 Sinn Fein members elected in 1918 refused to attend Westminster the Irish element was for all practical purposes removed at this point. After 1922 the separation of the Irish Republic left Northern Ireland with only 12 Westminster MPs, not more than two of whom were ever other than Unionist. Thus, whereas before 1918 the Conservative Party had normally suffered a handicap of around 65 (that is 84 minus 19) from Ireland, after 1922 they usually enjoyed an advantage of 8 to 12. Herein lay the real gain; the virtual disappearance of the Irish factor from Westminster in itself made it far more difficult for the non-Conservative forces to obtain a majority than previously.

If one turns to consider the regional distribution of Conservative support in the new constituency system one finds considerable continuity of strengths and weaknesses between the wars. A comparison based on the proportion of Conservative seats held in each region in the 1892–1910 period with that in the 1922–35 period points to an enduring pattern in which Wales, Scotland and the four northern counties and Yorkshire continued to be the party's weakest areas, and the counties south of the Wash–Severn line the strongest.[8] What modifications there were are best brought out by comparing the elections of 1900 and 1924 when, for England, Wales and Scotland, the party won 67 per cent of the seats on both occasions. If these victories are broken down into six broad regional groups it is clear that southern England, London and the Midlands remained the strongest and Wales, Scotland and the north the weakest (see table 12.4). By 1924 Conservatives had grown even more reliant upon southern and midland England. Their tightening grip on the south reflected, first, some spread of

TABLE 12.4. *Seats won by Conservatives in 1900 and 1924 (%)*

	London	Southern England	Midlands	Northern England	Scotland	Wales
1900	86.4	79.4	68.2	63.6	51.4	17.6
1924	62.9	90.9	73.6	50.1	50.7	25.7

middle-class residential population beyond London (hence a drop in their share within the capital itself), and second, the Conservatives' ability to take up the slack resulting from Liberal decline in East Anglia and the south-west, both areas in which Labour found it difficult to inherit fully the old radical vote.

Inevitably any regional perspective somewhat exaggerates the fundamental north–south divide; on the other hand if one looks at the spread of Conservatism socially the impression is more one of a nationally based party. On the basis of the occupational categories in the census of 1921 it has been found that 200 constituencies had a middle-class element of 20 per cent or above in their occupied male population.[9] Of these 200 the Conservative Party invariably won 130–80 during the 1918–31 period. While this was a valuable base it was by no means the key to their post-war electoral hegemony, for the middle classes had plainly shrunk as a proportion of the electorate. What was therefore vital for the Conservatives during the 1920s was their capacity to supplement their basic 130 with a further minimum 130 in the seats where the middle-class element fell below 20 per cent, thereby making an irreducible minimum of around 260 in the Commons, which rendered it difficult for any other single party to obtain a majority. What is remarkable is that, apart from 1923 and 1929, they usually held another 100 on top of this from the less middle-class areas. A breakdown of the Conservative victory in the 1924 general election illustrated in table 12.5 shows that the party's

TABLE 12.5. *Distribution of Conservative seats in 1924*
(England, Scotland and Wales)

Total	Middle class 20% or more	Middle class 10–19.9%	Middle class under 10%
409 (602)	169 (200)	236 (356)	4 (46)

Source: M. Kinnear, *The British Voter: an Atlas and Survey 1885–1964* (1969) p. 122–4.

massive command of the Commons rested upon successes in more than two-thirds of the constituencies where the middle-class element fell between 10 per cent and 19.9 per cent or, to put it another way, where the working class comprised 80–90 per cent.

The corollary of this spread of Conservative seats was dependence upon fully mobilizing their support in each social group by means of an efficient and comprehensive electoral machine. The traditional skill in doctoring the register of voters naturally became redundant under the new simplified system in which the bulk of the work was done by town clerks and clerks to the county councils. Registration gave way to a new emphasis, particularly on increasing the number of volunteer workers; this followed from the curtailing of expenditure and introduction of one-day polling in 1918 which threw most constituencies upon their own organizational resources on polling day. The party activist's role as intermediary between politician and voter grew further in importance as a result of the increase by two and a half times in the size of the electorate. Many were young voters whose loyalties were less deep or less rigid than those of pre-war voters; one indication of the difficulties this posed is the fall in turnout to 70–6 per cent during the 1920s against the 81–6 per cent in Edwardian elections. There are certainly grounds for thinking that the Conservatives responded more effectively to the challenge presented by this larger, relatively uncommitted electorate than either of their rivals. While the Liberal agents disappeared and Labour made do with union organizers, the Conservatives improved their existing system of training and examinations for agents, some 352 of whom, together with 99 women organizers, received training between 1924 and 1937.[10] Regular attention by professional staff enabled the party to get to grips with the new system of absent voting established in 1918 for those whose occupations kept them away from home; the routine, meticulous work of tracking down such people and ensuring postal votes for loyal supporters probably came more naturally to the clerically minded Conservative organizations than to their Labour rivals.

A new emphasis was also placed upon fund-raising activities and upon raising large numbers of small subscriptions. Indeed Conservatives from Baldwin down were now heard to criticize the party for relying too much on candidates wealthy enough to relieve constituency associations of any need to finance elections. Rather than widening their choice by adopting impecunious but able candidates, as Baldwin urged, it seems that some constituencies relieved their MPs of bills they normally paid; even this process did not go very far, for only a quarter to a third of local associations appear to have become financially independent by the 1930s.[11] The basic framework in the constituencies comprised a vigorous women's organization — which was partly a matter of absorbing membership from the Primrose League (which declined as a separate force after the war) and carrying on the League's tradition of social functions. Women's activities were also, no doubt, a valuable means of absorbing middle-class ex-Liberals now looking for a safe haven in a world of Labour governments. The consciously restrained approach of the Conservative leaders, which verged on the non-political in Baldwin's case, served admirably to consolidate middle-class support around Conservatism; this process culminated during 1931–35 when the participation of large parts of the Liberal Party in the National Government helped to blur the line between Conservative and Liberal.

Despite their organizational importance in the party women made an almost imperceptible advance against male hostility to them as full-time agents and MPs. While all parties were reluctant to nominate women, the Conservative share of women's candidatures in the 1920s was disproportionately small. At the best in 1924 a mere 12 out of 534 Conservative candidates were women, a sign of the selection boards' fear that since some voters disliked women politicians, a woman would be a handicap if chosen. This reality was partly obscured by the fact that the first woman to take her seat in the Commons was the Conservative Nancy Astor who, significantly, took over her husband's seat at Plymouth (Sutton) following his elevation to the peerage in 1919. Though resented by many, Lady Astor was tolerated as a 'character' in the House. She heralded no great change for there were never more than three women Conservative MPs during the 1920s; even 1931 with its exceptional victories in hopeless seats brought in only 13, and this was rarely equalled throughout the next half century.

Labour's Grass Roots 1918–29

Between the First World War and the 1930s the Labour Party turned itself from the rather loose federal structure it had originally been into a substantial parliamentary party supported by a strong central organization and a comprehensive framework of regional and local organization and membership. Much of the credit for this achievement must be ascribed to Arthur Henderson who held tight control over head office, the National Executive and its sub-committees until 1924 when he temporarily surrendered the party secretaryship. He was helped by the new national agent, Egerton Wake, who in 1918 appropriately replaced Arthur Peters, a man whose sympathies with Liberalism rendered him a hindrance to the expanding party. Central to Henderson's dominance was his co-operation with the trade unions whose financial contribution nationally and locally underpinned the whole structure. During the 1920s the union membership affiliated to the party — which was based very approximately on the number who paid the political levy — rose to 3.5 million, though the figure fell sharply to 2 million between 1927 and 1928 as a result of the Baldwin government's Trade Disputes Act which introduced the practice of 'contracting in' for the levy.

At constituency level union branches or trades councils were often instrumental in fighting election campaigns and selecting candidates. On the whole union-sponsored candidates held the safer seats, and even in difficult rural constituencies the key trade union frequently determined the choice. Dependence upon strong union branches explains the patchy but continuous growth of constituency organizations during the 1920s. The number of affiliated constituency parties rose year by year from 397 in 1918 to 626 by 1924, though the latter figure is inflated by some double affiliations. The three general elections in 1922–24 clearly provided a stimulus in that the 140 constituencies lacking a Labour party in 1921 had shrunk to 19 by 1924. Yet there remained a shortfall of up to 100 between affiliated parties and parliamentary contests which reflects the inability of young organizations to sustain expensive campaigns in the absence of strong union branches. Nevertheless the pattern of continuous expansion which began around 1917 was virtually complete by 1929 when the Labour Party fought on almost as broad a front as the Conservatives. The party's steadily rising share of the national poll is a direct measure of the additional candidates fielded; the average poll per contest, which hovered around the 40 per cent mark, reflects additional candidatures in weak constituencies in 1924 and 1929 which depresses the average figures (see table 12.6).

TABLE 12.6. *Labour growth at general elections*

	1918	1922	1923	1924	1929	1931
% total poll	22.2	29.5	30.5	33.0	37.1	30.6
Candidates	388	411	422	512	571	515
Average % poll per contest		40.0	41.0	38.2	39.3	33.0

The dramatic interruption in this pattern of growth in 1931 diverted attention from the flaws in the party's organizational base during the 1920s and it is to these that we must now turn. In the first place it is clear that many constituency parties were little more than nominal, and that the pattern of individual membership projected in 1918 always remained an elusive goal rather than an achievement. Frequently local Labour parties comprised simply the delegates of local union branches plus some socialist societies' representatives. After 1918 in the industrial north-east, Lancashire, Scotland and Wales the old trades councils had frequently adopted the title of 'Divisional Labour Party'; consequently at local level the party remained an umbrella organization outside the real centres of power as it had been before 1914. It is not surprising that the desired mass membership was rarely attained. In 1928, when separate figures became available, individual party membership stood at 215,000; though no doubt a considerable improvement on pre-war strength this suggests a constituency average of around 350 only. Even this must be qualified by the knowledge that 1928 was a buoyant time for Labour — now anticipating victory over a fading Baldwin administration — and that all parties' official figures tend to exaggerate real membership. Although Conservative figures were not published, local evidence suggests a massive advantage in membership; by 1929 the Glasgow Conservatives, for example, enjoyed an average of 2,000 per constituency. A brighter sign for Labour was the recruitment of women; some working-class towns like Woolwich and Barrow claimed around 1,000 women members by 1924, though these had been unusually well organized localities before 1914 and remained exceptional in the 1920s: at this time individual membership was often far more female than male in composition. Also among the seats with over 200 women members were mixed industrial and middle-class towns such as York, Colchester, Gloucester and Newport, in each of which Labour either won or ran the Conservatives very close in 1929; they were in fact the crucial battleground if the party's total of 288 seats in 1929 was to be turned into an overall majority of 308. In this struggle the disproportionately middle-class Labour women's sections had a vital part to play in taking on the Conservative organization on more equal terms.

It may be thought that individual membership was insignificant in view of the huge affiliated union membership and that the unions somehow endowed Labour with all the apparatus of a mass political party; yet this was by no means the case. For one thing the affiliation to the party of an arbitrary number of union members meant much less, in terms of individual commitment, than taking out direct membership; indeed recent studies suggest that many of those who pay the political levy are unaware that they are doing so. Also, although total union membership reached a peak of over 8 millions in 1920, thereafter until 1934 it steadily declined to almost half that number, so that it was a wasting asset for much of the period. What is most important is that while a trade-union-based organization was perfectly adequate for mobilizing voters in overwhelmingly unionized working-class constituencies this could guarantee only a hard core of MPs; for a party whose path to a majority necessitated winning the more mixed seats this could never be a satisfactory substitute for the efficient machine built up by the Conservatives. Moreover, although the unions were a vital source of funds they remained somewhat inflexible about how the money was deployed. Henderson, who was acutely aware of the need to channel resources through headquarters into needy and marginal areas, never obtained the funds he believed to be necessary. Against the opposition of a number of union leaders he managed to persuade Conference in 1920 to raise the levy from 2d per member to 3d, and this produced £40–50,000 a year. In 1923 he resurrected the fighting fund to assist impecunious constituencies which had been abolished in 1919. Although some £20,000 was thereby paid out in 1924 this still fell short of Henderson's objective of equalizing the expenditure of the richer and poorer constituencies. Seats fought by the miners, for example, spent on average 50 per cent more on elections in the early 1920s though they could have managed on less than most. Because the trade unions felt reluctant to allow headquarters unlimited powers to redistribute the movement's resources Labour continued to enjoy abundance in its safest seats but failed to make good the deficiencies in areas where it had to make gains. A crucial consequence of this failure to tap resources fully was the poor provision of full-time agents. In 1920 the number stood at 112; it rose to 133 in 1922 and tailed off to 113 by 1924, though it was supplemented by 20–30 agents employed largely by the Miners Federation. By 1929 a maximum of 169 had been recorded, but this fell back to 136 by 1935. Again these agents were concentrated largely in safe seats. Only a total of 300–400 full-time professional agents would have placed the party on an equal footing with its rival.

One partial exception to these remarks is the example of the London Labour Party. Under Herbert Morrison's leadership the LLP's activity was characterized by the channeling of funds directly from the Transport and General Workers Union to the central control point, and by less reliance on major meetings and more on the thorough doorstep canvass in which women members came into their own. Even in some most unpromising seats the LLP established effective organizations, and claimed high membership figures – 2,000 in the case of South Poplar for instance. Mastery of the canvass, which was particularly appropriate for the huge suburban housing estates around London, was regarded as a key factor in the remarkable Labour gains in such places as North Camberwell in 1922 and Mitcham in 1923. 'The new school of Labour politicians is a scientific school', Morrison claimed. 'It knows that noisy tub-thumping does not make up for careful organisation.'[12]

Morrison's hyperbole did highlight another characteristic of Labour's approach to elections during the inter-war years. After 1918 Henderson made great use of regular regional conferences and rallies, and for these, as for parliamentary elections, he relied heavily upon obtaining star speakers. The price was unduly heavy speaking engagements for Henderson himself (who thought nothing of giving a two-hour oration at a by-election) but also for MacDonald. The party's reliance upon the Victorian radical techniques of inspirational rallies and whistle-stop tours, at which MacDonald undoubtedly excelled, is all of a piece with the relative neglect of individual mass membership and efficient local machinery. For although Conservatives also held big rallies this was never such a central part of their approach to the electorate. Their leaders, usually less proficient with the Gladstonian oration, showed, especially in Baldwin's case, considerable facility with the quieter technique of the radio broadcast; and their larger membership, and efficiency with transport, the canvass and the postal vote were far better calculated to mobilize their support from the enlarged electorate of relatively uncommitted voters than was Labour's traditional radical revivalism. This has sometimes been lost sight of by writers who attribute the Liberal decline to an inherent inability to master the techniques for mobilizing the post-1918 mass electorate, inhibitions from which the more democratic Labour Party should in theory have been free. Yet if there was a basic division in approach it would seem, in practice, to have been between the Conservative Party on the one hand, and, on the other, the Labour and Liberal parties whose strengths and weaknesses betrayed a common Victorian origin.

The Realignment of the Working Class

In the past it was assumed that the central feature of popular politics between the wars was the emergence of social class as the basic determinant of political allegiance, a development that in itself would account for the replacement of the Liberals by Labour as the party of the working class. As a broad description of what happened this sketch has much to commend it, but as an explanation it does not take us very far. We have already considered the strong empirical grounds for thinking that the shift to a class-based pattern had already occurred before the First World War. Even for the inter-war years an interpretation of the role of class depends very much on the perspective adopted, whether for example, one studies the Labour vote in terms of its class origin, or whether one examines the total working-class vote in terms of its party loyalty. In the former instance studies of post-1945 voters suggest that among Labour supporters 87 per cent were working class and 13 per cent middle class; however, of the working class electorate only slightly over 60 per cent supported the Labour Party in the 1945–51 period.[13] During 1918–39 the proportion must have been considerably lower than this. For what actually happened in this period was that Labour progressively pushed up its share of the total poll so that by 1929 it had reached

37 per cent, but it stuck around this ceiling; after the drop in 1931 the party was only barely able to exceed this figure with 38 per cent in 1935. It has been rightly pointed out that the pattern was something less than a sudden and complete breakthrough resulting from the incorporation of millions of new voters in 1918;[14] such drastic transformations can occur as the near eclipse of the Irish Nationalists and the rise of Sinn Fein from none to 73 seats during 1916–18 shows. Yet in Britain the working class, markedly less monolithic than the middle class after 1918, failed to conform at all neatly to a pattern of class allegiance.

An estimate of working-class support for the Labour Party may be obtained from the 1929 figures if one makes an assumption that 76 per cent of the 22,648,000 who actually voted were working class; this leaves 17,212,000 as against a Labour poll of 8,389,000. One cannot be sure what proportion of Labour votes were middle class, but if 13 per cent is taken as a maximum and none at all as the minimum, then Labour's share of the working-class vote would fall within the range 42–8 per cent in 1929. At other inter-war elections except for 1935 the proportion would of course have been lower. It must be doubtful, in the light of such (admittedly approximate) calculations, whether Labour was any more effective in winning the working-class vote after 1918 than the Liberals had been before 1914. Since the Liberals had been able to draw more strongly on the middle-class electorate they had been more successful, on occasion, in obtaining overall majorities.

Thus we have more than one problem to explain. Why was there a steady and impressive rise in Labour support? And why did it stick at a fairly low ceiling around 37 per cent even after recovering from the check administered in 1931? We have argued earlier that there was so much continuity between pre-war Liberal and post-war Labour support that the explanation for the replacement of one party by the other must be essentially chronological–historical. An alternative approach would involve adopting a structural explanation, namely that while pre-1914 Liberal voters largely continued to support their old party, Labour's new strength was derived from newly enfranchised and, by implication, different working-class voters. However, these approaches are by no means mutually exclusive. Elements of each are combined in the idea of the political generation as an explanation for the pattern of political change. Clearly the regular arrival of a fresh set of young voters and the removal by death of older ones constitutes a structural transformation of the electorate; but the chronological–historical element is also implicit in that each new generation experiences a different set of political circumstances; young voters have been found to be less set in their loyalty to party than their elders and more impressionable in the face of events. The formation of their political attitudes, therefore, tends to reflect the political conditions that are paramount in the years when they are growing to adulthood and political consciousness.[15] One study of voters alive in 1960 has highlighted the fluctuation between political generations by isolating the allegiance of those who voted for the first time in 1935, of whom 45 per cent supported Labour, those who voted for the first time in 1945, of whom 61 per cent supported Labour, and those who voted for the first time in 1955, of whom 48 per cent supported Labour.[16]

Which were likely to have been the critical formative influences making for political generations between the wars? Those born around 1900 — and consequently voting for the first time in the early 1920s — experienced a traumatic political apprenticeship in the First World War and post-war chaos, which, in view of the sorry conclusion of Lloyd George's Coalition in 1922 may well have disrupted Liberal allegiance more severely than among the older generations. The generation born around 1914–18 grew to political awareness in the late 1920s and early 1930s; it is a matter for speculation whether for them the discrediting of MacDonald's second government weighed more or less heavily than the fact that by this time Labour was plainly the only real alternative government.

In what sense did national events and trends help to mould a generation relatively predisposed to Labour sympathies? We have noted already the groundswell of trade union membership which doubled from 4 to 8 millions between 1914 and 1920, and the accelerating industrial militancy during the latter half of the war. In 1917 the number of working days lost in strikes doubled to 5.8 million; but the real explosion came in 1919, with 21 million days lost, in 1920, with 35 million, and in 1921 with 86 million. What stoked up this outburst was the maintenance of full wartime employment by the post-war boom until the summer of 1920, and the abandonment of compulsory arbitration procedures by the government. At this stage men sensed that although wages were higher than before the war they had missed the real fruits of victory. Union leaders felt that their patriotic restraint had not been fully reciprocated by the employers who had reaped vast profits, and so they now declined responsibility for holding back their members' demands. These were years of rising expectations which, during 1920–21, suddenly seemed unlikely to be fulfilled. Though few can be said to have been directly influenced by the Russian Revolution, the comparison did serve to highlight a belief that Britain alone was slipping back into the *status quo*. The hurried Coupon Election soon came to be regarded as a tactic to hamstring the working man's new power; and the impression of the Coalition as a conspiracy of employers to deceive the workers gained credence from the neat defusing of demands for public ownership by timely wage concessions and the Sankey Commission. By the summer of 1921 unemployment had leapt to 2 million or 18 per cent of the insured workforce, and union membership soon began its inexorable downward slide as long-term unemployment took its toll. This turn of events was significant in several ways; it induced an embattled defensiveness in the labour movement which lasted until the Second World War; and in the short run it generated a sense of betrayal which spilled over into the 1922 general election.

The fusion of Conservative and some Liberal forces in the Coalition after 1918 drove many working men to see Labour as the natural alternative for them; indeed during 1915–22 Lloyd George had established himself in the eyes of their leaders as an enemy more dangerous, because cleverer and more unscrupulous, than the Conservatives, an interpretation vociferously reinforced by the Liberal recruits to Labour. Meanwhile the independent Liberal Party became bereft of those politicians most in tune with labour aspirations, and seemed to have nothing of relevance to say; in so far as it won back the coalitionists it appeared less congenial to labour. Though it developed constructive industrial policies along the lines of the wartime Whitley Councils, no policy was likely to be as effective electorally as an attitude; and in a period of sharply rising unemployment and dashed expectations the Liberal stance of impartiality between the two sides of industry inevitably appeared evasive and insincere. In this way the 1920s were an instrumental phase in severing the Liberal Party from its traditional working-class base; indeed the years from 1918 to 1924 were possibly more important in this respect than 1914–18, which is usually taken as the decisive period. In this process the significance of the Labour government of 1924 cannot be overestimated; for however brief its life, it made the Liberals redundant at a stroke for the working classes.

The culmination came with the General Strike of 1926. While the parliamentary Labour Party disliked the strike almost as much as the Liberals they did not make the mistake of saying so. Sir

John Simon's rash pronouncement that the strike was illegal appeared to commit his party to the government's side especially as Asquith concurred at least to the extent of believing it to be a threat to parliamentary government. When Lloyd George dissociated himself from this view he provoked the clash that brought him the leadership of the party. Yet after all that had happened his credentials were too besmirched for him to restore his party's standing with the working class. It is noticeable that although the Liberals often gained ground they continued to lose working-class seats to Labour at each election during the 1920s.

Another perspective on the remaking of the electoral alignment during the 1920s lies in municipal politics. Indeed, at this level, where Labour's advance was particularly rapid, the pre-1914 relationship between Labour and Liberalism broke down almost entirely. The first post-war local elections held in November 1919 gave an indication of the change of mood since the Coupon Election; outside London Labour gained 400 seats, and in the London boroughs its candidates were elected for 572 out of 1,362 seats. These gains were not only of a higher order than pre-war advances, they were also improved upon in almost every subsequent year between the wars. Much of the ground was gained at Liberal expense; indeed Liberal inability to survive at local level was plainly marked by a steady fall in municipal candidatures, which continued unabated even when the party was enjoying revivals in parliamentary elections. In this light the revival engineered by Lloyd George during 1926–29 looks particularly fragile. The six by-election gains were largely in traditional Liberal seats where the Labour challenge was abnormally weak; elsewhere the party's vote continued to fall back. As the Labour organizers observed the 'revival' was essentially an ephemeral phenomenon puffed up by the publicity attaching to the arrival of Lloyd George's 'circus' in certain favourable areas rather than a firmly entrenched gain.[17] At the general election in 1929 only 24 of the 43 existing Liberal seats were held; 33 of the 35 gains were at Conservative expense, while 17 of the 19 losses went to Labour. Thus the slide away from the Liberals in working-class areas manifested in municipal activity was repeated in the parliamentary contests notwithstanding a revival.

This working-class realignment was partly a cause and partly a consequence of the collaboration of middle-class Liberals with Conservatives in anti-socialist pacts which took such forms as a Citizens Party in Bristol, a Municipal Association in Hull, or a Progressive Party in Sheffield. While such combinations checked

Labour's attainment of majority control in many cities during the 1920s they left Liberals holding working-class wards which were highly vulnerable to Labour, and merely turned the Liberals into a Conservative force in the long run. For the party could not be sustained by an appeal for cautious, Conservative votes at the municipal level and for radical anti-Conservative votes at the parliamentary level. The confusion was compounded by the growing fluctuations in the number of candidates which had the inevitable effect of breaking the habit of voting Liberal and obliging erstwhile supporters to make an alternative choice. Radical Liberals were often antagonized by the appearance of ex-coalitionists as Liberal or National Liberal candidates in 1922–23, while the more right-wing and traditionalist supporters withdrew into the Conservative camp in great numbers in 1924. Each subsequent revival began from a lower level and never recouped the losses of 1918. The attrition of the traditional Liberal constituency culminated in 1931–35 when the Liberal MPs — apart from Lloyd George and his family — were absorbed into the National Government, in the case of the Simonites on a permanent basis. After a short interruption Labour then resumed its absorption of the remnants of industrial Liberalism.

The 1920s were also a formative period for other elements within the electorate such as the Irish, hitherto a pillar of the Liberal vote. Though largely working class the Irish had displayed a reluctance to vote Labour. Yet the war shattered the Liberal–Nationalist alliance, and as early as 1919 the leading Irish politician in Britain, T. P. O'Connor, had begun to urge Irish voters to back Labour; the new alignment was formalized in 1924 when MacDonald made him a privy councillor. On O'Connor's resignation from his Scotland (Liverpool) constituency his successor simply received the Labour nomination. Wherever Irish working men were numerous as in Liverpool or Glasgow they came to be a bastion of Labour strength — but as Catholics rather than simply as working men. For the transition from one party to another occurred during the early 1920s when Labour was a staunch Home Rule party free of association with the Easter Rebellion or the 'Black and Tans' policy; Labour could thus inherit one role within the traditional sectarian pattern of politics which in places like Liverpool and Glasgow still had much life in it.

Similarly there was no sudden collapse of 'Nonconformity' but rather a political realignment of many Nonconformists to Labour's advantage. Ever since the settlement of certain Nonconformist grievances in the 1860s there had been a gradual drift from radicalism to Conservatism especially among Wesleyans; and by 1914 groups like Quakers had grown so high in the social scale and so close to the establishment view as to be largely patriotic volunteers despite their reputation for pacifism. Conversely those Nonconformists whose sympathies were engaged by the anti-war movement and who had been ardent social reformers often migrated via the ILP to the Labour Party afterwards. By 1924 86 Labour parliamentary candidates were Nonconformists (as against 120 Liberals) and 45 Labour MPs were Nonconformists (as against only 21 Liberals).[18] However, Liberal support among middle-class Nonconformists did remain relatively firm, so much so that the relationship was still discernible in 1960.[19] The big shift occurred among working men. One modern study of voters alive in 1960 who had reached voting age before 1914 suggests that whereas working-class Anglicans of their generation were evenly divided between Conservative and non-Conservative allegiance, working-class Nonconformists split 4:1 against the Conservatives.[20] Although this pattern had largely died out among new voters after 1945, for inter-war voters religious traditions remained politically relevant. In County Durham, for example, the smoothness of the transfer of loyalties from Liberal to Labour after the war owed much to the pervading Methodist tradition common to both. A generation before 1914 Durham Methodists had adopted both the secular ideology of radicalism and the institutionalized politics of the miners' lodges. Their mobilization in the post-1918 Labour Party therefore involved little perceptible 'conversion'; for adherence to Labour did not imply adopting socialism except in the general ethical sense in which they were already socialists.

What such shifts did imply was a certain moderation in objectives and methods which characterized the labour movement in general, not just the Nonconformist element in it. It has been rightly observed that notwithstanding the grievance of unemployment, manual workers during the 1920s and 1930s displayed remarkably little predilection for a drastic soak-the-rich policy, but tended rather to compare their own situation with that of other workingmen.[21] Their apparently limited aspirations were surely of a piece with their politics; for their characteristic claim — faithfully reflected by the Labour Party — was that the working man was entitled to work, and failing that, maintenance, not that the distribution of wealth in society should be fundamentally altered. Essentially the party appealed to the self-respect of the working class rather than to any militant sense of class consciousness. This is consistent with Labour's steady accumulation of support up to 1929 which nevertheless fell short of two-fifths of the total vote. Despite its stance as, in essence, the party of the working class at a point in time when the working class came into its own electorally, Labour failed to overturn the existing pattern of approximately class-based loyalties; the persistence of substantial working-class Conservatism ensured that. What Labour did accomplish was the inheritance of one sector within the pattern of political allegiance that had been established before the First World War.

Whatever the underlying explanation it is undeniable that Labour suffered a check after 1929, dropping to no more than 30 per cent in 1931. The political origins of this debacle will be considered later; here we shall note only the electoral nature of the setback. Of course, with a mere 52 MPs returned in 1931 Labour's voters were grossly under-represented. The net loss of 236 is explicable if one remembers that in 1929 the system had worked in the party's favour in giving it more seats than the Conservatives for slightly fewer votes; four out of ten Labour seats had been won on a minority vote and often by very slender margins. In these circumstances a slight shift of votes was bound to be disproportionately damaging. The by-elections of 1929–31, in contrast to those of the first MacDonald government, brought substantial falls in the Labour poll, a reflection of its inadequate response to mounting unemployment. This in itself heralded a defeat at the next general election; but the landslide was compounded by a withdrawal of Liberal candidates (down from 513 in 1929 to 173), which left Labour facing far more straight fights than before. Even in the presence of a Liberal the Conservatives now managed to concentrate the non-Labour vote on themselves. There is, however, a tradition that the special arrangements inspired by the National Government led to the defeat while Labour's supporters actually remained loyal in 1931. There is limited evidence for this, most conspicuously in Glamorgan and Monmouthshire where Labour held on to almost all its seats and frequently improved its share of the poll as a result of Liberal or Conservative withdrawals. This, however, was by no means typical. In north-east England there occurred a major shift towards National Government candidates, especially on Tyneside and in Durham where Labour lost votes both absolutely and proportionately: it lost 14 seats and retained only two. Nationwide the turnout stood at 76 per cent as in 1929; but with an electorate greater by a million the Labour poll fell from 8,389,000 to 6,649,000. By the standards of British elections this undoubtedly represented an abnormal collapse of support. Subsequently the party's own enquiry identified as the chief cause the public impression that its leaders had run away from the financial crisis in contrast to MacDonald, Snowden and Thomas who had helped to form the National Government. Four years later, despite the advantage of being the sole effective alternative government, the party retrieved only its 1929 level of support; thus was consolidated a pattern that only the passage of a generation and the Second World War would disrupt.

Chapter 13

The Eclipse of the Extremes
1931–1939

> ... you are following the very traditions of Disraeli
> himself adapted to the present day.
> *Stanley Baldwin at Cambridge, 1924*

Labour, Socialism and Keynesianism

Whereas during the 1920s the Labour Party under MacDonald had generally been regarded as moderate and respectable, in the 1930s it enjoyed a, largely undeserved, reputation for extremism and irresponsibility; it was even accused of harbouring undemocratic, totalitarian tendencies in view of the admiration for the Soviet system of centralized planning shown by some socialists. Ironically the party devoted considerable energy to dissociating itself from Marxism and purging Communists from its ranks. In reality the Labour movement remained characteristically parliamentarian – perhaps deferentially so – in approach. Its objective was never to challenge the basis of the political system or the economic structure so much as to master the machinery of government with a view to securing the maximum concessions for working people. It placed upon the state a general obligation to provide work, or failing that, maintenance for those in need of it, but it was for years unclear about whether this entailed drastic and comprehensive economic controls by the state. Though the movement had always included a large part of British socialism it was not socialist as a whole, except in a limited sense; and despite the frequent use of the fashionable idea of 'planning' in Labour circles during the 1930s, the gradual evolution of a coherent Labour economic policy owed as much to Keynesian and Fabian thinking as to socialism.

In the immediate aftermath of 1918 even socialists often regarded wartime controls as a unique experiment rather than as a pointer to future strategy; libertarian socialists like C.D.H. Cole and Clifford Allen were convinced that state collectivism had merely helped to shore up a decaying capitalism, and therefore looked more to workers' control than to centralized state planning. However, by 1923, in the face of mounting unemployment, the ILP was in retreat from guild socialism, and began to concentrate upon the techniques for managing the economy. The ILP's *The Socialist Programme* of 1923 displayed an underconsumptionist approach in the emphasis it laid upon raising and stabilizing the demand for the products of industry by a more equal distribution of incomes. Indeed the ILP had already begun to study Keynesian ideas to some effect: it identified a scientific credit policy as the means of moderating the fluctuations in the economy;[1] and unemployment was ascribed basically to inadequate purchasing power which was itself a consequence of insufficiency of bank loans. Thus, state management of banks and credit seemed to the ILP crucial for economic planning; and the extension of control over other industries was similarly seen in the light of what each would contribute to costs, prices, production levels and so forth.

This is worth stressing because it was at variance with the woolly imprecision of official Labour Party thinking at the time. For notwithstanding the 1918 constitution and *Labour and the New Social Order* the party had yet to think out the implications of economic planning or even the mechanics of imposing control. However, throughout the 1920s the ILP and other critics failed to push the party to a more definite economic policy. If anything Labour backed away from precise, radical notions such as the capital levy, for example, as being inconsistent with its electoral appeal. As a result MacDonald arrived in office unexpectedly in January 1924 without an economic strategy except in so far as he shared with other governments of the 1920s a conviction that the solution to unemployment would be found in the restoration of the export markets for British capital and staple industries; this required a stabilization of the world economy and a return to a high level of trade. This was, of course, hopelessly flawed, for even when international trade did climb back to pre-war levels Britain could not reclaim her former share. Moreover, Britain's capacity to stimulate world trade and to counter the general drift to protectionism and international indebtedness was severely circumscribed. While the United States declined to play this role the most that British governments could do was try to whittle down

German reparations, and MacDonald enjoyed some success in this with the Dawes Plan of 1924.

Despite the common ground that existed between the various governments in Britain the political debate was increasingly, and quite misleadingly, cast in terms of 'capitalism' versus 'socialism'; the House of Commons even treated itself to a debate on this theme in 1923; yet this was a choice that was never in fact available. The real alternatives were between the more orthodox capitalist solutions of restoring British trade and balancing the budget, and the ideas of the reformist, radical capitalists. The latter were not the property of a single group, but influenced a miscellaneous collection of people including Keynes, Lloyd George, Sir Oswald Mosley, the ILP and Political and Economic Planning (PEP). They offered various mixtures of public works schemes funded by budgetary deficits, devaluation of the pound, cheap money policies, and tariff protection, all of which were designed to reduce unemployment by increasing the demand for British-made goods. Placing the emphasis on stimulating the domestic market, they effectively abandoned futile attempts to manage the world economy. In marked contrast MacDonald and Philip Snowden remained rooted in an optimistic nineteenth-century belief in maximizing commercial intercourse. As Chancellor in 1924 Snowden produced a model Gladstonian budget in which he devoted a modest surplus to reducing duties on food items, and subsequently permitted himself only a niggardly grant towards public works schemes. For nine months the Labour movement was too awed and delighted at the spectacle of a Labour Chancellor as orthodox master of the Treasury to challenge effectively the basic policy pursued.

However, once in opposition again the party ventilated its doubts as to the wisdom of accepting office without a parliamentary majority sufficient to enact a radical economic programme. Remarkably, the party leaders managed to escape any such commitment, or being tied to any definite economic strategy before their return to office in 1929. In accomplishing this they were helped by the manner of their departure from office in 1924 which fostered the illusion that capitalist conspiracies had ejected a socialist administration. However, much the most important means of deflecting criticism was provided quite fortuitously by the General Strike of 1926.

The crucial decision to entrust the General Council of the TUC with the responsibility for a general strike strategy had been made during the absence of several of the moderate leaders who were involved in MacDonald's government. Yet the moderates were willing to risk a general strike even if they hoped it would be unnecessary in the last resort. The explanation lies in the reaction of men like Ernest Bevin, leader of the Transport and General Workers Union, to the fall of the Labour government. They now anticipated widespread conflict with the employers backed by a Conservative government. This diagnosis was soundly based in that the decision in 1925 to restore the pound to its pre-war level of $4.87 could be sustained only if there followed a general reduction of costs, and therefore of wages, in British industry. This appraisal led Bevin to approach a general strike as a defensive measure against the expected attack on workers' wages generally, and not simply as an unselfish act to stand by the miners. This is why 1926 saw both a general strike *and* a miners' strike. For the wider objective of checking general wage reductions was at least partially attained. Fortunately for both the General Council and MacDonald, who gave no effective support to the strike, the immediate outcome did not produce a reaction against the moderate leadership as might have been expected; if anything it strengthened their hold by discrediting the advocates of industrial action, and helped to concentrate the energies of the trade unions into parliamentary channels.

In an industrial sense the General Strike was not of great significance, for it marked the end of a long period of declining militancy; union membership had been falling steadily for five years *before* 1926 — a reflection of substantial long-term unemployment. On the other hand the strike had a considerable political significance, stemming from the provocative Trades Disputes Act passed by Baldwin's government in 1927 which made sympathetic strikes illegal, banned civil servants from membership of a union affiliated to the TUC, and introduced the procedure for contracting out of the payment of the political levy. These restrictions were, perhaps, of no great practical importance, for the party's income was only temporarily reduced, and the provision against sympathetic strikes was never invoked during the 19 years of the Act's life. Yet it became a symbol of the common grievance of the industrial and the political wings of the Labour movement, and facilitated the task of the unions in harnessing their resources to parliamentary ends. Consequently between 1925 and 1929 attention was considerably distracted from the problems of 1924 and precise economic objectives for the future; it seemed sufficient simply to secure the return of a new Labour government.

Thus, when the ILP began to flourish its proposals in *The Living Wage* in 1926, MacDonald merely condemned its authors as extremists — a singular demonstration of the authority now attaching to the leader. Similarly when Sir Oswald Mosley (Labour MP for Smethwick) urged him to adopt a clear and precise economic programme, he too was swept aside in preference for the usual general statement of party attitudes.[2] Quite the most serious threat to MacDonald's lofty generalities was represented by Lloyd George who succeeded in making unemployment the major issue in 1929 — though to Labour's benefit rather than his own. Since 1926 Lloyd George had been rebuilding his bridges to radicalism. Old colleagues like Charles Masterman, Manchester radicals like E. D. Simon, Ramsay Muir and Ted Scott, and an important collection of radical economists and academics including Hubert Henderson, Walter Layton, J. M. Keynes, William Beveridge and J. A. Hobson had pooled ideas through the Liberal Summer Schools and Lloyd George's Liberal Industrial Enquiry which generated the famous Liberal Yellow Book *Britain's Industrial Future* in 1928. This document bore the Keynesian imprint in its proposed use of the Bank of England's control of credit to stimulate trade and in its major schemes of public works by deficit financing. What was impressive, apart from the intellectual underpinning, was the detail with which the proposals had been considered. It was calculated that every £1 million invested in road-building would generate 5,000 man-years of employment. In the first year some 350,000 extra jobs were to be created by such means. This was the basis of Lloyd George's claim that he could reduce unemployment, which stood at 1.1 million in June 1929, to normal proportions within a year.

Thus in complete contrast to MacDonald, Lloyd George had a definite idea of how he would proceed if returned to office. Why was Labour's response to Keynesianism so ambivalent in the 1920s? Some swallowed uncritically the Snowden–Treasury arguments against deficit finance. Some thought of public works in terms of the traditional efforts of local authorities — both inadequate and humiliating; they had not yet grasped the scale of Keynes' proposals or the underlying justification. Moreover, it was comfortingly easy to dismiss them as palliatives designed to shore up a system in fatal decline; socialists correctly saw that in so far as Keynesian methods could create full employment under private enterprise they would undermine a central part of their own case. In the long run Labour was in fact to opt for Keynesianism rather than socialism, but the process was a gradual one and somewhat obscured by the trauma of 1931. For the time being it was sufficient to adopt MacDonald's line, partly out of conviction, but also as a matter of tactics, and dismiss the Liberal campaign as a typical Lloyd George stunt by a man notorious for unfulfilled promises. Yet the basic vacillation and confusion were evident in the party's 'Appeal to the Nation', which boldly promised to deal with unemployment by schemes that 'have been before the country for years before the Liberal Party — in the hope of reviving its declining fortunes — appropriated some of them and proclaimed them as original'; the real position was given away in the lame admission that 'the most important attack upon unemployment is to restore prosperity to the depressed industries'.

MacDonald's eloquent exposition of socialism for years before 1929 only served after 1931 to reveal him to his erstwhile colleagues as a humbug. Yet he can be defended partly on the grounds that the movement itself willingly placed its confidence in him, as his triumph over his critics at party conferences as late as 1928 shows;[3] and partly on the grounds of the continuity of his political thought and objectives over 20 years which mitigates any charge of unprincipled opportunism. For MacDonald socialism had always been a distant conclusion to the eventual transformation of society which he never expected to see; it was as much spiritual as political. In so far as he envisaged a governmental route to socialism he believed, not as a Marxist, that it would emerge from the crisis and collapse of the existing system, but as a Fabian, that it would grow from the steady evolution, even success, of the system. Meanwhile the Labour Party was the proper vehicle for guiding society to socialistic solutions with the consent of both workers and the middle classes.

MacDonald, however, left himself exposed to periods of economic depression in which the only practical justification for holding office lay in the party's capacity to protect working people from the effects of unemployment. The absence of a short- to medium-term policy for handling unemployment itself proved to be the fatal flaw. Both in 1924 and 1929 the lack of a parliamentary majority was adopted as an alibi for the failure to attempt any steps towards socialism; but this could not entirely conceal the fact that neither government had such intentions. Nor is it plausible to argue that MacDonald's actions were entirely circumscribed by the magnitude of the economic problem facing him when he entered office in 1929. Unemployment was 1.3 million in November 1929, 1.7 million in April 1930, and 2 million by July 1930. Yet the Prime Minister, finding foreign affairs more congenial, divided responsibility for economic matters between Snowden at the Treasury and J.H. Thomas, who as Lord Privy Seal held a brief for unemployment but was denied real executive powers and civil service backup. MacDonald only compounded this original mistake by proliferating extra committees such as his Economic Advisory Council. Only Mosley, a junior minister under Thomas, supplied the government with a coherent programme in February 1930 in a memorandum that envisaged deliberate expansion of purchasing power, restrictions upon imports, and public control of banking so as to finance industrial development. Although it seems that MacDonald had grown privately sceptical of Snowden's faith in balanced budgets and free trade, he did nothing to check the Cabinet's endorsement of the Treasury view: public works schemes would take a long time to bring into operation; they were inherently uneconomic, and since no idle reserves existed, they would only damage private industry by robbing it of investment. Mosley resigned, and Thomas escaped to the Colonial Office to be replaced by Vernon Hartshorn, upon whom the Prime Minister showered pathetic letters entreating him to do his job and put 'pressure on industries to put themselves in order'.[4]

Yet another economic and political strategy was available to MacDonald in seeking the co-operation of Lloyd George, who could marshall both the extra votes in the Commons and the intellectual artillery to cope with the Treasury – in return for a sustained attack on unemployment. Since the election Lloyd George had been constantly on the Prime Minister's doorstep bearing ideas and proposals, anxious to mould his policy. It is now clear from MacDonald's own papers that he played Lloyd George shrewdly by keeping him and his advisers involved in protracted negotiations on relatively trivial matters with no intention of reaching an overall agreement on economic management;[5] even the Bill to reform the electoral system by introducing the alternative vote, which was seen as contrary to Labour's interests, was emasculated safely by the Lords before the government fell.[6] All this served the purpose of keeping Lloyd George from alliance with anyone else. Natural caution and pride made MacDonald hesitate to allow the Liberal leader into his government on any terms.

It has been argued that the Keynesian remedies of Lloyd George or Mosley were not valid alternatives in view of the failure of similar policies in the United States to overcome the depression there. This is, however, to overlook the fact that the slump in

America was of far graver proportions than that in Britain; in fact the substantial reduction in unemployment achieved by President Roosevelt suggests the possibilities open to British governments for stimulating an economy that was comparatively lightly affected.

Thus for various reasons MacDonald missed his opportunities until in August 1931 the collapse of international banking faced him with a real crisis at last. In accordance with the Treasury view that the priority was to restore confidence and avoid a devaluation, Snowden drew up a list of reductions in expenditure totalling £78.5 million, including a 10 per cent cut in unemployment benefit, so as to balance the budget. Although the Cabinet accepted this reluctantly by 12 votes to 9, the General Council of the TUC flatly rejected the proposals; this led to a retreat by the waverers, notably Henderson who perceived the danger of alienating the industrial wing from the politicians. As a result the government broke up on 23 August, but was replaced immediately by a National Government with MacDonald as Premier and Snowden as Chancellor.

Inevitably MacDonald's severance in 1931 from the party he had done so much to build up produced a reaction against his style of leadership; and some critics like Stafford Cripps and Harold Laski cast doubt on the possibility of ever achieving socialism through a parliamentary system. However, it was not Parliament that had blocked socialism. Nor was the alternative strategy of mobilizing working-class power to overawe Parliament seriously proposed; the trade unions would have been the last to lend themselves to such a course. Instead the party kept its reappraisal within the gradualist, parliamentary framework, but sought a more precise and feasible left-wing policy than before.

In the long run the chief effect, supported by the union leaders, was to shift the party towards Keynesianism as the most satisfactory way of managing or 'planning' the economy. Even before the fall of the government the TUC's General Council, led by Ernest Bevin, had adopted the Keynesian view that attempts to defend the exchange rate were futile; they declined to accept the necessity of waiting for capitalism either to collapse or to recover its health as a precondition for socialism; instead they sought ways of creating jobs in the short to medium term; and in rejecting retrenchment and further deflation they had been fortified by the conviction that alternatives did exist. By 1933 this approach had crystallized in a specific commendation by the TUC of the New Deal programmes of President Roosevelt as worthy of emulation.[7]

Its priorities were now a programme of public works financed out of national credit, a 40-hour maximum working week, the raising of the school-leaving age to 16 and the prohibition of labour by those under 16. This was seized upon by socialists as proof that the unions, lacking a theoretical framework, had been seduced by reformist capitalism. Many on the left now grew less flexible than they had been in the 1920s; for the emergence of fascist regimes out of the ruins of European capitalism fostered a conviction that economic strategies like the New Deal were merely doomed attempts to stave off fundamental change. However, the bulk of the party's leaders appreciated the significance of the Rooseveltian revolution in radically extending the power of the state at the expense of private capitalism. Although they often took to describing their policy as 'socialist planning' they meant by this Keynesian techniques for managing an economy in which only limited sectors would be under public ownership; in *For Socialism and Peace* (1934) nationalization proposals included coal, gas, electricity, water, transport, agriculture, iron and steel, shipping, shipbuilding, engineering textiles, chemicals, insurance and banking. Attacks by political opponents and the eloquence of the socialists gave this lengthened list undue prominence; but between 1935 and 1939 the party concentrated upon a short selection of public utilities and ailing industries where opposition to public ownership from vested interests would be slight. Nationalization remained a matter of limited attempts to staunch the worst wounds in the system, leaving four-fifths of industry in private hands. The extent of the nationalization proposals was thus less important than the evolution of a definite procedure for taking over and running industries. The chief architect of this was Herbert Morrison, the one minister of 1929–31, apart from Addison, to have demonstrated a real grasp of the practicalities. His London Transport Bill established the principles of compensation for the dispossessed private owners, and the operation of publicly owned industries by small boards of experts and businessmen selected by the minister and responsible to him rather than to Parliament or the employees. Although the exclusion of workers' participation and trade union representation drew severe criticism from Bevin both in 1930 and subsequently, Morrison's blueprint survived without serious amendment as a guide to Labour's nationalization programme after 1945; it was a form of state collectivism inspired by the need for efficient servicing of a mixed economy and represented a return to the ideas of the Webbs.

The National Government and Liberal Toryism

The National Governments of 1931 to 1940 have figured so prominently in left-wing demonology that one tends to overlook the outrage of the far right at having what they regarded as an effete liberal administration foisted upon them when a proper Conservative one was easily attainable. A true interpretation of the period requires an appreciation of both perspectives. There is no question that these governments were, in policy and tone if not in personnel, thoroughly Conservative; the point is that they represented the triumph of a particular type of Conservatism. In this fact lay the reason for turning what was originally intended as a temporary expedient into a long-term fixture.

In accepting the royal invitation to form a coalition in August 1931 MacDonald, Baldwin and Sir Herbert Samuel, then acting Liberal leader, all appear to have contemplated co-operation for a matter of weeks or months only in order to undertake unpopular measures necessary to balance the budget and restore confidence; they would fight the next election separately. However, this expectation disappeared with extraordinary speed. In view of the perfectly adequate majority in the Commons, the three-year term still remaining, and the demoralized condition of the opposition, the decision to hold a general election on 27 October 1931 seemed an unnecessary diversion from the new government's task. The obvious explanation is that the circumstances provided the Conservatives with an irresistible opportunity to take advantage of Labour's disarray, and that MacDonald was unable to resist being used by them for a national appeal as Lloyd George had been used in 1918. However, this is less than a complete explanation. For one thing MacDonald himself does not seem to have required such encouragement. Although he told Samuel on 18 September that there was no justification for a dissolution, he had been encouraging Baldwin to that course for some time before:

> How long can this Government continue? My own impression is, not very long, and, indeed, if we could get such a state of financial stability as would bear what undoubtedly would be the shock of an election, I would not stand in the way of a Dissolution.[8]

By the 14th he was confessing to the King his fear of going to the country after taking the necessary economic measures for, 'the feeling of national unity will ebb away'.[9] Since Baldwin was under pressure to ditch MacDonald at the earliest opportunity it was clear that unless the special arrangements of August were put on a permanent footing his career might end abruptly. MacDonald was not ambitious any longer; he simply had nothing to live for now but politics, and no effective role in politics except within Baldwin's alliance.

The other part of the explanation is that many Conservatives were appalled at the prospect of another coalition. Yet Baldwin himself had fundamental reasons for refusing to lead an unencumbered Conservative Party. For despite his role in destroying the Coalition in 1922 Baldwin actually liked coalitions — provided that Lloyd George had no part in them (he must have thought it divine intervention that immured the 'Goat' in hospital with a serious operation during the formation of the National Government in 1931). In harnessing MacDonald and the Liberals to the 554-seat landslide for the government Baldwin executed more than a short-term electoral manoeuvre: he imposed his control over the Conservative Party by emasculating his own right wing. For the massive increase in Conservative MPs from the 258 of 1929 to the 471 of 1931 radically altered the composition of the party. It has been estimated that 100 MPs owed their seats directly to withdrawals of Liberal candidates.[10] At least 150 were unlikely to have been elected on a purely Conservative ticket; their capacity to survive at the 1935 election, as many of them did, rested very much upon the credibility of a national policy in the eyes of erstwhile Labour and Liberal voters. While Conservatives could have governed without winning all the industrial working-class constituencies captured in 1931 and 1935, without them Baldwin would have been deprived of support for his liberal, Disraelian brand of politics. Thus the origins of the National Governments lie in Baldwin's attempts during the 1920s to lead his party from slightly to the left of its centre; the relative security of his position during the 1930s is a measure of his success.

Baldwin was particularly well equipped to ease the Conservatives through a period when their chief opposition came from a party claiming to represent the working class. A wide range of Labour politicians recognized him as a man separated from them more by background than by principles. His own son, Oliver, joined the Labour Party in 1923; and Baldwin's own experience of harmonious industrial relations in the family firm contributed to his relaxed attitude towards the working class. He not only displayed a greater willingness than most of his colleagues to treat Labour

MPs as equals, but even reproached his own party for restricting its choice of candidates to the small proportion of the population wealthy enough to finance their political careers. By comparison all the alternative Conservative leaders in the 1920s — Austen Chamberlain, Curzon, Birkenhead, Balfour, Churchill — were remote and aloof. Neville Chamberlain, implored by Baldwin in 1927 not to address the Labour members as though they were dirt, replied: 'the fact is that intellectually, with a few exceptions, they are dirt'.[11]

Yet Baldwin's 1924—29 premiership had shown how difficult it could be to stick to the relaxed relationship with working-class leaders which he favoured. In 1925 he had had to use a prime ministerial veto in Cabinet to kill a bill prepared by MacQuisten, a backbencher, which attacked the unions' political levy. Similarly he had deliberately used a subsidy to maintain miners' wages in 1925 while the Samuel Commission was at work; the cabinet papers now show that this was not because of any unreadiness to meet the emergency, for the machinery was virtually complete in 1925;[12] it was a political decision to buy nine months in the hope of avoiding a general strike altogether. When this failed Baldwin seemed to pass the peak of his influence; and gave way to the pressure for restrictive legislation on trade unions in 1927.

The other major element in Baldwin's brand of Conservatism was represented by the catalogue of social reforms enacted by Chamberlain while at the Ministry of Health: the 1925 Widows, Orphans and Old Age Contributory Pensions Act, the Unemployment Insurance Act and the Local Government Act of 1929 which abolished the Poor Law Unions and introduced block grants for local authorities. This at least reversed the negativism of 1920—22 and gave the Conservatives a constructive position in social matters which they had not had since the 1870s. After 1931 there was no reversal of the Baldwinian approach despite the impression of financial severity cultivated by the National Government. After embarking on a strategy of orthodoxy and deflation the government devalued in 1931 and actually ran modest budget deficits from 1932 onwards; by 1934 the expenditure cuts necessitated by the crisis had been removed; and the Chancellor, Neville Chamberlain, deliberately promoted low interest rates — to reduce national debt charges — which stimulated the boom in house-building during the 1930s. Doctrinaire reliance upon market forces was most conspicuous in ship-building whose capacity dropped dramatically; in iron and steel this was masked by the establishment of new plant; and in coal many inefficient mines were kept in operation by means of a quota system for production and fixed prices. Positive intervention in the economy went beyond the protective tariffs of 1931 and 1932 which left three-quarters of all imports paying duties. For example use was made of Labour's Agricultural Marketing Act to fix quotas for imports, and production was bolstered by subsidies and marketing boards which cost £100 million per annum by 1934. In contrast a niggardly £2 million was made available for public schemes under the 1934 Depressed Areas Act, though in 1937 the Chancellor introduced remission of rent, rates and taxation for companies moving into such areas. The willingness of Baldwin's ministers to impose rationalization through the state where private enterprise seemed inadequate or inappropriate was shown in the creation of the Central Electricity Board in 1926 and in the granting of a charter to the BBC in the same year. This approach continued under the National Governments, which revived Morrison's plan for a London Passenger Transport Board in 1933 and merged the private airlines into a public body, the British Overseas Airways Corporation, in 1939. All in all these measures of empirical nationalization, of piecemeal social welfare, and of economic pump-priming effected a steady shift in the Conservative position during the 1930s so that it was separated from that of the Labour leaders more by emphasis and rhetoric than by substance. Its performance fell well short of the expectations of bodies like Political and Economic Planning set up in 1931, and the Next Five Years Group of 1935; representative of elements within all three parties they continued to propagate the Keynesian strategy for operating capitalism with high economic growth, full employment and social welfare. While there was no intellectual acceptance of their proposals by Neville Chamberlain, they ensured that the inheritance of the younger Conservatives such as R. A. Butler and Harold Macmillan would be broadly similar to that of their Labour rivals after the Second World War.

Baldwin's ability to reassure rather than to provoke was also calculated to win over the relatively uncommitted elements among the voters, notably women who, as a result of the Equal Franchise Act of 1928 (another of Baldwin's liberal successes in the teeth of Cabinet opposition) now formed 52 per cent of the electorate. For the new voters, male and female, and less politically committed than the smaller pre-1918 electorate, Baldwin was an ideal leader, radiating a wholesome, non-political appeal. A more distinct element, perceived as vital by Conservative tacticians, was the regular Liberal voter and those apt to surge back to the Liberals in the elections of 1923 and 1929. Attempts to attract wavering Liberals took various forms. In the first stage the entire parliamentary Liberal Party, except Lloyd George and his family group, joined the National Government in 1931. When in 1932 the Samuelites resigned over tariffs Sir John Simon retained about half the MPs, who fought the 1935 election at National Liberals. Simon's only virtue as Foreign Secretary in 1931–35 was as the embodiment of Liberal influence on the government. While there is no evidence that the politicians believed the voters to be pacifists, they did try to court popularity from disarmament and the League of Nations, both symbols of the will for peace; hence their fear of being blamed for the failure of the Disarmament Conference at Geneva, chaired by Arthur Henderson,[13] and their concern to stay on terms with Lord Robert Cecil and the League of Nations Union which urged voters to support candidates most likely to back the League.[14] Rightly or wrongly Liberals were thought to be especially keen on the League and disarmament. Therefore Baldwin took care to advance the popular and seemingly liberal Anthony Eden to the status of cabinet minister with responsibility for League affairs; and when Simon was replaced it was to Sir Samuel Hoare, a Conservative with relatively liberal credentials, that the Foreign Office fell. The success of all this was marked by the willingness of the Samuelites to vote for the government's defence estimates in 1935. Yet the price had to be paid in terms of criticism from the right who intensely resented Simon for his apparent willingness to sacrifice British sovereignty through the League of Nations and for allowing the Soviet Union to join in 1934. This demeaning pursuit of the League was, in the critics' view, practised by both Hoare and Eden whom they accused of abandoning Britain's vital interest in good relations with Mussolini as a result of his invasion of Abyssinia. In addition, if the National Government's liberal tendencies were ever in doubt Winston Churchill vociferously reminded Liberals what a real Tory policy on defence or India should be. Everything, in short, served Baldwin's purpose of entrenching him on the middle ground from which neither the Liberals nor Labour could dislodge him.

Baldwin's liberal credentials were most severely tested by controversies over imperial affairs. Indeed he could well have been overthrown but for the division of his right-wing critics between the Indian cause and the United Empire Campaign, both of which dogged him throughout the late 1920s and early 1930s. In retrospect Baldwin emerges as the key figure in leading the Conservatives away from their traditional role as defenders of Empire, and in this sense his leadership represented a sharp break with that of Bonar Law which had been so closely associated with resistance to Irish Home Rule. Though an MP before 1914 Baldwin had been too obscure to be associated with that desperate stand, and like Hoare he simply could not share the sense of trauma at losing Ireland. It was Baldwin who dropped the 'Unionist' tag in referring to his party; and he expressed his patriotism infrequently in imperial terms, preferring to cast it in the form of a romantic celebration of all things English.

In the case of India Baldwin took up where the Lloyd George Coalition had left off. Those Conservatives who were most closely involved in Indian policy – Edward Wood (Lord Irwin), Hoare and Baldwin himself – largely shared the liberal assumption that western-educated Indians ought not to be excluded indefinitely from government because their active collaboration was necessary both to the maintenance of British rule and to eventual self-rule. The Montagu–Chelmsford reforms of 1919 had already created in India an electorate of 5 million with powers over certain reserved topics at provincial level. These reforms were due for revision in 1929, but Baldwin anticipated this by appointing a Commission under Simon in 1928. Unfortunately Indians were not included in the Commission, whose usefulness was completely destroyed by the famous Civil Disobedience campaign launched by Gandhi. In order to regain the initiative Lord Irwin, now Viceroy, issued an important declaration in October 1929 to the effect that dominion status was 'the natural issue of India's constitutional progress', and initiated the first of the Round Table Conferences. Irwin provoked a storm of protest from the Conservative right wing, especially when his policy culminated in the Gandhi–Irwin Pact of 1931 – a demoralizing blow to the morale of the British administrators. At home the Secretary of State, Hoare, followed up with the massive dose of reform (the 1935 Government of India Act), which extended virtual self-government at provincial level and created a franchise for 30 million people. It was this approach that decisively alienated Churchill from Baldwin after 1929, and led him to resign from the shadow Cabinet in January 1931 so as to be free to attack official policy. Although the critics attracted only 40–50 votes in the Commons, their support in the party was much more widespread and open. At a meeting of the National Union's Central Council in February 1933 the Cabinet's policy was challenged and upheld by only 189 to 165 votes; and it was flatly repudiated by both the Conservative women and the Junior

Imperial League. At the 1934 party conference the India rebels lost the vote by only 543 to 520.

Baldwin managed to live with such a bitter and long-running controversy partly because the leading India rebels failed to combine with the protectionists under Lords Rothermere and Beaverbrook. Since the party's defeat in 1929 they had waged a campaign for 'Empire Free Trade' in their newspapers, in the party organization, and even at by-elections. A decisive clash occurred at the St George's (Westminster) by-election in March 1931 in which Baldwin's candidate, Duff Cooper, triumphed over his Empire Free Trade rival. Although Rothermere contributed financially to the India Defence League (a backbench Churchillian group), there was little chance of the rigid free trader, Churchill, reciprocating by lending support for protectionism. The greatest danger to Baldwin was probably Neville Chamberlain whom the press barons offered to back as alternative leader in 1931. The same motive led Rothermere to adopt Sir Oswald Mosley as a suitable battering ram in the early 1930s, also without success.

Thus, in the light of the controversies through the 1925–35 period Baldwin's distaste for a purely Conservative administration is entirely explicable. His centrist, liberal, conciliatory brand of politics, which had been initiated in the mid-1920s, checked in the later 1920s, and nearly destroyed along with his own leadership during 1929–31, was continued under the aegis of the National Governments. Only by effecting a modification in the balance within the party could Baldwin hope to lead Conservatism in the way he wanted. Consequently, as early as 1932 he began to present the National Government as Britain's long-term bulwark against dictatorships of right and left – an increasingly credible picture now that Europe was falling under totalitarian regimes. By 1934–35, with the financial crisis clearly over and the economy showing signs of recovery Baldwin had no difficulty in rallying his party to the 'national' strategy if only as the best means of preserving the country's stability from a resurgent left.

The Threat from the British Union of Fascists

By deliberately seeking the central ground of politics Baldwin ran the risk of driving his opponents in the party to an alternative leadership outside the National Government. In the early 1930s the most compelling and coherent alternative was that offered by the British Union of Fascists under Sir Oswald Mosley. Not only did Mosley appear to have a bolder grasp of economic and social problems than the conventional politicians, he and his movement also posed a dire electoral challenge to the National Government, and thus for some years threatened to undermine Baldwin's entire strategy. With hindsight it is comfortingly easy to assume the inevitability of the BUF's failure, and to attribute its loss of momentum after 1934 to the public reaction against the anti-semitism and the violence associated with the notorious BUF rally at Olympia in June of that year. Yet the underlying reason for the BUF's decline almost certainly lay in the modest economic revival in 1934. It was this that gave the government the confidence to risk a general election in November 1935. Fascism was only likely to succeed as a revolutionary movement if it enjoyed the oppor-tunity to step in to save a collapsing and discredited capitalist democracy from communism, but by 1935 this was clearly not going to materialize in Britain. However, since there was scarcely time for the BUF to re-orientate itself around a parliamentary strategy before the general election, Mosley decided to abstain, and the National Government escaped unscathed.

Yet it was not until 1936 that the government felt confident enough that the fascists were losing public sympathy to take legislative action to curtail their activities by means of the Public Order Act which banned political uniforms and empowered the police to ban marches for three-month periods. Up to that time the politicians were in fact highly apprehensive of Mosley's capacity to win adherents right across the political spectrum; and it is the threat he posed to the conventional party system which must be explained. In particular the reaction of those on the right of British politics to the apparent rise of fascism in Britain was more complicated than might be supposed. In the Commons debate on Mosley's Olympia rally in June 1934 Conservative, not Labour, members were the most prominent contributors; and despite the reputation of this debate as a turning-point in BUF fortunes relatively few of them actually expressed total disapproval of the BUF. In fact a number of Conservative and National Labour members readily admitted to some sympathy with Mosley as a man who had to 'sow his wild oats'; some condemned him but made a point of praising 'the thousands of young men who have joined the Blackshirt Movement. They are among the best elements in this country.'[15] Conscious of the vulnerability of urban, working-class seats won in 1931 to be defended at an election a year or two away, they felt alarmed at seeing large numbers of younger people going over to the BUF 'in shoals'. Research on fascist grass-roots support is limited and BUF membership figures are still unavailable; therefore the claim that 500 branches existed by 1936 may considerably exaggerate fascist strength. But something of significance may be discerned from the distribution of the parliamentary constituencies the BUF planned to contest by 1936–39: 39 in and around London, 16 in Lancashire, 12 in Yorkshire, 6 in the Midlands, 3 in Wales. Fascist campaigning in the northern towns was designed to win over traditional working-class Conservatism by a nationalist–protectionist appeal; in areas of declining industry this must have seemed a potent threat to the Conservative Party and to Baldwin's strategy in particular; it serves to remind us that the impression of the BUF as an East End of London anti-Jewish movement is only part of the picture. Certainly the politicians were torn between resentment of Mosley as an electoral rival who could deliver their seats to Labour, and admiration for his capacity to hold meetings in areas where, they claimed, left-wing disruption normally made it impossible for them to do so. Thus Olympia actually confirmed the truth of Mosley's boast that he could conduct political rallies anywhere; the possibility that he would continue to gain ground made for a hesitant response as yet by the party. In the event their fears were not realized because Mosley, evidently deterred by the poor showing his infant New Party had made in 1931, decided to abstain from the 1935 general election.

Those close to the Conservative establishment were more suspicious of Mosley as a divisive force exploited by his patron Rothermere. They shared with many politicians a deep distrust of a man who could change his party allegiance as often as he had done in a rather short career, especially when he had 'betrayed his class' by joining the Labour Party. In addition there existed an ideological deterrent. While some shared Mosley's anti-democratic sentiments and despaired of the effete Baldwinian leadership, they saw no great need for an extra-parliamentary force so long as the pillars of society, particularly the monarchy, the Church, and to a lesser extent even Parliament, remained intact. Economically much of what Mosley had to say was an extension of tariff reform and imperial development perfectly congenial to Conservatives. Yet there was a radical edge to his ideas. He sharply distinguished between those capitalists who manufactured goods and those who were devoted to finance, insurance and trade. He often attacked the latter on the grounds that they helped Britain's competitors and imposed the bankrupt policies of nineteenth-century liberalism on Britain in their own narrow interests. His willingness to exploit the power of the state at the expense of private enterprise further alienated Conservatives, especially as the economy showed distinct signs of climbing out of the depression; Britain had escaped the inflation that had devastated middle-class savings elsewhere and thus opened them to radical economic alternatives. Mosley's wartime experience and his six years in the Labour Party had not been for nothing; they had left him with a conviction that the pathetic conditions of life of most British people could be improved if the resources of society were brought fully into play. This radicalism would only be acceptable on the right when the only alternative was the radicalism of the far left.

This quality in Mosley's thinking which enabled him to address himself coherently to the central question of unemployment largely accounts for the appreciation of him by some socialist politicians such as Aneurin Bevan and James Maxton in 1930 who saw him as a complete contrast to the ineffectual MacDonald. John Strachey and the ex-Labour MP John Becket even followed him after 1931. However, the bulk of the Labour movement was alienated by Mosley's abrupt abandonment of the party after failing to carry the conference with him in the autumn of 1930 and by his intervention in the Ashton by-election which cost Labour the seat. Thereafter he had to contend with systematic opposition wherever Labour was strong. After Hitler's rise to power the trade unions, hitherto inclined to regard the BUF simply as an unofficial arm of the National Government, increasingly identified it as part of an international phenomenon; noting the tendency of fascist regimes to suppress trade unions they threw their weight against any attempts to win over working men in areas of declining industry.

In the final analysis the inability of the BUF to become a major force at the expense of the existing parties may be ascribed to three causes. First, the relatively light impact of the depression upon Britain which spared the middle classes from inflation and permitted a rising standard of living for many working-class families. This left the main institutional pillars of society, enhanced by victory in the First World War, resilient and popular at least by comparison with most of the rest of Europe. Secondly the timing was unfortunate. In 1931 the New Party was too young to mount an effective challenge, and in 1934-35 economic revival checked a slide towards the BUF; the uncommitted voters and the neglected lower middle classes were swept up by the National Government thus depriving Mosley of his natural constituency.

Thirdly Mosley's thesis that Britain should concentrate on a self-contained empire leaving the inward-looking Nazi Germany to do the same in east–central Europe, while attractive at the start of the 1930s, had waned by 1939 and left him exposed as a potential agent of Hitler by that time.

The Left, Rearmament and Public Opinion

After the trauma of 1931 the forces on the left on politics gave way to fissiparous tendencies with the result that they largely failed to rally an effective opposition to the National Governments, despite the fact that the dominant problems, unemployment and defence, ought to have worked to their advantage. At the centre of the Labour Party in this period lay a leadership vacuum. Of the founding fathers only Henderson, Clynes and Lansbury still occupied prominent positions in the movement, though this facilitated the emergence of three men from the second rank, Herbert Morrison, Ernest Bevin and Hugh Dalton, who were to become key figures for the next 20 years. In the Commons after the electoral holocaust of 1931 the party numbered a mere 52 members (including the ILP), of whom 26 represented the Miners Federation; for the most part they had been loyal to MacDonald and were still too confused to give a strong lead now that he had gone. Only three MPs had any ministerial experience, and so Lansbury by default became party leader and Clement Attlee his deputy. When in 1935 Attlee succeeded to the leadership his modesty and inconspicuous efficiency seemed qualifications enough. Though from a middle-class background he had no history except within the Labour movement; having worked his way up through local government in London Attlee was a safer choice than the more brilliant figures or the intellectuals recruited from other parties. Hence Herbert Morrison (who was his senior as a minister and his superior as party organizer and public speaker) was passed over. The small size and mediocrity of the parliamentary party robbed it of the dominance it had enjoyed through the National Executive Committee since 1918; whereas on average 16 of the NEC's 23 members had been MPs in 1918–31, only three were MPs in 1931–35. Consequently with each major institution of the party – NEC, parliamentary party and the National Joint Council – dominated by cautious, defensive trade unionists it proved difficult to come to terms with both the socialists and the rebellious movements among the rank and file.

Union defensiveness was caused by the continued drop in membership to 4.5 million by 1934. Although this left a huge slice of the working class outside union organization they were not recruited in substantial numbers by rival bodies such as the ILP, the Socialist League or the Communist Party; membership of the latter did rise from 2,500 in 1930 to 6,000 in 1931 and to 18,000 by 1939, but this reflected middle-class concern about fascism rather than working-class allegiance. The most serious threat to the unions came from Wal Hannington's National Unemployed Workers Movement, which at its peak in 1931–33 managed to mobilize 50,000 men; even this must be set against the total of almost 3 million unemployed among the insured population at this time. Despite the apprehension of the orthodox leaders of labour, the methods of the NUWM tended to be limited to hunger marches and petitions, and its objectives to be confined to the restoration of the cuts in unemployment benefit and abolition of the means test. In neither sense, therefore, was it really radical, let alone subversive; what violence accompanied its meetings was half-hearted and unorganized, and the movement fizzled out in 1933 in an anti-climax reminiscent of Chartism. It is a tribute to the political apathy of the 1930s, or perhaps to the cushioning effects of welfare benefits and falling prices, that the Labour Party could afford to shun the NUWM without danger to itself. Loss of working-class support to the National Government was a much more serious concern.

The party leaders bore even more lightly the severance of ties with the ILP in 1932, after which the latter went into headlong decline. However, the split led some ILP members to join the new Socialist League, a small but vigorous intellectual elite including G.D.H. Cole, Sir Stafford Cripps, Harold Laski, Sir Charles Trevelyan, R.H. Tawney, D.N. Pritt, Ellen Wilkinson and Aneurin Bevan. Though designed as a research and propaganda group within the Labour Party the Socialist League rapidly ran into the same problem as the ILP of developing a rival programme to that of the party. It also became embroiled from 1933 in attempts to persuade the party of the virtues of a United Front strategy against fascism incorporating the Communist Party, which from 1935 was seeking affiliation to the Labour Party. These efforts were decisively rebuffed by annual Labour conferences.

In fact the only effective challenge to the centrist leadership in the 1930s — the Constituency Parties Movement — emerged outside the conventional left-wing forces. This was essentially a spontaneous expression of rank and file frustration at their effective exclusion from power in the party since 1918. In the original constitution the constituency activists had enjoyed a certain role through the generous representation of the ILP on the NEC. However, the ILP had gradually ceased to play a prominent part. Moreover, the reforms of 1918, while allowing the constituency parties to nominate candidates for five of the 23 places on the NEC, left the choice to the vote of the whole conference, which in effect meant the block votes of the larger unions. Yet the constituencies were now the one expanding section of the movement; individual membership rose to 419,000 in 1935. At this point a campaign for constitutional reform led by Ben Greene emerged particularly in the southern constituencies. As a body of loyal party workers at the heart of the movement the Constituency Parties Movement could not be brushed aside like the socialist societies even though much of its strength was concentrated in areas where Labour representation remained slight. In 1937 conference agreed to raise constituency representation from five to seven and to allow them to be elected separately. Although this coup had not been engineered by the left, the movement had enjoyed, to its embarrassment, the support of Cripps since 1936; certainly its immediate effect was to strengthen the influence of the left since Cripps, Laski and Pritt were among those elected from the constituency parties to the NEC.

Throughout the inter-war period the controversies between the left and the leadership were largely fought in the realm of defence and foreign policy with the left gradually losing the initiative. During the 1920s Labour had been strongly placed to criticize those who had imposed a punitive settlement on Germany at Versailles for the satisfaction of France. In adopting the view that it was a blunder to fix 'war guilt' upon Germany and to squeeze reparations from her, and in condemning the armaments race as a major cause of war in 1914, the party was well within the mainstream of British thinking. In principle Labour went somewhat further in that it advocated a drastic revision of the Versailles Treaty on the ground that it had been an imperialist peace that deprived Germany of colonial and economic assets and flouted the principle of nationality where it would have worked in Germany's favour as on the borders of Czechoslovakia and Poland. However, in practice Labour and Conservative governments operated a bi-partisan policy during the 1920s involving strictly limited steps towards the appeasement of German grievances — a downward revision of reparations, assistance with the currency, persuading the French to quit the Ruhr, and an early evacuation of the Rheineland. Appeasement thus stopped well short of accepting the right to racial unity of all Germans, or of permitting Germany's re-establishment as a major military power.

One consequence of their attitude towards Versailles was an initial hostility by many Labour politicians to the League of Nations on the grounds that it was a vehicle for the victorious powers to apply sanctions to preserve an advantageous *status quo*. Pacifists, both Christian and socialist in inspiration, urged unilateral disarmament as a surer way to permanent peace than embroilment in League affairs. This position was never accepted by the parliamentary party although its members regularly voted against the defence estimates, and the party conference in 1922 and 1926 passed resolutions opposing any participation in wars. However, these decisions represented the high-water mark of left-wing pacifism which progressively gave way to the more pragmatic approach of Henderson, Bevin, Dalton and Attlee who argued in favour of 'collective security'; this meant elevating the League of Nations to a place of central importance in foreign policy and through it applying sanctions — economic and if necessary military — against aggressor states; therefore for Dalton and Bevin there were strict limits to British disarmament and a point where rearmament would become necessary. In spite of the impression of fundamental differences of principle between the pacifist left and the Conservative right, the position of the Labour leaders closely approached that of the Conservative and National Governments. By 1922 expenditure on the armed forces had been cut back to £110 million — from £600 million in 1920 — and remained around that level until 1935 when both parties decided that rearmament was necessary.

The pace of disarmament and appeasement has sometimes been explained in terms of an all-pervading pacifism in inter-war British society. This involves demonstrating first that the public was pacifist and second that the awareness of this moulded official policy. Certainly the late 1920s and early 1930s saw some striking manifestations such as the anti-war publications, notably Robert Graves' *Goodbye To All That* (1929) and Vera Brittain's *Testament of Youth* (1933). No doubt the success of such volumes a decade after the war tells us something about the mood of the 1920s and 1930s; but they do not point to a general pacifism so much as to a repudiation, particularly by some of the middle classes, of the kind of appeal that had been used to justify war in 1914–18. A similar significance may be placed upon the famous Oxford Union debate in 1934 on the proposition that 'this House will in no circumstances fight for its King and Country'; in condemning politicians' manipulation of the people in one set of circumstances they did not necessarily indicate a refusal to fight when a proper cause arose, as it did for many when the Spanish Civil War broke out. Nor are the findings of the more important Peace Ballot of 1934 to be interpreted as proof of pacifism. The immediate background to the ballot was Germany's withdrawal from the Disarmament Conference in 1933. This called into question the effectiveness of the League of Nations which had been widely, if vaguely, regarded as the best means of avoiding war. To demonstrate support for the League and collective security the League of Nations Union therefore conducted a poll in which 11.5 million people voted. While an overwhelming majority favoured the reduction of arms by international agreement even to the point of their elimination, they were also prepared to face a situation in which the reverse occurred. Some 6.7 million voted for applying sanctions including military ones against aggressor states who flouted arbitration by the League; only 2.3 million opposed this. Thus support for the League ought not to be equated with pacifism; there clearly existed public support for resistance to the dictators in the early 1930s, as was strikingly demonstrated by the extremely hostile reaction to the Hoare-Laval Pact of 1935 which offered a partition of Abyssinia to the advantage of Mussolini.

Indeed any idea of the National Government being tightly constrained in its foreign and defence policy by the public's adamant refusal to contemplate war and rearmament is a travesty. The classic piece of evidence used to substantiate this view was the East Fulham by-election of October 1934 when a Conservative majority of 14,000 was turned into a Labour majority of 4,800 supposedly because disarmament was offered by the latter and 'warmongering' by the former.[16] However, this interpretation has been largely discredited by critical examination of the evidence. In the first place the constituency was far from being a safe Conservative seat: the 14,000 majority reflected only the special circumstances of 1931; in 1929 East Fulham returned a Conservative by 1,700, and in 1935 by 1,000. It was therefore by no means remarkable that it fell to the opposition in a mid-term by-election. Nor was the by-election fought primarily over defence, but rather on domestic economy and housing questions which were ably exploited by an attractive, middle-of-the-road candidate who apparently won over the bulk of the Liberal vote in the absence of a Liberal candidate. Moreover, even if East Fulham could be interpreted as a pacifist vote, it would have to be set against the comfortable Conservative victories in seats where their candidates frankly espoused rearmament such as Basingstoke and Twickenham in 1934 and Aberdeen South in 1935.

In any case there appears to be no good evidence that the government was sufficiently impressed by the election at the time to allow its defence policy to be determined by fear of public opinion. Endowed with the massive mandate of 1931 the Cabinet had already displayed a willingness to disappoint expectations on the economic front, and it seems unlikely that they would have shied away from a vital policy merely because it would bring unpopularity. In fact the chief restraint on defence in the early 1930s and after 1935 when rearmament began was imposed by Neville Chamberlain as Chancellor of the Exchequer: and his central arguments were the economic ones of the Treasury. He refused to allow his nearly balanced budgets to be jeopardized by a major increase in defence spending; the expansion of one sector would inevitably weaken other sectors of the economy and would force the government into massive borrowing. In 1934 the report of the Defence Requirements Committee urged that Germany not Japan should be regarded as the most likely enemy, and the army and air force expanded with that in mind. Under Chamberlain's influence the Cabinet opted for building up the RAF as a deterrent force, thereby restricting the proposed expenditure increases to £59 million rather than £97 million as originally suggested.

In the same hesitant way and at much the same time the Labour leaders also moved into a position of cautious support for rearmament. Despite the leadership of the elderly Lansbury the pacifists were steadily undermined from the early 1930s — initially by Japanese aggression in Manchuria which led both the TUC and the NEC in 1933 to advocate an economic boycott. The advent of Hitler to power also altered attitudes by putting fascism firmly into an international framework. Hitherto much had been made of the unwisdom of putting arms into the hands of the National Government, a view that received short shrift from men like Bevin. In 1934 Henderson carried the conference by 1.5 million to 670,000 on a resolution favouring collective security through the League. This led to the resignations of Cripps, of Arthur Ponsonby as leader in the Lords, and finally of Lansbury. However, the outbreak of the Spanish Civil War in July 1936 was to have the most powerful effect of all in that it led many of those like Trevelyan and Cripps, usually most opposed to intervention, to demand active support by Britain for the Spanish Republicans. By 1937 the party had abandoned opposition to armaments to the extent of ceasing to vote against the defence estimates. By 1939 opposition and government had reached a common view of the war against the dictators as a justified one.

The General Election of 1935 and its Aftermath

During the early 1930s only the more nervous members of the National Government seriously expected to be swept out of existence at the next election. A predictable Labour recovery did take place after 1931. Individual membership rose by 100,000 during 1933 when it reached 380,000, but the momentum was hardly sustained in 1935 when it levelled out at 419,000. By-elections showed the Labour poll returning to and sometimes exceeding the 1929 level. However, two gains in 1932, two in 1933 and four in 1934 represented rather limited successes amid 40 by-elections in which the government held on to the bulk of its vast 1931 gains; spectacular losses like East Fulham were not indicative of a general trend of opinion. When the depression reached its nadir in 1932–33 the opposition should have reaped the electoral dividends; yet they were the opposition precisely because of their inability to cope with the depression. In addition by July 1935 when unemployment fell below 2 million the growing sense of recovery deprived them of a central line of attack. The government pointed to the construction of one million houses since 1931, the restoration of the 1931 salary cuts, and the tax relief in Chamberlain's 1935 budget; and during the election he took the opportunity to announce extra funds for road-building to offset attacks upon his parsimony towards the unemployed. On only one occasion had the government run into serious opposition from the unemployed. In 1934 it decided to remove unemployment assistance from the Public Assistance Committees and administer it on a uniform basis through a central body, the Unemployment Assistance Board; when in January 1935 it became clear that the new uniform scales would reduce the income of many families there arose a rare display of outrage throughout the country. Thereupon the new scales were promptly dropped; and Baldwin took care to get the election safely out of the way well before revised scales were implemented in 1936. In so far as there was a safe time for an election it was the autumn of 1935 only a few months after the King's jubilee. Still saddled with the charge of having run away from the financial crisis in 1931 the Labour leaders found it difficult to erase the impression that if they returned to office the crisis would return with them; it seemed unwise to jeopardize the modest improvements achieved under Chamberlain's unimaginative management.

The only alternative line of attack for the opposition lay in questions of peace and rearmament. Now some historians, usually as part of a defence of Baldwin's handling of rearmament, still insist that the general election of 1935 was fought on foreign and defence policy, and thereby might be held to have furnished the Prime Minister with a 'mandate' for rearmament.[17] Yet this has never been demonstrated. An explanation on these lines would argue that the Labour Party benefited from its anti-armaments stance in 1934 but failed in 1935 because public opinion had veered round to support of rearmament. We have already seen how dubious the first part of this argument is. To say that rearmament was an issue in 1935 is to assume that the main parties adopted clear and opposed views that could be perceived by the voters; for no item of policy, however intrinsically important, becomes an issue that turns votes unless the parties manage to articulate it clearly. While we know that substantial differences did exist between, say, Churchill at one extreme and Cripps at the other, the views of Attlee–Bevin–Dalton and Baldwin–Chamberlain–Simon were never far apart and had been steadily converging on one another. Far from unequivocally exhorting the electors to accept a rearmament programme Baldwin insisted that 'there will be no great armaments' and that the Cabinet intended only to 'repair gaps in our defences'. Both sets of party leaders were striving to edge their followers and the country towards a modest rearmament programme; neither wished to make a point of advocating it, but they would not go out of their way to resist it. They sought to express what seemed to be the generally accept-able view that Britain must possess whatever weapons were necessary to enable her to play an effective part in collective security through the League. Indeed in so far as any clear message emerged from the 1935 election it was the central importance attached to the League, which of course united the political parties. Instead of trying sharply to differentiate their views on defence, leaders of both parties preferred to concentrate on domestic questions. Thus rearmament never grew into an issue in 1935, and no mandate was either sought or given. In a thickening international atmosphere the public were doubtless not alarmed by limited doses of rearmament, and took refuge in confidence in the League.

The Labour Party devoted much of its effort to rebutting

charges of extremism in domestic and economic affairs which had been sedulously cultivated by National Government supporters. It was easy to point to connections between British socialism and some of the policies of Stalinist Russia whose economic planning was frankly admired by the Webbs and others. At the election the Communist Party exacerbated matters by publishing its manifesto on the same day as Labour and emphasizing that all its candidates but two had been withdrawn so as not to jeopardize the return of a Labour government. Since 1934 the Labour Party had gone to the lengths of organizing a series of 'Peace and Freedom' meetings to emphasize its commitment to parliamentary democracy and to dispel fears of totalitarian sympathies. Unfortunately the prominent resignations of Cripps, Lansbury and Ponsonby so close to the election drew more attention to the left. The death of the reassuringly moderate Henderson in 1935 robbed the party of a familiar face; and Attlee had too short a period as leader and too faint a personality to make a useful impact before or during the election. It proved difficult to present the party as an effective ruling group while MacDonald remained to call into question the fitness of his former colleagues to govern. Fitness in office was thus a far more damaging cry in the 1930s than it had been in the 1920s.

There are grounds for thinking that the popular reputations of the rival parties had been moulded by the mass media well before the election. Apart from sporadic right-wing criticism the only consistent opposition the National Government had to face in the press came from the radical *Daily Chronicle* and the Labour *Daily Herald*; not until 1938 when the *Daily Mirror* swung to Labour did the balance shift significantly. Perhaps more important were the cinema newsreels which by the 1930s catered to a huge working-class audience; these were invariably calculated to foster an optimistic, patriotic view of current events in which ministers received the bulk of the coverage for their gallant efforts against the odds; the tendency to minimize the controversial aspects of current affairs would have hampered any opposition whatever its complexion. Similarly analysis of the newsreels, programmes and personnel of the BBC during 1932–35 suggests a distinct bias in favour of ministerial achievement and neglect of opposition views.[18] The gradual effect of all this upon the public perception of politicians is to be distinguished from the direct and immediate advantage that probably accrued to the government from Baldwin's mastery of the technique of reassuring radio broadcasts in contrast to the more formal and stilted messages delivered by Attlee.

In these circumstances the comfortable survival of the National Government, still allied with the Simonite Liberals and National Labour remnants, is quite explicable. With a net gain of 94 seats in 1935 the Labour total reached 158, almost three times its 1931 figure, but nowhere near the 288 of 1929. Despite an average swing of 9.4 per cent to Labour the government held 435 seats, 388 of which were Conservative. In areas like the West Riding, Durham, Northumberland and southern Scotland, barely touched by economic recovery, the swing exceeded this; but in the buoyant West Midlands it was only half the national average. In Birmingham where 6 of the 12 seats had fallen to Labour in 1929, none did so now. Many industrial working-class constituencies – all three in Salford, all four in Newcastle – returned National Government candidates; even Jarrow was but narrowly recovered by Ellen Wilkinson. The true extent of Baldwin's success may be discerned in the 40 seats that enjoyed a straight Conservative–Labour contest in 1929, 1931 and 1935; here the swing away from Labour between 1929 and 1931 had been 15.1 per cent and the swing in their favour between 1931 and 1935 only 9.9 per cent, so that roughly a third of the lost support continued to adhere to the National Government. In the 32 seats with a three-cornered contest in the three elections Labour candidates almost recovered their 1929 vote; however, the redistribution of part of the Liberal vote in favour of Conservative and National Liberal candidates kept them well ahead. This underlines Baldwin's key achievement in claiming the middle ground. Although the Labour share of the national poll (38 per cent) narrowly exceeded that of 1929 (37 per cent) it brought 130 fewer seats because of the concentration of non-Labour votes on National candidates where previously they had been more evenly divided between Conservative and Liberal. Having been boosted by the electoral system in the 1920s Labour was thus seriously under-represented by it in the 1930s.

Between 1935 and the outbreak of the Second World War there were no clear indications of a major change in the *status quo*. During 1936–38 the government suffered swings to Labour in by-elections but they were usually below 10 per cent, which suggests a certain stability in partisan allegiance. The growing polarization of opinion for and against appeasement, which was to manifest itself in the emergence of 'Popular Front' candidates opposing the Munich settlement, had evidently not yet been translated into party terms. Such candidates challenged unsuccessfully at Oxford in October 1938 and at Bridgewater in November where a hitherto safe Conservative seat fell. However, these seem to have been special cases, and as yet no consistent trend against Chamberlain's conduct of foreign affairs had emerged. The chief division was within the Conservative ranks; for example the Duchess of Atholl resigned her seat to fight a by-election in December only to lose narrowly to an official Conservative who backed Chamberlain. Opinion polls which were now being conducted by Mass Observation indicated a certain bewilderment among voters on foreign policy questions with inevitable fluctuations in attitudes towards the government, but no substantial movement in favour of one party; the chief effect of the undoubted public concern at the approach of war was to raise turnout on both sides.

Thus on the available evidence one is bound to conclude that any general election held up to 1939 would have resulted in a further term for the National Government; the seeds of the 1945 landslide still lay dormant. This curiously unexciting conclusion to a decade marked by trauma and extremism reflects the skill of both Conservative and Labour leaders in emasculating their respective radicals, isolated on the peripheries; and further, the success of one of the two schools of moderation in outmanoeuvring the other on the central ground of British politics.

Epilogue

Between the outbreak of war in September 1939 and the general election of July 1945 political fortunes in Britain changed drastically in favour of the Labour Party. As early as 1943 the opinion polls — a novelty that most politicians disregarded as yet — pointed to a huge Labour lead of 16 per cent. And despite the prestige of the Prime Minister, Churchill, this advantage was only narrowed to a comfortable 6 per cent on polling day which gave Labour 393 seats and an overall majority for the first time. The 1945 election thus decisively ended the chronic imbalance in the party system in which the Conservatives had been so dominant since 1918. The result was essentially a defeat for the Conservative Party rather than Churchill; for Conservatives were still widely labelled the 'Guilty Men'[1] whose pursuit of appeasement had left the country unprepared for war. By the summer of 1945 the public seemed interested chiefly in domestic matters, especially housing and social welfare which the Beveridge Report had crystallized and publicized two years earlier. In fact politics in the post-1945 era was to revolve more than ever around questions of social policy and economic management. In 1945 this gave Labour the inestimable advantage of being able to speak with greater credibility and conviction on precisely the topics which the voters believed to be most important. Moreover, the Labour Party could no longer be written off as dangerous or unfit to govern as in the 1930s. Its leading figures, particularly, Attlee, Morrison and Bevin, had served with distinction in the wartime coalition since 1940. Although their economic and social policies had not changed significantly between 1935 and 1945, they were no longer regarded with apprehension, partly, perhaps, because of the reassuring wartime experience with state organization and the feeling for equality of sacrifice engendered by the emergency; in short the mood of 1945 was very close to what one historian has called 'Mr Attlee's Consensus'.[2] In addition the electorate itself had changed considerably since the last election in 1935. As many as one in five electors were voting for the first time, and of these 61 per cent are estimated to have supported the Labour Party — a reflection, no doubt, of their education during the depression and the rule of the National Governments. Thus long-term trends as well as immediate pressures worked strongly in the party's favour at this time.

The 15 years after 1945 marked the apogee of the political system which had evolved gradually from late Victorian politics. By this stage the need for fundamental change appeared to have come to an end. By 1928 the political system had managed to absorb the bulk of the adult population as citizens without becoming unstable, and it had been tested in the depression without succumbing to anti-parliamentary forces. Subsequent modifications, such as the elimination of the university franchise and the remaining business voters, or the enfranchisement of eighteen year olds, proved to be relatively uncontentious by comparison with the great Victorian reforms. By 1945 this parliamentary democracy had produced a system characterized by two evenly balanced parties, one broadly representative of labour and one of property. To most Victorians this would have sounded an alarming recipe for instability; yet in most respects change had been so heavily masked by continuity and consensus that this was by no means a justified fear.

In the institutional sphere the period witnessed a steady but not spectacular diminution in the role and authority of ordinary MPs and of Parliament, and a tendency for power to be concentrated further in the Cabinet, in cabinet committees, and in the Prime Minister, his personal entourage and leading civil servants. In this respect Lloyd George's premiership was probably a turning-point; for although none would confess to emulating his methods, his successors invariably repeated his habit of creating independent sources of advice and extending the powers of patronage. One might have expected that the rise of a party whose roots lay outside Parliament would have led to drastic modifications in the system. In practice, however, Labour was a guardian of parliamentary tradition except in so far as it tended to undermine the House of Lords. In principle Labour's policy was the policy of its Conference; but in practice the relationship of leaders and followers was not far removed from that between the National Liberal Federation and the parliamentary Liberals in the late nineteenth century. Once in office a Prime Minister like Attlee was hardly less powerful *vis-à-vis* his party than his Conservative equivalent. The difference was that Labour showed much less respect towards its leaders but was nonetheless very loyal and indulgent to them, while the Conservatives, though more deferential, were consistently ruthless in disposing of leaders who were felt to be beyond their useful life. In terms of personnel the two parties, though rather different, grew more alike. In the parliamentary Labour Party the proportion of working-class members shrank steadily after 1945. On the Conservative side the middle classes also advanced as the landed aristocracy faded imperceptibly. The latter had begun their prolonged retreat from national government back in 1889 by opting for county councils as a more congenial sphere of activity. After the Parliament Act of 1911 and the rise of the Labour Party they inevitably acquiesced when Lord Curzon was passed over in 1923 despite being the obvious choice as Prime Minister.

In policy and administration the post-1945 era also witnessed a surprising coalescence between the parties. For while the Liberal Party came near to dropping through the trap-door of history, the governments of both major parties tended to reflect the influence of two 'Liberals' — J.M. Keynes and William Beveridge. Conservatives made no attempt to dismantle the social reforms that came to be known as the 'Welfare State'. And both parties had emerged from the war in agreement with Keynes' premise that a comprehensive welfare system depended upon the maintenance of fairly full employment by the government; nor did they have to contend with a recalcitrant Treasury in applying Keynesian methods of economic management. The maintenance of employment helped to blunt socialist objections to the economic system, as did the Attlee government's nationalization programme. This proved much less controversial than expected because it left 80 per cent of industry privately run, relieved business of a number of unprofitable utilities, gave compensation to the dispossessed, and involved a system of running public industries that Conservatives found broadly acceptable.

Perhaps the chief architect of mid-twentieth-century Conservatism was Stanley Baldwin, though he is unlikely to be generally regarded as such for some time. Yet it was during the 1920s that he prepared his party to surrender the Imperial cause which had been the pillar of late Victorian Conservatism, a process that culminated in the rapid dismantling of the Empire in the 1950s and 1960s and Britain's application to join the European Economic Community. After Baldwin Conservatives invariably chose their leaders from their more liberal or innovating figures like Sir

Anthony Eden, R.A. Butler and Harold Macmillan, or Edward Heath and Reginald Maudling.

Finally there is the electoral dimension to political change that has figured so prominently in these pages. In retrospect the displacement of the traditional Liberal Party by Labour as the major governing party on the left during 1914–29 proved to be a remarkably smooth one. This was a consequence of the intellectual and electoral overlap between the two. By the Second World War Labour had emerged as the standard-bearer of the key elements in radical Victorian politics: it incorporated the Gladstonian tradition in foreign affairs; it was a party of causes; it maintained libertarian principles; and it propagated improvement through social reform. Equally significant is the social–geographical distribution of Labour strength in the country after 1945. Though relying on its large working-class vote Labour had not come near to extinguishing working-class Conservatism; by 1945 the party had won over sufficient middle-class and suburban support to make it a national party on the Liberal model. Just as 50 years earlier non-Conservative representation was concentrated in Wales, Scotland, the four northern counties and Yorkshire; London and, to a lesser extent, Lancashire were still the major volatile regions which each party had to win for an overall majority. The only real difference between the nineteenth- and twentieth-century patterns is that Labour was a more urban party than the Liberals, and could not recapture the old radical strength in south-west England, the Scottish highlands or East Anglia, though it often did in rural Wales. With these qualifications, however, modern elections provide a striking demonstration of the continuity of appeal by the parties of Attlee and Asquith.

Notes

CHAPTER 1: *Party and Participation 1867–1900*

1 Brian Harrison, *Separate Spheres: the Opposition to Women's Suffrage in Britain* (1978), pp. 59–64, 71.
2 J. R. Vincent, 'The Electoral Sociology of Rochdale', *Economic History Review*, 16 (1963–64), pp. 79–81.
3 N. Blewett, 'The Franchise in the United Kingdom 1885–1918', *Past and Present*, 32 (1965), pp. 33–4.
5 ibid., pp. 46–7.
5 R. J. Olney, *Lincolnshire Politics 1832–85* (1973), pp. 158–81.
6 G. E. Mingay, *The Gentry* (1976), pp. 79, 172, 177; F. M. L. Thompson, *English Landed Society in the Nineteenth Century* (1963), p. 342.
7 T. J. Nossiter, *Influence, Opinion and Political Idioms in Reformed England* (1975), pp. 48–9.
8 ibid., p. 53.
9 J. Howarth, 'The Liberal Revival in Northamptonshire 1885–95', *Historical Journal*, 12 (1969), pp. 90–1.
10 Countess of Warwick, *Joseph Arch: the story of his life told by himself* (1898), p. 329.
11 P. F. Clarke, *Lancashire and the New Liberalism* (1971), p. 251.
12 Charles Roberts, *The Radical Countess: the history of the life of Rosalind Countess of Carlisle* (1962), p. 85.
13 Patrick Joyce, 'The Factory Politics of Lancashire in the later Nineteenth Century', *Historical Journal*, 18 (1975), pp. 533–41.
14 ibid., pp. 541–3.
15 Nossiter, *Influence, Opinion and Political Idioms*, pp. 125–8.
16 Surviving two-member boroughs were Bath, Blackburn, Bolton, Brighton, Derby, Devonport, Halifax, Ipswich, Leicester, Newcastle, Northampton, Norwich, Oldham, Plymouth, Portsmouth, Preston, Southampton, Stockport, Sunderland, York, Merthyr Tydfil and Dundee.
17 Derek Fraser, *Urban Politics in Victorian England* (1976), pp. 115–24.

18 L. Kitchen, 'The 1892 Election in the Tyneside Area' (Newcastle M. Litt. thesis, unpublished, 1979), pp. 268, 284.

19 Leeds Liberal Federation Executive Committee Minutes 1894–1924; Keighley Conservative Association Minutes 1885–1904.

20 J. A. Garrard, 'Parties, Members and Voters After 1867: a local study', *Historical Journal*, 20 (1977), p. 151.

21 NUCCA Conference Minutes, 1897.

22 Quoted in the *Campaign Guide* (1892) published by the Conservative Party.

23 W. L. Guttsman, *The British Political Elite* (1965), p. 104.

24 R. Pumphrey, 'The Introduction of Industrialists into the British Peerage', *American Historical Review*, 65 (1959–60), p. 7.

25 H. H. Asquith, *Memories and Reflections* (1928), vol. II, p. 105.

CHAPTER 2: *The Evolution of the Gladstonian Liberal Party 1867–95*

1 In full, the Society for the Liberation of Religion from State Patronage and Control.

2 Henry Pelling, *America and the British Left* (1956), pp. 16–27.

3 C. Harvie, *The Lights of Liberalism: University Liberals and the Challenge of Democracy* (1976), pp. 112–14.

4 Robert Spence Watson, *The National Liberal Federation 1877–1906* (1907), pp. 3–4.

5 D. A. Hamer (ed.), *Joseph Chamberlain: The Radical Programme* (1971 edn), pp. xxii–xxv.

6 T. W. Heyck, 'Home Rule, Radicalism and the Liberal Party 1886–95', *Journal of British Studies*, 13 (1974), p. 69.

7 Michael Barker, *Gladstone and Radicalism 1885–94* (1975), p. 24.

8 P. C. Griffiths, 'The Caucus and the Liberal Party in 1886', *History*, 61 (1976), p. 192.

9 Barker, *Gladstone and Radicalism*, p. 75.

10 Quoted in D. A. Hamer, *John Morley* (1968), p. 236.

CHAPTER 3: *The Conservative Revival 1874–1900*

1 *Times*, 6 June 1865.

2 Balfour to Salisbury, 27 August 1891, J. P. Cornford, 'Parliamentary Foundations of the Hotel Cecil', R. Robson (ed.), *Ideas and Institutions of Victorian Britain* (1967), p. 296.

3 *Conservative Annual Conference Report*, 1867, fol. 3–4.

4 NUCCA Conference Minutes, 23 July 1880.

5 NUCCA Conference Minutes, 14 November 1882.

6 R. E. Quinault, 'Lord Randolph Churchill and Tory Democracy 1880–85', *Historial Journal*, 22 (1979), pp. 144–5.

7 National Union (Pamphlet No. 24, 1873), p. 4.

8 Quinault, 'Randolph Churchill', pp. 152, 158–9.

9 Peter Marsh, *The Discipline of Popular Government* (1978), p. 152.

10 R. B. McDowell, *British Conservatism 1832–1914* (1959); Samuel Beer, *Modern British Politics* (1965).

11 R. J. Olney, *Lincolnshire Politics 1832–85* (1973), pp. 188–9, 217.

12 G. Stedman Jones, *Outcast London* (1971), pp. 202–6, 215, 326.

13 *Campaign Guide* (1892).

14 *Campaign Guide* (1892 and 1895).

15 Marsh, *The Discipline of Popular Government*, p. 160.

16 J. P. D. Dunbabin, 'The Politics of the Establishment of County Councils', *Historical Journal*, 6 (1963), pp. 228–36.

17 Stedman Jones, *Outcast London*, pp. 227–30.

18 Quoted in Dunbabin, 'County Councils', pp. 239–40.

CHAPTER 4: *The Social Roots Of Political Change in Late Victorian Britain*

1 T. J. Nossiter, *Influence, Opinion and Political Idioms in Reformed England* (1975), pp. 177–92.

2 H. M. Pelling, *Social Geography of British Elections 1885–1910* (1967), p. 415.

3 Quoted in R. J. Olney, *Lincolnshire Politics 1832–85* (1973), p. 229.

4 See Raphael Samuel, *Village Life and Labour* (1975) on Headington Quarry in Oxfordshire.

5 Peter Marsh, *The Discipline of Popular Government* (1978), p. 207.

6 Olney, *Lincolnshire Politics*, p. 214.

7 Karl Marx 'The Chartists', *New York Daily Tribune*, 25 August 1852.

8 Pelling, *Social Geography of British Elections*, p. 419.

9 Countess of Warwick, *Joseph Arch: the story of his life told by himself* (1898), p. 55.

10 Frank Gray, *Confessions of a Candidate* (1925), pp. 9–10.

11 J. R. Vincent, *Pollbooks: How Victorians Voted* (1967), p. 45.

12 Ramsay MacDonald, *The Socialist Movement* (1911), p. 93.

13 NUCCA Annual Conference Minutes, 13–14 November 1892.

14 C. Green, 'Birmingham's Politics 1873–91: the Local Basis of Change', *Midland History*, 2 (1973), p. 92.

15 Quoted in A. McKenzie and A. Silver, *Angels in Marble* (1968), p. 60.

16 R. Price, *An Imperial War and the British Working Class* (1972), pp. 200–28.

17 National Urban pamphlet no. 3 (1892), 'Promise Versus Performance'.
18 *Campaign Guide* (Conservative Party) (1892), 'Labour Problems'.
19 Countess of Warwick, *Joseph Arch*, p. 255.
20 *Campaign Notes* (Conservative Party), *(1901), p. 516.*
21 Green, 'Birmingham's Politics 1873—91', p. 91.
22 ibid.
23 Nossiter, *Influence, Opinion and Political Idioms*, pp. 163—7, 147—8.

CHAPTER 5: *The Edwardian Crises 1895—1914*

1 H.A.Tulloch, 'Changing British Attitudes Towards America in the 1880s', *Historical Journal*, 20 (1977).
2 H.C.G.Matthew, R.I.McKibbin and J.A.Kay, 'The franchise factor in the rise of the Labour Party', *English Historical Review*, 91 (1976), pp. 742—3.
3 Minutes of the Society of Certificated and Associated Liberal Agents, 1895—1945.
4 For a valuable discussion of the problem see A.J. Lee, *The Origins of the Popular Press 1855—1914* (1976); and S.E. Koss, *Fleeet Street Radical: A.G. Gardiner and the Daily News* (1973), p. 40.
5 S.E. Koss, 'Wesleyanism and Empire', *Historical Journal*, 18 (1975).
6 Correspondence for 1897—98 in C.P. Trevelyan Papers, vol. 4; M.D. Pugh, 'Yorkshire and the New Liberalism?', *Journal of Modern History*, 50 (1978), p. 1142; L. Kitchen, 'The 1892 Election in the Tyneside Area' (Newcastle M. Litt. thesis, unpublished, 1979), pp. 70—1.
7 M. Barker, *Gladstone and Radicalism* (1975), pp. 50, 89—96, 197—8.
8 C.P. Trevelyan to Herbert Samuel, 2 October 1898, Trevelyan Papers, 4.
9 T. Boyle, 'The Liberal Imperialists, 1892—1906', *Bulletin of the Institute of Historical Research*, 52 (1979), pp. 51—5.
10 R.B. Haldane to Rosebery, 24 April 1895, Rosebery Papers, 24.
11 Peter Cain, 'Political Economy in Edwardian England: the Tariff Reform Controversy', A. O'Day (ed.), *The Edwardian Age* (1979), p. 37.
12 Contemporary estimates after the 1906 election suggested that the MPs comprised 11—16 free traders, 32 Balfourites and 109 tariff reformers, though historians have thought this an exaggeration of protectionist strength.
13 R. Rempel, *Unionists Divided* (1972), pp. 94—5.
14 G.R. Searle, 'Critics of Edwardian Society: the case of the Radical Right', in O'Day (ed.), *The Edwardian Age*.
15 He had been parliamentary secretary at the Board of Trade 1902—05 and had worked for a firm of merchant bankers and become a partner in a Glasgow iron merchant's company.

16 Lord Oxford and Asquith, *Memories and Reflections 1852–1927* (1928), vol. 1, p. 202.
17 H.H. Asquith to W.S. Churchill, 12 September 1913.
18 See P.F. Clarke, *Lancashire and the New Liberalism* (1971), p. 387.
19 J. Liddington and J. Norris, *One Hand Tied Behind Us: the Rise of the Women's Suffrage Movement* (1979), pp. 193, 205, 219.
20 Paul Thompson, *The Edwardians: the remaking of British society* (1975), pp. 240–64.
21 D. Lloyd George, *Better Times: Speeches on the Social Question* (1910).

CHAPTER 6: *Edwardian Progressivism*

1 See, for example, J.R. Vincent, 'The Electoral Sociology of Rochdale', *Economic History Review*, 16 (1963–64), p. 85.
2 Published as Charles Booth, *Life and Labour of the People of London*, 17 vols (1902–04); B.S. Rowntree, *Poverty: a Study of Town Life* (1901).
3 J.M. Robertson, *The Meaning of Liberalism* (1912), p. 64.
4 P.F. Clarke, *Lancashire and the New Liberalism* (1971), p. 223.
5 Herbert Gladstone Papers 46106, memorandum, 6 September 1903.
6 C.P. Trevelyan to W.S. Churchill, draft, undated, December 1903, Trevelyan Papers 13.
7 Bruce K. Murray, *The People's Budget 1909–10* (1980), pp. 112–21.
8 Notably the British Medical Association, friendly societies and insurance companies with their armies of collectors. Part I of the Act provided health insurance and Part II unemployment insurance for three groups of workers.
9 A.E. Pease to Herbert Samuel, 19 August 1908, Samuel Papers A/155 (III).
10 Runciman Papers 21, Runciman to Asquith (copy) 27 February 1908, and 63, Crawshaw to Runciman 2 April 1912.
11 See Lloyd George Papers C/21/1/17.
12 W.D. Rubinstein, 'Wealth, Elites and the Class Structure of Modern Britain', *Past and Present*, 76 (1977); and 'The Victorian Middle classes: Wealth, Occupation and Geography', *Economic History Review*, 30 (1977).
13 See Runciman Papers 66 and 74.
14 H.V. Emy, *Liberals, Radicals and Social Politics 1892–1914* (1973), p. 219.
15 Leslie Scott to Lloyd George, 29 September 1913, Lloyd George Papers C/8/2/1.
16 P. Poirier, *The Advent of the Labour Party* (1958), p. 110.
17 Memorandum, MacDonald Papers 30/69/5/81.

CHAPTER 7: *The Electoral Struggle 1906—14*

1 Roy Gregory, *The Miners and British Politics 1906—14* (1968), p. 189.
2 Neal Blewett, 'The Franchise in the United Kingdom 1885—1918', *Past and Present*, 32 (1965), pp. 30—42.
3 *The Labour Leader*, 18 July 1912.
4 CAB 37/108/148, 16 November 1911.
5 Gregory, *The Miners and British Politics*, p. 9.
6 J. Blackley to Walter Runciman, 15 September 1906, Runciman Papers 14.
7 T. Catterall, 2 July 1903, C.P. Trevelyan Papers 13.
8 Labour Party Archives, LP/EL/08.
9 Alexander Murray to Lord Knollys (copy), 7 November 1906, and 'Memorandum on the Socialist and Labour Movements in Scotland', by D.A. Wood and W. Webster, Elibank Papers 8801.
10 P.F. Clarke, 'The Electoral Position of the Liberal and Labour Parties 1910—14', *English Historical Review*, 90 (1975), pp. 829—35.
11 Alan Sykes, *Tariff Reform in British Politics 1903—13* (1979), p. 273.
12 Austen Chamberlain, 9 March 1910, Chamberlain Papers AC/8/8/15.
13 Josiah Wedgwood to Ramsay MacDonald, 12 June 1913, MacDonald Papers 30/69/5/23.
14 Private Memorandum, 3 March 1914, MacDonald Papers 30/69/8/1.
15 George Young to C.P. Trevelyan, 28 June 1906, Trevelyan Papers 16.
16 J. Cochrane Shanks to D. Lloyd George, 9 February 1914, Lloyd George Papers C/10/3/19.
17 Mrs L. Bulley to Mrs Lloyd George, Lloyd George Papers C/10/1/68.
18 Catherine Marshall to Arthur Henderson, 14 October 1912, Marshall Papers.
19 Undated memorandum, J.A. Pease Papers 88.
20 Asquith Papers 23, fol. 298.
21 Trevelyan to Walter Runciman, 25 March 1912, Runciman Papers 63.
22 Lloyd George to Christopher Addison (copy), 11 November 1913, Lloyd George Papers C/10/2/24.
23 Trevelyan to Walter Runciman, 3 November 1913 Runciman Papers 82.

CHAPTER 8: *The Impact of the Great War on British Politics*

1 Ponsonby to W.S. Churchill, 31 July 1914, Churchill Papers.
2 E.I. David (ed.), *Inside Asquith's Cabinet: from the Diaries of Sir Charles Hobhouse* (1977), pp. 179—80.
3 A. Bonar Law to H.H. Asquith, 2 August 1919, quoted on R. Blake, *The Unknown Prime Prime Minister* (1955), p. 222.
4 The Union of Democratic Control had been founded in August 1914 by

MacDonald, E.D. Morel, C.P. Trevelyan, Arthur Ponsonby and Norman Angell and was dedicated to restoring parliamentary control of foreign policy.

5 *The Times*, 18 September 1914.

6 David French, 'The Military Background to the "Shell Crisis" of May 1915', *Journal of Strategic Studies*, 2 (1979), pp. 199—200.

7 Bonar Law Papers 36/1/12, 14, 18 for correspondence with Lord Crewe on this point.

8 Bonar Law to Curzon (copy), 29 January 1915, and memoranda by Curzon and Long in Balfour Papers 49693.

9 Richard Denman to C. P. Trevelyan, 28 May 1915, quoted in M. Swartz, *The Union of Democratic Control in British Politics During the First World War* (1971), p. 66.

10 C. P. Scott's Diary, 3 September 1915.

11 Report of Proceedings of the National Union Special Conference, 30 November 1917.

12 M. D. Pugh, *Electoral Reform in War and Peace 1906—18* (1978), pp. 98—9, 103—35, 156—7.

13 Notes on the Report of the Speaker's Conference, 3 February 1917, Steel-Maitland Papers 202.

14 F. E. Guest to Lloyd George, 20 July 1918, Lloyd George Papers F/21/2/28.

15 I. G. Hunter, 'Working Class Representatives on Elective Local Authorities on Tyneside 1883—1921' (unpublished Newcastle M. Litt. thesis 1979), pp. 115—38.

16 ibid., pp. 124—5.

17 Annual Conference Reports, Labour Party Archives.

18 Labour Party Archives, ORG/14/1 & 2.

CHAPTER 9: *A Mass Electorate at War*

1 Quoted in P. F. Clarke, *Liberals and Social Democrats* (1978), p. 175.

2 Philip Gibbs, quoted in P. Knightley, *The First Casualty* (1978) p. 97.

3 Diary of Miss K. M. B. Alexander (aged 11), 29 February 1916; Peter Liddle's 1914—18 Personal Experience Archives presently held within Sunderland Polytechnic.

4 See M. D. Pugh, *Women's Suffrage in Britain 1867—1928* (Historical Association G97, 1980).

5 M. D. Pugh, *Electoral Reform in War and Peace 1906—18* (1978), pp. 84—6, 136—54.

6 G. Slater (ed.), *My Warrior Sons: the Borton Family Diary 1914—18* (1970), p. 51; also M. Moynihan (ed.), *A Place Called Armageddon* (1975), pp. 134—59.

7 Julian Grenfell to Lady E. Desborough, 17 October 1914.

8 M. Moynihan (ed.), *People at War 1914—18* (1973), p. 48.

9 H. J. Odell to his mother, 30 August 1917; Peter Liddle, Personal Experience Archives.

10 H. J. Odell to his mother, 13 January 1918; Peter Liddle, ibid.

11 S. Sassoon, *Seigfried's Journey* (1946), p. 51.

12 D. Englander and J. Osborne, 'Jack, Tommy and Henry Dubb: the Armed Forces and the Working Class', *Historical Journal*, 21 (1978), pp. 603—5.

13 ibid., p. 620.

14 Addison Papers, vol. 80.

15 Stansgate Papers, 40/1.

16 R. B. MacCallum and A. Readman, *The British General Election of 1945* (1947), p. 239.

17 J. Davidson to Arthur Ponsonby, 29 December 1918, Ponsonby Papers 667.

18 MacDonald Papers 30/69/7/51.

19 G. Morgan to Arthur Ponsonby, 20 December 1917, Ponsonby Papers 666.

20 A. Rowntree to Arthur Ponsonby, 3 January 1919, Ponsonby Papers 667; K. O. Morgan, *Consensus and Disunity: the Lloyd George Coalition Government 1916—22* (1979), pp. 152—3; D. Marquand, *Ramsay MacDonald* (1977), p. 235.

21 Report by S. Higgenbotham, 17 January 1919, MacDonald Papers 30/69/7/51.

22 ibid.; A. Rowntree to Arthur Ponsonby, 3 January 1919, Ponsonby Papers 667.

CHAPTER 10: *Party, Ideology and the State in the Great War*

1 See A. J. P. Taylor, *English History 1914—45* (1970), pp. 57, 64—5, 98—101, 113.

2 David French, 'Some Aspects of Social and Economic Planning for War in Great Britain 1905—15' (University of London Ph.D. thesis 1978), pp. 63—5.

3 David French, 'The Military Background to the "Shell Crisis" of May 1915', *Journal of Strategic Studies*, 2 (1979), pp. 192—7.

4 CAB 42/1/21, 25 January 1915.

5 French, 'Some Aspects of Social and Economic Planning', p. 160.

6 17 February 1915 (French, ibid., p. 176).

7 Alan Sykes, *Tariff Reform in British Politics 1903—13* (1979), p. 278.

8 J. Turner, 'The British Commonwealth Union and the General Election of 1918', *English Historical Review*, 93 (1978), pp. 530—9.

9   Rodney Lowe, 'The Erosion of State Intervention in Britain 1917–24', *Economic History Review*, 31, 2 (1978), p. 278.

10 K. O. Morgan, *Consensus and Disunity: the Lloyd George Coalition Government 1916–22* (1979), pp. 105–7.

11 H. C. Deb., 23 June 1921, c. 1600.

12 J. M. McEwen, 'The Coupon Election of 1918 and the Unionist Members of Parliament', *Journal of Modern History*, 34 (1962), pp. 298–302.

13 J. O. Stubbs, 'The Impact of the Great War on the Conservative Party', in G. Peele and C. Cook (eds), *The Politics of Reappraisal* (1975), p. 34.

14 C. P. Scott's Diary, 11–12 December 1917.

15 C. P. Trevelyan, *From Liberalism to Labour* (1921), p. 17.

16 C. V. Wedgwood, *The Last of the Radicals* (1951), p. 154.

17 Addison to Arthur Henderson (copy), 19 November 1923, Addison Papers 82.

18 Kenneth and Jane Morgan, *Portrait of a Progressive* (1980), pp. 182–7.

19 C. P. Trevelyan, *From Liberalism to Labour* (1921).

20 W. Wedgwood Benn to A. Munro (copy), 25 January 1927, Stansgate Papers 85/1.

CHAPTER 11: *The Elevation of Labour and the Restoration of Party Politics 1918–24*

1   M. Kinnear, *The Fall of Lloyd George* (1973), pp. 79–85.

2   John Ramsden, *The Age of Balfour and Baldwin* (1978), pp. 134–5.

3   M. Cowling, *The Impact of Labour* (1971), pp. 72–5.

4   Kinnear, *The Fall of Lloyd George*, pp. 89–90.

5   K. Middlemas and J. Barnes, *Baldwin* (1969), p. 216.

6   Lloyd George to C. P. Scott 27 December 1923, quoted in R. Douglas, *The History of the Liberal Party 1895–1970* (1971), p. 175.

7   MacDonald's Diary 7 June 1920, quoted in D. Marquand, *Ramsay MacDonald* (1977), p. 268.

8   Sir Keith Feiling, *Life of Neville Chamberlain* (1946), p. 111.

9   Middlemas and Barnes, *Baldwin*, p. 268.

10 MacDonald's Diary 26 September 1924.

11 Middlemas and Barnes, *Baldwin*, p. 273.

CHAPTER 12: *Origins of the Conservative Electoral Hegemony 1918–31*

1   For 1922 the total poll can be recalculated by estimating the likely vote in the 42 Conservative seats uncontested and in the 14 Liberal and Labour ones on the basis of subsequent performances; this would raise the Conservative share by around 3%, from 38% to 41%.

2   MacDonald Papers PRO 30/69/5/166.

3   M. Kinnear, *The British Voter: an Atlas and Survey 1885–1964* (1969), pp. 70–1.

4   They were: Cambridge 2; Oxford 2; London 1; Combined English Universities 1; Wales 1; Combined Scottish Universities 3: Dublin 2; National University 1; Belfast 1.

5   Memorandum dated October 1916, Steel-Maitland Papers 202.

6   Col. R. A. Sanders Diary, 15 June 1917.

7   Memorandum on seats by Walter Long (copy), 19 January 1918, Long Papers.

8   J. P. D. Dunbabin, 'British elections in the nineteenth and twentieth century: a regional approach', *English Historical Review*, 95 (1980), pp. 244–5.

9   Kinnear, *The British Voter*, pp. 122–4.

10 John Ramsden, *The Age of Balfour and Baldwin 1902–40* (1978), p. 239.

11 ibid., p. 249.

12 R. I. McKibbin, *The Evolution of the Labour Party 1910–24* (1974), p. 145.

13 Mark Abrams, 'Social Class and British Politics', in Lewis A. Coser (ed.), *Political Sociology* (1966), pp. 206–71.

14 Dunbabin, 'British Elections', p. 243.

15 D. Butler and D. Stokes, *Political Change in Britain* (1971 edn), pp. 65–89.

16 ibid., p. 77.

17 MacDonald Papers PRO 30/69/5/160.

18 S. E. Koss, *Nonconformity in Modern British Politics* (1975), p. 234.

19 Butler and Stokes, *Political Change in Britain*, p. 163.

20 ibid., pp. 166–7.

21 W. G. Runciman, *Relative Deprivation and Social Justice* (1972 edn), p. 82.

CHAPTER 13: *The Eclipse of the Extremes 1931–39*

1   A. Oldfield, 'The Independent Labour Party and Planning 1920–26', *International Review of Social History*, 21 (1976), p. 21.

2   D. Marquand, *Ramsay MacDonald* (1977), pp. 478–9.

3   Quoted in R. Skidelsky, *Politicians and the Slump* (1967), p. 241.

4   MacDonald to V. Hartshorn (copy), 20 December 1930; MacDonald to Graham (copy), 2 October 1930, MacDonald Papers 30/69/5/174.

5   See correspondence of MacDonald and Lloyd George, Snowden and Hartshorn, autumn 1930, MacDonald Papers 30/69/5/174, and for 1931 MacDonald Papers 30/69/5/175.

6 MacDonald Papers 30/69/5/166, memoranda and correspondence on electoral reform 1929—30.

7 B. C. Malament, 'British Labour and Roosevelt's New Deal: the Response of the Left and the Unions', *Journal of British Studies* (Spring, 1978), pp. 158—9.

8 MacDonald to Baldwin (copy), 5 September 1931, MacDonald Papers 30/69/5/180.

9 MacDonald to the King (copy), 14 September 1931, MacDonald Papers 30/69/5/180.

10 C. T. Stannage, 'The General Election of 1935' (Cambridge Ph.D. thesis 1973), pp. 30—1.

11 Quoted in David Dilks, *The Conservatives*, ed. Lord Butler (1977), p. 312.

12 A. Mason, 'The Government and the General Strike, 1926', *International Review of Social History*, 14 (1969), pp. 3—8.

13 M. Cowling, *The Impact of Hitler* (1975), p. 63.

14 ibid., p. 81.

15 H. C. Deb., 14 June 1934, c. 2018.

16 See K. Middlemas and J. Barnes, *Baldwin* (1969), pp. 744—7, 764, 791.

17 ibid., pp. 863—8; Dilks, *The Conservatives*, p. 366.

18 Stannage, 'The General Election of 1935', pp. 287—99.

EPILOGUE

1 The title of a book by Michael Foot, Frank Owen and Peter Howard which went through ten impressions in July 1940.

2 Paul Addison, *The Road to 1945* (1975).

Guide to Further Reading

CHAPTER 1: *Party and Participation 1867—1900*

Mid to late Victorian attitudes towards the franchise and representative government are perceptively revealed in F. B. Smith, *The Making of the Second Reform Act* (1967); Brian Harrison, *Separate Spheres: the Opposition to Women's Suffrage in Britain* (1978); and Walter Bagehot, *The English Constitution* (1867, reprinted 1963). Specifically on franchise changes see C. Seymour, *Electoral Reform in England and Wales 1832—85* (1915); the indispensable article by Neal Blewett, 'The Franchise in the United Kingdom 1885—1918', *Past and Present*, 32 (1965); and G. A. Jones, 'Further Thoughts on the Franchise', *Past and Present*, 34 (1966).

Much the most valuable single volume on the operation of the political system in the country is H. J. Hanham's *Elections and Party Management: politics in the time of Disraeli and Gladstone* (1959). Excellent insights into particular aspects of elections at this time are to be found in: R. Kelley, 'Midlothian: a study in politics and ideas', *Victorian Studies*, 4 (1960); Trevor Lloyd, *The General Election of 1880* (1968); D. Richter, 'The Role of Mob Riot in Victorian Elections', *Victorian Studies*, 15 (1971); C. C. O'Leary, *The Elimination of Corrupt Practices in British Elections* (1962); and W. B. Gwyn, *Democracy and the Cost of Politics in Britain* (1962).

A highly perceptive analysis of the gradual shift from local to national patterns in both county and borough constituencies is T. J. Nossiter's *Influence, Opinion and Political Idioms in Reformed England: case studies from the north-east* (1975). On largely rural developments the following are useful: R. J. Olney, *Lincolnshire Politics 1832—85* (1973); J. Howarth, 'The Liberal Revival in Northamptonshire 1885—95', *Historical Journal*, 12 (1969). On urban changes there are two important and stimulating contributions: J. A. Garrard shows the response of the parliamentarians to the new electorate in 'Parties, Members and Voters After 1867', *Historical Journal*, 20 (1977); Patrick Joyce argues for the continuing strength of non-political voting behaviour after 1867 in 'The Factory Politics of Lancashire in the later Nineteenth Century', *Historical Journal*, 18 (1975), and in *Work, Society and*

Politics (1980). Useful on the extension of party influence are Derek Fraser, *Urban Politics in Victorian England* (1976); and Trevor Lloyd, 'Uncontested Seats in British General Elections 1852–1910', *Historical Journal*, 8 (1965).

W. L. Guttsman's *The British Political Elite* (1965) analyses the changing social composition of the parties. Valuable studies of the tightening party control at Westminster are Hugh Berrington's 'Partisanship and Dissidence in the Nineteenth Century House of Commons', *Parliamentary Affairs*, 21 (1967–68); and P. Fraser's 'The Growth of Ministerial Control in the Nineteenth Century House of Commons', *English Historical Review*, 75 (1960). There are three interesting articles on the role of the whips in honours and fund-raising: H. J. Hanham, 'The Sale of Honours in Late Victorian England', *Victorian Studies*, 3 (1960); R. Pumphrey, 'The Introduction of Industrialists into the British Peerage', *American Historical Review*, 65 (1959–60); and Trevor Lloyd, 'The Whip as Paymaster: Herbert Gladstone and party organisation', *English Historical Review*, 89 (1974).

CHAPTER 2: *The Evolution of the Gladstonian Liberal Party 1867–95*

The seminal work here is J. R. Vincent, *The Formation of the British Liberal Party 1857–68* (1966). A number of works shed interesting light on the development of Liberal attitudes and policies: F. B. Smith, *The Making of the Second Reform Act* (1967); R. T. Shannon, *Gladstone and the Bulgarian Agitation 1876* (1963); C. Harvie, *The Lights of Liberalism: University Liberals and the Challenge of Democracy* (1976); Ian Bradley, *The Optimists: themes and personalities in Victorian Liberalism* (1980); H. Pelling, *America and the British Left* (1956); A. Briggs, *Victorian People* (1954); H. A. Tulloch, 'Changing British Attitudes Towards America in the 1880's', *Historical Journal*, 20 (1977).

The local fabric of Liberalism is lucidly analysed in D. A. Hamer's *The Politics of Electoral Pressure* (1977). Also valuable on the local basis of party organization are: R. Spence Watson, *The National Liberal Federation 1877–1906* (1907); B. McGill, 'Francis Schnadhorst and Liberal Party Organisation', *Journal of Modern History*, 34 (1962); C. D. H. Howard, 'Joseph Chamberlain and the Unauthorised Programme', *English Historical Review*, 65 (1950); D. A. Hamer (ed.), *Joseph Chamberlain: the Radical Programme* (1971); K. O. Morgan, *Wales in British Politics* (1970); James Hunter, 'The Politics of Highland Land Reform 1873–95', *Scottish Historical Review*, 53 (1974).

Several works examine the relationship between the parliamentary leadership and the wider party. There is a detailed study of Gladstone's final decade in Michael Barker, *Gladstone and Radicalism 1885–94* (1975), and a wide-ranging treatment in D. A. Hamer's *Liberal Politics in the Age of Gladstone and Rosebery* (1972), though the latter book seems to me to mislead by emphasizing the negative aspects above all else. There are two important corrective articles by T. W. Heyck, 'Home Rule, Radicalism and the Liberal Party 1886–95', *Journal of British Studies*, 13 (1974); and P. C. Griffiths, 'The Caucus and the Liberal Party in 1886', *History*, 61 (1976). The most penetrating analysis of the parliamentarians' motives in 1886, and particularly the tactical calculations of Chamberlain, Gladstone and Hartington, is A. B. Cooke and J. R. Vincent, *The Governing Passion* (1974). The importance of 1886 in the evolution of the party is also brought out in: J. G. Kellas, 'The Liberal Party in Scotland 1876–95', *Scottish Historical Review*, 44 (1965); D. C. Savage, 'Scottish Politics 1885–86', *Scottish Historical Review*, 40 (1961); Janet Howarth, 'The Liberal Revival in Northamptonshire 1880–95', *Historical Journal*, 12 (1969); D. Southgate, *The Passing of the Whigs* (1962).

Two useful biographies are: E. J. Feuchtwanger, *Gladstone* (1975); and D. A. Hamer, *John Morley: Liberal Intellectual in Politics* (1968). There is an excellent recent biography of Chamberlain by Richard Jay, *Joseph Chamberlain: a political study* (1981). Also on the Liberal Unionists see: M. Hurst, *Joseph Chamberlain and Liberal Reunion 1887* (1967); Peter Fraser, *Joseph Chamberlain* (1966); 'The Liberal Unionist Alliance: Chamberlain, Hartington and the Conservatives 1886–1905', *English Historical Review*, 77 (1962); and Denis Judd, *Radical Joe* (1977).

CHAPTER 3: *The Conservative Revival 1874–1900*

Several general works on the Conservative Party cover this period though none are particularly strong on the Salisbury era: Robert Blake, *The Conservative Party from Peel to Churchill* (1970); D. Southgate (ed.), *The Conservative Leadership 1832–1932* (1974); and Lord Butler (ed.), *The Conservatives* (1977).

All previous works are superceded by Peter Marsh's *The Discipline of Popular Government: Lord Salisbury's Domestic Statecraft 1881–1902* (1978) which fills a major gap; the author emphasizes the adaptive qualities of Salisbury rather than the inflexibility. See also the useful revisionary article by R. E. Quinault, 'Lord Randolph Churchill and Tory Democracy 1880–85', *Historical Journal*, 22 (1979); Viscount Chilston, *Chief Whip* (1961); Andrew Jones, *The Politics of Reform 1884* (1972); M. E. Chadwick, 'The Role of Redistribution in the Making of the Third Reform Act', *Historical Journal*, 19 (1976); A. B. Cooke and J. R. Vincent, *The Governing Passion* (1974).

There are several stimulating works on Conservative strength in the country: J. P. Cornford's seminal article, 'The Transformation of Conservatism in the late Nineteenth Century', *Victorian Studies*, 7 (1963), and 'Parliamentary Foundations of the Hotel Cecil', in R. Robson (ed.), *Ideas and Institu-*

tions of Victorian Britain (1967); H. J. Hanham, *Elections and Party Management: politics in the time of Disraeli and Gladstone* (1959); J. P. D. Dunbabin, 'Parliamentary Elections in Great Britain 1868–1900: a psephologocal note', *English Historical Review*, 81 (1966). Valuable on party organization are: E. J. Feuchtwanger, *Disraeli, Democracy and the Tory Party* (1968); R. T. McKenzie, *British Political Parties* (1955); D. W. Urwin, 'The Development of Conservative Party Organisation in Scotland Before 1912', *Scottish Historical Review*, 44 (1965); and Janet Robb, *The Primrose League 1883–1906* (1942).

Salisbury's ideas are examined in Paul Smith's *Lord Salisbury on Politics* (1972); M. Pinto-Duschinsky, *The Political Thought of Lord Salisbury* (1967); and in a wider context in the following: Noel O'Sullivan, *Conservatism* (1976); Samuel Beer, *Modern British Politics* (1965); and R. B. McDowell, *British Conservatism 1832–1914* (1959).

On domestic policy the key book that cuts through the Disraelian mythology is Paul Smith's *Disraelian Conservatism and Social Reform* (1967). There is no similar work for the 20 years after Disraeli, though Marsh, in *The Discipline of Popular Government*, throws light on this period. Useful on particular aspects are: J. E. B. Munson, 'The Unionist Coalition and Education 1895–1902', *Historical Journal*, 20 (1977); J. P. D. Dunbabin, 'The Politics of the Establishment of County Councils', *Historical Journal*, 6 (1963); Peter Davis, 'The Liberal Unionist Party and the Irish Policy of Lord Salisbury's Government 1886–92', *Historical Journal*, 18 (1975). See also chapter 2 for works on Chamberlain and Liberal Unionism. Among the biographies the following are useful: R. Rhodes James, *Lord Randolph Churchill* (1960); Viscount Chilston, *W. H. Smith* (1965); T. J. Spinner, *George Joachim Goschen* (1973); S. H. Zebel, *Balfour* (1973); and R. Taylor, *Salisbury* (1975).

CHAPTER 4: *The Social Roots of Political Change in Late Victorian Britain*

Henry Pelling's *Social Geography of British Elections 1885–1910* (1967) is an invaluable guide to the themes treated in this chapter. There are several other original interpretations of popular politics in this period. T. J. Nossiter, *Influence, Opinion and Political Idioms in Reformed England* (1975) is the best analysis of the breakdown of traditional, deferential patterns of politics; H. J. Hanham's *Elections and Party Management: politics in the time of Disraeli and Gladstone* (1959) is essential reading; J. R. Vincent's *Pollbooks: How Victorians Voted* (1967) throws fascinating light on the occupational basis of party support before 1872. See also two articles by J. P. D. Dunbabin, 'Parliamentary Elections in Great Britain 1868–1900', *English Historical Review*, 81 (1966); and 'British Elections in the Nineteenth and Twentieth Century: a Regional Approach', *English Historical Review*, 95 (1980).

A number of works help to bring out the political significance of particular issues: Brian Harrison's excellent *Drink and the Victorians* (1971); J.S. Hurt, *Elementary Schooling and the Working Classes 1860–1918* (1979); Alan Simon, 'Church Disestablishment as a Factor in the General Election of 1885', *Historical Journal*, 18 (1975); Ian Sellers, *Nineteenth Century Non-conformity* (1977); K.S. Inglis, *Churches and the Working Classes in Victorian England* (1963); S.E. Koss, 'Wesleyanism and Empire', *Historical Journal*, 18 (1975); H. Pelling and K.O. Morgan, 'Wales and the Boer War', *Welsh History Review*, 4 (1968–69); J.A. Garrard, *The English and Immigration 1880–1910* (1971); and Catherine Jones, *Immigration and Social Policy in Britain* (1977).

The social context of rural politics is admirably reconstructed in Raphael Samuel (ed.), *Village Life and Labour* (1975); and in Flora Thompson's classic account, *Lark Rise to Candleford* (1939, reprinted 1973). There are several works on the political manifestations of agricultural areas by J.P.D. Dunbabin, *Rural Discontent in Nineteenth Century Britain* (1974); and 'The Revolt of the Field: the Agricultural Labourers' Movement in the 1870's', *Past and Present*, 26 (1963). See also: F.M.L. Thompson, 'Land and Politics in England in the Nineteenth Century', *Transactions of the Royal Historical Society*, 15 (1965); Roy Douglas, *Land, People and Politics* (1976); Countess of Warwick, *Joseph Arch: the story of his life told by himself* (1898); P. Horn, 'Agricultural Trade Unionism and Emigration 1872–81', *Historical Journal*, 15 (1972); R.J. Olney, *Lincolnshire Politics 1832–85* (1973); L. Marion Springhall, *Labouring Life in Norfolk Villages 1834–1914* (1936); F.M.L. Thompson, *English Landed Society in the Nineteenth Century* (1968); G. Mingay, *The Gentry* (1978); and T.W. Fletcher, 'The Great Depression of British Agriculture 1873–1896', *Economic History Review*, 13 (1961).

On the attitudes of urban working-class people towards politics see three stimulating works: Robert Tressel, *The Ragged Trousered Philanthropists* (1955, reprinted 1967); Stephen Reynolds, *Seems So! A Working Class View of Politics* (1911); and Robert Roberts, *The Classic Slum* (1971). The hostility to authority indicated in the latter two volumes is discussed by Henry Pelling in 'The Working Class and the origins of the Welfare State' in a valuable collection of essays, *Popular Politics and Society in Late Victorian Britain* (1968). Much incidental light is thrown upon political attitudes in: R. Moore, *Pitmen, Preachers and Politics* (1974), which examines Methodist mining villages in Durham; Paul Thompson, *The Edwardians* (1975), an excellent social history based on oral sources; G. Stedman Jones, *Outcast London* (1971); and S. Meacham, *A Life Apart* (1977).

On industrial aspects of working-class history there is an excellent wide-ranging survey by E.H. Hunt, *British Labour History 1815–1914* (1981); for more detailed work see H.A. Clegg, A. Fox and A.F. Thompson, *A History of British Trade Unions Since 1889*, vol. 1 (1964); E. H. Phelps Brown, *The Growth of British Industrial Relations* (1965); A. E. P. Duffy, 'New Unionism in Britain 1889—90: a reappraisal', *Economic History Review*, 14 (1961—62); Henry Pelling, *A History of British Trade Unionism* (1963). Aspects of labour politics are explored in: Royden Harrison, *Before the Socialists: Studies in Labour and Politics 1861—81* (1965); R. Moore, *The Emergence of the Labour Party 1880—1924* (1978); Henry Pelling, *Origins of the Labour Party* (1954); A. Briggs and J. Saville (eds), *Essays in Labour History*, vol. 1 (1967), vol. 2 (1971); K. Willis, 'The Introduction and Critical Reception of Marxist Thought in Britain 1850—1900', *Historical Journal*, 20 (1977). The idea of an elite within the working class has been vigorously debated by historians: E. J. Hobsbawm's 'The Labour Aristocracy in Nineteenth Century Britain', in *Labouring Men* (1968) is critically examined in Henry Pelling's 'The Concept of the Labour Aristocracy', in *Popular Politics*; detailed studies are: R. G. Gray, *The Labour Aristocracy in Victorian Edinburgh* (1976); and G. Crossick, *An Artisan Elite in Victorian Society: Kentish London* (1978). The recent broad treatment from a Marxist viewpoint, Keith Burgess, *The Challenge of Labour* (1980), should be compared with the volume by Hunt above. The reality of working-class Liberalism is brought out in several local studies: D. Rubinstein, 'The ILP and the Yorkshire Miners: the Barnsley By-election 1897', *International Review of Social History*, 1 (1978); K. O. Fox, 'Labour and Merthyr's Khaki Election of 1900', *Welsh History Review*, 2 (1964—65). On the working-class and socialist press see the essays by Victoria Berridge and Deian Hopkin in G. Boyce (ed.), *Newspaper History: from the seventeenth century to the present day* (1978).

For a broad interpretative consideration of working-class Conservatism see Frank Parkin, 'Working Class Conservatives', *British Journal of Sociology*, 18 (1967); and A. J. Lee, 'Conservatism, Traditionalism and the British Working Class', in D. E. Martin and D. Rubinstein (eds), *Ideology and the Labour Movement* (1979). There are several original contributions based on local studies: Patrick Joyce, *Work, Society and Politics* (1980); R. L. Greenall, 'Popular Conservatism in Salford 1868—1886', *Northern History*, 9 (1974); J. A. Garrard, 'Parties, Members and Voters after 1867: a local study', *Historical Journal*, 20 (1977); C. Green, 'Birmingham's Politics 1873—91', *Midland History*, 2 (1973). R. T. McKenzie and A. Silver's, *Angels In Marble* (1968) contains interesting material on the Conservative appeal to the working class. Henry Pelling sceptically examines popular attitudes in 'British Labour and British Imperialism', *Popular Politics*; while Richard Price, *An Imperial War and the British Working Class* (1972), argues strongly, if unconvincingly, that imperialist sentiment was to be found only in higher social levels. Also helpful on some aspects of popular Conservatism are Hanhan, *Elections and Party Management*, and Robb, *The Primrose League 1883—1906*.

The lower middle class is considered, *inter alia*, in the works cited above by Nossiter, Vincent, Price and Paul Thompson. G. Crossick (ed.), *The Lower Middle Class in Britain 1870–1914* (1977), is a pioneering collection of essays. A useful recent study of one major group is G. L. Anderson's *Victorian Clerks* (1976). For a general discussion see Arno Mayer's 'The Lower Middle Class as a Historical Problem', *Journal of Modern History*, 47 (1975), and for an amiable contemporary spoof, George and Weedon Grossmith, *The Diary of a Nobody* (1892, reprinted 1965).

CHAPTER 5: *The Edwardian Crises 1895–1914*

A valuable analysis of the ideas of the leading Liberal Imperialists is H. C. G. Matthew, *The Liberal Imperialists: the ideas and politics of a post-Gladstonian elite* (1973); for an attempt to estimate the strength of such sentiment in the Liberal ranks see T. Boyle, 'The Liberal Imperialists 1892–1906', *Bulletin of the Institute of Historical Research*, 52 (1979).

Michael Barker's *Gladstone and Radicalism: the reconstruction of Liberal policy 1885–94* (1975) attempts to find links between Gladstonianism and New Liberalism; it should be compared with the very different picture in D. A. Hamer, *John Morley: intellectual in politics* (1968). K. O. Morgan's *The Age of Lloyd George* (1971) provides an excellent introduction to the problems of this period; also useful on the high politics are Peter Stansky's *Ambitions and Strategies: the struggle for the Liberal leadership in the 1890's* (1964); and R. R. James, *Rosebery* (1963).

For a splendid, readable analysis of attitudes stimulated by the obsession with national decadence see G. R. Searle's *The Quest For National Efficiency* (1971). The themes and problems raised by Searle are considered further in several interesting volumes: I. F. Clarke, *Voices Prophesying War 1763–1984* (1966); B. Semmel, *Imperialism and Social Reform* (1960); R. Scally, *The Origins of the Lloyd George Coalition: the politics of social imperialism 1900–1918* (1975); A. Gollin, *Proconsul in Politics* (1966); and a contemporary work of propaganda, Arnold White's *Efficiency and Empire* (reprinted 1973, ed. G. R. Searle).

Alan Sykes, *Tariff Reform in British Politics 1903–13* (1979) is an excellent, scholarly study that emphasizes the difficulties faced by the constructive protectionists in the party. A useful general guide to the arguments on tariffs is provided in Peter Cain, 'Political Economy in Edwardian England: the Tariff Reform Controversy', in A. O'Day (ed.), *The Edwardian Age* (1979). The internal factionalism among Conservatives after 1903 is examined in several works: R. Rempel, *Unionists Divided: Arthur Balfour, Joseph Chamberlain and the Unionist Free Traders* (1972); S. H. Zebel, 'Joseph Chamberlain and the Genesis of the Tariff Reform Campaign',

Journal of British Studies, 7 (1967); P. Fraser, 'Unionism and Tariff Reform: the Crisis of 1906', *Historical Journal*, 5 (1962); N. Blewett, 'Free Fooders, Balfourites, Whole Hoggers: Factionalism within the Unionist Party 1906–10', *Historical Journal*, 11 (1968).

For the Edwardian crisis from the Conservative side see Robert Blake, *The Unknown Prime Minister: the life and times of Andrew Bonar Law* (1955), and D. Southgate, *The Conservative Leadership* (1974). A stimulating view that puts the period in perspective is G. R. Searle's essay 'Critics of Edwardian Society: the case of the Radical Right', in O'Day, *The Edwardian Age*. This, along with Paul Thompson's *The Edwardians: the re-making of British society* (1975), which uses oral evidence, and J. B. Priestley's *The Edwardians* (1970), serves as a corrective to the exaggerated and misleading impression given in George Dangerfield's *The Strange Death of Liberal England* (1935), and, to a lesser extent, in S. Hynes, *The Edwardian Turn of Mind* (1968). The suffragettes are placed in perspective in Andrew Rosen's, *Rise Up Women!* (1974), a critical study of the WSPU, and M. D. Pugh, *Women's Suffrage in Britain 1867–1928* (Historical Association pamphlet 1980). On the nature of Edwardian working-class action see Henry Pelling, 'The Labour Unrest 1911–14', in his *Popular Politics and Society in Late Victorian Britain* (1968), and R. Roberts, *The Classic Slum* (1971), an interesting autobiographical account of the period.

CHAPTER 6: *Edwardian Progressivism*

The key attempts to restate Liberalism around the turn of the century are: L. T. Hobhouse, *Democracy and Reaction* (1904, reprinted 1972, ed. P. F. Clarke), and *The Labour Movement* (1912, reprinted 1974, ed. P. Poirier); J. A. Hobson, *The Crisis of Liberalism* (1909, reprinted 1974, ed. P. F. Clarke); Herbert Samuel, *Liberalism* (1902); C. F. G. Masterman, *The Condition of England* (1912); J. M. Robertson, *The Meaning of Liberalism* (1912). For a popularization of the New Liberalism see Lloyd George's collection of 1909 speeches, *Better Times: speeches on the social question* (1910).

Some excellent secondary works on the evolution of Liberal thinking have appeared in recent years: M. Richter, *The Politics of Conscience* (1964); M. Freeden, *The New Liberalism* (1978); P. F. Clarke, 'The Progressive Movement in England', *Transactions of the Royal Historical Society*, 24 (1974), and *Liberals and Social Democrats* (1978). For a general account that sets the New Liberalism in context see David Manning, *Liberalism* (1976); and for a useful cross-party treatment of attitudes towards the state among other aspects see Rodney Barker, *Political Ideas in Modern Britain* (1978).

There is an interesting and convincing exploration of the connections between ideas and political practice in H. V. Emy, *Liberals, Radicals and*

Social Politics 1892—1914 (1973), and 'The Impact of Financial Policy on English Party Politics Before 1914', *Historical Journal*, 15 (1972); also useful here is the detailed analysis in Bruce Murray's *The People's Budget 1909—10* (1980), and the short overview in J. R. Hay, *The Origins of the Liberal Welfare Reforms 1906—14* (1975). On the land question see H. V. Emy, 'Lloyd George as a Social Reformer: the Land Campaign', in A. J. P. Taylor (ed.), *Lloyd George: Twelve Essays* (1971); and Roy Douglas, 'God Gave the Land to the People', in A.J.A. Morris (ed.), *Edwardian Radicalism 1900—1914* (1974). Useful studies of three rather different adherents of the New Liberalism are: E. I. David, 'The New Liberalism of Charles Masterman', in K. D. Brown (ed.), *Essays in Anti-Labour History* (1974); S. E. Koss, *Sir John Brunner: Radical Plutocrat* (1970); and S.E. Koss, *Fleet Street Radical: A. G. Gardiner and the Daily News* (1973). In addition to the collections of essays on the Edwardian period edited by Morris, Brown and Taylor cited above, the following are useful and readable: K. O. Morgan, *The Age of Lloyd George* (1971), which ranges from 1890 to 1929; and Alan O'Day (ed.), *The Edwardian Age* (1979). For biographical treatment see John Grigg, *Lloyd George: the People's Champion 1902—11* (1978); Roy Jenkins, *Asquith* (1964); S. E. Koss, *Asquith* (1976); Lucy Masterman, *C. F. G. Masterman* (1939); and R. S. Churchill, *Winston S. Churchill: the Young Statesman 1901—14* (1967).

Essential on the Liberal—Labour alliance are Frank Bealey, 'The Electoral Arrangement Between the Labour Representation Committee and the Liberal Party', *Journal of Modern History* (December 1956); Frank Bealey and H. Pelling, *Labour and Politics 1900—1906* (1958). The most persuasive explanation of Labour ideology in the 1900s may be found in several works by Rodney Barker: 'Socialism and Progressivism in the Political Thought of Ramsay MacDonald', in Morris, *Edwardian Radicalism*; and *Education and Politics 1900—51* (1972). For a hostile critique see Ralph Miliband's *Parliamentary Socialism* (1961); and for a valuable examination of the role of the Fabians, A. M. McBriar, *Fabian Socialism and English politics 1884—1918* (1966). K. D. Brown's *Labour and Unemployment 1900—14* (1971) demonstrates the limitations on the parliamentary party's ability to influence government policy. There is a recent short account of the party in Roger Moore's *The Emergence of the Labour Party 1880—1924* (1978). Although there are still, unavoidably, gaps in Labour biography several excellent volumes have appeared in the 1970s. David Marquand's *Ramsay MacDonald* (1977) puts its subject in the Progressive tradition and demonstrates his consistency of thought and objectives. Two admirable works on Hardie tend to emphasize his Lib—Lab traditions: K. O. Morgan, *Keir Hardie: radical and socialist* (1975); and I. S. McLean, *Keir Hardie* (1975). Fred Reid in *James Keir Hardie* (1978) does argue for a more distinctively socialist ideology for his subject.

CHAPTER 7: *The Electoral Struggle 1906—14*

The most original and compelling interpretation of pre-1914 electoral politics is P. F. Clarke's *Lancashire and the New Liberalism* (1971), which argues for the adaptation of Liberalism to a working-class electorate and for the arrival of class-based politics before rather than after the First World War. Several other published studies of the regions are available though many more exist as postgraduate theses: Paul Thompson's *Socialists, Liberals and Labour: the struggle for London 1885—1914* reaches conclusions quite inconsistent, in my view, with the evidence in the book which tends to confirm Clarke's line of argument; A. W. Purdue, 'Arthur Henderson and Liberal, Liberal— Labour and Labour Politics in North-East England 1892—1903', *Northern History*, 11 (1975); K. O. Morgan, 'The New Liberalism and the Challenge of Labour: the Welsh Experience 1885—1929', *Welsh History Review*, 6 (1973); M. D. Pugh, 'Yorkshire and the New Liberalism?', *Journal of Modern History*, 50 (1978). There are Nuffield-type studies of the general elections of 1906 in A. K. Russell's *Liberal Landslide* (1973); and of 1910 in Neal Blewett's invaluable *The Peers, the Parties and the People* (1972), whose findings tend to corroborate Clarke's case.

R. I. McKibbin's *The Evolution of the Labour Party 1910—24* (1974) accepts the ideological cohesion of Labour and Liberalism but argues lucidly that a politicized working class could not be contained within the alliance; Henry Pelling also argues for the long-term importance of social changes in his essay 'Labour and the Downfall of Liberalism', in *Popular Politics and Society in Late Victorian Britain* (1968); similarly Roy Gregory's *The Miners and British Politics 1906—14* (1968) argues for a collapse of the politics of the pact.

A number of writers have examined the problems encountered by the electoral pact strategy particularly after 1910: M. Petter, 'The Progressive Alliance', *History*, 58 (1973); R. I. McKibbin, 'James Ramsay MacDonald and the Problem of the Independence of the Labour Party 1910—14', *Journal of Modern History*, 42 (1970); Roy Douglas, 'Labour in Decline', in K. D. Brown (ed.), *Essays in Anti-Labour History* (1974); M. D. Pugh, *Electoral Reform in War and Peace 1906—18* (1978), and 'New Light on Edwardian Voters: the Model Elections of 1906—12', *Bulletin of the Institute of Historical Research*, 51 (1978). Finally a convincing case for Liberal vitality on the eve of war is made by P. F. Clarke from an analysis of the 1911—14 by-elections in 'The electoral position of the Liberal and Labour Parties 1910—14', *English Historical Review*, 90 (1975).

An important attack on the new orthodoxy has come from H. C. G. Matthew, R. I. McKibbin and J. A. Kay, 'The franchise factor in the rise of the Labour Party', *English Historical Review*, 91 (1976); a similar line is pursued in C. Chamberlain, 'The Growth of Support for the Labour Party in Britain',

British Journal of Sociology, 24 (1973). Another area of debate is opening up on the municipal elections front: C. Cook, 'Labour and the Downfall of the Liberal Party 1906—14', in A. Sked and C. Cook (eds), *Crisis and Controversy: Essays in Honour of A. J. P. Taylor* (1976).

CHAPTER 8: *The Impact of the Great War on British Politics*

Zara Steiner's *Britain and the Origins of the First World War* (1977) is a superb synthesis, treating domestic political aspects as well as diplomatic and military; detailed essays on foreign policy are to be found in F. H. Hinsley (ed.), *British Foreign Policy Under Sir Edward Grey* (1977); for military preparations and thinking see John Gooch's *The Plans of War* (1974), and the short, masterly study by Michael Howard, *The Continental Commitment* (1972).

Useful analysis of the weakness of radical criticism of foreign and defence policy may be found in: Howard Weinroth, 'The British Radicals and the Balance of Power 1902—14', *Historical Journal*, 13 (1970), and 'Left-wing Opposition to Naval Armaments in Britain before 1914', *Journal of Contemporary History*, 6 (1971); M. Swartz, 'A Study in Futility: the British Radicals at the Outbreak of the First World War', in A. J. A. Morris (ed.), *Edwardian Radicalism* (1974); A. J. A. Morris, *Radicalism Against War 1906—14* (1972), and 'Haldane's Army Reforms 1906—08: the Deception of the Radicals', *History*, 56, 189 (1971).

Cameron Hazelhurst's *Politicians at War* (1971) provides a readable and detailed examination of the Cabinet's decision for war and the high politics of the first nine months; also useful is E. I. David (ed.), *Inside Asquith's Cabinet: from the diaries of Sir Charles Hobhouse* (1977). The strains and stresses on the Liberals are fully exposed in Trevor Wilson (ed.), *The Political Diaries of C. P. Scott 1911—28* (1970); B. McGill, 'Asquith's Predicament 1914—18', *Journal of Modern History*, 39 (1967); and M. Howard, *War and the Liberal Conscience* (1978). Trevor Wilson's fine, readable analysis, *The Downfall of the Liberal Party 1914—35* (1966), tends to place the blame on Lloyd George; it sees the 1915 Coalition in terms of the shells crisis and party warfare; S. E. Koss, *Lord Haldane: Scapegoat for Liberalism* (1969), finds an improbable explanation in a conspiracy; Lord Beaverbrook's *Politicians and the War* (1928) was for long an influential account because of the author's supposedly close involvement in the events; M. D. Pugh, 'Asquith, Bonar Law and the First Coalition', *Historical Journal*, 17 (1974), interprets the crisis as collusion between Law and Asquith at the expense of their parties; and David French, 'The Military Background to the Shell Crisis of May 1915', *Journal of Strategic Studies*, 2 (1979), demonstrates the vulnerability of politicians to miscalculations by the generals. Lord

Hankey's *The Supreme Command 1914–18* (1961) is perceptive about the strengths and weaknesses of both Asquith and Lloyd George as wartime premiers. The nature of Liberal disintegration is analysed in E. I. David, 'The Liberal Party Divided 1916–18', *Historical Journal*, 13 (1970); J. M. McEwen, 'The Liberal Party and the Irish Question During the First World War', *Journal of British Studies*, 12 (1972); and J. Gooch, 'The Maurice Debate', *Journal of Contemporary History*, 3 (1968).

A. J. P. Taylor provides a lively overview in 'Politics in the First World War', and 'Lloyd George: Rise and Fall', in *Politics in Wartime* (1964). For accounts of the December 1916 crisis sympathetic to Lloyd George see Peter Lowe, 'The Rise to the Premiership', in A. J. P. Taylor (ed.), *Lloyd George: Twelve Essays* (1971); P. Rowland, *Lloyd George* (1975); and K. O. Morgan, *Lloyd George* (1974). A. J. P. Taylor's *Beaverbrook* (1972) throws light on Conservative motivation as does Austen Chamberlain, *Down the Years* (1935). Roy Jenkins, *Asquith* (1964) and S. E. Koss, *Asquith* (1976) are more hostile. An excellent analysis of the new coalition government is K. O. Morgan's 'Lloyd George's Premiership', *Historical Journal*, 13 (1970). Other aspects are examined in J. Turner, *Lloyd George's Secretariat* (1980); P. A. Lockwood, 'Milner's Entry into the War Cabinet', *Historical Journal*, 7 (1964); J. F. Naylor, 'The Establishment of the Cabinet Secretariat', *Historical Journal*, 14 (1971); and J. Ehrman, 'Lloyd George and Churchill as War Leaders', *Transactions of the Royal Historical Society*, 11 (1961). On relations with the Conservatives Robert Blake's *The Unknown Prime Minister* (1955) is the best volume. For an examination of how the Conservatives were led via franchise reform to the 1918 election see M. D. Pugh, *Electoral Reform in War and Peace 1906–18* (1978); D. Close, 'The Collapse of Resistance to Democracy: Conservatives, Adult Suffrage and Second Chamber Reform 1911–28', *Historical Journal*, 20 (1977); and D. Rolfe, 'Origins of Mr. Speaker's Conference during the First World War', *History*, 64 (1979).

M. Swartz, *The Union of Democratic Control in British Politics during the First World War* (1971), is good on the shifting allegiances of Liberal and Labour opponents of the war; see also D. Marquand's *Ramsay MacDonald* (1977) and C. Howard's 'MacDonald, Henderson and the Labour Party in 1914', *Historical Journal*, 20 (1977). Essential reading on Labour's wartime activity is Royden Harrison, 'The War Emergency Workers National Committee', in A. Briggs and J. Saville (eds), *Essays in Labour History 1886–1924* (1971); for the local level see A. Clinton's 'Trades Councils during the First World War', *International Review of Social History*, 15 (1970); and for a typically pragmatic trade union leader see A. Bullock, *The Life and Times of Ernest Bevin*, vol. 1 (1960). An important article on Labour's turning point is J. M. Winter, 'Arthur Henderson, the Russian Revolution and the Reconstruction of the Labour Party', *Historical Journal*, 15 (1972); the same author's *Socialism and the Challenge of War* (1974) analyses the growing role played by the Webbs and other middle-class socialists in the party at this time. The best treatment of the organizational breakthrough is R. I. McKibbin's indispensable *The Evolution of the Labour Party 1910–24* (1974).

CHAPTER 9: *A Mass Electorate at War*

There is an interesting examination of pre-war attitudes in I. F. Clarke, *Voices Prophesying War 1763–1984* (1966); and a credible explanation for contradictory attitudes towards the army in Anne Summers, 'Militarism in Britain Before the Great War', *History Workshop Journal*, 2 (1976). C. Haste's, *Keep the Home Fires Burning* (1977) is a general survey of domestic propaganda in wartime. Specialist studies are: M. L. Sanders, 'Wellington House and British Propaganda during the First World War', *Historical Journal*, 18 (1975); D. G. Wright, 'The Great War, Government Propaganda and English Men of Letters', *Literature and History*, 7 (1978); D. Hopkin, 'Domestic Censorship in the First World War', *Journal of Contemporary History*, 5 (1970); C. Lovelace, 'British Press Censorship during the First World War', in G. Boyce (ed.), *Newspaper History* (1978); and P. Knightley, *The First Casualty* (1978).

K. G. Robbins analyses the whole range of anti-war activity in *The Abolition of War* (1976); see also M. Swartz, *The Union of Democratic Control in British Politics during the First World War* (1971), and H. Hanak, 'The Union of Democratic Control', *Bulletin of the Institute of Historical Research*, 36 (1963). An excellent, dispassionate analysis of conscientious objection is John Rae, *Conscience and Politics* (1971). Also helpful on the anti-war forces are A. Marwick, *Clifford Allen: the Open Conspirator* (1964); S. E. Koss, *Nonconformity in Modern British Politics* (1975); A. J. A. Morris, *Charles Trevelyan* (1977); and A. J. P. Taylor, *The Trouble Makers* (1957).

J. M. Winter argues convincingly for improving wartime living standards in 'The Impact of the First World War on Civilian Health in Britain', *Economic History Review*, 30 (1977); see also A. Marwick, *The Deluge* (1965); R. Mitchison, *British Population Growth Since 1860* (1977); and Robert Roberts, *The Classic Slum* (1971). On radical tendencies among trade unions see James Hinton, *The First Shop Stewards Movement* (1973), and S. R. White, 'The Leeds Soviet', *International Review of Social History*, 19 (1974); the narrow base of radicalism is well brought out by I. S. McLean, 'Red Clydeside 1915–19', in J. Stevenson and R. Quinault (eds), *Popular Protest and Public Order* (1974), and for a union leader hostile to the shop stewards movement see A. Bullock, *The Life and Times of Ernest Bevin*, vol. 1 (1960). C. Wrigley, *Lloyd George and the British Labour Movement* (1976) provides a detailed account of union–government relations.

On the response of men to the call for volunteers see R. Douglas, 'Voluntary Enlistment in the First World War', *Journal of Modern History*, 42 (1970); and the superb account by Martin Middlebrook, *The First Day on the Somme* (1971). In addition to the latter there are some stimulating recent examinations of battle experience and the attitudes of the men: John Keegan, *The Face of Battle* (1976); and Denis Winter, *Death's Men: soldiers of the Great War* (1978). Evidence of discontent in the army and its political significance is analysed in a valuable article by D. Englander and J. Osborne, 'Jack, Tommy and Henry Dubb: the Armed Forces and the Working Class', *Historical Journal*, 21 (1978); see also G. Dallas and D. Gill, 'The Mutiny at Etaples Base in 1917', *Past and Present*, 69 (1975); and a general account of trench life in John Ellis, *Eye Deep in Hell* (1976).

On the Coupon Election there are some useful publications on the circumstances in which it was fought: R. Douglas, 'The Background to the Coupon Election Arrangements', *English Historical Review*, 86 (1971); T. Wilson, *The Downfall of the Liberal Party 1914–35* (1966), and 'The Coupon and the British General Election of 1918', *Journal of Modern History*, 36 (1964); B. McGill, 'Lloyd George's Timing of the 1918 Election', *Journal of British Studies*, 14 (1974); M. D. Pugh, *Electoral Reform in War and Peace 1906–18* (1978). For further reading see the bibliography for chapter 8.

CHAPTER 10: *Party, Ideology and the State in the Great War*

There are useful general accounts of the questions raised in this chapter in S. Pollard, *The Development of the British Economy 1914–67* (1962); and C. L. Mowat, *Britain Between the Wars 1918–40* (1955). E. M. H. Lloyd's *Experiments in State Control at the War Office and the Ministry of Food* (1924) expresses a contemporary civil servant's enthusiasm for controls and sees political ideology as the obstacle; more recent secondary works in a similar vein are A. Marwick, *The Deluge* (1965), and A. J. P. Taylor, *English History 1914–45* (1965). An essential corrective to all this for the early phase of the war is David French's, 'Some Aspects of Social and Economic Planning for War in Great Britain 1905–15' (London University Ph.D. thesis, 1978), to be published in 1982 as *Business As Usual: British Economic Planning for a war against Germany 1905–15*. For the later stages the fragility of Lloyd George's system is well analysed in Rodney Lowe, 'The Erosion of State Intervention in Britain 1917–24', *Economic History Review*, 31 (1978); see also R. H. Tawney, 'The Abolition of Economic Controls 1918–21', *Economic History Review*, 13 (1943); and P. K. Cline, 'Eric Geddes and the Experiment with Businessmen in Government 1915–22', in K. D. Brown (ed.), *Essays in Anti-Labour History* (1974).

The optimistic view of the impact of war on social policy is lucidly stated by Richard Titmuss in *Essays on the Welfare State* (1958) and in the controversial study by S. Andreski, *Military Organisation and Society* (1954). This view has never recovered from the criticism offered in P. Abrams, 'The Failure of Social Reform 1918–20', *Past and Present*, 24 (1963). A useful summary is A. Marwick, 'The Impact of the First World War on British Society', *Journal of Contemporary History*, 3 (1968). P. B. Johnston's *Land Fit for Heroes* (1968) is a detailed examination of the reconstruction ideology, and P. F. Clarke's *Liberals and Social Democrats* (1979) throws valuable light on the alienation of progressives from Lloyd George. Against a strong tide K. O. Morgan, *Consensus and Disunity: the Lloyd George Coalition 1918–22* (1979) attempts to defend the liberal, reforming credentials of its subject.

The general volumes on the Conservative Party by Blake, Beer, Butler, Southgate and Ramsden tend to overlook either the war or ideas. One has to turn to more specialist studies. One essay that tends to ascribe to the war much that existed already is J. O. Stubbs, 'The Impact of the Great War on the Conservative Party', in G. Peele and C. Cook (eds), *The Politics of Reappraisal* (1975). The role of business pressure is examined in J. Turner, 'The British Commonwealth Union and the General Election of 1918', *English Historical Review*, 93 (1978); and for changes in party personnel see the useful article by J. M. McEwen, 'The Coupon Election of 1918 and Unionist Members of Parliament', *Journal of Modern History*, 34 (1962). R. Scally, *Origins of the Lloyd George Coalition: the politics of social imperialism* (1975), probably exaggerates the coherence of the phenomenon but is a valuable treatment of right-wing interventionist elements within the party and on its peripheries. The ideas of one right-wing breakaway from the Conservatives are considered in D. Rubinstein, 'Henry Page-Croft and the National Party 1917–22', *Journal of Contemporary History* 9, (1974).

An excellent analysis of wartime socialism especially Webbian is J. M. Winter's *Socialism and the Challenge of War* (1974); on the decline of the ILP see A. Marwick, 'The ILP in the Nineteen Twenties', *Bulletin of the Institute of Historical Research*, 35 (1962), and R. E. Dowse, *Left in the Centre* (1966). The most cogent and forceful statement of the view that Clause IV was without significance is in R. I. McKibbin's *The Evolution of the Labour Party 1910–24* (1974). A persuasive and credible explanation of the positive value of the socialist commitment is Rodney Barker's 'Political Myth: Ramsay MacDonald and the Labour Party', *History*, 61 (1976). The elements of continuity between pre- and post-war Labour politics are well brought out in R. I. McKibbin, 'Arthur Henderson as Labour Leader', *International Review of Social History*, 23 (1978). For the motives behind Liberal changes of allegiance see the invaluable book by C. A. Cline, *Recruits to Labour* (1963); also on this theme are: C. P. Trevelyan, *From Liberalism to Labour* (1921); A. J. A. Morris, *Charles Trevelyan* (1977); and Jane and Kenneth Morgan, *Portrait of a Progressive: the political career of Viscount Addison* (1980).

CHAPTER 11: *The Elevation of Labour and the Restoration of Party Politics 1918–24*

Maurice Cowling's *The Impact of Labour 1920–24* (1971) analyses in detail politicians' motivations and strategies after the war. The Conservatives' detachment from Lloyd George is well brought out in R. Blake, *The Unknown Prime Minister* (1955) and M. Kinnear, *The Fall of Lloyd George* (1973). Also useful on the Conservatives are R. Blake, *The Conservative Party from Peel to Churchil* (1970); Lord Butler (ed.), *The Conservatives* (1977); D. Southgate (ed.), *The Conservative Leadership 1832–1932* (1974); J. Ramsden, *The Age of Balfour and Baldwin 1902–40* (1978); K. Middlemas and J. Barnes, *Baldwin* (1969).

The collapse of the Coalition is examined sympathetically from the Liberal side in K. O. Morgan, *Consensus and Disunity: the Lloyd George Coalition Government 1918–22* (1979). Also valuable is the same author's essay 'Lloyd George's Stage Army: the Coalition Liberals', in A. J. P. Taylor (ed.), *Lloyd George: Twelve Essays* (1974). John Campbell's *Lloyd George: The Goat in the Wilderness* (1977) is a very readable account of his post-war career, sympathetic to its subject. More 'Asquithian' versions are Trevor Wilson, *The Downfall of the Liberal Party 1914–35* (1966); R. Douglas, *The History of the Liberal Party 1895–1970* (1971); Roy Jenkins, *Asquith* (1964); and S. E. Koss, *Asquith* (1976).

David Marquand's *Ramsay MacDonald* (1977) is a credible account of Labour's approach to office after the war; a hostile view of Labour's search for respectability within the system is Ralph Miliband's *Parliamentary Socialism* (1961); for an interesting study of direct action in the Labour movement see L. J. MacFarlane's 'Hands Off Russia: British Labour and the Russo-Polish War 1920', *Past and Present*, 38 (1967). Also useful are C. L. Mowat, 'Ramsay MacDonald and the Labour Party', A. Briggs and John Saville, *Essays in Labour History 1886–1923* (1971); G. D. H. Cole's *A History of the Labour Party from 1914* (1948); R. Lyman, *The First Labour Government* (1957); C. Cook and J. Ramsden (eds), *By-Elections in British Politics* (1975).

CHAPTER 12: *Origins of the Conservative Electoral Hegemony 1918–31*

David Butler's *The Electoral System in Britain 1918–51* (1953) provides a good introduction to the subject. There is a valuable discussion of the effects of different voting systems in Enid Lakeman, *Voting in Democracies* (1955), reprinted as *How Democracies Vote* (1959). A sign of the growing academic interest in and concern about the British system is S. E. Finer (ed.), *Adversary Politics and Electoral Reform*. On the emergence of the post-1918 constituency pattern and attempted modifications of the electoral system see M. D. Pugh, *Electoral Reform in War and Peace 1906–18* (1978), and 'Political Parties and the Campaign for Proportional Representation 1905–14', *Parliamentary Affairs*, 33 (1980).

Students will find general elections brought to life in Michael Kinnear's *The British Voter: an Atlas and Survey since 1885* (1969). For evidence on Conservative organization centrally and locally John Ramsden, *The Age of Balfour and Baldwin 1902–40* (1978) is essential reading. For Labour there is a more interpretative treatment which also provides important evidence in R. I. McKibbin, *The Evolution of the Labour Party 1910–24* (1974); much of the evidence is, in fact, inconsistent with the assumptions made about party responses to a mass electorate in the important article by H. C. G. Matthew, R. I. McKibbin and J. A. Kay, 'The Franchise Factor in the Rise of the Labour Party', *English Historical Review*, 91 (1976). A useful corrective on Labour Party membership and related themes is I. S. McLean, 'Party Organisation', in C. Cook and I. Taylor (eds), *The Labour Party* (1980). Also interesting because of its subject's role as an organizer is B. Donoughue and G. W. Jones, *Herbert Morrison: portrait of a politician* (1973).

On the realignment of voters during the twentieth century David Butler and Donald Stokes, *Political Change in Britain* (1969) is fascinating and essential, though flawed by the assumption that class-based politics must have arisen *after* the First World War. C. Cook's *The Age of Alignment* (1975) charts party fortunes in the general elections of the 1920s, and the same author examines the municipal pattern in 'Liberals, Labour and Local Elections', in C. Cook and G. Peele (eds), *The Politics of Reappraisal* (1975). Robert Moore's *Pitmen, Preachers and Politics* (1974), is an illuminating study of shifting allegiance among Methodist working men in Durham; the declining role of the Free Churches in national politics is examined in S. E. Koss, *Nonconformity in Modern British Politics* (1975). W. G. Runciman's *Relative Deprivation and Social Justice* (1966) offers, *inter alia*, an original interpretation of the defensive nature of working-class politics in the inter-war years. Also useful on changing party fortunes are C. Cook and J. Ramsden (eds), *By-Elections in British Politics* (1973); and Trevor Wilson, *The Downfall of the Liberal Party 1914–35* (1966).

CHAPTER 13: *The Eclipse of the Extremes 1931–39*

Among the many publications on inter-war economic problems and policies the following are particularly useful: P. Fearon, *The Origins and Nature of the Great Slump 1929–32* (1979); D. Winch, *Economies and Policy: an Historical Study* (1969); K. J. Hancock, 'The Reduction of Unemployment as a Problem of Public Policy 1920–29', *Economic History Review*, 15 (1962–3); and C. L. Mowat, *Britain Between the Wars 1918–40* (1955).

A credible account of the evolution of Labour's policy and programme during the twentieth century is David Howell's *British Social Democracy* (1976). Two valuable studies of attitudes to economic questions by Adrian Oldfield are 'The Independent Labour Party and Planning 1920—26', *International Review of Social History*, 21 (1976), and 'The Labour Party and Planning — 1934 or 1918?', *Bulletin of the Society for the Study of Labour History*, 25 (1972). The reluctant acceptance of Keynesianism is analysed in Barbara Malament's important article, 'British Labour and Roosevelt's New Deal: the Response of the Left and the Unions', *Journal of British Studies*, (Spring 1978); and in Henry Pelling, *America and the British Left* (1956). The best recent interpretation of the 1931 crisis which argues that there were economic and political alternatives available to the MacDonald government during 1929—31 is Robert Skidelsky's *Politicians and the Slump* (1967); there is a rebuttal, on the grounds that Keynesianism did not succeed in countries where it was tried, in R. I. McKibbin, 'The Economic Policy of the Second Labour Government', *Past and Present*, 36 (1975). Also useful are: B. Donoughue and G. W. Jones, *Herbert Morrison: portrait of a politician* (1973); David Maraquand, *Ramsay MacDonald* (1977); A. Bullock, *The Life and Times of Ernest Bevin* (1960); R. Bassett, *1931: Political Crisis* (1958); and S. Beer, *Modern British Politics* (1965).

A perceptive treatment of the Conservative leaders in the National Government is to be found in David Dilks' section in Lord Butler (ed.), *The Conservatives* (1977); see also David Butler (ed.), *Coalitions in British Politics* (1978). Baldwin receives sympathetic handling in John Ramsden, *The Age of Balfour and Baldwin 1902—40* (1979), and in the monumentally tedious and pedestrian biography by K. Middlemas and J. Barnes, *Baldwin: a biography* (1969). J. A. Cross, *Sir Samuel Hoare* (1977) throws useful light on an important liberal Conservative. The boundaries between liberal and right-wing Toryism are also drawn in Gillian Peele's essay on India in G. Peel and C. Cook (eds), *The Politics of Reappraisal* (1975); A. Marwick, 'Middle Opinion in the Thirties: Planning, Progress and Political Agreement', *English Historical Review*, 79 (1965); and R. R. James, *Churchill: a study in failure 1900—39* (1970). On the fascist challenge Robert Skidelsky's sympathetic biography *Oswald Mosley* (1975) interprets its subject as an authoritarian modernizer. Also useful on this aspect are: R. Benewick, *The Fascist Movement in Britain* (1972); K. Lunn and R. C. Thurlow's collection of essays, *British Fascism* (1980); and C. Cook and J. Stevenson, *The Slump: society and politics in the depression* (1977).

A number of recent publications explore the reasons for the weakness of the left in the 1930s. Ben Pimlott's *Labour and the Left in the 1930s* (1977) is useful on the Socialist League and the Constituency Parties Movement; John Stevenson emphasizes the absence of radical inclinations among the unemployed in two essays, 'Myth and Reality: Britain in the 1930's', in A.

Sked and C. Cook (eds), *Crisis and Controversy* (1976), and 'The Politics of Violence', in G. Peele and C. Cook (eds), *The Politics of Reappraisal* (1975); the erosion of the pacifist left's influence on Labour foreign policy is explained in John Naylor's *Labour's International Policy* (1969), and in H. R. Winkler, 'The Emergency of a Labour Foreign Policy in Great Britain 1918−29', *Journal of Modern History*, 28 (1956).

The traditional, Baldwinian view of public opinion and rearmament is exploded in C. T. Stannage's, 'The East Fulham By-Election', *Historical Journal*, 14 (1971). A balanced and critical study of one manifestation of opinion is Martin Ceadel's, 'The First British Referendum: the Peace Ballot 1934−35', *English Historical Review*, 95 (1980): for a more wide-ranging study see the same author's *Pacifism in Britain 1914−45* (1980). Other works which examine the political calculations behind rearmament are: M. Cowling, *The Impact of Hitler* (1975); F. Coughlan, 'Armaments, Economic Policy and Appeasement: the Background to British Foreign Policy 1931−37', *History*, 57 (1972); J. P. D. Dunbabin, 'British Rearmament in the 1930's: a chronology and review', *Historical Journal*, 17 (1975). The essential work on changing political allegiance in the mid-1930s is C. T. Stannage, 'The General Election of 1935' (Cambridge Ph.D. thesis, 1973), now published as *Baldwin Thwarts the Opposition* (1980). Other useful studies of opinion in the last years of peace are: Nicholas Pronay's two articles on 'British Newsreels in the 1930's', *History*, 56 (1971) and 57 (1972); I. S. McLean, 'Oxford and Bridgewater', in C. Cook and J. Ramsden (eds), *By-Elections in British Politics* (1975); R. Eatwell, 'Munich, Public Opinion and the Popular Front', *Journal of Contemporary History*, 6 (1971).

ADDENDA

The following were published too late for inclusion in the first printing:
Chapters 2 and 4
D. W. Bebbington, *The Nonconformist Conscience: Chapel and Politics 1870−1914* (1982) is a short survey which students will find very useful.
Chapters 4 and 6
David Clark, *Colne Valley: Radicalism to Socialism* (1981) is an interesting and persuasive interpretation of the early Labour Movement in terms of 'ethical socialism' and individualism.
Chapters 5 and 6
D. J. Dutton, 'The Unionist Party and Social Reform 1906−14', *Historical Journal*, 24 (1981), discusses Edwardian Conservative thoughts on coming to terms with the working class.
Chapter 10
Kathleen Burke (ed.), *War and the State: the Transformation of British Government 1914−19* (1982) comprises seven critical essays by specialists on the expansion of government intervention and the reasons for post-war contraction.

Index